WORLDVIEW
for
CHRISTIAN WITNESS

CHARLES H. KRAFT

WILLIAM CAREY
LIBRARY

Worldview for Christian Witness
Copyright © 2008 by Charles H. Kraft

All rights reserved.

No part of this work may be reproduced or transmitted in any form or by any means—for example, electronic or mechanical, including photocopying and recording—without prior written permission of the publisher.

All scripture quotations, unless otherwise indicated, are taken from the *Good News Bible* © 1994 published by the Bible Societies/HarperCollins Publishers Ltd., *UK Good News Bible* © American Bible Society 1966, 1971, 1976, 1992. Used with permission.

Cover: Anthony Fisher
Typesetting: Jeff Simons
Editorial Manager: Naomi Bradley

Published by
William Carey Library
1605 E. Elizabeth St.
Pasadena, CA 91104
www.missionbooks.org

William Carey Library is a ministry of the
U.S. Center for World Mission
www.uscwm.org

Printed in the United States of America

Library of Congress Cataloging-in-Publication Data

Kraft, Charles H.
　Worldview for Christian witness / Charles H. Kraft.
　　　p. cm.
　Includes bibliographical references.
　ISBN 978-0-87808-520-0
　1. Missions. 2. Anthropology of religion. 3. Christianity and culture. I. Title.
　BV2063.K73 2008
　140--dc22
　　　　　　　　　　　　2007027355

Contents

Introduction 7

PART I: THE PERSPECTIVE

Chapter 1	Why Should Christians Study Worldview?	11
Chapter 2	People, Worldview & Change	33
Chapter 3	Critical Realism	55
Chapter 4	Current Approaches of Non-anthropologists	75
Chapter 5	Other Approaches: Anthropological	105
Chapter 6	Worldview, Religion & Subsystems	129

PART II: CHARACTERISTICS OF WORLDVIEWS

Chapter 7	Functions of Worldview	151
Chapter 8	Universals: Categorization, Person/Group	167
Chapter 9	Worldview Universals: Relationship, Causality	187
Chapter 10	Universals: Time/Event, Space/Material World	207
Chapter 11	Worldview Orientations & Types	231
Chapter 12	Worldview Configurations	251
Chapter 13	Discovering Worldview	297
Chapter 14	What Are We Taking to the World?	325
Chapter 15	How Are Worldviews Changed?	343

PART III: WORLDVIEW CHANGE

Chapter 16	Obstacles & Opportunities in Worldview Change: Person/Group	371
Chapter 17	Obstacles & Opportunities in Worldview Change II: Categorization, Causality, Time, Space, Relationship	405
Chapter 18	Patterns of Worldview Change	425
Chapter 19	Strategies for Constructive Change	463
Chapter 20	Reaching Peoples of Three Types	481
Chapter 21	Wrapping Things Up	501

Appendix A	History of the Concept of Worldview in American Anthropology	507
Appendix B	Additional Worldview Configurations	527
Appendix C	Additional Folklore for Discovering Worldview Myths	537
Bibliography		549
Index		555

Introduction

From the earliest days of formal anthropological study in the latter half of the nineteenth century it has been the habit of anthropologists to compare cultures. It was by then obvious that different peoples approach the problems of life in quite different ways. Why the differences, it was asked, and which approaches are best?

So the customs of various peoples were compared. The first assumption made by those who made the comparisons was that our western customs are clearly "superior" to those of other peoples. So they used their data to try to discover how we got to be this way (i.e., superior). With an evolutionary bias in their minds, the early observers made comparisons between western and non-western cultures with the assumption that what they were seeing in other cultures were the stages western peoples had gone through on their way to our present superior position. Non-western customs and beliefs were assumed to show us what our ancestors once practiced but then grew out of.

This assumption was a worldview assumption widely held even by scholars during the latter half of the nineteenth century. It was tied into western concepts of development often referred to as social evolutionism. Unfortunately, though most scholars claim to have abandoned assumptions of western superiority and social evolutionism, at least at the conscious level, some aspects of this theory are still widely held unconsciously by scholars and often quite consciously at the popular level.

Further study by those concerned with culture, however, led to a change in the worldview assumption of most anthropologists. The data now seemed to support the conclusion that western approaches to life are not necessarily better than those of non-western peoples. Nor are the practices of other peoples indicative of the stages our ancestors went through. Rather, different cultures represent different creative approaches to life—each with areas of strength and areas of weakness.

So anthropologists turned to studying more and more cultures while consciously fighting the ethnocentrism that assumes that our way of life is superior to theirs. In the process it became clear that the ways of life of the various peoples of the world are each quite respectable. They are also very complex.

The complexity of cultures lies in at least two areas. First, there is the complex structuring of each of the vast array of components of which life is made up. People need to communicate so there is language. And language is always complex. People need to be regulated so there are rules and enforcers of rules, concepts of propriety and social pressure to keep people in line. And all of the social customs going to make up these patterns are complex.

People need food, clothing, shelter and techniques for obtaining and maintaining these necessities. So there are complex cultural patterns to govern those aspects of life, likewise with the patterns governing family relationships, economics, religion, art, education and all the rest. All such cultural patterns are complex. They are also closely interrelated with each other.

Secondly, though, it has become clear that each of these areas of cultural patterning consists of surface level behavior and underlying ("deep level") assumptions. The latter—the assumptions—we call worldview. Worldview is beneath the surface of cultural behavior, with most of it below the level of a people's awareness and often difficult for outsiders to discover.

So as we attempt to compare cultures, we need to compare them at two levels. The early anthropologists and most contemporary travelers tend to compare largely at the surface level. The diversity of different cultures on the surface is very interesting. If, however, we are to really understand the significance of those surface level differences, we need to understand the deep level assumptions and values on the basis of which people operate that surface level behavior.

It is at this point that the comparative study of worldview helps us. When we look at other people's assumptions and compare them with ours, we become aware of at least two things:

1. There is a great variety of underlying assumptions and values held by the various peoples of the world and
2. Our own worldview assumptions aren't the only ones that make sense. We can, therefore, perhaps learn something more about REALITY as God sees it by taking seriously the insights of those of other societies.

True, we all see dimly. Yet through looking at cultural (worldview) data concerning how other peoples see, we can learn to see more than the limited perspectives of our own worldview allow us to see. In this way we can get insight into both the strengths and weaknesses of our own perspectives.

One thing that becomes clear is that the area under consideration in this book is of great importance to most of the peoples of the world, including biblical peoples. And, I believe, this area is also very important to God. For it is at the deepest level of our assumptions that God wants to reach us. Though it is only through a relationship with (not simply knowledge about) God that we are saved, the things we understand cognitively about Him and His workings either support our relationship or detract from it.

This text is an attempt to raise to our awareness the whole area of basic assumptions and to help us to deal with them, both within ourselves and within those to whom God calls us. In this, however, our aim is to get beyond simple awareness to the place where we can use our insights to bring more unbelievers into the Kingdom and enable more believers to grow in their faith and faithfulness.

May God bless this effort to that end.

South Pasadena, CA
June 2008

PART I:

THE PERSPECTIVE

Chapter 1

Why Should Christians Study Worldview?

The concept of worldview is being used today in quite a number of Christian circles. Understandably, this has resulted in several different understandings of the concept and its significance. We frequently hear terms like "Christian worldview," "the worldview of secular humanists," "African worldview," "American worldview," and the like.

Representative of the ways in which non-anthropologists have used this term are books by James Sire (3rd edition, 1997), Ninian Smart (1983), and David Naugle (2002) that we will look at in chapter 4. Sire's book is entitled, *The Universe Next Door* with the subtitle, *A Basic Worldview Catalog*. Smart's title is *Worldviews: Cross-cultural Explorations of Human Beliefs*. Naugle, then, attempts "The History of a Concept." Each of these, and several other books and articles that use the term "worldview," have a much more limited view of what the term includes than do those of us who come from an anthropological perspective. Though Sire's definition is useful (see below), each of these authors tend to limit the concept pretty much to religious and/or philosophical assumptions.

Smart uses the word "worldview" throughout his treatment. But his aim is not to deal with the broad area in view when anthropologists use the term, but simply to provide "a good introduction to the modem study of religion" (1983: vii). He moves in our direction, however, when he states that he seeks to "pay attention to all the major forces of belief and feeling which animate our world" (ibid). Naugle, then, is more concerned with the history of the concept than with defining it. It is, however, clear that his understanding of the term is the narrower one that most Christian authors have in view. His is, however, a fascinating, though heavy, discussion of the concept as used mostly by philosophers, though he does briefly discuss a couple of anthropologists. In an appendix of "books on the Christian worldview not addressed in this volume," though, he lists several who are dealing with the concept from a "social science" perspective.

Sire comes closer to our broader concept by defining worldview as "a set of presuppositions (assumptions which may be true, partially true or entirely false) which we hold (consciously or subconsciously, consistently or inconsistently) about the basic makeup of our world" (1997: 16). His discussion is, however, focused on religious and philosophical concepts that challenge biblical Christian theism in the West. We will deal with Sire and Smart in more detail in chapter 4.

This kind of treatment is of great value. And I will contend especially in chapter 9 that Sire has focused on the most important (at least for us Christians) facet of worldview—causality. As we shall see, however, when we come at the concept of worldview from an anthropological perspective, we have a much broader range of issues to deal with. Though concepts we in the West regularly label "religious" or "philosophical" play important parts in worldview, especially as they deal with causality, so do concepts of relationship, time/event, space/material world, categorization and person-group. That is, the whole range of assumptions underlying cultural behavior is in focus here, not simply those underlying the topics that have attracted the attention of philosophers and theologians.

Embracing this broader view, I define worldview as the totality of the culturally structured images and assumptions (including value and commitment or allegiance assumptions) in terms of which a people both perceive and respond to reality. Worldview is not separate from culture. It is included in culture as the structuring of the deepest level pictures and presuppositions on which people base their lives.

"Worldview" in Culture and Life

Though we will go into more detail later concerning the relationships between worldview and culture, I here introduce two fundamental concepts that are foundational to our whole presentation.

1. The first of these is to see culture as consisting of two levels: surface and deep. At the surface level of human life, we observe people behaving in certain ways. This surface-level behavior consists most often of the habitual activity of people behaving according to the patterns and processes of their culture. Underlying these patterns and processes, however, there is at least one level of assumptions. These assumptions are structured in relation to each other and in relation to the surface-level structures to form the deep level of culture. We call this deep level of culture "worldview."

SURFACE LEVEL CULTURE
Patterned/structured behavior, usually habitual, often visible.
DEEP LEVEL CULTURE (WORLDVIEW)
Patterned/structured assumptions (including values and commitments), also usually habitual, usually invisible. There is possibly more than one level of assumptions.

Figure 1.1. Surface and Deep Level Culture

2. The second foundational concept is **the distinction we need to make between cultural (including worldview) structuring and *people***. I will go into more detail on this in chapter 2, but for now I want to emphasize the fact that *behaving is a "people thing," not a cultural thing*. It is people who behave, people who do things. Culture doesn't do anything. It just sits there. Culture is like the script of a drama. It is learned and (mostly) followed by the players but does nothing itself. I, in contrast with many both within and outside of anthropological circles, *use the term culture strictly as the label for the patterns and structures that people follow, never for the people themselves*. When we speak of culture, then, we are speaking of the *patterns* that people ordinarily follow when they behave.

And just as behaving is a "people thing," not a structure thing, so assuming is a people thing. People, however, not only tend to behave according to the cultural patterns they have been taught, they also "perform" their assuming according to deep level cultural patterns (i.e., worldview). Like every other aspect of culture, worldview does not do anything. Any supposed power of worldview lies in the *habits* of people. *People*, not worldview, do the things that get done. Worldview, however, is that part of culture to which people look (unconsciously) to provide the bases and underlying structuring for their actions.

As detailed in chapter 2, I believe we must make a clear distinction between people and culture. People are the actors, culture the script. When we are discussing activity, then, we are discussing people, not culture. When we are discussing the patterns (the lines of the script) ordinarily followed by people as a matter of habit, we are referring to culture.

A worldview is a part of the patterns, the script. It is the deepest level of culture. It provides the basic assumptions on which a people act. Like a script, it simply "sits there" like our roads and paths do, waiting for someone to drive or walk along them.

People are the active agents. They ordinarily drive or walk along the roads and paths passed on to them by their parents and other elders. But sometimes they elect to drive or walk where there are not yet roads or paths. And sometimes, other people recognize that the new way seems better than the old way and so they "pave" the alternate way to make it a permanent part of the cultural configuration. In such a way, new patterns (paths) are developed in human life and become a part of the cultural patterns passed on to the next generation.

CULTURAL STRUCTURE	PERSONAL BEHAVING
Cultural patterns, structure and the processes associated with cultural patterning Like an actor's script There is cultural structuring of human behavior and assumptions (worldviews)	The personal behavior, largely habitual, that people engage in Like the actor in a drama People, not culture, think (a cognitive dimension), feel (an affective dimension), evaluate (an evaluative dimension) and "habit"

Figure 1.2. Cultural Structure and Personal Behaving

Five Critical Characteristics of Worldviews

Among the most important characteristics of worldviews are the following five:

1. Worldview assumptions or premises are *learned by people as children and, therefore, are not reasoned out but assumed to be true without prior proof.* The basic assumptions of a society are taught to each new generation so persuasively that these assumptions seem absolute and are seldom questioned. People then interpret their life experiences in terms of these assumptions and feel they are proven. Since they are assumptions, acceded to largely unconsciously by the members of the society, they are simply accepted by adults as well as children without the requirement that someone prove them. They are thus deeply imbedded in the structure of the culture and serve as the basis for the acting out of surface-level behavior.

To illustrate, let's look at a *people's definition of life*. A basic question to ask is, when does life begin? The answer for most of the peoples of the world is assumed rather than proved. People in one society grow up with the assumption that life begins at birth. Those in another society may assume another starting point before or at birth, or at some point after birth. The Kamwe of northeastern Nigeria, like many peoples, make a distinction between the start of biological life and the start of human life. For them, a baby isn't to be regarded as fully human until about a year and a half to two years after birth. For many peoples (including the Jews), life as a full-fledged human, as opposed to mere biological existence, starts at the naming of the child—for Jews on the eighth day.

For many peoples, the life of a newborn is but the continuation or restarting of the life of someone who has already lived several lives and died at the end of the last one. For many, the life of humans is seen as quite different from that of animals and plants. For others (e.g., most of the peoples of India) all life is seen as of the same type. This belief is called "Monism." Furthermore, because of the assumed process of reincarnation, even animals are not to be killed lest one inadvertently kill a relative. These are assumptions widely held by peoples of different societies. Seldom, if ever, does it occur to anyone in the societies involved to try to prove such assumptions objectively. The trust people have in those who taught them is regarded as sufficient proof.

Assumptions concerning disease provide another example. Americans assume that disease is caused by germs. Recently when I "caught" a cold, (or did the cold "catch" me?), I assumed what my American elders had taught me—that I came in contact with some germs that got into my system and caused the cold.

When I got to Nigeria, though, I came into contact with people whose parents taught them differently. These people learned, not about germs but about spirits as the cause of disease. When we would discuss our differing points of view, they would contend that their theory handles the situation better because it explains that it was the choice of a personal spirit to attack one person but to leave another alone. The germ theory attempts to explain that aspect of disease simply in terms of the *chance* that a given germ came along at a time when the person's resistance was low. This theory isn't very convincing to a traditional Nigerian because it doesn't adequately explain why when two people are exposed to the same germ, often only one gets sick.

They, like I, had been taught theory as fact. We could argue with them that our theory is more "scientific" than theirs. But is it? What we often don't take into account is the fact that our science is based on the assumption that if there is any reality beyond the physical world (e.g., a spirit world), it is irrelevant when dealing with causation. This, however, is a very challengeable assumption, especially from a biblical perspective.

Any argument between those who espouse these different theories of disease is complicated by the fact that, in terms of a broader view of reality, it may be that neither theory is entirely wrong, except when it is advanced as the whole truth. As is often true with worldview assumptions (and with the blind men and the elephant), each of these theories contains enough truth to be convincing with respect to that part of reality in focus. Each theory, however, fails to explain another part of reality. In this case might it not be true that spirits manipulate germs to bring about sickness, if not all of the time, at least some of the time? If so, at one level the illness is caused by germs but at another level by spirits.

In arguing his point, an American might say to the one who believes spirits are the cause, "I'll prove to you that the germ theory is the correct perspective. Here's some medicine. Take it and it will kill the germs and you'll be well." If the person gets well after taking the medicine, though, the non-American may simply conclude that the medicine is effective in getting rid of spirits. Many of the Kamwe did come to believe this about receiving injections by needle. When sick people were brought to our medical clinic, they were frequently given an injection of penicillin. This usually brought relief. On occasion, though, our supply of penicillin would run out and the ill ones were denied their shots. This led to no end of arguing between the patients, who demanded their shots even with empty syringes, and the dispensers who refused to give them unless there was medicine in the syringe. For, to the majority of the Kamwe, it was not the medicine in the syringe that brought health, it was the fact that the needle provided a way for the offending spirit to leave. Thus, to them, a shot with an empty syringe was just as valid as one that injected medicine into the person's system.

A third theory believed by many is that loss or damage causes disease to a person's soul. When a person is ill, they say that somebody has stolen the person's soul or that she/he has fallen and jarred the soul loose. To us westerners this seems like a very strange theory. But, like each of the other theories, it is taught convincingly, believed implicitly, and accepted as truth in each instance of illness (and of healing) by the people of certain societies. They, like us, then, interpret whatever happens as proving their assumption. All worldviews are like this.

2. Like all of culture, *a worldview is an organized system* consisting of several levels and types of assumptions, each relating to all others but serving a distinct function. We will have much to say about the organization of worldview in the following chapters so will not go into great detail here.

By way of illustration, though, let's look at a typical tribal worldview, that of the Kamwe of northeastern Nigeria. At the highest level is the worldview itself, organized into several parallel components that we will label "themes." The assumptions organized into each theme interact with and limit those in other themes to provide the overall structuring of the worldview. M. Kraft (1978) does not deal with all of the themes or paradigms of Kamwe worldview, but does treat three that she calls "supernaturalism," "mountain-orientation" and "guinea-corn complex." A complete description might include another four to ten or more themes. These themes are made up of the structuring of the assumptions related to the focuses of Kamwe life.

The Kamwe live in the Mandara Mountains and orient much of their life and even their language to those mountains. Their assumptions concerning the meaning of the mountains to their way of life are organized into a mountain-orientation theme. Their staple food is a sorghum called "guinea corn." This food is considered to be so essential both to physical and to social and spiritual life that the thousands of assumptions surrounding it form a second worldview theme. See chapter 12 for more detail on these and the following theme.

We will deal with the theme of Kamwe supernaturalism in more detail to show some of this theme's internal organization. Within the theme are sub-themes or paradigms made up of the assumptions concerning subjects such as the high God, evil spirits and ancestors. Each of these paradigms, then, will include assumptions concerning how humans are to relate to these beings.

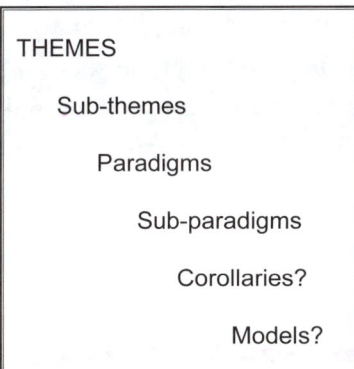

Figure 1.3. Themes and Their Smaller Components
(see Chapter 12)

A paradigm regarding the high God holds that he is all-powerful and positive toward humans but only to be consulted by humans in emergency situations. This is done in situations such as drought or warfare through clan and/or family rituals superintended by specified religious practitioners. Thousands of assumptions, some major, others less important underlie Kamwe understandings of and activities toward their high God. These assumptions can be viewed as organized into sub-themes, paradigms, sub-paradigms, corollaries and the like (see chapter 12). The assumptions underlying a given ritual, for example, might be seen as a sub-paradigm based on a corollary concerning the way in which a relationship with the deity may be restored if broken.

A second paradigm would consist of the assumptions concerning the realm of evil spirits perceived of as constantly interfering with human life to bring disease, accidents, infertility, severed relationships and all manner of other difficulty and calamity. The assumption that the high God is only to be appealed to in emergencies has as its corollary the assumption that to handle life's difficulties you deal with the evil spirits that are causing the problems. It is assumed, therefore, that it is crucial to please them through correct behavior and, when things go wrong, to discover why they are displeased and to appease them through reconciliation with the offended party and/or proper ritual.

Given the Kamwe perception of life, the paradigms concerning ancestors would probably fall under a theme dealing with the living rather than one dealing with supernatural beings and powers. The assumption is that ancestors, or at least some of them, are a part of the living community with responsibilities and privileges in the society. Certain of the ancestors, however, have been elevated to a status parallel to that of the evil spirits. These ancestors could be either good or evil, depending on how they are treated by the living. Whether, in a complete analysis of Kamwe worldview, these ancestors should be treated under the supernaturalism theme or under a human life theme will have to await further analysis. Whichever way it goes, there are thousands of assumptions that underlie Kamwe behavior related to the ancestors.

These few paragraphs should suffice to illustrate the fact that a worldview is organized and systematic. It is also very complex, not simply a miscellaneous collection of assumptions.

3. A people's worldview *provides them with a lens, model or map in terms of which reality is perceived and interpreted*. As we shall see, our perspective on life is influenced by a number of factors that may be likened to lenses through which we look out at what goes on around us. Those factors or lenses include worldview, experience, temperament, will and sin. The most pervasive and influential of these lenses is, however, worldview. Indeed, it may be argued that these other factors should be regarded as components of worldview rather than separable entities. With this in mind, we will speak of a worldview as if it were a single lens.

The vast majority of the assumptions we live with are not idiosyncratic. They are given to us by those who taught us our perspective. While our elders were teaching us, then, others of that generation taught others of our generation to look at things the same way. We and all others of our generation in our society, then, learned to view through that lens habitually. And to the end of our days we follow most of the pathways of interpretation we were taught.

Our way of viewing, however, became more than simply a lens to look through. It is almost as if there was a picture on the lens, a picture of what our society expects us to see through that lens. The perspective not only filters our view, but anticipates what we will see. *Worldview is, then, both a lens and a model or map of reality. We look at an event and fit it into what seems to be the most logical place in an already established pattern.* If, for example, typical Americans with a typical naturalistic American worldview see a person behaving under the influence of a demon, they will more than likely interpret what is happening as a psychological problem. For this is the slot, the place in the picture, provided by their worldview for such an occurrence.

If, however, traditional Africans observe a person manifesting a psychological problem, they are likely to interpret the event as demonic. For that is the part of a traditional African model of reality appropriate to such an event. If these persons are to allow for the possibility of that part of reality they have not been taught, they will have to "grow" another component to the model they have been taught. I know many Americans who have been successful in expanding their worldview to include the demonic possibility along with the psychological illness possibility. I know many others, though, who refuse to make such a change in their model of reality.

Figure 2.1 in chapter 2 is intended to be helpful in enabling us to picture some of the elements in the process we go through when we experience an event. As we go through life, we are exposed to an enormous number of experiences. Though this number is far less than the number of things that could have happened to us, we only notice a select number of the ones that do happen to us. For example, it is likely that angels are involved in many of the life experiences of a Christian (and, probably, of non-Christians as well). We are seldom, if ever, conscious of this involvement even if we believe it to be true. So we don't notice it. Nor do we notice many more visible events in our lives. And that part of our experience that we analyze and fit into or use to alter our model of reality is still smaller. Though we miss a lot, we tend to fit most of the rest into the already constructed picture provided by our society. What we cannot interpret easily from that perspective often gets ignored, sometimes is taken as a challenge to defend our present perspective but may be used to widen our model.

The model we live with, then, is the "map" that we usually follow to guide our assumptions and behavior. Just as a map has lines and labels symbolizing a view of reality, so our mental map provides the pattern, recipe or script that we are expected to use habitually as a socially approved guide over life's terrain.

4. Our worldview not only guides us in the commitments we make but *we are committed to our worldview* as well. Our commitment is not, however, equally strong to every part of our worldview. For example, we may assume that one type of car or clothing or cereal is better than another, and be easily convinced that another brand is just as good or better, unless we have expended some energy in defending the product against competing claims. Our commitment to an assumption grows when we defend it. So does the amount of embarrassment before others if we should give up that commitment. Think of how difficult it might be to get a Baptist who is a part of a group that has been arguing for immersion as the only correct mode of baptism to give up that commitment by agreeing that another form of baptism is just as valid as immersion.

For ordinary Americans, there is a high level of commitment to such assumptions as the validity of scientific support or lack of support for an idea, the unreality of invisible beings in the world, the germ theory of disease, the superiority of democracy over other forms of government, the right of a person to privacy and the like. We are strongly committed both to these concepts and to the assumptions that support them. They are, therefore, difficult for Americans to give up.

As mentioned above, when we are confronted with data that does not fit neatly into our picture of reality, we either ignore it or face the challenge to change. When some part of our present model is challenged, our first action is usually to defend it, especially if our commitment to it is high. A challenge to any part of our model of reality that we consider crucial is in many ways similar to a threat on our lives. We will, therefore, defend those parts tenaciously. Not only will Baptists strongly defend immersion, Americans will defend democracy, science, schooling, our concepts of privacy, tolerance and freedom. American Christians (especially those with theological training) will often even strongly contend for naturalistic rational explanations of events over spiritual explanations in spite of the predominance of the latter in scripture.

When an area of worldview considered crucial by a people is challenged in such a way that they see it as no longer tenable, the stakes are very high. The result is often widespread demoralization. Take, for example, the many peoples of the world (e.g., Anglo-Americans, many American Indian groups, the ancient Jews) who live(d) with the worldview assumption that they could not be defeated in war. When the unbelievable happened and they were defeated, they were forced either to change their assumption or to reinterpret the event in such a way that the defeat was not allowed to challenge the assumption. Many Americans have taken the latter course in interpreting the Vietnam War (which we did not win) as a "police action" rather than a bona fide war.

Many American Indian groups, however, found themselves unable (or unwilling) either to change their assumption or to reinterpret. They, therefore, became demoralized (due to this, plus other factors), stopped reproducing and died out. The ancient Jews assumed they were "the People of God." To them this meant, among other things, that God would always protect them, regardless of whether or not they obeyed Him. As we see throughout the Old Testament, though, this was not God's assumption, so He frequently brought judgment upon them when they disobeyed, even at the hands of pagans. Those Israelites who survived demoralization were able to do so by developing a broader understanding of the close relationship between their faithfulness to Him and His assistance in war.

Even without such intense pressure to reconsider assumptions, a people may feel pressure to question some portion of their worldview when, for example, they become aware of alternative explanations or assumptions that seem to work just as well as or better than their own and cannot be simply explained away. Such a situation may occur either with or without outside pressure. This type of situation is widespread in non-western societies, enhanced by the pressure of western schools. Under such pressure, assumptions concerning agriculture, disease, God, the spirit world, and a myriad of other concepts are being altered, replaced, or otherwise accommodated.

Our ability to handle challenges to worldview assumptions, then, is directly related to the amount of our investment in and our commitment to them. Assumptions to which we are minimally committed (e.g., that a given type of toothpaste or soap is the best) may be reasonably easy to alter or change. Those to which we are committed in a major way, though, are a different story, especially if we have expended effort to defend them. The amount of social pressure exerted by a community against a given change is calibrated to the amount of commitment of the community to the given assumption. The desire and ability of any given individual to choose against that pressure relates to a number of individual factors. Among these are one's personal security, the amount of personal benefit foreseen, the amount of freedom allowed the individual by her/his significant others, the possibility of escape from the person's social environment if things go wrong and the like.

5. Of all the problems that occur when people of different societies come into contact with each other, *those arising from differences in worldview are the most difficult to deal with.* Since worldview is a matter of assumptions, most of which are unconscious, it seldom occurs to the members of a social group that there may be people in the world who do not share their assumptions—unless they travel or are otherwise made aware of such differences.

Being surrounded by behavior based on other assumptions is a major reason why people find themselves experiencing culture shock (better, "culture stress"). If we are living in another society, not only are the people of that society behaving on the basis of different assumptions than ours, they may not even understand why we are having a problem since to them the way they are behaving is quite natural. This can throw us off balance both because our assumptions aren't working, and because we get no help from them in adjusting to their assumptions since it never occurs to them that we are having a problem.

I was told once of a student from Asia who had such a problem in the States. Not only was he struggling with culture stress in general, but he was going hungry as well. He was living with an American family and eating every meal with them. In his society it is considered polite to take only a small amount of food during a meal and then to turn down additional food when it is offered. According to his assumptions, one must turn down such offers of food three times and then, with a show of reluctance, only accept it when it is offered the fourth time. So when the hostess offered him food, he said, "No, thank you." He responded that way again when she offered it the second time. Then she didn't offer it again. So he was getting thin and didn't know what to do.

On the basis of his cultural assumptions, he felt that this American family was greedy, not wanting to give him enough food to eat. Meanwhile, they were quite concerned because he wasn't eating and was losing weight. They thought he didn't like their food. Still, since the assumptions each of them were working from were quite unconscious, neither he nor they realized that their problem was a deep-level assumption problem. And until they found out, they had no idea what was happening. He didn't know that it was not normal for an American hostess to offer food more than twice. And she didn't know that he expected her to offer it at least four times. She was assuming that he was really not interested in more food when he refused it. He, of course, assumed that she knew she must continue to press it upon him before he would do what he really wanted to do—accept more food.

Not only do worldview differences result in culture stress problems, they are the underlying cause of most of the problems we face as we attempt to communicate Christianity cross-culturally. The gospel is intended to influence and change people personally and also structurally at the deepest possible level—the worldview level. A Christian commitment is intended to result in deep, basic changes in worldview assumptions. Worldview provides the guidelines in terms of which people assign meanings. In addition to the personal commitment, it is these meanings that are to be the primary focus of Christian change.

Not infrequently, the process goes afoul, however, since we tend to tangle up Christian assumptions with those of our own society, often quite unconsciously. In our attempts to discover and remedy such a problem we need to become conscious of which of our assumptions stem from our Christian commitment and which from our cultural conditioning. It is one of the aims of this volume to assist us in this process. Another aim is to provide tools that will better enable us to learn and to work productively in terms of the worldview of those to whom we are called.

Ten Reasons Why Christians Should Study Worldview

If we are serious about effectively evangelizing and discipling the peoples of the world, it is incumbent upon us to learn as much as possible about those people. Understanding what are the basic assumptions in terms of which they operate, then, must be high on our priority list. Following are ten reasons why I believe the study of worldview can be of help to us in this quest.

1. *A peoples' worldview includes the most basic assumptions, values and allegiances of that people.* This "deep level" of culture affects and underlies all surface level behavior. We might picture the surface of a lake on which appeared a colored liquid that didn't seem to come from anything visible on the surface. To deal with whatever was causing this surface-level phenomenon, we would want to check to see if there might be something under the water that was leaking the colored substance. So it is with cultural behavior—to discover why people behave in the ways they do, we must look beneath the surface to the things the people believe and assume. We have noted above the differences in western and many non-western concepts of life and of what to do about disease.

These deep-level assumptions (presuppositions, beliefs), values and allegiances (commitments, loyalties) are largely unconscious, having been learned from childhood as if they were the only possible assumptions. They are, therefore, simply assumed without proof.

2. *A people's basic perceptions and picturing of reality stem from their worldview*. We "see" (understand) and know in terms of our worldview. In the West, for example, we tend to picture the universe and most of what is in it as a machine that runs according to predictable rules and principles. Whether we think of the sun, moon and stars or of weather or of tides, this mechanical model seems to pervade. Our organizational and governmental structures are also expected to function as if they were machines. Western medicine has made great strides by working with our physical bodies as if they also are machines. Spinning off from this picture of reality are such things as our concern for being on time and doing things efficiently. For example, we schedule appointments with people as if both they and we were machines, without regard for the fact that the quality of personal relationships may be adversely affected by our time orientation. And, in the name of efficiency, our manufacturing companies often show little regard for the meaningfulness of what their workers do. They simply have their workers mass produce their products with little or no concern that their employees feel that what they do is meaningful.

Furthermore, our western worldview assumptions elevate material things over non-material, the physical over the spiritual, the visible over the invisible, science over religion, knowledge over experience, mind over emotion, for most, job over family. As we know, though, there are societies that choose the opposite on each of these issues.

For example, in place of our western mechanistic picturing of the universe, many societies see it as personal, capricious and not always predictable. Though it is likely that both picturings are valid but for different parts of the universe (e.g., mechanical for the material universe, personal for the spiritual), it is rare to find a society that has the two pictures balanced. With or without balance, though, it is these deep-level picturings of how things are or ought to be that provide the basis for surface-level behavior.

3. *All human interpretation is based on worldview assumptions*. Whenever we observe something, whether it is something merely standing there or something happening to us or to someone else, we automatically assign meaning and value to it. Such meanings and evaluations are both felt and reasoned. They are, however, done "reflexively," habitually and without thinking, on the basis of our worldview assumptions. These unproven assumptions underlie all of our thinking, feeling and evaluating, as well as our more overt behavior.

We even interpret scripture on the basis of our worldview assumptions. This means that biblical hermeneutics, the study of biblical interpretation, is a subtopic under the study of worldview. We are not, however, locked into the assumptions we learned as children. We can, with enough effort, learn new, hopefully more accurate assumptions and use them to replace inaccurate ones in our interpretations of the Bible. This is especially necessary since the Bible is a cross-cultural book. For example, it is important for us westerners in reading about the Samaritan woman (John 4) to suppress our natural tendency to interpret her as an immoral woman since in her society it would have been barrenness, not immorality, that would have caused her condition. Likewise, with the interpretation of David's sins in his affair with Bathsheba. Though our western tendency (based on western assumptions) is to see adultery as David's big sin, we need to recognize that the major problem, the one that Nathan pointed out, was misuse of power, with murder and adultery as "secondary" sins.

4. *People ordinarily follow their worldview habitually and unconsciously.* The worldview assumptions underlying our behavior are mostly quite unconscious to us, though we may become aware of certain of them (e.g., materialistic and/or naturalistic assumptions). We were taught these assumptions, values and commitments before we knew anything about alternate possibilities with which they could be compared. This meant that we accepted or, rather, imbibed what we were taught as absolute, the only right way.

Such unconscious acceptance as the only right way, then, led to the development of habits of assuming, thinking, feeling and behaving that felt natural to us and were without any competing concepts or behaviors. So we never had opportunity to choose between one concept or behavior and another. There was only one choice with regard to any given issue. So the habits got developed under the best possible circumstances for habit development and they became very strong. In fact, most of them became so strong that we would never change them even if at a later date we are presented with alternative assumptions that seem more reasonable than the ones we learned early in life.

5. *We must understand a people's worldview to understand them.* Though we can learn a lot about a people by observing their surface-level behavior, we will never know them deeply until we learn the deep-level assumptions and motivations behind their behavior. Without knowing such assumptions and motives, our tendency is to attribute to the people of another society the assumptions and motivations appropriate to the way we have been taught to behave as members of our own society. Thus, I had difficulty when I first arrived in northern Nigeria and noted that as we traveled along the road many of the men would raise their fists in the air.

In keeping with the assumptions of my society related to such a gesture, I interpreted their behavior as meaning anger toward us. I soon learned, however, that the assumption of their society, on which their behavior was based, was that such a gesture should be interpreted as a respectful greeting.

In order to properly understand the people to whom we go, we need to deal both with their worldview and with ours. It is important to learn as much as possible about each and to recognize the fact that we have two enormous problems to deal with: first, learning their assumptions and second, overcoming our assumptions in our relationships with them. Since, however, so much of what makes both their and our behavior intelligible lies at the deep worldview level, there is much understanding available to us if we study these basic assumptions and much misunderstanding in store if we don't. As outsiders, then, we need to learn how to discover their deep understandings and to compensate in our dealings with them for our own habits of interpretation.

6. It is important for us as Christians to understand our own worldview. As Christians we are just as much a part of our societies as are non-Christians. This means we are just as pervasively affected by culture and worldview, as are non-Christians. There is no escaping the influence of cultural patterning on our lives. Whatever we do, say or think is intimately related to the basic assumptions on the basis of which we behave.

As we grew up, we learned the patterns taught us by our parents and other significant others. In the process, we made these patterns ours, and the basis for our habitual behavior. If in the process we attempted to make changes in our basic assumptions and habits, for example, as a result of our conversion to Christ, we did so with those patterns and habits as the starting points. And for many, this process of change has been very difficult.

Change in worldview and the habits based on it is particularly difficult in areas where there is conflict between the assumptions, values and commitments of the society around us and those required by God. Discouragement is high, therefore, among Christians who have been promised that in Christ they will automatically become new creatures (2 Cor. 5:17) who then discover that attaining that newness involves intense struggle against deeply held basic assumptions and values and the habits based on them. The old assumptions and habits seem "natural" and right, the new ones a bit extreme and even the stuff of which fanaticism is made.

Yet, Christian growth toward maturity is eminently a matter of worldview change. And the more conscious we can be of the nature of what God expects and how to bring that about, the more actively we can participate with God in the process.

7. The basic cognitive underpinnings of Christianity are matters of worldview springing from our faith, not simply of surface-level religion. Jesus came to bring a faith, not simply another religion. Indeed, as I attempt to show later in this volume, I believe the word "religion" to be a very misleading term when applied to Christianity. Our relationship to God through Christ is intended to affect all of our behavior, not simply the religious part. For religion is a surface thing. When, then, it is simply our religious behavior that gets changed, we have missed the essence of what was intended by the One who said, "I have come in order that you might have life—life in all its fullness" (John 10:10).

The essence of Christianity is life lived as it was intended to be lived, in a personal faith-relationship with God through Jesus Christ, a relationship that starts with a new allegiance (to Jesus, not to a religious system) and is to be expressed in every area of the Christian's life. This truth and the other basic truths that spin off from it are to become worldview-level assumptions for Christians, yeast that is expected to leaven the whole of our lives. Any tendency to reduce such an all-encompassing approach to mere adherence to a system of doctrines and rituals (=religion) is a travesty. True Christianity involves the most basic of changes in worldview allegiances, values and assumptions springing from the deepest level of faith-commitment to Jesus Christ. The surface-level religious structures in terms of which this faith is expressed are to spring from this deep level faith-commitment.

8. We need to understand the relationships of Christianity to a person/group's worldview. Some Christians (e.g., Sire and Naugle to be dealt with in later chapters) are fond of referring to "a" or "*the* Christian worldview." What they are referring to are a set of specifically Christian understandings and perspectives that function within the broader thing that an anthropologist would label worldview. Though I would agree that most, if not all, of the commitments, beliefs and values they point to should be foundational to a Christian's experience, I contend that their concept of worldview is too limited. Their concept also tends to minimize the variety of worldview assumptions possible among committed Christians from different societies.

Our position, then, is that the cultural thing we call worldview is much broader than that selection of assumptions in focus when popular writers and lecturers speak of "Christian worldview." From our perspective, then, there is no such thing as a thoroughly Christian worldview, though there are thoroughly Christian people who live according to many different worldviews. That is, people can be Christian, structures cannot (see below). *There are, however, specifically Christian* **perspectives** *intended to be introduced into the worldview of every people.* These would include assumptions concerning who God is, who Jesus is, how we are to be related to God and Jesus, how we are to live our lives under their leading and the like. Each of these assumptions, then, is to be lived out in ways appropriate to the person's society. There are, however, a great many other worldview assumptions (e.g., concepts of time, space and categorization) in any given worldview that will remain essentially the same after a person's conversion with no need to be replaced by Christian assumptions.

So there definitely are Christian assumptions, values, commitments, perspectives, concepts and understandings that are intended to be introduced into the worldviews of the Christians of every people group. But there is no such thing as an all-encompassing Christian worldview structure that is intended to compete with the totality of a society's worldview with the aim of replacing it entirely.

9. Worldview understandings of cause/power and person/group are especially important for Christians to probe. Among the worldview concerns found in every society, those dealing with causality and person/group are the ones that tend to be challenged most by the assumptions endorsed in the scriptures. For example, it is typical of most of the societies of the world to concern themselves with appeasing evil spirit beings rather than with relating to the supreme God and depending on Him to protect us from the evil spirits (see chapter nine). For Christians in these societies, it is crucial that they adopt the latter perspective in place of their traditional practice. Christianity likewise challenges people's attitudes toward others, especially those of outgroups. It is usually in these areas that the most basic changes are required during Christian conversion and growth. Assumptions concerning time, space and categorization (the other universals we will deal with) are usually far less in need of change.

10. Worldviews can be changed but seldom (if ever) exchanged or replaced. Indeed, certain changes in worldview are required of us as we grow up. For example, children who doubt their mothers' explanation of where babies come from are expected to develop better understandings based on more accurate assumptions as they grow up. The experience of growing up brings many such expected changes in worldview. So do experiences such as study, exposure to people of other societies and any number of the more challenging aspects of life. Note, however, that it is parts (paradigms) of a worldview that get changed, not the whole worldview. This is also true when adults make worldview changes.

Though it is usually much easier to make changes in surface-level behavior than in worldview, those who interact with the world around them will make many deep-level changes and adjustments as well. They will, however, usually find it easier to make small changes than larger ones, to make changes in matters they consider peripheral than to make changes in more central issues and to make changes in assumptions that are less highly committed to than in those to which their commitment is high.

An important factor for cross-cultural witnesses to recognize is that it is extremely difficult for outsiders to influence change in highly valued assumptions, values and allegiances. Allegiances are particularly difficult to change, unless they are weak allegiances. When we approach people with an appeal for a commitment to Christ, we are challenging whatever allegiance they are already into. If, then, there is to be any change, they alone (not we) can make it. We can only witness to and recommend given options. Much depends, therefore, on our personal relationship with them and their trust in us.

Change of worldview is a person thing. Any "power" of culture (including worldview) is not in the patterns themselves but in the habits of those who follow them (see chapter two). So change in either surface culture or worldview is a matter of people changing their habits. A script does not change itself. If it is to be changed, it is the people who use it that make the changes. Since culture and worldview do not have life in and of themselves, they cannot change themselves. Like scripts, those who use them give life to the patterns they provide—usually by habitually following them, sometimes by altering the old patterns or by creating new ones.

One reason worldview patterns and the resultant habits are so difficult to change is that they were largely learned unconsciously. Before we learned of alternative possibilities for perceiving and relating to the world, we were led to believe that the way our elders taught us was the only proper way. And the principle seems to be that the less conscious we are of the conditioning, the stronger its grip on us.

Thus, for western Christians, a constant problem is the strength of the naturalistic conditioning we received early in life. As a result of that conditioning we learned to look at all of life as if God is not involved in any of it, with the possible exception of some of the things done on Sunday or an occasional miracle when He steps in to overrule some natural rule.

We learned such assumptions so early and so strongly and integrated them into our lives so thoroughly at a time when we were aware of no possible alternative perspectives that their ramifications and effects are extremely difficult to ferret out, even when we are strongly committed to doing so. It is common, therefore, to run into Christians who have made very little progress in the process of worldview transformation required of those who would conform themselves to the image of Jesus Christ.

Is There a Single Christian Worldview?

In concluding this chapter, it would be well to briefly state my position with regard to whether or not there is a single Christian worldview. We have indicated in several ways that the coming of Christianity is intended to bring about change at the deepest level of a people's cultural assumptions. A major concern of Christian growth is, therefore, the development of those assumptions and the automatic habitual behavior appropriate to them.

The worldview assumptions, however, are a part of the structuring necessary to support the personal activity of a Christian. *It is the person who is Christian, not the assumptions.* People can be Christians but not roads or scripts, each of which can, however, be produced in ways that enhance rather than detract from usage by Christians. This point may seem picky. But it has potentially great ramifications, especially for cross-cultural communication of Christianity. What I am saying is that in terms of the distinction made at the beginning of this chapter between the personal and the structural (Figure 1.2), it is only the personal side that could as a whole be labeled Christian. That is, there could be a Christian society (=people), but not a Christian culture (=structure).

On the structure side, we could point to both surface and deep-level structures that would support and enable Christian behavior. But it is primarily the *use* of those structures by people who follow Jesus, not merely the existence of the structures themselves, that would be Christian or non-Christian. And any of the structures that could be used by Christians for Christian purposes can also be used by non-Christians for deceptive or other non-Christian purposes. It would, therefore, be misleading to call such structures "Christian." Furthermore, the vast majority of cultural structures (including worldview) used by any society would be neutral rather than specifically Christian or non-Christian and, therefore, not needing to be changed when the people in that society become Christian.

Though I agree that certain structures and assumptions are more usable for Christian purposes than others, I do not believe there is a single Christian worldview. If there were, Christians of all societies would need to have a single approach both to things like moral values and to things like time, space and categorization in order to be considered Christian. There are those who speak of a Christian worldview (e.g., Sire 1997, 2004; Schaeffer 1976, Naugle 2002). They are not understanding, however, the all-encompassing nature of worldview in the anthropological sense. They are speaking of the influx of Christian assumptions, values and allegiances into a worldview as if that input constituted the whole worldview. This is far from the case.

I believe there are biblical principles—I like to call them Kingdom Principles—that we as Christians should incorporate into our own cultural behavior and to encourage our converts to introduce into their lives. But the totality of these principles is far less than any given worldview, though the effect of their introduction into the lives of the members of a society should "flavor" the culture as a whole. And, since God has shown Himself in the scriptures as desirous of working with people *within*, rather than *against* their culture (see Acts 15 and Gen. 12ff), we speak of the need for Christian worldview principles to be "inserted" into every culture rather than a "Christian worldview" that competes with cultural worldviews and would be designed to "bomb them out of the water."

Christian Africans, Christian Asians, Christian Europeans and the multitude of committed Christians from the other societies of the world simply do not see most things the same way, in spite of their commitment to Christ. The question is, should they? My answer is, no. There will be certain very important similarities brought about by the fact that all Christians from whatever society commit themselves to the same Lord and to most of the same assumptions (doctrines) supporting that commitment. But most of the differences in worldview, as in surface level cultural behavior, remain—unless, of course, in the process of becoming Christian, these people also change their culture (e.g., became westernized). This latter is not, however, a Christian requirement.

Jesus had a worldview (see Kraft 1989, ch. 9). It consisted of His "Kingdom Perspectives" integrated into His first century Jewish worldview. Our task is to follow His example by integrating those same perspectives into our cultural worldview. We are, then, to assume Christian assumptions and to live habitually by them, each within his/her own cultural context, just as Jesus did within His context.

Chapter 2

People, Worldview & Change

Anthropologists as well as non-professionals are often careless in the way they use the word "culture." Usually they (rightly) use the word to refer to cultural structures. But not infrequently they (inaccurately) use the word to refer to the *people* who live their lives according to a given set of cultural structures. Even professional anthropologists who should know better are fond of making statements such as, "Most of the world's cultures believe in a vast number of supernatural beings and powers." What they should have said is that, "Most of the world's *peoples*..." or, more technically, "Most of the world's *societies* believe in a vast number of supernatural beings and powers."

With regard to culture (including worldview), I consider it extremely important to distinguish between culture and people. People who speak of a culture as if it were a pseudo-personal entity that goes around doing things to people, have let themselves fall into a kind of cultural determinism that implies little or no room for human choice. For example, a statement such as, "Indian culture used to require people to burn widows," is very misleading, for it attributes to cultural structures the power to determine individual choices. The truth is that it was Indian *people*, in accordance with the cultural guidelines taught to them, who required people to practice this custom.

The "social penalty," (that is, a penalty imposed by *people*, not by culture) for not practicing the custom could be stiff. So most people, out of fear of the penalty, would follow the custom. But note that it is a penalty imposed by *people*, not by some impersonal entity called culture. And such a custom could be resisted by anyone with enough courage to choose to risk the social penalty by refusing to go along with the custom. Though the custom is ordinarily followed and the penalty for not following it is harsh, persons could choose to not follow it.

For culture is not a person. It does not *do* anything. Only people do things. The fact that people ordinarily do what they do by following the cultural "tracks" laid down for them should not lead us to treat culture itself as something possessing a life of its own (that is, able to do things on its own).

The Person Factor

As we study the cultural structuring called worldview, therefore, we dare not ignore or minimize what I will call "the person factor." Culture, including worldview, is not a being; it is a structure, a complex of patterns. Culture is like the roads we drive on or the script an actor uses—there to be used for whatever purpose the user chooses. The roads don't do anything, nor does an actor's script, they simply lie there where they were produced, waiting for people to make whatever use they care to of them.

We may say, in a shorthand kind of way, "That road goes to San Francisco." But the fact is the road *doesn't* go to SF. It actually goes nowhere. It just sits there while *people* use it to go to SF or to somewhere else. Or they go to SF some other way, either because the usual way is blocked or simply because they choose to do things differently for a change.

Statements such as, "Most of the world's cultures believe in supernatural beings..." or "Indian culture used to require people to burn widows" are equivalent to saying, "That road goes to SF," or "The rain kept her from going shopping." But in reality it was not a road going or the rain preventing the lady from shopping. It was, rather, people making choices that brought about the effects. This should be clear from the fact that people can get to SF by means other than the road or that many people are not kept from shopping because of rain.

We may not consider the distinction I am making to be very important, but such imprecision in the way we use the term "culture" can be misleading and unconsciously influence the way we think about the ability of persons to assert themselves. It can lead us to assume that culture determines much of life and thus discourage us from even trying to get people to change their beliefs and/or behavior.

Culture is like a complex of roads. Like roads, it just sits there while people make use of it to get places in life. The people who use a given set of cultural structures make choices concerning which of the cultural roads to follow to get to any given place. Most of the time they will follow their habits, usually the things they have been taught, to do routine things and to get to familiar places. But from time to time they will choose to be creative, to alter their habitual pattern, and to do something in a different way than they've done it before. I regularly drive a certain route to and from my office. But every once in awhile, either because I have to do an errand or just because I want to vary my practice, I choose against my habit and take a different route.

To return to our other picture, culture (including worldview) is like the script an actor uses to prepare for a performance. The actor memorizes the script very much like we memorize our cultural patterns as children. The major differences lie in the fact that culture is much more complex than any script and that the actor is much more conscious of the memorizing process than we are as children as we learn our cultural script.

When acting, the actor follows the script most of the time, but not always. He or she will change the script from time to time for a variety of reasons. We, like the actor, will also make changes in our use of cultural structures during our lifetime. Either actors will forget, or other actors will forget their parts and they will have to adjust, or they will use their creativity to attempt to improve on the author's plan. Or something else unexpected will happen (e.g., someone misses a cue, a part of the set falls down). For whatever reason, the actor creates a different way rather than following by habit the script he/she has learned.

In life, people are always creating new ways to do things, either because they forgot "their lines," or because something new occurred (i.e., something not anticipated by those from whom they learned the cultural behavior), or because somebody else goofed, or because they thought up what they feel to be a better approach or, not infrequently, because they never learned the socially acceptable behavior in the first place. All of these types of things happen to people in everyday life, forcing or tempting them to improvise and to follow a different script or road.

Most of this book will focus on the script or road we call worldview. In this chapter, though, we will focus on the actor.

Self and Other

When Robert Redfield first defined and suggested the importance of worldview (1953; see also Appendix A), he theorized how worldview originated in people's minds. He suggested that people started with what he called "Self" and looked out on what he called "Not-self," renamed by Kearney "Other." The perception of Other, then, he labeled "world view" (two words). I am in essential agreement with Redfield that this is how worldviews are developed.

As this Self observes the Other, that Self structures his/her perceptions of Other. The resulting structuring, then, we call worldview. The Self I call "Person." Though most of our attention in this text will be devoted to the characteristics and structuring of what the person sees, this chapter focuses on the very interesting person who does the seeing.

It is this Self or person that is in view here. We may validly ask, what is that person's reaction to the "Other" he/she is observing? And is this a learned reaction? If so, how was it learned? Is this person's reaction the same as that of others of his/her group? If so, how did it get to be that way? And is the reaction an objective one or is our person biased in some way? If so, what are the biases and where did they come from?

First of all, persons tend to see things as others in their groups see them. So when we speak of persons looking out at "Other," we are speaking of persons in groups, not simply of disconnected individuals. Though persons generate many individual perceptions that differ from those of their group, they ordinarily perceive in ways remarkably like the perceptions of the others in their group. Worldview, then, is a group thing, produced by people in concert with others as they look out at Reality.

So, when referring to the viewer, I prefer to use the term "Person/Group" instead of the too individualistic term Self. With regard to Other, then, we recognize that that term is divisible into several categories. For one thing, Self can observe Self. So the subject Self can view the object Self. In my terms, a Person or Group can observe self or other Person/Group. This Person/Group can also, however, perceive each of the other things we term "Universals." These were listed in chapter one, along with Person/Group, as Classification/Categorization, Causality, Time/Event, Space/Material and Relationship.

Learning a Worldview

Worldview is learned along with the rest of one's language and culture. And most of our learning of worldview is subconscious. Learning theorists inform us that most of what we will live with is taken in during our first six years. And there is quite a bit of evidence that much learning takes place even before birth.

Starting in the womb and continuing, mostly unconsciously, throughout our early childhood we "choose" our parents' worldview. The use of the word "choose" to label the beginning of this process may seem strange, since we begin it quite unconsciously and without any alternative choice except, perhaps, to eventually reject some parts of our parents' perspective. But I will state it this way in lieu of a better way and also contend that many of our other choices throughout life are equally subconscious. This choice, or series of choices leading to the formation of our worldview, starts in the womb and continues throughout life, becoming more conscious as we get older.

We may picture the initial process by using a computer analogy, saying that we as babies are getting "formatted" or "initialized" or, rather, that we are formatting ourselves. This process would seem to involve the developing of enough experience on the part of the child to enable him or her by analogy to interpret later experiences. As the child grows, of course, verbal instruction becomes important, but probably never as important as subconscious and sub-verbal learning.

What we are taught is what our parents' generation regards as most valuable. The fact that most of this learning is subconscious and without significant alternate possibilities is, I think, very important. For the concepts, attitudes, values, assumptions and approaches to life we learn subconsciously at a very young age are probably the things we most deeply imbibe and are, therefore, the most difficult to change.

I have mentioned that certain changes in worldview assumptions are expected as we grow up. Our early childish theories concerning why things are the way they are get replaced by more mature understandings or we pay a high social price. Whether we're talking about Santa Claus or Easter Bunny or where babies come from, changes in worldview assumptions are expected as we mature.

Changes in worldview happen between generations whenever there is a problem in the transmission of worldview assumptions from elders to children. These transmission problems are the result of factors such as the following:

- The people of one generation are never completely successful in passing on their insights and values to the following generation,
- The young learners of the next generation are never completely successful in learning what they are taught,
- Learners make mistakes in the learning process (as do teachers).

In addition, people make changes in their assumptions when they discover that their circumstances are sufficiently different from that of their parents that the perspectives and strategies they learned from their parents don't work. In such cases, people have to create new perspectives and approaches, changing both surface-level behavior and, though usually to a lesser extent, worldview. See chapter 5 and chapters 14-19 for more on worldview change.

What Are We Taught to See?

We have noted that it is through the process of being taught our culture, and especially the worldview of our culture, that we are trained to see as the other members of our society see. Our question here concerns what we are taught to see. I want to make four points in this regard.

1. *We are taught to interpret in culturally approved ways and rewarded when we conform.* Though a certain number of people choose to be non-conformists, most people go along with the tide. In secular western society, those who get excited about religion tend to fall into the non-conformist category and pay a social penalty for it. Artistic people also pay a penalty because they tend not to conform to our society's focus on rational, mechanical, and scientific ("left brain") pursuits.

2. *We are taught to see selectively.* There are certain things in focus in any given society and certain things that are out of focus. Material, economic, and political things tend to be very much in focus for westerners. The existence and influence of spiritual beings, however, is an aspect of REALITY that most Anglo-Americans learn to ignore or deny. Until recently, the destructive influence of industrial pollutants on the atmosphere was also ignored, as was the fact that the high mobility and urban sprawl required of the American workforce is destructive to family life. An aspect of our life that is still largely blurred is the fact that contemporary schooling usually trains the mind without teaching us how to live. Thus we tend to produce adults who may know how to think but often don't know how to live.

3. *We unconsciously accept things that confirm what we've been taught.* In considering how to relate to new experience or information, we almost always accept those things that confirm what we have been taught (i.e., are compatible with our formatting). We usually reject (at least, at first) most or all of any position that would raise questions about our present perspective. Because the perspective we have been taught is usually naturalistic, even many committed and spiritually minded Christians reject contemporary miracles, though they usually strongly contend that the biblical accounts of miracles are factual. To hold this view, they have developed the theory (often unconsciously) that God has changed his method of operation since the first couple of centuries of the church. Since they have not experienced miraculous things, they assume that God must work differently today than he did in biblical times.

4. *As pointed out by Paul, we see REALITY only dimly and partially* (1 Cor. 13:12), that is, we see through "lenses" or "filters." The following diagram attempts to portray some of these lenses and to label them. Note that the number of influences (indicated by the number of arrows), lessens as we go from one side of the chart to the other. There are, for example, a much greater number of things that happen than there are things we are taught to believe possible. What we eventually focus on when we analyze and construct our view of reality, then, comes from much less than what we believe or have experienced.

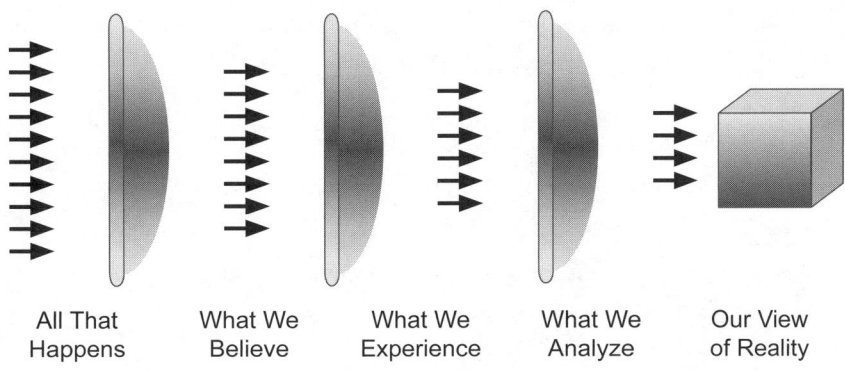

Figure 2.1. Components That Go to Make Up Our View of Reality

People Things

People are complex. We seem to need structure, both in behavior and in assumptions. Our minds seem to both require this structuring and to consistently impose it on our perceptions of life around us, and our part in it. An important part of that structuring seems to result from *focus*. We seem to need to be able to sort out the variety of things that come into our experience and to focus on certain of them to the exclusion of others. For example, we will note that most non-western peoples tend to focus on spirits as the cause of many things in human life, while westerners focus on "natural" (as opposed to supernatural) causation.

Both the *structuring* of perceptions and the *choice of focus* are matters of worldview. As persons we unconsciously choose our parents structuring and focus and then choose to work largely within the limitations of that structuring and focus. We "habituate" the structure and focus and largely live by those habitual ways of perceiving.

Though we will concern ourselves with the important place of habit (see below) in the way people operate in relation to worldview, habit is not the whole story. If it were, there would be no change as we grow older and are exposed to alternative possibilities. As it is, we can choose change as we grow up, creating thereby worldview patterns and focuses slightly or greatly different from those of our parents.

People are often seen as consisting of bodies plus four non-material facets: spirit, mind, emotions and will. As people

- We are physical beings, living in physical bodies,
- We are spiritual beings, relating to God and others with our spirits,
- We are cognitive beings, thinking and reasoning with our minds,
- We are affective beings, feeling with our emotions and
- We are volitional beings, choosing with our wills.

Worldview is a cognitive thing. We structure our perceptions cognitively. Then we express ourselves cognitively in different ways, depending on the worldview assumptions we have concerning cognitive activity. Three primary "cognitive styles" have been identified: concrete-relational, conceptual and intuitive in an excellent treatment by David Hesselgrave (1978:199-234).

1. In the West, we assume a "conceptual" way of thinking and reasoning. We assume that our thoughts are to be lined up in linear fashion (as I am trying to do here) that we call a "logical order," building toward a conclusion that can be expressed as a generalization derived from the points made. We focus on what we call logic, often unaware that there may be other logics. And we generalize with the assumption that if people know the general concept, they can apply it specifically in their own lives. Western schooling has moved many non-westerners into this style of thinking.

2. Most of the non-western world (and, I believe, many in the West), however, think, reason and argue differently. Probably what Hesselgrave calls "concrete-relational" thinking is the most frequently occurring type. The object here is to create a picture of reality with the relational dimensions of that reality in focus. The biblical books of Hebrews and James are good illustrations of this way of thinking. Hesselgrave says:

> In verbal communication, the concrete relational thinker tends to express, inform and persuade by referring to symbols, stories, events, objects and so forth, rather than to general propositions and principles. But he is especially prone to rely on non-verbal communication of all types—gesture and sign language, music and the plastic arts, ritual and drama, and image projection (1978:223).

3. The third cognitive style is what we may call "intuitive." This style depends on direct insight, not reason. A person will depend on creative flashes of insight to gain understanding. The peoples of the Indian subcontinent are noted for this kind of thinking.

Each of these cognitive styles is justified in people's thinking by their worldview assumptions. But our emotions are also involved in our approach to worldview. We have feelings, often deep feelings, about our way of thinking and the worldview structuring that underlies it. We value our way of looking at and thinking about things and usually develop a high commitment to it. We thus continue to choose to perceive in our habitual ways and defend these perceptions as the right ones.

In addition to *having* feelings about our worldviews, we also structure our feelings or, at least, our ways of feeling according to our worldview. Nordic peoples and Japanese, for example, are noted for not showing their emotions while Italians and Africans are noted for just the opposite. At the worldview level, these peoples believe their way of expressing (or not expressing) emotion is the right way. At the behavior level, then, they have developed habits of showing or not showing emotion according to what they believe is right.

We also govern the ways in which we use our wills to make choices and commitments according to our worldview structuring. Some make major choices only after they have taken time to reason out all the alternatives they can think of. Others make them quickly on the basis of intuition alone. Either way, there is a correspondence to deep-level worldview assumptions.

The way in which the spirit part of us functions is a bit more difficult to pinpoint. This is the part that connects us with God and, I believe, with other people. How and why we do such connecting is, however, also structured by worldview assumptions underlying our convictions concerning how we, God and others ought to relate.

In addition, a large number of other people factors such as **motivation, preferences, evaluation** and others relate to the continuance or change of worldview perspectives. Suffice it to say, though, that whatever the relationships may be, it is *people* who are active in relation to worldview while worldview itself, being structural, is passive, though providing parameters within which people usually function.

The Personal and the Cultural

In chapter one we showed two diagrams designed to show four distinctions in the relationship between people and culture, including worldview. We distinguished between surface and deep cultural structuring and between people and culture/worldview. In the chapters that follow, we will go into more detail concerning the worldview part of that structuring. Now, though, we will look at the personal side of the chart.

Before we turn to a discussion of the unshaded part of the following chart, note that overall it is intended to point out two kinds of phenomena:

1. The differences between what people do and the cultural structuring in terms of which they ordinarily do it and

2. The close relationship between what people do and the cultural structures they have learned. Note that the labels on the personal (left) side of the chart are mostly verbs while those on the culture people who are active, not the structures in terms of which they act. The structures, like an actor's script, are, however, very important to a people's activity since the "lines" are carefully learned and provide the limits within which people ordinarily function.

	PERSONAL BEHAVING	CULTURAL STRUCTURING

S U R F A C E	**BEHAVING**
	
	Habitual Behaving
	    Overt (Doing, Speaking,
	        Emoting)
	    Covert (Thinking, Feeling)
	
	Creative Behaving
	    Overt (Doing, Speaking,
	        Emoting)
	    Covert (Thinking, Feeling)
		PATTERNS OF BEHAVIOR
		
		Overt Customs that Pattern Doing, Speaking, Emoting, etc.
		
		Covert Customs that Pattern Thinking, Feeling, etc.

D E E P	**ASSUMING**
	(Usually Habitual, Often Creative)
	
	PRIMARY-LEVEL ASSUMING
	    Willing (Choosing)
	    Emoting
	    Reasoning
	    Assuming Motivations
	    Assuming Predispositions
	
	ASSIGNING MEANING
	    Interpreting
	    Evaluating
	
	RESPONDING TO ASSIGNED MEANINGS
	    Explaining
	    Committing/Pledging Allegiance
	    Relating
	    Adapting
	    Seeking Psychological Reinforcement
	    Striving Toward Integration/ Consistency
		PATTERNS OF WV ASSUMPTIONS
		
		PATTERNS UNDERLYING PRIMARY BEHAVIOR
		    Willing (Choosing)
		    Emoting
		    Reasoning
		    Deciding Motivation
		    Being Predisposed
		
		PATTERNS OF MEANING ASSIGNMENT
		    Ways of Interpreting
		    Ways of Evaluating/Validating
		
		PATTERNS OF RESPONSE TO MEANING
		    Ways of Explaining
		    Ways of Committing/Pledging Allegiance
		    Ways of Relating
		    Ways of Adapting
		    Ways of Getting Psychological Reinforcement
		    Ways of Integrating/Attaining Consistency

Figure 2.2. The Personal and the Cultural

We may think of cultural structuring as providing an endless number of customs, each, like roads, with boundaries on either side. The activity of driving (that is, living) is ordinarily done by people within the boundaries of those roads (the customs), but not always. Sometimes people drive off the roads, whether by ignorance, by mistake or because they want to do something different. In so doing, they exercise their creativity (even when they make mistakes). When they drive on the roads, they are demonstrating the habitual nature of most cultural behavior.

Though anthropologists have tended to spend most of their time discussing the structural side of cultural behavior, *it is the personal activity that is the most interesting*. The fact that we learn cultural patterns at an early age and seldom deviate from them is well established. The habits, mostly unconscious, that keep us following the cultural patterns and the choices we make, both consciously and unconsciously, when we deviate from those patterns are, however, at least as important to study as the relatively static patterns themselves.

Note the close relationship between each of the patterns on the right side of the chart and the activities of persons (implemented by habit) listed on the left. At the deep level, note that people ordinarily conduct activities such as willing (choosing), emoting, "habiting," interpreting, evaluating, explaining, adapting and the like according to the patterns for willing (choosing), emoting, etc. listed on the right side of the chart.

Looking now at the unshaded quadrant of the chart, note that the whole quadrant is labeled "Assuming." *The basic activity of people at the worldview level is to assume.* As pointed out on the chart, such personal activities are ordinarily engaged in habitually and in accordance with the customs of the society. On occasion, though, we creatively choose a different option than the one ordinarily practiced by the members of our society or we interpret or explain or emote or adapt differently (creatively). Such creative responses, then, result in individual changes in cultural behavior and, if they are imitated by others, can result in changes of the cultural patterning for larger or smaller groups within the society.

Worldview and Habit

Cultural (including worldview) patterns, then, do not force people to follow them. It is *force of habit* that keeps us following custom. The "power" that keeps people following their cultural script most of the time is the power of habit, not any ability that culture possesses in and of itself to empower. Though culture and worldview often seem bigger than all of us and to "have a life of their own," that life and empowerment do not exist within culture but within human beings who function largely by force of habit. We are creatures of habit. We do things in certain ways not simply because significant others taught us to do them that way, but because we have gotten into the habit of doing them that way. We internalized the patterns and developed habits to keep us within the guidelines.

Worldview structuring provides the patterns that those who are significant in our lives teach and model for us. Most of these patterns, then, we adopt and "habituate" quite unconsciously, with or without modification. Some of what is modeled or explained we eventually reject. Not much of what we learn in our early years is rejected, however. It is largely assimilated at the unconscious level and practiced automatically without our being conscious of the presence of the patterns and habits that keep us following the cultural tracks. For that reason we ordinarily follow the patterns of our culture, but not always.

As we have stated, culture/worldview is like an actor's script or the roads on which we drive. We habitually drive on the road, but we sometimes deviate from our course. I was riding with a driver in France once who developed a creative alternative to staying on the road by driving on the sidewalk for several hundred yards to skirt a traffic jam! It was a bit frightening, and I expected a policeman to arrive at any time to enforce the "drive only on the road" rule. But our driver got away with it.

The same is true of the cultural roads that are laid out for us. We, like the French driver, ordinarily follow them, but not always. Sometimes we change our behavior. We may choose on occasion or permanently to eat with our left hand or to dress in a way considered strange by our group or to regularly eat food considered "foreign" by our subgroup. And even a habit can be changed with some effort. If the change is considered serious, however, others in the society will exert great pressure on us to get us to conform. If the deviation is not considered serious, little or no social pressure may be exerted to get us back in line. And we will pay little or no social penalty for such changes. When I decided to deviate from my lifelong practice of shaving and to grow a beard and mustache, little pressure was exerted on me (except by my wife) to return to the usual custom of my peer group. The change was considered important enough for me to pay a slight social penalty but not a large one. And, since I myself did not like the change, I soon reverted to my previous habit of shaving.

Driving on the sidewalk is, however, considered a large and unacceptable deviation, both in France and in America. Should I (or the French driver) adopt that creative alternative as a regular practice, it would only be a matter of time before we found ourselves in trouble with the police. For it is their job to keep people from those kinds of alternate cultural behavior considered dangerous by the society. Police pressure to conform is one of the highest forms of social pressure in western societies; a form only resorted to in extreme cases.

One of the most pressing reasons for changing our habitual behavior, and the worldview assumptions that underlie it, is when we find ourselves living in another society, surrounded by a world of people who have learned worldview and cultural patterns different from ours. Learning their habitual perspectives and customs is a big problem, but it is only part of the difficulty. The greatest problem is learning to counter our own habits of perceiving, acting and reacting.

For example, while living in northern Nigeria, I learned that it is insulting for an adult to receive something from another person if it is offered with the left hand. This is the "road" or "script" they customarily follow in such situations, so I had to learn to follow it while living in that part of the world. In fact, I learned that pattern so well that I have often found myself practicing the Nigerian custom in America where it is not required! Fortunately, there is no penalty I have to pay for this slight deviation, since it breaks no American cultural rule, though it may seem strange to anyone who observes me moving something from one hand to the other before giving it to someone.

Worldview, People and Cultural Change

For solid change to happen throughout a culture, people must make basic changes in the worldview of that culture. Just as a tree can only grow as well as the roots allow it to, so a culture and the society that lives by that culture can only function as well as their "worldview-habits" allow them to. But change in worldview-habits, though basic, needs to be accompanied by a change in behavior if the process is to be complete. Changes in both the cultural structuring of basic assumptions and in the personal living out of those assumptions need to take place. But these changes do not always need to take place in the same order.

A people's ability to function well depends both on the solidness of the worldview assumptions on which they base their lives and on their willingness to carry out the activities indicated by those assumptions. But in some cases the understanding will change first, followed by the behavior, in others the behavior will be changed, followed by the assumptions to undergird the behavior. It is a sad but common thing, however, for people to change their assumptions without changing their behavior to match.

Jesus knew this. When He wanted to get across important points, He aimed both at worldview and at consistency between belief and behavior. He sought to change both paradigm and practice. And He knew what our memory experts are just finding out (see Schacter 1996) that it is pictures and stories rather than words alone that enable people to really connect with and remember the message.

So, when someone asked, "Who is my neighbor?" he told them a story. He then asked, not the expected question, "Who was the neighbor?" This would have been a simple question about their worldview assumptions. Instead, he asked *who was being neighborly*, a more important question designed to challenge both their worldview and their behavior. He was leading them implicitly to reconsider and, hopefully, change a basic value down deep in their system and explicitly to change their behavior to match the worldview change. He wanted them to move first *to*, then *through* a paradigm shift into a practice shift, the practice of being neighborly, not just believing they should treat outcasts as neighbors. He said,

> You have heard that it was said, "Love your friends, hate your enemies." But now I tell you: love your enemies and pray for those who persecute you. ... If anyone slaps you on the right cheek, let him slap your left cheek too" (Matt. 5:43, 44, 39).

Paul and Philemon discussed a runaway slave. Philemon had become a Christian but was also a slave owner. His assumptions concerning what was proper treatment for a runaway slave were one thing. His assumptions concerning how to treat a fellow Christian were quite another thing. Paul challenged the one set of assumptions by asking Philemon to accept his slave back, but to recognize that now he is a Christian. Poor Philemon had to figure out on what basis he could accept back a runaway slave who was now a Christian. Could he treat a blatantly disobedient slave as a brother? Not without a radical change in both perspective and practice. Paul was pressuring Philemon in the direction of a worldview change issuing in an immediate change in behavior.

This is again planting the seeds for change at the deep worldview level but also requiring a change of practice. But suppose someone makes this one change at both worldview and behavior levels but does not make changes in related areas of assumption and practice. Suppose, for example, that a given group of people start loving and praying for their enemies but continue to look down on them, regarding them (as they did previously) as inferior to themselves and in the same class of people as those who are racially and/or culturally different whom they also look down on. If a person makes the one change but not the others, that person's worldview assumptions are no longer integrated and the foundations of his/her life become unbalanced.

To move to an actual example, I have interacted with several missionaries to Africa who, as best they can, love Africans. And they certainly pray much for them. But they have never gotten over their worldview assumption that Africans are inferior and bordering on subhuman. Indeed, from the way some of these people act and talk, I conclude that down deep in their subconscious they both hate Africans and resent the fact that they feel God has called them to serve in Africa. It looks as though these missionaries have changed certain assumptions but not changed others. Their behavior, then, comes across as very inconsistent and their assumptions unbalanced.

When people begin to change deep-level assumptions, it frequently throws things off balance. And any disequilibrium or unbalance at the center of one's cultural structuring tends to cause difficulty through the rest of that structuring. Such disequilibrium may follow on from any number of worldview changes that are not properly integrated, even if chosen voluntarily, as with those discussed above.

Something very bothersome to us is the fact that the introduction of Christianity has often resulted in unforeseen negative consequences, because it has threatened people at the deepest worldview level. It is a disturbing fact of life that even well meaning cross-cultural witnesses for Christ can introduce apparently good changes that turn out to be culturally as well as spiritually damaging. The enormous damage (both cultural and spiritual) that has been done through the influence of western schools introduced and run by missions in Africa and other non-western areas is a case in point. Though there are positive things learned in these schools, the African children, like western children, learn to assume that most of what they need to learn comes from teachers and books, rather than from parents and traditional leaders. Since African traditional education is based largely on learning from parents, western schools provide a direct challenge to that system, a challenge that few African families can successfully combat.

The children are put in school before they have finished learning from parents. This interrupts their traditional educational system, replacing it with a system based on different assumptions but not completely indoctrinating them into western cultural assumptions, especially in areas such as morality. So parental authority and their traditional standards for much of life are questioned or even refuted and they are left with confusion as to how they should behave except in the limited knowledge-oriented activities they have been taught in school. At both worldview and behavior levels, they are completely off balance. As one Nigerian put it, "We are like the fruit bat, neither bird nor animal."

By way of concrete illustration, note the effect of mission-founded boarding schools for Africans. The moral behavior of large numbers of the students in such schools provides a startling illustration of the results of the kind of disequilibrium brought by Christian missions. The essence of the problem lies in the challenge mounted by the new system to the traditional social control mechanisms. The introduction of Christianity within a western cultural package brings with it the assumptions underlying western social control mechanisms that contrast markedly with those of the worldview of the receiving peoples. Among these is the assumption that by the time children enter school, their consciences will have been trained in such a way that they are able to maintain high moral standards on their own, even when boys and girls are in constant unsupervised contact with each other throughout adolescence.

Traditionally, however, the young people's consciences were usually not so trained. Indeed, their training tended to be based on the assumption that premarital sexual morality is to be protected by the families of the girls, not by individual conscience. Furthermore, their cultural expectation (including that of the girls themselves) was that girls would be married and start bearing children soon after puberty, not that marriage, sexual activity and child bearing would be delayed by schooling. With the protective influence of family absent in the school setting, then, and the expectation that sexual activity would happen among adolescents whenever there was opportunity, the boarding schools and Christian youth in general become known for the prevalence of sexual activity and, unfortunately, for the frequent practice of abortions for the girls.

John Messenger (1959) documents such breakdown of morality as a result of these kinds of challenges to the basic assumptions of the Anang Ibibio, a tribal group living in southern Nigeria. Among other things, he points to the fact that the Christian God is presented as much less demanding and, therefore, less inclined to punish them than the Ibibio traditional god. Reportedly, then, they were attracted to the Christian God because He allowed them to do whatever they wanted to do with the only condition being that they repent afterwards. On the basis of this perception, the Ibibio Christians felt little compulsion to behave morally, since God would always forgive them. They thus gained for the Christian community a reputation for flagrant immorality. Given such results of Christian missions (and there are many situations like this), we can understand that there are at least a few valid reasons (among the invalid ones) for certain anthropologists to be critical of missionary work.

Such disequilibrium as that described above may be analyzed as stemming from challenges to worldview assumptions resulting in changes flowing from the assumptions to surface-level behavior. There are, however, unbalancing influences that seem to flow the other way as well, from changes in behavior to changes in worldview. One type of such an unbalancing influence comes about when non-western peoples feel coerced by such things as conditions of employment to change their marriage pattern. It is common, for example, for missionaries to Africa to require those in their employ as well as church members to be monogamous. When such changes in surface-level behavior are mandated as conditions of church membership and/or employment, the people often draw their own conclusions concerning why this is required. Such conclusions commonly result in one set of assumptions underlying their behavior in relation to the missionaries while the traditional assumptions continue to exist in their worldview. A disturbing amount of worldview confusion can result.

The requirement that Nigerian Christians (including mission employees) reject polygamy and become monogamous led even Christians to certain undesirable worldview assumptions concerning the Christian God. Among the assumptions I have heard are: God is against the real leaders of our society (since they are expected to have more than one wife), God is not in favor of women having help and companionship around the home, God wants men to be enslaved to a single wife (like whites seem to be), God favors divorce (since this is how polygamists are expected to get rid of their "extra" wives), God favors social irresponsibility and even prostitution. None of these conclusions is irrational or far-fetched from their point of view. Unfortunately, worldview change like this, mandated by those in power without their sympathetic understanding of the custom, frequently results from this kind of forced change in a surface-level custom.

Similarly, people who in the name of Christianity change from indigenous medicine to western medicine often come to assume that God condemns their medicine and endorses western medicine. And, if they get deeply enough into secularized medicine, they may even conclude (with most western medical personnel, including many Christians) that God is irrelevant to the healing process, since the medicine works either with or without reference to God.

People who in becoming Christian change from task-centered work (i.e., work to accomplish a task, followed by leisure) to working every day simply for the sake of working, often come to assume that God does not value their family and communal interactions and rituals, since these can no longer be maintained in the face of a daily work schedule. They will often assume that God wants them to be more oriented to money than to personal (family/clan) relationships. In addition, changing from traditional or traditional types of religious rituals to western rituals often leads to worldview assumptions that regard western rituals as more powerful in a magical way than their own. And so on.

We will deal with worldview change in greater detail toward the end of the book. Suffice it to say here that cross-cultural witnesses would do well to learn as much as possible about this whole area.

The Social Price of Change

Among the most important habitual assumptions we develop are those that push us to seek intimacy and recognition in social relationships. There seems to be a deep personal need for attention, preferably accompanied by acceptance and approval by the significant others in our lives. And we soon develop habits that conform our behavior to seeking such approval. As we note when observing children, the need for acceptance and approval from their parents are among their highest priorities.

The deeply ingrained felt need for such social approval stays with us throughout life, often keeping us from launching out into areas that we know or suspect will be socially disapproved by those with whom we want to continue a relationship. In my own life, even as an adult in my fifties, with great job security in an evangelical institution and a measure of prestige, I found it frightening to consider opening myself up to assumptions I had been taught to believe were charismatic, not evangelical. I did not consider Charismatics, "my kind of people" and reasoned that if I moved in this direction, I would probably be labeled "one of them" and, therefore, lose the approval of many of my non-charismatic, evangelical associates. "What would people say if they thought I had become charismatic?" I asked myself. "Will the people I consider 'my people' still respect me? Or would they say I had 'gone off the deep end?' Or worse yet, would they feel that I had joined the enemy?"

These were my thoughts as in 1982 I reached out to Charismatics to seek answers to some of the questions my evangelical perspective was not providing concerning the presence, power and continuing miraculous activity of God. To some extent, now that I have made the change, I am paying a social price, though not as great as I feared. There are certain places I am not invited to any more and certain people who now hold me at arm's length. They would like me to "come to my senses" (as Jesus' family wanted Him to—see Mark 3:31-32) and return to my previous belief and behavior. I have felt this change to be so valuable, however, that I refuse to revert in spite of the social cost.

Social approval is ordinarily conditioned on a person's behaving in ways that show a high degree of conformity to the cultural patterns and perspectives followed by his or her significant others. Social "enticements" are exerted to reward conformity and greater or lesser pressure is exerted to prevent deviance. These enticements and pressures, then, have a powerful effect on habit development and maintenance. For instance, those whose viewpoints differ widely from the majority in American society—rebels, communists, certain artists and members of certain religious groups—are likely to pay a social penalty except with those within their own select groups. They may be treated as "different," strange, or weird. That is, they are "marginalized" by society in an attempt to get them to conform.

Note, for example, the strength of social pressure in American society concerning church membership. This pressure is based on such worldview assumptions as that religion is fairly irrelevant to human life and that if we must be religious, we shouldn't get excited about it, we should keep it private. The first line of pressure, exerted by the "normal" people of our society is to not belong to a church at all. If one must belong to a church, however, the pressure is very strong in favor of those churches whose patterns of behavior are most like that of the non-Christian society around them. Society, even church society, exerts pressure for people to belong to certain "respectable" denominations—Presbyterian, Episcopal, Methodist, even certain Baptist groups. In this way it exerts pressure to keep even dedicated Christians from doing anything defined by the society at large as "weird."

Christian groups such as Pentecostals or Charismatics are, of course, considered by society to be "weird." Note that nearly every reference to these groups by the news media and especially in movies is negative and/or sarcastic. If members of these groups do not submit to the social pressure to conform exerted by those around them, often including family members, they are ignored and pushed to the margins of society. So they produce their own "ghetto," made up totally of their own kind of people in order to survive. But many within such ghettos live with a good bit of psychological uneasiness in the knowledge that they don't count in mainstream society. And many either leave the ghetto or seek to conform their church practices to those considered more socially respectable. There are now, for example, many Pentecostal congregations that have, under the influence of such social pressure, come to behave and worship very much like non-Pentecostals. As one member of such a Pentecostal church put it, "we might as well be Presbyterians!"

In a society like America, we learn from birth to view the universe naturalistically, to think rationally and follow the other patterns of our society's secular worldview until they have the force of habit. We habitually interpret and respond to all of life from these standpoints and find that our commitment to them runs very deep. This commitment makes it quite difficult to change certain worldview patterns. If we break out of such habits enough to commit ourselves to Christ, we stand in tension with a certain amount of the deistic view of life built into our western worldview. Given the tension and the challenge of altering habits, we often change much less than we ought.

The hopeful factor is our creativity. In spite of the depth and strength of our habits, we can change our perspectives and the behavior that accompanies them. Though we may not change to the extent of exchanging our original worldview for another, people have demonstrated over and over their ability to create major changes even at the deepest levels of worldview. The depths of Christian conversion are a case in point. Though, as noted, the changes may be less than they ought to be, or than we hoped they would be, for many they are radical, pervasive, affecting just about every area of belief and behavior. This is especially true for those brought up in secularism or one of the many other radically antichristian views of life.

Contrary to the opinions of behavioristic psychologists such as B.F. Skinner who claim that there is no such thing as free will, there is always some "room to wiggle;" some room, however small, for choice. Even if human behavior is 90 percent habitual, it is still 10 percent creative. Or if it is 95 percent habitual, there is still a 5 percent margin for creativity. I cannot estimate the percentages with any confidence. But whatever the ratio, I know that habitual behavior can be changed. I have seen it happen both in myself and in others!

We are not 100 percent determined by the perspectives and customs we have learned from our society. We can—by exercising our wills with the aid of the power of God—make changes both in our perspectives and in our behavior. We can also both recommend changes in others and introduce them to the power of God to enable them to make and maintain those changes.

Expected Changes

Our focus tends to be on the way people use their worldviews to produce continuity from generation to generation. From that perspective, change in worldview seems to be relatively unusual under ordinary circumstances. This is not true. Though there may be a social penalty to pay if we make certain changes, under other circumstances we are penalized if we don't change.

As mentioned, there are certain changes we are expected to make as we grow up. We expect children to believe in Santa Claus when they are young but to "outgrow" it. Likewise with their blind acceptance of all their parents and teachers tell them. Assumptions concerning who they are and what they will become usually are changed, sometimes for the worse. Assumptions concerning other people, concerning life crises, concerning taking responsibility, even concerning religion and thousands of other assumptions are expected to be changed during a person's movement toward maturity.

Other changes are made in response to less typical experiences. People may read the thinking of an expert or respected person on a given issue and change their perspective out of deference to that person's viewpoint. Or a trusted friend may let someone down, leading the one who is hurt to respond in bitterness toward other people. A person who feels frustrated over not achieving certain goals may develop a fatalistic or negative perspective toward life in general. One who witnesses what appears to be a miraculous intervention of God may choose to believe in miracles. One who experiences bereavement develops assumptions and behavior that enable him/her to comfort those suffering bereavement.

In each case there may or may not be social penalties to pay. In individualistic American society there is great latitude in most areas as long as people keep pretty much to themselves. This is especially true with regard to religious faith, for one's faith is seen as a private thing. But trying to convert others to one's perspective can bring harsh criticism, especially if one's new perspective seems to question the authority or accuracy of science and/or other "politically correct" perspectives.

It is the will to change a perspective that becomes crucial. One must decide to stand against inbred habit and social pressure to make an unpopular change of perspective permanent. This is difficult but not impossible. For what we are determined to do is ultimately more important than the cultural structures, the deeply ingrained habits, or the social pressures in our lives.

Chapter 3

Critical Realism

Each of us is taught to assume what our society assumes. These assumptions, then, we see as absolute, as if they are God's REALITY. This situation continues until we become aware of other points of view that we cannot reason away. When we are confronted by other points of view, our tendency is to defend the one taught us by parents, teachers and other "significant others" as the only right perspective, or at least the best of the alternatives. We feel that those who differ are wrong or settling for a lesser alternative. Such an attitude is an important part of our ethnocentrism.

Each society, unless demoralized, tends to absolutize its own positions. This is especially the case for us westerners and those of other societies who have imbibed westernization since so many western scientific achievements are so impressive. It appears as though we have hit on "capital R" Reality when our doctors can do what they do with surgical repair and replacement, when our space scientists can send vehicles to and beyond the moon (and get them back), when our engineers can build bridges, roads, airplanes, cars and an incredible number of other things. Such achievements are so impressive that, on the one hand, we feel we can trust everything scientists say and do and, on the other we cannot trust competing perspectives.

Large segments of western and westernized populations have made science (in all its forms) our religion with scientists as our priests. Whatever they say and do as scientists is thus taken as gospel truth and we trust that it's only a matter of time before they solve the remaining problems of humanity. This leads us to be deeply suspicious of alternative approaches based on different assumptions. For example, we have seen such dramatic medical advances through the research and practice of western medical scientists that we distrust approaches to healing based on prayer or such theories as chiropractic, osteopathy or acupressure.

Yet as Christians we know of wrong turns made by western scientists in areas such as evolution, exclusion of the miraculous in healing or of any divine intervention in human affairs and denial of the existence and activity of Satan and his hosts. Though medical scientists may do well in dealing with the physical aspects of health, they often are far less expert in dealing with the psychological and emotional needs of their patients and usually are completely oblivious to what goes on in the spirit realm. Unfortunately, most western Christians seem as blind as the scientific establishment with regard to the latter.

Whether scientists or lay people, however, from time to time we are forced to deal with alternative approaches to reality that we cannot rationalize away. This is especially true if we learn to view life from the perspective of another culture. Exposure to alternate views of life leads us to ask questions such as: How close is my perception to what is actually there?

When I ask this question, I often think of the glasses I wear. They are bifocals and give me at least two views of reality. They are made so that part of them helps me to see close up, another part to see things at a distance. When I look at close things through the top of the lenses, everything is blurred. Likewise, far things are blurred if I look at them through the bottom of the lenses, because that part of the lenses is meant for something about 18 inches in front of my eyes.

The question is, is what I'm looking at really like what I'm seeing? Or do my glasses alter or distort what is there? In our normal life experiences, is what we see what is really there? Or is our view distorted? If we see what is actually there, how come others see the same things differently?

Have you ever heard a report of the same event from two different people? Why are the reports different? Even sincere, honest, trustworthy people regularly describe similar experiences quite differently. Men and women regularly describe and interpret things differently. Two or three different people may describe the same automobile accident in quite different ways. In the scriptures we have four different gospels. Why are four inspired accounts not the same?

The fact of human variation in reporting and interpreting is such, however, that if Matthew, Mark, Luke and John had all written exactly the same thing, we would doubt the reliability of the Gospels. We would assume that somebody must have indoctrinated them into a single story so they all came out with the same account of their experiences with our Lord. But we know that when two or three or four people look at the same event, they come out with slightly or greatly different emphases, different focuses. Different things are important to different people. Some people see one set of things and don't see another set of things. Other people see that second set of things and miss the first set of things. That's the way human beings are.

The old story of the blind men and the elephant raises several of our issues in an interesting way. You'll remember that each of six blind men examined a different part of the elephant and then generalized from that experience that the whole animal was like the part they had touched.

One concluded that he was dealing with a hose, because the part he was holding—the trunk— seemed like a hose. Another concluded he was in contact with a tree-like being because he had grasped a leg. The others, then, drew their conclusions from their impressions of the elephant's tail, his side, his ear, or his tusks. And each would have been right if he concluded that his part was like a tree, a wall, a hose, a rope, a fan, or a spear. But each was wrong when he generalized about the whole animal on the basis of his limited experience with but one part of the beast.

Now this story has been used in many ways, to prove many points. I don't want to be thought of as buying into any of those other uses of the story. I simply want to make one point: there is a reality—in the story symbolized as an elephant—that lies beyond the small part of reality that we experience and interpret. People, however, tend to assume that their interpretations of their limited experiences enable them to conclude with certainty what the whole of reality is like. They each identify their own perception of the partial reality they have experienced with the total reality that is before them, most of which they have neither seen nor touched.

When paleontologists examine fossil remains and loudly proclaim that humans evolved through various stages without a Creator to guide the process, they are basing their conclusions on experience with only part of the elephant. When psychologists deny or ignore demonic interference in human emotional distress, they only see part of the elephant. When anthropologists declare that all moral standards are relative, they have based their conclusion on too narrow a view of reality. When the members of western societies ignore or make light of the whole spirit realm, focusing entirely on the material and human realms, they are missing at least one third of the reality they claim to be describing.

As we grew up, we imbibed our society's perspectives on reality (its worldview) as if it were absolute. Those perspectives seemed to be the right ones since they were without competitors and since they were taught to us by people we trusted to not mislead us. Along the way as we grew up we became aware of other, competing perspectives. We probably assumed, however, that our views were the right ones since we trusted those who taught them to us. So we defended them. As we grew and came in contact with more divergent views and practices, we either continued this habit of defending the views we were taught, or we opened ourselves up to appreciate and adopt at least certain other views.

This chapter is about such perspectives: ours and those of others, and the attitude we should take toward them. I have learned much on this subject from authors such as Ian Barbour (1974), Peter Berger (1966) and especially from my former colleague Paul Hiebert (1983, 1985, 1994).

Alternative Views of Reality

There are at least three ways of approaching the differences between how humans understand things. Each of them impacts us both individually and in terms of the worldview of our society. Each of them deals with that human perception, what I will call "small r reality," and what is actually there (as God sees it), what I will call "Reality with a capital R" or REALITY. I am indebted to Paul Hiebert (1985, 1994) for much of what follows. The positions are:

1. NAIVE REALISM (or Direct or Unmediated Realism)

Those who espouse this position believe that *with enough effort, we can see, interpret and understand exactly what is there.* That is, we can see things directly and interpret them as they actually are, rather than seeing them indirectly or in distorted fashion. Naive realists deny that there is any difference between their own position and what is absolutely right. Those who consider themselves experts especially would contend that they have a straight shot at REALITY and are able to see and understand it as it really is.

This is the traditional western approach, both in popular and in academic life. It assumes a real world that can be accurately observed and accurately described. A casual glance at a physical feature would seem to support these assumptions. If one sees a mountain, westerners assume the mountain is real. If there appears to be a mountain, it really exists. It is not just something in the observer's imagination. And if the mountain exists, a careful observer can be objective and describe that mountain as it really is. It is assumed that any hypothesis or theory of the observer can be proven to be true either by experiment or by logic. These theories, then, once "proven" are accepted as unchanging "laws" of nature, like the law of gravity or the laws of mathematics. They are believed to be unchanging and immutable.

This approach has resulted in scientific theories and philosophical propositions with the following characteristics:

1. Generalizations that are seen as parts of closed systems. All the parts of each system are understood to be tightly knit into a whole. No part of the system can be challenged without threatening the total structure. Whether it is a philosophical or a scientific system, these are systems of analysis that are set up as if they were eternal. We call them laws, propositions, basic truths.

We can illustrate from mathematics. When I was in elementary and high school, one of the most solid facts in our minds was that "two and two are four." We believed that implicitly. They couldn't equal anything else. That was solid, factual, a law of mathematics and of life. But we never examined the assumption underlying that belief. Then somebody came along with the so-called "new math" and said that under certain conditions two and two can equal eleven!

Those of us brought up under the old math thought this contention stupid. You could, we said, prove our answer on your fingers. But we never examined the underlying assumption accepted and taught in our society that all counting is done with a base of 10. That is, we count all the fingers from 1 to 10 and, in the process, give each a separate name, and then we start all over again at the next level (11 to 20) and at the next (21-30) and so on.

What we didn't realize (and, consequently, never questioned) was that there was an underlying assumption that led to our giving distinct names to ten items (the ten numbers) rather than to, say, five (like the Fulani of Nigeria and many other peoples) or to three (as with some American Indian groups), or to twenty. The Fulani system, for example, converts into ours as

1,	2,	3,	4,	5,	
11,	12,	13,	14,	15,	
21,	22,	23,	24,	25,	etc.

Thus, in their system, 3 digits plus 3 more digits turns out to be 11 (the first number in the second set).

In contemporary western mathematics, the digits are named by starting with 0. Thus, if your base is 3, you count three digits (0, 1, 2) and start over again, using the same three numbers in the next set (i.e., 10, 11, 12). Then you start over again at the next level (20, 21, 22), etc. Your system, then, looks like this:

0,	1,	2	
10,	11,	12	
20,	21,	22,	etc.

You only have three numbers in any set. Now take the 2 in the first set and add two digits to it from the second set, and what have you got? 11! (Though note that the twos mean different things. The 2 in the first set means the third digit, whereas the 2 we are adding means two additional digits.) So, if you assume a base of three, $2 + 2 = 11$.

When a group (whether a cultural group or a group of scientists) starts with an unconscious presupposition, such as the base 10 assumption, and builds its system on that assumption and others (equally unquestioned) derived from it, the resulting system tends to be fairly consistent internally but to be closed to other assumptions. The reason a system is closed is because the absoluteness of its validity is threatened if the validity of other presuppositions is admitted. This is why both cultural and scientific or philosophical or theological systems tend to be closed off by their adherents from other points of view.

Many of us have been brought up to understand Christian doctrine as a closed system and are carefully warned (often unconsciously) against doubting or even examining certain symbolic parts of the system. In my experience, the impression was given that my orthodoxy (and even, perhaps, my salvation) was in jeopardy if I ever questioned certain doctrines. Among them were the literalness of the early chapters of Genesis, conservative views of the authorship of various books of the Bible, the verbal plenary theory of inspiration, inerrancy, or any of a number of other doctrines (including at that time both a pre-tribulation rapture and the pre-millenial return of the Lord). These issues had been in focus during the modernist-fundamentalist debates of the early part of the twentieth century and we were expected to accept such conservative views as a package. We were taught that these conservative beliefs were so tightly tied together that questioning any of them would inevitably result in our becoming liberal and, therefore, lost to the cause of Christ. Those who decided to reject any of the conservative views, then, often rejected the whole package.

2. *Those who held to naïve realism, whether in mathematics or in theology, tended to become dogmatic.* Because the basic assumptions underlying our knowledge were not examined, we assumed that our knowledge was absolute, or nearly so. The old approach to mathematics that didn't examine the base 10 assumption was dogmatic. We were certain because we didn't even imagine another system. We claimed to operate under immutable and universal laws of mathematics. Any deviations from the system were considered wrong or heretical. If you say $2 + 2 = 5$, you are wrong. That's what everyone, including our teachers, always told us.

In Christian doctrine, likewise, only one way could be right—our way. For there are laws of doctrine as well, and we and our teachers are the ones who know them. Under this traditional approach the system (whether cultural, mathematical, theological, or some other) is regarded as an unchanging, final statement of fact. And philosophers, theologians, behavioral scientists, and all others who consider themselves scientists give themselves to the pursuit of "laws" of their disciplines that would parallel in absoluteness the laws of the physical sciences or mathematics. When, then, they discovered what they felt to be such immutable laws, they tended to become quite dogmatic about them.

The clear claim of this approach, then, is to deny that there is any difference between what the experts see and what actually exists. We have noted the dogmatism. There is also an elitism. Those who have studied the area in question or for some other reason are in power over others get to claim that their view is the correct one with all others being wrong. To refer back to the blind men and the elephant story, suppose the first of the blind men was either an expert on elephants or a person of high prestige. He might well have argued that all the rest were wrong, saying only he understood correctly. He could contend that he alone "sees" REALITY as God sees it. And, since his prestige was high, the others might have acquiesced, not realizing that his blindness, in spite of his expertise, made it likely that his judgment would be wrong.

Such a dogmatic attitude is commonly taken in real life by people whose exposure to ideas different from their own is minimal. Some of these claim God's authority for their ideas. This is also the usual attitude of those who are insecure about their own beliefs and understandings.

This view basically assumes that "my reality" is identical with God's REALITY. Anyone, therefore, who questions my point of view is clearly wrong. I once heard a pastor with this attitude say, while presenting his opinions concerning Jesus' Second Coming, "If you disagree with what I am saying, you're not disagreeing with me, you're disagreeing with God!" Though there are some things we as Christians will want to assert strongly and even commit our lives to, we need to be very careful that we don't claim to know the mind of God. And we should be especially careful in dealing with areas such as the Second Coming, where equally expert biblical scholars have differing interpretations.

Though we in western society are often guilty of taking this kind of a dogmatic point of view, many in a variety of scientific fields are now questioning it. See below.

2. *RELATIVISM (or Idealism or Intuitivism)*

A second approach to the reality problem is to go to the opposite extreme from the dogmatic attitude. Those who exalt relativism to the point where they attempt to absolutize it assert that nobody is completely wrong or right. "Anyone's way of doing things is just as good as anyone else's," they say. "Who are we to judge? Are we God to assert that we can decide which beliefs, customs, and perspectives are right and which are wrong?"

People who take this approach recognize (rightly, I think) that the way one person or one group understands things is not necessarily totally right, while the way another person or group understands the same things is not necessarily all wrong. But then they go to the extreme of postulating that any view of reality is valid as long as it is held sincerely. Their contention is that reality is not a given. That is, there is no REALITY or, if there is, it is irrelevant. "Capital R" Reality, they say, is but a mental construct produced by people in their minds.

The extreme position such as that held by many of the peoples of India maintains that whatever reality is attributed to psychological, spiritual, or even material things exists only because humans have created it, not because it really exists. Moral standards and religious and philosophical beliefs, for example, are only psychological constructs produced by people to meet psychological needs. They are not to be taken as perceptions of something more real than something else.

For many Indians even material objects such as mountains or elephants are seen as illusory. If someone thinks an elephant is a kind of tree, it is a kind of tree for that person. If someone else thinks it is a rope, it is a rope for him or her. To one person it's a tree, to another a rope, to another a wall, because the only reality is what is in our minds. The same holds true with moral standards.

Many westerners, including philosophers and social scientists who consider themselves relativists, would go a long way toward the extreme position in the conceptual and non-material realm. They would contend that values, morals, and religious or philosophical ideas are merely the products of human thought and capable of evolving into something better. They would, however, usually believe that material things such as mountains and elephants actually exist.

A major problem with this position is that, while denying absolutes, it absolutizes relativity! A statement such as "everything is relative" is a statement of an absolute. A relativistic position also breaks down with regard to such things as medicine (not every medicine is as good as every other), poison (some things are absolutely not to be ingested), gravity and other physical "laws" (they work absolutely) and many other aspects of reality.

3. CRITICAL REALISM (or Indirect or Mediated Realism)

The position I consider most accurate attempts to incorporate the truths of the above positions while avoiding the extremes. It holds that there are two realities. There is a REALITY "out there." The world outside ourselves does exist both materially and non-materially. It is Real. But there is also a perceptual reality inside our minds. That, too, is real, but it stems from the way we perceive things and is not to be equated with God's REALITY.

There are four basic assumptions underlying Critical Realism:

1. The assumption that there is a real, structured world that can be experienced in part by people. Critical Realism, like Naive Realism but unlike Indian mysticism, assumes a real world.

2. Critical Realism says, however, that we have to distinguish between that REALITY and the human perception of it.

3. But Critical Realism assumes that *REALITY is much bigger and more complex than we can grasp all at once.* Just as with the blindmen, the elephant was too big for them to grasp all at once. They could only perceive one part at a time—a tail, a leg, a side, a trunk. This led to their differing theories as to what the elephant was like.

4. Critical Realism *sees the observer as both very important and very limited in the observational process.* In fact, it's a frightening thing to reflect on all the different things that may be going through your minds as you read this material. You all come to it from your own points of view. And those differing perspectives may result in quite a variety of understandings of what is written here. And you (not I) will have the final say as to what I mean. Your part, then, becomes at least as important as mine in determining the reality of what I intend.

Before we go on to a more detailed presentation of the Critical Realist position, I want to summarize all three positions in chart form. The *little r* is used to indicate the reality in the person's mind. The *big R* indicates actual or objective REALITY, the REALITY that's out there in the world outside of our minds.

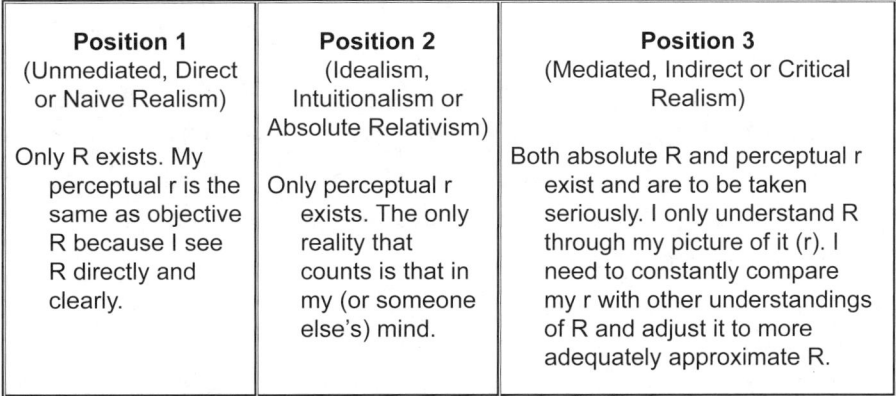

Position 1 (Unmediated, Direct or Naive Realism)	**Position 2** (Idealism, Intuitionalism or Absolute Relativism)	**Position 3** (Mediated, Indirect or Critical Realism)
Only R exists. My perceptual r is the same as objective R because I see R directly and clearly.	Only perceptual r exists. The only reality that counts is that in my (or someone else's) mind.	Both absolute R and perceptual r exist and are to be taken seriously. I only understand R through my picture of it (r). I need to constantly compare my r with other understandings of R and adjust it to more adequately approximate R.

Figure 3.1. Three Positions Concerning Reality

Limitations of Observers

Critical realism recognizes that observers are subject to certain limitations, some biological, some personal, some cultural, some spiritual:

1. First of all, *we are limited to our senses.* There are many things happening that are outside of our experience—some of them, indeed, are probably outside of any human's experience. But we can only experience what our senses give us.

2. Secondly, *we limit ourselves by being highly selective in choosing the data we consider.* We tend to screen out (unconsciously or consciously) data that we've been taught not to notice or that we aren't interested in or don't understand. In this presentation, you, the reader, are already involved in this selection process. You are accepting and understanding certain things and, probably, ignoring those things you don't understand. Some of the things I have said and may consider important will be things you don't understand and either ignore or, worse yet, misunderstand.

Such personal selectivity came to my attention rather strikingly several years ago. I was with my older daughter (ten or eleven years old at the time) when we were asked what color our car was. I said black, but she said red. I looked at her in amazement, saying, "Cheri, are you calling our car red?" "Yes, it's red," she said. So I took her outside and showed her the car, asking, "Is that car red?" She looked at it and said, "You're right, it's black." Then we looked inside the car. All the seats were red. She had identified the car by the part of it that she experienced most, the inside with its red seats. She was right for one part of the data, though I was right for another part of the data. Our perceptions were not only partial, they were selective. Unfortunately for my daughter, our society has arbitrarily chosen to identify cars by their outside color rather than their inside color. In terms of that arbitrary convention, then, she was "wrong."

3. In addition to the limitation of such personal selectivity, *there is the screening or filtering of reality produced by our society in accord with our cultural (worldview) patterns.* This is a broad-gauged type of limitation in which we learn as members of a society to notice certain things and to describe them in certain ways while ignoring other things. Many non-western peoples, for example, divide the color spectrum into three or five categories and/or assume that the universe is full of very active malevolent spirits and/or tend to regularly ignore the passage of time (including other commitments) if something meaningful is in process and/or consider every decision still negotiable even if a vote has been taken and a rule/law passed. Such practices result in culturally inculcated differences between the members of such societies and the members of western societies in what aspects of reality are noticed and how they are perceived.

In dealing with color, we in the West tend to make more distinctions than many peoples. But when it comes to spiritual beings, we tend to ignore or even deny their existence and have only a few terms in our language by which to identify them if we believe in them. Many of the world's peoples, however, see the world as populated with lots of spirits and have a large number of terms for the different types. When it comes to distinguishing heat and cold, I found that my western upbringing did not provide me with all of the categories I needed to be able to speak the Hausa language of northern Nigeria. As I found out by trial and error, they are taught to divide heat and cold into four categories, each with a specific word to label it: dry heat, damp heat, dry cold, damp cold.

4. In the fourth place, then, *we are influenced in our perceptions by the limitations and distortions imposed by human sinfulness.* Secular scientists, of course, usually ignore this factor. It is not a part of the reality that their subculture focuses on, though some seem to be noticing (e.g., Goldschmidt 1966; Menninger 1973).

Sinfulness undoubtedly affects perception at both individual and cultural levels in a multitude of ways. Among them would presumably be the many times when the selfish interests of persons or groups intrude into the way reality is understood. Whenever, for example, we perceive reality as endorsing our good at the expense of the good of others, we can assume that it is sin that is distorting our vision. Indeed, every perception of reality is tainted in some way by the sin factor.

The Critical Realist position starts, then, from the observation that, though we do observe REALITY, we do not see it directly. It goes on to point out that we strive to make sense of what we see by organizing our perceptions into a mental ordering that may be labeled by such terms as "mental map," "model," "picture of reality," or "perspective." This mental ordering consists of a more or less integrated understanding of reality built largely from the worldview system or systems we have been taught before we knew of any alternative perspectives. The perspective taught to us subconsciously while we were growing up has a big head start on any other perspective we may seek to adopt later on.

Change and Retention

In spite of the depth of worldview and the largely subconscious nature of it, we seem to always be in the process of modifying the perspectives we are taught. Though we will deal more fully with this topic later in this volume when we deal with worldview change, it will be helpful here (elaborating on what has been said in chapter two) to note several reasons for such modifications:

1. First, as mentioned in chapter 2, **children learn to change certain of their assumptions.** Probably all of us when we were young held incorrect ideas concerning various aspects of adult reality. Some of this came, of course, through imperfect understanding and/or lack of complete acceptance on our part as children. But some incorrect assumptions may have come from our parents' evasive or incorrect explanations of various aspects of life. Whether it was belief in Santa Claus or the Easter Bunny or how children come into the world, as we grew up we changed our worldview assumptions. The process of schooling, then, involves a considerable number of changes in our basic assumptions.

Thus, in addition to learning to retain most of our early-learned assumptions, we also learn the habit of changing assumptions to conform to new information coming from parents, teachers, books and life experiences.

2. As children, though, **we have also learned to be tenacious in conserving many, often trivial, assumptions that we've been taught.** I learned, for example, to regard General Motors cars as better than Fords, to support the Boston Red Sox professional baseball team, to consider my church better than other churches, to value living in the country and to hate cities plus a large number of other fairly trivial assumptions as I was growing up. I have tried to shake some of them, (e.g., supporting the Red Sox who seem to specialize in finding ways to lose) but to no avail.

3. But, as we experience life **we constantly test the assumptions we've learned in relation to that experience.** And some of those assumptions don't fit, since most of the perspectives we were taught by parents and teachers were designed to handle the problems of previous generations. We may not perceive these assumptions to be helpful in handling today's problems, so we modify them or replace them with other assumptions. Or we may hold onto certain unhelpful assumptions either because we can't think of an alternative or because we assume that by so doing we are honoring those who taught us.

4. When people are **introduced to a different assumption to explain some aspect of reality, they may accept it or reject it.** If people are convinced that the alternate assumption is more accurate or more helpful than their present one, they may go through a *paradigm shift*, a change in perspective. Or, they may refuse to deal with the new perception and "sweep it under the rug," acting as if they never had the experience. Or, they may keep at least part of the old perspective, either adapting it to the new experience or holding two conflicting assumptions without trying to reconcile the two.

5. ***Pressure for change of assumptions may even come from a perceived need to reconcile what one believes with what one practices.*** Probably all of us have aspects of our life in which we hold to an ideal but don't live up to it. Recognition of this fact can motivate us to make changes either in our behavior or in some of our assumptions. Hopefully, as Christians we are motivated to change our behavior whenever we find that a scriptural ideal is not what we are practicing.

Models and Perspectives are Small "r" Reality

Models, perspectives, grids, mental maps, paradigms and perceptions such as we are discussing here are to be understood as ways of seeing things (small r reality) rather than as absolute declarations about the essential nature of things. They are interpretations of REALITY (or parts of it) seen imperfectly and partially by human beings through lenses affected by culture, personality, experience, sin, and probably a myriad of other limiting and distorting factors. We cannot see/understand as God does, so we cannot speak of these perspectives as ultimately true or false (i.e., absolute), only as useful, appropriate, helpful, and, hopefully, adequate. From this perspective a model is a good or adequate one (at least in a tentative sense) if it seems to fit the data. We must, however, constantly review our data and evaluate our models in a search for greater adequacy of our understandings.

We must recognize, furthermore, that our models are always partial rather than complete. Only God fully sees REALITY and TRUTH. We see as partially as the blind men examining the elephant. The best we can claim, therefore, is glimpses of REALITY and TRUTH—glimpses that prove to be adequate in the living of life and that are revealed to be adequate in our preparation for eternity. We cannot, however, claim to know the totality of Truth in any area of life.

What we have, then, are tentative ways of perceiving Reality. Since our perceptions are tentative, they should be subject to constant reevaluation, change, refinement and replacement. Models of Reality are intended to be improved upon. Meanwhile, they are important to us in at least two ways:

They help us understand and relate to REALITY, whether that of the world around us or that of the realm that lies beyond human time and space.

In addition, such models provide for us maps for action, enabling us to chart our course in relation to both this world and the next.

The perspective (critical/mediated realism) being presented here may already have become your point of view. Or it may require a paradigm shift for you to accept it. In any event, you may notice that even in presenting this view I have at times tended to present it as *TRUTH* rather than (as the theory requires) simply a tentative perception of TRUTH.

This is easily done, and I need to apologize for it. But let me also take this opportunity to give two reasons why I think this has happened.

1. I suspect that I, like most others who advocate the critical realism paradigm, am actually in the category of those described above who actually hold within them two mutually incompatible perspectives. I'm afraid that I regularly switch back and forth between Critical Realism and Naive Realism. If so, you may detect in this chapter and elsewhere in the book touches of the dogmatism of the Naive Realism that I seek to avoid. Sorry. But look out for the same tendency in yourself.

2. Secondly, there seems to be something about an attempt to be persuasive that requires a high degree of certainty in the words and phrases used. Such certainty in vocabulary should be accepted as I intend it—as designed to present my ideas as persuasively as possible. It should not be interpreted as an unconscious repudiation of the position I am arguing for.

REALITY, reality and Worldview

All of what we have been saying concerning the two realities affects us as human beings and the structuring of our worldview at both individual and group levels. A worldview is made up of the agreed-upon perceptions of a group of people. It is, therefore, the agreed-upon "small r" reality of that group. The socially accepted assumptions, values, allegiances, picturings of reality, perspectives, patterns, etc. that we are taught by those who raise us are the shared legacy of our society and designed to lead us into seeing things as the adults of our society see them.

As pointed out at the beginning of this chapter, then, we are tempted to absolutize the assumptions we have been taught. It is easy to assume that our ancestors looked at a variety of perspectives and chose just the right ones to pass on to us. Given that we learned our worldview in a context in which there were no competing perspectives, we grew up regarding it as the only right way to look at things. If, then, we have occasion to live in another society and find out that the people around us are not making the same assumptions we are about life, we may go into what has been called "culture shock." This is the name that has been given to the off-balance, out-of-control feeling we ordinarily experience when life around us doesn't conform to the rules we have learned and we can't do anything about it.

If we are to survive in another society, we need to adopt a Critical Realist position with regard to both our worldview assumptions and those of the society in which we find ourselves. And in their context, we need to learn to operate as much as possible on their assumptions if we are going to survive.

Unfortunately, too many Christian witnesses have gone to other societies with a Naïve Realist approach. Their aim, then, is to convert the receptor people to their "correct" view of reality. They have so given themselves to Christ and the brand of Christianity they have embraced that they may see no alternative way of approaching the gospel. When faced with understandings of Christianity rooted in other worldviews, such people feel that gospel orthodoxy is being sacrificed. Historically, such Naïve Realist cross-cultural witnesses have set up western schools in non-western societies to teach the people "correct" understandings of Christianity and life in general. These schools and other western attempts to teach people to think our way have, of course, been very disruptive and given a very inaccurate picture of how Christianity is intended to relate to the cultural context in which it is to function.

In cross-cultural witness to Christian Truth, therefore, it is important for us to adopt a Critical Realist position. If we are to be true to our calling, we need to recognize that there is both an objective REALITY at God's level and a subjective reality at our human, cultural level. In every life situation, people within a given society share similar views of external REALITY. They, like us, are actually seeing capital R Reality, but taking a kind of photograph (a small r or perceptual picture) of the R with their minds and behaving in response/reaction *to that mental picture*, not in response to the actual REALITY that was observed. Thus the REALITY "out there" is mediated to their minds through a mental picture that they themselves have constructed and their reaction will be to *their interpretation of the REALITY*, rather than to the REALITY itself.

It is impossible to overstate this fact. In communication theory terms: people respond to the meanings they create, not to whatever the communicator had in mind. The job of the communicator, then, is to so frame the message that it will stimulate in the receptors the will and the ability to create meanings similar to those of the communicator. To do this, the communicator needs to learn to work from within the conceptual framework of the hearers. For they will construct their meanings from the materials in their own experience. So we have to learn to start where they are, not simply where we are to help them to connect with vital things we have come to communicate to them.

However, as we discuss Critical Realism, we need to refrain from assuming that what we are designating "capital R REALITY" is limited to God's eternal and absolute truths. Though those truths are included, they are only part of what is meant. When, for example, as teachers we look at a classroom full of students, we need to recognize that each student comes with her/his own set of issues and may or may not be listening to or comprehending what the teacher is saying. For the fact is that the REALITY as God knows it of what's going on in that classroom may be far different from the "small r" reality perceived by the teacher or anyone else in the classroom.

God understands what is going on in that classroom, including everything that is going on in the minds of the students and the teacher as well as what is being said by the teacher. The REALITY of that classroom, then, includes all that is actually going on, both consciously and unconsciously, in and between all of the participants. Such things as the backgrounds of the participants, their mental states, the perceptions and misperceptions, the motivations, the intentions, the peculiar influences of setting, the relationships between the participants and the like—all of these and much more enter into the REALITY of that event. Most of this is, however, beyond the ability of any of the participants to see and plays little or no part in their perceptual reality.

A Critical Realist view, further, enables us to explain both the differences between our perceptions and God's in the scriptures and the changes that take place as God leads us into clearer insight and further truth from scripture. Though material, psychological, social, and spiritual REALITY exist and are seen clearly by God, the mental pictures we construct of those parts of that REALITY that we observe and analyze cannot correspond with God's complete and clear view of it. Our pictures are constructed on the basis of the limited and distorted understandings provided by such things as our present and past experience, our psychological makeup, and our sociocultural training—all affected by sin.

Think of how wide the difference can get between the worldview structured perceptions of the people of one society and those of a group working from a radically different set of worldview assumptions. The Nigerian leaders I worked with, for example, found little attraction to Romans, a book that I think is marvelous, but a lot to James, Hebrews and the Old Testament, portions of scripture not so popular in America. Both Hebrew and Greek reasoning are found in the Bible. Though I tended to favor the more Greek approach of Paul's epistles, my leaders favored portions of the Bible couched in Hebrew thinking. I learned, however, that these culture-based preferences need not hinder either them or us from hearing

God. I do not, therefore, need to press them into my cultural preferences. I can start from the parts of scripture most agreeable to them.

In this experience as in all others we (and they) do observe "big R" REALITY, but we perceive or picture it as "small r" perceptions—in this case according to our preferences. Though the material we observe may be inspired scripture, our perception is always subjective, focused, limited, and partial. We always relate it to our own interests and may embellish it with our imaginations.

The upshot of Critical Realist thinking for Christians is to notice that though *we do not see absolutely, we can see and respond adequately*. Indeed, if humans do not perceive and respond to their perceptions adequately, they will not survive long or well. Inadequate responses to REALITY may lead to such things as physical death, psychological dysfunction, sociological destruction, and spiritual ruin. In the physical realm, those who violate the rules of REALITY by trying to fly without an airplane or by drinking poison tend to not live long or well. Those who violate psychological, social, or spiritual rules likewise forfeit the kind of existence they were meant to have.

With regard to Christian conversion, we can be thankful that, in spite of differences of interpretation of scripture, the message is clear enough to be adequate to lead us to salvation. The biblical revelation is a part of "big R" REALITY. Though we do not interpret even the Bible absolutely, God has provided the guidance and empowerment of the Holy Spirit to enable us to adjust our perceptions so that our responses can be adequate in the spiritual area.

Problems in Critical Realist Interpretation

Though we cannot understand absolutely, we need to learn as much as possible about REALITY and to adjust our perception of our own reality accordingly, both as individuals and as groups. To do this we must learn to be open to understandings that lie beyond those we and our group now have. We need to keep searching for new insight into REALITY and adjusting our perceptions to those new insights. This involves constant comparison between our present views and those we become aware of through other people, new experiences, books and other sources of input.

In some areas of life, comparisons and adjustments are comparatively easy. Physical and material things, for example, are more susceptible to such comparisons and adjustments than are the less tangible areas of life. Several years ago I was rushed to the hospital with an intense pain in my abdomen. The doctors diagnosed my problem as a ruptured peptic ulcer and proceeded to operate. Once inside they discovered that their diagnosis had been wrong. But they were close enough to the real problem to discover it and to remove a gangrenous appendix. Their perception had been wrong, but they were open to correction, adjusted their approach, and saved my life. Their adjusted perception turned out to be very close to the REALITY of that situation—perhaps as close as is humanly possible.

In many less tangible areas of life it is unfortunately not so easy to know whether what we are perceiving is as close to the REAL as was the adjusted perception of my doctors. In human relationships, for example, how can we know how a person really feels about us? Or in the realm of ideas, how can we know for sure just what is truth in any given area of thought? Or in the spiritual realm, can we really know what angels or demons are like? Or can we really know whether our interpretation of a given passage of scripture is the only absolutely correct one? Even Jesus claimed absolute truth only for His person (John 14:6), certainly not for our perceptions of Him.

Though some will accept a Critical Realist position with regard to natural things, they will claim that God has solved the problem in spiritual matters by providing us with his written Word. Certainly there we can be absolutely certain, they contend. I wish this were so. Unfortunately, even the fact that the scriptures themselves are inspired does not assure that our interpretations of them are always accurate. In fact, the wide diversity of interpretations of scripture testifies to the fact that even the way the REALITY of God's inspired Word is understood is subject to the perceptual reality of human interpretation.

Though God's written revelation may be labeled "capital R" REALITY, the human interpretations of it on which we depend are subject to all of the limitations that have just been discussed. We simply cannot legitimately assume with the Naive Realist that any human interpretation, even of scripture, is exactly the same as God's understanding. Yet there are certain human understandings that we regard as trustworthy enough that we commit ourselves to them in faith. For example: God loves us, He has redeemed us through His Son, Jesus is the Son of God, and we can be saved through faith in Him.

In spite of the solidness of our relationship with God and our commitment to Him, we have to settle for greater or lesser approximations in our understandings of God and His works. We, then, need to strive toward ever more adequate perceptions and responses without getting discouraged over the fact that we dare not claim absolute understandings even of those things we are willing to die for. I, for example, am giving my life to God on the basis of my understanding of who God is, what He has done, and what He expects of me. I have a high degree of certainty in each of these areas—a certainty I believe to be adequate to undergird my commitment. But I cannot claim the kind of absolute understanding that only God has of anything, even of the God I've given myself to.

Advantages to This Position

There are at least two great advantages to this position:

1. One is the potential for a lessening of dogmatism. The dogmatic person demands that one interpretation be set up as a "party line" that everyone follows. For that alone is truth. But if we recognize that the Bible itself teaches that we understand in a fuzzy, partial way (1 Cor. 13:12), we should be much less tempted to assert that our interpretations correspond exactly with God's point of view.

2. Another advantage is that this position provides us freedom to learn from others. If, for example, you and I disagree on a certain position, we can sit down and discuss the differences and learn from each other. As we both attempt to understand the REALITY that lies beyond our positions, we may decide that your position seems more accurate than mine in certain details, while mine seems to have the advantage in others. We can both learn by discussing and comparing, thereby possibly bringing both of our understandings into closer correspondence to REALITY, as well as growing spiritually in the process.

CHAPTER 4

CURRENT APPROACHES OF NON-ANTHROPOLOGISTS

As mentioned, the concept of worldview is quite widely spoken of and written about in our day, both popularly and academically. This fact results in a variety of approaches, many of which can be quite helpful. Though it would not be possible to deal with any significant number of such approaches, it will be helpful to look at a few of them. To that end I have chosen to focus on three non-anthropological approaches and four from an anthropological perspective. With one exception, the proponents of these positions affirm a Christian commitment. Each of these approaches has something to offer us in our quest to understand worldview and its various ramifications.

First, let's look at three approaches from non-anthropologists James Sire, Ninian Smart and David Naugle. In summarizing their thoughts, I will not always use quotation marks in the charts, though I will follow standard procedure in the text. In the charts, however, I have mixed their words with mine, using mostly theirs.

James Sire

James Sire, for many years an editor for InterVarsity Press, has written a very interesting book entitled *The Universe Next Door* (3rd. ed. 1997). He followed that book in 2004 with *Naming the Elephant* a shorter book reflecting on his more than thirty years of grappling with the concept of worldview. In the longer book (1997) he deals with ten philosophical positions that are currently vying for followers in America. He calls these positions worldviews, though he does not have as broad a concept of worldview as that advocated by anthropologists. Yet, recognizing that the term is widely used popularly in this narrower sense, there is much to be learned from Sire's treatment.

Sire's primary concern is to reach westerners with the gospel. To this end, he wants his readers to understand where their potential converts are coming from. The fact that Sire's focus is on varieties of worldview within the western context somewhat limits the value of his presentation for those whose concern is to understand the subject of worldview cross-culturally.

The worldviews he treats are not necessarily to be found outside of the West. The approach he takes to examining them and the questions he asks, however, could be of great value to those working outside of the limits of western perspectives. For that reason, I feel it is worth the time and energy it takes to outline Sire's approach.

Though Sire is looking at worldview from a philosophical perspective rather than an anthropological one, his definition is close enough to ours to be useful. His "refined" (2004) definition is

> A worldview is a commitment, a fundamental orientation of the heart, that can be expressed as a story or in a set of presuppositions (assumptions which may be true, partially true or entirely false) which we hold (consciously or subconsciously, consistently or inconsistently) about the basic constitution of reality, and that provides the foundation on which we live and move and have our being (2004:122).

Though I don't like calling a cultural structure a "commitment," I think he's on track calling it "a fundamental orientation." I would say worldview is a fundamental orientation to which *people* commit. The commitment is what people do with a worldview, not what the worldview is in and of itself. Nevertheless, I consider this a good statement. And he follows it up with another good statement that separates his perspective from that of many philosophically-oriented scholars for whom "propositional truth" is their major concern. He says,

> ... a worldview is not fundamentally a set of propositions or a web of beliefs. That is, it is not first and foremost a matter of the intellect. Nor is it fundamentally a matter of language or a semiotic system of narrative signs. The intellect is surely involved, and language is present as a tool of the intellect, but the essence of a worldview lies deep in the inner recesses of the human self. It is a matter of the soul and is represented more as a spiritual orientation, or perhaps disposition, than as a matter of mind alone (2004:127).

So, from Sire's point of view, we are dealing with something that is deeper than the intellect and deeper than language and symbols. True, it is expressed through intellectual statements (propositions) couched in language and symbols or in stories. But it is more basic than any statement or picturing that might be involved in articulating its content. Whether, then, we agree with him that it is a "spiritual orientation," I like his term "disposition" or mine "perspective," involving the minds of the person or group who have committed themselves to it but constituting a more total orientation than simply a mental one.

Turning now to Sire's ten "worldviews," he labels them as follows. Note that with two exceptions (eastern pantheistic monism and animism), he deals with perspectives that have grown up in the West.

1. Christian Theism	6. Theistic Existentialism
2. Deism	7. Eastern Pantheistic Monism
3. Naturalism	8. New Age
4. Nihilism	9. Animism
5. Atheistic Existentialism	10. Postmodernism

Figure 4.1. Sire's List of Worldview Perspectives

Many who deal with worldview from a popular perspective equate worldview with religion. Sire, to his credit, unlike Ninian Smart whose perspective is outlined below, largely resists this temptation. Having identified these ten perspectives, Sire generates a series of seven questions that he puts to each position. The questions are:

1. *What is prime reality—the really real?* Is it God, gods, the material cosmos, only humans?

2. *What is the nature of the world around us?* Is it created or autonomous, chaotic or orderly, matter or spirit? Also, do we emphasize a subjective or an objective relationship to the world?

3. *What is a human being?* Are we highly complex machines, sleeping gods, persons made in God's image, naked apes?

4. *What happens to a person at death?* Are we extinguished, transformed to a higher state, reincarnated or do we simply move into a shadowy existence somewhere?

5. *Why is it possible to know anything at all?* Is it because we are in the image of God or that consciousness and rationality developed during the process of evolution?

6. *How do we know what is right and wrong?* Is it because we are in the image of God, or are we simply to do what feels good, or do we develop such ideas in order to survive?

7. *What is the meaning of human history?* Is it to realize the purposes of God or the gods, to make a paradise on earth, to prepare for a life in community with God? (1997:17-18).

To these seven questions, then, Sire adds a short list of other issues that often arise within various ones of what he terms the "basic" worldviews. These are:

1. Who is in charge of this world—God or humans or no one at all?
2. Are we as human beings determined or free?
3. Are we alone the maker of values?
4. Is God really good?
5. Is God personal or impersonal?
6. Or does he exist at all? (1997:18).

Each of these is an important question. And the answers given by the proponents of each of the worldview perspectives listed above provide great insight into their perceptions of Reality. We can summarize Sire's analysis of each of the positions in chart form as follows:

CHRISTIAN THEISM - Evangelical orthodoxy.
1. God is infinite and personal (triune), transcendent and immanent, omniscient, sovereign and good.
2. God created the cosmos out of nothing to operate with a uniformity of cause and effect in an open system.
3. Human beings are created in the image of God and thus possess personality, self-transcendence, intelligence, morality, gregariousness and creativity.
4. Human beings can know both the world around them and God himself because God has built into them the capacity to do so and because he takes an active role in communicating with them.
5. Human beings were created good, but through the Fall the image of God became defaced, though not so ruined as to be incapable of restoration; through the work of Christ, God redeemed humanity and began the process of restoring people to goodness, though any given person may choose to reject that redemption.
6. For each person, death is either the gate to life with God and his people or the gate to eternal separation from the only thing that will ultimately fulfill human aspirations.
7. Ethics is transcendent and is based on the character of God as good (holy and loving).

Figure 4.2. Sire's Summary of Christian Theism

For Sire, of course, and for us as well, the above summary of what he calls "Christian Theism" provides the basis for evaluating all of the other positions. The perspective he points to next is Deism. This is a position more like ours than naturalistic perspectives (see below) but with significant differences. The key to this position is the view that God created everything then wound it up like a clock and left it (and us) to work things out on our own while, like a clock, the spring runs down. This was the understanding of several of the founders of the United States.

DEISM
- a name for a variety of perspectives exalting reason and distancing God. People: Locke, Voltaire, Pope
1. A transcendent God, as a First Cause, created the universe but then left it to run on its own. God is thus not immanent, not fully personal, not sovereign over human affairs, not providential.
2. The cosmos God created is determined because it is created as a uniformity of cause and effect in a closed system; no miracle possible.
3. Human beings, though personal, are a part of the clockwork of the universe.
4. The cosmos is understood to be in its normal state; it is not fallen or abnormal. We can know the universe, and we can determine what God is like by studying it.
5. Ethics is limited to general revelation; because the universe is normal, it reveals what is right.
6. History is linear, for the course of the cosmos was determined at creation.

Figure 4.3. Sire's Summary of Deism

The next view, naturalism, is the prevailing view of contemporary secularists. Because of the extreme view of many naturalists concerning matter, this position is also known as "materialism." Naturalists are typically atheists, assuming that the theory of macro evolution provides an adequate explanation of how the world and its contents got to be the way they are.

NATURALISM
- including secular humanism and Marxism. People: Descartes, La Mettrie, Sagan, G.G. Simpson, Lippmann
1. Matter exists eternally and is all there is. God does not exist.
2. The cosmos exists as a uniformity of cause and effect in a closed system.
3. Human beings are complex "machines;" personality is an interrelation of chemical and physical properties we do not yet fully understand.
4. Death is extinction of personality and individuality.
5. History is a linear stream of events linked by cause and effect but without an overarching purpose.
6. Ethics is related only to human beings.

Figure 4.4. Sire's Summary of Naturalism

Nihilism is, as Sire points out, more a feeling of hopelessness and a revolt against any positive view of life than a full-blown philosophy or worldview. It can be seen as an expected result of a thoroughgoing naturalistic/materialistic perspective. Without God and a purpose to history where is hope?

NIHILISM
More a feeling than a philosophy; shown mostly in art and literature. People: Samuel Beckett, Kafka, Heller, Vonnegut, Douglas Adams
1. Same as Naturalism but with feelings of despair added.
2. Despair and hopelessness from taking Naturalism to the extreme.
3. Human beings are conscious machines without the ability to effect their own destiny or do anything significant; therefore, human beings (as valuable beings) are dead.
4. Nothing has meaning. We might as well already be dead.
5. History is meaningless.
6. Everything is relative (and meaningless).

Figure 4.5. Sire's Summary of Nihilism

The first of two existentialist perspectives is the atheistic variety. To their credit, atheistic existentialists are trying to overcome the despair of nihilism. However, they never quite escape from naturalism, buying into naturalistic presuppositions such as the eternality of matter, the non-existence of God, the cosmos as a closed system of cause and effect and the ultimate meaninglessness of history.

ATHEISTIC EXISTENTIALISM Attempts to transcend Nihilism. People: Camus, Sartre, Heidegger
1. The cosmos is composed solely of matter, but to human beings reality appears in two forms—subjective and objective.
2. For human beings alone existence precedes essence; people make themselves who they are.
3. Each person is totally free as regards their nature and destiny.
4. The highly wrought and tightly organized objective world stands over against human beings and appears absurd.
5. In full recognition of and against the absurdity of the objective world, the authentic person must revolt and create value.

Figure 4.6. Sire's Summary of Atheistic Existentialism

Theistic existentialism is a breath of fresh air when compared to the above naturalistic positions. For, without denying the findings of science, it brings God into the equation in a big way to explain how things got to be as they are. This is the position of many Evangelicals. It came into existence under Barth, Brunner and others to counter the atheistic positions that western societies had fallen into (and still are in) in the 1930s and 40s often related to the events in Europe that developed into the Second World War. It picked up themes that had been espoused by Soren Kierkegaard two generations earlier to counter "a dead orthodoxy of a dead church" in Europe that had "lost its theology completely and had settled for watered-down gospel of morality and good works" (1997:106).

Though this position accepts the following presuppositions of Theism, its questioning of the historicity of biblical events weakens it badly.

God is infinite and personal (triune), transcendent and immanent, omniscient, sovereign and good. God created the cosmos from nothing to operate with a uniformity of cause and effect in an open system. Human beings are created in the image of God, can know something of God and the cosmos and can act significantly. God can and does communicate with us. We were created good but now are fallen and need to be restored by God through Christ. For human beings death is either the gate to life with God and his people or life forever separated from God. Ethics is transcendent and based on God's character (1997:107).

With these things going for it, Sire suggests that in many respects existential theism might be seen as "more a special set of emphases within theism than it is a separate worldview" (1997:107). This view, unlike theism, starts with "human nature and our relation to the cosmos and God" (ibid.). "With theism God is assumed certainly to be there and of a given character; then people are defined in relationship to God. Theistic existentialism arrives at the same conclusion, but it starts elsewhere" (1997:108).

Theistic existentialists have been put off by the apparent deadness of objectivity and turn rather to the importance of theological and historical data to the observer. To be true, then, something must be true to *me*. In a quest for life in Christian experience, many, under the influence of so-called "higher criticism," took the position that it really doesn't matter if the Bible is historically accurate. What matters is that the accounts are "religiously true." "So while the doctrine of the neo-orthodox theologians looks ... like the orthodoxy of Calvin ... the historical basis for the doctrines was discounted and the doctrines themselves began to be lifted out of history" (1997:114).

For example, theistic existentialists, starting from human doubt that supernatural events could have really occurred, question the historical underpinnings of doctrines such as Jesus' resurrection, creation, redemption, human bodily resurrection and the second coming of Jesus. Each of these is granted importance as a religious symbol but, it is contended, whether or not they really happened is not important.

We would contend, however, that "there must be an event if there is to be meaning." If Jesus actually rose from the dead, that means something. If He did not rise that would mean something else. So we refuse to give up the basis for our faith in historical reality even though we may admit that the personal meaning of these events to Christians is of supreme importance. We can also agree, with theistic existentialists, that coming to Christ must involve a "leap of faith" even if the history is real and that it is that leap of faith that saves, not our knowledge of the history. A position that contends that "meaning is created in the subjective world" does not have to go to the extreme of denying that there are "objective referents" supporting it (1997:115-16).

THEISTIC EXISTENTIALISM (Neo-orthodoxy) People: Barth, Brunner, Neibuhr, Bultmann, Kierkegaard, Buber		
1. Human beings are personal beings who, when they come to full consciousness, find themselves in an alien universe; whether or not God exists is a tough question to be solved not by reason but by faith.		
2. The personal is the valuable, relationships primary.		
3. Knowledge is subjectivity; the whole truth is often paradoxical.		
4. History as a record of events is uncertain and unimportant, but history as a model or type or myth to be made present and lived is of supreme importance.		
Sire contrasts Theistic Existentialism with Dead Orthodoxy as follows:		
	Dead Orthodoxy	Theistic Existentialism
Doctrine	Depersonalized (as in dead orthodoxy)	Personalized (as by a live theistic existentialism)
Sin	Breaking a rule	Betraying a relationship
Repentance	Admitting guilt	Sorrowing over personal betrayal
Forgiveness	Canceling a penalty	Renewing fellowship
Faith	Believing a set of propositions	Committing oneself to a person
Christian life	Obeying rules	Pleasing the Lord, a Person

Figure 4.7. Sire's Summary of Theistic Existentialism

Next, Sire turns to Eastern Pantheistic Monism, a perspective that has fascinated many in the West and formed one of the significant sources from which New Age has drawn. This is the most different of the perspectives so far discussed since it wipes out any distinction between person and cosmos advocating that we seek "oneness" with the cosmos and that reality is the experience of that oneness and involves the recognition that all else is illusion.

	EASTERN PANTHEISTIC MONISM
	Sire's focus is on the Hindu Advaita Vedanta system of Shankara, the most popular monistic perspective in the West. He does not treat Buddhism which is similar but differs in a key point—the nature of ultimate reality. Persons: Mahesh Yogi, Hesse
1.	Atman is Brahman; that is, the soul of each and every human being is the Soul of the cosmos.
2.	Some things are more one than others. Reality is a hierarchy of appearances or illusions, some of which are closer than others to being at one with the One. Matter is the least real; then vegetable life, then animal, and finally humanity which is also hierarchical, the guru being closer than other humans to pure being.
3.	Many (if not all) roads lead to the One. There are many paths from maya to reality. What is important is not doctrine but technique. Whatever road one follows, the aim is to get on the vibe level with reality, to turn one's soul to the harmony of the cosmos and ultimately to the one solid, non-harmonic, non-dual, Ultimate vibration—Brahman, the One.
4.	To realize one's oneness with the cosmos is to pass beyond personality. Human beings in their essence—their truest, fullest being—are impersonal.
5.	To realize one's oneness with the cosmos is to pass beyond knowledge. The principle of non-contradiction does not apply where ultimate reality is concerned. To be is not to know, since knowledge, like personality, demands duality—a knower and a known.
6.	To realize one's oneness with the cosmos is to pass beyond good and evil; the cosmos is perfect at every moment. No soul ever passes out of existence, though it has to go through whatever illusory forms its past action, its karma, requires. All soul is eternal, for all soul is essentially Soul and thus forever the One.
7.	Death is the end of individual, personal existence, but it changes nothing essential in an individual's nature. It is the end of a person but not the soul, Atman, which is indestructible. One is reincarnated into another life.
8.	To realize one's oneness with the One is to pass beyond time. Time is unreal. History is cyclical.

Figure 4.8. Sire's Summary of Eastern Pantheistic Monism

Next, we turn to animism, the worldview of the majority of the world's peoples. We will deal more fully with this perspective in later chapters but here simply present Sire's minimal treatment with a few additions. The key to animism is the recognition that animists are primarily concerned with the spirits, whether or not they believe in a high god. Many do believe in such a god but reason that he will be good to them so they need not pay much attention to him.

The spirits that fill the space between them and God, however, can cause them trouble if they are not treated right. They are capricious and demand attention. If they are treated right, they will bring blessing. If they are treated wrongly, though, they can cause great harm. Thus, the primary concern of animists is to keep the spirits happy by honoring them, feeding them and not upsetting them.

Such an awareness of spirits and their activities often leads to the development of techniques to try to control them. Shamans and priests often make a handsome living assisting people in their quest to gain the assistance of the spirits to bring blessing on themselves and their families (e.g., to bring fertility) or to bring misfortune on their enemies (e.g., through cursing). Magic is also used to manipulate what is often conceived of as impersonal power.

Animism, is a second of the perspectives from which New Age draws. The whole concept of "spirit guides" is derived from animistic thinking as are the various ways of contacting the dead.

ANIMISM
—the world's majority worldview (not developed by Sire beyond the following points).
1. The natural universe is inhabited by countless spiritual beings, often conceived in a rough hierarchy, the top of which is the Sky God (vaguely like theism's God but without his interest in human beings).
2. The spirits are to be focused on more than whatever Sky God there may be because the spirits can hurt us whereas the Sky God will probably be good to us.
3. These spiritual beings range in temperament from vicious and nasty to comic and beneficent.
4. For people to get by in life the evil spirits must be placated and the good ones wooed by gifts and offerings, ceremonies and incantations.
5. Witch doctors, sorcerers and shamans, through long, arduous training, have learned to control the spirit world to some extent, and ordinary people are much beholden to their power to cast out spirits of illness, drought and so forth.
6. Ultimately there is a unity to all of life—that is, the cosmos is a continuum of spirit and matter. Animals may be the ancestors of human beings, people may change into animals, trees and stones may have spirits in them.

Figure 4.9. Sire's Summary of Animism

New Age is an attempt to recognize the validity of a certain amount of science but in combination with Eastern religious ideas and animism. Unlike naturalism, the spirit world is taken seriously and the power of spirits (often seen as angels) is utilized to enable us to get where we want to go. Such power can make us rich or famous if that is the way we choose or can enable us to become more fully one with nature (Monism) if that's our choice. In any event, we can gain blessings such as health and healing, protection and other benefits through contact with the spirits and use of naturalistic medicines and healing practices. And we can develop a "cosmic consciousness" that takes us beyond normal space, time and moral reality.

A major attraction of New Age is the recognition, contrary to naturalism, that there is more to life and existence than science alone has given us. Thus, the promise of greater power is enticing. The old satanic promise that we can be gods also draws people.

This is a worldview that is still in flux with many competing perspectives that do not reconcile well with each other. So Sire asks,

> Can the New Age—with roots in three separate worldviews—be a unified system? Not really. Or, not yet. We are seeing this worldview in formation. Not all of the propositions [listed below] fit neatly together; still there is a large measure of agreement among the avant garde in virtually every area of culture that something like this description is a valid—or at least useful—way of looking at reality (1997:145).

> **NEW AGE**
> —animism with a naturalistic twist, roots in three worldviews (animism, naturalism and pantheism). People: Castaneda, Roszak, MacLaine, Lilly, Ferguson, Capra
>
> 1. Whatever the nature of being (idea or matter, energy or particle), the self is the kingpin—the prime reality. As human beings grow in their awareness and grasp of this fact, the human race is on the verge of a radical change in human nature; even now we see harbingers of transformed humanity and prototypes of the New Age.
>
> 2. The cosmos, while unified in the self, is manifested in two more dimensions: the visible universe, considered real and accessible through ordinary consciousness, and the invisible universe (or Mind at Large), also real and accessible through altered states of consciousness.
>
> 3. The core experience of the New Age is cosmic consciousness, in which ordinary categories of space, time and morality tend to disappear.
>
> 4. Physical death is not the end of the self but a transition to another stage of life via reincarnation. Under the experience of cosmic consciousness, the fear of death is removed.
>
> 5. Three distinct attitudes are taken to the metaphysical question of the nature of reality under the general framework of the New Age:
>   1) the occult version, in which the beings and things perceived in states of altered consciousness exist apart from the self that is conscious,
>   2) the psychedelic version, in which these things and beings are projections of the conscious self, and
>   3) the conceptual relativist version, in which the cosmic consciousness is the conscious activity of a mind using one of many non-ordinary models for
>
> 6. New age reflects every aspect of animism (see below), though often giving it a naturalistic twist—or demythologizing it by psychology.

Figure 4.10. Sire's Summary of New Age

Postmodernism, then, is the last of Sire's ten "worldviews." He calls this the latest form of naturalism. It is also a dive into subjectivism, relativism and to some extent despair. Sire states,

> No longer is there a single story, a metanarrative (in our terms a worldview), that holds western culture together. It is not just that there have long been many stories, each of which gives its binding power to the social group that takes it as its own. The naturalists have their story, the pantheists theirs, the Christians theirs, ad infinitum. With postmodernism no story can have any more credibility than any other. All stories are equally valid (1997:174)

Every concept, theory, description, command, moral standard, etc. is relative with no ground to stand on to evaluate one as against another. In terms of our discussion of reality, there is no capital R REALITY, only an infinite series of equally valid small r realities. And that is stated as an absolute truth!

To clarify the postmodern positions, Sire points to five contrasts between premodern, modern and postmodern understandings:

With regard to Justice:

There has been a movement from (1) a "premodern" concern for a just society based on revelation from a just God to (2) a "modern" attempt to use universal reason as the guide to justice to (3) a "postmodern" despair of any universal standard for justice. Society then moves from medieval hierarchy to Enlightenment democracy to post modern anarchy (1997:175)

With regard to Story:

[T]here is a movement from (1) the Christian "premodern" notion of a revealed determinate metanarrative to (2) the "modern" notion of the autonomy of a human reason with access to truth of correspondence to (3) the "postmodern" notion that we create truth as we construct languages that serve our purposes (1997:180-81). Another take on Story:

[W]e can trace a movement from (1) a "premodern" acceptance of a metanarrative written by God and revealed in scripture to (2) a "modern" metanarrative of universal reason yielding truth about reality to (3) a "postmodern" reduction of all metanarratives to power plays (1997:181).

With regard to Human Dignity:

[T]here is a shift from (1) the "premodern" theistic notion that human beings are dignified by being created in the image of God to (2) the "modern" notion that human beings are the product of their DNA template, which itself is the result of unplanned evolution based on chance mutations and the survival of the fittest, to (3) the "postmodern" notion of an insubstantial self constructed by the language it uses to describe itself (1997:182).

With regard to Ethics:

> [W]e recount the shift from (1) the 'premodern' theistic ethics based on the character of a transcendent God who is good and has revealed that goodness to us to (2) the 'modern' ethics based on a notion of universal human reason and experience and the human ability to discern objective right from wrong to (3) the 'postmodern' notion that morality is the multiplicity of languages used to describe right from wrong (1997:183).

Sire holds out little hope for the survival of postmodernism. He sees is as rife with internal contradictions—almost as many as in New Age—and often difficult to understand. It has influenced the disciplines of history and English literature but has but little impact on science since "Most scientists, whether naturalists or Christian theists, are critical realists" while "postmodernists are antirealists; they deny that there is any known or knowable connection between what we think and say with what is actually there" (1997:185). However, says Sire, "Postmodernism pulls the smiling mask of arrogance from the face of naturalism" (1997:189). Nevertheless, he finds three positive contributions stemming from the perspective:

> 1. [P]ostmodernism's critique of optimistic naturalism is often on target. Too much confidence has been placed in human reason and the scientific method (1997:187).

> 2. [T]he postmodern recognition that language is closely associated with power is also apt. We do tell "stories," believe "doctrines," hold "philosophies" because they give us or our community power over others. The public application of our definitions of madness does put people in mental health wards (ibid.).

> 3. [A]ttention to the social conditions under which we understand the world can alert us to our limited perspective as finite human beings. Society does mold us in many ways (1997:188).

But even these positive aspects of the perspective cannot overcome the fact that even the rejection of a "modern" or "premodern" story is a story. Secondly, the claim that we cannot access reality but only tell stories about it does not necessarily mean that we must deny that there is a reality that the story refers to. And third, "postmodernism's critique of the autonomy and sufficiency of human reason rests on the autonomy and sufficiency of human reason" (1997:188).

POSTMODERNISM - the latest form of naturalism. People: Nietzsche, Rorty, Foucault
1. The first question postmodernism addresses is not what is there or how we know what is there but how language functions to construct meaning itself. In other words, there has been a shift in "first things" from being to knowing to constructing meaning.
2. The truth about reality itself is forever hidden from us. All we can do is to tell stories. Postmodernists are antirealists; they deny that there is any known or knowable connection between what we think and say with what is actually there.
3. All narratives mask a play for power. Any one narrative used as a metanarrative is oppressive.
4. Human beings make themselves who they are by the languages they construct about themselves.
5. Ethics, like knowledge, is a linguistic construct. Social good is whatever society takes it to be.
6. The cutting edge of culture is literary theory.

Figure 4.11. Sire's Summary of Postmodernism

One could do a lot worse than to follow Sire's approach. Indeed, we will be dealing with most of these issues from a different approach later in this volume.

Ninian Smart

A second instructive non-anthropological approach is that of Ninian Smart of the University of California, Santa Barbara, in his book *Worldviews: Cross-cultural Explorations of Human Beliefs* (1983). For Smart, the term worldview is virtually synonymous with, or even a subcategory of *religion*. I differ with him at this point for at least two reasons: I reserve the term religion for surface-level cultural phenomena while using the term *worldview* for deep-level assumptions that underlie all of a culture. The second reason is that I believe Smart is using the label "religion" to cover assumptions and perspectives that are genuinely worldview issues. His approach, then, leaves one confused as to what is to be seen as religion and what to be seen as worldview. Do we have two terms that are synonymous or is there a distinction?

If we compare the following quotes with the longer one below, we can see a bit of Smart's confusion. We can, however, also see helpful insight. He says,

> I shall use worldviews in a general sense to refer to both religion and ideologies, and also to refer specifically to secular ideologies. ...The study of religions and secular worldviews—what I have termed "worldview analysis"—tries to depict the history and nature of the beliefs and symbols which form a deep part of the structure of human consciousness and society (1983:2).

I regard this as a reasonable statement. Later in the book, however, Smart makes the following statement in which he makes "worldview analysis" a subcategory of the study of religion.

> [A] main part of the modern study of religion may be called "worldview analysis"—the attempt to describe and understand human worldviews, especially those that have had widespread influence—ranging from varieties of Christianity and Buddhism to the more politically oriented systems of Islam and Marxism, and from ancient religions and philosophies such as Platonism and Confucianism to modern new religions in Africa and America. To see how they work we must relate ideas to symbols and to practices, so that worldview analysis is not merely a matter of listing beliefs. ... [for] belief, consciousness, and practice are bound together.
>
> An educated person should know about and have a feel for many things, but perhaps the most important is to have an understanding of some of the chief worldviews which have shaped, and are now shaping human culture and action. It is for this purpose that I here try to present some of the main elements and themes of the modern study of religion (1983:5-6).

The equating or confusing of religion and worldview is not uncommon among contemporary thinkers. I hope that one of the things this presentation will help us with is to see them as separable and separate.

Smart sees the world divided up into six "blocs of belief." These are:

1. The Modern West	4. Old Asia (India, Japan)
2. The Marxist Bloc	5. The Latin World
3. The Islamic Crescent	6. Black Africa and The Pacific

Figure 4.12. Smart's Six "Blocs of Belief"

For each of these blocs, Smart deals with six of what he terms "dimensions." These dimensions (1983:7-8) are:

Doctrinal—"a religion typically has a system of doctrines."	**Ritual**—"typically a religion has a ritual dimension."
Mythic—"typically a religion has a story or stories to tell."	**Experiential**—"ritual helps to express feelings ... and ... provide a context of dramatic experience ..."
Ethical—"a religion has an ethical dimension."	**Social**—"any tradition needs some kind of organization in order to perpetuate itself."

Figure 4.13. Smart's Six Dimensions of Religion

Smart also focuses on three features or influences that have affected each of the dimensions in recent times. The first of these is what he calls the *Rise of Nationalism*, defined as the concept "that every people should in principle have its own state," a concept that originated before the French Revolution but has been especially prominent since. He sees nationalism as "not quite a religion, but [having] some of the same characteristics" (1983:48).

Spinning off from this feature, then, are such things as national languages and national educational systems. "It is important," says Smart, "to see how religion and worldviews are often deeply involved in the national idea; the advent of nationalism represents a new backdrop against which religious attitudes and worldviews are thrown" (1983:49). Along with nationalism, then, comes the increasing interaction between the blocs, an interaction that makes the present situation exciting but also makes each worldview harder to neatly distinguish from others.

Secondly, Smart points to the importance of recognizing the *Contributions of The Past*. These have been formative of the present perspectives. Among such, he points to the ways in which western culture has been influenced by Hebrew, platonic, Egyptian, Gnostic and many other streams of thought coming from the past, including, of course, Christianity. Such influences are often there even if the given perspective was rejected.

The third of the influences that Smart feels need to be factored into any treatment of worldview is *Twentieth-Century Secular Humanism*. Though historically the West has been at least nominally Judeo-Christian,

> many people today feel that the day of traditional religion is past: the scientific outlook has no place for God, or for reincarnation, or for other central traditional preoccupations. ... in modern societies people increasingly are moving away from traditional religious patterns. ... What a person believes becomes his own private concern. ... There are more and more "religionless" people in modern society (1983:52).

Under this influence, the focus of people's attention is on humans, not on God. Human thought, especially scientific thought, becomes the measure of all things and "all true knowledge about the world is ultimately to be found through science, or at least within the framework of a scientific outlook" (1983:53). Smart sees atheistic existentialism as a spin-off from secular humanism. Marxism, however, he sees as distinct since "[s]cientific humanism favors liberty, a liberal outlook, and democratic institutions, and thus tends to be at odds with mainline Marxism" (1983:53).

In dealing with *the structure of worldviews*, Smart states, "The various belief-systems of the world have different pictures of the cosmos. We might think of the structures of these views as a triangle: at the apex is the cosmos, at one end of the base the self, at the other society" (1983:54).

Worldviews are formed in pictures through the interaction of these three variables. For the theist, "the cosmos is a divine creation which reveals God's glory" (1983:55). For animists the cosmos "has a more complex character: it has in it many various powers and beings which animate different parts of it" (ibid.). For Hindus "the cosmos has expanded and contracted repeatedly over vast periods of time" (1983:58). For Buddhists the cosmos "is a vast series of interconnected events, all of which are short-lived ... [and] without permanent substance" (1983:59). In contrast to all of these, materialists see even our minds as "a byproduct of the cosmos. The world was not created by God; God was created by us and we are created out of matter" (1983:60). In such ways, Smart sees the person and the society interacting with the cosmos and with each other.

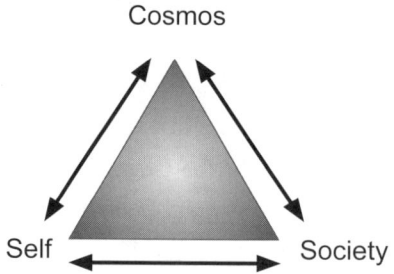

Figure 4.14. Smart's Triangle representing the dynamics of how people view the cosmos in relation to themselves and society

In transitioning from this general treatment of religions/worldviews, Sire makes explicit both his view of such perspectives and the motivation that spikes his interest. Stating his view of worldview perspectives, he says,

> These different pictures of the cosmos are affected partly by the human search for the truth -about what surrounds us, and partly by the quest for meaning. The human being sees the cosmos as a kind of mirror: can she read in its strange and beautiful features a reflection of herself? What light can the sun and the stars throw upon the directions of life? (1983:60).

His motivation is in view, then, as he speaks of the emergence of a "global city" and a "global civilization." He asks, how will we deal with the differences as we come into greater and greater interaction with those who see things differently?

> The varied worldviews as they come together in the global city pose vital questions about the future. Is human life to be exhausted in the struggle for material well-being? To what degree are we nourished by visions of the transcendent and of what lies somehow beyond the cosmos? What are the ways in which religion and science can live together, if in fact they can live together at all? How much will the traditional faiths change in their struggle to stay meaningful and believable to a world where human knowledge and technology are expanding so vastly?

> From one perspective the different worldviews are maps of how to live. From another they themselves depict those powers in human experience and the cosmos which stir people to action. Figuring out their meaning is thus one way of coming to see what will happen in

the complex emerging global civilization which is forming around us right now.

Central to the shape of traditional faiths, and central to the estimate of the spiritual power of human beings, are the patterns of religious experience which have irrupted into human life (1983:60-61).

Questions concerning the nature and functioning of the cosmos are to Smart central to his discussion of worldview. So he summarizes the various views of the cosmos and makes a series of contrasts. He contrasts theistic creationism with views that see the physical universe as basically spiritual (animism) and those that are quite unconcerned about its nature with materialist views. He mentions the so-called "big bang" theory of how the universe came into existence in contrast to the Buddhist view that the universe is essentially without substance but, rather, a series of short-lived but interconnected events and processes. In contrast to a Christian creationist view that the world was created once in its present form, he cites a Hindu view that "the cosmos has expanded and contracted repeatedly over vast periods of time, for God does not create once and for all, but rather, after periods of quiet and passivity He or She recreates the cosmos" (1983:58).

In an effort to point to the abovementioned "patterns of religious experience" with which the "global civilization" has to deal, Smart outlines five basic perspectives (1983:55-61) that I will summarize in the following charts:

THEISM (Christian, Jewish, Muslim)
1. The cosmos is created by God for his glory. It was created a finite time ago and is essentially good though marred by hostile spiritual forces.
2. Theists, except for deists, believe God continues to guide and sustain the cosmos.
3. Humans are created by God in his image and have a hope of salvation, a kind of blissful union with God.
4. For society there is a hope of founding a divine kingdom on earth.

Figure 4.15. Smart's Summary of Theism's View of the Cosmos

ANIMISM
1. The cosmos has in it many various powers and beings that animate different parts of it. It is full of powers and gods that are unseen but show themselves throughout nature.
2. Often a belief in a High God, but he is not so easily approached since he is exalted and remote, so not much attention paid to him.
3. Smart sees animism fading under the impact of missions and technology.
4. Yet a kind of "environmental animism" is emerging in which the cosmos is seen as containing powers and forces, including the human race, which need to live together in harmony.

Figure 4.16. Smart's Summary of Animism's View of the Cosmos

HINDUISM
1. Smart sees the Hindu view of the cosmos as two-tiered, on one level as the body of God, on the other as an illusion with ultimate reality beyond it.
2. Many gods but all manifestations of how the one divine Being manifests him or herself.
3. In Vedanta Hinduism, beyond the Creator (the soul of the cosmos) is unity—the highest experience. Through self-control and meditation, one can attain pure consciousness in which the self and the divine Being can become one. We can, thus, go beyond the cosmos which is maya, illusory anyway.
4. In Hindu thinking, the cosmos has expanded and contracted repeatedly over vast periods of time, for God does not create once and for all, but rather, after periods of quiet and passivity He or She recreates the cosmos.

Figure 4.17. Smart's Summary of Hindu Views of the Cosmos

BUDDHISM
1. No creator, no single all-powerful God. No ultimate beginning of things.
2. The cosmos is both uncreated and impermanent. It consists of a vast series of interconnected events, all of which are short-lived, a huge cloud of processes. It is itself without permanent substance, a kind of mirage.
3. The gods are not denied, just considered irrelevant to the highest aim of living things.
4. Nothing is eternal or changeless. The heart of the cosmos is empty, an emptiness seen when a person gains enlightenment, nirvana.
5. Everything, including me, is in flux. I wander from incarnation to incarnation with nothing permanent to me. Only if I see the true nature of emptiness and impermanence, usually through a kind of inner vision brought about by following various practices of meditation, shall I gain liberation.

Figure 4.18. Smart's Summary of the Buddhist View of the Cosmos

MATERIALISM (including Marxism and philosophical materialism)
1. We create God in our image, to serve our purposes.
2. The universe emerged from a "big bang." We are "created" out of matter.
3. For Marx culture and knowledge are essentially byproducts of material relations. Religion is an illusion, no need to postulate God to explain change and motion in matter, the inner contradictions in matter supply the dynamics for change.
4. Conscious states (mind) are nothing but specific kinds of physiological processes occurring in the brain and central nervous system. No non-material beings or human soul.

Figure 4.19. Smart's Summary of the Materialist View of the Cosmos

In an interesting paragraph, Smart likens the world's religious landscape to a jungle:

> The world of many small-scale peoples has been one in which the cosmos is a jungle—the many trees representing the gods and spirits. When Islam or Christianity comes along the jungle is leveled, so that one Tree can be planted, that Tree which represents the One God. The old jungle may put forth shoots and seedlings, and these (the old gods a little revived) are the saints of Europe, Mexico, and elsewhere. Hinduism, however, does not remove the jungle: it treats the many plants as leading inward to the One Tree which is to be found at the Center. Buddhism, by contrast, though it does

not remove the jungle, builds a road—the "eightfold path" which takes us to final liberation—around the jungle. Wander into the jungle if you wish, but that will not bring you further along the road (1983:57).

Again, we could do worse than following some of Smart's ideas, though he is not nearly as helpful to us as Sire. As mentioned, the rest of Smart's book deals mainly with surface-level religious behavior and is not, therefore, as relevant for our purposes as Sire's presentation.

David K. Naugle

David Naugle, a professor of philosophy at Dallas Baptist University has done the Christian community a great service in publishing a revision of his Ph.D. dissertation entitled *Worldview: The History of a Concept* (2002). In an enthusiastic blurb on the back of the book, William Abraham of Perkins School of Theology calls the book a "wonderfully clear and concise book" that is "Indispensable reading for anyone interested in the idea of worldview, this book fills a glaring gap in the literature and should become the standard work on the subject in English." It is also highly recommended by James Sire.

This book, like Sire's, advocates the narrower view of worldview that uses terms like "Christian worldview," or "biblical worldview" on the assumption that the basics of a Christian perspective constitute the whole of a worldview. As noted, I do not take that narrow a position, though I fully agree with most of what these advocates of what I would call an "evangelical Christian perspective" are saying with regard to that perspective.

Within its genre, this is a masterful work. Naugle traces the history within philosophy and to a lesser extent in other disciplines of the concept first labeled *Weltanschauung*. Though his primary concern is to deal with the views of Christian scholars, he covers the ground on the non-Christian side as well. Most of that material is, however, not of primary relevance to us. His theological and philosophical "reflections" in the later parts of the book, though, contain high quality insights from the perspective of a "Christian worldview" advocate.

I would like to register one disappointment before we look at some of Naugle's material. Though he has a brief section on "Worldview in Cultural Anthropology," in which he deals with Kearney and Redfield, he misses the insights of those of us within anthropology who deal with worldview from a Christian perspective. Interestingly, he provides an appendix of books on Christian worldview not addressed in his study. Books by Hiebert and both my wife and myself appear in that listing.

To his credit, Naugle regards Kearney's treatment of worldview as "one of the most complete worldview models available today in any discipline" (2002:244). Perhaps at some future date the broader approach we advocate here will be more recognized by Christian philosophers.

Turning to Naugle's approach, we note that his goal is "to demonstrate how to think about this notion [worldview] biblically" (2002:290). His method is to "naturalize" the concept within Christian discussion in order to harness it for Christian use, taking it away from its origins in non- and anti-Christian discourse. Though the concept is widely used outside of evangelical Christianity with relativistic connotations, when used to label Christian perspectives, it "must shed its relativist and subjectivist clothing and assume new objectivist attire" for, Naugle contends (and we would agree), "God's existence and character constitute the absolute value in the universe. He establishes and imparts meaning to everything. ... The expression 'Christian or biblical worldview,' therefore, does not imply a mere religious possibility or philosophical option, but suggests an absolutist perspective on life that is real, true, and good" (2002:266).

Though I don't feel that Naugle makes enough of it, he does take a critical realist position that allows for the relativities of Christian understandings as well as the absolutes in focus in the above quote (2002:321ff).

One intriguing part of Naugle's approach that risks missing the distinction I have tried to make between person and structure, is the way he connects worldview with the human heart. Perhaps support for this view would come from a look at alternative translations of the word translated "heart." Might it, along with the word translated "mind" often be better translated "perspective" as in Rom. 12:2 where the reference is to the "renewing of your perspective?" He says,

> ... the phenomenon of worldview itself must be comprehended in terms of the biblical doctrine of the heart. In other words, the heart of the matter of worldview is that worldview is a matter of the heart. ... [for] *into* the heart go the issues of life. Before the springs of life flow *out* of the heart, something must first and even continue to flow *into it*. ... Things are internalized *before* they are externalized. For, indeed, the life-shaping content of the heart is determined not only by nature or organic predispositions, but very much by nurture. ... [Then] *out* of the heart go the issues of life. Once the heart of an individual is formed by the powerful forces of

both nature and nurture, it constitutes the presuppositional basis of life. Presuppositions are those first principles that most people take for granted. ... They constitute the background logic for all thinking and doing. They do not rest upon other principles but are rested upon; they are not argued *to* but argued *from*. They are responsible for how the world appears and life is conducted. ...

From a scriptural point of view, therefore, the heart is responsible for how a man or woman sees the world. Indeed, what goes into the heart from the outside world eventually shapes its fundamental dispositions and determines what comes out of it as the springs of life. Consequently, the heart establishes the basic presuppositions of life and, because of its life-determining influence, must always be carefully guarded (2002:269-272).

Given Naugle's position with regard to Christian worldview, it is not surprising that he suggests that a part of spiritual warfare is a "warfare *over* worldviews." He sees,

... a megabattle between the forces of light and darkness over the identity or definition of the universe. A key strategem of the devil, who is the father of lies (John 8:44), is to conceal the true nature of things through the proliferation of multiple cosmic falsehoods in order to secure the blindness of the human heart and its ultimate spiritual perdition (2 Cor. 4:3-4). In the conflagration that has engulfed the universe, the truth about reality is satanically enshrouded in darkness, and a multitude of idolatries and fallacious conceptions of life, counterfeiting as wisdom and enlightenment, are put in its place. What better way for Satan to deflect the light of truth than by ... controlling what goes into the hearts of men and women, shaping their interests and ruling their lives. Worldviews are the basis for a zeitgeist and are at the center of this process. If this big-picture strategy succeeds, then there is only an occasional need for personal temptation to sin. How people get their jollies is of little interest to Satan if he has already captured and misdirected their hearts (2002:280-281).

Naugle provides a worldview interpretation of Rom. 1:21ff. He says, "Because people *are* sinful, they are religiously hostile toward God, have replaced the knowledge of him with false deities, and consequently have concocted erroneous explanations of reality" (2002:276). Anti-God worldviews, then, are the result of the effects of sin and idolatry on the human heart. Sin and error, then, are embedded in anti-God worldviews because they flow from sinful human hearts.

> What is certain ... is that the human heart in its fallen condition will continue to suppress the truth in unrighteousness and to manufacture surrogate gods and errant perspectives on the world. ... What is also certain is that spiritual warfare will continue, and it will continue to revolve around worldviews. The kingdom of Satan will capitalize on human pride and self-sufficiency as the source of idolatries and errors to insure the fact that the world's religious and philosophical environments are dominated by false notions that sustain deception and keep people from God and the truth (2002:284).

Later in this book we will deal with the issue of how to communicate for change at the worldview level. To see this, as Naugle sees it, as a matter of spiritual warfare is indeed helpful. For Satan himself is behind the lies that people believe and the worldview assumptions they hold based on those lies. In this regard, Naugle adds,

> Since Satan and the demons can manipulate men and women only to the extent that they are deceived, what better way to achieve this than by the promulgation of fallacious conceptions of reality through the conduit of the spirit of the age from which no one can escape? To top off this scheme, the principalities and powers under devilish management cleverly cover their tracks and operate in such a clandestine fashion so as to suggest their non-existence. [As C.S. Lewis put it] "They withdraw from sight into the men, elements, and institutions through which they make their power felt. To seem not to appear is part of their essence" (2002:283).

One valuable aspect of Naugle's approach is the section of the book in which he deals with the connections between worldview and a variety of aspects of human thinking. He deals there with worldview in relation to signs and symbols, narrative, reason, hermeneutics and epistemology. I have already referred to the critical realist position he takes in the area of epistemology. One more quote from this section will illustrate his treatment of worldview in relation to signs and symbols. Though he tends to personalize signs and symbols a bit more than I am comfortable with,

I like the statement.

> Behold, then, the power of signs and symbols across the whole spectrum of reality and human existence. They permeate the physical universe; they are germane to all aspects of culture; they are essential to human thought, cognition, and communication; they are efficacious instruments of either truth or falsehood; they create symbolic worlds in which people live, move, and have their being. Indeed, a certain string of symbols possesses unique cultural power and determines the meaning of life. Those symbols I would designate a worldview. As an individual's or culture's foundation and system of denotative signs, they are promulgated through countless communicative avenues and mysteriously find their way to the innermost regions of the heart. There they provide a foundation and interpretation of life. They inform the categories of consciousness. They are the putative object of faith and the basis for hope, however it may be conceived. They are embraced as true and offer a way of life. They are the essential source of individual and sociocultural security. They are personal and cultural structures that define human existence. Thus, when they are in crisis or are challenged, people respond anxiously, and even with hostility (2002:296).

When, toward the end of the book, Naugle summarizes his approach in a rather technical definition of worldview, this is what he comes up with:

> A worldview, then, is a semiotic system of narrative signs that creates the definitive symbolic universe which is responsible in the main for the shape of a variety of life-determining, human practices. It creates the channels in which the waters of reason flow. It establishes the horizons of an interpreter's point of view by which texts of all types are understood. It is that mental medium by which the world is known. The human heart is its home, and it provides a home for the human heart. At the end of the day it is hard to conceive of a more important human or cultural reality, theoretically or practically, than the semiotic system of narrative signs that makes up a worldview (2002:330).

Naugle's "final conclusion," then, is

> This examination of the role of worldview in Protestant evangelicalism, Roman Catholicism, and Eastern Orthodoxy; the massive philological and philosophical history of the concept; its prominent use in the natural and social sciences; its theological utility; and its impact as a semiotic system of narrative signs on reason, hermeneutics, and epistemology all lead to three simple conclusions. The first is that worldview has played an extraordinary role in modern and Christian thought. The second is that it is one of the central intellectual conceptions in recent times. The third is that it is a notion of utmost, if not final, human, cultural, and Christian significance (2002:344).

If this is not enough of a pep talk to launch us into what follows in this book, Naugle continues,

> After all, what could be more important or influential than the way an individual, a family, a community, a nation, or an entire culture conceptualizes reality? Is there anything more profound or powerful than the shape and content of human consciousness and its primary interpretation of the nature of things? When it comes to the deepest questions about human life and existence, does anything surpass the final implications of the answers supplied by one's essential *Weltanschauung*? Because of the divine design of human nature, each person in a native religious quest possesses an insatiable desire to understand the secret of life. A hunger and thirst, indeed, a burning fire rages to solve the riddle of the universe. There is a yearning in the very core of the heart to rest in some understanding of the alpha and omega of the human condition (2002:345).

With that we will conclude these brief presentations of three non-anthropological approaches to our subject. These will suffice to illustrate some of what is going on in other circles in their use of the concept of worldview. Though these approaches to the study of worldview differ markedly from mine, each has its value both to those outside the reach of this volume and to us who continue on with the emphasis that seems right for our purposes. Next we turn to the approaches of some other anthropologists.

CHAPTER 5

OTHER APPROACHES: ANTHROPOLOGICAL

Though we could find quite a number of anthropologists to summarize, I will restrict this section to four: Louis Luzbetak, David Burnett, Michael Kearney and Paul Hiebert. Burnett and Hiebert are evangelical Christians, Luzbetak a Roman Catholic. These three are also former missionaries.

The reader will notice that anthropologists approach our topic quite differently from the more popular approaches we have been surveying. For one thing, we are quite concerned about the structuring of worldview, especially in relation to the rest of culture, on the one hand, and the people who live according to that culture on the other.

Louis Luzbetak

Luzbetak is a Roman Catholic anthropologist who worked as a missionary in Papua New Guinea. After a long career as missionary, teacher and diplomat, he has now gone to be with the Lord after living to a ripe old age in retirement at the headquarters of the Society of the Divine Word in Techny, Illinois. His excellent anthropology text is titled, The Church and Cultures (1963, revised and enlarged 1988). The part of his 1988 book we will be focusing on is pages 225-291, the section concerning the integration of culture.

Luzbetak sees culture as made up of three levels:

1. ***The surface level*** of which he says,

> … the surface level of culture, [consists of]… the *forms* or "shapes" of behavior, the *who, what, where, when, how,* and *what kind*. These are the symbols *minus* their meanings.

The forms are the building blocks or "phonetics" of culture; they are "sounds" that can be described apart from the structure and meaning of the "language." Forms provide only a superficial (etic) understanding of the culture. By contrast, our concern in anthropology … is with an *emic* or an "insider's" understanding of symbols—the form as it is structured in the particular symbolic system and as such carries meaning (1988:225).

I have included this statement to give us a picture of Luzbetak's overall approach. I consider it a fairly good statement except for the implication that forms *contain* their meanings. This is a fairly common mistake made by anthropologists. Communication theory teaches us, however, that cultural forms *convey* but do not *contain* their meanings. Meanings are always in *people*, never in forms (see Kraft 1991). Words and other cultural forms are used to transmit messages from people who have meanings in themselves, to other people who create their own meanings on the basis of their interpretations of those cultural forms. These interpretations, then, are strongly influenced by the understandings of their cultural or subcultural group.

2. Secondly, Luzbetak sees **an intermediate level that he calls the "structural integration" level**. He points to such features of a culture as institutions and complexes as exhibiting this level, noting that in every culture we find contrasting and meaningful basic units of structure. These units are what we will later refer to as "categories," the items regarded by the people of a society as worthy of being classified or categorized.

Such contrasts as that between material, animal and humans or types of dances or kinds of automobiles fit into this category for Luzbetak. An important point that he raises is that in any given culture, whatever the units are, they are internally unique to that culture and related to each other in unique ways. Neither internally nor externally, then, can they be assumed to be the same as similar cultural forms in another culture. His key illustration is of an American high school education with all that it implies and means within the society (1988:236-7).

3. Luzbetak's third level, however, is the one that we are most interested in. He calls this **the level of "psychological integration"** and focuses first on what he calls the "mentality" of a people (1988: 249ff). He approaches his subject by asking,

> Of all the human potentialities in adjusting to life, why does a society choose certain more or less coherent ways of thought, attitude, and action and reject others? What is it that makes cultures into systems? What, in the last analysis, is responsible for such integration? The answer is the mentality of a society (1988:249).

Luzbetak notes that what is considered by a people to be true, valuable and useful in one part of life is likely to be so considered in all other parts as well. What he sees as making up the "*third* or *deep level* of culture," then, are "the *underlying* notions, values, and motives, ... the *starting points* of reasoning, reacting and acting ... the *basic* premises, emotionally charged attitudes and goals" (1988:250). Though he sees worldview as a subcategory of a people's mentality, what he says about mentality serves well to introduce what I see as the personal response to worldview structuring. The worldview as I see it is totally structural. It is *people not worldview* who reason, react and develop attitudes.

In an approach that we will come back to in chapter 11, Luzbetak refers to a classification of worldviews by Robert Brow (1966) into three groups "(1) those that regard existence as *meaningless*, e.g., atheistic world views; (2) those that regard existence as *meaningful*, namely theistic world views such as the Christian, Jewish, and Islamic; (3) the *irreligious* world views, such as those of humanists and communists" (1988:252-3).

Luzbetak goes on to characterize worldviews in a way I will criticize here and when we get to the discussion of Hiebert's approach. He falls into what anthropologists have labeled *superorganicism*. This is a view that implies that culture is a kind of organism with a life of its own, sometimes even with certain human characteristics (e.g., will, feelings, thinking), including the ability to "do things" to people. Notice this implication when Luzbetak says that worldview "is (1) cognitive, (2) emotional, and (3) motivational in nature" (1988:253). He then says, "The world view *tells* the society what and how it is to think about life and the world" and "A world view also *tells* the society how it is to feel about, evaluate, and react to the world and all reality" (emphasis mine). Such statements imply that worldview has the ability to do something, a view I strongly reject.

Luzbetak then goes on to discuss religion as one category and ideology and philosophy as another category under his concept of mentality. From my point of view, he shows quite a bit of confusion between worldview and these other categories, especially religion. And the way he defines ideology/philosophy is pretty much the same way that I define worldview. For example, he quotes Honigman approvingly,

> Ideology ... includes socially standardized beliefs about the universe and man's place in it; conceptions about the sources of illness and other sorts of danger, attitudes of belonging, allegiance, and identification; sentiments about persons, objects, places, and times; and, finally, values concerning what to do and what not to do (1959:589-90).

In spite of my criticisms of Luzbetak, his book is a goldmine of insight into both anthropological theory and its application to Christian mission. Among the insights he offers missionaries is that

> The worldview of a people is really the only medium through which a society is able to understand anything, including the gospel message and anything else that the Church may wish to communicate. It is the main measuring-rod of a people used for evaluating the gospel message, and, humanly speaking, it ultimately determines what will or will not move a society to accept and live the gospel (1988:284).

Another valuable contribution of Luzbetak is his discussion of themes and counter themes (1988:276-9, 286-91). We will return to the subject of themes and present Luzbetak's analysis of Middle Wahgi worldview in chapter 12. One helpful part of the earlier and shorter version of his book (1963) that he, unfortunately, omitted from the 1988 version is a list of topics that can usefully be investigated to discover worldview themes. These are based on F. Keesing, 1958:159-68. I present them here in chart form.

Luzbetak says, "A considerable amount of valuable clues to the underlying set of themes may be found by inquiring into the following:

1. The self-image of the society and whom the society considers to be 'a good person';
2. The violent resistance to certain innovations;
3. The native educational content and motivations, the constant lessons and warnings given to small children, the instructions given to the youths during the initiation rites;
4. Arguments between tribesmen, quarrels between husband and wife;
5. The scolding, reprimands, and praise given especially to the young;
6. The factors that contribute to a feeling of security;
7. The factors that contribute to a preferred status;
8. The content and motivation contained in the arguments of native agitators;
9. The reasons for dissatisfaction and criticism;
10. The object of violent hate and condemnation;
11. The assumptions, motivations, and general line of reasoning observed in tribal meetings and court sessions;
12. The behavior which the more severe sanctions aim to control;

13. The type of sanctions feared most;

14. The more serious worries;

15. The severest insults and the most painful type of ridicule;

16. Chief aspirations;

17. Occasions for war;

18. Motives for suicide" (1963:160).

David Burnett

David Burnett is British and a professor at All Nations Bible College in England. He has written what I consider the best popular presentation of worldview understandings from a Christian perspective. He has been a missionary and, like Luzbetak and Hiebert, has anthropological training. His book is titled, *Clash of Worlds: What Christians Can Do in a World of Cultures in Conflict* (second edition 2002).

This presentation is in some ways similar to that of James Sire, but with a worldwide and cross-cultural focus, in contrast to Sire's primarily American focus. For example, Burnett starts out with a series of questions to answer. These he fashions after those of Luzbetak listed above. He then lists my five major functions of worldview (Kraft 1979:54-56): explanatory, evaluative, providing psychological reinforcement, integrative and adaptive. We will come back to these functions in the chapters that follow. He has four aims in view: to help us to understand some contemporary worldviews, to help us to understand our own worldview, to try to understand the ways in which these worldviews are interacting and to learn principles that will help us in communicating the Christian gospel to those of other worldviews.

Burnett sees the world's worldviews divisible into five groupings: Secular (western), Primal (animistic), Hindu, Chinese and Islamic. For each of these worldviews he describes them, then deals with the approach of each to six key areas of life. They are

<ul><li>Cosmos—what is thenature of the universe?</li><li>Self—who are we?</li><li>Knowing—what is truth?</li></ul>	<ul><li>Community—what is society?</li><li>Time—what is time?</li><li>Value—what is good?</li></ul>

Figure 5.1. Burnett's Six Worldview Questions

Burnett then proceeds to discuss how each of his five worldviews deals with each of these six questions. He starts with a basic description of each of the worldviews. For much of what follows I want to thank one of our Fuller Ph.D. graduates, D. Michael Crow who provided a helpful summary of Burnett's treatment in a 1998 tutorial paper, based on Burnett's first edition (1992). The chapter on Buddhism is, however, new in the 2002 edition and the summary (Figure 5.5) my own.

The first of Burnett's worldview categories is the Secular or Western. From this perspective, the universe is seen as an enormous "machine" that can be studied. There's a dualism (called "Cartesian dualism") between mind and matter. Matter is the only valid subject of study. We only know what we can learn through the physical senses. Reason, not revelation, is the final judge of what is true. This perspective has spawned secular humanism, deism, atheism, Marxism and hedonism.

SECULAR (WESTERN) (Descartes, Locke)
Cosmos The cosmos is "matter only." The focus is on nature, a "closed" system without outside divine influence, that is consistent, orderly, evolutionary and based on cause and effect.
Self The body is a machine inhabited by a soul. The Self is molded by its environment. An individualistic, egalitarian view of humanity. There is no afterlife.
Knowing Knowledge is power. Knowledge comes through rational, empirical investigation of the universe. The emphasis is on the control of nature. This produces growth in technology.
Community The individual takes priority over the community. Associations are more important than kinship relations.
Time Time is linear (from infinite past to infinite future), non-repetitious, highly valued, measurable. Time takes precedence over socializing. It is progressive. Optimistic that the future can be controlled.
Value Ethics are relative, expedient. We live in a "closed system," that is situational. Ethics are for the sake of the individual not of society. Humans are in competition with nature and each other and aggressive in seeking control of their environment. Progress is assumed and valued.

Figure 5.2. Summary of Burnett's Overview of Secular Worldview

Burnett's evaluation of this worldview is that the loss of meaning and purpose that people who held this worldview feel is a major factor. There is no moral base for law. Secularism is headed either for totalitarianism or chaos. Some are seeking the transcendental in the face of absurdity and opening themselves up to evil spiritual beings to satisfy their quest for power.

Next he turns to Animism, with its many varieties the majority worldview in the world. He points out that animism antedates the great religions. There are many manifestations of animism (i.e., it is not a single religion), but the various forms of animism manifest many common themes, suggesting a single satanic mind behind them. Burnett estimates that at least 40% of the world, including many (most?) of the adherents of world religions fall into this category. I would put the figure much higher, perhaps double his 40% counting all of Hinduism, Buddhism, Shinto and shamanism plus the very large number of those who claim to belong to Islam and even Christianity (e.g., Latin American Roman Catholics) who regularly consult satanic spirits.

TRADITIONAL (ANIMISTIC)
Cosmos The universe is a unity. Non-matter is as real as matter. There is no dichotomy between the secular and the sacred. God is distant and alienated. Lesser nature spirits (in rivers, rocks, sun, moon, etc.) impact life in dangerous ways. We must harmonize with or be at war with nature.
Self Society is over the individual. Animism has a multiple soul concept and believes the soul. Shamans have supernatural power to heal. Ancestors are part of the living community with strong links to the living.
Knowing In a capricious world of spirits, follow the safe ways of the ancestors. Manipulate the spirit world. Every event has spiritual causes, discoverable through divination. Ancestors communicate through dreams and visions.
Community The individual finds significance in and through family, tribe and ancestors. The group takes priority over individual happiness. Age and experience are respected. Working includes socializing. Decision-making and ownership are group things.

Time
Time is past and present without significant attention to future. The focus is on past events dominated by myth. A socializing and event orientation. Little forward planning. Change and innovation are dangerous therefore follow tradition.
Value
Ethics are decided by the clan and the ancestors. Outsiders have no rights, so stealing from them is okay. Fertility is highly valued, the family must be perpetuated. Therefore, barrenness is a curse and not marrying anathema. Tradition takes priority over family. Unseen powers can be used for harm or for healing.

Figure 5.3. Summary of Burnett's Overview of Traditional Worldview

Burnett points out that the majority of purely animistic peoples live in isolation and contact with the outside world is traumatic. Their worldview is fragile and they easily convert to world religions, though usually carrying with them much of their animistic belief and practice. In reaction against the changes taking place, revitalization of the traditional religion may also occur.

Next Burnett turns to the most animistic of the world religions, Hinduism. The worldview underlying Hinduism developed from the primal worldview. Hinduism is essentially the faith of a single cultural unit with many variations. It is centered in belief in one indescribable force, impersonal and without any attributes—Brahman. A major theme is Monism—the belief that all life, whether animal, plant or human or spirit, is of the same essence. Another theme is that humans pass through endless reincarnations that can end through enlightenment.

HINDU
Cosmos
Brahman is the ultimate reality behind the illusion (*maya*) of the world. Reality consists of nature, spirits, and demons, and is unpredictable. The gods are manifestations of the Supreme Reality, Brahman.
Knowing
Wisdom is the mystical flash of inner insight or enlightenment. This is assisted by sacred sounds or mantras (e.g., *om, klam*) that are often names of Hindu deities (*Ram*, etc.).
Community
Rigid hierarchical caste is part of the monistic order from insects up to gods. There is no social mobility. Cooperation, not competition is the rule. There is a patron-client (dependency-loyalty) system. An emphasis on tolerance of diverse views rather than conversion.

Time
There is an endless cycle of growth and decay. The basic cycle is *kalpa*, the "Day of Brahman," 4.2 billion years. We are in year 51. Each person has thousands of rebirths. If a beggar or a baby dies it doesn't matter, they will be reborn.
Value
Monism has no absolute morality. People gain *karma* through caste duty. "Right" is conformity to the cosmic order (caste). Harmony has priority over justice. That is left to *karma*. The highest good is detachment from material and sensual pleasure through *yoga* knowledge, action, devotion, psychic experience or *tantrism* (the use of the sexual urge).

Figure 5.4. Summary of Burnett's Overview of Hindu Worldview

Hinduism has amazing resilience, endurance, plasticity, adaptability and power to assimilate. It is world-denying. It venerates saints. It sees the inner world as Brahman.

Next, Burnett turns to Theravada Buddhism. Of this worldview he says it is

> A vast body of doctrine, practice and culture that has grown up around the teaching of the person who became known as the Buddha. The declared aim of the Buddha's teaching is to assist all beings to eliminate the suffering caused by their foolish, false and selfish actions through achieving enlightenment. His teaching grew out of the prevailing worldview of north Indian society some time in the fifth or sixth century BC. ... [resulting] in a new and different worldview that stimulated the renewal of civilization in many parts of Asia (2002:86).

THERAVADA BUDDHISM
Cosmos
Buddha was not concerned with a "first cause" or an "absolute being," only practical things like individual human suffering and how to end it. "It is our attempt to attach ourselves to impermanent things to gain happiness that perpetuates *dukkha*" (suffering) (2002:90). Reincarnation in five or six states: gods, humans, animal, ghosts, hell-beings. Monism.
Self
Sees the Hindu *atman* not as eternal but as always in a state of flux. Perceptions, ideas, consciousness, body always in the process of change, yet we are the same person. When a person dies and is reborn (not reincarnated) they are neither the same person or a different person. "The nature of the rebirth results from [*karma*]... [meaning] 'volitional action' ... [that] may be relatively good or bad... [with] good or bad effects. ... According to Buddha, it was possible for a being to bring to an end the continuing cycle of births and rebirths by gaining an insight into the actual nature of reality" (2002:92).

Knowing
Knowledge or enlightenment comes through following the teachings of Buddha and through meditation. "Buddhist meditation ... aims to develop the mind, cleansing it of impurities and disturbances, worries, doubts and restlessness and cultivate the qualities of tranquility, joy, will and energy. ... lead[ing] finally to the attainment of the highest wisdom that sees the true nature of things, Nirvana" (2002:93).
Community
The quest for true realization is basically an individual quest. But Gautama formed monasteries (*Sangha*), communities of those who have renounced ordinary life to seek Nirvana. These provide support for members. Monks don't work but beg for food, depending on the surrounding community for their needs.
Time
Birth and rebirth never cease and time is simply the flow of these. People are not to get attached to time or to speculate about its nature or how things came to be.
Value
The "Middle Path" that leads to cessation of suffering is composed of eight elements: Right Understanding, Right Thought, Right Speech, Right Action, Right Livelihood, Right Effort, Right Mindfulness, Right Concentration. A monk commits himself to 227 precepts, lay people to the first five: Abstain from taking life, taking what is not given, misconduct in sensual action, false speech and liquor.

Figure 5.5. Summary of Burnett's Overview of Buddhist Worldview

As mentioned above, Buddhists are very animistic. Wherever Buddhism has gone, the lay people have tended to keep their gods and spirits in spite of the monks teaching them the Middle Way. Buddhism is not so much a philosophy as a practice. Buddhism is greatly syncretized wherever it exists. These syncretized forms are often referred to as folk Buddhism.

What Burnett calls the Chinese worldview is a syncretistic mix of Confucianism, Taoism, Buddhism with traditional religious ideas. The Chinese are now absorbing modernization.

CHINESE (Confucianism, Taoism, Buddhism)
Cosmos
Man and nature are inseparable and interdependent. Nature is alive, animate by *Tao* (the way, the principle of life), a monistic process pervading all. *Tao* is dualistic *yin/yang* (good-evil, male-female, hot-cold, etc.). Gods, spirits and ancestors inhabit and control the universe.
Self
The body is possessed by two souls: *hun*—the superior spirit, and *p'o*—the inferior, controller of one's animal nature. *Hun* may leave the body in a dream or in madness. Health occurs through balance of body and nature. At death, *hun* becomes an ancestor spirit.

Knowing
Tao is beyond knowing. One's fate may be learned through fortune-telling, divination, almanacs, geomancy and joss sticks.
Community
The family is supreme. One becomes more human in relations with others (*li*). Five relationships structure society: sovereign-subject, father-son, husband-wife, elder brother-younger, friend-friend. Filial piety a strong value in life and death (ancestor veneration). Loss of face is collective shame for family and community.
Time
Time stretches from present into past and future, with people in the middle. Not conceived of as abstract if used, as in the West, to explain or predict. Situations, involving time and space relationships, are seen as events for people to integrate with and adapt to rather than to change.
Value
Human nature as good, bad or neutral is unclear. One needs education to be a "superior" man. *Jen* (good faith, politeness, liberality, diligence, generosity) is all-important. Right relationships and social harmony are achieved when all do their duty according to their station in life (wu lun, the five basic relationships).

Figure 5.6. Summary of Burnett's Overview of Chinese Worldview

Unlike the capricious animist world, to the Chinese the cosmos, interpenetrated by the visible and the invisible, is stable and orderly (*Tao*). Structure gives durability, complexity, development. Chinese are world-affirming and pragmatic. The sage is venerated. *Tao* unites both worlds. Buddhism introduced deities and Communism introduced materialism.

The final worldview Burnett presents is the Islamic, which he sees as a radically monotheistic reaction against Arabic polytheism, strongly influenced by aberrant forms of Christianity and Judaism.

ISLAMIC
Cosmos
Belief in one God, one people, one worship. Everything occurs according to the will of Allah (fatalism). Allah is radically distinct from his creation and distant. There is war between good and evil spirits. Pray toward Mecca and go there on the Hajj. Observe Ramadan, the month of fasting.
Self
Humans are dependent on and must submit to Allah (Muslim = one who Submits) as a slave to his master. Must follow the "Five Pillars" and Shariah Law. After death some are chosen for sensual Paradise, others for torment in Hell.
Knowing
Divine revelation is all-important, not intellectual analysis or enlightenment. The Qur'an is holy and powerful even if memorized without understanding or used as a charm. It reveals God's law, not his character. He is unknowable.

Community
Islam is to be a religious-political state. Identity is with the extended family and religious community. Men are public and dominant; women are submissive and hidden. The Shariah community takes precedence over family obligations.
Time
Event rather than time oriented. Efficiency is disregarded in favor of relationships with people. Bargaining is social interaction. Change is resisted. Muslims look back to the golden age of Islam.
Value
Shariah law is seen as giving the answer to every ethical question, based on Muhammad's behavior. Honor revolves around sexual propriety. Shame must be avenged. Hospitality enhances one's reputation.

Figure 5.7. Summary of Burnett's Overview of Islamic Worldview

Burnett sees the externalness and rigidity of Islamic law as a problem leading to a failure to meet the inner needs of the heart. Mystic Sufism, involving one-third to one-half of Muslims enables people to experience a mystic relationship with Allah. Islam has undergone a recent revitalization due to oil money. Muslims are now seeking to spread an Islamic revolution in the decadent West.

After these characterizations of the various worldviews, Burnett moves into a discussion of worldview change, using principles derived from Tippett that we will use later in chapter 18 and then discussing in successive chapters New Religious Movements, Sects and Cults, New Age and Neo-Paganism (witchcraft). He follows these chapters with three chapters on communicating Christianity into non-Christian contexts. These are valuable discussions but beyond this part of our treatment. We will cover most of the ground he covers in the later chapters of this book.

Paul G. Hiebert

Paul Hiebert was my esteemed colleague in The School of World Mission, Fuller Seminary for thirteen years (1977-90). During that time, he and I alternated in teaching the worldview course in which we regularly referred to each other's ideas. We influenced each other and were influenced by some of the same authors, speakers, and colleagues. Some of the influences on each of us are outlined in Appendix A where the history of the worldview concept within anthropology is discussed.

In 1990 Hiebert moved to Trinity Evangelical Divinity School near Chicago where he has been ever since. Hiebert is brilliant and perceptive as well as "down to earth." He contributed a lot to our program while here at Fuller and we have missed him since he left. Though I differ from him in a couple of crucial points, I have learned a lot from him. And he serves the same Lord that I do and has the same concern that what we do by way of scholarly endeavor be available to be used in enhancing the cause of Christ worldwide.

Hiebert's approach to worldview is presented most fully in his 1985 book, *Anthropological Insights for Missionaries*, pages 45-49. An earlier, though less explicit presentation is in his 1983 (original publication 1976) text entitled, *Cultural Anthropology*.

There are important similarities in the way Hiebert and I approach worldview. For example, we both see worldview as the deep level of culture, with surface-culture subsystems of a culture "radiating" out from it, as in the following diagram:

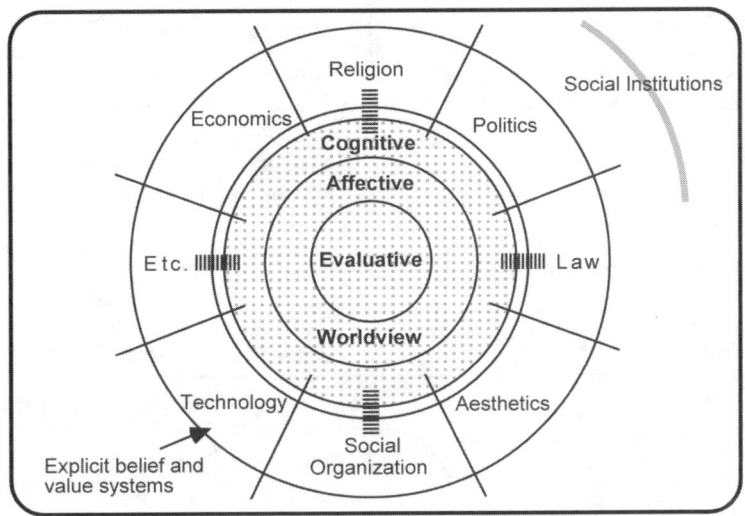

Figure 5.8. Hiebert's Model of Worldview (Hiebert 1985a:46)

The speckled inner three circles of the diagram represent worldview. The outer ring, with the names of cultural subsystems, then, represents surface-level culture. Though I agree with Hiebert that worldview is the "inner circle" of culture, I disagree that worldview has cognitive, affective and evaluative functions. For me, these are *human* functions, not characteristics of cultural/worldview structure.

A further illustration of Hiebert's approach is found in his anthropology text where he provides a detailed comparison/contrast between American and Indian worldview assumptions (1983:358-62). I'll not give the details of each contrast but his approach is evident from the titles of the topics he contrasts. In introducing the chart, he says,

Following are two examples of worldviews, one of middle-class Americans, the other of Indians of South Asia. ... Beginning with much the same types of human needs and experiences, the two groups have constructed two very different and contrasting perceptual worlds. For the sake of comparison, point-by-point, these assumptions have been simplified and forced into the same mold. Nevertheless, they do point out the basic differences that can exist between different world views (1983:357).

AN AMERICAN WORLDVIEW	AN INDIAN WORLDVIEW

Empiricism
   Absolutes
   Naturalism
   Linear Time
   Order & Immutability
   Knowledge
	Maya
	   Relativism
	   Supernaturalism
	   Cyclic Time
	   Mutability & Unpredictability
	   Wisdom

A Particularistic and Categorized World
   Equality
   Individualism
   Competition
	The Unity of All Things
	   Hierarchy
	   Specialization & Interdependence
	   Patron-Client Relationships

Natural & Moral Management
   Science & Technology
   Uniform Morality & Justice
   Missionary
	Karma or Cosmic Law
	   Samsara or Pilgrimage
	   Relative Morality
	   Inclusivism & Tolerance

Self-reliance
   Expanding Good
   Achievement Orientation
   Associational Groups
   Success & Progress
	Dharma or Functional Responsibility
	   Limited Good
	   Ascription Orientation
	   Jatis and Castes
	   Moksha (release from life)

Figure 5.9. Hiebert's American and Indian Worldview Contrasts (Hiebert 1983:357)

Hiebert and I are in essential agreement in our basic understandings of how worldview is defined and how people use it. He gives a similar list to mine of worldview functions: providing cognitive foundations in terms of which to *explain*, provide *emotional security*, *validate* our deepest cultural norms, *integrate* our culture and *monitor culture change* (1985:48). Though I don't see it in print, I think he also uses a list similar to mine or Kearney's concerning cultural universals.

Though some of the influences on Hiebert are similar to those in my background, there are a few that form the backdrop for some differences in our approaches. As can be seen from the discussion in Appendix A, the primary theoretical influence on Hiebert has been the anthropological perspective known within anthropology as "symbolic anthropology." Among the big names in this school are Mary Douglas, Victor Turner and Clifford Geertz. This involvement prods him to look for worldview insights in the symbolic behavior of humankind such as rituals, festivals and events involving religious symbolism. Though I agree that these aspects of culture should be studied to discover whatever we can learn from them concerning worldview assumptions, I have had virtually no input from that school of anthropology.

In addition to the general anthropological influences that form both of our backgrounds, my main influences have come from linguistics, communication theory and psychological anthropology. From this perspective, I am critical of symbolic anthropology as being so fascinated with certain surface culture phenomena (e.g., ritual) and their symbolisms that they do not give sufficient attention to the people part of cultural behavior. As a part of this focus, then, their approach to meaning seems to miss the fact that meaning is a people thing, not a structure thing.

An additional contrast between Hiebert and myself is the fact that he worked in India while I worked in Africa. This fact, I believe, prods Hiebert toward more of an identification of worldview with religion and the identification of cultural (especially religious) meanings with the forms in which they are expressed. The form-meaning dichotomy and its implications for contextualization seem easier to apply in analyzing African sociocultural phenomena, making the application of biblical principles easier as well. It seems that one can be more optimistic that African peoples will catch onto biblical teaching since it is based on worldviews similar to theirs. Having to deal with Indian monism and a worldview so radically different from either the West or the Bible without the input of communication theory, then, has resulted in some problems (from my point of view) in Hiebert's analysis of worldview (see below). Among other things, Hiebert has seemed to be much more cautious in advocating the incorporation of Indian cultural features in contextualized Christianity.

Hiebert, however, has probed more deeply than I in several areas. One of the diagrams he used to use in class (though I don't believe he has published it) shows two levels of analysis beneath the surface-level of culture.

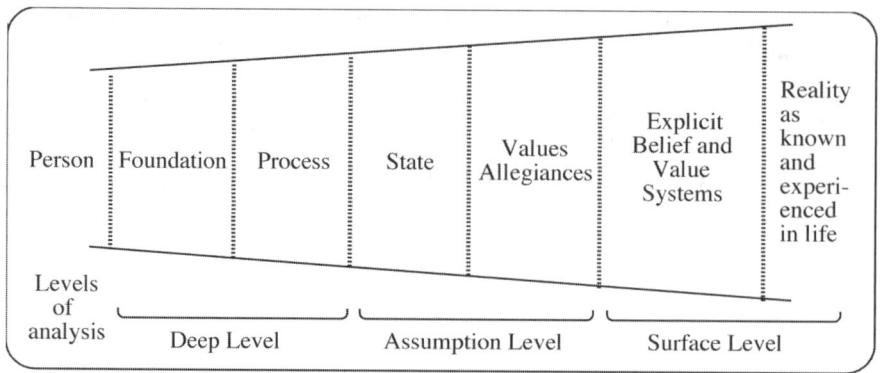

Figure 5.10. Hiebert's Three-Level Model of Worldview (Clinton 1986:68)

In a very valuable analysis and discussion of Hiebert's and my work on worldview, Yoshiyuki (Billy) Nishioka describes each level of Hiebert's chart as follows:

> The *Surface level* consists of realities as known and experienced in people's lives and of explicit belief and value systems represented in various cultural forms (symbols, behaviors, laws, and so on). They are visible aspects of culture out of which tacit assumption levels can be discovered. The *assumption level* includes values and allegiances as well as what Hiebert calls state. State refers to existential assumptions which are meaningfully integrated in terms of ontology, grids (time, space, scales, roles/status, social categories), causality and so on.
>
> At the deep level, the major concern is how knowledge is constructed. This level consists of *process* and *foundation*. The *process* indicates the modes in classifying process ... as well as taxonomic systems (scales, grids, reference points, linkages, and so on). The *foundation* refers to fundamental cognitive conditions or means for knowledge construction. The deepest level is foundation which includes epistemology (idealism, naïve realism, and critical realism), analogy (mechanical or organic, static or dynamic) and scale (empirical or transempirical, this worldly or other worldly ...).
>
> Hiebert seems not to identify this deep level with the worldview system itself, but rather orientations or processes by which certain particular worldviews are formed (Nishioka 1997:98).

That deepest level is of particular interest to me. Hiebert sees it as deeper than worldview. I would divide between the process level that I would see as lying in persons and the foundation level that I would see as a structural, worldview thing. Note that Hiebert is connecting our discussion of epistemology with a particular level of worldview. However we label or describe these things, the suggestion that there is another level of worldview structuring is intriguing.

He has also gone much more deeply into the area of epistemology than I have. Note that in chapter three I have spoken only of three epistemological understandings (naïve realism, idealism and critical realism). Hiebert, having influenced me considerably with that approach, has now expanded it, as follows:

POSITION	NATURE OF KNOWLEDGE	RELATIONSHIP BETWEEN SYSTEMS OF KNOWLEDGE	THE UMPIRE'S RESPONSE
ABSOLUTE IDEALISM	Reality exists in the mind. The external world is illusory (e.g., Vedantic and Advaita Hinduism)	Each system is an island to itself. Systems are incommensurable. Unity is possible only as everyone joins in the same system.	"My calling it makes it a strike. The game is in my mind."
CRITICAL IDEALISM	Reality exists in the mind. The external world is unknowable. Order is imposed on sense experience by the mind.	Each system is an island to itself. Systems are incommensurable. A common ground is found in human rationality, which is assumed to be the same for all humans.	"My calling it makes it a strike. My mind imposes order on the world."
NAÏVE IDEALISM/ NAÏVE REALISM	The external world is real. The mind can know it exactly, exhaustively, and without bias. Science is a photograph of reality. Knowledge and reality are equated uncritically.	Because knowledge is exact and potentially exhaustive, there can be only one unified theory. Various theories must be reduced to one. This leads to reductionism in the physical, psychological or sociocultural sphere.	"I call it the way it is. If it is a strike I call it a strike. If it is a ball I call it a ball."

CRITICAL REALISM	The external world is real. Our knowledge of it is partial but can be true. Science is a map or model. It is made up of successive paradigms that bring us to closer approximations of reality and absolute truth.	Each field in science presents a different blueprint of reality. These are complementary to one another. Integration is achieved, not by reducing them all to one model, but by seeing their inter-relationship. Each gives us partial insights into reality.	"I call it the way I see it, but there is a real pitch and an objective standard against which I must judge it. I can be shown to be right or wrong."
INSTRU-MENTALISM (PRAGMATISM)	The external world is real. We cannot know if our knowledge of it is true, but if it "does the job" we can use it. Science is a Rorschach response that makes no ontological claims to truth.	Because we make no truth claims for our theories or models, there can be no ontological contra-dictions between them. We can use apparently contradictory models in different situations so long as they work.	"I call it the way I see it, but there is no way to know if I am right or wrong."
DETERMINISM	The external world is real. We and our knowledge are determined by material causes, hence know-ledge can lay no claim to truth (or to meaning).	There is no problem with integration, for all systems of know-ledge are determined by external, non-rational factors such as infant experiences, emotional drives, and thought conditioning.	"I call it the way I am programmed to."

Figure 5.11. Hiebert's Taxonomy of Epistemological Positions (1994:23)

In his discussion of the above varieties of understanding, Hiebert invites us to ponder what each perspective looks like both in science and in theology. We probably all know Christians who, wholly or partially, fit into each of these categories. For me, Hiebert's brilliance is shown both in the ways in which he has analyzed the epistemological positions and in his use of a baseball umpire's approach to his job to illustrate each position.

1. To illustrate my difficulties with some of Hiebert's approach to worldview, I offer the following quote where, in a general discussion of culture, he states

Taken together, the basic assumptions about reality which lie behind the *beliefs and behavior of a culture* are sometimes called a worldview ... Because these assumptions are taken for granted, they are generally unexamined and therefore largely implicit. But they are reinforced by the deepest of feelings, and anyone who challenges them becomes the object of vehement attack. People believe that the world really is the way they see it. Rarely are they aware of the fact that the way they see it is molded by their world view (1985:45, emphasis mine).

This is a good statement and I agree with all but one thing. I have mentioned above that Luzbetak lets himself fall into superorganicism, the fallacy of personifying culture as if it were a being that is capable of having person-type activity. Hiebert, as we shall see, falls into the same error and signals it above when he speaks of the "beliefs and behavior *of a culture*" (italics mine), as if a culture can think and behave. As we have seen in chapter two, I assert strongly that culture is structure and pattern, not person. And only persons can think and behave.

Notice the same problem when Hiebert holds that worldview consists of three dimensions: cognitive (or existential), affective and evaluative, as if worldview thinks, feels and evaluates (see Figure 5.8, above). What he means is, I think, the same as I mean: that structured assumptions in these areas underlie how people assume and behave. This comes out in a statement such as, "Existential assumptions provide a culture with the fundamental cognitive structures people use to explain reality" (1985:45). But here, and in many other places in his writing, he has not been careful to distinguish between structure and people. He often uses the term "culture" (rightly) to refer to cultural structure, but also uses it often to refer to the people. This is confusing at best and misleading at worst.

One way of reconciling his approach with mine would be to say that by making this distinction as carefully as I try to, I am looking at the basic components: cultural/worldview structuring and people. This is a first step in dealing with the issue. Hiebert, however, is focused on a second step, where the people and the structures are brought together as people are making use of the structured worldview assumptions and thinking, feeling and evaluating according to them.

2. A second problem I have is with what comes across to me as a lack of a clear distinction between worldview and religion. Due to the influence of symbolic anthropology and, no doubt, his experience in India, Hiebert sees a very formative influence of religion on worldview. This comes out in

a statement in his 1983 cultural anthropology text where he says; "A world view provides people with their basic assumptions about reality. Religion provides them with the specific content of this reality" (1983: 371). If he still holds this view (and he may have changed), it seems to be confusing. I would say that the whole of surface-level culture, of which religion is but one of the components, manifests the specific content a people builds on its worldview assumptions.

As we will see in chapter six, to me, religion is a surface-level phenomenon that, along with politics, economics, family, education and several other subsystems of culture provide the more or less visible customs through which the worldview assumptions are played out. Though in many societies, religion does indeed have a greater influence on worldview than the other subsystems, we don't have to confuse the two, as I believe Hiebert does. See chapter six and 1996:52-5 for the way I work this out.

3. Another problem I have with Hiebert's approach is the way he, and symbolic anthropology in general, treat meaning. In a superb presentation on communication entitled "Cultural Differences and the Message" (1985:141-169), for example, one is left with the impression that the meanings to be conveyed are contained in the symbols (the cultural forms) employed. However, as communication theory makes clear, the meanings are never in the forms (symbols) themselves, they are always in the *people* who use the forms to *convey* them to others. Again, the important distinction between people and structure is not made clear. Indeed, in an article on form and meaning, he makes several statements such as, "There are a few symbols in which form and meaning cannot be separated" (1989:115), that show what I believe to be an erroneous understanding of the form-meaning relationship. See Kraft 1996:145-7 for a more complete treatment of my differences with Hiebert at this point.

In conclusion, as Nishioka (1997) points out, Hiebert participates in the strengths and weaknesses of the symbolic anthropologists (just as I participate in the strengths and weaknesses of the more cognitive and linguistic perspectives that have influenced me). I have pointed out above some of the weaknesses I see. I hope I have been clear concerning some of his strengths as well. I have the highest respect for Paul Hiebert as a person and as a scholar and do not lightly criticize his approach. I have learned a lot from him and highly recommend that the reader get into his writings firsthand. It will be well worth it.

Michael Kearney (pronounced Karniy)

Michael Kearney, a professor of anthropology at the University of California, Riverside, has written a masterful presentation of worldview theory from an anthropological point of view. His presentation is important to us because so much of my own approach is similar to and influenced by what Kearney has done. His 1984 book titled *World View* is, in my estimation, the best technical presentation of worldview theory from an anthropological point of view. And it is gratifying to note that Naugle, coming from a philosophical point of view, has a similar opinion. For he states that Kearney's book presents "one of the most complete worldview models available today in any discipline" (2002:244).

The book deals first with the history of the concept of worldview in anthropological writing, giving honor to Robert Redfield (1953) from whose approach Kearney draws heavily. He then goes on to present a comprehensive discussion of such topics as how worldviews are formed, how they are structured, how they relate to internal and external reality and the universal components of worldviews. This discussion is followed by two case studies.

> Kearney defines worldview from several angles as follows:
> The worldview of a people is their way of looking at reality. It consists of basic *assumptions and images* that provide a more or less coherent, though not necessarily accurate, way of thinking about the world. A worldview comprises images of Self and of all that is recognized as not-Self, plus ideas about relationships between them, as well as other ideas (1984:41).
>
> A worldview is ... an integrated combination of concepts, typical of a particular society, having to do with the nature of things human beings need to know to behave successfully. For the most part, insofar as they are aware of them, humans tend to regard their worldview images and assumptions about time, space, causality, etc., as absolute and true knowledge of reality (1984:46).

He adds, "a world view is a dynamic, more or less internally consistent system which demonstrates logical and structural regularities" (1984:52). On this subject, then, he points out that worldview is organized both internally due to a human propensity for logicality and consistency and externally because of the necessity to relate to the external environment.

Kearney's reference to "Self" in the first quote above identifies him as basing his approach on that of Robert Redfield (1953). Redfield became interested in analyzing how people view the universe around them. This led him to suggest that there are universal features analyzable in the worldview perspectives of all peoples. He asked, "What are the fundamental ways in which all people everywhere conceptually divide up and categorize the phenomena that they perceive?" (Kearney 1984:37).

In seeking these universals, Redfield suggested that people break reality down into a Self-Not-self dichotomy. Within this basic dichotomy, then, people divide Self into the "I" and the "me" and the Not-self into Human and Non-human. He further subcategorized Human into such divisions as old, young, male, female, we, they and Non-human into Nature and God. Redfield focused on a tripartite division of reality into Human, Nature and God. He wished to know in what characteristic way different peoples "confronted" the non-human (Nature and God). He noted that there is much variation in the central concerns of peoples, with some attending more to the Human, some more to Nature, and some more to "God, while others more evenly divide their concerns" (Kearney 1984:39)

Redfield then recognized that people also must relate to space and time, so he added these to his non-human category. This results in the following scheme:

Self	Not-Self
I	Human
me	Non-human
	Nature
	God
	Space
	Time

Figure 5.12. Redfield's Approach to Worldview Universals

Naugle helpfully summarizes Redfield's approach as follows:
To review Redfield's contribution, he sees the formation of worldviews as an innate human characteristic. Everyone shares the same world and everyone has a view of it, though these views are indeed different. For him the term "worldview" meant something specific; namely, how people at the center of things look out upon and see the universe, especially in terms of totals. With human observers at the center, a worldview organizes things in the cosmos and makes knowledge of them possible. It is also the way a person

orients himself or herself to everything else. Redfield desired to know what is true of all human beings and their worldviews—the common categories by which all people analyze the cosmos. So he developed a universal typology consisting of the self, others (human and non-human), space and time, life and death. Since each of these domains can be construed differently, worldviews can be markedly divergent. One startling contrast is between the primitive and civilized worldviews. Redfield offers a provocative description of the primitive outlook as unified, interdependent, and moral. This perspective has been eclipsed by modernity with its fragmented, amoral vision of the cosmos from which God, humanity, and nature are alienated. Redfield uses his knowledge of the primitive worldview as the basis for a critique, and proposes it as a constructive "postmodern" alternative to the tragedies of modern life (2002:249).

I have spent a bit of time on Redfield's approach to point out the basis from which Kearney and I develop our concern for and listing of worldview universals. Kearney starts with Redfield's Self-Not-self dichotomy but labels the latter, "Other," saying, "The first requirement for a world view is the presence of a *Self*—discernibly distinct from its environment, which I refer to as the *Other*" (1984:68). This distinction recognizes the fact that humans are aware of themselves as distinct from their environment but, of necessity, relate to that environment. Implied also is the fact that both Self and Other are made up of subcategories.

> Other, especially, is complex. Recognizing this, Kearney says, although we will retain the category of Other as a world-view universal, it must be remembered that, like the Self, it often refers to an unnamed domain that is composed of several named domains, each of which has a taxonomic status on the same order as the Self, all of these domains being subordinate to the ultimate domain of "universe" (1984:71).

Once a conscious Self and an environment have been recognized, the next universal Kearney identifies is Relationship—referring to the relationship between Self and the various components of Other. Within Other, then, Kearney accepts Redfield's universals: Space and Time, adding Causality (to cover Redfield's God and Nature categories) and Classification but omitting Self as object (a serious omission from my point of view).

Kearney's scheme, then, can be pictured thus:

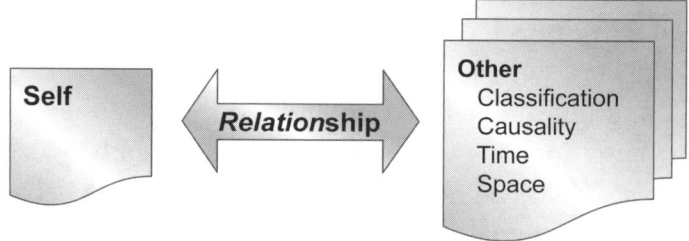

Figure 5.13. Kearney's Universals

In my approach, as you will see as we continue, I have renamed Kearney's Self Person/Group and entered it on both sides of Relationship. I have also done away with the Other label since it is unnecessary as long as we deal with each of its parts. My scheme, then, looks like this:

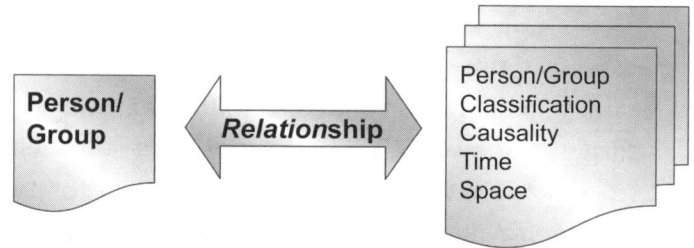

Figure 5.14. My Revision of Kearney's Universals

Kearney, working out of a mild Marxist "cultural materialist" paradigm, is committed to the belief that external reality shapes thought more than vice-versa. Yet in his concern for worldview, though he knocks the idealist position (that mind shapes reality), he seems not so much to be attempting to prove the materialist position as to discover how reality and thought shape each other.

Kearney's book is a milestone in worldview studies and we are all indebted to him for writing it, though we cannot agree with the materialist assumptions of his own worldview. These do not intrude enough to do major damage to his presentation, however. So I highly recommend the book to those who wish to pursue further study of worldview theory.

With that introduction to non-anthropological and anthropological approaches to the study of worldview, we now turn to a continuation of the approach we started with in chapters one through three.

Chapter 6

Worldview, Religion & Subsystems

Terminology can be a problem. And terminology can be affected by worldview assumptions. In the case of the term "religion"[1] we have, I believe, a terminology problem rooted in a worldview problem. Our western worldview divides life into quite a number of rather non-overlapping compartments such as: politics, economics, education, religion, family, play, work and the like.

Most societies have no such word or any single compartment of life designed to encapsulate the beliefs and practices we call "religious." They have, rather, a constant recognition, consciously and unconsciously, of the presence and activities of supernatural beings in all aspects of life. This recognition is, of course, based on a worldview-level set of assumptions. To reduce their perspective and practice to the limited thing we call "religion" is a great disservice to them and very misleading to us. It smacks of a kind of ethnocentrism that demands that their pervasively supernaturalistic approach to life be compressed into our concept of "religion." I, therefore, reject the term "religion" as a label for anything as central as what we are discussing, though I will use it for an aspect of surface-level culture parallel to politics, economics, education and others.

Though as anthropologists we seek to be aware of the influence of our assumptions and to overcome them as much as possible, we do not always succeed, especially in areas that are out of focus in our own experience. Generations of western anthropologists, adventurers, business people and others who traveled outside the Euro-American context came in contact with people who believed they lived in a world heavily populated by spirits. Whether or not these travelers were themselves committed to some religious faith, the involvement with the spirit world of the non-westerners they encountered most easily fit for them into the western category, "religion."

---

[1] I will regularly put quotation marks around the term "religion" to indicate that I consider the validity of using the term questionable. It is a term used within western societies to label one of the compartments into which we have segmented our lives. It has, therefore, no validity as a label for Christianity or any other perspective intended to affect all areas of life. Christianity is intended to affect people at the deep worldview level, not to be a surface-level thing called "religion."

The rituals, taboos, dedications, concepts of invisible beings and the like all reminded westerners of the behavior called "religion" of many in western societies.

However, in western societies, our religious commitments and behavior often show up very little in what we consider the non-religious aspects of our lives, all of the behavior of many non-western peoples seemed to be strongly affected by what looked to westerners like religion. Another way of saying this is to assert that most non-western peoples are thoroughly supernaturalistic in their beliefs and behavior. They are traditionally quite conscious at all times of the spirit world and its interactions with humans. Whether at work or play, in seeking answers to health questions or in normal family life, these peoples live with a consciousness that appears "religious" to westerners.

Under the influence of this western compartmentalized view of life, then, just about all the travelers, including most anthropologists, came to label "religious" those things in the lives of non-westerners that looked to westerners like religious behavior. From such labeling, then, came frequently made statements such as, "Non-western peoples are pervasively religious" or "Religion is at the core of most non-western cultures."

Problems

As time went on and we learned more and more about the cultures of humans and the societies that operate them, a series of problems began to become apparent, some of them simply terminological, some of them perceptual.

One thing that was obvious to many is the fact that whatever the behavior in question is to be called, it is much more important to and pervasive in non-western societies than usually in the West. Most anthropologists have traditionally dealt with non-western societies, usually small-scale societies that were pervasively supernaturalistic. They were, therefore, able to continually see what they defined as "religious" influences throughout those societies. The focus on non-western, small-scale societies plus the western habit of labeling a supernaturalistic orientation "religion," however, put anthropologists into a strange position when they began to look at western societies.

In the early days of anthropological investigation, not much attention was paid to studying the West. But there came a time when American and British and German and Russian and other western societies began to be subjected to anthropological analysis. This meant that anthropologists had to begin asking questions concerning whether religious allegiance is the same as or different from allegiance to, say, atheism or Communism or materialism or humanism or other political or philosophical ideologies. Given that most of the anthropological discussion of religions has dealt with supernaturalistic perspectives, could it be that non- (or anti-) supernaturalistic allegiances ("faiths") should be studied in the same way we study religion?

Anthropologists found that some societies had what they called "religion" (defined as involving attention to supernatural beings and power) at the core, while others had secularism, atheism or some other non-supernaturalistic system (e.g., Confucianism, some forms of Buddhism) as central to their belief and practice. Those who felt that religions and these other perspectives should be looked at in the same way, then, had to decide what to call the cultural facets they were studying. Should we call atheism or humanism religions? Or is there another term that would suit the situation better? Some chose to call them all "religion." These would assert, then, that all people are pervasively religious but that many of the "religions" of humankind are non-supernaturalistic.

The dilemma, then, is whether to use a label for what in the West is usually a fairly surfacy thing as the term for something that is very pervasive and deep for non-westerners. Many just ignored this problem, choosing to employ the "religion" label and simply to contend that most non-western peoples are pervasively religious. Others looked for a cover term that did not seem to imply supernaturalism. So they came up with terms such as, "ideology," "core values" or simply "values," "philosophy of life," "genius of a culture," "inner logic," "mentality" and eventually "worldview." Note Smart's attempt to handle the problem by treating religion (supernaturalistic) and ideology (non-supernaturalistic) as subcategories of worldview. He says, "I shall use *worldviews* in a general sense to refer to both religion and ideologies, and also to refer specifically to secular ideologies. ..." (1983:2).

It is only relatively recently (early 1950s) that anthropologists have begun to use the term worldview. In the beginning of the discipline, anthropologists focused primarily on the vast assortment of surface-level customs practiced by non-western peoples. Only gradually did they become aware of the importance of the multitude of assumptions and values lying behind these customs at what I call the "deep level" of culture that seemed to relate the customs coherently to each other. But, especially under the influence of a focus on psychological anthropology, some began to see a kind of personality or configuration (Benedict 1934) or core values (Hsu

1961) or themes (Opler 1945) as underlying people's customs (see Appendix A for a more complete treatment of this history).

Out of this concern comes a concern for what we are calling worldview—the basic assumptions underlying the surface-level behavior of a people.

Needed: Consistency and Clarity

Since a scientific approach to anthropological analysis requires consistency and comprehensiveness, it is scientifically untenable to analyze the societies of the world in two different ways, some with "religion" at the core, some with something else at the core. The alternatives would seem to be, then, either to call such perspectives as secularism "religions" or to use another term for that complex of assumptions that was being discovered as the underlying basis for cultural behavior. Redfield's (1953) pioneering work, however, began to expand the understanding of anthropologists to recognize that even in societies in which "religion" seemed to be at the core, there appear to be many deep-level, core assumptions that are not easily labeled "religious."

Among such are deep-level assumptions concerning relationships between people, concerning the nature of the universe, concerning whether time is linear, cyclical, pendular or whatever, concerning how space is to be used and organized, concerning whether the life of the various creatures on earth is of one kind or of different kinds. These and a myriad of other deep-level assumptions would seem to require a broader term, a term that might well cover religious assumptions as well but would not be limited to them.

Consistency and comprehensiveness, not to mention common sense, would seem to require, therefore, that we find a term that can include so-called "religious" assumptions (or pseudo-religious ones such as those underlying Communism), but that can also cover the assumptions concerning self, other, time, space and the like that Redfield and Kearney are pointing to. The best suggestion would seem to be to use the term Redfield himself suggested, "worldview," to label all the central assumptions, concepts, premises, and values to which the people of a sociocultural group commit themselves, whether or not they relate specifically to what westerners call "religion."

This is the approach taken here. We will consistently label as "worldview" the structuring of the central assumptions, values and commitments that lie at the heart of culture. By definition, then, these are the assumptions that affect all areas of surface structure.

Worldview and the Subsystems

At the surface level of culture there are several dimensions that we choose to call "subsystems." In the figure below I have only listed a few of the subsystems of culture: Economics, Politics, Religion, Social Structure and Material Culture. There are many more, such as Family, Education, Language and the like. The diagram is intended to indicate both that worldview-level assumptions affect every one of the subsystems and also that there is an influence of the surface-level subsystems on worldview. We will discuss this factor below.

We may diagram this fact as follows:

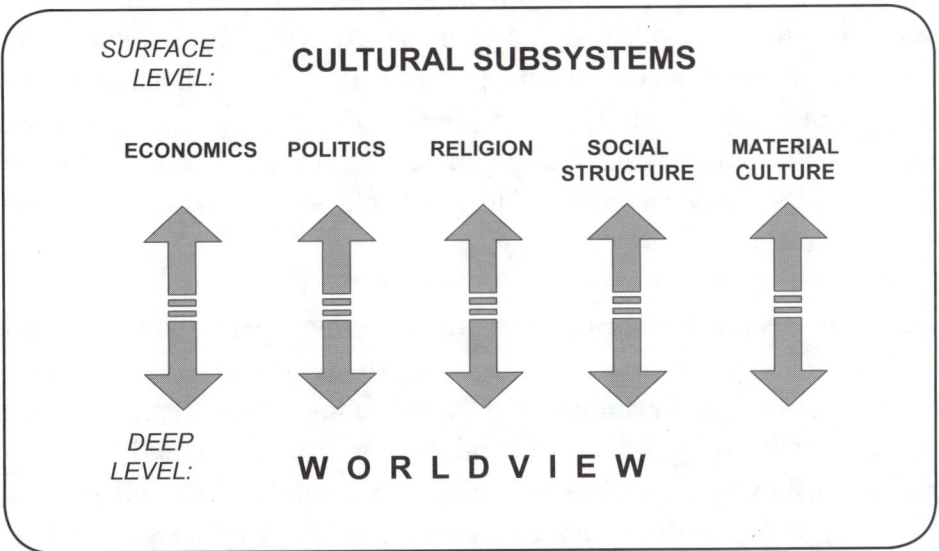

Figure 6.1. Relationship Between Worldview and Surface Culture

Note that, according to this analysis, religion is a surface-level phenomenon on a parallel with politics, economics and the rest. It, like each of the other subsystems derives culture-wide assumptions from the worldview. Each subsystem, however, represents at least three types of surface-level behavior that applies only to the subsystems (i.e., is subsystem-specific): habitual behavior, creative behavior and subsystem-specific assumptions.

The fact that we use the term *assumptions* at two levels can cause some confusion. We could speak of *beliefs* or *presuppositions* or use some other term, either at the worldview level or at the subsystem level. But neither of these words or others seem to convey what we mean as well as does the word *assumptions*. Note, however, that when we speak of assumptions that are "subsystem-specific," we are speaking of assumptions that only apply to the subsystem of which they are apart. These assumptions, unlike worldview assumptions, do not necessarily affect the whole of life as do worldview assumptions.

Most of what we as human beings do in our daily life is quite habitual. *Shopping*, for example, a facet of economic behavior involves an incredible amount of routine, here called habit or ritual. In America we go to a store, pick out some items, be they clothes or groceries, move to a counter where there is an employee of the store, wait until that person totals up our bill, pay the bill and leave to go home. All of this habitual behavior, and the thousands of smaller habits that make up each of these activities are based on certain assumptions that are specific to shopping. When, in any of a number of places around the world, one is expected to dicker for what one buys, then, there are other sets of habits and assumptions. Among them are the assumption that one will not pay the first price stated, that time will be spent in interpersonal interaction (in contrast with the western rather impersonal interaction) and that if you don't know the price or find it out in the process you'll get cheated, etc. The habits in the dickering ritual are built on these assumptions.

Within our families (the family subsystem), likewise, we habitually "perform" greeting rituals, dressing rituals, eating rituals and others—all based on assumptions specific to the subsystem in focus. Even the ways we think of each other are habitual. In the religion subsystem, then, we assume certain subsystem-specific things concerning how and when we should worship, where we should go to perform religious acts and what we are to believe. On the basis of these assumptions we carry out our religious behavior, usually habitually.

Intermixed with our habitual behavior is *creative behavior*. This is the most interesting behavior. We are creative when we go to a different grocery store than we usually go to, when we drive a different route to or from our workplace, when we change toothpaste or soap, when we try a new food or a new recipe, when we sit at a different place at table, when we change a routine dickering situation into a verbal adventure, when we dress differently or change our hair style, when we decide to worship on Saturday rather than Sunday or to sing in church sitting down when everyone else is standing. And all such behavior is predicated on the assumption that we have the freedom to act that way within the guidelines of the assumptions specific to the given subsystem (and within the larger guidelines of our worldview)—unless, of course, we choose to challenge those assumptions by engaging in creative behavior outside of them and risking social pressure to conform.

The following diagram may help us to picture the place of creative behavior, habitual behavior and subsystem-specific assumptions at the surface level in the subsystems:

ECONOMICS SUBSYSTEM	FAMILY SUBSYSTEM	RELIGION SUBSYSTEM
Creative Behavior	Creative Behavior	Creative Behavior
Habitual Behavior (Ritual)	Habitual Behavior (Ritual)	Habitual Behavior (Ritual)
Subsystem-Specific Assumptions	Subsystem-Specific Assumptions	Subsystem-Specific Assumptions

Figure 6.2. Internal Structuring of the Subsystems

Though there are assumptions that apply specifically to each of the subsystems of surface-level culture, the assumptions labeled worldview assumptions apply to all of the subsystems. Given that there are both types of assumptions, the question is how to tell them apart. *The rule is: if the assumption underlies all or nearly all of the subsystems, it is worldview. If it applies only to one subsystem, it is a subsystem assumption.*

For example, in America, individualism applies to all the subsystems. We are individualistic in family, economics, education, religion, etc. Worshiping is, however, for most of us religion-specific unless, of course, we are able to really incorporate into our worldview the admonition of Rom. 12:1-2, in which worship is defined as the presenting of our whole selves, presumably at all times, to God. If we learn to worship that way, we have moved a subsystem assumption concerning worship to the worldview level.

Further, if a people assume that supernatural beings and power affect every area of life, that assumption is a worldview assumption, not merely an assumption that falls into the subsystem called religion. On the other hand, if a people assumes that the only right place to worship is in a building called a "church" and the only right time to worship is on Sunday, these assumptions are specific to the surface-level subsystem called "religion." These assumptions, then, are paralleled by such assumptions of devotees of other religions within the same society that worship should be conducted in another way, in another type of building on Saturday or on Friday or at some other time. In western societies, large numbers of people will be characterized by naturalistic (usually dominated by so-called "scientific") assumptions at the worldview level accompanied by a few supernaturalistic assumptions (such as a belief in God). Though they may be regular churchgoers or synagogue-goers, the influence of their religious assumptions is pretty well restricted to the religion segment of their lives, rather than affecting their total behavior.

To show the contrast between these two kinds of assumptions, it will be helpful to chart some examples of each kind of assumption, first for the United States, then for Kamwe. There is a more detailed presentation of each of these worldviews in chapter 12.

WORLDVIEW ASSUMPTIONS—U.S.	SUBSYSTEM ASSUMPTIONS—U.S.
Individualism	**Economics** Buy and sell impersonally Prices fixed One is entitled to all he/she can make
Secular-Humanism (Naturalism)	
Democratic Government	
Look to government for protection & security	**Family** Small family best for economic reasons Live in a house with many rooms Mother and father sleep together Parents provide for children Children go to school
Enough effort brings success	
Time is money—efficiency	
Knowledge is power	**Religion** Go to church on Sunday Sit quietly during sermon Put money in the offering plate
Scientism	
Capitalism	**Politics** Primaries to select presidential candidates Two government "houses"—Senate and House of Representatives State governments as well as national

Figure 6.3. American Worldview and Subsystem Assumptions

WV ASSUMPTIONS—KAMWE	SUBSYSTEM ASSUMPTIONS—KAMWE
Supernaturalism—high God, many spirits Appease evil spirits to live well The mountains give strength and protection Guinea corn means life and health Family relationships provide social security Kinship relationships central to life	**Economic** Each extended family provides for all of its own needs—food, clothing Buy and sell personally **Family** The larger the family, the better Live in compound consisting of several one-room huts built close to the mountain, if possible Polygamy a good idea—every woman to be married Children learn how to be adults by associating with parents—girls learn from mother, boys from father Ancestral spirits have family responsibilities **Religion** Rituals can bring rain during drought Only call on God in time of great need Diviners can determine matters of health, guilt of offending party **Politics** Senior male in family of chief is chief of the village Chief of the tradesmen has great power because linked to the spirits

Figure 6.4. Kamwe Worldview and Subsystem Assumptions

Worldview, Religion and Commitment

It should be clear by now that worldview and the subsystems, including religion, are on different levels. These levels were pictured on the chart in chapter 2 as surface and deep. Something else that was pictured there is the difference between cultural structuring and personal behaving. It is important to refer to each of those dimensions here.

We have said that culture, including worldview, is structure. To this point we have dealt primarily with that structuring without referring overtly to the fact that it is the personal behavior based on that structuring that is the crucial component of Christianity. *For biblical Christianity is intended to be a faith, not a structure—a matter of personal commitment, not of performing religious rituals. In fact, I believe it is very misleading to refer to biblical Christianity as a religion.*

This being true, though, people have made a religion to express that faith. So, at one level, Christianity is a religion. This is necessary, since all human behavior will be expressed in cultural forms and religion is an organization of cultural forms. But, in spite of the need for such structuring in order to express Christian meanings, I believe God never intended our faith, our commitment to be *simply* a set of cultural forms like what people call "religion."

If ours is simply a *religion*, we can speak of *adapting* it to whatever culture it is introduced into. And, indeed, it has often happened that Christian witnesses have simply carried their cultural religion to other peoples and taught them to worship and behave like those in the home country who call themselves Christians. This is unfortunate, even if within those foreign cultural forms many in the receiving societies come to meaningful saving faith in Christ. We can rejoice that the foreignness did not prevent them from coming to faith.

What we often see is so-called "Christian" forms (i.e., the cultural forms used in the practice of Christianity in the home country) introduced into the cultures of the world with slight modifications to accommodate to the receiving culture. This is the way religions are moved from culture to culture. They are *adapted* to be sure but always carry with them a significant amount of the cultural forms in which they are expressed in the home society. Whatever their culture, when people become Muslims they are required to pray in a certain way and in a certain direction and to dress as those in medieval Arabia dressed. Buddhists and Hindus have to obey the food taboos instituted by their founders. Sincere Jews are to dress according to Jewish custom and participate in characteristically Jewish rituals.

Religions, then, are made up of a set of cultural forms. These forms can be adapted and adjusted when taken to new societies. But they are givens if people are to participate in that religion. With true, biblical Christianity, however, it is not the adaptation of a cultural system that is in focus when the faith is taken across cultures. It is what we call *contextualization* of the faith. Contextualization of Christianity is the expression of Christian meanings and allegiance in the cultural forms of the receiving peoples. These forms, then, are intended to be subservient to the *meanings and allegiance* and may remain the same as they were previous to the coming of Christianity, or they may be adapted, though some forms will be discarded. But the major change required of those who come to Christ will be in the meanings conveyed and the commitment/allegiance chosen, not in the forms imported into the society.

Jesus said He came to bring life (John 10:10). Does this mean He came to add one more religion to the list of the religions of the world? Or does it mean He was bringing something that differs from the religions and that, therefore, can be conveyed even through traditional cultural forms, including those cultural forms that are identified with the religion of the people who use them?

Christianity is intended to be a faith, not simply a religion. It is to be something expressed on the personal behavior side of our chart more than simply a set of structured worldview assumptions, as important as those are as a foundation for the faith.

This understanding of Christianity is the one the Apostle Paul was arguing for in Acts 15 when he advocated that Gentiles not be required to adopt Jewish custom in order to follow Jesus. Paul had learned this approach by watching God give the Holy Spirit to Gentile converts on the basis of their faith alone, in spite of the fact that they had made no attempt to convert to Jewish culture. Though the(?) it was the practice of the early Christians to? seek to win people on the basis of a conversion to Christ plus Jewish culture, the Holy Spirit broke their rule and endorsed Gentile cultures as adequate vehicles for Gentile interaction with God. The culture in which Jesus met His followers was not to be the cultural norm for the expression of Christianity. By contrast, Muslims worldwide are expected to adopt many features of the culture of their founder.

God expects, then, that the focus will be on the *relationship* between the converts and Himself, rather than on the *cultural forms* in terms of which that relationship is expressed. It became clear to those who agreed with Paul that what God wants is not a certain set of cultural forms but a faith response that can be expressed in a multiplicity of cultural forms. The battle for the Christians of the early centuries, then, was to be over whether one worshipped Caesar, calling him Lord, or whether one worshipped Jesus as Lord—not over whether one practiced the religious forms followed by the Jewish Christians.

If ours is simply a "form religion," it can be adapted but not contextualized, it can be in competition with other forms of religion but not flow through those forms because by definition it seeks to replace those forms. But biblical Christianity is not simply a set of cultural forms. Cultural Christianity, however, is. And we get tangled up in our discussions because when we refer to Christianity, it is often not clear whether we are speaking of essential, biblical Christianity or of the traditional religion of western societies that is also called Christianity. In my book *Christianity in Culture* (1979) I have attempted to make this distinction by spelling biblical Christianity with a capital C and cultural christianity with a small c.

Essential biblical Christianity requires none of the original cultural forms. That's how it came to be in history that it was "captured" by the West and is now considered western even though its origin is not western. Essential Christianity is an allegiance, a relationship, from which flow a series of meanings that are intended to be expressed through the cultural forms of any culture. These forms are intended, then, to be chosen for their appropriateness to convey proper biblical meanings in the receptors' contexts.

I believe, then, that we should make a clear distinction between religion or, rather, *a religion* and a faith. What I mean by "a faith" is a commitment to someone or something, supported by a set of deep worldview-level assumptions. For most of the world, such a faith involves commitment to a God, gods or spirits. In the West, rather than committing to Christ, the majority of people both outside and inside of the church seem to have made their primary commitment to human achievement, especially scientific, economic or political achievement supported by human scientific, economic or political structures. This faith, then, called "scientific humanism" serves as the real religion of most westerners.

A religion, then, is a set of cultural forms in terms of which a faith is expressed. As indicated above, these cultural forms are at surface-level in any given cultural structuring, as opposed to the worldview-level assumptions that underlie a faith. The surface-level forms are, however, designed to express the worldview-level understandings of the faith. The practicing of the religious forms may be the expression of a deep-level commitment to a God, gods, spirits, our families, or material wealth, or it may simply be seen as ritual by means of which one gains merit with a supernatural being or magically controls some supernatural power. The forms may be seen as valuable and powerful in and of themselves and, indeed, may be the object of a people's commitment. That is, a people may, in their religious life, in reality be pledging allegiance to the religious forms themselves rather than to any being or thing that exists beyond the forms.

Often, then, this commitment to a religion is regarded as a part of a people's cultural identity, part and parcel of their commitment to the culture itself, to the customs that distinguish them from others. But it is usually accompanied by commitment to beings as well—both human beings within the society such as family members and spirit beings outside the society. Our commitment to the people we love, then, may differ significantly from our commitment to our customs. Likewise, if we commit ourselves to God, gods or spirits, beings that are not culture-bound, these commitments are of a different order than our commitment to the culture or our commitment to some of the people who share our culture with us. So we live with a hierarchy of commitments. And Jesus expects His people to make Him their No. 1 commitment (Matt. 10:37-8; Luke 14:26-7).

People can, of course, commit themselves to ideas as well as to beings. In such a case, the commitment is to something inside the culture. It is not to beings such as family who are not in the culture but are a part of the society that uses the culture. Nor is it a commitment to someone outside the culture such as God, a god or a spirit.

The point is, we have in the world both religions and faiths or commitments. Religions are structure. Faiths are personal/group commitments. These are two very different things, though a faith is ordinarily expressed in cultural structures that are called religion. This fact confuses some people, especially if the term "religious faith" is used to distinguish the religious type of faith from, say, faith in a government, in an economic system, in a family, in oneself or the like. To make the point that there is a difference between these two things, let's look at ten of the contrasts between them.

RELIGION (STRUCTURAL)	A FAITH (PERSONAL)
Structural, Cultural/Worldview	Personal/Group/Social
Rituals, Rules	Relationship
Beliefs	Commitment/Allegiance
Perform	Obey
Adapt	Contextualize
Borrow/Accept/Imitate (e.g., worship forms of the source culture)	Create/Grow (e.g., cultural forms of the receiving culture)
"One size fits all"	Cultural varieties of expression
Like a tree, must be transplanted	Like a seed that gets planted
Like a loaf of bread that gets passed on	Like yeast that gets put into raw dough
An Institution	A Fellowship

Figure 6.5. Ten Contrasts between Religion and a Faith.

A religion is a cultural and worldview structure, centered around a certain kind and number of rituals accompanied by rules and regulations. There are system-specific beliefs on the basis of which the religion is practiced and lived, and a focus on performance of the rituals. Though the structures and beliefs can be *adapted* when taken into a context different from their original context, the aim of taking a religion into another context is lead people to accept and imitate the performance of those practicing that religion.

A faith, on the other hand, is personal, centered around a relationship, usually with one or more supernatural beings, based on a person's commitment to that being or, alternatively, a commitment to an idea, an idol, a structure or a living being. There are beliefs underlying the commitment, to be sure, and these assumptions are worldview-level. But the allegiance itself is not simply an intellectual thing, it is a matter of a person's will to commit oneself to that something or someone outside of oneself. Commitment, therefore, is a person thing, not a structure thing. It is person, not culture in spite of the fact that it results in cultural behavior, as do all commitments. Though the relationship is primary, a faith is usually ritualized, even if it is just a commitment to an idea. The focus of a faith is on obedience, not just belief, within whatever cultural structures are available, with the aim of creating and growing in that faith-obedience.

It is well-known that there are rituals conducted in worship of God, gods or other beings with which people have established a relationship. There are, however, also academic, economic and political rituals performed by those with a religion-like commitment (faith) to certain ideas and theories.

By way of an example of a non-religious commitment and accompanying ritual, I will recount an experience one of my graduate students went through at a secular university where I was teaching. He was seeking entrance into a Ph.D. program in political science. One of the rituals required for such entrance is an oral exam where the candidate is grilled concerning his/her knowledge of the field. The student came to my office soon after he finished that ritual and reported that he had done well in the question and answer part of the exam but that he was stunned when they commented that they were not sure he should be admitted to the program because they questioned his *commitment* to political science! He remarked that he could understand someone asking about his commitment to Christ, to Christianity or to some other religion, but not to an academic discipline such as political science. I remarked that he should have known by now that for these professors, political science is their religion and that they consider themselves the priests of that religion and were leery of allowing someone into its mysteries whose commitment was suspect.

The thing committed to may be any part of the culture, including an academic discipline or the cultural forms of a religion with or without a commitment to supernatural beings. This fact may confuse some people if they fail to understand the difference I am making between structural things such as religion and the personal thing called allegiance or commitment. Since people are entirely immersed in culture, however, they will automatically express whatever allegiances they have in cultural ways.

I have said "allegiances," in the plural. To this point I have been speaking of *an* allegiance or commitment, as if people have only one. In reality, though, each person has many allegiances. And the allegiances that are directed toward supernatural beings or religious structures may not even be at the top of the list. For many of the peoples of the world, for example, allegiance to family is their primary allegiance. All other commitments or loyalties are secondary to that one. What Jesus intends, however, is that our allegiance to Him be primary with all other allegiances, including family, secondary to that.

Different Peoples Have Different Emphases

We have emphasized that the assumptions that make up a people's worldview lie behind the kinds of surface-level behavior of that people. But we have not yet made the point that the amount of focus on any given area of surface-level behavior will have a great deal to do with the proportion of worldview assumptions that relate to that area. Societies do not give equal value or pay equal attention to their various subsystems.

For example, many people do spend a high proportion of their time and energy (not to mention money) carrying out religious activities. On the other hand, Anglo-Americans may be dominated to a similar extent by economic activities. Others (e.g., traditional Chinese) seem to be dominated more by family concerns than by either "religion" or economics.

In each of these situations we can see a surface-level *sociocultural specialization*. In any given society, as with any given individual, greater attention is given to certain things than to others. Just as individuals specialize, then, so do groups of individuals (societies). Certain peoples give more attention to "religious" matters, other peoples to economic matters, others to family.

This being the case, we would expect to find a corresponding "imbalance" at the worldview level. We can expect that the surface level behavior a people specializes in will have a greater influence on the core assumptions, values and allegiances (worldview) than the behavior they do not emphasize as much. The principle is, *the greater the attention to a given surface-level focus, the greater the number of assumptions at the worldview-level that relate to that focus.*

I mentioned above the possibility of a person redefining the society's meaning of worship in his/her life according to Rom. 12:1-2. If that happens, an assumption that had been at the religion subsystem (surface) level gets redefined, expanded and "buried" in the worldview, thus becoming a principle that affects all of life, not just one's surface-level religious practice. An important change thus occurs at the worldview level, expanding the influence of a person's religious involvement on that person's worldview. Such a process is, of course, what we recommend to all who seek to grow in their relationship to Christ.

For another example, suppose a person who has not been particularly concerned about environmental issues becomes converted to that cause. As she or he gains more insight and develops greater commitment to that cause, the assumptions and values that once were either surface-level or even entirely absent, become governing principles for the person's whole life. They thus become worldview-level assumptions and values and a/the major determinant of the focus of that person's life, influencing many, if not all, of the subsystems in that person's cultural experience.

In this way we see that conversion to a perspective affects a person greatly at the worldview level. This links with the fact, noted earlier, that a sincere commitment to Christianity (or any other life involvement) deeply affects a person's worldview, not simply the surface-level religious behavior.

On the societal level, our society biases us in favor of certain worldview emphases by pressuring us to be more focused on certain areas than on others. Our preoccupation in western societies with the material world, for example, shows up in our language when we speak of intangible things such as time as if it were a material substance. We speak of "long" or "short" time as if time were a material thing that can be measured like a rope or a river or a road. We speak of "wasting" time or "saving" time as if it were food or money that can be stored or thrown away. We pay laborers for their time as if it were a commodity that can be bought or sold.

One of the things such an emphasis suggests to us is that what we call "time" is valuable to us. This, then, becomes a consideration at the worldview level. Another is that material world concepts in some way govern our perception of a non-material concept like time. Values from the space/material worldview universal are influential on the "territory" covered by the time/event universal in Anglo-American worldview.

A similar thing happens, of course, with peoples who spend much of their time in surface-level religious pursuits. Supernaturalistic peoples tend to perceive of the universe in personalistic and spiritual terms, as opposed to western understandings that the universe is like a machine. When such peoples talk about what we consider the physical environment, then, it is often not clear to us if they are talking about physical substance or spiritual beings. We see a tree or a river as physical. These peoples often see them as primarily spiritual.

To summarize what I am getting at, the influences between worldview and surface-level assumptions and behavior move both ways. There is obviously an influence coming from worldview "up" to the surface on surface-level behavior. But there are as well, important influences moving "down" from the surface into the worldview. And we can expect to find in the worldview of a society that spends much of its time in religious activity, a lot of worldview assumptions dealing with the matters that support that activity. Likewise, we can expect to find in the worldview of a society that spends much of its time concerned with economic activity, a lot of worldview assumptions dealing with matters that support that activity. That is, the more surface-level activity in any given subsystem, the greater the influence of that focus on the worldview and, through the worldview, on the rest of the subsystems.

If, for example, a people spend approximately one-third of their waking time and energy in religious activity, we can expect a high percentage (not necessarily one-third) of their worldview assumptions to relate to the values underlying that religious behavior. And these assumptions will, along with the rest of the worldview assumptions, percolate up into all the surface-level subsystems, not just the religion subsystem. The following diagrams are intended to picture two configurations designed to show the approximate percentage of surface-level behavior devoted to each of several subsystems.

The differences between the emphases of a *supernaturalistically-oriented society* and one (e.g., western) *focused primarily on material culture and economics* might be pictured thus (with the amount of space allowed for each subsystem representing the amount of emphasis):

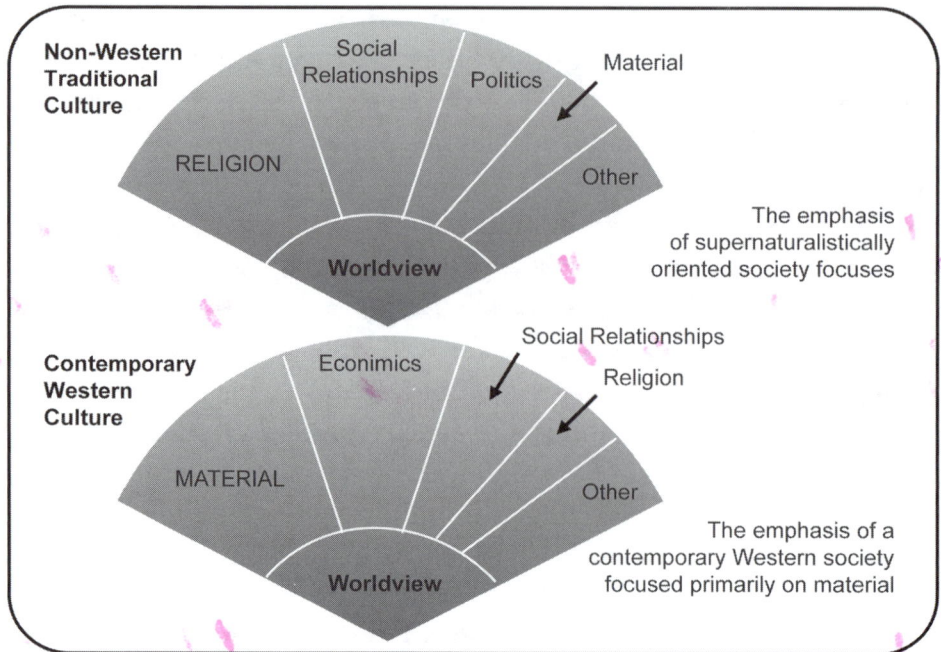

Worldview (adapted from Nishioka 1997:91)

As illustrated, the primary concerns of a people dominate the surface level of their culture. These same areas, then, will influence the worldview more than will the other subsystems. In cultures where supernaturalism is a primary focus, we find that the religious subsystem influences the worldview more than, say, the economics or the concern for the material world or some other aspect of the culture as a whole. In western societies, though, we find that subsystems dealing with economics and the control of the material world influence the worldview more than the religious and social relationships subsystems. Such differences in focus suggest that we may characterize different societies as centered around a supernaturalistically-oriented worldview or a materialistically-oriented worldview or a social relationship-oriented worldview.

Worldview Schizophrenia[2]

In smaller, relatively tightly knit societies, worldview assumptions, values, and allegiances (commitments) usually vary little from member to member and from subgroup to subgroup. In larger, less tightly knit

---

2 Though technically it is improper to refer to Multiple Personality Disorder (now renamed Dissociative Identity Disorder) as schizophrenia, the fact that MPD/DID is thus labeled in popular usage leads me to use it here instead of the more cumbersome "worldview MPD" or worse, "worldview DID." I hope I will be forgiven for making this choice.

societies, such as that of America, however, there may be considerable variation in worldview assumptions from subgroup to subgroup and even from individual to individual.

Though there is, apparently, always some allowed range of variation at the worldview level, that range tends to be wider in proportion to the size of a society, the duration and intensity of contact with other societies and the amount of diversity within the society. As we would predict, then, smaller societies with little contact with other groups tend to exhibit a smaller range of allowed variation, while larger societies with greater contact with outside groups will show a wider range of variation.

Indeed, in large, diverse societies with strong outside influences, the tendency is for their people to experience a good bit of conflict at the worldview level between competing assumptions, allegiances and values. Such competition results in many people in such societies assimilating at least an important portion of one or more worldviews in addition to the one they learned as children. These, then, are often only partially reconciled with each other, leading to a situation where a person or group applies one worldview perspective in one set of circumstances and another, at least partially contradictory, set of assumptions in other circumstances.

Foreign students studying in the United States commonly are forced to apply western assumptions in their school and social activities among Americans but they commonly revert to their home worldview when they are with their own people. A considerable amount of confusion is, however, normal for the newly arrived. For example, many Asian students, for whom quoting a professor or author at length in research papers is highly valued at home, are surprised to find themselves accused of plagiarism and/or a lack of original thinking in American graduate schools.

Though I deny that there is a Christian worldview, the insertion of Christian values by westerners into an American worldview results in a similar type of worldview schizophrenia. For we have been carefully taught to interpret events (in keeping with what is normal in our society) from a naturalistic perspective. But, as Christians, we espouse Christian supernaturalistic values. We may, therefore, in keeping with our Christian commitment, assume that God is involved in any given event but not be sure just how He is involved.

To illustrate, picture an American Christian driving along a highway and narrowly avoiding an accident. How does she/he react? Influenced by the naturalistic American worldview into which we have been trained, our response is likely to be some such statement as, "Boy, was I lucky!" Our Christian perspective, which we have probably only partly assimilated, however, brings to our attention the fact that God is involved in every such event to protect us from harm (Rom. 8:28). An appropriate reflexive response stemming from that assumption, then, would be something like, "Thank you, God."

Such differences in our automatic (habitual) response to such a situation come from competing values at the worldview level within us. Some of us will have so integrated our lives around our Christian assumptions that we will automatically say, "Thank you, God. You saved me from that accident. You protected me," rather than "Boy, was I lucky!" But many of us will show less integration of our Christian values and sometimes go one way and sometimes the other. Such experiences bring to our attention the conflict between worldview assumptions going on within us.

Some internationals may even have parts of three or more sets of worldview assumptions competing within them—those they were brought up with, western assumptions taught them in western schools, and Christian assumptions (possibly infected by a western perspective). The whole thing can get quite complicated.

PART II:

CHARACTERISTICS OF WORLDVIEWS

Chapter 7

Functions of Worldview

At this point in our study we turn a corner from a general introduction to a more specific treatment of certain characteristics of worldviews. The first of these is what I will call the *functions* of worldview. This is a focus on the way people *use* worldview assumptions. An understanding of how worldview functions will help us considerably in our attempt to gain insight into the concept of worldview and the part it plays in the cultural life of a people.

Since it is *people* using worldview, not worldview doing something by itself, we will label these *the functions served by worldview*, with the understanding that these functions only occur when people use their worldview. To deal with these functions, we will treat each of the items on the worldview structure side of Figure 2.2 concerning personal behavior and cultural structuring.

Worldviews provide guidelines for at least four types of primary behavior and seven types of derivative behavior. With regard to primary behavior, people act according to worldview assumptions to do such basic things as willing (choosing), emoting, thinking and what I will call "habiting" (doing things habitually). The derivative behavior, then, is divided into the assumptions that pattern meaning assignment and those that pattern people's responses to that assignment. Interpreting and evaluating fit into the former category, with the latter made up of such things as committing/pledging allegiance, explaining, relating, adapting and integrating the various components of life.

Assumptions Underlying Primary Behavior

The first set of patterns provided by a worldview is that for the *structuring of deep, underlying "primary" behavior*. At a very basic level, we will or choose things. We also think, express emotions, and reason. In these and all other activities, then, we have underlying motivations and predispositions. This may not be an exhaustive listing of primary behavior, but it will serve to establish the point that at this very deep level, there is worldview structuring.

1. Patterning the Way We Use Our Wills. We are taught the socially approved ways of choosing and deciding. Though no society could endorse total individualism, those that pattern toward the individualistic end of the spectrum tend to teach their children to assert their wills individualistically in most areas of life. In such societies, parents set before their children the need to "grow up" to "stand on their own two feet," making their own choices according to the worldview assumptions of the society.

In societies whose ideas lie toward the group-oriented end of the spectrum, then, the patterns taught to the children keep the concerns of the society as a whole in sharper focus than those of any given individual. Traditional Japanese assume, for example, that it is "sweet" and, therefore, ideal for a person to always be dependent on his/her family. They expect their children to continue to use their willpower to depend on and conform to the group even after they are grown. "It is the one who wanders away from the group that gets in trouble," they are taught.

Learning to use our wills to obey—people, rules, traditions and the like—is usually a strong emphasis in child rearing. We are taught what kinds of things we can choose for ourselves and what things others will choose for us. We are taught how to make decisions—whether to sit down and reason things out or to follow our intuition or to ask someone else's advice or to pray, or some combination of such choices. In these and a multitude of other ways, worldview assumptions are used to guide our wills as we choose.

2. Patterning the Use of Emotions. All societies structure the use of emotion. In few, if any, is it considered proper to simply express any emotion at any time. Though some allow great latitude in emotional expression, some are very repressive. It is worldview assumptions concerning the proper expression of emotions that lie behind such customs.

What is considered appropriate for one group (say, women) in the expression of emotion may be considered inappropriate for another group. In Anglo-American society, for example, women are allowed much more freedom than men in crying and in openly expressing joy, sorrow, even pain. It is proverbial that oriental peoples hide their emotions in public.

Those of us whose ancestors came from northern Europe are usually quite repressed in our emotional expression, especially those of us who are male. Even males whose ancestors came from southern Europe, however, may be quite emotional.

Which emotions can be shown as well as how they may be shown are patterned, and each according to worldview guidelines. Expression of happiness may be allowed but not sadness under most circumstances.

For many peoples, grief is to be "stuffed." Though in many societies, it is expressed loudly, especially by the women. And professional "criers" are customary at funerals in some societies. Assumptions concerning emotional expression in different situations are common. In Euro-American societies, loud expressions of joy or sorrow are allowed at athletic events, but complete silence is expected in church, at least during the sermon.

Due to differences in the worldview assumptions lying beneath the emotional expressions of the various societies of the world, it is common for people from one society to not be able to "read" the emotional expressions of another people. Westerners have been so bad at reading the emotions of Asians that we commonly refer to Asians as "inscrutable" and are commonly misled when we try to read their emotions. I am told, however, that Asians can usually read the emotions of their own people. Yet even they cannot read emotions that are not expressed.

3. Patterning of Logic and Reason. People in different societies reason differently. Westerners (especially western men) are known for what is called "linear logic." We tend to reason more or less "in a straight line," building our case point by point toward what we consider a logical conclusion. "If such and such is true, then it follows that such and such is also true," we say. We then tend to make rather sweeping generalizations on the basis either of logic or of a few experiences that we feel point in the direction of the generalization. This is our "cognitive style."

Many of the peoples of the world, however, reason "contextually." They see each event encased in a context that is different from any other context. The uniqueness of each context, then, makes each event unique and difficult to generalize from. Contextual thinkers will tend to tell story after story, often in great detail, to develop the unique features of the event in its context, allowing the hearers to infer the proper conclusions rather than making what we would consider logical point after logical point to build their case. The writers of the books of Hebrews and James plus many of the Old Testament authors, especially the prophets, demonstrate a Hebrew form of contextual reasoning.

Then there is intuitive thinking in which the person simply "knows" without going through a reasoning process or developing a case through elaborately discussing the contextual factors. There seem to be many intuitive thinkers in even American society, while Indian societies tend to produce a majority of such thinking. Then there are those who "hear from the Lord," prophets and others functioning in the spiritual gifts of "word of knowledge," "word of wisdom" and prophecy. Their divinely guided insights seem to be intuitive rather than linear or contextual.

Whether it is linear reasoning, contextual reasoning, intuitive insight or some other type, worldview assumptions pattern the ways in which a given people are expected to come to conclusions. It is worldview assumptions that lie behind what I believe is an overemphasis on rational thought as the proper way to truth in much of western society.

4. Worldview Assumptions Also Affect and Pattern Motivation. What motivates people to behave in certain ways differs from society to society according to differential patterning at the worldview level. Though there are certain basic biologically-based motivators (e.g., the need for food, water, sleep, sex, exercise), there are also socially inculcated wants (e.g., desire for prestige, wealth, comfort, freedom from trouble) that motivate people in powerful ways.

What these motivations are and the strength of each are based on worldview assumptions. What one is expected to do about them, then, is also patterned by worldview. It is worldview assumptions, for example, that make comfort and wealth such powerful motivations in western societies. There are many societies in the world for which comfort has not traditionally been a high value. For many of the peoples of the world, peaceful relationships between members of their group are a high value—even to the extent that people are not motivated to seek guilt and punishment if an infraction has occurred but, rather, to seek reconciliation without punishment.

In the communication of Christianity, we are fond of helping witnesses to look for "felt needs." People are usually motivated to seek to meet such needs, especially if they are not being met. Though many of these needs may be physical (e.g., food, water), those in the spiritual realm are of particular interest to us. I have heard, for example, that the gospel presented to the peoples of India was not perceived to be of much relevance when presented as a gospel of peace or of eternal salvation. When, however, it was presented as offering forgiveness, the receptivity of the people greatly increased. Apparently this appealed to a felt need that was not being met on the basis of their traditional worldview assumptions.

5. Even the Types and Expressions of Predispositions are Patterned by Worldview. Such attitudes as optimism or pessimism, a positive outlook on life or a negative one, idealism, negativism or realism are based on worldview assumptions and expressed differently from society to society.

Though certain people in every society will manifest each of these attitudes, some societies will teach their children in such a way that the vast majority of them will look on the positive side of things most of the time. There have been societies, for example, who lived in lush surroundings in which all of their needs were met and no enemies threatened whose outlook on life, as structured by basic worldview assumptions, was, as we say, "through rosy tinted glasses." On the other hand, especially in response to the negative impact of modernization, there are now a large number of small-scale societies whose emotional stance is rather totally pessimistic. Their children no longer obey their parents, nor do they help on the farms now that they go to western schools. Crime is rampant because the old structures of social control no longer work. And overall, the predominant emotion is demoralization. Over history, a number of such societies have sunk into extinction.

Patterning the Assignment of Meaning

The next two worldview functions relate to the *patterning of the assignment of meaning*. Assigning meaning is perhaps the most frequent activity human beings engage in. It is important to recognize, as I have detailed in Kraft 1991, that meaning is assigned by people. Meaning is not inherent in the vehicles we use to convey it.

The cultural vehicles we use are called *cultural forms* or *symbols*. Words are cultural forms. So are gestures, material artifacts, rituals and any other of the millions of items and structures that make up a culture. As we live our lives, we see, hear or think about these items and assign them meaning. As you read these words, for example, *you* are assigning them the meanings that occur to you on the basis of what is internal to you. That is, you are employing the worldview structuring that you have developed on the basis of what you have been taught modified by the adjustments you have made on the basis of your life experiences to enable you to make sense out of what you are reading.

I, of course, have certain meanings I would like you to assimilate. But the fact is, once the words have left me, I have no control over how you will understand them (unless, of course, I am the teacher of a class using this book as a text and have a chance to further negotiate with you orally over my intentions). The way you or I assign meaning to any set of words or actions involves us in interpreting and evaluating.

1. Interpreting. We have been taught how to interpret. For example, in the West it is common for us to interpret landscapes and flowers as beautiful. We interpret them that way in accord with the way we have been taught. In many societies, however, "beautiful" is not a word the people would use for landscapes and flowers. They have not been taught to assume such things are beautiful. As Americans we have the saying, "beauty is in the eye of the beholder." This saying recognizes that beauty is a matter of interpretation by the observer. So is everything else in life.

But interpretation is done according to social convention. And social convention is quite predictable to those within a society because it is governed by worldview guidelines that have been learned by the members of that society. Indeed, people would find it impossible to communicate if it were not for this predictability. Say, for example, I was lecturing in English concerning dogs. But every time I used the word "dog," some in the audience thought of sheep, some of houses, some of airplanes, some of people. Only those who interpreted the word "dog" to signify a canine animal would have interpreted what I said as I intended. Within the cultural systems in which English is used, people have learned and, therefore, agree to habitually assign to the word "dog" essentially the same meaning. Only because each member of a language community habitually assigns approximately the same meaning to each combination of sounds can they understand each other.

An additional interesting factor is that we ordinarily assign meaning primarily on the basis of how we feel about what we observe or hear and only secondarily on the basis of how we reason. So the structuring of emotion described above has a lot to do with how we interpret. And the reason-based presentations we are accustomed to in school and church are often much less effective than we have been led to believe unless the hearers are strongly motivated (an emotion) to receive what is being said.

We say, then, that the assignment of meaning is a matter of personal interpretation, strongly affected by the person's feelings, usually done habitually according to social agreements concerning how to interpret cultural forms. And these people-agreements are, for the most part, quite predictable to those who know the worldview of the speaker, since they are based on the worldview structuring of assumptions they have been taught.

There's a sense in which all that we say and illustrate concerning worldview applies to this interpretation function. This being true, we will not further elaborate on this function here, allowing the following discussion to fill in additional details concerning it.

2. *Evaluating*. As we interpret, we also evaluate, again usually on the basis of how we feel toward what we are observing or hearing. Indeed, the evaluating of the meaning is an extremely important part of the assignment of meaning. In the evaluational part of meaning assignment, feeling is even more important than in basic interpretation. For we learn to feel differently about different words and other cultural items and the people who present them. When I say the word "dog," for example, not only do hearers think of a canine animal, they react positively, negatively or neutrally to that thought. People either like dogs (or a dog), dislike them or are neutral toward them. Whatever the evaluation, it becomes a part of the way they assign meaning.

Culturally, Anglo-Americans are taught to assume that dogs can be pets, even "man's best friend," that they can be allowed to live in our homes, that we are to feed them, that it is appropriate for children to play with them, that some of them are to be trained to be fierce and to act as "watchdogs," and the like. These assumptions inform our evaluation of dogs in general or any given dog. In northeastern Nigeria, people thought it strange that we kept a dog in the house, fed him and let our children play with him. Their worldview assumptions, on the basis of which they evaluated our behavior, led them to feel that dogs should not be treated kindly. They are expected to forage for their own food and they are kicked when they get too close to people or their living quarters. Their main contact with children is to clean up their bottoms after they have defecated.

The evaluational part of meaning assignment concerning "dog" (and thousands of other concepts and items) will be quite different for these Nigerians than for an Anglo-American. The reason, of course, is that the basic worldview assumptions they have been taught are so different from the ones we have been taught.

Evaluational assumptions provide the bases for judgments concerning what is good and what is not good. Typical areas in which these assumptions are applied are esthetics (e.g., judgments as to what is visually or aurally pleasing), ethics (e.g., judgments as to what is moral and what immoral), economics (e.g., judgments as to what ought to be more or less expensive), human character (e.g., judgments concerning proper versus improper or admirable versus criticizable conduct and/or character traits), and the like. Values may be technically referred to as "normative" or "ethical" postulates (Hoebel 1972).

In teaching children how to evaluate, a people (unless demoralized) gives them the impression that their approach is right, and any other approach is at least inferior, maybe even wrong. For example, the assumption that our American way is best is deeply embedded in our American worldview(s). Visitors to our country may rightly be concerned, therefore, about the way we Americans assume that our approach to life, our politics, our economics, our religion, are endorsed by God. Some of us realize that this system is not endorsed by God. Yet a naïve perspective on the part of American Christians simply says, "It is our way, therefore it must be the best way. We are Christians, therefore, our way must be God's way and our culture a Christian culture." Thus, many people assume that God Himself is in favor of democracy and capitalism. They may even assume that God created our society, giving us permission to take this land away from the Indians and to establish this kind of government and to develop the ability in technology and in warfare that put us in our present place of power and prominence in the world.

But such considerations should lead us as Christians to ask serious questions about how God evaluates things. For we are pledged to attempt to see things from His perspective, to value what He values, to stand against what He stands against. Because of this we may be required by our commitment to a Christian perspective to reevaluate and to modify and/or replace some of the evaluations provided by our American worldview.

Christians of other societies are called to do the same thing. Their worldviews may (like ours) lead them to approve of things that God does not approve of and/or to ignore things that God advocates. It seems clear, for example, that God is in favor of both truth and *love* (Eph. 4:15). To American Christians who often have a tendency to be so blunt in speaking the truth that we are unloving, God says, "Speak the *truth* in love." To many politeness-oriented peoples, however, He may want to emphasize the other part of the verse, commanding them to "Speak the truth in love." For their temptation is often to be so polite (loving) toward people that they regularly accommodate what they say to the expectations of the other person (especially if that person is a social superior) and, therefore, may be careless about being truthful.

Most cross-cultural problems stem from such differences in meaning assignment. Indeed, the examples of cross-cultural differences in understanding we have already given and will give in the following chapters all relate to this aspect of worldview. When we go into another society, we are accountable for their assumptions, not ours. To the extent that we can assign meaning according to their assumptions, rather than ours, to that extent we can understand and function properly within their world. Learning their language and culture, however, means learning their assumptions.

Patterning the Responses to Assigned Meaning

The next seven worldview functions relate to the patterning of how people *respond to the meanings they assign*. These patterns include ways of explaining, pledging allegiance, relating, adapting, regulating, getting psychological reinforcement and integrating.

1. Patterns of explaining. Explanatory assumptions concern the way things are or are supposed to be. They include basic assumptions (often articulated in myths, proverbs and/or other folklore) concerning God (e.g., God exists versus God does not exist, God is distant and unconcerned versus God is close and involved with His creation), concerning the universe (e.g., the universe is like a machine versus the universe is like a person; the universe is predictable versus the universe is capricious and unpredictable; the universe is controllable by humans versus the universe is to be submitted to by humans; the universe is centered around the world versus the universe is centered around the sun), concerning the nature of human beings (e.g., human nature is essentially good, sinful, or neutral), and the like. The various assumptions concerning disease that we have discussed also fit in here. These assumptions are sometimes technically referred to as "cosmological" or "existential" postulates (Hoebel 1972).

If, for example, the worldview assumption is that the world is mechanistic (as in western societies), explanations of how and why things happen will tend to focus on the place of impersonal cause and effect, without reference to any involvement of personal spiritual beings in the process. For many societies, however, their worldview assumptions lead them to explain as the activity of personal spirits most of the same phenomena that westerners attribute to impersonal causes.

Our Christian perspective, of course, holds that God has created and is sustaining the universe. But we may not know just how much He depends on impersonal forces (e.g., cause and effect, "laws" of nature) for the day-to-day operation of things and how much He assigns to spiritual beings. Not knowing this may lead us to wonder whether mechanistic or spiritistic worldview explanations are more accurate. Or might one be the explanation in certain situations and the other in other situations? In any event, the worldview of one's society embodies the socially approved explanations of all such phenomena. A major part of the confusion we may experience at this point comes from the fact that as Christians we have committed ourselves to a perspective other than that of our society—a perspective that at least partially contradicts western assumptions in areas such as this.

In addition to explanations concerning the origin and nature of the universe, we look to worldview assumptions for explanations of such things as how people, animals, plants, geographical phenomena, etc. got here and what we should expect of them. Explanations provided by science, history, myth, legend, and the like fit in here. Whether such explanations can be proven to be accurate or not is irrelevant. If they are assumed by a people, they are a part of their worldview. And worldview assumptions need not be totally accurate to be believed as long as they are close enough to REALITY to enable the people to live and function.

2. Patterns of pledging allegiance. A worldview provides a society's recommended stances in terms of which people develop and prioritize allegiances. It thus enables people to sort out, arrange, and make differential commitments to the things we assume, value, and do. That is, we don't simply assume, believe, value, or relate to everything in the same way. We assume, believe, and relate with some degree of intensity, committing ourselves quite strongly to certain of our beliefs, values, and behaviors, but quite weakly to others. We commit ourselves to some degree to whatever we value, most strongly to those things we value most highly. We are likely, for example, to be less strongly committed to the brand of toothpaste we use (even though we may use it because we believe it to be the best on the market) than we are to our parents (even though we may see faults in them).

It is likely that all peoples are provided by their worldviews with a prescribed (or at least strongly recommended) ultimate allegiance. For Americans this is likely to be one's self, with allegiances to job (for men), family (especially for mothers), reputation, wealth, and the like high enough on the list to sometimes vie for first place. Other allegiances may be to nation, God, traditions, children, money, comfort, a hobby. American men learn that allegiance to their job (and through that to money and comfort) is to take precedence over anything except self. American women traditionally were taught to put husband and children either before or after self. Now many put job ahead of or equal to family. God is not usually a high priority for the members of American society. Those of us who attempt to put Him first have to fight a good bit of social pressure, much of which has been assimilated and works from inside of ourselves.

For members of other societies, the culturally prescribed primary allegiance is often family, clan or other such kinship grouping, with other potential commitments such as the above sometimes replacing it in the lives of certain members of the group (especially the more westernized). For many peoples (e.g., many Muslims) their religion is also high.

For Christians, of course, we are expected to give our primary allegiance to God with other commitments falling into line behind that supreme one. The requirement that God be first necessitates a worldview change for us that is both difficult to initiate and difficult to maintain. We experience constantly in our own lives and see throughout the scriptures the tendency for those who have once put God first to replace Him with someone or something else (e.g., family, job, self-interests of one kind or another, other gods). Such replacement is labeled idolatry in the scriptures and thoroughly condemned.

How we have prioritized our allegiances becomes most obvious when we are forced to choose between them. To test the way in which allegiances are ordered we may ask the question, "If such-and-such an allegiance conflicted with such-and-such, which would one choose?" To discover which are the highest allegiances we may ask the question, "Which of these commitments would one die for?" Beyond the highest priority items, a society may or may not recommend an ordering of the lesser ones.

Americans frequently have to prioritize allegiances in choosing between job and family, between self-interest and the best interests of loved ones (e.g., spouse, parents, children, friends), between self and community, and for Christians between God and any of these. For non-westerners the need to choose between allegiance to God and that to community is often excruciatingly difficult. Our real commitments are often most obvious when such choices are made unconsciously—as when during wartime most Christian citizens of a nation unconsciously agree to put allegiance to nation above an allegiance to their Christian brothers who are fighting for the enemy nation.

In this regard, it is interesting to ask people from various societies the old conundrum concerning the capsizing of a boat in which you, your wife and your mother were riding. The problem is, given that neither of the women can swim, you can only rescue one of them. The question is, "Which one would you rescue and which one would you allow to drown?" The way a person chooses shows how he/she prioritizes those two allegiances. Anglo-Americans usually say they would rescue the wife. For the mother is old and the wife is needed for the sake of the children. Many non-westerners, however, without hesitation opt for saving the mother, reasoning that one can always find another wife but not another mother. In response to this problem, however, a Japanese student once told me he could not make that choice—he'd just have to drown with both of them! He could not, he said, face life with the shame of having let either wife or mother drown.

Most of our allegiances are, however, much less spectacular, though they, too, are likely to come into conflict with competing possibilities in situations of culture contact. We are committed via our worldview to the values, structures, and practices of our society. The degree to which we believe in the betterness of these values, structures, and practices is a measure of the intensity of our commitment to them. Note how strongly we Anglo-Americans are committed to the betterness of our cultural practices, whether technological (e.g., labor-saving devices), social (e.g., courtship and marriage practices, "equality" of women), political (e.g., democracy), or educational (e.g., schools), not only for ourselves but for the other peoples of the world as well. In general, the more intense the commitment of groups or individuals to an assumption, value, or practice, the less likely they are to change it. If, on the other hand, they become dissatisfied with the custom and/or discover an attractive alternative, the strength of their allegiance is likely to lessen, and they, therefore, become more open to the possibility of change.

3. *Patterns of relating*. A worldview provides assumptions concerning how people are to relate to one another. Perhaps most peoples (following their worldview) assume that it is good for people and groups within the society to relate cooperatively with each other. Working together, then, would be seen as good, and competing with each other as bad. People are taught according to worldview patterns how men should relate to women, how youth should relate to their elders, how people of low prestige should relate to those of higher prestige, how one occupational group should relate to another, how followers should relate to leaders and so on.

Relating to outsiders is a different matter for most peoples. A worldview includes assumptions concerning who is in our "ingroup" and, therefore, to be treated as one of "us" and who is in our "outgroup" and to be treated differently. Various outgroups, then, are to be ignored, treated with reserve or treated as enemies.

Even our relationships with animals, plants and other parts of the material universe are patterned by worldview assumptions. Are we to dominate the world around us or to submit to it? Likewise, with relationships to any invisible beings and powers a people believe in. Relationships to ideas, moral values and rules and regulations are also patterned. Since we believe such and such, how should we behave? And if we don't behave as we are taught to, what will be the penalty?

A society is in difficulty when the relationships between the various potentially competing groups within the society are not well-managed. Within American society, for example, we seem to have allowed individual and group competitiveness to get out of hand. We have learned how to achieve through competition. In many ways our greatness rests on our ability to compete. We have, however, gotten to the point where our competitiveness is ripping us apart socially. We encourage boys and men to compete against other boys and men (and, increasingly, even against women—and vice versa), young people against adults, business against business, labor against management, and even church against church. "If we don't compete," we say, "how will we get anywhere?" Some of us may "get somewhere" in our careers by using time and energy that should have been devoted to our families and other important relationships. Families do not compete well with careers. And the social cohesion or our society is breaking down because many have let this aspect of life get out of hand.

Another relational area that we Americans have allowed to get out of hand is that between us and the world of nature. We have assumed that natural resources such as air, water, trees, land, oil and animals are there to be used and that there is no limit to them. We are discovering, however, that they are limited and that they have become polluted, used up, overused or otherwise exploited to the point that our future is in danger. If we are to survive, we need to alter our assumptions and behavior in this area also.

4. Patterns of adapting. People are not always able to handle everything that comes their way by following the guidelines of their worldview. Often this is because the worldview their parents taught them was adapted to their parents' generation, not to theirs. So there are within a worldview assumptions concerning what to do when we perceive that things are not as we believe they ought to be. When this happens, the most frequent first approach seems to be to attempt to handle it without altering our assumptions. We try to keep our present worldview intact by interpreting what we see in such a way that it either is conformed to our worldview or dismissed as unreal.

On occasion, however, either because of personal and/or group openness or because of the persistence of an uncongenial perception that we find ourselves unable to deny, we may choose to make a change in some aspect of our worldview. Non-charismatic western Christians who have learned to assume that God no longer heals people via direct miracles as He did in biblical times may, for example, choose to make such a change in their worldview as a result of seeing one or more miraculous healings. Or they may attempt to preserve the old perspective by explaining the miracles away. Likewise, non-westerners under constant pressure from the teaching of western naturalistic interpretations of reality may choose to replace part or all of their supernaturalistic assumptions with naturalistic ones.

Or, persons and groups faced with experiences that challenge their worldview may attempt to retain two sets of contradictory or partially contradictory assumptions and thus to live their lives with the kind of worldview schizophrenia spoken of in the previous chapter. Whatever the result, though, people ordinarily follow the assumptions concerning change patterned by their worldview when any of their worldview assumptions are challenged.

In this regard our values and allegiances come strongly into play. We are committed so strongly to certain things that we would rather "fight than switch" if they are called into question. We may close our eyes to any other evidence to protect such assumptions. On the other hand, there are behaviors and assumptions that are not that important to us. So, if faced with evidence that change would be a good idea, we change.

If the challenges are too great and/or for some other reason the worldview assumptions are unable to handle the pressures for change, a people can lose confidence in their worldview. When this happens, and it is happening more and more in our day especially in tribal societies, there is breakdown at the worldview level that commonly issues in demoralization. Such demoralization is manifested in symptoms such as psychological, social, and moral breakdown and, unless it is checked and reversed, in cultural disintegration.

5. *A fifth function of worldview lies in the fact that it provides assumptions on the basis of which life can be regulated.* All peoples have cultural mechanisms for social control. These mechanisms are built on worldview assumptions concerning what is appropriate behavior and what is to be done to keep people in line. We are aware of laws with penalties if we break them. There are police in Euro-American societies to see to it that people don't get away with breaking the law.

The most effective regulation of behavior, however, comes from the inbuilt concepts of what is right and what is wrong and the fear of social consequences we feel if we overstep the culturally defined boundaries set up for us by our society. We learn at an early age what the expectations are of our family and other people of significance in our lives. And these expectations become regulating assumptions for us. Fear of being shunned or of gossip, or of some other form of discipline, then, motivates us to stay in line. If we overstep, internal feelings of guilt or shame beset us to motivate us to get back in line.

An Anglo-American cheats his employer out of a large sum of money. A Korean youngster fails to show respect to an elder. A Japanese drives over the speed limit. A northern Nigerian offers something to an adult with his left hand. An American burps in public. A Chinese eats a meal and fails to burp. These and a multitude of other behaviors are disapproved by societies on the basis of their worldview assumptions. And fear of some social penalty, also prescribed by worldview assumptions, keeps most people from such behaviors.

Note that the regulation of cultural behavior is especially person-oriented. It is social regulation, not cultural regulation. We are not so much regulated by the worldview assumptions themselves as by the people who apply these assumptions to us or by the internal personal application of the principles to ourselves. The worldview assumptions that we should obey our parents or obey the law are taught to us but it is usually the fear of what our parents or a policeman might do if we don't obey that keeps us in line. It is usually that fear of persons, more than the rule itself that influences our behavior. But, as with all culture, it is the agreed-upon worldview assumption that lies behind the fact that a person fears to do or not do certain things and that groups enforce penalties when the rules are broken.

6. Further, when things seem to be in order at the worldview level, people can relax psychologically. We can refer to this function as providing psychological reinforcement. On the basis of worldview assumptions, we know what to do in life when faced with normal and most abnormal situations. We usually know what to do in such things as transitions and crises, as well as in everyday life situations.

When we're trying to make a decision, for example, we work on the basis of the underlying assumptions we have been taught concerning how to go about decision-making. And we do that, usually without concern over other possible ways to arrive at the answer we seek. Do we sit and think about it, or go and discuss that decision with somebody else, or pray about it, or do all of these things? Whenever the question is, "What is the proper thing to do now?," our decision will usually be based on our worldview assumptions concerning how to do it. And when we do the expected thing, when we follow our worldview assumptions, we relax with the feeling that we have done the right thing.

A baby is about to be born. We have been taught to assume that it is proper to do thus and so. We do it and are psychologically at ease, because we have done the proper thing. Someone is to get married. Someone is ill. Someone has died. We or someone in our group knows what to do. We do it and relax. We have fulfilled the expectations of ourselves and the other members of our society—expectations that have been taught to us along with the instructions concerning what to do in each situation.

Often what is expected is a ritual. The ritual may be religious or secular, elaborate or simple. It may involve many people or only a single individual. *Passage rituals* such as those that commonly are prescribed at times such as birth, naming, puberty, marriage, retirement, and death are one kind. *Crisis rituals* such as those surrounding illness, accident, failure, and decision-making may be similar to or dissimilar from passage rituals. Many less obvious rituals also occur, however, and are just as governed by worldview. The ritual of food refusal may be cited, as may rituals of greeting, of giving and receiving, of buying and selling, of eating, of playing, of interacting with those of higher, lower, or equal status, of sleeping, of courtship, of arguing, of leaving or returning home, etc. All of these and more are prescribed by a society and embedded in its worldview assumptions. And people feel satisfied when they conform to such assumptions.

7. A final function of worldview is an integrative function. The fact that groups of people assume an incredibly large number of the same things provides a kind of glue holding a society together. Thus, when one aspect of a people's life is changed or challenged, that fact has ramifications for many of the other aspects of the society. When, for example, western schools are introduced into tribal societies, massive breakdown of family and other social relationships occurs. Likewise, when gold or oil is discovered in a an (?) area populated by a traditional people, the whole society gets thrown out of cultural equilibrium.

Positively, people with a common worldview tend to apply the same principles and values in all areas of life. If, for example, their worldview value in one area of life is (like Anglo-Americans) individualism, they are likely to be individualistic in virtually all areas of life. They integrate their whole life and culture around such a principle. If, on the other hand, (like many non-western peoples) their worldview principle is communalism in one area of life, they are likely to practice communalism in virtually all areas of life. Likewise with other core values, such as freedom, hierarchy, male/female dominance, materialism, supernaturalism/ naturalism, past/present/future time orientation, competitiveness, conformity, and the like.

Though such common assumptions push sociocultural life and structures toward integration, however, it is doubtful that any culture is or ever was perfectly integrated. Most seem to be integrated well enough that anything that is changed in the worldview automatically produces ramifications throughout the rest of the culture. This is because the whole of the culture is centered in the same worldview assumptions. The worldview, then, functions within culture much like a radio transmitter. Anything fed into it, whether normal operations or changed procedures, gets broadcast throughout the rest of the culture.

These are some of the major functions of worldview. There may be more, possibly many more, but this will provide a start.

Chapter 8

Universals: Categorization, Person/Group

A study of a sizeable sampling of the worldviews of the various peoples of the world leads to the conclusion that there are several categories of assumptions to be found in every worldview. These are what we, following Kearney 1984 and Redfield 1953, have labeled "worldview universals." They apply to those areas of life that seem to be dealt with by all peoples and concerning which all peoples have assumptions, values and commitments.

We may speak of six worldview universals. These are:

1. Categorization/Classification, Logic
2. Person/Group
3. Causality
4. Time/Event
5. Space/Material World
6. Relationship

Though I have largely followed Kearney in suggesting these six, I have labeled some of them differently and, I think, expanded a bit on his approach (see Kearney 1984). See Figure 5.13 for a chart of Kearney's universals. Comparing his with mine, note that I have dropped out the category he calls "Other," since its only function is as a cover term for the six categories. My scheme, then, looks like this:

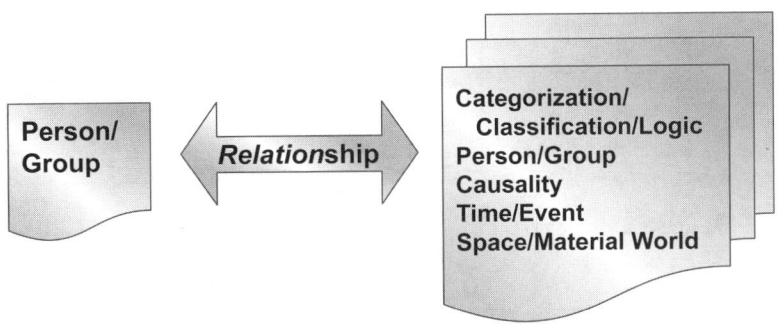

Figure 8.1. My Lineup of Worldview Universals.

Note that "person/group" (replacing Kearney's "self") appears on the chart both as the subject that is observing and relating to the "other" (made up of the five universals in the right-hand column) and as an object of the observing and relating. This addition to Kearney goes back to Redfield's insight that persons (Self) observe themselves as well as the rest of what Kearney calls Other. I agree that persons and groups relate to other persons and groups. Persons also observe themselves and relate internally to themselves. Groups, likewise, can observe and relate to themselves internally as well as to other groups.

The content of each universal focuses on a different concern. Time, for example, is a very different thing than cause or categorization. Likewise, persons and groups are very different from space. The "material" in each universal, however, relates to and interpenetrates the others to a greater or lesser extent. We will see this especially below when discussing categorization, noting that we categorize time, we categorize space, we categorize people, we categorize causes, even relationships.

The following diagram attempts to combine the material on worldview functions from the previous chapter with that on the universals of worldview. A worldview may be seen as:

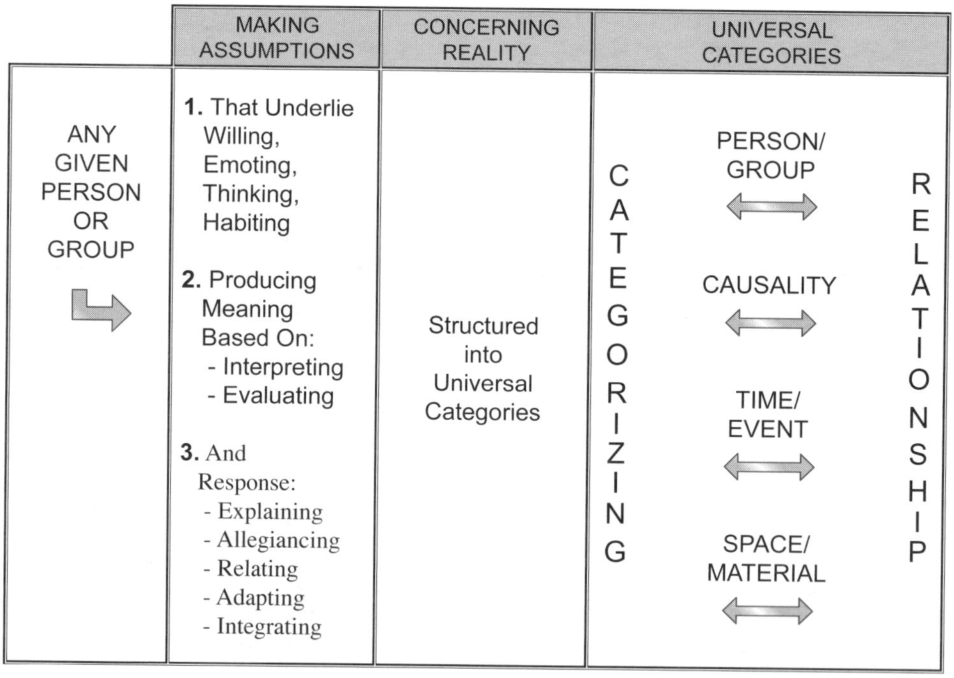

ANY GIVEN PERSON OR GROUP ⇨	MAKING ASSUMPTIONS	CONCERNING REALITY		UNIVERSAL CATEGORIES	
	1. That Underlie Willing, Emoting, Thinking, Habiting 2. Producing Meaning Based On: - Interpreting - Evaluating 3. And Response: - Explaining - Allegiancing - Relating - Adapting - Integrating	Structured into Universal Categories	C A T E G O R I Z I N G	PERSON/ GROUP ⇔ CAUSALITY ⇔ TIME/ EVENT ⇔ SPACE/ MATERIAL ⇔	R E L A T I O N S H I P

Figure 8.2. Flowchart of Worldview Functions and Universals

We now turn to the first universal, the one I call "categorization."

Categorization (Classification, Logic)

As with all of the universals, we start with people or groups looking outward toward reality (Kearney's "Other") and focusing in on something. In this case, the focus is on dividing up that reality into groups of things that the person/group considers similar and distinguishing these things from those other things that the person/group considers different.

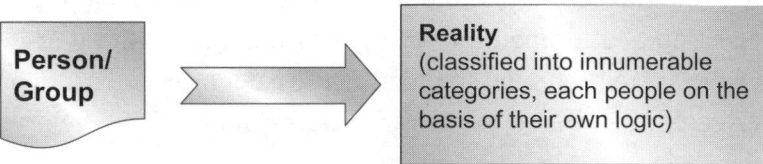

Figure 8.3. Person/Group Looks at Reality and Categorizes It

All people have assumptions in terms of which they classify, categorize and reason (in terms of their patterns of logic). Every worldview, therefore, provides ways of dividing up the various components of reality and classifying or categorizing them. We are taught to see things as being alike or different, in the same grouping as certain other things or in different groupings from them. So we lump together what we see as belonging together.

Kearney observes,

> all peoples name objects and conceptually include them into larger more general groupings. The study of worldview is to a great extent the analysis of the major categories of reality recognized by a people and the criteria by which they group the contents of these categories together. The way in which a people categorize the major areas of their conceptual world constitutes an important part of the framework of their worldview. And, as we will see, the arrangement of the major categories in the Classification universal depends on and in turn influences the contents of the other worldview universals (1984:78).

There is something built into us as human beings that seems to require that we classify things. There are, however, sizeable differences between how the people of one society classify things and how those of another arrange the same things. Some of those differences in the logic of classification are illustrated below. Though categorization is largely arbitrary, the various ways in which it is done seem to be fairly "adequate solutions to the problem of cognitively organizing the phenomenal world" (Kearney 1984:81). Humans seem to need to organize things but there are a variety of ways in which we do it. However, once the categories have been established, they are no longer arbitrary for those within the system. For there needs to be a fairly high level of agreement on categories as well as on labels (e.g., language labels) if a people are to understand each other.

People classify plants, animals, people, things, material objects, social categories, natural and supernatural entities, the visible and the invisible. All are labeled and lumped into categories together with other items and entities believed to be similar to them. These categories, then, are paralleled by other categories made up of other items and entities believed to be dissimilar from those in other categories.

People also categorize all of the material dealt with under each of the other five universals. Thus, all peoples classify people, both as individuals and as groups. We also classify time and space and things that cause things. Whatever we notice gets put into categories with other things we notice.

Though this fact is significant in itself, it is even more useful as an indicator of the importance a people places on various concepts. For, as Kearney points out,

> the attributes of domains are as important in defining them as are the contents. For example, it is possible that two people may conceptually group the following items: ghosts, spirits, the Devil. Knowing this grouping alone tells us little about their respective world views. However, if we know that for one person these items are grouped together as elements of folk tales and superstitions, while for another they are sources of sickness and sin, we then gain insight into the associated dimensions of Causality and Relationship in their respective world views (1984:82).

Another illustration of the importance for worldview study of the content of terms used in classifying a people's perception of reality lies in the use of terms like "family," and "ancestor." It is probable that all peoples conceive of both family and ancestor in contrast to categories such as non-family and non-ancestor. For some peoples the family will consist of a small number of people, basically father, mother and children but definitely not including ancestors. For others, however, the category family consists of a large number of relatives (perhaps as many as 50-60 or more), including at least certain ancestors who have died physically but are understood to be still functioning as members of the family with certain important responsibilities (e.g., assuring fertility, mediating with spirits).

Apart from the importance of such contrasts, the fact that concepts such as this are designated by linguistic terms demonstrates that a people's language is an important source of insight into worldview. Indeed, we may say that a people's language provides the most obvious clues to a people's system of categorization, though not infrequently the linguistic classification and the logic of a people will not correspond exactly.

To understand the place of language in pointing to worldview classification, consider the following types of classification required by the languages people speak: English and many other languages classify most nouns as either singular or plural. There are some languages that divide nouns into singular, plural and trial (i.e., threes). Many languages mark nouns as masculine or feminine, many add neuter, many others don't make such divisions at all. Many sort nouns into even more categories. The Bantu languages of Africa, for example, may show as many as fifteen or more "genders" called "noun classes." In the West we ordinarily divide time into past, present, and future. In contrast, many Melanesian peoples divide time into "now time" and "myth time." Many peoples regard the life of plants, animals, people, and spiritual beings as qualitatively different, while others regard all life as of the same nature and quality. In western societies we speak of animate and inanimate objects, though many peoples regard all objects as possessing life.

Though it has been demonstrated that the various colors we label are parts of a continuum, each social group labels certain points on that continuum to represent by words in the language. Underlying such labeling are, of course, worldview assumptions and values. These have been worked out sometime in the past and are now "imposed" on children as we grow up and learn many of the things considered important by our ancestors in the process of learning our language. In many small-scale societies, the people learn that only three color distinctions are to be made at what might be called the "primary" level. These usually translate as "dark," "light" and "colorful." Though there will usually be second or third-level distinctions such as, "dark like night" versus "dark like those trees," the worldview assumption that three distinctions is enough for most purposes is what people operate on most often. For many other peoples, their worldview as represented in their language requires that the color spectrum to be divided up into five, seven, nine or, as in English, eleven categories (note that it is usually an odd number).

Luzbetak points to the complexity of our western classification of motor vehicles, a complexity that would cause a tribal person who had never been to the city a headache were he/she to attempt to master it. Were someone from outside our western societies to study what our vocabulary says about our values, they would easily conclude that the classification of motor vehicles is to us at least as important as things pertaining to camels are to Arabs who are reputed to have over a thousand terms in their vocabulary related to camels. Luzbetak says,

> Some technologically simpler societies view all motor vehicles as forming only one category of objects, while our feeling tells us that passenger cars, station wagons, buses, and trucks are "essentially" different and that, in fact, further distinctions and subdistinctions ought to be made. For example, our concept of "truck" calls for such further differentiations as "van," "pick-up truck," "dump truck," and "semi." Each of these would be broken into still further subcategories based for instance on differences in load capacity, number of wheels, usage (e.g., cement mixer, fire truck, tank truck, cattle truck), manufacturer, and model. "Passenger cars" have an even more complex hierarchical taxonomy. Our culture tells us not only the hierarchical arrangement of motor vehicles but "essential" contrasting features involved as well (1988:227).

In these and a myriad of other ways people divide up and compartmentalize the reality around them. Humans seem to have an inherent drive to categorize in their desire to understand reality. And the way we categorize and the values we put on the various categories affect every aspect of how we perceive, think, and behave. Westerners, for example, tend to categorize the spirit world along with fairies, elves, and other mythical beings that we do not take seriously. This evaluation affects our attitudes toward spirit beings and tends to block our attempts to take angels and demons seriously, even though as Christians we claim to accept anything we find in the Bible, including spirit beings.

The Logic Behind Classification

The importance of logic in this universal becomes apparent when we recognize that it is not only the classifications themselves that are a part of a worldview. *The assumptions underlying the way the items or aspects of reality are classified are themselves worldview assumptions.* That is, we divide things up according to the logic we have been taught. And that logic itself is a worldview phenomenon that differs from people to people.

It might be discussed whether logic is a subcategory of the categorization universal as I have it here. It might be contended that this represents *a deeper level of worldview*, like Hiebert's "Deep" level, in which he suggests we find "process" (see chapter 5). I will not argue for or against this possibility but will suggest, as I have in chapter 5, that there may be a deeper level here that subsequent analyses will be able to clearly delineate.

An exercise we like to do in class sometimes can be used to demonstrate this fact. We ask people of various societies to place the following 21 items in categories appropriate to their logic and to label the categories. I give in the charts below the results of how seven actual groups of people classified the items. See if you can figure out the logic behind each classification. The 21 items are:

DEER	ROCK	MAN
ANGELS	BACTERIA	FLIES
TREE	WATER	TURTLE
WOMAN	DEMONS	COW
GRASS	FISH	VIRUS
BIRD	WHALE	BOY
GERMS	GOD	BUSH

Figure 8.4. Twenty-One Items to Classify

Group 1						
Inanimate	*Sort of Plant*	*Plant*	*Animal*	*Animal with Spirit*	*Super Animal*	*Creator God*
Rock Water	Virus Bacteria Germs	Bush Tree Grass	Flies Bird Cow Whale Fish Deer Turtle	Man Boy Woman	Demons Angels	God

Figure 8.5. Group 1 Classification

Group 2 (Maasai of East Africa)			
Most Valued	*Public Domain*	*Things That Can Kill You*	*Authority*
Woman Cow	Fish Tree Bush Rock Grass Turtle Deer Bird Water	Bacteria Virus Flies Demons God Angels Germs	Boy Man Whale

Figure 8.6. Group 2 Classification (Maasai of East Africa)

Group 3 (Anglo-American)					
Super-Natural	*Human*	*Animate Nature*	*Inanimate Nature*	*Animals*	*Micro-biology*
God Angels Demons	Man Woman Boy	Tree Bush Grass	Water Rock	Deer Cow Turtle Fish Flies Bird Whale	Virus Bacteria Germs

Figure 8.7. Group 3 Classification (Anglo-American)

Group 4				
Living Organisms Plants - Animals	*Humans*	*No Name*	*Supernatural*	*Non-Living Organisms*
Tree Deer Grass Cow Bush Fish Flies Whale Bird Turtle	Boy Woman Man	Virus Bacteria Germs	Angels God Demons	Water Rock

Figure 8.8. Group 4 Classification

Group 5						
Plants	Mammals	Insects	Spiritual	Micro-Scopic	Inanimate	Amphibian/Reptile/Fish
Tree Grass Bush	Deer Boy Cow Woman Man Whale	Flies	Angels God Demons	Virus Bacteria Germs	Rock Water	Fish Turtle Bird

Figure 8.9. Group 5 Classification

Group 6				
Earthy	Supernatural	Human	Creature	Cause of Sickness
Tree Grass Bush Rock Water	God Demons Angels	Boy Woman Man	Cow Deer Fish Bird Whale Turtle Flies	Virus Bacteria Germs

Figure 8.10. Group 6 Classification

Group 7				
Immovable Things in a Group	Human Beings Together	Animals Together	Spiritual Beings	Parasites, Cause Disease
Bush Tree Grass Rock Water	Man Woman Boy	Cow Deer Bird Turtle Fish Flies Whale	God Angels Demons	Bacteria Virus Germs

Figure 8.11. Group 7 Classification

Ethnoscience/Ethnosemantics and Categorizing

Much of what we have learned about the ways in which people categorize the materials in their world comes from those whose theoretical orientation is called "ethnoscience," "ethnosemantics" or "cognitive anthropology." Two books by James Spradley (1979, 1980) are especially helpful in the use of this perspective in discovering worldview. Spradley has in each of these volumes carefully spelled out the steps a person can take to discover the patterns of classification underlying the behavior of a given society.

As noted in Appendix A, my theoretical position has been greatly influenced by the application of insights from the field of linguistics to the study of culture. I find, therefore, the ethnoscience approach, since it is greatly influenced by linguistics, to be very helpful in dealing with this universal. Since categorization is in many ways the basic universal, ethnosemantic insight can be helpful in probing the other universals as well. The aim of ethnoscientists is to enable us to see the world from an "emic" perspective, the point of view of the insider. This perspective assumes that finding out how a people classifies reality enables us to understand how they view the world.

To bring this about, these anthropologists analyze what are called "semantic domains." A cultural domain is a cultural category that contrasts with other domains and includes other, smaller categories. By gathering vocabulary items relating to various domains of cultural life and classifying them, ethnoscientists gain considerable insight into how people view the world. Among the kinds of things studied have been kinship terms, color terms, botanical terms, medical terms and a large number of other domains.

Kearney, who is mildly negative toward ethnosemantics has the following to say by way of summary of their approach:

> Ethnosemantics as such has been essentially the study of the internal ordering of groups of nouns—mainly folk taxonomies and paradigms—in different languages. Ethnosemantic studies also have several other general features in common: (1) They take as their subject matter areas of culture content that are defined as such by native criteria, rather than by analytic categories of theoretical anthropology. (2) They attempt to discover units and dimensions of meaning within these domains, again according to principles inherent in the native systems. (3) As of yet, most of the applications of these approaches have been to relatively small and finite ethnosemantic domains, such as kin terms, aspects of folk medicine, ethnobotany, or ethnocuisine. (4) They do not, for the most part, investigate how the idea systems relate to behavior, or how they change through time (1984:32).

The approach has been accused of enabling people to systematically go about investigating trivia. Though there is some validity to that criticism, the carefully worked out approach of Spradley can be very helpful. He instructs us well concerning what questions to ask and how to organize the information we get. Though I don't believe a study of classification alone tells us all we want to know about a people's worldview, ethnosemantic studies have provided us with much valuable insight into how people categorize reality. Since I will be dealing with his approach in more detail in chapter 13, I will leave the discussion at that for now.

Person/Group

The second universal I'd like to deal with is what I choose to call *Person-Group*. The way the human universe is perceived and both its internal and external relationships need to be understood in the same way by all the members of a society if they are to interact and communicate effectively. So a worldview provides perspectives by means of which people can assume this understanding.

As with all worldview assumptions, we learn them as children from our elders. This process, being a process of interaction between the learner and those who know the assumptions is a Person/Group thing and thus fits under this universal. We will not go into detail here but simply point out that in a multitude of ways, most of which are subconscious, children listen and observe adult behavior and learn the assumptions and values of their elders. On occasion, then, these assumptions are dealt with at the conscious level.

On the basis of Person/Group worldview assumptions we 1) conceive of ourselves and 2) relate to the various persons and groups in our lives. Under this universal, then, we have a two-fold task on our hands since we are dealing both with the *perceiving* person/group, the person or group who observes and reacts, and the *perceived* person/group, the person or group who is observed and reacted to.

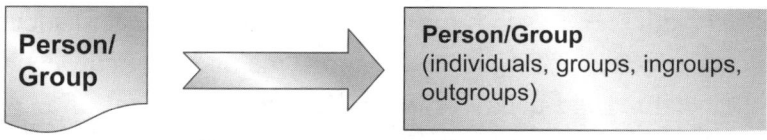

Figure 8.12. Person/Group Looks Out on Person/Group, Classifies, Evaluates, and Responds to Them

Under this category we first need to deal with the *focus* of the person/group doing the observing (that of the P/G on the left side of the above chart). People of different societies are trained into differences of focus. In some societies, for example, few people in observing another person will focus on the color of that one's skin. In others, that will be a primary focus. In some societies the focus in finding out about another person will be on who that person's family is, in others, what is the person's occupation. We are taught whether to see people primarily as individuals, as in America, or primarily as groups, as in many other societies. Various societies will teach their children to focus on how people are dressed, what kind of house they live in, what kind of car they drive, whether they are of a royal family or of an outcaste family.

As we look out on the human environment, we have been taught to distinguish between people we consider the "us" (our ingroup) and the "them" (our outgroup) and to relate to each differently. As we thus focus on people, we *evaluate* them, as the ancient Jews did in dividing their human environment into Jews ("us") and Gentiles (everyone else). We also evaluate people according to categories such as "good" and "bad," "tall" or "short," "fat" or "skinny," "white," "black," "yellow" or "red," etc. And these evaluations, whether positive, neutral or negative, will be largely those we have been taught as we were growing up.

In addition, a worldview will provide assumptions concerning how a human being is to be defined and how one ought to behave in the various contexts of which he or she is a part. Concepts of the ideal person, concepts of status and role, concepts of the proper relationships between people of different social classes, age groups, sexes, ethnic groups, and the like are thus defined by one's worldview.

We are taught the characteristics of good people and bad, of rich and poor, of leaders and followers, of wise and unwise, of respectable and not respectable. We are taught what is appropriate for men and what for women, what for adults and what for children, what for youth, what for parents, what for grandparents, what for various statuses and occupations. We are taught, then, whether people are expected to dominate the physical environment (as in western societies) or to submit to it (as in many non-western societies).

Whatever a society deems necessary for its members to know concerning people, their nature and behavior is codified in this aspect of a society's worldview. In what follows, we will look at a series of topics appropriate to this area. This list is far from exhaustive, but can suggest the range of the content of this important universal. Among them will be individual and group, definition of person, human nature, status and role, male and female and relationships.

Individual and Group

A very basic consideration within this universal is whether a society is individual-oriented or group-oriented. Societies may be plotted on a scale from extremely individualistic to extremely group-oriented. Most societies will be somewhere between those extremes. For extremely individualistic people, the individual is the reality and the group is seen as merely a collection of individuals, mostly connected by fairly weak ties. For extremely group-oriented people, though, the group is the reality and the ties between people, especially those in the same kinship group, are extremely strong.

One of the major differences between the assumptions of individualistic people and group-oriented people concerns how decisions are made. In highly individualistic societies, it is assumed that each individual will make his or her own choices in a large number of areas. In America, for example, individuals are expected to choose their own occupations, their own marriage partners, clothing, schools (after high school), whether or not to have children and how many(,) and on and on.

In group-oriented societies, less of these choices (sometimes none of them) are made individually. Who one marries, what one's job will be, even children are assumed to be the concern of the extended family. As with most cultural things, there is logic to support such assumptions. From the point of view of these peoples, the older, more mature members of the society should be the ones responsible for the big decisions in the life of younger, less mature persons.

When faced with major decisions such as whether or not to adopt a new faith or a new method of farming, a typical pattern in group-oriented societies would involve the older, male leaders meeting on the one hand with each other and, on the other, with the leaders under them to thoroughly discuss the potential change. In this way, the matter gets discussed within each extended family and what Homer Barnett (1953) calls a "multi-individual" decision is made either to adopt the change or to reject it. Though the leaders of lower status and the women often do not appear to outsiders to participate in the final decision, they have usually been polled and had their opportunity for input within the family. The decision carefully discussed and planned at lower levels, then, is announced (not decided) by the higher-level leaders when a consensus has been reached. In this way, whole tribal groups have converted to Christianity, Islam, Hinduism or some other faith either freely or in the face of social, political or military pressure.

Wise advocates of sociocultural change do their best to discover the underlying worldview assumptions of the people concerning how decisions for change are to be made. Clues to what these assumptions are may be obtained from observation of social activities such as court cases. Other clues may be available in the folklore of the people.

In our day, many of the group-oriented societies of the world have been greatly affected by individualistic ideas introduced through western schools and other western influences. Often, largely through the schooling process, a system of attaining prestige and influence has been set up in competition with the traditional system. This means that many younger men who would not traditionally have had much to say at the higher social levels have attained a prestige through schooling that, even over time, they would not have been able to attain via traditional patterns. These who are literate and much more knowledgeable about the outside world than the older traditional leaders, then, have certain advantages in relation to sociocultural (including political and economic) processes stemming from western influence. They are also more individualistic and likely to make or participate in decisions without adequately consulting the traditional leaders.

There is, then, a great deal of conflict between worldview-level assumptions created by the adoption of western approaches to life on the part of tribal and peasant peoples. And not a few such conflicts develop in highly industrialized but still quite communal societies such as Japan, Korea and China, both internally and in their interactions with the individualistic West.

Definition of Person

Our worldviews provide us with assumptions governing how we are to see ourselves and others. As children and youth in certain societies, the prescribed pattern is to see oneself as far less important than one's elders. Exceptions to such a rule exist, however, for those destined to assume prestigious positions such as chief, king or prince. These children may become aware of their importance at an early age. The assumptions come to the surface if we ask the question, "How is a child supposed to act?" or "How does the seven-year-old heir to the throne act?"

In other societies and with many western individualistic parents, the children seem to rule from an early age. Such parents assume that children should be allowed to do whatever they want largely without adult interference unless the child is in danger.

In traditional societies, principles of kinship are the most important factors in defining oneself and others. Kinship—who one's family and relatives are—is the glue that holds these societies together and that defines people's statuses and relationships within their communities. Socially approved perceptions of oneself and of others are embodied in kinship terms such as "mother," "father," "son," "daughter," "cousin," etc. Kinship systems and terms seem to have the main social function of supporting an individual's claim to power, authority, and property by linking the individual with a requisite ancestor. In addition, they aid in establishing governing rules of incest prohibition, who marries whom, ultimate responsibility for children and channeling of the inheritance of land, goods, and formal authority.

Americans tend to have a weak sense of descent and kinship. We tend to lose track of our ancestry beyond our grandparents. In other societies, many take pride in and find a sense of self-worth in knowing past and ancient family lines. Korean and Japanese, for example, talk much of family histories and compare them. The older families tend to command more respect. In most kinship-oriented societies, descent is of crucial importance in defining who one is.

In ancient Hebrew culture the recording of genealogies tracing kinship relationships into the deep past, played an important part in their acquiring of power, property, and family responsibility. In contrast with modern America, the Jews usually did not travel over long distances and choose wives from families totally unknown to their parents.

In many societies property and wealth are important to defining personhood. One born into a wealthy family may automatically be accorded greater worth than one born "on the wrong side of the tracks." What is defined as wealth may, however, enter into the equation. A former student of mine who served as a missionary in Papua New Guinea recounts the fact that the people he worked among felt sorry for him because he did not own any pigs or land. In their society, one could not be a full adult male if one did not own pigs and land. So, in their pity for this missionary, the people gave him a pig and a small plot of land so they could regard him as a full-fledged grown male.

Whether through status, kinship definitions, wealth or other means, how we and others define ourselves is crucial to our personhood. Perceptions and evaluations of ourselves as individuals, as parts of groups, as male or female, as younger or older, as Christians or non-Christians, as winners or losers, or whatever, influence just about every aspect of our lives. And lurking in the background of these evaluations is the question of whether we and others think of ourselves in terms of *being* (who we are) or *doing* (what we do).

In Anglo-American society, we tend to evaluate ourselves on the basis of what we do rather than on the basis of who we *are*. Indeed, someone has said that we are not really "human beings." Instead we are "human doings!" When evaluations are made on the basis of family, there is more of an emphasis on a person's *being*. When the evaluations are made on the basis of occupation or achievements, then, the emphasis is more on one's *doing*. When we try to see ourselves from God's perspective, we need to recognize that He evaluates us on the basis of who we are (being), not on what we do (doing). We are a part of the family of God. We can, then, rejoice in who we are even when what we have done in our life is not that spectacular.

Human Nature

In addition, a worldview will provide assumptions concerning how human nature is to be defined and how we ought to behave in relation to whatever is within us. Are we basically good? Or evil? Or neutral? Whatever our conclusion, how should we act?

If human nature is basically good, how do we explain the evil that we see many involved in? Are there spiritual or biological or social influences that explain the evil? In American society, there are those who claim that humans are basically good but that our cultural structures incline us toward evil. Evangelical Christians, of course, see in us a propensity to sin. We thus find our assumptions in conflict with those of many of our compatriots.

Recognizing that there is evil or weakness or whatever in human nature leads different people to take different courses to remedy the problem. The ancient Greeks felt that the problem with humans is ignorance. The answer, therefore, is to increase knowledge. Unfortunately, this seems to be the theory that contemporary western societies have adopted. The fact that generations of experimenting with this education solution has not come close to solving the problem doesn't seem to deter our society from continuing on this pathway, following a bankrupt theory.

Many societies do not seem to philosophize over whether humans are good or bad. They do, however, have to deal with the problems caused by whatever the problem is. For most of the smaller societies of the world, and for some of the larger ones (e.g., Asian societies), the way to solve the problem is seen in careful adherence to tradition, an approach that is increasingly being interfered with by the forces of westernization. The rules and regulations of tradition provide the basis for social control and, often, when not interfered with are quite effective. Kinship relationships are usually the most obvious enforcers of the tradition. The worldview assumptions lying behind the norms, then, are assumptions concerning how persons are to interact within kinship groupings. Where such assumptions are often not so effective is when one kinship group gets into conflict with another.

Biblical Christianity, of course, sees the problem of human nature as a moral one, not to be solved by education or tradition or biologically-oriented techniques such as biofeedback or psychologically-oriented techniques such as psychotherapy. The spiritual inheritance of sin affects us all. Human nature is, therefore, not bad or good but infected. And the biblical answer that we need to work into our worldviews involves dealing with the problem through a relationship with our Creator and Redeemer.

Status and Role

Every worldview has assumptions concerning the relative positions of persons in relation to each other and the value of those positions. We call these positions *statuses* and refer to how people are expected to behave in those positions their *roles*. Statuses and roles always go together. Any given person will occupy several statuses and function in their roles during his or her lifetime. A male, for example, is born into the position called "son" and may, in addition, be a brother, a husband, a father, uncle, grandfather; a female is born a daughter and may be a sister, wife, mother, aunt, grandmother. To these kinship statuses and roles may be added those that are associated with jobs, with wealth, with schooling, with membership in clubs, with politics and others.

Cultural groups define the expectations that go along with these statuses and roles quite differently. In many, perhaps most, societies, it is assumed that males will be dominant over females. In most societies, then, the family inheritance will be transmitted through at least certain of the males. We call these societies *patrilineal*. In many of the world's societies, however, the status and role of transmitter of the family inheritance is assumed to be that of the women. We call such societies *matrilineal*.

Though in western societies, we expect to *achieve* our position in life, for many of the world's peoples, the status with its accompanying roles is *assigned*. That is, if a person is born into a royal family, the position he or she will occupy in life will be royal. If a person is born into the family of a carpenter, the position of carpenter is assigned. Along with the position, then, goes a certain amount of power or powerlessness.

Underlying all such assignments, then, are worldview assumptions that, when learned by the people of the society, both predict what they will become and give them a sense of the "rightness" of their practice.

As an example, let us look at some of the differences between a university professor in the United States and in China. Though both Chinese and American professors have high status, it is culturally acceptable in the U.S. for students to question what their professor is saying or teaching. In traditional Chinese society, however, students are expected to accept what their professor is presenting without question (at least publicly). In both societies, students also assume certain forms of behavior from professors. In traditional Chinese society, students are allowed to mention, discuss, and seek advice from their professors for personal problems having nothing to do with school. In the U.S. most professors would rather not have anything to do with a student's personal problems, nor would students expect them to. Worldview assumptions are markers by which an individual knows the proper demeanor and role to display. They also aid others in knowing what proper behavior to expect from this individual. Worldview assumptions also validate the assignment of power and the value of persons.

Male and Female

As near as we can tell, men and women are genuinely different in a wide variety of ways, ranging from biological differences to cognitive, emotional and psychological differences. This fact, however, does not in itself explain the variety of worldview assumptions around the world concerning how each should view and relate to the other. In many societies, the status of women is not high. Their power may, however, be even greater than that of men if one grants that the often invisible power of *influence* may be greater than the visible power of *authority*.

Much that goes on in the various societies of the world pertaining to the views of and relationships between the sexes can be explained on the theory that men fear women or at least stand in awe of them because of their reproductive powers. The seclusion that is often mandated for women related to their menstrual periods and childbearing, for example, may have originated with such fear on the part of men. Likewise, the strong taboos in some societies that keep women secluded in their homes and/or excluded from political, economic or educational activities.

In America we make a big deal about men and women being "equal." But the worldview assumptions underlying our concept of equality should be examined carefully before we assume that we have done a good thing in striving for equality between the sexes. There are many kinds of equality possible. For example, we could speak of equality of prestige, equality of opportunity, equality of achievement and so forth, any of which could be possible without the requirement that the genders perform the same tasks in order to be equal. That is, people in any of these and many other areas could be thoroughly equal though thoroughly different. We could have chosen to define equality as referring to the genders fulfilling themselves in terms of their uniqueness so that first-class men would be uniquely male and first-class women would be uniquely female and the equality be a matter of fulfillment rather than of sameness. We have not chosen that alternative, however, so for Americans equality means "sameness."

Though the equality movement has meant a great deal to women in terms of the freedom they have to accomplish tasks outside the home, women and our society in general have, I believe, paid a very high price. For example, in spite of the growing evidence that men and women are cognitively different, we put both boys and girls through the same schooling, holding both accountable for the same material. The material is presented, however, in formats pervasively influenced by male type thinking and reasoning. It is a tribute to the flexibility of women that they have achieved well in such a system. In the process, though, they have been forced to learn to think like men. Thus, the equality of which we speak is an equality of sameness, based on one sex being required to achieve on the playing field governed by the ideas of the other.

What could have happened, if we had learned to examine our underlying assumptions and decided to be fair to women, would have been to develop a concept of "thoroughly equal but radically different." Had this been done, I believe we could have produced first-class men and first-class women. What we have instead, is first and second-class "men," many of whom are second-class because, as females they have not done as well as males on a male playing field. Many women, of course, have achieved first-class status in spite of this hindrance but often have paid a high price emotionally, psychologically and, I believe, spiritually. And they are a great threat to the males they are competing with.

A major social problem that the striving for this kind of "equality" has raised is that it greatly increases competition between men and women. While in most traditional societies there have been strong social strictures to keep men and women from competing against each other, in America we train our children to compete. From earliest school days, boys compete with girls for attention (from teachers), for grades, for approval. Because girls are usually more constitutionally compliant and conscientious, then, they tend to get the most approval from teachers. This leads to many boys "dropping out" or "acting out" because they see that they can never make it in the competitive system. Then, of course, as boys when we grow up, we marry one of these creatures we have competed with at a disadvantage for so many years. As adults, then, we either learn how to stop competing and start cooperating or experience continual marital disharmony leading all too often to divorce. And we never quite know what the problem is because we don't learn to examine our basic worldview assumptions.

One more example: In America we learn to assume that one major thing will be required of men as we grow up, but four major things of women. For men, the assumption is that we will have "made it" in life if we do well in a career. Women, however, have to be sexy, get married, have a career and produce at least one child to feel that they have "made it." Though these four requirements are very demanding, they are fairly well defined, even though largely unconscious, and provide tremendous drive for a woman to succeed at each of them. The equivalent for a man is success in his career. This usually comes much later than most or all of the four come for women, leading to great dissatisfaction, often for many years, on the part of males in our society and a crushing blow if we never find success in our career. Add to this the competition we men experience from women both in growing up and, often, in our careers, and we can understand a bit of why men are in such bad shape in American society.

This discussion of person/group assumptions has important ramifications for Christians because a serious Christian commitment often brings us into conflict with the way our society teaches us to treat other human beings. As mentioned, westerners are taught to be quite competitive in relation to others. Yet the Bible commands us to love and to seek the best for all others, even those who threaten us or misuse us. The Bible sets higher ideas for us than those advocated by our worldview. We need power greater than merely human power to follow these ideas. It is God's power that provides us with the means to transform human attitudes and behavior so we can live close to biblical ideas and standards.

Chapter 9

Worldview Universals: Relationship, Causality

Relationships

All people make assumptions concerning relationships between people and our social environment (other people), between people and our physical environment, between people and animals, between people and time and between people and the spirit world. In Redfield's and Kearney's terms: between Self and Other. In my terms, of course, that Other is divided into these other objects of our relationships.

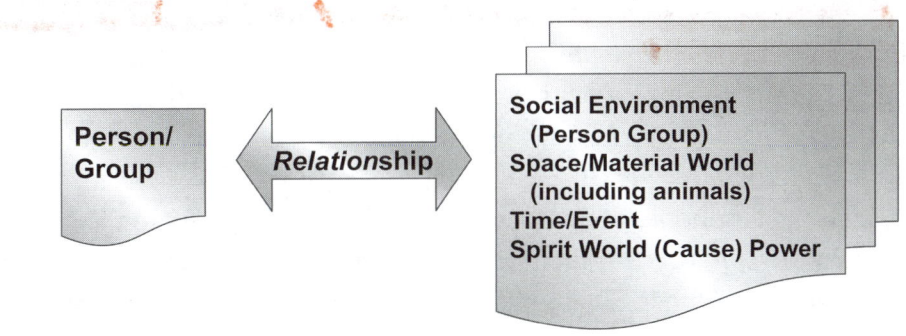

Figure 9.1. Person/Group Relates to Other Made Up of Social Environment, Space/Material World, Time/Event, Spirit World

Much of what falls under this universal either has been said above concerning Person/Group or will be said as we deal with the other universals. However, the focus is different here. When, for example, we spoke above about assumptions concerning who is in our ingroup and who is in our outgroup, we were focused on the *content* of those groups. Here we speak of the ways in which we are taught to relate to ingroup and outgroup. The usual assumption is, of course, that we relate positively to our ingroup and negatively to outgroups. The members of those groups are parts of our social environment that we value differently and, therefore, relate to differently.

Relating to Our Social Environment

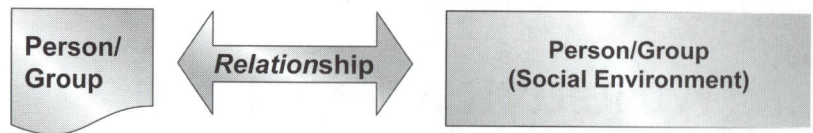

Figure 9.2. Person/Group Relating to Person/Group (Social Environment)

Our ingroup consists initially of the members of our family. We learn from conception to have a special relationship with our mother, a relationship that under normal circumstances goes through years of growth and change as we are born, cared for by her during childhood and adolescence and then move out on our own. We have special relationships of a different nature, then, with father, brothers, sisters, aunts, uncles, cousins, grandparents and any others that are included in our extended family. For societies that have a tight kinship structure, these relationships may be carefully prescribed. For other societies, the relationships may be more varied.

Certain assumptions concerning emotions accompany terms such as "mother" and "father." In addition to respect, it is assumed that there will be feelings of warmth and love engendered, at least toward mother. For many societies, the assumption is that there will be feelings of distance between child and father, however. In East Asian societies, it is common for there to be a strong emotional bond between mother and son, even to the extent that when the son marries, there is tension (often great tension) between his wife and his mother. Though the relationship between father and first son may not be a warm one, the expectations that the first son will carry on the family line create in many societies a respectful closeness between father and first son, often to the detriment of any closeness between father and other sons.

We base our treatment of other people on what we've been taught concerning how to relate to our ingroup and our outgroup. Those in our ingroup are ordinarily treated well. Those in our outgroup, however, are usually not treated with the same kind of respect and are often exploited. On the basis of such definitions of ingroup and outgroup, then, moral and social behavior such as that taught in the Ten Commandments is interpreted. The commandments say, don't steal, don't commit adultery, don't murder, don't covet, and so on. Each of the commands prohibits an activity against members of the ingroup.

For example, in spite of the mistranslation in the standard versions of scripture, the commandment is against "murder," not a command against every kind of "killing." The fact that Jesus later expanded the command does not give us warrant to read more into the command than was originally there. "Murder" is the unwarranted killing of one of the ingroup. Other kinds of killing, such as warfare and capital punishment, are not spoken against until later when Jesus presents a higher ideal. Likewise, stealing is defined as taking property from one of the ingroup. Yet taking things from enemies is seldom considered stealing, being viewed, rather, as the right of the victor.

One type of ingroup relationship that is often found in small-scale societies is what is called a "joking relationship." This is frequently between a grandchild and a grandparent or between a woman and her husband's younger brother. It often involves the participants in playing jokes on each other. In the case of a woman and a younger brother-in-law, the custom may allow them to tease each other about intimate (e.g., sexual) things, though not to have sexual relations.

Another type of ingroup relationship often found is called "avoidance." In various societies it is assumed to be improper for one to pronounce the name of one's mother, or for one to be in the same room as one's mother-in-law, or for a wife to speak to her father-in-law, or for a brother and sister to be in the same room alone.

Relating to Our Physical Environment
(Space/Material World)

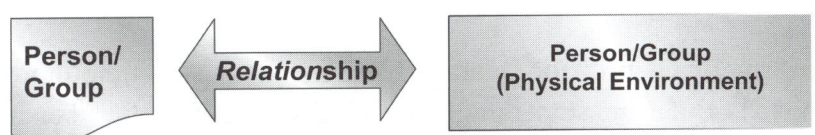

Figure 9.3. Person/Group Relating to Space/Material
(Physical Environment)

How one is to relate to the physical environment is also specified. As westerners we learn to assume that we are to dominate the physical environment. In many non-western societies, however, people learn that it is proper for them to seek harmony with the environment or to submit to it.

In Japan, for example, the basic traditional attitude is one of acceptance of life and nature as is. Nature is not something to be defiled and/or conquered. Traditional assumptions lead Japanese to feel that there is something very unnatural about the western compulsion to reshape the natural or preexisting environment. Japanese seek harmony between humans and nature as well as between humans and other humans. The ideal is that there be a symbiotic existence between persons and their natural and social environments. Nature is viewed as having given birth to and now nurturing humankind. One of the cores of Shinto belief is that everything in nature has its own spirit and is thus worthy of acceptance as is. Japanese seek to preserve nature and avoid wastefulness while using space to meet the needs of humans.

In America, we have not been pressed to make the most out of our physical resources until recently. Only now are we becoming aware that natural resources may not be inexhaustible. Our air and water have gotten polluted, some of our land worn out, our forests disappearing, oil supplies depleting and warnings of global warming have begun to come to our awareness. The ability of such warnings to bring necessary changes in our worldview assumptions seems, however, to be limited. We are still a consumer nation with the attitude that we can get away with exploiting our environment forever without serious consequences. And anyway, we believe, if there is a problem, our scientists will take care of it.

Relating to Time/Event

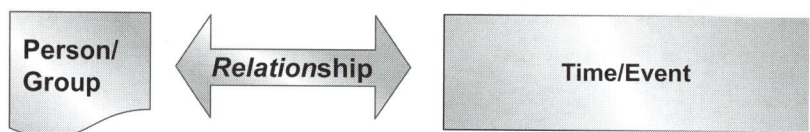

Figure 9.4. Person/Group Relating to Time/Event

We Americans probably tend to see ourselves using time more than relating to it. But using something is a relationship, especially when we use it in such a way that we virtually enslave ourselves to it. I have mentioned earlier that we assume time is some sort of a commodity, like money that we can spend or save or like water that we can waste or like a rope that is long or short.

We Americans tend to relate to time by parceling it out to be used for various activities. We use time for working, for sleeping, for leisure, for eating, relating to it often as if we are the master and it is a servant. However, when we schedule things too closely and run our lives by the clock, it seems that we are the servants and time is the master.

Conflict comes when we need to interact with people but only allow a certain amount of time for such interaction. In such situations, the needs of persons are often sacrificed for the sake of other time commitments, often giving the impression that our relationship to time is more important than our relationship with that person. Such is often the case within our families, leading often to wayward children who feel they have been cheated out of their right to more of their parents' time.

In many societies, and sometimes in the West, it is more typical for people to get engulfed in *events* that may go on and on, without regard to the amount of time being expended. Traditional societies tend to be what we call, "event-oriented" rather than "time-oriented." See chapter 10 for more on this subject. Suffice it to say here that an event-orientation involves a rather different relationship to time, since it takes little cognizance of the "quantity" of time expended in favor of a focus (usually quite unconscious) on quality of interpersonal relationships or other meaningful activity that continues until it no longer is meaningful, rather than until a given time on a clock is reached.

For westerners, an illustration of time-orientation versus event-orientation comes from the way certain athletic contests relate to time. Football, whether gridiron or soccer, basketball and hockey are timed by the clock so that every game involves the same amount of playing time, not counting time-outs. Baseball and tennis, however, are event-oriented with the amount of time expended in the activity longer or shorter depending on what goes on within the time rather than simply on the time measured by the clock.

Other time relationships occur between people and history or between people and the future. For many of the peoples of the world, their history is seen as the basis for their present behavior. For others, working toward and for the future is a major motivation. Such attitudes toward time imply relationships with time.

There are person/group relationships with time involved in a woman's monthly menstrual cycle as well and in our relationships to the seasons. And in the necessity that I pay my bills at the beginning of every month. And in the times we get up in the morning and go to bed at night. And in our weekly attendance at church.

We might ask what God's relationship to time is. Certainly, He is above time. But in Jesus, He submitted to the limitations of time. And in His interactions with us, He chooses our frame of reference as the context within which He works, thus submitting to the limitations of time.

Relating to the Spirit World

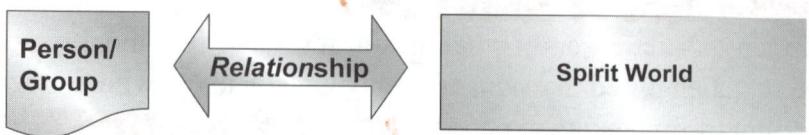

Figure 9.5. Person/Group Relating to Spirit World

People also need to relate to the spirit beings that populate the air. Nearly everyone outside the West recognizes the presence of spirit beings that can cause problems. The Bible also takes the spirit world seriously. In addition, most of the peoples of the world recognize that there is a High God from whom ultimate power flows. The question is how people relate to these beings.

The most common pattern worldwide is one or another form of what we call "animism." Animists are very tuned in to the spirit world. They know that spirits exist and typically assume that at least some of the spirits exercise control over territory and over nature. Humans, then, need to recognize their authority and to keep them happy. It is assumed that if the spirits are not kept happy, they can take revenge by causing misfortune, hindering fertility (e.g., of land, animals, people) and in other ways. Thus, people relate to the spirits through such things as sacrifices (to appease them if they have caused trouble), through divination (to learn things not knowable naturally) and by being very careful not to break taboos or defile sacred places or objects.

Relationships with the spirit world are typically carried out through a shaman, a priest or other specialists in dealing with the spirit world. Thus, there is a human-to-human relationship involved as well as the human to spirit relationship.

The recognition that spirits are near to and constantly interacting with humans is very common. In addition to this recognition, many believe that some of the spirits are the spirits of their physically dead ancestors. These ancestral spirits, then, are assumed to participate in the daily activities of the physically living members of the community in which the ancestors were once physically alive. They are understood to still be a part of the living community, without bodies but with greater power than when they had bodies. The ancestral spirits, then, have certain responsibilities to the community, typically with regard to fertility, while those still with physical bodies have certain responsibilities toward the ancestors (e.g., to provide food and drink for them, especially at festival times). These so-called ancestor spirits are, of course, demons masquerading as ancestors.

Spirits, whether ordinary demons or ancestral demons, are believed to be open to influence by humans, especially by the shamans. Often when misfortune strikes a person, that person or another representing him/her will appeal to the shaman to learn from the spirits if the misfortune was due to revenge by someone who resorted to using a spirit to pay the person back. If the shaman discerns that it was revenge, he/she will determine what has to be done to stop the problem plus, perhaps, to return spirit-caused revenge to the other person. In cases such as this, the relationship between humans and the spirits is supposedly one of human control over the spirit to do the bidding of the one seeking knowledge and/or revenge. In reality, of course, it is the spirit that is in control, deceiving the shaman or other person into thinking that he/she is in control.

For us as Christians, our relationship with the spirit world is one that links us directly with God through Jesus Christ. Rather than relating to the spirits by appeasing them, we have the right to relate to God directly and to the rest of the spirit world indirectly. God Himself started the relationship with humans through covenants and established it once and for all in Jesus, the God-Man, who forever links God with us. Contrary to the worldviews of most of the peoples of the world, the initiation of this relationship was taken by God Himself. It requires *response* from humans, not the initiating of the relationship. The relationship, then, enables humans to have enough power at their disposal to counter that of the evil spirit beings that most of the world is so conscious of. This power is invested in us by God in the presence of the indwelling Holy Spirit. We don't have to appease the lesser spirits, then, only to learn to work with the Holy Spirit, employing God's power to defeat them. What an enormous advantage this gives us in relating to the spirit world!

Causality

A third area addressed by every people according to worldview guidelines is the matter of causality. I'm speaking here of matters surrounding such questions as, What causes things? And what power lies behind such causation? What forces are at work in the universe? And what results do they bring about? Are the forces personal, impersonal, or both? The answers provided have names like God, gods, spirits, demons, luck, fate, karma, chance, cause and effect, political and economic structures, the power of persons inherent in such things as status and role, and so on.

Causality refers to the process by which some person, quality, power, or agency brings about something else. It is universally believed that if something happens, there is some cause. The study of causality is the study of the differing perceptions of causes, effects and the connections between them.

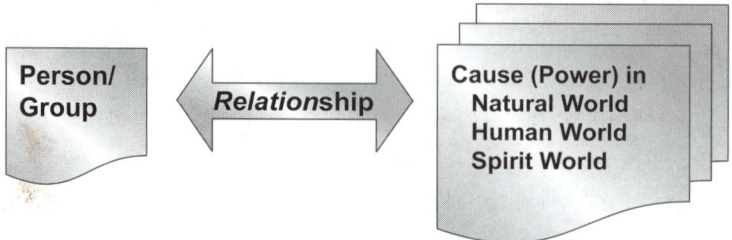

Figure 9.6. Person/Group Observes and Relates to Cause in Natural, Human and Spiritual Spheres

There are at least three major spheres or domains within which questions of causality and power need to be treated. They are the natural world, the human world and the spirit world and the relationships between them. Different societies pay differing amounts of attention to these three areas of life. Western peoples pay great attention to causation in the natural world and little if any attention to the possibility that some natural-world events may have a spirit-world origin. In many non-western societies the proportions seem to be reversed. Biblical societies were much more like contemporary non-western peoples than like western societies in this regard.

The area of causality and power, especially that that relates to the spirit realm, is the part of worldview most likely to undergo change for those who accept the gospel message. Whatever their former belief and commitment, as Christians, they commit themselves to the Power above all powers—God. Depending on where they come from, acceptance of and commitment to this God entails a more or less radical change in their view of and relation to spiritual power in the universe.

Though the focus of western peoples tends to be on natural and human causality, most of the world's peoples are more aware than we westerners are of the existence of the spirit world. They understand at least some of the ways in which spirits are involved in human life and are actively seeking greater spiritual power to cope with the exigencies of life. We need, therefore, to follow Jesus' example by focusing in ministry on the presence and application of His spiritual power in the human context. Though much of western Christian ministry has been carried out primarily with human power, it is one of the aims of this section to help us learn to counter our worldview in this area and to move into more spiritual power in Christian witness.

Natural World Causality

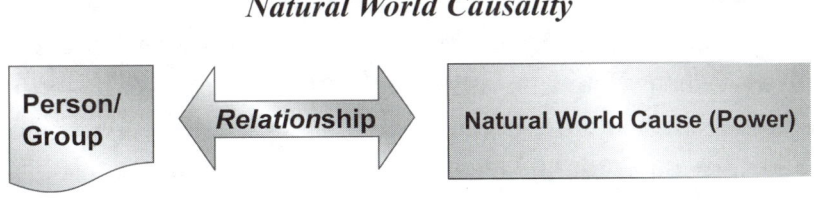

Figure 9.7. Person/Group Observes and Relates to Natural World Cause or Power

Natural world causality includes such things as weather, physical laws such as the law of gravity, heat, cold, electricity, water power, leverage, speed and the like. All of these things impinge on human life to bring about a variety of things, many evaluated as good, many evaluated as bad. Everyone experiences the effects caused by natural laws and weather patterns. When one pushes or pulls an object, one exerts a force to affect it in a certain way. When one lifts something or drops something, one experiences the effects of gravity. When one sweats because it is hot or shivers because it is cold, one experiences the effects of the natural world phenomena called heat or cold.

But the relationships of the natural world to the human world are subject to radically differing perceptions among the peoples of the world. People differ as to whether the natural world is to be submitted to or conquered. Likewise, there are different perceptions concerning the nature of the universe, whether it is like a machine, working according to mechanical "laws" or controlled by personal beings, capricious and only as predictable as personal (often spirit) beings are. Furthermore, people differ in their perceptions as to how things got started and how they continue, with westerners tending to explain in terms of mechanical laws and even "chance," while many other peoples attribute much to the activity of spirits.

The cause of such forces as gravity, motion, acceleration, leverage, heat, cold, friction and any number of other effects may or may not be noted by a people. Many peoples do not seem to be interested in such matters. "They simply happen, that's all," they may say if we should ask them. For their attitude to the world around them is one of simple submission to what exists without questioning it. Westerners, however, are often more interested both in what or who causes such things and in taking control of them if at all possible.

We in the West speak of "laws" or principles in terms of which the processes we observe in the natural world operate. Many of these are the laws of physics such as those listed above. These processes are seen by us as the workings of a machine and we don't simply want to submit to them, we want to learn to control them. We want to control leverage in order to move heavy objects, control heat and cold to make it warm when it's cold outside and cool when it's hot outside, control gravity and other aeronautically important physical forces in order to enable our planes to fly and so forth.

Other peoples interpret the phenomena of nature, not as the workings of a machine, but as the result of personal beings (spirits) that populate the universe. They believe that there are many and varied spiritual beings or forces linked to phenomena such as weather patterns, gravity, sea tides the sun and the moon. They hold that some or all of the forces we call "natural" are alive, and, therefore, that the universe is an organic, personal or semi-personal entity rather than a machine.

How a people see the world, whether as a machine or as organic, has a lot to do with how that people relate to the world. Those who see the way the world operates as predictable relate to it in one way. Those who see it as personal, capricious and, therefore, unpredictable relate to it in quite a different way. We might see the contrast as between those who say, "Natural law causes what goes on in the world, therefore we seek to control those natural laws" versus those who say, "Spirits cause what goes on, therefore I must try to keep in harmony with the spirits and, if possible to control them."

Those who see the world as largely predictable without personal beings involved have great trouble interpreting events such as hurricanes, tornadoes, volcanic eruptions, earthquakes and the like. Insurance agencies, not knowing how to place blame call them "acts of God!" Those who see the universe as personal and capricious have little or no difficulty in explaining what lies behind such tragedies but give their attention to trying to influence or control the spirits rather than trying to make predictable the natural events in order to control them.

Human Causality

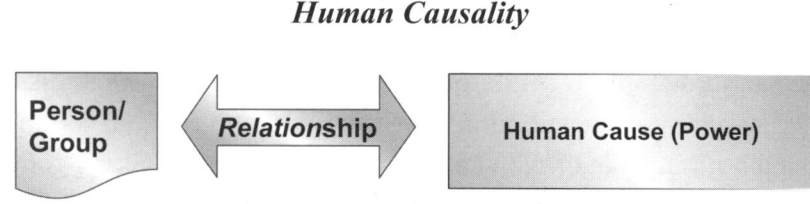

Figure 9.8. Person/Group Observes and Relates to Human Cause or Power

The area of Human Causality covers the power exercised by humans over the natural world, over other humans and over spirit beings and forces. Under this heading come the political, social and economic dynamics that seem to allow certain humans to pressure others in certain directions. Differences in status and role figure prominently in this area, as does the place of human will in interpersonal relationships between those of unequal power. Can a human being be forced to do things against his or her will? Any power that humans seem to have over supernatural beings and forces also comes under this heading.

In the human world, such things as status, talents and abilities, knowledge, political and/or social position, prestige, the ability to persuade, the ability to procreate, the ability to kill and the like come under scrutiny. Through procreation, humans are able to cause new humans to come into existence. Through teaching, humans are able to influence (cause) children to learn their culture.

Such human things as status, prestige, political or social position enable people to exercise power over others. For example, a person who has the status of father or leader, or who is wealthy, highly schooled or very knowledgeable may exercise great power over those within his or her sphere of influence. Such people cause to happen, or at least influence things in the human sphere.

People differ in their perception of what is allowable in the exercise of power in the human sphere. For example, age gives automatic status and power in many societies, though in the West and among certain Eskimo groups, aged people are looked on as liabilities and forced out of the ordinary affairs of the society. It is usually assumed that in tribal societies political power is the prerogative of the oldest male in a kin group. In large scale societies, however, political power may be inherited as with kings, or it may be the result of elections as in democracies or in certain societies such power is the prize attained through revolution. Social status with all its prerogatives is often assigned to those born into certain families. In other societies, such status and perhaps leadership position may be gained through educational or financial attainments.

Few people in their traditional state would admit the kind of power we in the West allow our youth to influence large crowds, to set standards of dress, music, freedom and the like. Nor would most traditional peoples allow middle-aged adults to treat their parents like many in American society do when we put them away in retirement homes to await a lonely death. For such peoples, age increases rather than decreases prestige. And with death and ancestorhood, one's power and ability to cause things to happen in the human sphere is enormously increased.

Supernatural Causality

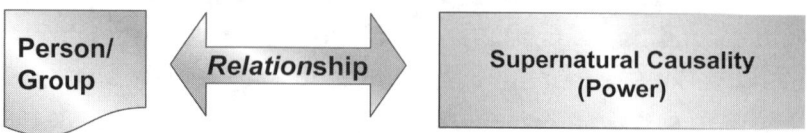

Figure 9.9. Person/Group Observes and Relates to Supernatural Cause or Power

The area of supernatural causality, then, deals with concepts of cause attributed to supernatural beings and powers. Among the questions to deal with under this heading are, Is there a Supreme Cause? If so, is the cause personal or impersonal? And is he/it all-powerful or subject to limitations? If there are limitations, what are they? Are human and angelic "free will" among the factors that limit him? Is there a hierarchy of spirit beings? What power do spirit beings have in human life? And what power do spirit beings have over each other? Is weather purely a natural phenomenon or are spirit beings involved in the weather? And can humans exert any control over spirit beings? If so, under what conditions?

Most of the peoples of the world are supernaturalistic, believing that there is a world of invisible spirit beings and that those beings impinge on human life and activity producing certain results in the human world and the world of nature. Many believe in impersonal forces such as fate, karma or chance. Many peoples also assume that certain physical objects contain impersonal spiritual power often technically referred to as "mana"). Such power, whether personal or impersonal, is often seen to be either good or evil. Evil spirits are blamed for sickness, accidents and other negative events.

Above the spirits a good God is often understood to exist. That God may be seen as the creator and/or the ultimate source of power. But he is usually thought to be distant and difficult to approach. He is, therefore, often almost completely ignored. Meanwhile, attention is devoted to appeasing the evil spirits to prevent them from causing harm or to stop harm that is already in progress. Such a supernaturalism theme is labeled "animism."

Christian supernaturalism, of course, posits the God of the Bible as the Creator and Sustainer of the universe. He is also the Source of all power. He is, however, approachable and, though offended by human sin, basically positive toward us. Though omnipotent, He has given humans a certain amount of free will in relation to which He has put certain limitations on Himself. Apparently, Satan, the head of the evil spiritual kingdom, has a certain amount of self-determination as well, at least enough to enable him to rebel in the first place and to continue to carry out his warfare against God. Evil spirits, called demons, can under certain circumstances influence and even indwell humans. Working in the power of Jesus Christ, humans can expel demons from other humans.

Differing Emphases

Different societies pay differing amounts of attention to the natural, human and spirit realms. Western peoples pay great attention to the natural world and little if any attention to the spirit world even though most North Americans claim to believe in God. As mentioned, in many non-western societies the situation seems to be reversed, with great attention given to the spirit world and less to the natural world. Biblical societies were much more like contemporary non-western peoples than like western societies in this regard.

It may be helpful to diagram the approximate proportions of attention given by these three types of societies to each of the three areas or spheres of causality outlined above. Though any chart such as this is greatly oversimplified, my intent is to portray the fact that biblical and "2/3 World" societies give about the same amount of attention to each of the three areas of causality, while western peoples give much less attention to the spirit sphere and much more attention to the nature sphere than either of the other sets of societies.

BIBLICAL SOCIETIES	2/3 WORLD SOCIETIES	WESTERN SOCIETIES
Spirit Sphere (God in primary focus)	Spirit Sphere (Spirits in primary focus)	Spirit (God) Sphere
		Human Sphere
Human Sphere	Human Sphere	Natural/Material World Sphere
Natural/Material World Sphere	Natural/Material World Sphere	

Figure 9.10. Comparisons of Emphasis Between Three Different Types of Societies

That the contrast is so great between our society, on the one hand, and both biblical and 2/3 world societies on the other suggests at least two interesting facts:

The lack of development within our western worldview of an understanding of spirit beings and powers, including God, makes it very difficult for us to understand either the Bible or the concerns of non-western peoples in this area; and

It is usually easier for non-western peoples both to understand and to receive God's message directly from the biblical accounts than from westerners. The Bible is more on their wavelength than we westerners are and this is for worldview reasons.

Note, however, that, even though the percentages of attention devoted to the spirit world in biblical and 2/3 World societies may be roughly similar, there is one major difference between them. Though God's people often devolved to what I have labeled above as the 2/3 World position, the focus in the Bible is squarely on God while in the 2/3 World the focus is usually more on spirits than on God. This leads, as noted above, to a primary concern on the part of animistic peoples to appease the spirits that can harm them rather than (as taught in the Bible) to appeal for help to the God who is above the spirits. When animists come to Christ, then, it is important to give attention to the need for change in this area of their worldview. This change is, however, often less of a problem than that caused by a secularized presentation of the gospel by westerners to people who are much more aware of spiritual reality than the westerners who brought the gospel to them.

The area of causality and power is the part of worldview most likely to undergo change for those who accept the gospel message. For westerners, conversion means belief in and commitment to a God who either wasn't believed in before or was only vaguely seen. Turning to a fully biblical Christianity for westerners, then, means also moving into believing in the spirit world and spiritual warfare against the evil spirit world, including working in God's power for healing and deliverance. This latter, especially, requires great change for most of us. For people converted out of an animistic background, the change from a focus on the spirits to a focus on God can be a very great change.

For true Christians, of course, the power above all powers is God. And He requires of us both knowledge of and commitment to Himself. Acceptance of Him, then, entails a radical change in one's view of and relation to the Supreme power in the universe and the lesser evil and good powers. The communication of the gospel has as its aim the bringing about of belief in and total allegiance to the one true God, a belief and allegiance that replaces all competing beliefs and allegiances. Such belief and allegiance usually involves great change.

As we study the peoples of the world, we find that most of the world's peoples are seeking greater spiritual power to cope with the exigencies of life. The spiritual power part of biblical Christianity, then, is the part of our message most likely to be attractive to such peoples. following Jesus' example, we ought to be using spiritual power as a primary method of blessing and communicating to those whom God loves. They are more likely to be open to Christian witness that focuses on power demonstrations and power encounters than on attempts to change their philosophy or theology.

Determinism

When dealing with cause, the question arises, How determinative is any given causal factor? When we lift or move inanimate objects, we can say that the determination is complete. That is, we by means of our strength and effort have determined that the object we lifted or moved ended up where we willed it to end up. When we influence people, however, we have to reckon with a force in the other person that we often refer to as "free will." The presence of this factor leads to quite a bit of discussion concerning how much of any given effect on a human being may be *caused* by another and how much is the result of the receiving person's choice.

Determinism, in one form or another, holds that humans are totally or almost totally devoid of freedom of choice. All human behavior to the determinist is simply predictable response to past or present situations with little or no "free will" involved. The success of scientists in discovering causes of certain behavior and in some cases being able to use such knowledge to cause and/or control human behavior leads some to generalize that all human behavior is caused and/or controlled by factors outside human choice.

Philosophical determinism is the theory that human interaction can be reduced to relationships between biological, chemical, or physical entities. This assumption is fundamental to much of modern sociobiology, neuropsychology, and medicine. The behavioral determinism of psychologist B. F. Skinner reduces all internal psychological states to publicly observable behavior. His stimulus-response account also uses modern statistical and probabilistic analyses of causation.

Philosophical determinism is similar to fatalism and the theological concept of radical predestination. However, it does not share with these concepts the assumption that some outside being or force is ultimately responsible for the causation.

No one seems to be a hard-core determinist. Even if history takes place by absolute necessity and is indeed absolutely determined, we have no way of knowing that. Our only access to history is observation of a sequence of things that happen. We may be able to trace partial causes back one or two steps, but cannot be sure, naturalistically speaking, just how great the causal effect may be of one thing or event on another.

As Christians, we can listen with interest to those arguing in favor of a determinism, whether it be natural, psychological, sociocultural or spiritual. We can, however, observe that those who argue that we are determined do not seem to be totally determined themselves. They seem to have enough free will and creativity to come up with their ideas, even though those ideas deny the free will and creativity they are using. Before scientists discovered that there are a number of biological, psychological and sociocultural constraints on our freedom, many people believed that humans had a great deal more freedom than it now appears we do. Even though we must admit such constraints, however, there still remains a measure of freedom and creativity that we believe God has invested us with.

Religious Ritual and Magic

Human beings are often not content to simply allow themselves to be pushed around by the various causes in our lives. People thus try to control nature, other human beings and even spirits. The activities used to assert such control are based on worldview-level assumptions concerning what can and cannot be done.

In the West, of course, we have learned well how to exert power over the material universe through science and technology. We have worldview assumptions on the basis of which we assert that we have a right to do this. In the human realm, again based on worldview assumptions, we use techniques such as persuasion, commanding on the basis of status, political processes, law, police and any number of other means to attempt to exert control over others. For many, even prayer is an attempt to get God to manipulate people or circumstances.

Throughout the world, the number one approach to attempting to exert power over natural, human and spiritual phenomena is through control of certain spiritual beings and powers. The peoples of many societies invest large amounts of time, energy and money in "religious" activities in attempts to make use of spirit beings and powers to serve their ends. It is assumed that by doing certain things, those powers will serve us.

I have mentioned the fact that many use the services of shamans or priests to get the help they want from spirit powers. These "experts" will often do things themselves to control the spirits. Or they will advise their clients as to what to do. The following discussion of some of the principles on which shamans and animistic peoples in general work does not distinguish between what the shaman does and what ordinary people do.

Appeals to spirits may be direct, as when a shaman invites a spirit to take him/her over or when an appeal is made for information about, say, one who supposedly has put a curse on the client's family. Or such an appeal may be indirect, as when a Kamwe diviner studies and draws conclusions from the tracks made in the sand by the crabs he uses to discover the spirit world's answer to a question.

Another form of direct control of power is based on the assumption that certain rituals or other behavior can automatically bring about a desired result. This kind of practice is called "magic." In this case, the assumption is that there is a kind of impersonal power that can be mechanically controlled through the ritual. I will assert right here that I am convinced that such a belief is inaccurate and that what is happening is that personal spirits with a desire to deceive are going along with the assumption and making the result happen often enough to keep people believing in the process.

The role of magic and other types of manipulation of spirits vary from society to society. For some, techniques to control spirits occupy a central position in primary rituals involving the well-being of an entire community. For other people groups, such activities are largely private acts. Black magic, sorcery or witchcraft may be used destructively to bring misfortune or death through use of magical techniques, such as spells or charms.

So-called "white magic" is believed to be beneficial and is used by peoples in all parts of the world to ward off attacks as well as to prevent natural calamities. Magical healing is among its aspects. Much of white magic is directly concerned with the productive activities of a particular society (e.g., fertility of women, agricultural and animal fertility. For many people this involves fishing and/or agricultural magic. Love charms are also considered white magic.

In casting spells, the appropriate use of words is considered sufficient to release or activate a power. The importance of such words is variable. In some Melanesian and Polynesian societies the precise wording of a spell is a crucial part of the magic. Other societies, such as the Azande of the Sudan, lay less stress on wording, being content with conveying the spell's general meaning. For the Azande, magical objects such as special woods and roots are of greater significance than the words. The objects used in magic are regarded as repositories for or symbols of the powers engaged, or, as with the destruction of wax figures of victims in sorcery, symbolically connected to the aims of the magic.

Magical acts may be performed by individuals on their own behalf, or a magician with specialized knowledge of the rites may be consulted. In some societies associations of magical specialists exist. Magical knowledge is sometimes bought and sold or can be passed on through inheritance. The magician, both in the preparation and the performance of a rite, may need to be aware of a complex set of rules and restrictions, such as food taboos, that may influence the efficacy and safety of the magic.

As with the so-called automatic efficacy of the rituals used in magic, there is a large amount of deceit at work in the assumption that people can control spirits. Satan, however, gets a lot of mileage out of that bit of deceit. For, if people can believe they are in control when, in fact, they are being controlled, Satan wins. He is smart enough, though, to allow enough success to keep people believing even when the techniques fail. And overall, he keeps both those administering the help and those seeking it, strongly in his grip. One thing that is of interest in this regard, however, is the fact that in many societies, shamans know they will someday experience a miserable death. And they understand that the misery they will go through will be part of the price they will have to pay to the spirits for allowing them the power they have used during their lifetimes.

The Eternal God as Ultimate Cause

As Christians, we believe and, therefore, assume, that the God of the Bible is both the Creator and the Sustainer of the universe. He is, therefore, the Ultimate Cause, the Source of all causality and power. As we know, philosophers have argued endlessly over whether or not God exists and whether or not we could know it if He either does or does not exist. A major problem in such discussions is that they have taken place among westerners whose assumptions were weak at best concerning the spirit world. The research capability and sensibilities of westerners may have been attuned carefully to the physical world (scientists) or the world of thought (philosophers), but there was a whole realm of Reality that they neither knew nor fully believed in (with the exception, often, of God). And Satan and his helpers are wise enough to keep themselves from being obvious to those who don't believe they exist. So they very seldom get discovered by scientific or philosophical/theological research.

The scientists' approach was (and is) "empiricism." This is the assumption that if something can be experienced with our senses, it is real and can be studied. The physical world fits into that category, spiritual reality does not (from their point of view). The philosophers' approach is "reason." But that reason is so thoroughly affected by western worldview assumptions that is it no wonder that, as westerners, they missed spiritual reality, again except for the fact that some of them believed in God.

For those of us who have stepped out, often against our own worldview assumptions, and met God, committed ourselves to Him and made the necessary changes in our worldview, we have no doubts about the Ultimate Cause and Sustainer. We simply say, "Amen" to the arguments for the existence of God based on causality, design and purpose in the universe. Though we may have questions about such things as the age of the earth, fossils, the antiquity of humans, etc., we know that whatever was done, it was done by God. Something this complicated has to have been made by an "Intelligent Designer." No one who was not determined to believe that the universe got here by chance would accept such a lie.

Though we may have the Creator question settled, other questions arise concerning Cause when we contemplate the existence of a "natural" world full of catastrophes caused by weather (e.g., earthquakes, tornadoes, drought, famine), evil events caused by humans (e.g., wars, murders, rapes), disease caused by germs or spirits (who created germs?), accidents (does God not care enough to protect us?) and the like. There are, I believe, no answers to these questions unless we assume what the Bible assumes—that there is an evil spirit world headed by Satan that has a degree of autonomy and is out to do as much damage as possible to what God has created and the creatures He loves.

We certainly find no answer if we assume that God can do anything He wants to at anytime He wants to. We speak of His omnipotence, omniscience and omnipresence. We seldom speak of the fact that He has limited Himself in certain ways by allowing us and, apparently, Satan, some freedom to choose. We know He doesn't always get His own way from scriptures such as 2 Pet. 3:9 where we are told that "God is not willing that any should perish." The fact that many will go to Hell is indication that what God wills is limited by something—in this case, the choices of humans to not follow Him.

So, put a frail creature, created in God's image but infected by a sin nature that inclines us to disobey in the middle of a conflict between God and Satan and we've got problems. Problems arise from the fact that 1) A primary tactic of our enemy is to do everything he can to mess up God's prized creatures in order to get at God. 2) Still another problem arises from the fact that we are predisposed by our sin nature to rebel and disobey and so find it easy to side with our enemy. 3) Another problem arises from the fact that Satan and his hosts work invisibly so we can't see them and oppose them openly as we would like to. 4) A further problem that we westerners have is that our worldview just about cripples us in our attempts to understand what is going on in the spirit world.

However, the Great Original Cause is there and is positive toward us. And He invites us to participate with Him in acts of spiritual warfare through prayer both to protect ourselves and to go on the offensive against the enemy. God has set up the universe to operate according to rules—physical rules, psychological rules, spiritual rules. All humans and all spirits and all nature have to obey these rules. We have learned quite a few of the rules concerning physical reality, some concerning human reality but few concerning spiritual reality. I believe, however, that just as there are sciences applying to the physical world and sciences applying to the human world, so there are sciences applying to the spirit world. And we have a lot to learn.

I'll leave this subject here but recommend that you read Kraft and DeBord 2000 for more on the rules for the interaction between the spirit and the human worlds.

Chapter 10

Universals: Time/Event, Space/Material World

Time/Event

The kind of focus a people will have in the area of Time/Event is another part of life structured by worldview. All worldviews provide guidelines for people in this area. People have certain assumptions concerning time and organize their concepts in what they consider to be an appropriate way to deal with daily, weekly, monthly, yearly, seasonal, and other recurring events. The passage of time is also noted—though seldom quantified as precisely into seconds, minutes, and hours as in the West. Something is done to remember important events in the past (history, myth), to understand present events, and to anticipate future events. But the worldview assumptions underlying the way such events are treated vary considerably from society to society.

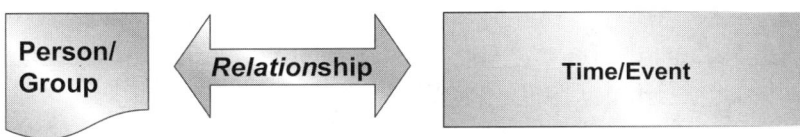

Figure 10.1. Person/Group Observes and Conceptualizes Time/Event

Not infrequently the worldview focus is on the *quality of an event* rather than on the quantity of time "consumed" by that event. Western travelers have often observed that "these people have no sense of time." As usual, such a comment is only accurate if one assumes that our cultural structuring of time is the only valid one. The truth is, those people are simply more concerned with what is happening—be that a conversation or a public meeting—than with how long it goes on. From their point of view, it may not be appropriate for a meeting to start until the right people are there. Nor should it end if something significant is happening. We often refer to such a focus as an "event orientation" as opposed to our own western "time orientation."

Differences in assumptions concerning time can underlie the most frustrating experiences for the cross-cultural worker. Luzbetak highlights some of the frustrations in the following quote:

> The value attached to time will ... be an endless source of culture jolts. What does it mean to hurry? When is a person on time? When is he prompt? What should the missionary's reaction be when someone fails to keep an appointment? How long may the missionary keep one waiting? How serious must the reason be before the missionary may be disturbed? When may one be disturbed while reading, eating, recreating, entertaining a guest, resting, sleeping? The answers to all these questions will be found to be closely associated with the culturally defined value attached to time. E.T. Hall describes how a band of South Pacific natives once called on an American official at two o'clock in the morning for a relatively insignificant matter ...
>
> After almost four years in New Guinea I discovered that my nickname was "Padre Wait-A-Minute." ... Words like "exactly" and "punctually" may mean one thing to the missionary and quite another to his flock, and the value attached to exactness and punctuality, as the missionary understands these terms, may differ considerably from the value the local people attach to such exactness and punctuality. ... "Long-range" planning in the United States may be only "short-term" planning in China. A "leisurely" pace in the United States may be "top speed" and "on the double" in Trinidad, Haiti, or the Orient (1970:88-9).

In the West, we set rather strict time limits on most of our activities. Western Christianity has often short-circuited the possibility of Christians genuinely relating to God in corporate worship by structuring church meetings more as timed happenings than as events—activities that get cut off when "the time is up," even if something important is going on. Like other types of lovemaking, worship takes time because it is intended to be an event in which the quality of the relationship experienced is to take precedence over the time expended in the activity. One wonders if God is pleased with the way we limit our time with Him on Sunday mornings.

Unfortunately, we Evangelicals have tended to lessen the quality of our worship in the interests of keeping the time of our meetings short. Evangelicals have a lot to learn from Pentecostals and Charismatics in the area of spending quality time in worship. And there is often a direct relationship between the quality of worship and the effective exercise of spiritual power in a community of believers.

A Brief History of Western Time

Kearney alerts us to some changes that have happened in history that have resulted in the approach to time that we in industrialized societies take.

> Americans and other industrialized peoples tend to pay attention to small segments of time, and to have common terms for them. Until late in the Middle Ages, European clocks did not have minute hands, and presumably people then were not greatly concerned with organizing their affairs so accurately. It was around 1345 that hours were commonly divided into sixty minutes and minutes into sixty seconds. With this conscious harnessing of time it acquired a meaning and value equivalent to work and commodities. As Benjamin Franklin expressed it later ... "time is money"; it can be "bought," and "spent," "saved," and "wasted." Consequently, people in industrial societies talk and think about time more precisely and literally (1984:104).

Kinds of Time

For a start to our discussion of time, we turn to the reigning expert on time, Edward T. Hall. His books, *The Silent Language* (1959), and *The Dance of Life* (1983) are the "state of the art" when it comes to dealing with time. In the latter book, he starts out by saying,

> Some things are not easily bent to simple linear description. Time is one of them. There are serious misconceptions about time, the first of which is that time is singular. Time is not just an immutable constant, as Newton supposed, but a cluster of concepts, events, and rhythms covering an extremely wide range of phenomena (1983:14).

Hall then goes on to describe nine kinds of time (1983:13-27). I will only list seven of his nine:

1. Biological Time. This is the kind of time that gets disrupted when we fly to distant places and experience jet lag. Hall speaks of the dismay one feels when in a meeting in a place where the time is 10-12 hours different from home "one is overwhelmed by fatigue" because the body feels it has been up all night, in spite of what the clock on the wall shows. Other facets of biological time relate to our life cycle and the process of aging, a women's menstrual cycle and her reproductive "biological clock" and the like.

2. Personal Time. This is the subjective way in which "people experience the flow of time in different contexts, settings, and emotional and psychological states" (1983:19). At certain times, we feel that time is flying, while at other times it seems to be dragging. As Kearney says, "Everyone experiences differences in [the perceived rate] under different conditions, say, the last day of vacation versus time in the dentist's chair" (1984:102).

3. Physical Time. This is time measured precisely according to the sun's "annual pilgrimage from south to north and then back to south again" (Hall 1983:20).

4. Metaphysical Time. This is the time of horoscopes and astrology. Hall doesn't know what to do with this kind of time, but admits that it is very real for many of the peoples of the world.

5. Micro Time. This is time as defined by any specific society. Various illustrations will be given as we go along. One important patterning of micro time is what is called "monochronic" time, the practice of tending to one thing at a time (as is our custom in North America). This use of time is in contrast to "polychronic" time, which "stresses involvement of people and completion of transactions rather than adherence to preset schedules" (1983:46). Those with this mindset working, say, in a Latin American office, are often tending to several persons and things at the same time. North Americans, waiting for an appointment in such an office are frequently frustrated, since we are culturally conditioned to wait for one person's business to be completed before we step forward, yet we observe that people coming after us simply interrupt and get taken care of.

6. Sacred Time. This is myth time. Westerners have difficulty understanding this kind of time because we see time in terms of substance. Hall says,

> ...this type of time is imaginary—one is *in* the time. It is repeatable and reversible, and it does not change. In mythic time people do not age, for they are magic. This kind of time is like a story; it is not supposed to be like ordinary clock time and everyone knows that it isn't ... When American Indian people participate in ceremonies, they are in the ceremony and in the ceremony's time. They cease to exist in ordinary time (1983:25-6).

7. Profane Time. This is the kind of time we know best, with time divided into minutes and hours, days, weeks and months, years, decades and centuries.

Images of Time

There are a variety of images of time. Many of the assumptions concerning time may be revealed in the pictures people conceive of in their minds when they deal with time. Americans, for example, seem to visualize time as a river in which we are swimming upstream toward the future. The Ancient Greeks, however, saw time as a stream in which people stand looking downstream at the past, with the future behind them. For the Greeks it was the past that lay ahead of them when they "looked" at time whereas for us we "look ahead" to the future and picture the past as behind us.

At least certain New Guineans seem to see time as a small oval ("memory time") surrounded by a larger oval (mythological time) that encompasses all that is beyond memory, whether past or future.

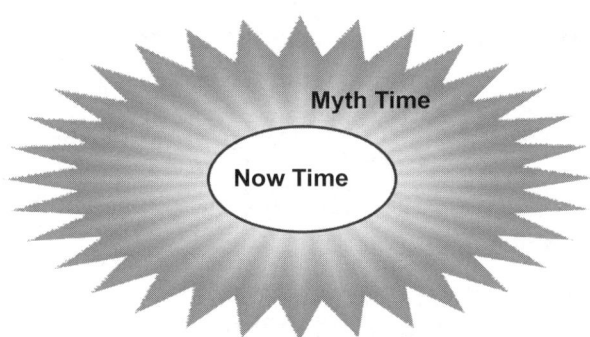

Figure 10.2. New Guinean Now Time and Myth Time Illustrated

Hall attempts to picture the time concepts of three tribal groups. Referring to E.E. Evans-Pritchard's work with the Nuer of East Africa (1940), Hall describes the Nuer view as that of a large wheel on which each of the spokes is a channel through which kin and groups moved.

> ...in Nuer time one knew the wheel was moving, but it had the appearance of standing still as generations fed in at the hub slowly worked their way up to the top of the spoke at the rim. The Nuer realized that time moved ... [but] for them only the generations moved (Hall 1983:79).

Hall then turns to the Tiv of Nigeria, basing his discussion on the work of Paul Bohannan (1953). For the Tiv,

> ...time was somewhat like a series of enclosed rooms, each containing a different activity. The walls of time, like the hollow conduits of the Nuer, seem to have been relatively fixed. "Time rooms" could not be moved about or shuffled, nor was the activity in those rooms to be changed or interrupted, as occurs in [Euro-American] cultures. Once inside one of their time-activity chambers, both the Tiv and their activity were inviolate. Like the time clock in a vault, they were sealed in and safe from interruptions (Hall 1983:79).

Turning to the Quiche of Guatemala and basing his discussion on the work of Barbara Tedlock (1981), Hall describes a system built around two calendars, one of which he calls "civil," consisting of eighteen twenty-day months, accounting for 360 days "with five days remaining." Of the other, he says,

> There are 260 days to the religious calendar, which has no months but is an assemblage of twenty combinations. These two calendars interlock like two rotating gears to produce the Calendar Round, which only repeats itself once every fifty-two years.
>
> ... the Quiche 260-day calendar, like the wheel which it resembles, has no beginning and no end.
>
> ... To the Maya, the sacred 260-day calendar provides the base on which an elaborate system of divination is built. Each day has special characteristics and it takes a shaman-diviner to provide a proper interpretation of the day (Hall 1983:81- 82).

It is common to speak of *linear time* and *cyclical time*. Kearney uses the term, *oscillating* instead of cyclical and says it is the most common view of time in human societies. He argues that

> ...it is often inappropriate to refer to a primary concern with repetitive events as a cyclical sense of time. The word *cyclical* implies that something is circular and revolves. But in the traditional societies to which a cyclical notion of time is usually attributed, circular motion is virtually absent (1984:98).

E.R. Leach has argued that what has been called cyclical is better imaged as a zigzag motion. He adds very helpfully,

> ...in some primitive societies it would seem that the time process is not experienced as a "succession of epochal durations" at all; there is no sense of going on and on in the same direction, or round and round the same wheel. On the contrary, time is experienced as something discontinuous, a repetition of repeated reversal, and a sequence of oscillations between polar opposites: night and day, winter and summer, drought and flood, age and youth, life and death. In such a scheme the past had no "depth" to it, all past is equally past; it is simply the opposite of now (1966:126).

Some have suggested the image of a *pendulum* as appropriate to this understanding of time.

Figure 10.3 – Pendulum Representation of Time

As for linear time, the image of a river mentioned above applies to this type. Linear is the term used to label the most widespread western concept of time. Though I believe the term gives an overly simplistic picture of western time, "the essential thing about a linear image of time is that time is one-way and irreversible" (Kearney 1984:100). Kearney says linear time was "an unintentional invention of the ancient Hebrews" who saw things beginning at Creation and proceeding through the events of their history inexorably toward whenever God calls history to a halt. Such a view, then, results in a strong emphasis on history.

Personally, I don't like the linearity image. It seems to me too simplistic, implying that the only thing that is happening to time is steady movement forward. I suggest in its place the picture of a *spiral* to cover what we see in the Bible—time conceived of as repetitive but also as moving in a given direction. For me, the concept of spiral captures both the directionality of time that, I believe, the scripture advocates and the fact that there are seasons and cycles to be accounted for as well.

Figure 10.4 – Spiral Representation of Time

We see from this small sampling of the variety of approaches to time, a bit of the complexity of trying to deal with time cross-culturally. Whether we see time as a river with ourselves facing one way or the other, or as an oval within an oval, or as tunnels resembling the spokes of a large wheel, or as divisible into separate rooms or as some combination of two calendars, or as linear, or as oscillating, or as spiraling, or in some other way, we see enormous difficulties in trying to understand one concept from the perspective of another.

Past, Present or Future

In terms of our western concern for past, present or future, it has been observed that different societies assume that one or the other of these three is more important than the others. In an important study of values of five groups, Florence Kluckhohn and F.L. Strodtbeck found that Anglos had a strong future orientation, Spanish Americans, on the other hand, are described as living in a "timeless present." More traditional societies, then, are often described as having an orientation toward the past and the preservation of their traditions.

Kearney defines a *future-orientation* as meaning "that one thinks of future events and conditions that have not yet come to pass more than one senses the immediacy of events that are actually occurring, or than one thinks of past times (1984:95). He sees this orientation among Anglo-Americans as related to Calvinism and issuing in "hard work, success in business and austere living" for the sake of gaining favor with God. Putting off present gratification for the sake of some future "good" is characteristic of a future-orientation. He sees present day Anglo-Americans becoming less future-oriented and more oriented toward present gratification.

Though we Anglo-Americans may be characterized as future-oriented, ours is but what Kearney calls, "a shallow range of concern."

We tend to think ahead only within the span of [our] own lifetime, or the next few generations. Thus, although [we] are good at short-range planning, [we] are not effective at preparing for the distant future. The current environmental crises in this country are largely the result of very efficient short-term planning for exploiting resources, but without regard for the long-range consequences. Our concern with the past is also shallow (1984:102).

What matters to a *present-oriented* person or group is what they are experiencing right now. Though for a future-oriented person, a schedule of future appointments is a real thing, "not so for a present-oriented person who may be confronted by another, immediate event demanding his or her attention while en route to an as yet unreal appointment" (Kearney 1984:96). Hall illustrates a present-oriented situation from among the Navaho by describing a possible event involving the giving of a horse to a Navaho horse-lover. He points out that if one were to promise a Navajo a great horse sometime later in the year, the "face would fall and he would turn around and walk away," whereas if one were to offer that man an old dilapidated horse right now, "the Navajo would beam and shake your hand and jump on his new horse and ride away." Hall then comments, "only the immediate gift has reality; a promise of future benefits is not even worth thinking about" (1959:33).

The Chinese are known for their *past-orientation*. Kluckhohn and Strodtbeck state that "the Chinese attitude [is] that nothing new ever happened in the Present or would happen in the Future; it had all happened before in the far distant Past" (1961:14). The attention of traditional Chinese is continually focused on such past-oriented things as ancestors, filial piety, family tradition and "an almost compulsive concern with record keeping and history" (Kearney 1984:97).

Language and Time

Though not all of a people's worldview assumptions concerning time will be signaled by various parts of their language, some will. With regard to time expressions, in English, a worldview assumption becomes evident when we note that we speak of an abstract thing like time by using terms whose primary usage relates to material things such as "long," "short," "spend," "waste" and the like. The worldview-level assumption is that time is like a substance. And we further concretize it by dividing it up into seconds, minutes and hours, as if we were marking out inches and feet on a yardstick.

When we find a fairly large number of references in the speech of a people or their writing relating to any given topic, we are right to assume that that topic is of importance to a people. Reading an American newspaper, book or magazine and looking for references to time would convince one that time is fairly important to Anglo-Americans.

Another indication in language of worldview concern appears from the distinctions one is forced to make by the language. The fact that English forces us to make distinctions between past, present and future indicates that dividing time in this way is assumed (at the worldview level) to be important by the speakers of English. We can conclude the same with regard to the necessity that we distinguish males from females in our pronouns, but only in the singular.

Dividing time in the western way is not as important to the Hausa of Northern Nigeria. In the Hausa language we have a "completive aspect" specifying that the action is completed, a "continuous aspect," a "habitual aspect" and a "future aspect" (the closest they come to a tense). A completive aspect expression, though usually used to refer to past action, is just as easily used in present or future time. In isolation, then, the expression *na tafi* could be translated, "I went away," "I go away (right now)" or "I will have gone away (by this time tomorrow)." The time of the action is specified by other words in the context, e.g., "yesterday, *na tafi*" or "by this time tomorrow, *na tafi*" or simply "*na tafi*" (= "I leave" in the present). This and other features of the grammatical patterns of Hausa support the observation, clear from other things in their cultural life, that Hausa people are less concerned about past, present or future divisions of time than of the kind of activity a person is involved in (indicated by the aspect of the pronoun).

One important use of language to discover worldview is to listen to and read folklore. Proverbs often contain time references such as in English, "A stitch in time saves nine" (referring to knitting and recommending that one take the time to repair something lest it become a bigger problem later) and "The early bird catches the worm" (recommending that one get places promptly). Myths, tales and fables will often depict situations in which assumptions concerning time are indicated. We will deal with folklore in more detail in chapter 13.

History

What people do with regard to past time is a function of worldview assumptions. Whether the past is highly valued, as with the Chinese, or virtually ignored, as with many with the "oscillating time" orientation mentioned above are worldview matters.

How history is recorded is of interest. In biblical times, the Jews indicated some of their history through erecting "stones of remembrance" (Josh. 4:4-7; 20-23), some of it, then, was to be given orally at Passover time, some of it was remembered through names given to children (e.g., Ichabod: 1 Sam. 4:21; Beriah: 1 Chron. 7:23). Names were also given to wells and towns and their names changed on occasion to update the history. Biblical history has, of course, also been written. But most of it had been handed down orally for at least a generation, and some for many generations before it was committed to writing.

Measuring history in equal periods of time such as years, months and days, as we are used to, is not everybody's custom. We see in the Old Testament, for example that the Jews recorded history unevenly, with clusters of important events recorded in fairly detailed fashion followed by longer or shorter periods of time before the next set of events. Thus, we learn quite a bit about certain of the events in Abraham's life (Gen 12-23), comparatively little about Isaac (Gen 24-27, most of which is about Jacob and Esau), more about Jacob (Gen 28-35), then a lot about certain events in Joseph's life (Gen 37, 39-50), and then nothing until Moses comes along, when we get great detail concerning certain of the events of his life. The whole Old Testament presents history in this uneven fashion. This is a kind of event-oriented approach to history and contrasts with our time-oriented approach.

We can picture the contrast between these approaches by indicating events with hyphens with the spaces representing gaps in the record:

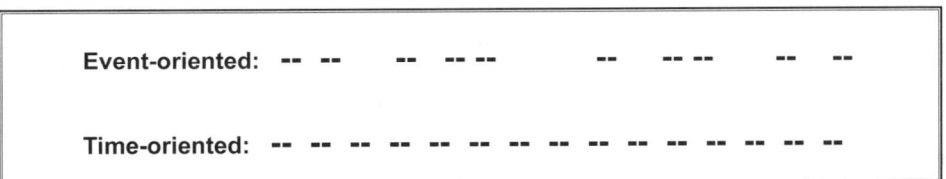

Figure 10.5. Time-Oriented Versus Event-Oriented History

Conventional Use of Time

Concepts of lateness are an interesting thing in Euro-American worldviews. The question is when do we arrive for an appointment or a get-together in given situations? And at what point are we expected to apologize if we arrive late? In the United States, if we have a ten o'clock appointment with a doctor or dentist, or with the owner of the business we work in or the president of the university we go to, at what time do we arrive? Probably a little ahead of ten o'clock. If we arrive even a few minutes late, we apologize. If we're invited to an informal get-together "at sevenish," however, and we arrive as much as half an hour late, we may not feel we need to apologize.

Africans and the peoples of many other parts of the world, including Latin America may give themselves quite a bit more leeway, even in the more formal situations. And they may feel no impulse to apologize for being late among their own people and little impulse even in America.

On another issue, when someone calls and we answer, "I'll be there in a minute," what do we mean? What did Father Luzbetak mean when he said to the New Guineans, "Wait a minute?" And some are fond of saying, "Just a second!" As Americans, we know enough to not take any of these expressions literally. Foreigners might get caught, however, as have more than one non-American, when someone said, "Why don't you come over some time," or "We'll have to get together sometime," and they showed up at the person's home without having made prior arrangements.

Getting used to a society's formal and informal uses of time can be challenging. Many is the expatriate in African contexts who, having learned that meetings always start at least an hour late, then turned up an hour late and found that the meeting had started somewhere near "on time." The challenge is to discover the assumptions underlying this and all other time-related behavior.

Space / Material Universe

All people have worldview assumptions in terms of which they conceive of and arrange their relationships with space and material objects. And, as Hall says, just about everything we humans are and do "is associated with the experience of space" (1969:181).

Cosmological questions concerning the material universe, how it got here, how to arrange ourselves in relation to it and the like are one important concern of the worldview assumptions of all peoples. Everyone notices and develops ideas concerning the "macrospace" of the cosmos—how to conceive of the world, the sun, moon and stars, space and material in general. We also, however, concern ourselves with the "microspace" of how to arrange buildings, how to arrange the space within and between buildings, how to structure interpersonal standing space, sleeping space, eating space, or how to conceive of and relate to geographical features or the universe as a whole. In addition, we are concerned with the value people put on material objects. The material world is important to us at many levels.

But, as we would expect, the assumptions of each group will differ from those of others. Should we dominate nature or submit to it? Should we live in one place or should we move around? Should we sleep all in one room or should we sleep in separate rooms? These and millions of other questions regarding space and the material universe around us are answered in terms of worldview assumptions. Our guiding perspective is this:

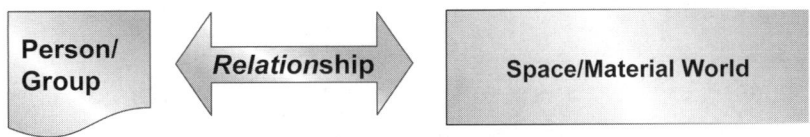

Figure 10.6. Person/Group Looks Out on and Creates Assumptions Concerning Space and the Material World

Though the matter of space and concern for the material world may seem less important than some of the other universals, there are several considerations that are of major importance to us as Christians. The lure of materialism is certainly one. It has badly skewed our American perspective and is infecting the rest of the world at an alarming rate. We are a people of things! Another is that our church sanctuaries are seldom set up to facilitate anything but lectures. They tend to be arranged as if they were large classrooms in which everything significant is expected to happen in the front with the audience expected to be spectators rather than participants. What does this say about our assumptions concerning what will go on in church?

As indicated above, there are many aspects of space to be dealt with. We will start with the broadest—cosmology—and work toward the more intimate aspects in a discussion of what has been labeled "proxemics."

Language and Assumptions Concerning Space

As with Time, there are interesting indications in language highlighting deep-level assumptions concerning space. The materialistic emphases of western societies would lead us to expect to find a very large number of vocabulary items dealing with the material world. This is indeed the case, whether we observe ordinary conversations about moving from one place to another involving terms like "street" or "freeway," that refer to ways in which we have organized our space for easy (?) access with our vehicles or whether we eavesdrop on conversations concerning buying or decorating a home or whether we take note of the thousands and thousands of vocabulary items that designate the scientific and/or technological entities that make up the parts of the universe that scientists spend their time studying and engineers spend their time manipulating. There is no doubt that the material universe and its contents are of high interest to westerners.

The interest of westerners in the material universe as represented in our language, then, becomes formative for our children as they learn the language. The result of language learning, says Hall, is like the programming of a computer, for

> ... man's very perception of the world about him is programmed by the language he speaks, just as a computer is programmed. Like the computer, man's mind will register and structure external reality only in accordance with the program. Since two languages often program the same class of events quite differently, no belief or philosophical system should be considered apart from language (1969:2).

A concern for the space in which a people live that differs greatly from western concepts is evidenced in the Kamwe language of northeastern Nigeria. Without getting into grammatical details, suffice it to say that one cannot make any comment about coming or going without using verbs that require reference to whether the movement is toward the mountains or away from them, uphill or downhill. Additional reference to whether one is moving toward or away from the river is sometimes also required. Such required reference to local geographical features in the Kamwe language are major features of their world and thus of their worldview. For those of us coming from a European language background, this makes the language very difficult to learn.

Cosmology

Cosmology is the study of the universe, dealing with such things as its origin, structure and relationships. As usual, there are quite an array of differing cultural assumptions concerning the universe. Though some have seen cosmology as virtually synonymous with worldview, we use the term in a more restricted sense here. One reason for equating cosmology with worldview is the fact that for many of the peoples of the world, the primary fact of the universe is that it is populated by personal spirits. This fact virtually eclipses all else in their perception of the universe.

A cosmology seeks to account for how the universe came into existence and what we should do now that we are a part of it. Though not every people is concerned about origins, most seem to ask cosmic questions such as, How did the universe come into existence? Where did we come from and where are we going? What are we here for? How should we relate to the world around us? The myths of a people typically articulate their view of the answers to these concerns. At this point we need to remind ourselves that the term "myth" is being used here in its technical sense to refer to any people's attempts to answer the above questions, whether accurate (factual) or inaccurate. Calling such explanations "myth" (as they are called in the literature) does not mean that they could not be factual. From this technical usage, biblical explanations are myth even though they are true.

For Christians, then, the Bible is our source of the answers to these questions. The Bible provides our myth—the only revealed one and, therefore, the only true one. So, we assert that an omnipotent God created the universe and put us in it with a primary concern to relate to Him and, under His guidance, to populate and take care of the world in which He put us. No frills to our myth. But let's look at some others.

Raymond Scupin and Christopher DeCorse (1998) summarize two of these myths. First *Navajo*:

> The Navajo Indians believe that the Holy People, supernatural and sacred, lived below ground in twelve lower worlds. A massive underground flood forced the Holy People to crawl through a hollow reed to the surface of the earth, where they created the universe. A deity named Changing Woman gave birth to the Hero Twins, called Monster Slayer and Child of the Waters. Human mortals, called Earth Surface People, emerged and First Man and First Woman were formed from the ears of white and yellow corn (1998:20-21).

The perspective of *Tao* in China and elsewhere in Asia is presented by Scupin and DeCorse as follows:

> In the tradition of Taoism, male and female principles known as yin and yang are the spiritual and material sources for the origins of humans and other living forms. Yin is considered the passive, negative, feminine force or principle in the universe, the source of cold and darkness, whereas yang is the active, positive, masculine

force or principle, the source of heat and light. Taoists believe that the interaction of these two opposite principles brought forth the universe and all living forms out of chaos (1998:21).

These authors go on to note several *Greek* views, saying,

> ... the ancient Greeks had various mythological explanations for the origin of humans. One early view was that Prometheus fashioned humans out of water and earth. Another had Zeus ordering Pyrrha, the inventor of fire, to throw stones behind his back; these stones became men and women. Later Greek cosmological views considered evolutionary ideas. Thales of Miletus (c. 636-546 B.C.) argued that life originated in the sea and that humans initially were fishlike, eventually moving onto dry land and evolving into mammals. A few hundred years later, Aristotle (384-322 B.C.) suggested another early theory of creation through evolution. Based on comparative physiology and anatomy, his argument stated that life had evolved from simple lower forms to complex higher forms, such as humans (1998:21).

Naturalistic western myth, of course, has the world coming into existence at some very distant point of time through a "big bang." This myth does not, however, explain where the materials contributing to the big bang came from, though some scientists are willing to accept a First Cause as the originator of those materials and even see Intelligent Design in the universe and its creatures. Most, though, in their determination to keep from postulating a God, prefer to believe the impossible—that humans evolved from animals which had evolved from lower animals all the way back to an original single cell. Such a scheme is statistically laughable unless there is an Intelligent Designer guiding the process, a theory that some are willing to accept.

Given a cosmos, what is our relationship to it? As we have seen, worldview assumptions lead one people to submit to their surroundings, another to attempt to master them. Or, do people worship or otherwise use sun, moon and stars as if they were powerful beings? In any event, the physical space provided by our universe becomes the venue or the object of the dramas of life in which we engage. To conduct those dramas, we must organize our environment.

Organizing Space

All peoples organize their space. For some the construction and arrangement of buildings is done largely along rectangular lines. This is the predominant custom in the West. In the part of Nigeria where we lived, the organizing principle for homes is circular. The huts were round and one-roomed, the collection of huts we called a "compound," consisting of all the huts in which a family lived and interacted, then, was encircled by grass mats or a kind of cactus.

In the parts of America where cities and towns were planned, again, the predominant structuring of buildings and roads is rectangular. In New England, where I was brought up, though we arranged our homes more or less according to rectangular patterns, the myth was that our roads were designed to follow cow paths, for they seem to wander all over the place. For us, since these roads never did seem to go in straight lines, we always gave directions in terms of "turn left" or "turn right," never, as I found they did in the Midwest, "go north two blocks and turn west." When I was first given directions in terms of north and west, I had no idea how to proceed since I had not learned to think in those terms. They would have been virtually meaningless in New England, since most of our roads went north at one time and west at another, perhaps meandering south somewhere along the way as well!

Internally, buildings may be large with many rooms within them, as in the West, or single-roomed as we found in Nigeria. And different societies use the space inside buildings differently. Our Anglo-American use of space within our homes relates strongly to our concepts of privacy. Indeed, in Nigeria we found ourselves being misunderstood because we demanded privacy when going to the toilet. The rural Nigerians in our area went to the "bush" to relieve themselves. We went inside our home. This led to the question, "Why do you whites want to save all that stuff? We just get rid of it in the bush!"

Hall notes that people in western societies did not always organize our homes as we do today. He points out that

> …rooms had no fixed functions in European houses until the eighteenth century. Members of the family had no privacy as we know it today. There were no spaces that were sacred or specialized. Strangers came and went at will, while beds and tables were set up and taken down according to the moods and appetites of the occupants. … In the eighteenth century, the house altered its form. … the function of a room was indicated by its name—bedroom,

living room, dining room. Rooms were arranged to open into a corridor or hall, like houses into a street. No longer did the occupants pass through one room into another (1969:104).

The rooms in western homes are decorated so that furniture stands around the edges with the center kept open. It is nearly the opposite in Japan, according to Hall, who, in pointing out that the Japanese moveable fireplace (*hibachi*) is in the center of the room, suggest that

> ... its location carries with it an emotional tone that is as strong, if not stronger, than our concept of hearth. As an old priest once explained, "To really know the Japanese you have to have spent some cold winter evenings snuggled together around the hibachi. Everybody sits together. A common quilt covers not only the hibachi but everyone's lap as well. In this way the heat is held in. It's when your hands touch and you feel the warmth of their bodies and everyone feels together—that's when you get to know the Japanese. That is the real Japan!" In psychological terms there is positive reinforcement toward the center of the room and negative reinforcement toward the edges ... Is it any wonder then that the Japanese have been known to say that our rooms look bare (because the centers are bare) (1969:150).

Another aspect of the Japanese perspective on housing comes out in the feeling many Japanese have that we Americans are being unkind to our children, especially when they are very young, by putting them in their own rooms to sleep. Babies, according to Japanese assumptions, should always sleep with their mothers. From their point of view, isolating a young child in his or her own crib in his or her own room is cruel.

Still another Japanese housing assumption that conflicts with western concepts is that to Japanese a floor is clean space, therefore one should take off her or his shoes when walking across it. In the West, we tend to assume the floor is dirty (by definition, whether it is or not), therefore, we keep our shoes on. Walking on a Japanese floor, especially if it is covered with a *tatami* mat with one's shoes on is, however, the equivalent of walking on the couch in an Anglo-American home with one's shoes on!

Outside the home, then, in America Anglo-Americans like to have a plot of grass that we call a "yard" (British "garden") between our house and the street. In Latin America, however, the house is built right up to the sidewalk but within the structure is an open space called a *patio*. In Nigeria, in order to make our home seem more comfortable, we planted grass in front of the house. This led to questions from the Nigerians, similar to the questions they asked about the flowers we liked to plant and nurture—"Can you eat that grass/flower?" We finally didn't like the reputation our front yard grass gave us for doing something useless like planting something we couldn't eat that required constant mowing to keep it low enough so the snakes couldn't hide in it. So we took out the grass and planted a front yard crop of peanuts! Those could be eaten and, therefore, were worth tending in the eyes of the Nigerians. (We never did change our toilet habits though!)

One interesting housing pattern, common in Papua New Guinea, is what is called a "longhouse." This is a single dwelling, long and rectangular, in which several families or, in some cases, the women and children of several families all live. In the latter case, the men live together in another place. It is obvious that this type of arrangement, like each of the other housing patterns, has a significant impact on the social interactions and behavior of the people who live there. Spradley and McCurdy comment, "When an entire community lives in a single longhouse, interaction between families is more frequent and intimate. Children interact with many different adults and their care and nurturance is spread among many people" (1975:206). Such an arrangement results in quite a different experience for both the children and the adults than does living in modern American suburbia in nuclear family homes.

Though there is much more that could be said about housing, the patterning of cities and towns, multistoried buildings, the arrangement of furniture, road and path patterns and the like, we will stop here and simply remind ourselves again that underlying all such patterns are deep-level worldview assumptions.

Attitudes Toward Material

The attitude toward material, especially of the kind that is considered to be wealth, is of special interest to us as Christians. What is considered wealth has varied greatly from society to society, though modernization has influenced most people in the direction of money as the primary standard of wealth. We know of peoples in the South Pacific for whom cowrie shells were the measure and peoples in West Africa who used iron bars and others who used cloth and many people simply traded goods for goods in a system called "barter." But what they used is not the point. It is their attitude toward material that is the worldview issue.

For some people, the possession of material wealth means that it is to be displayed. For others, it is to be hidden. In times past, there were even people living in the Pacific Northwest of the United States who sought to gain significance in their societies by destroying their wealth. For the ancient Hebrews, those who had wealth were assumed to be favored by God while poverty was a sign of a negative attitude on God's part. Such a view is not uncommon today.

In the U.S. it is homes, cars, electronic equipment and a myriad of other material things that are looked at as signifying wealth. Other peoples have measured their wealth in cattle, size of family, size of farm or in other ways that may or may not have to do with material possessions.

Proxemics

One of the more interesting areas of spatial assumptions is the study of proxemics. Hall's definition is "the interrelated observations and theories of man's use of space as a specialized elaboration of culture" (1969:1). Though there are many aspects to Hall's treatment of proxemics, the one I want to focus on here is the way we organize space as we relate to others.

Hall finds that there are four main distances between people as we interact with one another (1969:113-29). He calls them "intimate, personal, social and public." Hall's basic description of these distances is for Anglo-Americans. I will start there and make comments concerning contrasting uses of space.

Intimate Space "is the distance of love-making and wrestling, comforting and protecting." In this use of space, Anglo-Americans are in bodily contact in what he calls the "close phase," and from 6 to 18 inches apart in the "far phase." When people other than one's spouse or girl or boyfriend get within this space, one gets very uncomfortable, as when a Latin American interacts with an Anglo-American using his preferred personal space distance of 12 inches. Using intimate distance in public is socially disapproved but is required in subways, busses and elevators.

> The use of intimate distance in public is not considered proper by adult, middle-class Americans even though their young may be observed intimately involved with each other in automobiles and on beaches. Crowded subways and buses may bring strangers into what would ordinarily be classed as intimate spatial relations, but subway riders have defensive devices which take the real intimacy out of intimate space in public conveyances. The basic tactic is to be

as immobile as possible and, when part of the trunk or extremities touches another person, withdraw if possible. ... In elevators the hands are kept at the side or used to steady the body by grasping a railing. The eyes are fixed on infinity and are not brought to bear on anyone for more than a passing glance (1969:118).

Personal Distance is the second of Hall's categories. The close phase of this category is for Anglo-Americans 18 to 24 inches and the far phase two and a half to four feet. This is the distance of casual conversation, allowing for a spouse, but not someone else's spouse, to be within the close range but for a more formal interaction to be held at the far phase. Some of the greatest culture shocks for Anglo-Americans come when people of another society "invade" our personal space by getting inside of our 18-inch "capsule." Indeed, in another place Hall refers to a conversation he once observed between a Latin American and an Anglo-American that started out at one end of a hallway and ended at the other end as the Latin continually "closed in" to about 12 inches (his comfortable personal distance) on the Anglo-American who kept stepping back to his comfortable 18 inches. All the while, then, the Latin interpreted the North American as "standoffish" and the North American interpreted the Latin as "pushy."

Social Distance is the distance outside what someone has called the "limit of domination." The close phase of social distance runs from four to seven feet and the far phase from seven to twelve feet. Hall says,

> Impersonal business occurs at this distance, and in the close phase there is more involvement than in the distant phase. People who work together tend to use close social distance. It is also a very common distance for people who are attending a casual social gathering. To stand back and look down at a person at this distance has a domineering effect, as when a man talks to his secretary or receptionist. ...

Business and social discourse conducted at the far end of social distance has a more formal character than if it occurs inside the close phase. Desks in the offices of important people are large enough to hold visitors at the far phase of social distance. Even in an office with standard-size desks, the chair opposite is eight or nine feet away from the man behind the desk (1969:121-2).

Public Distance is the distance of public speaking. The close phase is 12 to 25 feet and the far phase more than 25 feet. Relationships at this distance are quite formal and impersonal and when we get beyond 30 feet the voice (without amplification) loses the ability to convey subtle shades unless exaggerated as actors learn to do. Subtleties of facial expression and movement are also lost.

When the use of space involves people of the opposite sex, things can become annoying or even embarrassing. When, for example, a woman who is only a casual acquaintance stands in the man's personal or, worse yet, intimate space, the man can be embarrassed and/or turned on sexually. In many societies, the fact that the people have divided themselves up into what I'll call "men's community" and "women's community" means that they will seldom, if ever, occupy the same territory, whether in the home or at play or moving from place to place or in public meetings. In northeastern Nigeria, for example, the women's huts are pretty much out of bounds for men, and when they dance, it is men with men and women with women, when they walk, say, to market, it is men walking with men and women with women and in church, the men sit on one side, the women on the other.

Concepts of privacy are closely related to concepts of territoriality. In America, we feel free to "take" privacy whenever we need it. We go into our homes, into our rooms, into bathrooms and take privacy by closing the door. In many societies, however, privacy is not so much something someone "takes" as something others "give" or grant to a person. On several occasions, walking with a friend along a Nigerian path, the person I was with stopped and motioned me to stop. After awhile, another man would join us and my friend would feign surprise that that person had appeared. What had happened is that my friend saw the other man relieving himself in the bush, waited for him to finish (granting him his privacy) and then acted surprised as that man joined us on the path, as if my friend hadn't seen him until that moment.

Many westerners living in tribal areas just can't get used to the fact that "their" people think nothing of staring in their windows or even walking into their house without knocking, calling or in any way obtaining permission. While visiting in a rural area of Papua New Guinea once, I was intrigued to find that the missionaries had built their home with a kind of viewing platform along one side of it to accommodate the "starers" who frequently came by to observe the missionaries' strange customs. The viewing platform was along the side of the house where the kitchen and dining area were. The back of the house where the bathroom and sleeping rooms were was quite effectively blocked off to allow no viewing.

Spiritual Power Through Objects

One final space/material world consideration is that spiritual power is often conveyed through material objects. It is the custom with many of the world's peoples to dedicate work implements and religious objects to their spirits or gods as they are made. Thus, South Pacific peoples regularly dedicated canoes as they were made. Likewise, in many societies with cooking utensils and other household items and axes and other work implements. Amulets and fetishes, often worn by people are routinely dedicated to spirits. Many missionaries, anthropologists and travelers have purchased such items, taken them home and experienced various kinds of spirit-induced hardships in their lives. Often, however, they had no idea that the reason was that they had invited evil spirits to live in their homes with them. Those of us who are savvy to such things usually simply claim the power of Jesus Christ over most objects to break enemy power and have no difficulty, though I recommend destroying objects that have no other purpose than to serve enemy spirits.

The use of oil that has been blessed (Jas 5:14) and healing through the use of personal objects like Paul's handkerchiefs (Acts 19:12) and Jesus' garment (Matt. 9:20) are scriptural examples of the use of material objects to convey spiritual power. Objects, buildings and even geographical areas can be invested either with God's power or with that of the enemy through blessing and cursing. Throughout the Old Testament, we see the understanding that various territories belong to various gods. This fact is recognized in Dan. 10:13, 20-21 where high-level demonic beings are named for the territory they control: "prince of Persia" and "prince of Greece." To minister effectively in areas in which humans have given control to demons, therefore, the power of the evil spirit in charge must be broken. See Kraft 1997, 2000, 2005 for more on space and spiritual power.

Though there is much more that could be said about space or time, we will leave the discussion here and move on to other things.

Chapter 11

Worldview Orientations & Types

We move now from a discussion of worldview universals to a discussion of worldview orientations and types. What I mean by "orientations," as will be clarified below, is the predisposition of a people to one or another set of assumptions within a given universal. We will note below that certain people groups gravitate toward a group orientation rather than an individualistic orientation, or a supernaturalistic focus rather than a naturalistic focus.

With this discussion as a backdrop, then, we will turn to a discussion of three "types" of worldview on the basis of their handling of causality. So we will deal with orientations and types in relation to the universals we have just been discussing before, in chapter 12, we turn to the specifics of various worldviews.

Worldview Orientations

There are certain competing orientations toward life that all peoples seem to have to choose between. Among them are choices between an individualistic orientation and a group orientation, that we may call "groupism," between naturalism and supernaturalism, between an absolutistic attitude versus a pluralistic attitude toward cultural differences. We can plot each of these competing orientations or focuses on the scale below and estimate the place of any given society between the options.

Note, however, that these various competing orientations fall into different universals. If we were to classify a society according to whether it was more individualistic or more groupistic, we would be classifying them in terms of their focus in the Person/Group universal. If, though, we classified the same society according to whether it was more naturalistic or supernaturalistic, we would be classifying them in terms of their focus in the Causality universal. Four of the universals (P/G, Causality, Time, Space) would seem to be amenable to such classification of focus. We exclude Categorization and Relationship since these universals apply to every one of the orientations any group would choose to focus on.

It would be nice to be able to produce a comprehensive listing of all of the possible orientations abroad in the world today that occur in the views of Reality. Failing this, we settle for a few scales such as those pictured below on which we may plot the predominant tendencies of any given society in each area and to estimate a people's level of concern for each. It appears as though the nature of life itself requires all societies to choose their orientation with regard to certain types of assumptions and values. Plotting their choices like this should help us to be clearer concerning what we mean whenever we use terms like "supernaturalistic," or "individualistic" as we go along.

Note the suggested scale from 3 at one end through B (for Balanced) to 3 at the other end. The way we could label a people, then, might be I-2, for a group that is fairly individualistic, S-3 for a group that is highly supernaturalistic. I have included a couple of subcategories in the chart below (e.g., Dependency-Independency). More such subcategories could be added. Some of them are discussed below.

PERSON / GROUP UNIVERSAL		
GROUPISM	←3-----2-----1-----B-----1-----2-----3→	INDIVIDUALISM
DEPENDENCY	←3-----2-----1-----B-----1-----2-----3→	INDEPENDENCY
SECURITY	←3-----2-----1-----B-----1-----2-----3→	FREEDOM
CAUSALITY UNIVERSAL		
SUPERNATURALISM	←3-----2-----1-----B-----1-----2-----3→	NATURALISM
PERSONALISTIC	←3-----2-----1-----B-----1-----2-----3→	MECHANISTIC
SPACE / MATERIAL UNIVERSAL		
ANTIMATERIALISM	←3-----2-----1-----B-----1-----2-----3→	MATERIALISM
MATERIAL AN ILLUSION	←3-----2-----1-----B-----1-----2-----3→	MATERIAL REAL
WEALTH RELATIONAL	←3-----2-----1-----B-----1-----2-----3→	WEALTH MATERIAL
TIME / EVENT UNIVERSAL		
EVENT-ORIENTED	←3-----2-----1-----B-----1-----2-----3→	TIME-ORIENTED
CONTEXTUAL LOGIC	←3-----2-----1-----B-----1-----2-----3→	LINEAR LOGIC
HISTORY AS MYTH	←3-----2-----1-----B-----1-----2-----3→	HISTORY AS FACT

Figure 11.1. Scales of Cultural Orientations [B = Balanced]

A chart such as this can alert us to a couple of general things that we will factor in at various points below. One is that characteristics of a people such as Dependency and a Security orientation tend to go with Groupism. Likewise, a Mechanistic view of Causality tends to go with Naturalism. A second thing to notice is that societies that are group-oriented tend to be supernaturalistic and event-oriented, as well, with many of the societies of India adding an antimaterialism perspective. Most of the societies outside of India, however, would plot at the Material Real end of the Space/Material World scale, though they would share with Indian societies the groupism, supernaturalism and event-orientation.

Person / Group Criteria

To briefly indicate what we mean by these terms, the *groupism-individualism* scale is meant to plot whether a society is relatively more prone to favor the desires and concerns of individuals over those of the society as a whole or vice-versa. An individualistic society will give individuals a great deal more latitude for freedom of action than a "groupistic" society while the latter will regularly choose to honor what they deem to be the good of the group over that of the individual in any conflict of interest between the two. Anglo-American society scores well over toward the individualism end, say about an I-2 or 3, while any number of small-scale tribal societies would score G-2 or 3.

Going along with individualism-groupism will often be what may be called an (a?) *dependency-independency* scale. This is the degree to which a society chooses to condition its members to assert independence from or dependence on their significant others (such as family members) when they are adults. As we have already indicated, American society trains its members to function as much as possible independently of others, even of family, while Japanese society tends toward the dependency extreme, at least within the family. Again, Anglo-Americans would score I-2 to 3 and Japanese D-2 to 3 within the family with, perhaps a less dependent D-1 in many other aspects of life.

A *security-freedom* scale, then, could be added to measure whether the institutions of a society (such as family, government) are designed to provide as much freedom as possible or as much security as possible for their members. An important American worldview value concerning women, for example, could be stated as, "women are so valuable that they must be as free as possible." The corresponding assumption in many other societies is, however, that "women are so valuable that they must be as secure as possible." Many of the marriage and family customs of traditional societies spin off from such a value. Among them are brideprice, arranged marriage, assured marriage, even if in a polygamous relationship, and customs designed to protect wives and children.

The choices made by different societies in the independency-dependency area and the freedom-security area may closely relate to the choices they make in the individualism-groupism area, or they may be at least partly independent. That is, probably most societies that are highly individualistic are also highly oriented toward individual independence and freedom. There are, however, societies that provide high levels of security with accompanying high levels of independency (e.g., Papua New Guinea) and those that expect their members to use their independency to conform to the group they choose to belong to (e.g., American youth).

The terms *publicism* and *privatism* can be used, and a scale constructed, to include such concepts as the assumption that land can be owned privately (as opposed to being held by family, clan or larger social entity). It could also include the value, strongly held by Anglo-American society, that there is an area of life called "personal" (usually including such things as religion, sexual activity, family, salary and even age) that is very private. In many societies (e.g., many African), each of these areas of what are private to Anglo-Americans are well known to nearly everyone who has much contact with a person. As mentioned in chapter 10, privacy in such societies is something given to a person by others, not something demanded by the person her/himself.

Another scale labeled *absolutistic-pluralistic* might be constructed to measure a society's tolerance for sociocultural diversity. There are many societies whose ethnocentrism leads them to assume that their ways are absolutely superior. There are, of course, others (e.g., Indian societies, many American anthropologists) that go completely to the relativistic extreme in which all views are accorded equal validity (at least in theory).

Causality Criteria

The *supernaturalism-naturalism* scale is designed to indicate a society's orientation with respect to belief in and activity toward an unseen spirit world. Those societies that assume the activity of spirits in nearly every human event plot close to the extreme left of the chart. Those, like secular American, that assume a naturalistic (i.e., non-supernatural) cause for everything plot to the right, perhaps as far as N-2 for most people, N-3 for some. Those that assume a balance between naturalistic (including both human and material world) cause and supernatural cause would plot near the middle, at B.

The *personalistic-mechanistic* scale is designed to plot where a society fits with regard to the predominant analogy concerning the way the universe is made up and expected to function. Euro-Americans tend to see the universe more like a machine than like a person. Within the universe, then, organizations are expected to operate according to "machine principles" such as efficiency and simplicity. People within organizations are seen simply as part of the machinery, to be hired and fired according to how well they function within that machine. Even the human body is seen as a machine, with parts that sometimes need repair and replacement. For much of the world, however, the universe and its contents are seen as more like persons than like machines, often with something like a will of its own, capricious and unpredictable, like people.

Space / Material World Criteria

The *antimaterialism-materialism* scale can be used to label both the attitude toward material and the material world of dedicated Christians and the rather extreme view of Indian *maya*—seeing material as an illusion. Both groups would plot to the left end of the scale, though western Christians, even with heroic attempts to reject materialistic values, would probably never come close to Indians in denying the reality of the material world. Philosophic Indians would plot far to the left on the subscale *material as illusion-material as real* in contrast to the views of most of the rest of the world, even those as supernaturalistically-oriented as Indians.

Most of the societies and subsocieties of Euro-America would, of course, score high on Materialism and those within Euro-America who plot toward the antimaterialistic end of the scale would have quite a different kind of antimaterialism than that found in India. And many non-western societies are very materialistic (even though supernaturalistic) in the sense that they see material prosperity as the reward of spiritual beings for their faithfulness.

With regard to the definition of wealth, for westerners wealth is measured by the material goods a person possesses. In many societies, however, it is the person with a large family who is considered wealthy. A grandfather, perhaps with several wives, surrounded by many children and many grandchildren, for example, is considered the wealthiest person in town. Such a society would plot way to the left on the scale dealing with whether wealth is relational or material—just the opposite of the way a western society would plot.

Time / Event Criteria

We speak of "time-oriented" and "event-oriented" societies. The reference, as we have mentioned earlier, is to peoples who place a high value on schedules oriented to time categories and those who orient themselves more to personal relationships and/or the quality of what happens during a given period of time (history/myth). We also mentioned the connection between linear logic and time-oriented thinking, paralleled by the fact that people who are event-oriented tend more to reasoning contextually.

As noted above, some societies would plot pretty far to one side or the other of the chart on every issue. Contemporary Anglo-American society, for example, would plot much toward the right end of each of the scales, while traditional African societies would tend to be toward the left in every area except perhaps materialism. This would mean that we Anglo-Americans tend to be very individualistic, independent, freedom-oriented, naturalistic, materialistic and mechanistic in our view of the universe. Typical traditional Africans, on the other hand, would tend to be "groupistic," dependent, supernaturalistic, moderately materialistic though with a supernaturalistic interpretation behind their assumptions concerning material prosperity, and personalistic in their view of the universe.

Though all such plotting on scales like these would be quite inadequate and oversimplified as a means of dealing with the specifics of any society, such typing might be helpful in indicating certain rather prominent contrasts. It enables us, further, to show movement in a given direction over a period of time. The younger generations of many non-western societies, for example, that were traditionally toward the left extreme in most of the areas labeled, are now moving rather rapidly toward the right under the influences of westernization.

Three Worldview Types

With the above attempt to point to worldview orientations, we are equipped to develop a typology of worldviews. There are several ways to do this. One would be to attempt to divide worldview types into two categories, using any of the dichotomies listed above. Thus, we could divide peoples on the basis of their predominant Person/Group orientation into group-oriented societies and individualistic societies. Or we could choose to classify societies on the basis of their Causality orientation into supernaturalistic societies or naturalistic societies. Or we could focus on the attitude of societies toward the material world and classify them as antimaterialistic societies or materialistic societies. Or we could divide people on the basis of their Time orientation into event-oriented societies and time-oriented societies. Each of these approaches would give us a fairly clear picture of groups at the extremes of our dichotomies.

Or we could attempt to develop types of societies by grouping, say, those societies showing all of the characteristics on the left of the chart in contrast to all those characterized by focusing on the criteria on the right side of the chart.

Or other criteria might have been selected such as, kinship structure, or economic or political philosophies. If social organization were chosen, our typology would divide peoples into such groupings as kinship, peasant, industrial and post-industrial (see Shaw 1988). These groupings would also work well if economics is our focus. A political focus, then, would divide people into various kinds of democratic philosophies, totalitarian philosophies and perhaps several other types of political worldview assumptions (see Smart 1983).

Classifying According to Causality

I have decided to choose the Causality dimension but to divide the material into three, rather than two, categories. I have chosen spiritual causality as the focal issue because I believe this is the most basic worldview concern of the majority of the world's peoples. Around causality, then, swirl the other worldview concerns plus all of surface level culture. I will contend, therefore, that, though religious terms are often used to identify the various approaches to spiritual causality, we are not simply dealing with religion. For a people's concern for causality is basic not only to a people's religion but to the whole of a people's life, pervading the thinking and, therefore, the total cultural behavior of a people.

The fact that spiritual causality is so basic to many of the peoples of the world leads a large percentage of those who discuss world cultures and worldviews to consider religion to be the "core" of human culture. For this concern of non-western peoples for what causes the circumstances of life is often most obvious in what secular westerners label their religious theories and practices. I contend, however, that a concern for cause is much more than a religious subject since this concern springs up in politics, economics, family and every other facet of a people's life. It is thus a worldview matter, not simply a religious matter. The difference, as we have seen, between a worldview theme and a religious value is the fact that the former plays out through the whole culture. A religious value (e.g., church on Sunday, a special type of music in church or synagogue), however, is limited to a single dimension of surface-level culture— religion. I am contending that causality thinking pervades the total life, not merely the religious behavior, of every people.

To attempt to lump all (or most) of the worldviews in the world into three types puts us in great danger of oversimplification. It does, however, make our subject more manageable. And it turns our attention to the facet of worldview that we as Christians are most interested in—how peoples conceive of and relate to supernatural beings and power.

I will call the three worldview types, Theistic Causality, Animistic Causality and Naturalistic Causality. Each of these types, then, has several subtypes. The following chart shows some of the subtypes.

THEISTIC CAUSALITY	ANIMISTIC CAUSALITY	NATURALISTIC CAUSALITY
CHARACTERISTICS: A High God who is active in the human context The primary attention of humans should be directed toward God. In the biblical version, spirits are active but subservient.	CHARACTERISTICS: There may or may not be a High God, but he is relatively inactive in the human context. Spirits/deities are very active and the primary attention of humans is directed toward them)	CHARACTERISTICS: Supernatural beings and power are largely non-issues or denied. Atheistic/ Agnostic. Assume this is the only world there is or, at least, that we should concern ourselves with.
EXAMPLES: Judaism (book) Islam (book) Christianity (book) [Deism] [Secular Theism (including much of evangelical Christianity)] Theistic Existentialism Biblical	EXAMPLES: Hinduism Folk Faiths (including most traditional peoples, Muslims and Buddhists, plus many Jews & Christians) Shinto Eastern Mysticism New Age	EXAMPLES: Buddhism (book) Confucianism Secular Humanism [Secular Theism (including much of evangelical Christianity)] [Deism] Materialism/Communism Atheistic Existentialism Nihilism

Figure 11.2. Three Worldview Causality Types

I place under the **Theism** category any group that gives major attention to a High God as ultimate cause and authority. This is a supernaturalistic perspective, holding that God has created the world and all that is in it and is actively involved with His creation. The biblical version of this perspective recognizes the reality of the spirit-world, with the spirits subservient to the High God, though actively involved with humans.

Note that there are "book" or official varieties of the theistic versions of Judaism, Islam and Christianity. However, most of the adherents of these perspectives fall into the animism category. Likewise, with Buddhism, it is officially atheistic but with most of its adherents animistic. Deism and Secular Theism are special cases, officially theistic but with adherents ranging from those who at least nod in the direction of God to those who are rather thoroughgoing secularists. These varieties will be discussed more fully below as we describe the three types in more detail.

Christians, Jews or Muslims live among people with Animistic or Naturalistic worldviews and are often strongly influenced by such assumptions. Their worldviews, then, vary from fairly pure Theism (orthodox) to quite syncretistic Animism or Naturalism. Many of their worldview assumptions will be the same as those of the people around them, except for those assumptions that flow from their concepts of the relationship of God to the beings and elements of the universe.

Under *Animism*, then, I place any group for whom the spirit world is the primary focus of their concern for causation, whether or not they also believe in a high god. This perspective, though it may hold that there is a High God, with or without His being Creator, sees this god is uninvolved with humans. Characteristic of this perspective is belief in a multitude of gods and/or spirits that are the active supernaturals in the universe, constantly interacting with humans and other parts of the creation. Many of these gods/spirits are seen as malevolent and in need of constant attention through rituals believed to prevent them from harming people or to stop them from continuing to interfere in human life. Person/Group assumptions of this group are usually well toward the Groupism end of the spectrum; though they may be Materialistic, it is usually a supernaturally-oriented materialism; concepts of Time are usually at the Event end of the spectrum. By far the majority of the world's peoples hold to this type of worldview.

Under *Naturalism* I place any group for whom supernatural beings and power are largely non-issues or denied. Such worldviews are either atheistic or agnostic concerning the existence of supernatural beings. They predicate that this is the only world there is or, at least, that we should concern ourselves with. They may or may not show concern for where we came from and where we're going. If they do, paradigms such as biological evolution and reincarnation may be in vogue.

I have opted for the term "Naturalistic," rather than such terms as "secularistic" or "materialistic" or "humanistic" (which I treat as subcategories) in order to highlight the fact that each of the varieties under that label focus on "natural" as opposed to supernatural causation. Natural causation, then, is that of natural laws, including, from their point of view, naturalistic evolution, plus the causation of humans governed by human nature with little or no reference to or belief in supernatural beings and power. It seems to be enough for Euro-Americans (including the Nacirema discussed in chapter 12) to accept explanations based on cause and effect, evolution, a universe that works like a machine and an unconcern for how things came into existence or what (Who) keeps them running.

Categorizing worldviews according to these criteria places large numbers of westerners (including most who call themselves Christians) and Chinese in the Naturalism category. Most of the tribal peoples of the world, then, along with those involved in folk varieties of Islam, Judaism and Christianity fit into the Animism category with pockets of people in most societies who espouse orthodox Christianity, Judaism and Islam fitting into the Theism category. In chapter 12, The Nacirema (Americans) are of the Naturalism type, while the Egyptian Muslims are Theistic and the Middle Wahgi and Kamwe are Animistic.

One further preliminary comment relates to the fact that in the modern world there is a good bit of inter-influencing of perspectives going on. This is apparent in the fact that Eastern Mysticism and New Age varieties of animism occur in populations known for secular humanism, such as in the United States. Christian or Muslim theistic assumptions, then, easily get mixed with animistic ones in places like Africa, Latin America and elsewhere. And many westerners who would strongly contend that they fit into the biblical theistic category really live according to secular theistic or even secular humanistic worldview assumptions in almost every area of their lives.

Animism

Animism is by far the majority causality perspective across the world. Under this rubric we include Hinduism and Shinto, approaches to life embraced by large numbers of people in India and Japan. These understandings of causality are animistic to the core. What we term folk religions, then, are the traditional understandings of the majority of tribal peoples around the world plus those of the vast majority of the people who claim to base their lives on the monotheistic perspectives of Islam, Judaism and Christianity. In addition, varieties of Indian and Asian animism, especially in the various forms of expression known as New Age also fit into animism. These perspectives have made significant inroads into western nations traditionally committed to naturalistic secularism.

To animists the universe is populated by spirits, many of which are dangerous and must be kept happy if human life is to go on with a minimum of hindrance. Appeasing the dangerous spirits is, therefore, a primary concern of animists. There often is a creator God or gods in animistic systems, but he/she/they is/are reckoned to be good and, therefore, not dangerous. It is the dangerous ones that need to be dealt with. Sacrifices and rituals of various kinds are, therefore, devised to ward off the spirits and/or to keep them happy. In addition, it is believed that at least certain persons can manipulate certain spirits to gain blessing or to curse enemies.

The western distinction between "natural" and "supernatural" is irrelevant to animists, since for them what westerners call "supernatural" beings and powers are a part of the natural world. The spirits are all around, in trees, rocks, rivers, mountains, the sea, in and outside of their homes, showing anger in storms, infertility, droughts and famine but at other times, demonstrating their pleasure by making things go well.

Intense interaction between humans and spirits is assumed, as is the ability of at least certain humans to manipulate and to some extent to control the spirits. Shamans and diviners often make a handsome living, therefore, as animists appeal to them for insight into the activities of the spirits. Witches and sorcerers, then, learn how to use spirit power to get revenge for their clients against those who have hurt them.

Ancestral spirits are often a part of an animistic system, as are a belief in reincarnation and a tendency toward fatalism. Hinduism, for example, the world's most prominent animistic system, is strong on reincarnation and the fatalistic concept of *karma*. Many of the traditional belief systems of smaller African societies, however, also include reincarnation, fatalism and a strong concern for the activity of ancestors in influencing the lives of the living.

Animists feel a strong connection between themselves and what we call the "natural" world. Totemic ideas are common about the close connection between a given animal or plant and a given people. Often it is believed that the animal or plant was the root from which the people sprang. Harmony with nature is often a high value, even to the extent that it is/was the custom in some societies for hunters to apologize to any animal they kill(ed).

For animists, the issue is spiritual power—how to keep bad spirits from hurting them, how to enlist good or even bad spirits to help them. Rituals are developed, therefore, to assure such things as protection, fertility, healing, good relationships, wealth, good grades, happy marriages and all the other good things of life. There are also rituals (often divination and/or magic) to discover who has hurt someone and to take revenge on that person. Seeking blessing and avoiding cursing are big items for animists.

The Shona of Zimbabwe can serve as an example of an animistic society.[3] They have a creator god that is distant and non-concerned with the everyday workings of the people. If this creator god does become involved,

---

3   My thanks for this material to Dr. Steven M. Whitmer, a missionary to Zimbabwe who was working on his Ph.D. at Fuller Seminary as I was writing an earlier version of this book. He has now completed his degree and is teaching at Hope International University in Southern California.

it is because of extremes in social disobedience. He is likely to punish the tribe or family involved by sending drought, plague, or perhaps a series of coordinated lion attacks. Even in such events, however, it is usually to the spirit world that people direct their attention to solve the problem. For this purpose, there are a number of patterns of interaction with different classes of spirits. There are special spirits that look after environmental concerns. Family matters, on the other hand, are normally handled by ancestral spirits.

Subthemes and paradigms of causation are typified by assumptions like: Death is never natural but caused by some personal, family, or clan transgression; drought is caused by offense to the "sky" spirit; or if the ancestors are not consulted before the bride is selected, she will be barren. In this kind of society, hundreds of such supernaturalistic subthemes and paradigms combine to affect every aspect of life and culture.

It is interesting to note that animistic thinking is amazingly similar the world over, especially the assumption that the High God is favorable to us but that the spirits can harm us, therefore we should do whatever we can to appease them. The fact that people in widely diverse locations share such an assumption suggests to me that there is a single mastermind, Satan, behind animism, and that he has found a single way of reasoning to appeal to most of the people of the world. It will be good to keep this in mind as we discuss a Christian approach to animistic peoples. I would suggest that we also note that there is much truth in animistic thinking. Satan is a deceiver, true. But deception is not the same as lying. A deceiver makes clever use of truth, mixing it with lies, to suck people into his schemes.

Animism provides the backdrop for the whole Old Testament and much of the New. The peoples whom God instructed Israel to wipe out were all animists who had given themselves over to the kinds of perversions alluded to in Rom. 1 and 2. These peoples had had their chance to turn to God but had consistently refused and so their time of judgment came as Israel took over the Promised Land. Israel, however, was also full of animistic tendencies. These worldview assumptions showed themselves every time they entered the territory of a given god and felt they had to be polite to that god, giving deference, even worship to that god. The logic is this, when you enter the territory governed by a given god or spirit, you need to show deference to that god or spirit by sacrificing to it to keep it from harming you. And if you don't know quite how to keep given spirits happy, you need to have experts, specialists or priests of these gods, to enable you to keep from offending them.

An interesting example of this belief is recorded in 2 Kings 17:24-41. In this passage we are told of a problem that developed for the new Assyrian settlers who had been relocated by their emperor in the cities of the former Northern Kingdom of Israel, known as Samaria. The Assyrians had carried off many of the Israelites and resettled them in Assyria. In exchange, they resettled many Assyrians in Israel. But these settlers were attacked by lions and some of them were killed (v 25). To explain this problem, the Assyrians concluded that "the people [that the emperor] had settled in the cities of Samaria did not know the law of the god of that land, and so the god had sent lions, which were killing them" (v 26). With this understanding, a typical animistic strategy was developed. The emperor commanded that one of the Israelite priests who had been taken to Assyria should be sent back to Israel (Samaria) to "teach the people the law of the god of that land" (v 27). "So an Israelite priest who had been deported from Samaria went and lived in Bethel, where he taught the people how to worship the Lord" (v 28). And the strategy apparently worked.

Unfortunately, there is enough truth in animistic understandings that many people get confused. There are, for example, territorial spirits working under Satan, ruling over every part of the earth not specifically occupied by God's people. These spirits, then, are able to deceive people who sacrifice to them by treating them well for a time. The greater truth that God seeks to get across to His people is, however, that if we put Him and His Kingdom first, He will take care of the evil spirits assigned to harm us.

In summary, we can chart a number of the features of animism as follows:

CHARACTERISTICS	ANIMISTIC CAUSALITY
Ultimate Cause	Spirits/gods (God, perhaps there but ignored)
Approach	Appease spirits/gods Manipulate spirits thru magic, ritual
Primary concern of people	Spiritual power to handle life's vagaries
Strategies to meet that concern	Magic, ritual (e.g., divination)
Specialists	Shamans, priests
Technique for finding answers	Try to discover secrets through divination

Figure 11.3. Characteristics of Animistic Causality

Naturalism

The second of our categories is Naturalism. If there is a God, this view holds, He is more or less irrelevant and can be ignored. Atheists, of course, deny the existence of God, at least until they find themselves in a crisis. Secular theists such as liberal Christians and many who would call themselves conservative Christians, live largely ignoring God, as if comfort and material things are the essence of life. They would not say that God doesn't exist but would act like it, as if there is no one who holds us accountable. Secular theism with a nod toward God pervades both liberal and conservative churches with a form of godliness that for all practical purposes denies His presence and power (2 Tim. 3:5).

Secular humanism is focused squarely on human activity and accomplishment. Science is the "religion" of humanism and scientists are its priests. From this point of view, human beings are the measure of all things, values are relative (in theory, though often not in practice), religion is okay if it fills some need for you, it's good to get as much "education" as you can get and to make as much money as possible so you and your family can be comfortable and to accomplish as much as you can in life since "we only go around once."

Naturalism in general holds that we are here by chance due to "natural" processes (e.g., evolution) with only the barest minimum of moral guidelines (e.g., don't hurt anyone else if you can help it, love everyone, be tolerant) and these without any real foundation. Nearly everything is relative, especially religion, but most anything that feels good is okay to do as long as it doesn't hurt anyone else. But tolerance is absolutized.

Secular humanism holds that we should focus on those things that are "good" for people (according to some rootless definition of "good"). At the other end of naturalistic thinking, however, is nihilism that despairs of anything worthy of the label "good" in human life. In between is materialism, advocating that "Whoever has the most toys, wins." Keep up with the neighbors in housing, cars, boats, and vacations. Earn as big a salary as possible because "we deserve to be happy, we deserve comfort, we deserve health, we deserve love."

Book Buddhism, then, is focused squarely on human attitudes and activity and concerned with balance. Life is made up of the "yin" and the "yang." These elements "are diametrically opposed in character, and yet are equally essential for the existence of the universe. Associated with yang are the positive elements, such as heaven, light, heat, masculinity, life, and strength. Yin includes the opposite elements: earth, darkness, cold, femininity, death, and weakness" (Burnett 1992:92). One is to work to gain merit which, if enough, enables one to escape the misery of human life into "nirvana," nothingness.

Secularism is tolerant of just about everything except views that hold that there are absolutes, especially in the name of God or Christianity. It asks, "How do we know that one position is any better than any other?" And if none is better, then let's tolerate every idea, every commitment except those who claim that someone is wrong. Intolerance, then, is seen as hate and love is defined as letting anyone do anything as long as it doesn't hurt someone else. There is no devil, no absolute rules, no God, so "watch out for those intolerant (usually conservative Christian) people who think they know better than others and, therefore, want to cram their ideas down other people's throats."

The roots of secular humanism lie in human beings being impressed with what humans can do. While once those who invented things exclaimed, "What has God wrought?" the focus of naturalism is on what humans have invented, discovered, manufactured and devised. We have conquered many diseases, sent people into space (and gotten them back), made devices to enable us to travel far and fast, sent voice and pictures over vast distances, simplified nearly every menial task and increased knowledge to a dizzying degree. And have bought the Greek lie that the problem with humans is ignorance, therefore increase knowledge. So we push knowledge and secularism and tolerance in our schools and in the process destroy our families and give the impression that knowledge and freedom from restrictions are what life is all about.

This is a comparatively modern worldview in many ways. Yet, in its glorification of humanity it perpetuates the fallacy that Satan first foisted on Adam and Eve—that with a certain amount of knowledge, we will be like God. And in its disregard of moral absolutes, this view buys into the hedonism that preceded the fall of Rome and many other kingdoms.

In summary, we can chart a number of the features of naturalism as follows:

CHARACTERISTICS	NATURALISTIC CAUSALITY
Ultimate Cause	Chance Evolution Human beings
Approach	Human effort
Primary concern of people	Ability to handle life's vagaries through science
Strategies to meet that concern	Gain knowledge, for knowledge is power Science gives power over nature

Specialists	Scientists Engineers Politicians
Technique for finding answers	Schooling

Figure 11.4. Characteristics of Naturalistic Causality

Theism

As mentioned, the focal point of theism is the importance of God and the relationship of humans to Him. In Orthodox Judaism, Islam, Christianity and biblical theism, there is a belief in spirits, but God is in control and human effort is to be expended primarily in relating to Him, not in relating to the lesser spirits. God is seen as interested in humans who He created and governs. Humans, then, are to obey Him, pray to Him and witness for Him.

But orthodoxy is not the only kind of theism. As mentioned above, there are "secular theists." They assume that God is there. But their lives are basically the same as those we call naturalists or secularists except that secular theists go to church, synagogue or mosque and may be quite serious in their quest to learn about God, theology and other aspects of their faith. These folks have a commitment to their God and to their cultural or subcultural ways of expressing that commitment and often can articulate that commitment very well. Their focus is, however, largely a matter of "knowledge about" rather than relationship with their God. And *a knowledge focus secularizes*.

Unfortunately, much of what is done in evangelical Christian churches, Bible schools and seminaries falls into this category since the stock in trade is largely the passing on of knowledge about the commitment rather than an enhancing of that commitment. And life as it is lived is pretty much the same as that of those who devote their time to understanding other subject matter. In Christian secular theism, the spirit world and Jesus' emphasis on spiritual warfare is largely ignored, leaving people spiritually crippled with nothing except self to serve in their partnership with Jesus. Since scriptural prayer is a partnership in warfare, a lack of involvement with Jesus in fighting enemy forces results in largely emasculated prayer. All that is left is secular, knowledge-oriented Christianity.

Theism of whatever variety postulates absolutes, though secular theism and deism may ignore or downplay them. Deism sees God as the cosmic clock maker who created the world, wound it up and has left it and us to do our best until the clockworks wear out. Though He started things, now we are pretty much on our own. Theistic secularism, without meaning to, often amounts to about the same thing. God is there and we can pray to Him, but don't expect much because He basically ignores us. Whether in its Calvinistic variety where God does whatever He wants to do and most everything is predetermined, or in more Wesleyan varieties where we have to strive to perfect ourselves in hopes that God will notice us, or in theistic existentialism, God is far off and not much concerned.

Biblical Christianity, of course, has God close, positive toward us and involved in our everyday life. He seeks to work in partnership with us, His choice creatures, with us obeying Him and He loving, guiding and empowering us to work with Him to accomplish His purposes here on earth. The only kind of Christianity in the scriptures is charismatic Christianity, with people "flowing" in the gifts of the Holy Spirit, signs and wonders occurring regularly, people being brought to Christ, healed, freed from demons and growing in their relationship with Jesus and with each other.

In biblical Christianity, we are both to pray to Him and to work with Him to make His Kingdom come, His will be done on earth as it is in heaven (Matt. 6:10). For this to happen, He enlists us in His army to fight the enemy from a base of close relationship, righteousness, truth, peace and faith(fulness) (Eph 6:13-18), empowered by Him to wield the sword of the Spirit according to His guidance.

In summary, we can chart a number of the features of theism as follows:

CHARACTERISTICS	THEISTIC CAUSALITY
Ultimate Cause	God
Approach	Worship, ritual
Primary concern of people	Ability to handle life's vagaries Afterlife
Strategy for meeting that concern	Obeying God Relationship with God
Specialists	Priests, prophets, pastors
Techniques for finding answers	Prayer Book (Bible/Koran) study Hearing God ("words of knowledge") Prophecy

Figure 11.5. Characteristics of Theistic Causality

At this point, let's draw some contrasts between the three types of worldview:

Contrasts Between the Worldview Types

ANIMISM	NATURALISM	THEISM
Spirits pervade the world, influencing or controlling everything	No supernatural beings or power	God created all, sustains all and is in charge of all
Maybe a God but ignore Him	If there is a God, who cares?	We are accountable to God
Fear of spirits governs life	Chance governs life	God governs life
Appease spirits to keep them happy Attempt to manipulate spirits	Everything by chance	Appeal to God to control spirits
Deal with life's unknowns by manipulating spirits Seek control over spirits by use of magic, ritual, taboo	Manipulate world by technology Seek control through scientific knowledge	Submit to God's control Work with Him to accomplish His will
Focus on material things to be gained thru manipulating spirits & with their help manipulating humans	Focus on material things to be gained through hard work	Material things to be used for God
Need shamans to deal with spirits	Need scientists to find new ways to control the universe	Need pastors, priests, prophets to lead us & intercede for us
Non-literate transmission of insights	Need books to transmit knowledge	Sacred book(s) —Bible, Koran, Torah
Spirits govern territories		Biblical—spirits over territories (Dan 10:13)
Seek to live in harmony with the world of spirits and nature	Seek to conquer natural obstructions thru human effort	We are caretakers of nature, to use it responsibly
No ultimate truth, so seek to use spiritual power to gain advantage over others	No ultimate truth, so adapt to society's changing values	Follow written truth
Morality governed by fear of the spirits	Morals relative	Moral accountability to God

Figure 11.6. Contrasts Between the Three Types of Worldviews

In conclusion, I'd like to chart one more set of contrasts. Since there is quite a range of understandings under the theism heading, it will be helpful to indicate some of the major differences between biblical theism and more generalized theism.

THEISM	BIBLICAL THEISM
God distant (Judaism, Islam), even harsh (Islam)	God above but also close and loving
Human prophets and (for Christians) a weak Jesus are mediators	Sinless Jesus the Mediator
Holy book(s) revered but often not followed	Bible revered and followed
Miracles rare or have ceased	Miracles frequent
God basically outside of us	Holy Spirit active inside of us
Impressive rituals but weak in power	Humans work in great spiritual authority and power

Figure 11.7. Contrasts Between Ordinary Theism and Biblical Theism

With this background, we turn to examples of the contents of several worldviews in chapter 12.

CHAPTER 12

WORLDVIEW CONFIGURATIONS[4]

Internal Structuring of Worldviews

An early concern in American anthropology for what we now call worldview came from what has been called the Culture and Personality school. Ruth Benedict and Margaret Mead are among the better-known representatives of this approach. These scholars began to see a kind of personality in each culture. This developed into various theories concerning what was called modal personality, the preferred type of personality of any given society. Some of the research from this perspective involved a quest to discover and describe what was labeled a people's national character.

Benedict became famous for her 1934 volume *Patterns of Culture* in which she described three societies in terms of what she considered their basic personality type, each of which she labeled with a name from Greek literature. She called the Pueblo peoples (including Hopi) "Appolonian" because of an impressive list of traits pointing to a preference for an orderly and routine way of life. By way of contrast, she portrayed the Kwakiutl of the northwest coast of the U.S. as "Dionysian," a people who seek "to escape from the humdrum round of daily life and to achieve excess, ecstasy, or unusual psychic states" (Barnouw 1979:61). She found a further contrasting configuration in the Dobu of Papua New Guinea whom she characterizes as "paranoid" and of whom she said, "Life in Dobu fosters the extreme forms of animosity and malignancy which most societies have minimized by their institutions"(1934:172).

Treating peoples like this, in terms of one central motif came to be known as Configurationism. This term refers to the view of sociocultural entities that pictures every (or nearly every) part of each as supporting, manifesting and focused on a single core value. For example, Francis Hsu (1961) did a fascinating article on American culture that contended that self-reliance is the American core value with everything else in American life supporting and relating to that single value. Though the insights such studies conveyed is impressive, they come across as quite simplistic to those who really get to know the people thus labeled. Cultural behavior is not so easily categorized.

---
4   With thanks again to Dr. Steven M. Whitmer, for valuable assistance in preparing this chapter.

Themes, Subthemes and Paradigms

Considering the configurationist approach too simplistic, Morris Opler (1945) opted for an approach that is both less simplistic and less neat. He outlined a perspective that sees each culture (I would say worldview) focused on a small number basic assumptions that he called "themes." He suggests that each culture (worldview) contains from half a dozen to a dozen or more such mutually interacting and limiting complexes of assumptions. He defines a theme as "a postulate or position, declared or implied, and usually controlling behavior or stimulating activity, which is tacitly approved or openly promoted in a society" (1945:198).

In what follows, we will use this concept of theme, perhaps a bit differently than Opler originally conceived it, as the major internal component of a worldview. We will also postulate the relationship of themes to two other "smaller" constructs—subthemes and paradigms—that I see functioning internally as parts of worldviews.

As mentioned, I see Themes as the largest of the three subentities we are postulating as making up a worldview. Themes can be represented as statements or picturings (images) of high-level, overarching values and assumptions that can usually be stated as propositions. Themes seem to contain, interact with and integrate what I see as the next levels down, Subthemes and Paradigms, with a good possibility that we could add Subparadigms and perhaps Models, Metaphors Small Picturings, Analogies, and other smaller entities to the list if we wanted to "slice" things thinner.

Though we see Themes as the major subdivisions within worldviews, we should not think of them as dividing up the "territory" of a worldview into equal divisions. As Thomas Williams says, paraphrasing Opler, "themes are not always in a perfect balance with one another … on occasion, one theme plays a more predominant role than others in the culture, particularly during times of great change in culture" (1972:223). Perhaps it is such predominant themes that Benedict and Hsu were pointing to as producing the "personality" of a culture. As Opler pointed out, then, themes "bump into" each other and produce limits for each other.

For example, the individualism theme in Anglo-American culture has often been pointed to as defining our culture, giving it a kind of individualistic personality. Among our major worldview values, however, especially for Christians, are strong concerns for family and for helping those who are less fortunate than we are. Such themes, subthemes and paradigms are the ones that "bump into" and limit our individualism, if we let them.

To illustrate briefly, a typical theme and some of its subthemes and paradigms in certain animistic, supernaturalistic societies might be:

THEME
God and spirits exist, with God above all, all-powerful but unconcerned, and spirits a major concern of humans.
SUBTHEMES
God can be appealed to if the situation is really bad; There are good and evil spirits; Spirits are very much involved in human affairs; etc.
PARADIGMS
Appeal to God only as a last resort; Evil spirits can hurt us, therefore appease them; Evil spirits can be appeased through sacrifices; etc.

Figure 12.1. Illustration of Theme, Subthemes and Paradigms for an Animistic, Supernaturalistic Society

A typical theme and some of its subthemes and paradigms in a naturalistic society might be:

THEME
If there is a God, He's more or less irrelevant since Natural Law covers all the bases.
SUBTHEMES
We can act as if God doesn't exist; Human thinking and activity is all we can count on; Natural Law is discoverable through science; etc.
PARADIGMS
Everything is (or someday will be) explainable in terms of cause and effect; Scientific research can provide the answer to all human problems; The more we learn, the more we will be able to control the presently not understood factors in life; etc.

Figure 12.2. Illustration of Theme, Subthemes and Paradigms for a Naturalistic Society

Another American theme and some of its subthemes and paradigms might be charted this way:

THEME
Money and/or material possessions are the measure of success.
SUBTHEMES Time is money; More "education" (=schooling) means more earning power; The more money one earns, the more prestige one has; etc.
PARADIGMS The value of a person can be calculated in terms of net monetary worth; Need to "keep up with the Joneses" in home, cars, clothes, etc.; Don't waste much time on non-monetary pursuits

Figure 12.3. Another American Illustration of Theme, Subthemes and Paradigms

Examples of a Thematic Analysis of Worldview

Following are anthropological analyses of the worldviews of five human societies: The Middle Wahgi of Papua New Guinea, the Kamwe of northern Nigeria, the "Nacirema" (American) of North America, the Egyptian Muslims and the Hakka of Taiwan. Each analysis is brief and incomplete but indicative of at least certain of the deep level presuppositions and values of these peoples. And each represents an attempt to study and to systematically analyze the core of a culture, its worldview. There are several further examples of worldviews analyzed in this way in Appendix B

A major purpose of this chapter is to help us reflect on what, with the background that we have, we would do in actually strategizing to win to Christ peoples with value systems like these. What should be the first step, the second step, the third step, etc.?

With regard to such strategizing, some of the most difficult problems arise in trying to deal with one's own worldview. I assume that those reading this are either westerners or very westernized through having spent many years in western schools. Often the distance between the worldviews of non-westernized peoples and Christian values seems shorter than the distance between western worldviews and Christianity (especially if we are Americans).

We look first at two animistic worldviews, Middle Wahgi and Kamwe:

I. MIDDLE WAHGI WORLDVIEW
(Papua New Guinea)
(from Luzbetak 1963, 1970:164-166, 143-4; 1988:287-289, 232)

From Luzbetak's data, but organizing it in our way, we can portray three of the Middle Wahgi themes with accompanying subthemes and paradigms. I have added, then, at some points, indications of surface-level practices (not a part of the worldview) based on the themes, subthemes and paradigms. These surface-level practices built on the worldview-level assumptions and images are recorded in the boxes below. Note that there are a relatively small number of key assumptions that underlie a fairly sizable segment of cultural behavior. These key assumptions are the right place to facilitate transformational culture change.

THEME I: The Clan is Everything

SUBTHEME A: The Ultimate Norm for Good and Bad is the Clan.

Paradigm 1: Outsiders don't have rights. They can be put up with, they can be exploited, they can be stolen from, they can be murdered, etc.

Paradigm 2: The clan is always right.

Paradigm 3: Personal rights and advantages are subservient to that of the clan. In this society the group is the reality; individuals are abstract or subsidiary entities.

Practices Associated With Paradigm 3:
1. No personal advantage is to be sought at the expense of the clan.
2. Women should be satisfied with their relatively inferior status, for they thereby serve the clan.
3. Forced marriages occur primarily for the good of the group—e.g., to strengthen a friendship that exists between two clans.
4. An individual may be expected to confess a crime that he did not commit so that the culprit, who is more vital for clan-life, might escape imprisonment.

SUBTHEME B: Security is Found in the Clan Alone.

Paradigm 1: Group prosperity and prestige is all-important.

Practices Associated With Paradigm 1:
1. Brotherly cooperation is expected of all clan-members at all crises and important phases of life—e.g., by contributing to the bridewealth, helping another in constructing a house, participating in the various customs associated with a birth, engagement, wedding, funeral.
2. Selfishness is frowned upon; sharing one's fortune or success with others is expected.
3. Willingness to defend one's clan and to die for it if necessary is a basic obligation. Bravery in battle is regarded as a great virtue; cowardice in battle may constitute an impediment to marriage.
4. Since the good of the clan has precedence over personal good, competition within the clan is frowned upon. On the other hand, competition is expected between clans—e.g., in outdoing another clan during a festival or football game.

Paradigm 2: Every member of the clan is vitally important to the group.

Practices Associated With Paradigm 2:
1. An offense to one member is an offense to all.
2. The group assumes the guilt and consequences of the actions of the individual members—e.g., feuding, hostage taking.
3. The education of the young is the responsibility of all.
4. The clan will go to war for the sake of any single individual whose life is threatened.

SUBTHEME C: Successful Living Consists in Close Cooperation Among All Members of the Clan, Living as Well as Departed and Still Unborn.

Paradigm 1: Cooperation among the living is emphasized.

Practices Associated With Paradigm 1:
1. Games are mainly recreational and educational rather than competitive unless the games are between distinct clans.
2. Instructions given during the initiation of the youth emphasize the importance of cooperation.
3. Not individual action but group action brings results.
4. See several of the following practices as well.

Paradigm 2: The use of pork symbolizes this reciprocity.

Practices Associated With Paradigm 2:
1. Pork is to be shared with family friends and groups.
2. When pork is shared it is understood that those participating in the feast will have to reciprocate when the occasion arises.

[For additional Paradigms see under Ancestral Reverence]

THEME II: ANCESTRAL REVERENCE

SUBTHEME A: The Ancestors are a Part of the Living Community with Privileges and Responsibilities in Relation to the Physically Alive.

Paradigm 1: The living members of the clan are utterly dependent on the departed; the very survival of the living depends on the all-powerful deceased relatives of the other world—e.g., health, sickness, gardens, successful birth, victory in battle, etc.

Practices Associated With Paradigm 1:
1. Traditional ceremonial dances, mock battles with traditional enemies, feasts, and pit sacrifices are not only social affairs but also religious, aiming to please the dead and to win their favor.
2. Elaborate funeral and memorial rites, chopping off fingers to prove one's sympathy for the departed, consultation of spirit-mediums, and other practices reflect the utter dependence of the living on the power and influence of the departed.

Paradigm 2: The departed members of the clan are utterly dependent on the living for their happiness in the land of the ancestors, the other world.

Practices Associated With Paradigm 2:
1. The departed constantly threaten the living with all sorts of misfortunes so that the living would be mindful of them.
2. The Middle Wahgi ancestor reverence is based on fear.
3. The happiness of the dead depends especially on the number of pigs sacrificed in their honor. Pig sacrifices take place on a small as well as large scale.

Paradigm 3: A major function of the ancestors is to support tradition.

Practices Associated With Paradigm 3:
1. Disregard of tradition by one or a few members may bring down the anger of the ancestors on all.
2. The ancestors are to be consulted before anything new can be introduced into the society.

SUBTHEME B: Keeping the Ancestors Content is One of the Most Important Aspects of Life.

Paradigm 1: People must learn and properly use appropriate rituals and ceremonies whenever they are required.

Practices Associated With Paradigm 1:
1. Great attention is given to learning and practicing rituals precisely lest the ancestors be upset and take revenge.
2. Experts such as spirit-mediums who know the rituals are highly regarded.

Paradigm 2: *The well-being of the clan members depends on the ancestors.*

Paradigm 3: *The relationship of people with their ancestors is all-important.*

THEME III: THE PIG IS ESSENTIAL TO LIFE

SUBTHEME A: *Man's Most Important Material Possession is the Pig.*

Paradigm 1: *Material wealth is measured in pigs.*

> **Practices Associated With Paradigm 1:**
> 1. Pigs form the most important part of the family wealth.
> 2. Pigs are exchanged for the precious pearl shell that served as traditional money.
> 3. The number and quality of pigs give the owner prestige while a pigless adult would be the equivalent of a penniless tramp.
> 4. The prestige of a tribe among other tribes depends largely on the number of pigs it has and many tribal battles are fought over pigs.

Paradigm 2: *All important social relationships involve pigs.*

> **Practices Associated With Paradigm 2:**
> 1. An exchange of pork seals friendships (a friend is called "a fellow porkeater"), between individuals, families, lineages, and larger social groups.
> 2. Distribution of pork climaxes all major festivities, such as birth ceremonies, engagements, weddings, food-exchange between friendly groups and truces between traditional enemies.
> 3. The pig is the chief source of security for the individual, family, and social group economically, socially and religiously.
> 4. Without pigs it would be impossible for a boy to be initiated into the tribe and thus become a full-fledged member of his social group.
> 5. It is impossible to acquire a wife except with pigs as an essential, if not main, part of the bridewealth.
> 6. A woman's value is measured by her skill in caring for pigs.
> 7. The skill of caring for pigs forms the major part of the training of a woman by her future mother-in-law during her trial-marriage and is the subject of the main test that a future bride must pass.

SUBTHEME B: *Without the Pig, Life Would be Impossible.*

Paradigm 1: *The pig is intermeshed with practically every aspect of life.*

> **Practices Associated With Paradigm 1:**
> 1. Although pork is eaten on a feast-or-famine basis, it is the main and usually the only source of animal protein in the native diet.
> 2. See the other practices listed above.

Paradigm 2: *Without the pig religion would be impossible.*

Practices Associated With Paradigm 2:
1. Every religious ceremony requires pig-sacrifice.
2. The ancestors require pork to appease them.

SUBTHEME C: Pig Sacrifices are Crucial to Keeping the Ancestors Content.

Paradigm 1: *The ancestors, especially recently deceased relatives, are pork-hungry and, therefore the pig must be sacrificed to keep them from causing trouble.*

Practice Associated With Paradigm 1:
1. When a pig is sacrificed, special morsels and the souls of the pigs are set aside for the ancestors.

Paradigm 2: *No child can be born into the world successfully without pig-sacrifices.*
Paradigm 3: *No tribal battle is won except through pig-sacrifices.*
Paradigm 4: *Often the only cure for a serious illness is a pig sacrifice.*

II. KAMWE WORLDVIEW (Nigeria)
(from Marguerite G. Kraft 1978)

From Marguerite Kraft's analysis of Kamwe worldview we can point to five themes with several subthemes under each (though she did not present her study in these terms). Her analysis is presented in terms of the relationships between the family unit which she sees as central and four conceptual domains that are of great importance to Kamwe people. These relationships may be diagrammed as follows:

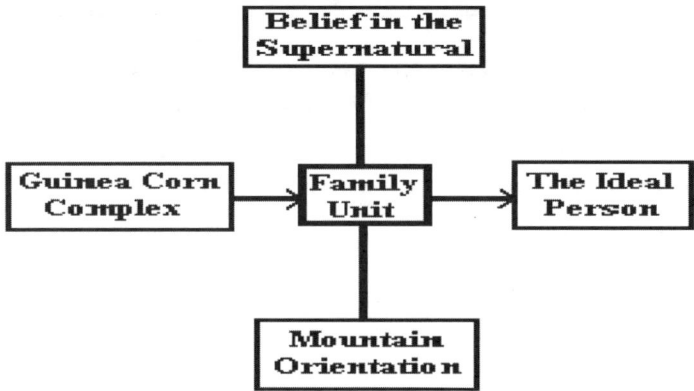

Figure 12.1 Relationships Between Kamwe Family and Four Conceptual Domains.

Here, however, we will treat each of the five dimensions as a separate theme, recognizing as always that within the worldview are multiple interrelationships between them.

THEME I: THE FAMILY

SUBTHEME A: The (Extended) Family is the Ground of All Human Existence.

Paradigm 1: The family is the most important person-group relationship.
Paradigm 2: Authority is in the family ancestors and elders.
Paradigm 3: Land for farming and building a house is obtained (leased) through the family.
Paradigm 4: Interpersonal unity is conceived of in terms of extended family relationships.
Paradigm 5: One's family is seen as his/her most valuable possession.
Paradigm 6: One's daily relationships with the family are paramount.
Paradigm 7: It is as a family group that one relates to other groups and to the outside world.
Paradigm 8: Order is seen as family-based.
Paradigm 9: The family is seen as the ideal of beauty and security, without which there would be no meaning in life.
Paradigm 10: The family is the basic economic unit.
Paradigm 11: The family is the significant group for relating to the unseen.
Paradigm 12: The family is the basic political unit.
Paradigm 13: The family is the center of social life and obligations.

THEME II: MOUNTAIN ORIENTATION

SUBTHEME A: Our Clan's Mountain is the Source of Our Identity.

Paradigm 1: Our ancestors came from the mountains.
Paradigm 2: Our mountain is where our ancestors are buried.
Paradigm 3: In our language, all terms related to going, coming and other movements reflect position in relation to mountains.

SUBTHEME B: Our God is in or at Least Associated with Our Mountain.

SUBTHEME C: Our Mountain is Our Source of Safety.

Paradigm 1: Our homes are built along the mountain with the man's side of the compound on the uphill side.

SUBTHEME D: Our Mountain is the Source of the Necessities of Life (e.g., building materials, medicines, grinding stones, firewood).

THEME III: GUINEA CORN COMPLEX

SUBTHEME A: *Guinea Corn Means Life.*

Practices Associated with Subtheme A:
1. Guinea Corn is treated as a person with great respect.

SUBTHEME B: *Guinea Corn Came from God.*

Paradigm 1: It is sacred.

Practices Associated with Paradigm 1:
1. Numerous taboos are attached to the planting, harvesting and pounding of guinea corn.
2. No act of eating is a meal without guinea corn.

SUBTHEME C: *The Use of Guinea Corn Maintains and/or Restores Relationships with Other People.*

Practices Associated with Subtheme C:
1. To forgive or assure good relationships with another, a small amount is chewed and spit out.
2. Rituals involving such spitting of guinea corn are a part of marriage ceremonies.

SUBTHEME D: *Guinea Corn is Necessary to Assure or Reestablish a Relationship with God.*

Practices Associated with Subtheme D:
1. Nearly all rituals seeking blessing from God involve guinea corn and/or guinea corn beer.
2. A small amount is thrown to the wind before eating to thank God for the food.

THEME IV: SUPERNATURALISM

SUBTHEME A: The Universe Includes Invisible as Well as Visible Beings in Constant Interaction with Each Other on the Same Plane (Cosmology).

> *Paradigm 1:* There is a high God.
> **Subparadigm a:** *God is good but distant.*
> **Subparadigm b**: *He is a person, a protector, very kind, never to blame for evil, dependable but never interfering and not to be called on except when desperate.*

Practices Associated with Paradigm 1:
"God is called on not only in times of great need: planting, marriage, birth, sickness, etc., but also in times of great thankfulness: harvest, health and recovery after a long illness, etc. ... God's name is also mentioned often when an appeasement sacrifice is made to the evil spirits or the ancestor spirits. This may be a recognition of the importance of God, the order he has made in the universe and the subjection of the lesser deities to him" (M. G. Kraft, 1978:43).

> *Paradigm 2:* There are good and bad spirits plus ancestral spirits in addition to God.
> *Paradigm 3:* Spirits can live in people (a vwe spirit).
> **Subparadigm a**: *This spirit lives only within people.*
> **Subparadigm b**: *One is born with this spirit, inheriting it through the maternal line.*

Practices Associated with Subparadigm b:
This is one reason why a very careful check is made into the bride-to-be's mother's line before the marriage is finalized. People suspected of having a vwe spirit are treated very carefully.

> **Subparadigm c**: *This spirit is with a person all his/her life.*
> *Paradigm 4:* Ancestral spirits work in correlation with and as part of the extended family.
> **Subparadigm a**: *Ancestor spirits reside in the afterworld, located deep inside the earth.*
> **Subparadigm b**: *The spirit of a person who dies is believed to remain near his home and grave and must be fed food and drink along with the family for several days.*
> **Subparadigm c**: *At a libation ceremony held seven to nine days after burial other spirits come to welcome the new ancestor spirit into the place of the spirits of the dead.*
> **Subparadigm d**: *These spirits may communicate with the living in dreams and may return and cause evil.*
> **Subparadigm e**: *A ceremony at the grave of the father will clear up this matter.*
> **Subparadigm f**: *The ancestors can bring about misfortune if these are*

not upheld. (When one has a problem, the medium may inform him that he is not following the advice his father gave him. The Kamwe are very conscious of the influence of the ancestors in their lives.)

Subparadigm g: *If one is living according to tradition, the presence of the ancestors is very supportive and comforting. (The ancestors have set the standard of behavior and the values of the society.)*

SUBTHEME B: Human Survival is Dependent on Maintaining Good Relationships with the Spirit World (Causation).

Paradigm 1: *There are spirits that cause both good and evil.*
Subparadigm a: *Sickness and trouble are both elements of evil.*
Subparadigm b: *Sickness may have one or more unseen causes: evil spirits, the vwe spirit in another person, poisoning through sorcery or the punishment by an ancestor for disobeying tradition*
Subparadigm c: *People can protect themselves from attacks by spirit beings through the use of charms on their persons and in their fields and by faithfully performing the proper rituals.*

Practices Associated with Paradigm 1:
1. Sacrifices prescribed by diviners are the usual recommendation for the person to get well except in the case of the vwe spirit.
2. In the case of the vwe spirit, the victim, with help from a diviner, discovers who caused the sickness and takes revenge.

Paradigm 2: *Evil spirits are only a partial cause of trouble and sickness.*
Paradigm 3: *Humans are the remainder of the cause because of their behavior toward or relationships with the invisible forces.*
Subparadigm a: *The good and evil spirits ... reside in certain big trees, rivers, stones, mountains, caves, and pools. ... One must be very careful not to touch anything close to their dwelling place.*
Subparadigm b: *Spirits often appear in the form of very old men, big snakes, tiny babies, or white mice.*
Subparadigm c: *He/she may have misfortune as a result of seeing the spirit.*
Subparadigm d: *If a person is not frightened on these occasions, he will be blessed by the spirit.*

Subparadigm e: *When one sees a spirit he must collect all kinds of things that man eats, uses, and plants, and place them at the place where he saw the spirit.*[5]

Subparadigm f: *He may see the spirit again later in a dream.*

Subparadigm g: *When an evil spirit causes an illness the patient must make a specific sacrifice of appeasement at a specific place in order to get well.*

Subparadigm h: *If he is too afraid or sick to go, the specialist for getting rid of spirits or a relative may go in his place.*

THEME V: ONE SHOULD STRIVE TO BE AN IDEAL PERSON

SUBTHEME A: *The Most Important Personal Qualities are Kindness and Good Character, Generosity, Possession of Riches, Hard Work, Discipline, Showing Honor/Respect, Good Health, Living in Harmony, Peace and Unity.*

SUBTHEME B: *These Character Traits are to be Taught Through Proverbs, Singing and the Influence of Group Life, Including Techniques of Social Control.*

> **Practices Associated with Theme V:**
> "Since the Kamwe place so much importance on personal relationships, one of the domains that is prominent in the worldview is the ideal person. ... though the personal standards are high, the people have the beautiful characteristic of acceptance of each other in the real world."

When choosing a bride, the family will carefully seek all of the following qualities. But once she is chosen "there is no attempt to make her over. The Kamwe, like most face-to-face type societies, are very perceptive of an individual's personal character. But this perceptiveness is used to build a relationship rather than" to damage it (M. G. Kraft, 1978:52).

---

[5] The basic attitude seems to be that although seeing a spirit might result in good, the fear that it may result in evil causes the Kamwe to prefer not to chance it.

===

III. "NACIREMA" WORLDVIEW (United States)
(From Kluckhohn 1949; Williams 1972:225-226 [after DuBois 1955]; Spradley & McCurdy 1975:488-490 [after R. Lynd 1939] and Stewart 1971)

This analysis is an attempt to present a general picture of the actual, as opposed to an ideal Anglo-American worldview. It is a synthesis of the analyses of several authors plus my own observations, resulting in eight major themes: Secular Humanism, Individualism, Competition, Materialism, Mechanical Universe, Progress, Equality and The American Way.

I do not consider this a complete representation of all that Anglo-American worldview contains. I doubt that any such complete picture could be worked out. And other analyses, focusing on other or additional themes might be just as valid as this one. I have not attempted, for example, to represent the incursions of New Age and Postmodernism in American life. What becomes mainstream of those issues can be added at a future date. This analysis should, however, give us a reasonable picture of the majority worldview of the United States.

It might surprise us, given the long presence of Christianity within American society, that many of the assumptions and values indicated in this presentation look like the antitheses of Christian values. Though Christians form an important subculture, it is the secular worldview taught in our schools that is in focus here. And a fairly generalized form of that.

Though several of my sources were written quite a few years ago, it is interesting to note how many of the insights of those authors are still reasonably accurate. This fact speaks of the durability of worldview assumptions, values and commitments over long periods of time, in spite of very rapid culture change on the surface-level of the culture.

I trust that for Americans and for non-Americans alike, this outline of American worldview assumptions and values will give us better insight into this very prestigious and influential way of life. Whether you are an American or not, what should our strategy be to win Americans? And what should the strategy of Anglo-Americans who are greatly influenced by this worldview be to win any of the other peoples whose worldviews are outlined above and below? What changes would a given people need to make and in what order?

For Americans, and for others too, I would suggest that a lack of important changes in our internalized American worldview might be the major reason for a lack of both Christian maturity and the ability to understand and witness to people of other worldviews. The statement is sometimes made about us that "You can take an American out of America, but you can't take America out of the American." It is probably also true that "You can take a Korean (or Nigerian or Indonesian or whatever country you may be from) out of Korea (or wherever), but you can't take Korea (or Nigerian, etc.) out of the Korean (or Nigerian, etc.). We wish it weren't so, but it usually is a sad fact that many Christians go to other parts of the world more characterized by their culture and its deep-seated worldview than by their Christianity.

THEME I: SECULAR HUMANISM: HUMAN BEINGS ARE TO WORK OUT OUR OWN LIVES WITHOUT DIVINE ASSISTANCE.

SUBTHEME A: Humankind is Master of the Universe. We Are to Control the Universe, Not Allow it to Control Us.

SUBTHEME B: Rationalism: Humans Can Reason Our Way to Correct Answers to Our Problems.

> **Paradigm 1:** The thing that distinguishes humans from beasts is that we are rational.
> **Paradigm 2:** Humans can be trusted, if left alone, to guide our conduct wisely ("Cult of the common man").
> **Subparadigm a**: All we need is enough knowledge.
> **Subparadigm b**: Knowledge produces character.

SUBTHEME C: Schooling ("education") is Important Since the Basic Problem with Humans is Lack of Knowledge.

> **Paradigm 1:** Seek knowledge by attaining the highest level of schooling possible.
> **Paradigm 2:** Children must go to school, at least through high school and, if possible, to college.
> **Paradigm 3:** Formal education prepares children for their work careers and activities and so is to be strongly encouraged.
> **Paradigm 4:** Even subjects that seem irrelevant to life are valuable since they teach children how to think and reason.

SUBTHEME D: Science and Technology Will Provide the Answers to Whatever Problems We Still Face.

> **Paradigm 1:** They have done such spectacular things in the past, it's just a matter of time till they've fixed everything.

Paradigm 2: Our future depends on science and scientific advancement.

SUBTHEME E: We Cannot Depend on Religion to Help Us Get Where We Need to Go.

Paradigm 1: We distrust churches and "spiritual" solutions to problems.
  Subparadigm a: So we keep ourselves ignorant of Christian answers.
  Subparadigm b: Our ignorance, though, leaves us curious about and often open to alternative spiritual systems.
Paradigm 2: Belonging to a church can help socially.
  Subparadigm a: It may give business contacts.
  Subparadigm b: It makes you look morally good.
Paradigm 3: A faith may help us psychologically.
  Subparadigm a: It can "prop us up" when we need emotional and psychological support to face life.
  Subparadigm b: But we should never get fanatic about religion.
Paradigm 4: Basically, all religions get you to the same place.

THEME II: INDIVIDUALISM: INDIVIDUALISM IS THE LAW ON WHICH THE UNIVERSE WORKS (SURVIVAL OF THE FITTEST).

SUBTHEME A: Achievement-Orientation: We Must Achieve if We are to Get Anywhere in Life.

Paradigm 1: We put doing above being.
  Subparadigm a: What we do is more important than who we are.
  Subparadigm b: Our prestige lies in our accomplishments.
  Subparadigm c: Achievement has to be visible and measurable.

> **Practices Associated with Subparadigm c:**
> 1. Americans believe that no single person can master the universe, so people must work together to meet their immediate tasks, to enable them to later cope with larger efforts.

  Subparadigm d: We have to achieve "on our own." We can't simply depend on family name or family help.
Paradigm 2: Seek prestige and power in a career.
  Subparadigm a: Don't seek prestige and power openly.
  Subparadigm b: Our value is indicated by our salary-level.
  Subparadigm c: Don't show off wealth.
  Subparadigm d: Cooperate with others but only to get ahead of them.

Subparadigm e: *Mobility: Gladly move if a better position is available.*
Subparadigm f: *Work is a drag. Seek leisure and recreation.*
Paradigm 3: *The individual is more important than the family.*
    Subparadigm a: *Seek power as an individual, not simply for the sake of the family.*
    Subparadigm b: *Be committed to family but don't let them. interfere with your achievement goals.*
    Subparadigm c: *When older members are no longer productive, cast them aside.*

SUBTHEME B: Effort Optimism: Everyone Can Get There if He/She Works Hard Enough.

Paradigm 1: *Conquest—Men need to conquer to feel good about themselves (e.g., athletics, job, women).*
Paradigm 2: *Everyone can make it to the top if he/she works hard.*
Paradigm 3: *Every woman can be as beautiful as a movie star if she works at it.*

SUBTHEME C: Seek Freedom: It is Everyone's Right To Be Free.

Paradigm 1: *It's not fair for men to be freer than women. So women have a right to be just as free.*
Paradigm 2: *Rules and obligations are a pain.*
    Subparadigm a: *Children tie us down, so get them into school as soon as possible and "on their own" as soon as possible.*
    Subparadigm b: *Break speed limits and other rules to prove you are free and can get away with it.*

SUBTHEME D: Tolerance: Whatever Anyone Does or Thinks is Alright as Long as it Doesn't Hurt Anyone.

Paradigm 1: *Do "Whatever turns you on."*
Paradigm 2: *Accept everyone, whatever race, religion, sexual orientation or political stripe.*
    Subparadigm a: *Especially in religion or philosophy, there is no right or wrong, so accept everyone's beliefs and lifestyle.*
    Subparadigm b: *Exotic religious beliefs and practices are especially intriguing. So experiment with them.*
Paradigm 3: *But don't tolerate those who stand for absolutes.*
    Subparadigm a: *They are arrogant, thinking they know something others don't.*
Paradigm 4: *Express your individuality by experimenting with behavior not approved by the previous generation.*

> **Subparadigm a**: *Test others' capacity to tolerate by changing such things as personal appearance, sexual behavior, dropping out of school, music styles or otherwise refusing to behave as your parents and other adults want you to.*

SUBTHEME E: Personal Insecurity: We Need to Prove Ourselves to Feel Good about Ourselves.

> **Paradigm 1:** *Men need to prove themselves by doing well in a career.*
> > **Subparadigm a**: *Not marriage, family or anything else compares with job in giving prestige and satisfaction.*
> > **Subparadigm b**: *Achieving in sports or music can help but those credentials are only temporary.*
> **Paradigm 2:** *Women need to prove themselves in four ways: by being sexy, getting married, having a career and having at least one child.*
> > **Subparadigm a**: *But staying home to raise children is considered drudgery.*
> > **Subparadigm b**: *Get the children taken care of or in school as soon as possible so you can get back to your career.*
> **Paradigm 3:** *We fear intimacy, so share ourselves with others only superficially.*
> **Paradigm 4:** *Lest we be thought strange we conform to our peer group.*

SUBTHEME F: We Value Youthfulness and Dread Aging.

> **Paradigm 1:** *Youthful is good, young is best.*

Practices Associated with Paradigm 1:
1. American cultural heroes are young, strong, handsome, and healthy.

> **Paradigm 2:** *Adults try to look and act younger than they are.*
> > **Subparadigm a**: *Women don't like to reveal their ages.*
> > **Subparadigm b**: *Many adults "work out" to keep themselves looking young.*
> **Paradigm 3:** *We fear aging, infirmity and death.*
> > **Subparadigm a**: *People seldom prepare for death.*
> > **Subparadigm b**: *We take all kinds of pills to heal or prevent illness.*

SUBTHEME G: We Are Preoccupied With Leisure.

> **Paradigm 1:** *We live for weekends.*
> **Paradigm 2:** *The leisure industry is booming.*

SUBTHEME H: *We Have Different Standards for Men's and Women's Expression of Emotion.*

> ***Paradigm 1:*** *Women are allowed to cry but men are not.*
> > **Subparadigm a***: Men are allowed only anger—if we fear or feel shamed or rejected, it comes out in anger*
> > **Subparadigm b***: Men are to stuff or rechannel all other negative emotions.*
> > **Subparadigm c***: Men cannot resist when a woman cries.*
> ***Paradigm 2:*** *Men are allowed to express positive emotion at athletic events and the like.*

THEME III: COMPETITION: COMPETITION IS A WAY OF LIFE FOR US, WHETHER BETWEEN INDIVIDUALS OR GROUPS.

SUBTHEME A: *We Compete Individual Against Individual.*

> ***Paradigm 1:*** *As children we learn to compete for the attention of parents and teachers.*
> ***Paradigm 2:*** *We compete for grades in school (boys against boys, girls against girls, boys against girls).*
> ***Paradigm 3:*** *We compete in athletics—only the winner is honored.*
> ***Paradigm 4:*** *Men and women compete with each other in marriages.*
> ***Paradigm 5:*** *We compete with others to get where we're going in our careers.*

SUBTHEME B: *Youth Compete Against the Previous Generation.*

> ***Paradigm 1:*** *All expertise comes from outside the home—from teachers and other "experts," never from parents.*
> ***Paradigm 2:*** *Never trust anyone over 30.*

SUBTHEME C: *Competition Between Businesses is of the Essence of Capitalism.*

> ***Paradigm 1:*** *Businesses have to "beat the competition" to make money.*
> ***Paradigm 2:*** *Military logistics shape basic strategy for business and any other competitive venture (e.g., athletics).*

Practices Associated with Paradigm 2:
1. American wars are to be prepared for by first building bases, filling them with equipment, and then starting to fight. Unless all is lost, Americans do not assume that personal heroism should be emphasized over providing proper supplies and equipment for fighting.
2. Usually there are three times or more "support" troops than "combat" troops.

SUBTHEME D: *The Political Process is Competitive.*

> ***Paradigm 1:*** *Loyalty to one's party in competition with whatever the other party offers is more important than the good of the constituency.*

SUBTHEME E: *Hostility Toward Authority Figures.*

Practices Associated with Subtheme E:
1. Americans resist authority symbols, for these accentuate status differences, rather than conformity and team work.

> ***Paradigm 1:*** *We don't trust bigness or fame.*
>   **Subparadigm a***: We envy the successful but don't trust them.*
> ***Paradigm 2:*** *We distrust institutions, whether business or political.*
>   **Subparadigm a***: Especially don't trust politicians.*

SUBTHEME F: *But People Must at Least Appear to be Working Together to Accomplish the Greater Good (Teamwork).*

THEME IV: MATERIALISM: MONEY AND MATERIAL WEALTH ARE THE MEASURES OF HUMAN SUCCESS AND VALUE.

SUBTHEME A: *Material Gain Equates with Well-Being.*

> ***Paradigm 1:*** *A high standard of living is the goal of life.*

Practices Associated with Paradigm 1:
1. Americans equate economic prosperity and social progress and expect that they have a right to demand a high level of living and consumption of goods.
2. This right is supported by health insurance, social welfare plans and operations, and political hostility toward economic and professional interest groups, organizations and plans that threaten to limit a high standard of living.

> ***Paradigm 2:*** *Success in material goods carries a moral sanction.*

Practices Associated with Paradigm 2:
1. Americans believe they have a right to be physically comfortable, after working hard, for virtue in daily labor carries the reward of attaining desired goods.
2. Since the amount of "good" (e.g., goods, benefits, respect, accomplishment, etc.) available in the world is limitless, we are to strive to obtain as much of it as possible without fear of defrauding anyone else.

SUBTHEME B: The More Money One Earns, the More Prestige and Status One Has.

Paradigm 1: Success is shown through material possessions such as home, cars, recreational vehicle, etc.
Paradigm 2: Need to "keep up with the Joneses" in home, cars, clothes, etc.
Paradigm 3: The value of a person can be calculated in terms of net monetary worth.

SUBTHEME C: Money and Material Wealth are Symbols of Power.

Paradigm 1: The wealthy have more clout wherever they go.

SUBTHEME D: The More "Education" (=Schooling) One Gets, the More Prestige and Earning Power One Has.

Paradigm 1: Schooling is automatically education.
Paradigm 2: An "educated" person can think well.
Paradigm 3: An "educated" person is more trustworthy than one who hasn't gone far in school.
Paradigm 4: The gaining of academic degrees proves one's worth.

SUBTHEME E: We Must Work to Maintain and Improve Our Economic Position.

Paradigm 1: Work is valuable for its own sake.

Practices Associated with Paradigm 1
1. Americans stress work activity as so necessary that even recreation and leisure must be work to be good.

Paradigm 2: Manual labor is dignified.

Practices Associated with Paradigm 2:
1. Americans feel that hard work with one's hands and body is of superior worth and will "pay off" in material well-being.

Paradigm 3: Everyone should try to be successful.
Paradigm 4: Vigor and impatience is valued.

Practices Associated with Paradigm 4:
1. Americans stress specific action now, even at the expense of planning.

Paradigm 5: No one deserves to have that for which he/she has not worked.

SUBTHEME F: *Time is Money.*

    Paradigm 1: Don't waste much time on non-monetary pursuits.

THEME V: MECHANICAL UNIVERSE: THE UNIVERSE AND ALL IN IT FUNCTION LIKE MACHINES.

SUBTHEME A: *The Universe Functions by Predictable Machine-Like Physical Laws.*

    Paradigm 1: Physical laws and processes are predictable and replicable.
        Subparadigm a: They work according to mathematical and scientific principles.
        Subparadigm b: Those laws and principles are discoverable through scientific research.

SUBTHEME B: *Our Bodies Function According to Machine-Like Physical Laws Also.*

    Paradigm 1: Repairs and replacements can be made on human bodies just like with machines.

SUBTHEME C: *Our Minds and Emotions Function According to Rules Also.*

    Paradigm 1: They too can be studied scientifically.
    Paradigm 2: All that might be considered spiritual is really just psychological.

THEME VI: PROGRESS: CHANGE USUALLY GOES IN THE RIGHT DIRECTION AND, THEREFORE, IS GOOD.

SUBTHEME A: *We are Optimistic that Humans are Capable of Great Improvement.*

    Paradigm 1: Life would not be tolerable if we did not believe in progress and know that things are getting better, in spite of how things often seem.
    Paradigm 2: Science and technology can solve all problems.
        Subparadigm a: Medical discoveries have done away with many diseases and will eventually do away with all of them.
        Subparadigm b: We can send people into space and get them back, so we can do anything through science.
    Paradigm 3: Physical and social barriers are unwelcome.

> **Practices Associated with Paradigm 3:**
> Americans tend to believe there are social, physical and other barriers to be overcome in our efforts to master life's problems. When doors are closed, we'll fight to get them opened.

SUBTHEME B: *The Evolutionary Process is Inevitable.*

> ***Paradigm 1:*** *Just as biological evolution got us here, social evolution will take us continually to new heights.*
> ***Paradigm 2:*** *Change is usually in the direction of betterment.*

SUBTHEME C: *Distrust Past (Traditional) Answers for Contemporary Problems.*

> ***Paradigm 1:*** *Today is a new day, so look for new answers.*
> ***Paradigm 2:*** *New discoveries promise a new future.*
> ***Paradigm 3:*** *Especially don't trust Christianity.*

THEME VII: EQUALITY: ALL PEOPLE ARE MEANT TO BE EQUAL.

SUBTHEME A: *All Should Have Equal Opportunity to Achieve.*

> ***Paradigm 1:*** *Though not everyone has equal ability, each should be given equal opportunity to do their best.*
> ***Paradigm 2:*** *Everybody is entitled to ("deserves") the good things of life.*

SUBTHEME B: *Equality Means Everyone Should Compete in the Same Way.*

> ***Paradigm 1:*** *Equality means "sameness."*
> > **Subparadigm a**: *Difference means inferiority.*
> > **Subparadigm b**: *Differences should be stamped out.*
>
> ***Paradigm 2:*** *We teach all the same things in all the same ways to boys and girls, to those who are "left-brained" and those who are "right-brained."*
> > **Subparadigm a**: *Men and women should think and reason alike, so we teach girls to reason like boys.*
> > **Subparadigm b**: *There is only one standard for intelligence.*

SUBTHEME C: *Self-Achievement has the Goal of Similarity.*

> **Practices Associated with Subtheme C:**
> 1. Americans strive individually to achieve the end of being similar to others in the society.

SUBTHEME D: *We Should Tolerate Differences but Work Toward Conformity.*

THEME VIII: THE AMERICAN WAY: OUR WAY IS THE BEST WAY YET DEVISED.

SUBTHEME A: The United States is the Best and Greatest Nation on Earth and Will Always Remain So.

Paradigm 1: We have achieved this position and deserve it.

Paradigm 2: Democracy, as discovered and perfected by the American people, is the ultimate form of living together.

Subparadigm a: We have a right to be proud to be Americans.

Subparadigm b: Democracy is right for everyone in the world.

Subparadigm c: We believe everyone in the world envies us and really wants to be like us.

Paradigm 3: The American judicial system insures justice to every man, rich or poor.

Paradigm 4: Patriotism and public service are noble efforts.

SUBTHEME B: America is a Land of Unlimited Opportunity, and People Get Pretty Much What They Work for in this Country.

Paradigm 1: There is an infinite amount of good (e.g., goods, opportunity, honor, etc.) for people to achieve.

Paradigm 2: Poverty is deplorable and should be abolished.

SUBTHEME C: We Are a Practical People.

Paradigm 1: Do whatever works.

Paradigm 2: We borrow ideas from anywhere.

SUBTHEME D: The Family is Our Basic Institution and the Sacred Core of Our National Life.

Paradigm 1: Women are the finest of God's creation.

Paradigm 2: Children are a blessing.

Paradigm 3: But our occupation determines where we live, how often we move and where the children go to school.

SUBTHEME E: Capitalism is the Best Economic System.

Paradigm 1: It's the fairest system for all concerned.

Paradigm 2: Competition in business is the best way to determine who should continue and who should quit.

SUBTHEME F: Politics Should be Everyone's Business.

Paradigm 1: Everyone is capable of understanding the issues and casting an intelligent vote.
Paradigm 2: We can freely criticize our leaders.

SUBTHEME G: We Cannot be Defeated in War.

Paradigm 1: If it looks like we were defeated (e.g., Vietnam), it wasn't a real war.

SUBTHEME H: We are a Sympathetic and Generous People.

Paradigm 1: We give to the needy, we help other nations in war.
Paradigm 2: Pain, brutality, and death are not to be tolerated either at home or abroad.

> **Practices Associated with Paradigm 2:**
> 1. Americans tend to be repelled by poverty, misery, cruelty, and physical suffering, since these all interfere with attainment of a material well-being.

Paradigm 3: We give money but impersonally.
    Subparadigm a: We can't stand to face the needy in person.
    Subparadigm b: We hate to give time and energy, so we "buy" our way out by giving money.

SUBTHEME I: We are a Nation of Joiners.

Paradigm 1: We belong to various organizations for various reasons.
    Subparadigm a: This makes up for a lack of close extended family relationships.
    Subparadigm b: Such memberships give us good contacts for friendship, business, recreation.
Paradigm 2: It is good to belong to a church to make a good impression on those around us.
    Subparadigm a: But don't get carried away and become a fanatic.
    Subparadigm b: And do not proselytize.

IV. EGYPTIAN SUNNI MUSLIM WORLDVIEW
[From a term paper by Eric Brockhoff & Jim Neergaard, students in the School of World Mission, Fuller Seminary, Winter 2000]

THEME I: ALLAH IS GOD AND THERE MUST BE TOTAL SUBMISSION TO HIM

SUBTHEME A: The Quran is the Very Word of Allah.

Paradigm 1: The Quran is Allah's final revelation, and it perfects the truth.
Paradigm 2: Since this book covers all subjects, it provides Divine guidance for daily living.

SUBTHEME B: Muhammad is the Last Prophet and Messenger of Allah.

Paradigm 1: Through him, Islam was completed and perfected.
Paradigm 2: His life serves as a model for all humankind.

SUBTHEME C: The Five Pillars of Islam are Required by Allah.

Paradigm 1: They will transform one's life when performed regularly, correctly and sincerely.
Paradigm 2: This process brings life into harmony with the wishes of Allah.

> **Practices Associated With Paradigms 1 and 2:**
> 1. Every act of worship requires the recital of the creed "There is no god except Allah, Muhammad is the messenger of Allah."
> 2. It is compulsory to offer prayer five times a day as a practical demonstration of faith. Its benefits are immeasurable.
> 3. It is compulsory to give alms to the poor, oppressed, disabled or other welfare recipients. It is an equitable sharing of the wealth and is an act of worship.
> 4. To develop a believer's moral and spiritual standards by keeping him away from vices such as extravagance, greed and selfishness each Muslim must fast yearly during the month of Ramadan.
> 5. The Pilgrimage to the mosque in Mecca should be performed at least once in a believer's lifetime if he can afford it. It symbolizes unity, equality and humility.

SUBTHEME D: The Community (Umma) of Allah is a Community of Brotherhood and Peace.

Paradigm 1: This community consists of all people who respond to the Muslim witness and submit to the Shari'a Law of Islam.

SUBTHEME E: *Shari'a Law is the Path that Leads Men Into Submission.*

> ***Paradigm 1:*** *Shari'a is applicable to every aspect of human action.*
> ***Paradigm 2:*** *Shari'a guides man to conduct his total life in line with Allah's divine will.*
> ***Paradigm 3:*** *Shari'a is the foundation for affairs of politics, economy, and social conduct, as well as moral standards and methods and modes of worship.*

SUBTHEME F: *Allah Determines Everything.*

> ***Paradigm 1:*** *The will of Allah is always done.*
> ***Paradigm 2:*** *Whether good things or bad things take place, they are ultimately all within the will of Allah.*

THEME II: ISLAMIC REVIVALISM IS A MOVEMENT TO RETURN TO TRUE ISLAM

SUBTHEME A: *Egypt's Social Decline and Military Defeats Are Due to Their Departure from Islam's Straight Path and Following a Western Secular Path.*

SUBTHEME B: *The Renewal of Egypt's Society Requires A Return to Islam.*

SUBTHEME C: *Modern Science and Technology are Acceptable in Egypt if They are Subordinated to Islamic Belief and Values.*

SUBTHEME D: *The Process of Reislamization Requires Organizations of Trained Muslims Who Will Struggle Against Corruption and Social Injustice and Lead Others in the Same Way.*

SUBTHEME E: *Islamic Revivalism is a Fulfillment of Prophecy.*

THEME III: SUPERNATURAL POWER AND "BARAKA" (BLESSINGS) ARE ESSENTIAL FOR DAILY LIVING [6]

SUBTHEME A: *There are Supernatural Beings and Power That Can Help or Harm You.*

> ***Paradigm 1:*** *Helpful beings include Allah, angels, and deceased saints and ancestors.*
> ***Paradigm 2:*** *Harmful beings include the devil (Iblis), jinn, and evil spirits.*

---

[6] This theme is generally categorized by western scholars as Folk Islam, much of which has been influenced by or absorbed into Islam from pre-Islamic practices of the Arabs.

> **Practices Associated with Subtheme A:**
> 1. In order to obtain a blessing or to seek relief from trouble or evil, one can visit the shrine built over the graves of especially holy people.
> 2. Avoid stepping into space known to be occupied by jinn no matter how well protected with charms one may be.

> *Paradigm 3:* Various kinds of impersonal powers include charms and amulets, magic, astrology, and the evil eye.

> **Practices Associated with Paradigm 3:**
> 1. The wearing of an amulet as a lucky charm to ward off evil spirits.
> 2. Warding off the "evil eye" by displaying a representation of the eye on a house or car.
> 3. Using the names of Allah in a magical way.
> 4. Drinking water from a source that is thought to have magical powers.
> 5. Drinking water that has had a piece of paper with a Quranic verse written on it dissolved in the water.

SUBTHEME B: *"Fate" is an Almost Ultimate Force, Against Which There is No Redress.*

SUBTHEME C: *For Healing, the Traditional Healer is the Source of Greatest Power.*

THEME IV: IN DEALING WITH OTHERS, HONOR IS GREATLY VALUED, WHILE SHAME IS TO BE AVOIDED AT ALL COSTS.

SUBTHEME A: *One Must Always Strive to Save Face Since it is the Outward Appearance of Honor.*

> *Paradigm 1:* Daily living consists largely of navigating successfully between honor and shame.
> *Paradigm 2:* Lying and cheating are not primarily moral matters.

> **Practices Associated with Paradigms 1 and 2:**
> 1. If it comes to saving face, either one's own or somebody else's, lying or cheating becomes a duty.
> 2. If you have to promise something you can't deliver, just bluff your way, relying on postponements and additional promises to deliver, which provides additional time in which a human connection might emerge and save the day.
> 3. It is not only acceptable, but expected, to express words of kindness and demonstrate acts of generosity towards others, even if you are plotting against that other person.

SUBTHEME B: *Honor May be Derived from a Variety of Sources, Including a Person's Lineage, Age, Generosity, Success, Hard Work, Wealth, and Personal Piety.*

SUBTHEME C: *Shame is a Social Phenomenon and Comes from Being a "Bad" Person.*

> *Paradigm 1:* One may be a "bad" person and lose esteem in a variety of ways; the most important of which would be to let down one's family or religion.

SUBTHEME D: *Sexuality is the Cornerstone of Honor and the Likeliest Cause of Shame.*

> *Paradigm 1:* The moral reputation of a daughter or sister is a critical component of a family's honor. A woman with a bad reputation can bring shame to her family.

Practices Associated with Paradigm 1:
1. A woman must avoid any situation that will create a sense of impropriety.
2. A daughter or sister who loses her virginity outside of marriage, will be killed by males in her family as a means of preserving their honor.

SUBTHEME E: *The Dynamics of a Person Being Shamed is a Mechanism for Social Control.*

> *Paradigm 1:* This is often accomplished by gossip.
> *Paradigm 2:* What people say, or what they might say, is a strong constraint on one's actions.
> *Paradigm 3:* Preserving appearance, or creating an image, is very important.

THEME V: FAMILY AND KINSHIP ARE THE PRIMARY SOCIAL UNIT

SUBTHEME A: *These Function On Mutual Interdependence.*

SUBTHEME B: *The Extended Family Offers Family Members a Sense of Belonging and Security, and is the Basic Building Block of Society.*

> *Paradigm 1:* A person's full name identifies father, grandfather, and tribal origin.
> *Paradigm 2:* The strongest links and associations in the extended family are forged through the father's relatives or kin.
> *Paradigm 3:* A blood-bond is very strong and demands one's first loyalty in all circumstance.
> *Paradigm 4:* The worst possible situation is to be kinless, for any reason whatever.

SUBTHEME C: Collectivism is of Far Greater Importance Than Individualism.

Paradigm 1: Privacy is not valued and never sought.
Paradigm 2: Conformity is the norm.
Paradigm 3: The greatest pressure for conformity comes from the extended family.
Paradigm 4: Marriage is traditionally the uniting of two families rather than two individuals.
Paradigm 5: Intermarriages contribute to family solidarity.

SUBTHEME D: Women Have an Unchangeable Assigned Role in the Family and Society.

Paradigm 1: Women live and function primarily in different realms than men.
Paradigm 2: Women are to function in the private environment of the home and family.
Paradigm 3: They have very limited responsibilities and movement in the public arena.
Paradigm 4: The husband has authority over his wife and she must be obedient to him. As younger family members defer to the older, so women defer to men.
Paradigm 5: Modesty is a virtue and it is a woman's responsibility to be especially modest in matters of dress.

> **Practices Associated with Paradigm 5:**
> 1. Modest apparel includes the covering of a woman's hair and veil for her face.

Paradigm 6: The woman's primary responsibilities are the maintenance of the home and the raising of the children.

V. HAKKA (TAIWAN) WORLDVIEW
(From a Ph.D. Dissertation by Patrick Tsang – March 2002)

THEME 1: ANCESTRAL REVERENCE

This theme explains the origin of the people, connects them with their Chung Yuan past (as a part of the Han tribe) and affirms who they are as well as their values and traditions such as filial piety and the structure of lineage, etc. This is the major theme, providing them with a sense of who they are and running through nearly every domain of their social life.

SUBTHEME A: Ancestor Veneration is the Center of Our Life as a Community.

Paradigm 1: Lineage and family ancestral hall is the center of community life

Practices Associated With Paradigm 1:
1. Every village must have an ancestral hall as the center.
2. Every clan in a village should have their clan ancestral hall.
3. Important meetings are held in the ancestral hall.
4. Important ceremonies and celebrations are held in the ancestral hall, e.g., marriage, Chinese New Year, etc.
5. Clan or communal ancestor veneration is held in the ancestral hall.
6. Pun Tsoi, the communal meal, is served in front of the ancestral hall.
7. The immigrants make regular visits back to their own town in order to participate in ancestral veneration or attend festivities.
8. The young Hakka immigrants are all looking forward to visiting their home village. Ancestral worship is the first thing they do when they go back.

Paradigm 2: The family and ancestor shrine is the center of family life.

Practices Associated With Paradigm 2:
1. Every Hakka immigrant has an ancestor shrine and tablet set up in their home.
2. Most of the immigrant families offer incense to the ancestor every day and other items such as fruit on a weekly or bi-weekly basis. Meat and wine are offered on important days and festivals.
3. When they have needs, they come to pray before the ancestor shrine.
4. For the immigrants, the only thing they have not given up is the ancestral veneration and ancestral tablet.

SUBTHEME B: *"Always Remember the Spring When You Have a Drink of Water."*

Paradigm 1: *We must never forget our ancestors.*

Practices Associated With Paradigm 1:
1. Set up an ancestor shrine and an ancestor's tablet at home for regular veneration and offerings.
2. Tell your children about the achievements of the ancestors and the sacrifices they have made.
3. Pay grave visits and ancestor veneration on the appointed dates.
4. In joyous days and festivals, always remember your ancestors by burning incense, candles and food offering.
5. Nearly all family events will involve some form of ancestral honor.

Paradigm 2: *Keeping our genealogy is our important duty.*

Practices Associated With Paradigm 2:
1. Treasure your genealogy and pass it on to your descendents.
2. The genealogy tells you who your ancestors are.
3. We must travel back to our ancestral hall and put in the names of our sons.
4. Every Hakka must know where is their lineage ancestral hall where the primary copy of the genealogy is kept.

Paradigm 3: *Keeping our traditions and model our life after our ancestors life is part of remembering our ancestors.*

Practices Associated With Paradigm 3:
1. The heroic acts and sacrifices made by the ancestors are major parts of lineage stories and genealogy content.
2. Those ancestors who have made contributions to the lineage by earning honors or contributing ancestral properties are remembered in special ways in memory hall.
3. Children are told not to bring shame to their family name.

SUBTHEME C: *Paying Respect and Reverence to Our Ancestors is One of Our Most Important Duties.*

Paradigm 1: *Our ancestors deserve our respect.*

Practices Associated With Paradigm 1:
1. We have received our life and all the ancestral inheritance from them.
2. They have taken good care of us when they were still alive.
3. They are still helping us in the other world.

Paradigm 2: Those who do not pay respect to their ancestors are irresponsible.

Practices Associated With Paradigm 2:
1. People who don't pay back their debts are scum of the world and those who forget their ancestors are even worse.
2. Myths and folklore about bad things that happen to those who neglect their ancestors.

SUBTHEME D: Ancestors are Always Good to Us Unless We Are Unfaithful to Them.

Paradigm 1: Filial piety and service is our unquestionable responsibility.

Practices Associated With Paradigm 1:
1. "Don't ask why. It is your duty."
2. "It doesn't matter if you believe it or not. You must pay respect to your ancestors and your parents because it is your responsibility."
3. Myths and folklore about deities show that they reward those who fulfill their filial duties.

Paradigm 2: If something good happens, it is because of the blessing of the ancestors.

Practices Associated With Paradigm 2:
1. First thing you do when something good happens is give thanks to the ancestors who give you luck or help you to achieve.
2. If a wish comes true, it must be with the ancestor's help.

Paradigm 3: If something bad happens it must be our fault or neglect.

Practices Associated With Paradigm 3:
1. "How could your parents do things to harm you? They can only help you."
2. "Your parents are those you should trust and so are your ancestors."
3. "It must be your fault. You should make it up to the ancestors."
4. There are a lot of myths and stories about ancestor spirits who turned into evil ghosts (or hungry ghosts) because their descendants neglected them.

SUBTHEME E: *Ancestors Think, Feel and Have Needs Like Everyone Else.*

Paradigm 1: We should make them happy by bringing honor and glory to them.

Practices Associated With Paradigm 1:
1. Human foods are offered to ancestors.
2. Paper items of things we use, like clothing, car, money etc., are burnt as an offering to our ancestors.
3. "If you can bring honor to your parents by doing well in examinations, then it will also bring honor to your ancestors."
4. "You should treat your ancestors like yourselves."

Paradigm 2: Our ancestors would like to see the clan united and living in harmony.

Practices Associated With Paradigm 2:
1. "If a family has harmony among the members, the family will prosper. If not, it will cause a lot of strife and arguments."
2. Ancestors are parents of past generations, therefore they would behave like our parents who want to see their descendants live in harmony and in solidarity.
3. Every branch of the lineage must have someone to attend ancestral veneration on important days and events, this will show to our ancestors that we are united and in good form.
4. Myths about ancestors visiting them in dreams to complain about the disunity and fights among lineage members.
5. Inside the village communal hall, on top of the image of the Chinese dragon, there is a red paper with four Chinese words: kindness, closeness, harmony and love.

Paradigm 3: Our ancestors should be involved in important occasions and celebrations of the clan.

Practices Associated With Paradigm 3:
1. "Would you want to be left out? Surely, our ancestors would not like to be left out."
2. The ancestors are a part of the family and family should join together in important events.
3. All important occasions and celebrations, no matter whether familial or communal, are causes to have ancestral veneration.

Paradigm 4: We should maintain good relationships with ancestors.

Practices Associated With Paradigm 4:
1. Ancestors are always good to us. If they are not happy, it must be something we have done.
2. If our ancestors are happy, they will work harder to help us.
3. "Don't make your ancestors angry, or they will turn their eyes away from you and not watch out for you."
4. Myths about those who have good relationships with the ancestors being blessed with material goods and becoming prosperous.

Paradigm 5: *We should ensure that the ancestors are living in comfort and have every need met.*

> **Practices Associated With Paradigm 5**:
> 1. As we have physical needs, our ancestors have needs too.
> 2. "The grave is the house of our ancestors. It must be a place with good fung shui."
> 3. "We offer incense and vegetarian food regularly. On special days, we offer candles and meats."
> 4. Paper clothes and appliances are burnt to meet the needs of our ancestors.

THEME II: LINEAGE/CLAN IS WHERE YOU BELONG

This theme validates and reinforces the importance of the Hakka lineage system and clan relationship. The clan, an extended family, is the basic familial unit. It is where one is nurtured, accepted, affirmed and taken care of. This is where the personal identity of Hakka comes from. The clan is your family.

SUBTHEME A: *The Interest of the Lineage is Supreme.*

Paradigm 1: *Personal rights and interests are subservient to those of the clan.*

> **Practices Associated With Paradigm 1:**
> 1. Duties and responsibilities to your family and lineage are more important than personal choice and happiness.
> 2. The Hakkas are a high group people and individualism is not highly valued.
> 3. They are encouraged to sacrifice their personal interests for the sake of the family or clan.
> 4. A young woman gives up her right for marriage in order to help the family to raise her five younger brothers and sisters. She does this as a personal decision and her act is commended.

Paradigm 2: *Lineage interest is your interest too.*

> **Practices Associated With Paradigm 2**:
> 1. We share in the glory and prosperity of our lineage.
> 2. We all have an equal share in the benefits of the ancestral properties.
> 3. "If one of the lineage members gets rich or into position of influence, he would certainly help us."
> 4. There are many myths and folklore about people who are faithful in helping their lineage members and rewarded by the gods.

Paradigm 3: *We must submit to the lineage elders and follow the traditions of the clan.*

> **Practices Associated With Paradigm 3:**
> 1. "We must respect the elders of our lineage. They are looking after our interests."
> 2. "They are older and more seasoned, we should listen to them."
> 3. "This is the way our people do things and the elders just make sure things are done in the right way."

SUBTHEME B: The Lineage is Our Family.

Paradigm 1: *Within the lineage, we are a family.*

> **Practices Associated With Paradigm 1:**
> 1. We always address the other clan member with kinship terms.
> 2. A Hakka's first commitment is always to one's own clan.
> 3. If a clan member comes to visit, you must offer hospitality.
> 4. If a clan member needs help, you must do your best to help.
> 5. It is important to remember the code of your generation, so that you know how to address and relate to the other clan members.

Paradigm 2: *Lineage members take care of each other.*

> **Practices Associated With Paradigm 2:**
> 1. Lineage members (and village members) take care of one another and share responsibility for what happens to each other.
> 2. We have a moral responsibility for the well-being of one another.
> 3. There are many stories and myths about distant lineage members offering help in critical situations.

Paradigm 3: *We are tied together by our lineage or covenant alliance.*

> **Practices Associated With Paradigm 3:**
> 1. There is a common heritage due to blood ties and/or the lineage's alliance (for a multi-lineage village).
> 2. "We are in the same family just like staying on the same boat."
> 3. Many examples of people who are faithful to their lineage even in hopeless situations.

Paradigm 4: *Looking out only for your individual interest is a selfish act.*

> **Practices Associated With Paradigm 4:**
> 1. The ancestors are not pleased when we are selfish.
> 2. Selfishness is bad and sharing is good among the lineage.
> 3. Eating pun tsoi together. We share the same food with one another.
> 4. The heroes are enshrined in the hall of heroes because they didn't look out for their own interests but the interests of the community and the country.
> 5. If you are selfish, no one will remember you.

SUBTHEME C: *Close Cooperation and Good Relationships Among the Lineage Members are Important for Successful Living.*

Paradigm 1: Lineage members should treat each other as kin.

Practices Associated With Paradigm 1:
1. We always address the other lineage members with a kinship term.
2. Blood is thicker than anything.
3. Friends are good but not as important as your own people (lineage).
4. Friends are for a good time but clans are for life.
5. Sharing and mutuality are expected between clan members even if you do not know the other person personally.

Paradigm 2: A strong lineage is good for everyone.

Practices Associated With Paradigm 2:
1. Many stories and myths about people being persecuted by other lineages and receiving help from fellow lineage members.
2. It is important to demonstrate our strength and number in the parade of the Tin Hau Festival.
3. If our lineage receives honor, everyone is honored.

Paradigm 3: A united lineage is important for our interest and success.

Practices Associated With Paradigm 3:
1. Everyone is encouraged to join the grave visitations and community events. If one cannot come, one must make sure at least one family member shows up.
2. Eating pun tsoi together.
3. When you have an important event to celebrate, like a wedding or the birth of a child, you should celebrate together with the members of your lineage.

SUBTHEME D: *Outside the Lineage You Cannot Find Real Security and Acceptance.*

Paradigm 1: Lineage members are those you can trust.

Practices Associated With Paradigm 1:
1. We always address other lineage members with a kinship term.
2. Your own lineage or your own village people are those you can trust.
3. You don't need to make friends with other lineage members because they are your kin.

Paradigm 2: Be careful with outsiders.

> **Practices Associated With Paradigm 2:**
> 1. People who do not belong to my clan (or village) cannot be trusted.
> 2. If a stranger enters the village, we must keep an eye on that person.
> 3. Stories about outside people trying to do harm to the unity and well being of the lineage or village in covert ways.
> 4. Always watch out when you leave your own village.

Paradigm 3: Outsiders have no rights among us.

> **Practices Associated With Paradigm 3:**
> 1. You always question strangers concerning why they have come into the village.
> 2. You cannot use force or violence toward your fellow clan members or villagers but you can do so if that person is an outsider.
> 3. "We don't like strange people coming into our village."
> 4. "This is our land. Why should you come in?"

THEME III: TEMPORAL WELL-BEING IS THE SUPREME GOAL OF LIFE

This theme motivates people to seek security and improvement. It also validates the lifestyle and temporal goals of the Hakka. Physical and material well-being are important aspects in life. Religion is looked upon as a means to help one to achieve well-being in life whether it is physical, emotional or social well-being. Religion, other than ancestor worship, must be useful. If it is not useful, it is viewed as useless.

SUBTHEME A: Material Goods are Important for a Person's Well-Being.

Paradigm 1: Work hard to assure your well-being.

> **Practices Associated With Paradigm 1:**
> 1. Hard work is an important virtue and laziness is a big vice.
> 2. You must also be careful about spiritual matters. Be watchful about fung shui and other taboos.
> 3. If you don't earn enough in good days, you will suffer in the rainy days.
> 4. If you don't save enough when you are young and able, you won't have enough when you get old.
> 5. In a Hakka village, every one works! Young or old, men and women, no exceptions.

Paradigm 2: *Academic achievements bring well-being into your life.*

Practices Associated With Paradigm 2:
1. Nearly every Hakka student ranks academic achievement as their top goal.
2. Getting high degrees and achievement not only brings honor to your ancestors and family, it will also bring you wealth and security.
3. "No one can take away what you have learnt. Isn't it true?"
4. "Money is good but it could be used up, but education always helps."

Paradigm 3: *Material well-being is a measure of success.*

Practices Associated With Paradigm 3:
1. In stories, folklore and myth, material riches are always good and an evidence of being blessed.
2. "Study hard and one day you could be rich."
3. "You can find gold in your books."
4. There are four goals in life: Honor, beauty, riches and status.
5. On the right-hand side of the Tin Hau Temple, there is the hall of eternal security. Inside the hall, the deities of literature and martial arts are worshipped. With academic achievement and military might, one can have eternal security.

SUBTHEME B: *Transempirical Matters Can be Important for Your Well-Being.*

Paradigm 1: *Ensure you do not offend your ancestors or any spiritual beings.*

Practices Associated With Paradigm 1:
1. "It never hurts to pay honor to one more god, but it would be bad if you neglect one."
2. Animism abounds. Trees and places become objects of worship.
3. Next to the ancestor's grave, there is always a shrine for the local gods/ghosts.
4. Before you make an offering and veneration at your ancestor's grave, you must make paper offerings to the hungry ghosts in the area.
5. There is a sign by the door of the Tin Hau Temple: Blessed territory. If you enter the temple, you will be blessed.
6. The ancient tree is worshipped because of its longevity and the location of the tree.

Paradigm 2: *Give offerings to any deity that can give blessings to you.*

Practices Associated With Paradigm 2:
1. People worship all kinds of idols. One family I visited had twenty idols in their house.
2. If any deity has potency, then give offerings to it.
3. "If they can help you, why not make offerings to them?"
4. Stories and myths about deities helping those who make tributes to them.

Paradigm 3: Geomancy concerning our dwelling place and our ancestor's grave is crucial to our well-being.

> **Practices Associated With Paradigm 3:**
> 1. "If our ancestors live well and have power, they can take better care of us."
> 2. "We are tied to our ancestors, therefore if they are blessed, we will be blessed."
> 3. "Fung shui is very important. It can harm you or bless you. If your house has good fung shui, then blessings and fortune will be yours.
> 4. Many fights among the lineages are about fung shui of their village or their ancestor's grave.
> 5. Bad fung shui or if damage is done to good fung shui are valid reasons to protest even with violent means.
> 6. The goddess in Tin Hau Temple of Shap Pat Heung has such potency because of the fung shui of the location.

SUBTHEME C: Social Relationships Are Important to Well-Being.

Paradigm 1: Unity and solidarity among the clan members are very important.

> **Practices Associated With Paradigm 1:**
> 1. We always address the other clan members with kinship terms.
> 2. You should always say good things before other people.
> 3. Attending celebrations and rituals with other clan members are important.

Paradigm 2: Harmony is important in familial relationships.

> **Practices Associated With Paradigm 2:**
> 1. "If a family has harmony among the members, the family will prosper. If not, it will cause a lot of strife and arguments."
> 2. There is harmony even among the deities. The Tin Hau also welcomes other idols and deities to be her guests in her temple.
> 3. Every branch of the lineage must have someone to attend the ancestral veneration on important days and events. That will show to our ancestors that we are united and on good terms.
> 4. In the ancestral hall, deities worshipped by the lineage members are welcomed on condition that they cannot take the central position. For the sake of harmony, people make a lot of accommodations.
> 5. Inside the village communal hall, on top of the image of the Chinese dragon, there is a red paper with four Chinese words: kindness, closeness, harmony and love.

THEME IV: ZHONG (FAITHFUL ALLEGIANCE) IS THE HIGHEST VIRTUE

To the Hakka mind, zhong (faithful allegiance) means more than trustworthiness. It includes the meaning of total commitment. Although zhong is listed at the top of all Chinese virtues, the Hakka people have put a special focus on this virtue. This is the ideal they have set for themselves.

SUBTHEME A: *Zhong is Important in All Aspects of Relationship.*

Paradigm 1: One must be faithful to one's ancestor.

Practices Associated With Paradigm 1:
1. We always address the other clan member with a kinship term.
2. The worst sins of all are neglecting one's ancestors and lack of filial piety.
3. "Our ancestors are faithful to us, they leave us the land and the property, we must be faithful to them."
4. The ancestor shrine and tablet must be put in a prominent place in the house so we won't neglect to pay honor to the ancestors.

Paradigm 2: One must be faithful to one's lineage and family members.

Practices Associated With Paradigm 2:
1. On the two sides of the entrance to the village communal hall, there are two parallel sentences. One says: Faith allegiance that is open to the sun and the moon. The second says: Righteousness (Chinese stress that righteousness is a matter of responsibility and acts instead of an attribute) connects the North with the South.
2. On the left hand side of the Tin Hau Temple (the more important position) is the hall of heroes. Those who pledge their faithful allegiance to their people and the country have the highest honor.
3. Betraying one's own lineage and people is the worst sin one can commit.

Paradigm 3: One must be faithful to one's friends.

Practices Associated With Paradigm 3:
1. All the Hakka immigrants named faithfulness as the major criterion for friendship and betrayal as grounds for the termination of friendship.
2. One must be willing to share things and spend time with your friends.
3. One must take care of one's friends.

SUBTHEME B: *Those Who Have the Virtue of Zhong will be Honored.*

Paradigm 1: Those who are faithful to the country or clan are honored.

Practices Associated With Paradigm 1:
1. Those who die for the common cause of the community and the country will be honored and remembered in the Hall of Heroes.
2. Chinese history and folklore are full of past heroes who have the virtue of zhong.
3. Kwan Kun, a general who was defeated and beheaded by his enemy, is a commonly worshipped deity. He is famous for his faithful allegiance to his master.
4. Within a lineage, nearly all mistakes and trespasses can be forgiven except betrayal, which is lack of faithful allegiance.

Paradigm 2: *Those who are faithful to the Confucian ideology and social order will be rewarded.*

Practices Associated With Paradigm 2:
1. Many myths and folklore have affirmed this paradigm.
2. The lineage system, the folk religious system and the political system are all supported by Confucian ideology and in turn are affirmed by the Confucian social order.
3. All honor is given to any deities or persons if they agree to pledge faithful allegiance to the ideology and social order.

THEME V: RECIPROCITY IS THE RULE OF ALL RELATIONSHIPS

Reciprocity applies to relationships in both the empirical world and the spiritual world.

SUBTHEME A: *Reciprocity in All Social Relationships.*

Practices Associated With Subtheme A:
1. We should take care of our parents because they have taken care of us.
2. If you continue to take care of them after they pass away, they will continue to take care of you in their own way.
3. Favors and help are like debts that must be paid back.
4. If someone is good to you, you must return the favors.
5. If someone gives you a gift, then you have to return with one. Therefore, there is no need to give a gift to a close friend. Otherwise people would feel obligated to return the favor.
6. Relatives should give gifts to one another in order to maintain close relationships.

SUBTHEME B: *Reciprocity in Relationships in Transempirical Matters.*

Practices Associated With Subtheme B:
1. If a god or goddess answers your prayers and wishes, you should be thankful and make an offering to them.
2. If your prayer is not answered, then you have no obligation. But if you make an offering to them first, then they are obligated to help you.
3. If you behave well, you will have merit and that should bring you good fortune as a reward.
4. If you do something bad, you put yourself in danger of reaping bad fortune as the result.

THEME VI: THE IDEAL PERSON IS ONE WHO IS BOTH VIRTUOUS IN CHARACTER AND SUCCESSFUL IN SOCIETY

The Hakka immigrants share the same view as the Old Testament Jews that a good person will be rewarded with temporal blessings and a bad one will be punished with poverty and bad fortune. Being virtuous and not successful is something difficult for them to accept. They encourage their children to pursue both at the same time. They do not see the two as conflicting values.

SUBTHEME A: An Ideal Person Must Be Virtuous.

Practices Associated With Subtheme A:
1. We should seek virtues like filial piety, morality, kindness, generosity, righteousness, etc.
2. A willingness to make sacrifices for the sake of the country, society and others are important virtues.
3. All heroes must be virtuous. The highest virtue is faithful allegiance unto death. It is being virtuous without demanding temporal rewards.

SUBTHEME B: An Ideal Person Must be Successful.

Practices Associated With Subtheme B:
1. Achievement and success in this world is an important goal of life.
2. Hakka are upwardly mobile people despite their disadvantaged situation.
3. Hakka seek to be successful in everything they do.
4. Hakka have two basic goals for life: success in political and academic pursuits and success in material gains.
5. All heroes must be virtuous. The highest virtue is faithful allegiance unto death. It is being virtuous without demanding temporal rewards.

With this indication of how to picture worldview themes and their parts, we now turn to how to go about discovering a people's worldview.

Chapter 13

Discovering Worldview

We have learned the importance of dealing with worldview assumptions in relation to the communication of Christian messages. We have also seen examples of worldviews. If the worldview of the people we go to has been analyzed, then, we can gain much insight into the kinds of things we need to deal with in our attempts to understand and communicate. But what if there is no analysis and write-up of the worldview of the people to which we go? How do we go about seeking to discover the themes, subthemes and paradigms of such groups?

There are several areas to explore. Among them are insightful observation, literature (both written and oral), and songs. There are several forms of literature. Among them are stories, myths, proverbs, novels, movies and other types of written, oral and dramatized literature. We will look first at what I will call "insightful observation," then turn to several types of literature.

Insightful Observation

In previous chapters I have pointed to several things that can assist us in probing into the worldview assumptions of a society. The questions raised by Sire (see chapter 4) and the subjects for inquiry listed by Luzbetak (from Keesing) in chapter 5 would be good places to start, as would the shorter list of questions raised by Burnett in chapter 5.

In addition, James Spradley has written two books (with much the same content), *The Ethnographic Interview* (1979) and *Participant Observation* (1980) designed to provide a recipe for discovering worldview themes. These books specifically aim at providing students with step-by-step instructions as to how to carry out fieldwork research to discover what makes up a culture. Spradley, writes from the perspective of a school of anthropology called "ethnosemantics." This approach is especially good at helping us to discover the classification/categorization aspect of worldview. Spradley defines culture as "the acquired knowledge people use to interpret experience and generate behavior" (Spradley 1980:6). Since this definition of culture is so close to our definition of worldview, Spradley's approach to discovering cultural knowledge is especially helpful for our purposes.

Our approach to worldview discovery is the time-tested anthropological research method called "participant-observation." The object of this method is to observe insightfully the behavior of a people and, on this basis, to be able to deduce the principles on which their behavior is based. These principles are, of course, what we are calling worldview. In order to observe insightfully, it is necessary to learn how to get beyond our tendency to evaluate the behavior of other people ethnocentrically. It is also necessary to have our imaginations expanded through anthropological study of the range of human possibilities in any given area of culture. I assume that you, the readers, have already met these requirements.

As for the participant part of the research, anthropologists discovered long ago that they could not effectively study a people if they did not also participate with them at least in small ways in their approach to life. Anthropologists, then, attempt to live with the people they study and to participate with them in daily activities with the aim of learning how it feels to look at reality and to approach life in their way. If you have had this kind of experience, the process of attempting to observe insightfully will be enlivened by it. If not, you should do your best to imagine yourself looking at reality from their perspective.

The following steps should be helpful in enabling us to be reasonably effective in discovering the worldview assumptions and values underlying surface-level behavior:

1. **Be open to anything.** A basic problem we have in looking for other people's cultural assumptions is the fact that our imaginations have been so thoroughly conditioned by our own worldview. Anthropological study in which we look at the many varieties of dealing with perceived reality is designed to broaden our imaginations to be ready for just about anything we find.

2. Strongly **resist the temptation to attach our own assumptions to the behavior of the people we are studying**. Our interpretational reflexes have been so conditioned that without thinking, we automatically attach our meanings to their behavior. Thus, we regularly misinterpret the meanings of behavior such as the fist-shaking greeting of a Northern Nigerian or the casualness of many people in keeping time commitments or the practice of polygamy or the fact that some people stand so close to us when we converse with them or any of thousands of other such customs.

3. **Ask questions**. But be careful who you ask and what conclusions you draw from the answers you get. The surest way to get useful information is to first establish a friendship relationship with those from whom you seek information. Seeking information from people who may not be positively

disposed toward you is both impolite and likely to bring you information that is not trustworthy.

The first thing, then, is to find persons within the society who will answer your questions honestly about their cultural behavior. These persons will probably be those who have traveled outside of their home area and who, therefore, have an understanding of what it's like to be ignorant of the basics of the behavior going on around them. They should also be those with whom you have a friendship relationship that goes beyond their simply being sources of information for your research.

Two problems arise when we seek information from those who have little understanding of what it's like to be lost in another people's world. The first is "the politeness problem." For perhaps the majority of the peoples of the world, their main motivation in answering a question from an outsider, especially if they regard that person as a social superior, is to keep from offending. They, therefore, will try to figure out what answer the outsider expects and to give that to the person. The result is a polite answer that may not be a truthful answer.

The second problem is that people who have never been outside their own society may not understand that anyone could be so ignorant as to not know the answer to the questions being asked. For insiders who have learned their assumptions and behavior from childhood, they assume that everyone knows what they know. It is reasonable for them to assume, then, that outsiders who ask questions about basic things are trying to trap them or in some other way trying to get them to act against the best interests of their people.

Having said this, it must be noted that even people who have had experience outside their cultural context may fall into one or both of these problems. It is, therefore, a good idea to seek information about any given subject in more than one way. Ask questions concerning any given cultural pattern from several different angles and, if possible, from several different people. One of the things I have done in investigating Kamwe behavior and worldview is to have several people write for me on several subjects. When they turned in their writing, then, I did two additional things. First, I gave what one person wrote to another person for critique and filling in of gaps in the first person's material. Secondly, I interviewed the writers about what they had written, making my own notes to supplement what they had written. In this way I was able to get a much more comprehensive understanding of the cultural data than if I had simply asked one person.

4. In addition to asking questions, it is good to **gather folklore, the words of songs and other cultural data** generated by the people themselves. In

learning Hausa, we did just that, finding such materials a delightful way to get into both the language and the culture. I will speak of the value of these materials in more detail below.

Asking Questions

In chapters four and five we have presented three sets of questions that can be used in our quest to discover worldview themes, subthemes, paradigms, etc. James Sire (1997:17-18) provides a useful list of questions that designate categories of things to investigate. In interviewing the members of a society to discover their assumptions, each of Sire's questions could be broken down something like as follows:

What is prime reality—the really real?

- Is there a God or gods? What does the spirit world look like—angels, demons, individual spirits, territorial spirits, ancestor spirits? Are they arranged hierarchically? Are they predictable or capricious? Who interacts with the spirit world—priests, shamans, heads of households? Which spirits are approached and how and when—spirits, ancestors, God/gods?
- The material cosmos? Is there nothing beyond what we can see and sense? Is matter eternal? Can matter create and/or extend itself? What is the relationship between matter and humans?
- Only humans? Are humans the basic reality? Are we our own gods? What is our relationship to the material world? Is there a spirit world? If so, what is our relationship to it?

Who is in charge of this world?

- Is there a God in charge?
- If there is, is he/it personal or impersonal?
- If there is a God, is he really good?
- Are humans in charge?
- Is no one at all in charge?

What is the nature of the world around us?

- Is the world the result of creation or is it autonomous?
- Is it orderly or chaotic—like a machine or like a person?
- Is it matter or spirit?
- Should we emphasize a subjective or an objective relationship to the world?

What is a human being?

- Are we highly complex machines?
- Are we really gods?
- Are we created beings, made in God's image?
- Are we merely the products of unreasoning evolution?
- Are we as human beings determined or free?
- Are we alone the makers of values?

What happens to a person at death?

- Are we extinguished, simply blotted out?
- Are we transformed to a higher state?
- Are we reincarnated?
- Do we simply move into a shadowy existence somewhere?

How is it possible to know anything at all?

- Is it because we are in the image of God?
- Did consciousness and rationality develop during the process of evolution?
- Is what we think is knowledge simply an illusion?
- If we can know, can we know absolutely?

How do we know what is right and wrong?

- Is it because there is a God who has implanted such knowledge in us?
- Or are we simply to do what feels good as long as it doesn't hurt others?
- Or do we develop ideas of right and wrong in order to survive?

What is the meaning of human history?

- Is it to realize the purposes of God or the gods?
- Are we on our own to try to make something of human experience without the help of supernatural beings?
- Are we to live so as to prepare for a life in community with God?

If we turn to the approach to discovering worldview advocated by Luzbetak (after Keesing), we get a rather uneven, though helpful, set of considerations to ask about. The reason I call these uneven is because the considerations are at different levels: some easily yielding worldview assumptions (e.g., 8, 9), some seeking information about surface-level behavior (e.g., 4, 5, 6) that would need to be analyzed to enable one to discover the underlying assumptions. And some of these concerns may be more helpful in uncovering the worldview assumptions of tribal societies such as those of Papua New Guinea than they would be in studying more industrial societies. Many of them are combinable with the questions listed above and those below. The topics are:

1. The self-image of the society and whom the society considers to be "a good person." See the Kamwe analysis in chapter 12.
2. The violent resistance to certain innovations.
3. The native educational content and motivations. What is really learned?
4. The constant lessons and warnings given to small children.
5. The instructions given to the youths during the initiation rites.
6. Arguments between tribesmen, quarrels between husband and wife.
7. The scolding, reprimands, and praise given especially to the young.
8. The factors that contribute to a feeling of security.
9. The factors that contribute to a preferred status.
10. The content and motivation contained in the arguments of native agitators.
11. The reasons for dissatisfaction and criticism.
12. The objects of violent hate and condemnation.
13. The assumptions, motivations, and general line of reasoning observed in tribal meetings and court sessions.
14. The behavior that the more severe sanctions aim to control.
15. The type of sanctions feared most.
16. The more serious worries.
17. The severest insults and the most painful type of ridicule.
18. Chief aspirations.
19. Occasions for war.
20. Motives for suicide.

David Burnett, as we have seen, deals with six areas in his approach to worldview. Each of these implies one major, overriding question:

- Cosmos—what is the nature of the universe?
- Self—who are we?
- Knowing—what is truth?
- Community—what is society?
- Time—what is time?
- Value—what is good?

Studying Oral and Written Literature

One of the most productive ways of getting at worldview is to collect and study the literature of a people, both oral and written. These are the myths, folktales, proverbs, song lyrics, poems, riddles, novels, rituals and the like. In literate societies much, though not all of such materials are written. In "oral societies" (i.e., the majority of the societies of the world who live without a major focus on writing) the materials have to be collected by listening to story-telling and other forms of oral communication. Such materials are produced by the people themselves as expressions of concepts they value.

Myths are stories that provide a society's ultimate explanations of Reality as they perceive it. Note that we are using the term "myth" with its technical definition, not in the popular sense where the term refers to something that is untrue. Technically, the term "myth" is used for any type of ultimate explanation, whether true or not. For example, as Christians we believe the Genesis account of the creation of the world by God. This is our myth or explanation of how things came into being. We also believe that myth to be true, though there is some discussion concerning whether the way the story is presented is factual or not.

Other peoples have their myths concerning how the world got here. These often embody some truth presented in a fanciful story. To qualify as a myth, a story must explain some aspect of Reality from the point of view of the people, whether this is done factually or fancifully. Technically, then, much of the Bible is myth (we would say true and historically accurate myth), explaining as it does both the origin of the world and the origin of Israel, the ways in which God worked with and through His people, the way in which He brought about salvation and many other aspects of God's interactions with His creatures.

Myth tells how (usually through the deeds of supernatural beings) a reality came into existence, be it the whole of reality, the cosmos, or only a fragment of reality. Myths explain why the world is the way it is and how it relates to humankind. They explain and validate a society's culture and institutions and the activities of supernatural beings and powers. They provide an explanation or a model for how we are to relate to God (or a god), other human beings, and our biosphere. They reveal exemplary models for all human rites and all significant human activities: diet, marriage, work, education, art, wisdom, etc. Though a study of myths can be fascinating in and of itself, our purpose is to get from myths glimpses of worldview assumptions.

Tales, then, are often more fanciful, with animals (representing types of people) often playing major roles. In contrast to myths in which the actors are usually gods and supernatural beings, the participants in tales are heroes and animals often involved in miraculous events. And all the actors share the common trait that they do not belong to the everyday world (Eliade 1963:10). Even so, distinguishing between myths and tales is not always easy. Yet worldview assumptions and values, though often less in focus than in the myths, can usually be seen to underlie the behavior of the participants.

Proverbs are pithy encapsulations of a society's wisdom. In that wisdom, then, we can often glean insights into a people's perception of and interaction with reality. Collecting and analyzing proverbs is probably the single most helpful activity in the folklore area.

Riddles are clever little statements or problems, presented playfully, usually with set answers. They often provide insight into how people see certain aspects of reality. Though collecting and analyzing riddles is great fun, it is often difficult to figure out just what major assumptions and values are indicated.

Song Lyrics and Poetry can also provide insight into values and assumptions. Often in songs and poetry, assumptions and values are closer to the surface than with the other types of materials mentioned above. Think of the kinds of things stated in western songs concerning love, individualism, discouragement and other prominent emotions and how they show certain of the worldview assumptions of western people.

Novels, Biographies, Newspapers and Other Written Literature can give great insight into the worldview assumptions of literate peoples. So can *Movies, Television and Radio Programs*, though one must be careful to look for the views of the people beyond those of the directors and editors of these media presentations. Often, what we see and read in such "literature" is derived more from the fantasies of the movie directors or the authors of the novels than from the actual beliefs and behavior of the people.

What to Look For in Folklore

To underline the importance of collecting and studying folklore, I would like to point to at least seven ways in which oral (including TV, radio and movies) and written literature function to teach and reinforce a society's worldview assumptions. These things are important to recognize, especially when we realize that in oral societies, folklore is a primary means of educating the young.

1. Folklore, especially myth, provides a basis of common origins and identity. Myths typically deal with the origins of life and a variety of the components of life as perceived by a people.

2. Folklore answers questions about human destiny as seen by a people and what may help or alter it. Myths, tales, proverbs and song lyrics often deal with topics such as death, fatalism, cause and effect and other things relating to what life is all about.

3. Folklore reinforces basic assumptions of authority, respect, and rights to land or other material possessions. Relationships between parents and children, between social superiors and social inferiors and the rights and privileges of each class of people are often in focus in folklore.

4. Folklore often clearly pictures who are to be included and who are to be excluded, who are the "we" and who are the "they." Folklore often teaches that insiders be treated in one way, outsiders in another, often as those whom it is legitimate to exploit.

5. Folklore teaches and reinforces moral values. The values of a society are often shown quite explicitly in the ways in which the characters in folklore (often represented as animals in oral societies) are depicted, their behavior, their attitudes, how they relate to others, when and how they take revenge.

6. Folklore serves to illustrate ideal and sub-ideal behavior and the rewards and punishments that go along with either. African animal tales are especially useful in this area, since the various animals represent various types of people.

7. Folklore serves as encouragement in times of difficulty and uncertainty. Themes such as courage and bravery are the subjects of many myths and tales, pointing out to people a society's expectations in times of trouble.

What follows are a number of myths, tales, proverbs and other types of folklore that can serve to illustrate the kinds of material to collect and analyze. Additional examples of most of these categories of folklore are to be found in Appendix C.

Myths

Though myths provide important insights into how people think, it is often necessary to study quite a number of them before the perspective is clear. There are, however, a large number of written collections of myths and also a number of summaries of the teaching of the myths of the world to help us in our quest to discover worldview assumptions and values.

Concerning the study of myths, I quote here a helpful statement from a book entitled *African Mythology* by Geoffrey Parrinder (1967) pointing out what to expect in studying myths.

> In the mythologies of every continent there can be distinguished great myths, and others that are of less importance. Some myths dominate and show the character of the religious outlook, while others are less central, repetitive, and fanciful. All kinds of myths need to be taken into account, for altogether they show the values which the society holds dear.
>
> Most myths tell how something came to exist; man, the world, certain animals, social affairs. The myths make a 'sacred history' of the people. But naturally the creation of the world comes first and this myth influences others that follow. There could be no stories of creation of men or animals if there was not already a world created for them to enjoy. So the central myth, telling the beginnings of the world, shows that history had a beginning. Legendary events that came later show how the world was changed, and in particular the adventures of man, his discovery of sex, the obligation to work, the coming of death.
>
> Myths also tell about supernatural beings, gods and ancestors. The great heroes of the past provided models for human behavior later. But they show an end as well as a beginning. For although the Supreme Being and other spirits created and lived on earth, they also left it later on or disappeared. Man too begins and ends his life on earth (1967:16).

1. How Things Began

There are in the world a very large number of creation myths. Probably, every people has at least one. Some people have more than one. Many of the myths concerned with the earliest beginnings of a people are very interesting. But few are as helpful in displaying worldview assumptions as are myths in some of the other categories below. They often do show assumptions concerning God or their gods and spirits plus whether the people are even interested in how things began. At least some of the peoples of the world don't seem to be. They start, therefore, with the world and its contents already in place. They also usually clue the reader in on the kind of environment the people experience.

Most people assume that our world exists because of certain activities within the spirit world. For many, God or a god created the world good and was once close to His creatures. All went well for humans during that time. Our problems, then, are explained as resulting from someone making a mistake in early times. Had that mistake not happened, then, humankind would have continued to be immortal and to live eternally without the present need for purification.

A Kamwe origin myth from M. Kraft (1978:194-95) follows:

God created the heaven and the world. He lived in the heaven but the world was empty. After many years, woman was first created by God. God saw from heaven that woman was very lonely. He came down and asked the woman to go to heaven to live together with him. The woman refused saying that she preferred to live in the world rather than to go to heaven to live with God. Though she had trouble and was lonely, God did not force her to go and live with him. Instead, he made her his wife, came down and slept with her.

She gave birth to ten children, five boys, five girls. God provided food and shelter for the children but asked the woman if he could take them to heaven to rear. The woman refused saying that the world belonged to her, heaven belonged to God, so her children would stay in the world to populate it. God then asked if she would divide the children between them so he could put his share of the children in another part of the world. To this the woman agreed, giving three boys and two girls to God. She took more females for herself since she knew that males do not give birth. God took his share of the children to a different part of the world and blessed them with many good things.

The place where the woman lived is Mcakali. All the people of the world came from this woman who lived at Mcakali. The children of God were blessed with many good things, including the power to rule the children of the woman. They were given horses and spears to fight the children of the woman. But to the children of the woman God gave axes, hoes, and sickles for tilling the ground. Thus, even today it is a popular conception that the Kamwe should be farmers and the Fulani the rulers. Anybody who opposes this opposes the law of God.

The creation myth of the people of the Ralik chain of the Marshall Islands assumes water and an uncreated being (god) living in it. It also tells us about some of their gods and their assignments.

Long ago when all was water, Lowa, the uncreated, was alone in the sea. "Mmmmmm," he said, and islands rose out of the water. "Mmmmmm," he said, and reefs and sandbanks were created.

"Mmmmmm," he said, and plants appeared. Again he uttered the creative word, and birds came into being.

Then Lowa made four gods for the four directions in the sky and a white gull to fly encircling the heavens forever.

Iroijdrilik was the one who was to preside over the west, the land of Eb, and to be in charge of life and increase and all living things. Lokomran was put in charge of the east. The people say he is the one "who twists the daybreak." Lorok was given the south and told to regulate the winds. Lalilikian is the north-man, who brings death. Then Lowa sent a man into the world whose name is forgotten. This man put all the islands in a basket … and started to put them in order. He put the Carolines to the westward, where they are today, and arranged the Marshalls in two long chains in their proper order. One island fell out of the basket, but he did not stop to put it straight. This is Namorik, which is still out of line. The last two to be put in their places were Jaluit and Ebon. Then he threw away the basket. It floated here and there in the ocean, and then stopped and became the island named Kili. It is named this for the basket which formed it. …

Sometimes Iroijdrilik, the god of the west whose country is named Eb, sends his son to the island of Ebon to see how the people are faring. Ebon is named for Eb, and therefore Iroijdrilik takes special care of it. When the black tern flies over Ebon, crying out, the people believe this is a promise of plenty. The god remembers the island, and this is why, they say, Ebon produces more food than the other islands (Leach 1956:185-86).

2. How Sin Entered the World and God Left

A Kamwe myth I heard from an old chief concerns the coming of sin into the world. It recalls a time when God and his son lived on earth, fellowshipping with people, eating with them, sleeping in their homes. All was good then. No one lied, cheated, stole or ran off with another man's wife like they do now. But there came a time when God and his son were sharing a meal in a certain home. The woman who prepared the meal, however, had not washed her dishes properly. God's son ate from a dirty dish and died. This angered God greatly, so he went far away and has not been heard from since.

When the chief finished his story, he looked at me and asked, "White man, can you tell us where God has gone? We do sacrifices and prayers to him constantly but have no idea whether he hears us or not." What an opportunity this provided for witness!

There are many similar myths in Africa. One fairly frequent theme in West Africa is of a woman using a mortar and pestle to grind grain. In one myth the heavens are so low that as the woman lifts the pestle, it bangs against heaven and bothers God. In anger, then, God leaves the earth, retracting heaven to a distance from earth, and leaving humans to their own devices from that time to this.

3. Origin of Death

The Dinka of East Africa use the above theme to explain both why God left and why hard work, illness and death have come to humans. One assumption that is prominent in this kind of story is that, though God was once near us, now he is far away.

> Because the sky at first was so low, men and women had to be careful in hoeing the ground or pounding the grain not to touch God. Death had not yet come into the world, and God had given the first man and woman one grain of millet each day. This was enough for them and they were forbidden to grow or use any more. But one day the woman was greedy and chose to pound more grain than the ration. To do this she had to take a longer pestle, and when she raised it up

she hit the sky, and so God went far away. Since that day men have had to work hard for their food, they are often hungry, they cannot reach God easily, and illness and death have come to them. ...

The Dinka say that ... a rope hung originally within reach of man who could climb up it to God. But when the woman had offended God by hitting the sky, God sent a blue bird to cut the rope so that men could not get to him easily (Parrinder 1967:35).

An interesting myth from Madagascar points to the strength of the felt need for children and some of the reasons why children are beneficial.

One day God asked the first human couple who then lived in heaven what kind of death they wanted, that of the moon or that of the banana. Because the couple wondered in dismay about the implications of the two modes of death, God explained to them: the banana puts forth shoots which take its place and the moon itself comes back to life. The couple considered for a long time before they made the choice. If they elected to be childless they would avoid death, but they would also be very lonely, would themselves be forced to carry out all the work, and would not have anybody to work and strive for. Therefore they prayed to God for children, well aware of the consequences of their choice. And their prayer was granted. Since that time man's sojourn is short on this earth (Feldmann 1970:114-115).

4. How a People Got to Live Where They Live

A Kamwe myth concerning how three groups got their land is recorded by M. Kraft (1978:190-91):

The people of Metla came from Sukur. They came in a group. On their way to Metla some of them settled at Mogodi and the rest proceeded to Nkala. There were three groups, led by three brothers: Tizhe, Zira and Tumba. They called on the high priest to divide the family property. He divided it into three unequal portions and called the boys to make their choice. Tizhe, being the oldest, chose first and chose the largest portion, leaving Zira and Tumba with smaller portions. Tumba, who had the smallest portion became angry with his brothers, so when he came to his portion he named it Ghumci, meaning "Good-bye forever." His group, then, cut themselves completely off from the others. Even during the time of war, Tumba's group got no help from the others. However, they were able to drive off the people of Kamwendiva from their area. These people had to go to the northeast to settle.

5. The Need for Cooperation and Discipline

The high value Japanese put on cooperation and discipline is depicted in the well-known myth of *Saru-to-Kani* (the Ape and the Crab). Though this story may be variously interpreted by outsiders, in a Japanese context it is designed to reinforce cultural themes of community and cooperation. The crab agrees to an exchange to satisfy the ape, showing that group harmony is of higher priority than individual direction. Though the ape is stealing his persimmons, the crab invites his cooperation by motioning him to throw him down some of the fruit. This he does in a completely unacceptable way. So the crab (and friends) punish the ape whereupon the ape returns to acceptable conduct, inducing the crab to forgive him.

> A crab finds a rice cake and an ape finds a hard persimmon seed. The ape wanting something to eat right away begs the crab to make an exchange. The crab agrees and while the ape goes away eating his rice cake the crab plants the persimmon seed in the ground. Some time later, a tree filled with ripe and unripe persimmons appears. The ape comes back, climbs the tree and begins to eat the ripe persimmons. The crab watches the ape and motions him to throw some of the fruit down to him. The ape responds by hurling hard unripe persimmons at the crab thus injuring him. The next day the crab tells what happened to his friends: chestnut, bee, and rice mortar and the four of them plot revenge against the ape.

> The crab invites the ape to dinner at his home and, not suspecting anything, the ape comes. The ape is seated in front of a burning charcoal burner where the chestnut is hiding. Chestnut bursts open with heat into the eyes of the ape nearly blinding him. He runs into the kitchen to splash water on his eyes to relieve the burning when the bee darts out of a cupboard and stings the ape. As he makes his way out the door to escape, rice mortar falls off a shelf near the door and knocks the ape to the ground. The crab gets near and squeezes the ape's neck with his pincers. The ape remembering what he had earlier done to the crab, begs his forgiveness. The crab immediately forgives and lets go.

6. A Papua New Guinea Summary

PNG is an interesting place to look for stories displaying their assumptions and values. Though I have no myths to present, I offer the following summary to point out some of the features of PNG beliefs and then to discuss the phenomenon of the "cargo cult" mentality, rooted in their worldview assumptions, that produces interesting twists in their interpretations of western contact phenomena.

According to James Siers (1981) PNG beliefs

> Have always centered round the existence of spirit beings. These may be the gods and goddesses of mythology, the spirits of ancestors or the spirits of the sea and bush. Ghosts can return in human or animal form and be easily confused with real people or animals. Few of these spirits were benevolent by nature. They were mostly a crotchety lot who needed constant appeasement and propitiation by means of sacrifices and offerings to concentrate their attention on the job of looking after the living.

> Another belief which made life very worrying was that no event had a natural cause. A bad harvest, a death or an accident were never due to weather, illness or misfortune but to the anger of spirits or perhaps to sorcery, the activity of a living enemy. After any death put down to sorcery (and most were) a lot of energy would be spent on tracking down the offender and avenging the victim. …

> Though Melanesians have no creation story, there is a general idea that all people are descended from a common ancestor and therefore are brothers. There are many stories concerning two brothers, one good, one bad. The bad one's anti-social activities cause most of the world's troubles, including the release of the sea and the separation of islands. Sometimes one brother is white, and his crime lies in withholding goods which should be shared by all. This situation has to be righted by magic—the ritual of the cargo cult.

> When planes and ships were seen during World War II disgorging goods by the ton, it naturally seemed that there was sharp practice afoot; nobody could possible have come by so many possessions fairly. The answer was to do away with tradition, imitate the white man with his office, papers and airstrips, and the lost goods would be

delivered to their rightful owners. This idea spread not only in Papua New Guinea but throughout the Pacific. Though groups of cultists were later taken to Australia and shown that goods came from factories where people worked hard, they were still not convinced (1981:13).

This cargo cult phenomenon is based on a traditional worldview-level set of assumptions, leading to interpretations of the source of European material goods that are quite divergent from what we know as the reality of the situation. With no understanding of western invention and manufacturing processes, Melanesians (including PNG peoples) assume the goods come from God and are meant for all, but are withheld by the descendents of one of the brothers, the Europeans. The Melanesians, therefore, attempt to invoke spirit power in a variety of ways to gain what they deem to be rightfully theirs. For many, this means listening carefully to the missionaries in hopes that they will sooner or later divulge the secret that made it possible for them to get the goods.

Tales

Though I have included tales with myths in much of what I've said above, I want to illustrate this genre from a collection of Hausa folktales published in my book, *Teach Yourself Hausa* (1973).

1. Illustrating fatalism:
A hyena came upon a lizard stealing beans. He caught the lizard and was about to eat it when he spied a dog. He decided to take the lizard to his lair, then come back to get the dog. This he did, but when he returned, the dog was gone. Upon returning to his lair, the lizard also had fled. The hyena's conclusion: whatever you go after in this life, if you were not meant to have it, it would be better if you never tried to get it.

2. Illustrating the need to share good fortune:
Two men were walking when one found a sack of money. The second man exclaimed, "Wow, we're sure lucky today." The man who found the money replied, "Is it we who are lucky, or is it me who is lucky?" The second man answered, "Okay, so be it." As they walked further, some thieves accosted them. As they ran, the first man became tired because of the weight of the sack of money, exclaiming, "What a bad situation we're in now." The second man

retorted, "Is it we who are in a bad situation, or is it you who are in a bad situation?"

3. Illustrating the foolishness of pride:
Once upon a time a jackal was wandering around looking for food. He spied a crow with a bit of meat in his mouth and coveted it greatly. So he thought up a scheme for getting the meat. "Crow," he said, "the other day I heard you singing so sweetly. When can I ever hear your beautiful song again." The crow, pleased at hearing this, opened his mouth to sing. The meat fell to the ground and the jackal ran off with it.

4. Illustrating the resourcefulness of people with disabilities:
A young man out for a walk at night spied a blind man carrying a lantern. Amazed, he said, "Blind man, are you crazy, carrying a lantern like this? Aren't day and night the same for you?" "Indeed, they are the same," said the blind man. "It is not for my sake that I carry the lantern. It is to keep idiots like you from knocking me over!"

Proverbs

One of my favorite ways of getting at a people's assumptions is to study their proverbs. It is probable that all people have proverbs, though they are more in evidence with some people than with others. Among Northern Nigerians (and probably most other Africans), for example, a typical discussion or oral presentation is likely to involve several proverbs to support major points. It is likely that participants in societies that are not literate or that place little emphasis on literacy place greater emphasis on proverbs than those in societies that place more emphasis on literacy and school-type education.

We must be careful what we assume concerning the value of proverbs, however. Proverbs typically embody the assumptions concerning reality of a people as held at the time the proverb came into existence or was borrowed, not necessarily at the present time. For this reason, each assumption highlighted in a proverb needs to be tested with the people of today to see if the assumption is still valid. That assumption may have changed since the proverb came into existence. Probably because proverbial statements are usually creative, proverbs tend to continue to exist in a society even after the assumption of value they portray has changed.

Proverbs can also contradict one another. This may be the result of their application to different situations or may arise from the continuity of a proverb after the assumption it embodies has been changed. For example, we have in English two proverbs concerning the use of time that contradict each other: "Haste makes waste," and "A stitch in time saves nine."

I will illustrate the kind of things that can be discovered about Hausa assumptions by listing some of their proverbs taken again from *Teach Yourself Hausa* (1973). I label them according to the kinds of assumptions and values they portray. After these, I list several from other African societies followed by a group of Mexican American proverbs.

1. Exhorting to Proper Conduct:

- If one does no wrong, there is no regret.
- Rather than dancing a bad dance, one would be better advised to stay home.
- Leave the chicken in its feathers.
- The statement, "If I had only known" is like the back of one's head.

2. Exhorting Activity:

- God says, "Get up, let me help you."
- The value of good sense is making use of it.
- Keeping one's excrement in one's stomach doesn't keep one from hunger.

3. Exhorting Patience:

- Patience is the world's medicine.
- A patient person is a wealthy person.
- A patient person will cook a stone and drink the broth.
- Traveling slowly doesn't keep a person from arriving.

4. Stating Facts of Life:

- Nighttime is the cloak of evil.
- Even if your hand stinks, you wouldn't cut it off.
- Everyone who is great has someone greater than he.
- Your body will let you know its limits.
- Even an old anus doesn't get to rest.

5. Dealing With Cause and Effect:

- Thanks to the presence of chickens, a lizard gets the benefit of being able to drink water from a bowl.
- The one who already has meat is the one who has a right to look for fire.
- "Let's go see," calls the bluff of a liar.

6. Involving Comparisons:

- A chief's friend shares the advantages of a chief.
- Kindness is a bed to sleep on.
- God is the Chief of chiefs.
- The world is like a pregnant woman (i.e., you never know whether it will bring forth blessing or trouble).
- Seeing something is better than hearing about it.
- Truth is better than money.

7. Proverbs for More Specialized Situations:

- It is a worthless activity for a blind man to turn his head to look (i.e., he can't see anyway).
- Would one seek blood from a locust?
- It is as impossible as the Kano railway station (i.e., where there is always great confusion).
- A worthless one has chased away a useless one (i.e., rather than improving things, the next appointee has made things worse).
- If I make daylight for you, don't you make night for me.

Following are several additional topics displayed in proverbs from a variety of African societies, collected by Alta Jablow (1961). The society from which the proverb comes is noted after the proverb.

8. On Ignorance and Knowledge:

- It is not only one mother who can cook a nice soup (i.e., there are many good cooks) (Efik).
- If you have never drunk somebody else's mother's soup, you think only your mother's soup is good (Ga).
- A man is like a pepper; till you have chewed it, you do not know how hot it is (i.e., experiencing a person is the only way to get to know what he is really like) (Hausa).
- A man who has not seen the new moon before, calls the stars the Moon (i.e., only experience can enable people to rightly interpret) (Vai).

9. Dealing With Prudence:

- One is not sent up a ladder to then have the ladder drawn away from under him (i.e., one does not expect to be abandoned by those who assigned him a task) (Ga).
- Pull the child out of the water before you punish him (Vai).
- One does not set fire to the roof and then go to bed (Yoruba).
- One does not throw a stick after the snake is gone (Jabo).
- Should a man roof his house without first building the walls (Efik)?

10. Teaching That One Should Know His Place:

- Even if you sit on the bottom of the sea, you cannot be a fish (Vai).
- An egg cannot fight with a stone (Bura).
- You are not the crocodile's brother, though you swim well by his side (i.e., even though you might be closely associated with a mean person, you'll never be accepted by him as a brother) (Mende).
- If a crocodile deserts the water, he will find himself on a spear (i.e., stay close to your family lest you be mistreated by those who don't care to protect you) (Bura).

11. Concerning Endurance:

- An elephant does not grow in one day (Gio).
- Bit by bit the fly ate the dog's ear (Ga).
- If a man lives long enough, he shall have eaten a whole elephant (Vai).
- If there is a continual going to the well, one day there will be a smashing of the pitcher (i.e., accidents will happen) (Hausa).

12. Concerning Wealth:

- The pipe of the poor does not sound (i.e., no one listens to a person with no status) (Ga).
- An empty rice bag will not stand up (Loma).
- Wealth is the man; if you have nothing, no one loves you (Hausa).
- Being poor makes it hard to have friends but not impossible (Bura).
- The frog says, "I have nothing, but I have my hop" (i.e., everyone has something of value) (Vai).

13. On Being Content With One's Situation:

- An elephant never gets tired of carrying his tusks (i.e., one can never resent the weight of his family) (Vai).
- I have a pot, why then should I search for another? (Kru).
- One who cannot pick up an ant and wants to pick up an elephant will someday see his folly (Jabo).
- Salt does not praise itself that it is sweet (i.e., accept who you are) (Ga).

14. On Anger:

- Anger is a warmth that lights itself (Kru).
- One does not become so mad at his head that he wears his hat on his buttocks (Yoruba).
- If you have never been angry, you have never been born (Bassa).
- A frown is not a slap (Hausa).
- Sweetness walks with bitterness (Efik).

15. On Consequences:

- The ashes are the children of the fire (i.e., there are certain expectable consequences of certain behavior) (Bura).
- Today is the elder brother of tomorrow, and a heavy dew is the elder brother of rain (i.e., what happens at one time has roots in a previous time or set of circumstances) (Fan).
- The tail must follow the head (Kru).
- Beware of scattering ashes, the wind will blow them in your eye (Efik).

16. On Women:

- Regular work tires a woman, but totally wrecks a man (Fan).
- If you want peace, give ear to your wives' proposals (Fan).
- The old bachelor does his own cooking (i.e., if he is so foolish as to not have a wife, he has to take the consequences) (Mande).
- Who marries a beautiful woman marries torment (Mande).

In an article by Shelly Zormeier and Larry Samovar (2000) we find a helpful discussion of Mexican American proverbs, including a listing of some of them:

1. Advocating Collectivism:

- Better to be a fool with the crowd than wise by oneself
- A solitary soul neither sings nor cries (i.e., has no feelings).
- He who divides and shares is left with the best share.
- Bewail your poverty, and not alone.

2. Advocating Fatalism:

- God gives it and God takes it away.
- If God is going to give you something, it will come easy.
- He who is born to suffer will start from the cradle.
- He who is born to be a potted plant will not go beyond the porch (i.e., will not take risks).

3. Present-Time Orientation:

- Don't move the water; the river is already flooding (i.e., leave matters as they are).
- Give time to time (i.e., don't rush).
- There is more time to life.
- Tomorrow will be another day.
- Don't do today what you can put off until tomorrow.

4. A "Being" Orientation:

- He who lives a hurried life will soon die.
- Don't worry so much so you can last longer.
- He who gets drenched at dawn has the rest of the day to dry out (i.e., don't try to get things done too fast, the rest of the day is there to use).
- He who wants everything will lose everything.

5. Family Values:
- A tree that grows crooked cannot be straightened.
- Better to die on your feet than to live on your knees (i.e., stand up for your honor).
- A man is king in his home.

From such proverbs one can get considerable insight into at least some of the assumptions and values of the people who use them.

Riddles

As mentioned above, riddles, though fun, are often hard to figure out. They should not, however be ignored as we look for worldview assumptions. The thing most evident in riddles is the mental picturing of the world that they display. In my own work with Hausa riddles (Kraft 1975, 2001), I have been amazed at the sometimes radical differences between the view of reality shown in the Hausa riddles and my own picturing of reality. There are, however, many similarities as well.

Following are several Hausa riddles from my own collection, followed by several from Jablow. I am sorry these are all from Africa. Riddling is especially prominent in African societies. I have not had opportunity to look for them in other societies.

The way these riddles are used is by a person making the statement and waiting for someone in the group to identify what the riddler has in mind by giving what I have here called the "answer." Riddles such as these are especially helpful in teaching the young how to view reality creatively. Since the answers are often prescribed, some analysts have suggested that they provide a sort of "catechism" to be memorized by means of which the young learn their society's views.

1. Body Parts:

- A little bow behind an anthill. *Answer*: a fingernail.
- My brother travels with me but I can't hear him moving. *Answer*: my shadow.
- A trusty slave that will protect me from whatever comes my way. *Answer*: my hand.
- White roosters on a fence. *Answer*: teeth.

2. Fauna and Insects:

- I've given to you, why are you still staring at me? *Answer*: a dog.
- I washed my bowl clean and put it in the sun to dry, but it didn't dry. *Answer*: a dog's nose.
- The girls of our house don't go to the bush without clapping their hands. *Answer*: doves.
- God gave him a saddle but I won't mount it. *Answer:* a scorpion.

3. Flora:

- I went to the bush, the bush laughed at me. *Answer*: a field of growing cotton.
- The one close to this shade will be bothered by the heat of the sun. *Answer*: shade of a palm tree.
- The bush is full of the sound of movement in the grass but the big bull buffalo just lies there silently. *Answer*: an anthill or tree stump.
- The walk of a woman expecting twins. *Answer*: a pumpkin.
- I went to the bush, the living things didn't welcome me, only the dead things. *Answer*: dry leaves.

4. Celestial Bodies:

- The cattle are lying down with the bull standing over them. *Answer*: the moon and the stars.
- White food covering. *Answer*: the stars.
- A dye bowl that can't have a lid. *Answer*: the firmament.
- Shade that has no variation of color. *Answer*: dark overcast.

5. Miscellany:

- My father is in the hut, his beard is outside. *Answer*: the fire inside and the smoke that filters up through the thatched roof of a hut.
- One path that splits in two. *Answer*: a pair of pants.
- They fear him, even though his business is lying. *Answer*: the medicine man.
- A switch on the path that beats children and adults alike. *Answer*: hunger.

6. Additional Riddles from Jablow's Collection (1961):

- Water stands. *Answer*: sugar cane (Temne).
- Young men live, the old die. *Answer*: Leaves (Mende).
- It bears fruit that cannot be picked, when the fruit falls it cannot be gathered. *Answer*: Dew (Yoruba).
- A slender staff touches earth and heaven simultaneously. *Answer*: rainfall (Yoruba).

Epithets

To illustrate one more type of oral literature, we have in Hausa pithy kinds of sayings called "epithets." These are usually used as labels or a kind of nickname, showing an evaluation or attitude toward the people and the various other things that we relate to in life. In research for an article I published in 1976, I collected and classified over 500 of these sayings. A selection of these follows.

The way these are used is by a person saying the epithet rather than using the name of the person or thing. An example in English would be a person talking about his/her father and referring to him as "my old man" as in "my old man gave me a car for Christmas."

1. Occupations

- A teacher: a worthless person with a big turban.
- A judge: a forgetter of friendship.
- Other officials: bachelor elephant or far-sighted but bad tempered.

2. Various People

- An Igbo person: a slave of yams.
- An Angas person: one shave, one word.
- A Fulani person: cause a quarrel but you have already run.
- A young girl: your whole body is pleasant.

3. Personal Characteristics

- An important person: a grinding stone or a horse or an elephant's buttocks.
- A great man: an elephant's back.
- A generous person: a crow (raises someone else's child as his own) or a funeral bier (it carries everyone eventually).
- A father: a protective wall.

4. Food and Drink

- Gruel (a disliked food): with gruel in your stomach, you sleep hungry.
- Old cassava: "Stop! Eat me and you die!"
- Yams: southerners food.
- Palm wine: that which drives a boy crazy.

5. Material Objects and Implements

- A train: scissors through the bush or a crazy thing from Europe.
- A fire: preventer of a person putting his hand down.
- A kind of axe: a work finisher.
- An arrow: thing that causes one to cover one's stomach.
- A gun: a large drum.

6. Non-material Things

- Study: hinderer of work.
- An insuperable task: making a leper untie a donkey.
- A cock's crow at midnight: the remover of a bachelor's hope (i.e., to find a sex partner).
- Distant drumming: farting while standing up.

7. Natural Phenomena

- A storm: the breaker up of a party.
- Rainy season: giver of profit or preventer of work.
- Night: the hider of secrets.
- Early morning: the hindquarters of a hedgehog (black and white mixed).

8. Animals

- Vultures: those who wait for what they expect will come along.
- Lizard: rustler of the grass roof.
- Lion: chief of the bush.
- Jackal: professor of the bush.

9. Places (each major city has at least one nickname)

- Daura: ruler over the land.
- Zaria: entrance hut for those going out to see the world.
- Lagos: tobacco that one cannot give up.
- Kano: the great Hausa one.

Conclusion

Looking for worldview assumptions can be great fun, especially if one has or is able to gather a corpus of proverbs, myths, tales and other literature. Whatever conclusions one makes from such materials, however, need to be checked with data derived from participant observation and, if possible, the findings of others who have worked in the society.

Chapter 14

What Are We Taking to the World?

As we turn to the important subject of change, there are a number of crucial issues we need to look at. We know that the gospel is a high quality item. And since it is our Lord who has commanded us to take that gospel to all of the peoples of this world, we have no choice but to commit ourselves to witnessing for personal and worldview change. How we go about that witnessing, though, is of major concern to us. For we know from the experience of generations of missionaries that the gospel we take and the one our receptors are "hearing" may be two very different things. What we bring may be attractive to us and our people, but it may not come across that way to them.

So this chapter will be devoted to raising and answering three crucial questions I believe we must ask ourselves before we begin dealing with the principles for change. These questions are:

1. What right do we have to assume that we have something to offer other peoples?
2. What is it that we are supposed to take to them?
3. To whom should we be appealing?

What Right Do We Have?

I insist on asking this question first, especially because many in our day, both outside of the church and within it, are asking it. I have raised this issue in my discussion of the *ethicality* of Christian witness in my 1996 book, *Anthropology for Christian Witness*.

It's a bit scary to ask ourselves if what we are engaged in is legitimate. It's easy for us to simply assume that whatever we do, especially since we do it in God's name, must be legitimate. Yet experience is a hard master in this respect. For we frequently discover, if we look carefully, that many of the things we do, even though we do them in God's name, probably are not done in a way that God approves. So we raise the issue of legitimacy, even though we know we won't come up with definitive answers. We do this to help us learn to be more aware than many have been of the impact of the ministries we are engaged in.

In spite of the difficulty in dealing with this issue, I believe we can establish (at least to our own satisfaction), that it is legitimate to engage in Christian ministry, if we go about it in the right way. We cannot expect God to be any more satisfied with us than our receptors are if we go about trying to help them in inappropriate ways.

Secular anthropologists have been asking the legitimacy question for years concerning technical and humanitarian aid, but especially about missionaries. Their worldview assumptions, of course, have a lot to do with their skepticism about what we stand for. In an excellent chapter in his book *Traditional Societies and Technological Change*, George Foster points out that "professional aid looks very different to the recipient than to the donor" (1973:252). Such aid, Foster continues, "says, in essence, 'if you people will learn to do more things the way we do them, you will be better off'" (1973:253).

The "spiritual aid" we offer might well be viewed in the same way. The people we go to may not so much be focused on the good things we are offering them as on the implication that what they have been believing and doing is totally wrong. Whether in technical or spiritual areas, the things the people to whom we go are believing and the ways in which they are conducting their lives may be wrong. This is often the case. But there may be redeemable things also. Indeed, if we probe to worldview depth, we may find there some solid bases on which to build both our witness and a relationship with Christ.

I believe it was this kind of solid worldview base that God found in ancient Semitic culture when He first began His relationship with Abraham. Abraham's culture was a typical animistic culture. And his father, Terah, was an idolater. But their belief in a spirit world, probably with an unknown God at the top of it, provided a basis on which to build the relationship between Abraham and God. It was, I believe, to this kind of animistic base as well that the Apostle Paul appealed in his address on Mars Hill (Acts 17:16-34). The Greeks believed in many gods but were afraid they might miss one. So they regularly established altars to unknown gods to avoid neglecting any. Paul was able to use this fact from within their animistic worldview on which to base his presentation of the true God.

Perhaps, then, we can devise an approach to non-Christian worldviews that focuses on what is right in them rather than what is wrong with them. We need not be blind to where they are deficient, but by looking within them for what the Holy Spirit can use to build on, we may be better able to justify our mandate to communicate Christ to all the peoples of the world. And by recognizing that God didn't start with ideal understandings in reaching us, we may be able to allow ourselves to accept sub-ideal understandings as starting points on the part of those we seek to win.

In dealing with a much less complex area—the area of technological change—Foster suggests that we may be right or we may be dead wrong in recommending a change—especially when their custom fits their life situation better than our custom does. He adds, "It is wrong to assume that a method, because it is modern, scientific, and western, is better than a traditional one" (1973:254) if it is not appropriate to the receiving context. If it is not appropriate to that context can it be considered better?

In spiritual matters, if our experience of Christianity is largely secular with a meaningful relationship with God added (as is so often true in the West), are we doing well to import our style of Christianity into societies that are pervasively supernaturalistic? I believe this is what I was doing in Nigeria. And the results were very gratifying. Large numbers of Kamwe came into the churches. They found, however, little or no spiritual power there to deal with the many aspects of life that their worldview assigns to the spiritual dimension but, in western worldviews are treated as secular. So, in spite of their commitment to Christ, many of them continue to go to traditional shamans for protection, healing, blessing, concerns about fertility and other spiritual needs.

The complaint I'm voicing here is not a complaint against what biblical Christianity offers. It is against the secularizing and intellectualized forms of Christianity that we in the West (and our disciples in Korea and other parts of the two-thirds world) have learned to offer to peoples who, though not yet Christian, often have deeper spiritual insight than we do. It is not Christ that is found wanting, it is our brand of Christianity that doesn't connect either with where people are at or with the scriptures. It is the introduction of this type of Christianity that I am convinced is neither appropriate to scripture nor to the majority of the world's peoples, since their worldview base is animistic. Nor, I believe, is it ethical to assume that our approach is automatically the right thing to convert them to. To quote Foster again, "until we are sure they are wrong on a particular point, it is unwise and *morally wrong* to try to 'improve' them" (1973:254 emphasis mine).

With regard to Christian witness, I believe we must assume that God wants it to happen. He certainly has made this clear in the scriptures. The only questions in my mind, then, are those concerning how to do well our witness to the salvation Jesus offers, and to do it in such a way that people will understand and accept God's offer of genuine assistance with real problems they cannot effectively deal with without God. In addition to assuming that God wants witness, we can assume that the reason for His wanting witness flows from His concern that His prize creatures experience the relationship with Him that He created us for.

Three Crucial Considerations

Over the years, I have been asking myself what are the crucial dimensions of biblical Christianity. I have sensed that there is some major misemphasis within American understandings of our faith. But it has taken me awhile to put my finger on what the problem is. The first big step toward sorting things out came for me in 1982, when I was taken through an enormous paradigm shift into experiencing the power of God in a way that I had never before even imagined. I have written about this change in my book *Christianity With Power* (1989) and will not repeat the details here.

Suffice it to say that that initial experience has drastically changed my life. It happened as I, a faculty member in my 13th year at Fuller Seminary, attended a class entitled *Signs, Wonders and Church Growth*, taught by the late John Wimber. The first change was in the observing and experiencing of God's present healing activity. What we experienced was akin to what we had read about in the Gospels and Acts. People were being healed as we took Jesus seriously when He said, "Whoever has faith in me will do what I do" (John 14:12). This was mind-blowing enough for me, one who was brought up in a typical evangelical church where we learned a lot *about* Jesus but did precious little *with* Him.

But the overriding change in me has been in my *relationship* with Jesus. Working with Him in power to set captives free (Luke 4:18-19) has been gratifying beyond measure. But the relational closeness between myself and Jesus has been breathtaking. I only wish I had had these experiences before going to Nigeria. I would have taken a far different Christianity to them—a Christianity that I now consider "normal," rather than the subnormal Christianity I was practicing at the time. That was a good Christianity in most ways but at a far lower level than now. But two of what I now see as the three crucial dimensions of biblical Christianity were not in as clear focus as they would be now.

The *three crucial dimensions* as I see them now are: 1) Allegiance leading to a saving relationship with Jesus, 2) Knowledge of Truth leading to a meaningful understanding of God, and 3) Spiritual Power leading to spiritual and relational freedom. I contend that these are the three major components of biblical Christianity. And I note that most of the societies of the world are strong in their focus on two of them: Relationship and Spiritual Power. This recognition should help us with our quest to communicate to the peoples of the world at the worldview level.

Overemphasis On Knowledge

In recognizing the importance of these three dimensions, I will first deal with what I see as a western overemphasis on the Knowledge dimension. As we look at worldwide Christianity as it has either come from or been strongly influenced by the West, we note the importance of schools to the movement. And in these schools, we note important similarities to western schools. Not that schools are bad. Nor is education bad, though schools are far from the only vehicles of education. But the emphasis of western-type schools on knowledge and information needs to be examined in the light of what it does to a faith that, according to scripture, is primarily relational and to be *lived*, not just thought about.

What western schools are good at is getting students to think about the various issues raised. What they are not good at is helping people to relate to each other and to practice what they have studied. And we in the West and those in the Two-Thirds World who have attended western schools have learned well what schools are good at and have brought that into our Christian experience. What emerges, then, is what I will call an intellectualized *knowledge-about* Christianity that comes into the churches in intellectualized *knowledge-about* sermons and membership classes.

The process of westernization has been a process of secularization. And, whether in Euro-America or in non-western societies, this secularization has greatly affected Christians at the worldview level. Thus, Bishop Newbigin (1966) has stated what many of us have observed—that *Christian missions have been the greatest secularizing force in history*. This comes from a knowledge-about orientation promoted primarily through western schools. In mission schools, children have learned to value information above everything else, even when the information has been quite irrelevant to their everyday life. Then, in Bible schools and seminaries, present and prospective church leaders have learned the same thing—that information concerning the Bible and Christian theology are the most important things in our faith.

We have unwittingly fallen into a misunderstanding that goes back as far as the Greek philosophers: *that the thing wrong with humans is ignorance and the antidote is to provide more and more knowledge*. This, of course, is the theory on which our school system is based. And, I'm afraid we make the same mistake in seminaries, Bible schools and Christian colleges. We forgot that this assumption has never worked in the West because the basic problems with human beings are moral, not intellectual. And when exported this error has created incredible damage cross-culturally.

A proper cross-cultural perspective, then, demands that we take people's total behavior seriously—not just their thinking behavior. And a proper approach to mission demands that we focus on what God wants people to *do and assume*, not just on *thinking about* what He wants people to do and assume. Whether in scripture or in life, we observe that knowledge about how to do things is always to be subservient to living that knowledge.

As one who has been involved in cross-cultural witness for more than forty years, it came as a startling revelation to me following the events of 1982, to recognize that the approach I was advocating was a secular, powerless approach. *I was advocating a Christianity without power based on the contextualization of a powerless theology with the all-important relationship dimension of Christianity treated as a byproduct of good theology.* Students kept asking me where the Holy Spirit was in my approach, and I didn't know.

Sometimes we have used the word "truth" as a label for this knowledge-about dimension as in the phrase "truth encounters." This usage makes sense to westerners since we so often associate truth with information, facts, explanations and the like. But scripturally, truth, like knowledge, is something experienced, not merely something thought. It is not a theoretical thing.

There are at least three kinds of knowledge in human experience: observational knowledge, intellectual knowledge and experiential knowledge. And it is the third kind, experiential knowledge, that is usually in view in the scriptures.

So in the scriptures, when teaching takes place, it is done relationally, in interaction with disciples and mentorees. Students are guided into *experiential knowledge and truth.* Furthermore, the Hebrew worldview assumption behind the concept of knowing truth in scripture requires that those who learn something obey what they know in response to their relationship with the Giver of that knowledge. Knowing the truth carries a moral obligation to practice it in real life experience. A proper English rendering of John 8:32 would be "You'll experience and obey the truth and the truth will set you free." If we are to be scriptural, then, truth and knowledge need to be *experienced and obeyed, not just thought*. It is not biblical to simply understand any part of the gospel theoretically without obeying it. But we pretty well limit ourselves to classroom handling of scriptural truth and it is difficult to handle the experiencing and obeying dimension of truth in classrooms.

The relational dimension of truth comes out when Jesus says, "I am Way, the Truth and the Life" (John 14:6), meaning, "I am the One who will be true to you as you follow Me, the Way, and participate in My Life." Obedience to the truth, then, involves being true to the Giver of that truth by following Him as closely as possible in living, not simply in thinking.

Following is a chart of my view of the truth/knowledge/ understanding dimension of Christianity:

THE TRUTH / KNOWLEDGE DIMENSION
Primary Concern: Understanding
1. This dimension involves teaching led by the Holy Spirit (John 16:13). 2. Scripturally both truth and knowledge are experiential, not simply cognitive, and assuming obedience to what is known. 3. Truth and knowledge are learned by *doing* them, not simply by thinking them. 4. Truth provides antidotes for ignorance and error. 5. Though spiritual truth is pervasively relational and experiential (John 8:32), there is also a cognitive and informational dimension. 6. This dimension embodies truth and knowledge of all aspects of Christian experience. 7. We are to learn in this dimension about the contents of the other two dimensions. 8. We are expected to grow in this knowledge dimension as in all other dimensions of Christian experience. 9. Satanic and human lies are to be countered with God's truths. 10. Under this dimension, the church is to be experienced as a teaching place (mentoring, discipling, classroom). 11. Theology should be primarily experiential, with an important cognitive component.

14.1 – The Truth / Knowledge Dimension

The Most Important Dimension: Relationship

A glance at the scriptures shows us a different sort of Christianity than that taught in our classrooms. We see there that the major focus is not on knowledge-about, but on what I will call *relationship-with*. By this I mean to focus on relationships with God and with brothers and sisters in the faith. This relational dimension is something quite different from the knowledge-about dimension.

We see in scripture that the primary requirement of our gospel is that people commit themselves to God in a new allegiance. Jesus taught the primacy of such a relationship and modeled it even in the fact that He chose discipleship rather than classrooms as His method of teaching.

Not that we as Evangelicals have completely ignored the relationship dimension. We have been strong on the need for a relationship with Jesus Christ. Without this, there is no salvation. Sometimes we study conversion patterns. And we talk a lot about love and forgiveness and even sometimes practice them. Certain churches, then, are quite relational in their worship. People sing their love and commitment to God and relate to other worshipers as they do.

Yet we have often contented ourselves (both in our training institutions and in church) with increasing our knowledge about our relationships with God and His people, rather than working at developing the relationships themselves. *And our relationship with Christ (whether in church or in a Christian Bible school, college or seminary) tends to be treated as a byproduct of our knowledge about Him* when, in fact, relationship is an entirely different dimension from the knowledge-about dimension. And one never gets to a relationship simply through knowledge-about relating. We can only learn relationship by relating.

This relegating of the relationship dimension to the status of a byproduct has resulted in a tragedy widely recognized in American Christian circles. When seminary and Bible school students are inundated with information about Christianity, many neglect or even lose the very relationship with Christ that they came to our schools to nurture. Many students in Christian training institutions die spiritually even as they grow intellectually—and, I believe there is a close relationship between the knowledge orientation and the spiritual deaths.

I am contending, then, that relationship to God and to His people is the primary dimension of scriptural Christianity. This being true, it is important that we ask ourselves how well we are doing at communicating the centrality of this dimension. And how well are the structures we create contributing to growth in these relationships? Might tragedies like what happened in Rwanda be averted if Christians who may be doctrinally quite orthodox had experienced a more relational Christianity?

I'm asking, how can we better contextualize relational practices such as the Lord's supper, baptism, fellowship meetings, repentance and reconciliation and, in fact, the way Christianity is taught? Jesus chose to teach relationally, we choose to largely limit ourselves to classrooms. Even though most of the people we take the gospel to in the non-western world are highly relational, we still take classrooms.

So, Christianity within any society, if it is to be truly biblical, will need to focus squarely on what the Bible focuses on, regardless of what our western academic approaches focus on. Indeed, as we look cross-culturally, we note that relationship is the primary focus of most of the societies of the world. The bridge between the peoples of the world and the Bible becomes shorter when we focus on what the Bible focuses on rather than on western custom.

If we are to be scriptural in our efforts to communicate and contextualize Christianity, *we need to focus on culturally appropriate relating to God, not simply culturally appropriate thinking about God.* Contextualization of relationship, then, has to become a major focus of our teaching, writing and witnessing. A major focus of our preparation to take the gospel to the world, then, needs to be to learn what the contextualization of relationships is all about. I'm not sure we know.

In order to further describe and elaborate on what I'm saying, I present the following chart:

THE ALLEGIANCE / RELATIONSHIP DIMENSION
Primary Concern: Relationship
1. This is the most important of the three dimensions.
2. It starts with conversion—a commitment to Christ—to establish a saving relationship with God through Jesus Christ.
3. Its aim is to replace any other primary allegiance/relationship with commitment to Christ. All other allegiances are to be secondary to this one.
4. It continues as growth in one's relationship with Christ and with others expressed as loving God with one's whole heart and one's neighbor as oneself (Matt. 22:37-40).
5. It includes practicing all that the Bible teaches on subjects like love, obedience, faith(fulness), fellowship, the fruits of the Spirit, intimacy with Christ (e.g., John 15), forgiveness, repentance, reconciliation, indeed all the major doctrines.
6. True intimacy and relationship should not be confused with knowledge about intimacy and relationship.
7. Knowledge is to be experienced and obeyed in relationship.
8. Under this dimension, the church is to be experienced as family.
9. Witness to one's personal experience is key to communicating this dimension.
10. Discipleship is the way to teach this dimension.
11. Relationship is learned through relating.
12. Theology is experienced in discipleship, fellowship in which people experience being true to each other, worship and submission to God (Rom. 12:2).

14.2. The Allegiance/ Relationship Dimension

The Power / Freedom Dimension

Beyond the relationship dimension that we have neglected and the knowledge-about dimension that we have overemphasized, then, there is another dimension to Christianity that we as Evangelicals have almost completely ignored, and seldom worked to contextualize.

My Nigerian church leaders read in the Bible that Jesus worked powerfully to heal, deliver and set captives free. They also read that He passed this power on to His followers. But they saw none of this power in missionary Christianity. Nevertheless, they hoped that I could help them in dealing with their battles against evil spirits. But I couldn't.

I believed in Satan and demons, sort of, but was very happy to ignore the whole subject, just as my seminary professors had. I remembered that our systematic theology text had a section on Satan and demons. But the semester ended before we got to that part.

As we study scripture, we quickly become aware of the fact that Jesus, though totally relational, also concerned Himself with whether or not people were free. When He states His mission, He quotes (in Luke 4:18-19) from Isaiah 61:1-3 in which the focus is on setting captives free from their captivity.

Jesus was very conscious that life and ministry in His Kingdom involve a constant concern for dealing with the devastation brought about by our enemy, Satan. Jesus dealt with that devastation by using the power and authority given Him by God the Father to bring freedom. And He initiated His disciples (in a relational way) into the use of that power and authority. He also taught them that down through the ages, "Whoever has faith in me will do what I do"—that is, will work in that same power and authority (John 14:12).

This power dimension is not the primary dimension—relationship is primary. But if the power and authority dimension was as important to Jesus as the Bible shows, it should play a much greater role in evangelical Christianity than it has. This emphasis on the use of spiritual power to heal and deliver from demons is not a fad that should be gotten over. It is an attempt to rectify an omission by bringing scriptural balance to an unbalanced Evangelicalism.

What we Evangelicals often miss, is that Jesus' use of the power and authority of the Holy Spirit had two important purposes beyond simply helping people to feel better. The "Satanward" purpose (to use James Kallas' term—1966) was to "destroy the works of the enemy" (1 John 3:8). But the Godward purpose was to express the love of God in very tangible ways. Jesus, when ministering to people, always used His power to show

His love. Jesus' power, then, like His handling of truth and knowledge, is to support relationship.

Given, there have been excesses in some contemporary power ministries. But, if we ever hope to experience and proclaim a balanced Christianity, we dare not point to those excesses as a reason for ignoring something that was so much a part of Jesus' life and ministry. If Jesus wasn't afraid to risk the distortions and perversions of power ministry, we should not be, especially since He made it clear that His followers were to do what He did (John 14:12).

We note from various scriptures that all the world is under the strong influence of the evil one. For example, 1 John 5:19 says, "The whole world is under the rule of the evil one." 2 Cor. 4:4 speaks of the fact that people "do not believe because their minds have been kept in the dark by the evil god of this world." Eph. 2:2 refers to Satan as "the ruler of the spiritual powers in space, the spirit who now controls the people who disobey God." And Eph. 6:12 says, "We are not fighting against human beings but against the wicked spiritual forces in the heavenly world." Despite some teaching and writing that tries to de-emphasize the spiritual warfare aspect of scripture, we cannot avoid this theme if we take scripture seriously.

The presence of these statements in our scriptures suggests that bringing people to freedom should be as high on our list of priorities as it was on Jesus' list. If we take seriously Paul's statement in 2 Cor. 4:4 about the blindness of normal people, we have to ask ourselves, How can people whose minds have been blinded think well enough to respond to Jesus Christ for the purpose of entering into a saving relationship with Him? The worldview of most Evangelicals leads them to assume that people can think freely, hear the message and respond appropriately. But, whether at home or abroad, it is less often a lack of knowledge that hinders people from coming to Christ than a lack of freedom.

The people Jesus ministered to recognized that the biggest hindrances to a well-ordered life are caused by evil spirits. Most of the peoples of the world today (including many Americans) also know this. And many want to get closer to Jesus relationally but are hindered by a lack of spiritual freedom—a lack that can only be remedied by the freeing power of Jesus, usually through inner healing.

These facts make dealing with spiritual power a major issue for anyone who takes seriously scripture, on the one hand, and real life, on the other. Those who would imitate Jesus' approach need to cultivate the ability to identify spiritual illness and oppression and to work in Jesus' power to counter it. People who suffer for lack of spiritual power are not attracted to a powerless Christianity.

Like my Nigerian leaders, people throughout the world hear or read of a wonderful miracle worker who used to live and do spectacular things. And they are attracted to this Jesus because of His power to set them free. So they may come to our churches, but almost always are disappointed, seeing little or none of Jesus' power in most of the churches missionaries have planted worldwide.

Those who do join and stay with our churches, then, usually practice what I have called "dual allegiance Christianity" (Kraft and Kraft 1993). They go to church on Sunday, but to the shaman when they have problems, because there's no power in the church to deal with the oppression they experience and recognize as coming from evil spirits. They know they are not free and they often know why. And their reason is the same as the Bible's reason—there is a hierarchy of spirits in the universe that is making trouble for human beings.

A similar kind of dual allegiance happens in the West, of course, when we go with our problems first to our medical and psychological "shamans," paying little attention to God in the process. But we're not as savvy as most non-westerners are in identifying many of our problems as related to the spirit world.

As those committed to relevant Christian witness, we've been trying to learn to take other people's perspectives seriously. It's about time we began to take them seriously in the spiritual power area, especially when we notice that Jesus, in a power-oriented society, set us an example by working in spiritual power.

An incarnational, contextualized gospel, appropriate both to the receiving society and to the Bible, will both teach and do what Jesus did in the power dimension in contextually appropriate ways. We need to learn how to contextualize power as well as knowledge and relationship. See Kraft 2005.

Following is a summary chart of the spiritual power/freedom dimension:

POWER / FREEDOM DIMENSION
Primary Concern: Freedom
1. The power in focus here is spiritual power (not e.g., political, personal, etc.) This dimension recognizes that humans are held captive by Satan.
2. Jesus worked in the power of the Holy Spirit to set captives free (Luke 4:18, 19). He did nothing under the power of His own divinity (Phil. 2:5-8).
3. Jesus passed this power on to His followers (Luke 9:1; John 14:12; Acts 1:4-8) by giving them the same Holy Spirit that was the Source of His power.
4. Satanic power must be defeated with God's power (it cannot be defeated simply with truth or a correct allegiance, though these help).
5. Under this dimension, the church is experienced as both a hospital where wounds are healed, thus freeing people, and an army that attacks the enemy, defeating him both at ground level and at cosmic level.
6. Awareness of the power dimensions of Christianity needs to be taught both cognitively and, especially, experientially (as Jesus did).
7. Working in Jesus' power is learned through working in Jesus' power.
8. Theology is experienced as confronting and defeating the enemy in warfare resulting in freedom to grow in relationships and understanding.

14.3. The Power / Freedom Dimension

A composite diagram showing these three crucial dimensions of Christianity in their proper relationship to each other would be as follows. Note that the proper function of Truth/Knowledge and Spiritual Power is to support, not replace, Relationship. See Relationship, then, as a kind of table with these other dimensions as the legs of the table.

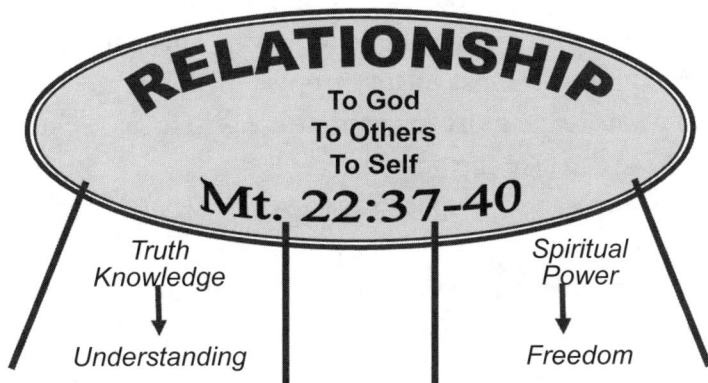

Figure 14.4 – Composite Picture of the Three Dimensions

Connecting With Our Receptors

Appropriateness of witness, then, will need to focus squarely on what scripture focuses on—a right relationship with God. This relationship, more than knowledge of doctrine, more than commitment to an institution, more than anything else Christianity has to offer needs to be in first place in our concern. As westerners and westernized Christians, however, we probably suffer from worldview and behavioral weakness in the relationship area (though some who come from non-western societies have better models to work from than we westerners do). And we are usually communicating into relationship-strong societies.

I discovered in witnessing to a non-western seeker, that as I led her to focus her attention on becoming a member of God's family (a relational model) rather than on our traditional American focus on being "born again" (a more individualistic model) or of getting certain doctrines straight (an intellectual model), she showed great interest in what I was recommending. I felt I was learning something important, since she seemed to respond positively out of a desire for a family kind of relationship with the God she only has known as a part of an antique institution. This was gratifying to me, given my growing awareness of the importance of the relationship dimension in Christian experience.

When we look at the worldview characteristics outlined in previous chapters, it is evident that there is a contrast between the American focus on knowledge and the focus of other societies on relationships and spiritual power. We note, then, from our concern for a biblical perspective, that the Bible is also strong on relationship and power. This parallel of emphases between the Bible and most of the peoples of the world should give us insight into what are the most appropriate areas to focus on in the societies to which we seek to take the gospel.

The knowledge-about emphasis has led to widespread nominalism and dual allegiance. Wherever people have really gotten into the relationship dimension of Christianity, in small groups here and there and in small-scale societies sometimes, biblical Christianity has become vital. And when that relational emphasis has been combined with experiences of God's power, faith in Christ has blossomed.

Case Studies

Does presenting the gospel to people in terms of these three dimensions work? I believe it does, and more effectively than the knowledge-about approach with schools as its basis. To attempt to prove my point, I will point to three cases, highlighted by George Otis, Jr. in his video Transformations (1999) and his book *The Twilight Labyrinth* (1997). In each of these cases, Christians, led by the Holy Spirit, began to do things that turned around a situation that was controlled by Satan. To do this they worked relationally and in spiritual power, not neglecting the knowledge base, but definitely keeping it balanced in relation to the other two dimensions.

The first of these three cases is Cali, Columbia, a city overrun by the famous Cali drug cartel, called in the Encyclopedia Britannica "the largest, richest and best-organized criminal organization in history" (Otis 1997:299). The second is Hemet, Calif., another drug, crime and gang center, so much under satanic influence that an Indian guru, Maharaj Yogi set up a Transcendental Meditation center there and the so-called Church of Scientology chose it for its headquarters. The third is Almolonga, Guatemala, where poverty, drunkenness, witchcraft, crime and idolatry had made it a place that everyone knew as evil.

Cali is a city of nearly two million in a country with, in 1993, the dubious distinction of having the highest homicide rate in the world (15,000 murders in the first six months alone!). In the early 1990s, a few of the pastors began to get together to pray for the city, thus starting a new relationship between pastors and between them and God and beginning to access the power of God for transformation. They didn't know how to pray or what to pray for so they asked God. Soon they had learned to divide the city into zones and to pray for the zones.

In 1995, then, they scheduled what turned out to be the first of several all-night prayer vigils, held in a civic auditorium that seats about 27,000. About 30,000 Christians, from all denominations turned out "to take a stand against the cartels and their unseen spiritual masters" (Otis 1997:299). Within 48 hours, then, the city went a whole day without a murder and over the next four months 900 police officers with connections to the cartel were fired. Soon the Columbian government declared all-out war on the cartel, attacked processing centers and shipping points and rounded up and imprisoned the seven top cartel leaders. The Christian community, then, overflowed a 60,000-seat soccer stadium for an all-night prayer vigil. In the months following that event specific political, social and spiritual strongholds in Cali's 22 administrative districts were mapped and targeted for specific prayer attacks. This resulted in "a dramatic loosening of the enemy's stranglehold on [the] community and nation" (1997:301). The government, including the president, became targets of investigation and many of them indicted.

In getting together in this way and employing God's power, the Christians of Cali have made an enormous impact both on the populace and on the government. So much so that they are granted free use of government facilities for their rallies. And God even rained on the annual, ten-day, debauchery-filled festival, forcing many of its events to be canceled (and this in December when it hardly ever rains in Cali!). Though there is still much to do, evangelical Christianity and the true Christ are now honored in Cali where once the drug lords ruled. The principles: unity of Christian leaders followed by unity (relationship) of the believers, prayer (relating in partnership with God) and the claiming of God's power to break that of the enemy.

In Hemet, Calif., Pastor Bob Beckett and his wife struggled for about seventeen years with their "emotional bags packed," waiting for a call to another place. God, however, challenged them to commit themselves to Hemet and they obeyed. They began to study and discover the truth of Paul's statement that our primary foes are not humans, but "the wicked spiritual forces in the heavenly world, the rulers, authorities, and cosmic powers of this dark age" (Eph 6:12). So, gathering pastors and intercessors to pray for the community and to take authority over it, Bob and his church began to attack the enemy. Again, the principles were relationship and the exercise of spiritual power. These were undergirded by united intercessory prayer and listening to God, plus a strategy based on the mapping of spiritual strongholds in the area and acts of spiritual warfare that have radically changed both the churches and the community.

Though there is still much to be done, the last decade has seen church attendance double (from 7% to 14% of the population) and dedicated Christians put into places of authority such as mayor, police chief, fire chief, 30% of law enforcement personnel plus a high percentage of the teachers and administrators in the schools. From incredible disunity and animosity between the churches, there is now great unity and working together among all denominations. Gang leaders and their whole gangs have been converted, drug trafficking stopped and the Transcendental Meditation center is gone. Beckett's book *Commitment to Conquer* (1977) details these and many more changes, starting with worldview changes on the part of pastors and intercessors and continuing with worldview and behavioral change on the part of congregations and community.

The story of Almolonga, Guatemala is even more spectacular than the two above examples. In the late 70s this city of 19,000 was known as a wasteplace where drunkenness, poverty, crime, idolatry and witchcraft ruled. The evil and degradation of the place was legendary. The people even stoned Christians! On one occasion, a pastor was confronted by a gun-wielding gangster who thrust the gun into the pastor's mouth. But as he prayed for protection and the trigger pulled, the hammer clicked harmlessly and the pastor was let go. This and other such events led the pastors to begin to unite, to gather people for prayer and to take authority over their city. The movement grew, then, blessed by God as the Christians worked in relation to other Christians and to God (involving, of course, repentance and the "cleaning up" of their own acts) and, exercising their authority and God's power, experienced a marvelous series of signs and wonders.

The result is that by the turn of the century, about 93% of the citizens of Almolonga could call themselves evangelical Christians, their soil that was considered worthless twenty years ago is yielding incredible crops (including carrots the size of a person's arm) the envy of the whole nation, idolatry and witchcraft are virtually gone (an amazing thing in Latin America), Christian festivals have replaced pagan ones, Christians are now in official positions in the city, the twenty-six bars have been reduced to three and many of them turned into churches, of which there are now twenty-four and they closed the last jail in 1994 because they didn't need it anymore. The Christians, having learned what God can do if they cooperate, continue to fast and pray in unity with each other, and God keeps honoring them with manifestations of His power and love.

Lessons to Learn

We see, then, that in each of these communities, presentations of the gospel that speak to worldview themes relating to relationship, understanding and spiritual power, if done in the right way can have spectacular results. The knowledge dimensions enables the leaders to know that the right way is the way that focuses on a close relationship with God and a working together in power with Him to bring about transformation. That working together in power, then, involves using prayer in partnership with God as both a way of gaining more understanding and an act of warfare to accomplish His goals. Just as power-oriented peoples around the world have learned to war against the true God in partnership with our enemy, Satan (in the form of their pagan gods and spirits), so we Christians can learn to work in a partnership relationship with each other and with the true God in obedience, prayer, repentance, worship, reconciliation and faithfulness to defeat that enemy.

It is this balanced message that we should be taking to the peoples of the world in Jesus' name. In the scriptures we see nothing of the academic approach western Christians have taken to the world. The use and propagation of truth and knowledge are always subjugated to and in support of the relationship and power dimensions of the faith. If, then, we are to be faithful to Jesus and to scripture, we need to learn to present His messages in His way.

Learning to take our message relationally and in power, then, often involves worldview change on the part of those who take it. To enable the message of Christ to bring change in the worldviews of others, may involve us in some important worldview changes of our own. In each of the examples above, the Christian community, including in many cases the leaders themselves, had to undergo worldview change from their older understandings of how to conduct Christian activities. These understandings depended on the structures and schemes they had learned in their knowledge-based training programs, with accompanying divisions between denominations.

In order to bring about change, they had to first focus on bringing about cooperation within the Christian community, especially among the pastors, the spiritual leaders of that community. This took prayer and the claiming of God's power, starting with just a few of the leaders, to enable them to put away theological and personal differences. In each case the pastors first and then their congregations repaired their relationships with God and with each other. They focused, then, on repentance to God and to each other and then on united prayer, taking authority over the enemy and asserting the power of God to break through the human divisions, on the one hand, and the occult activity of the enemy and those who served him, on the other. Thus their focus was on relational truth and the power of the Holy Spirit rather than on mere knowledge and academic truth. And a powerful act of God was the result.

We might say that these leaders and their followers developed a "spiritual warfare worldview." Such a worldview is characterized by love and unity within the community plus fierce attacks on the satanic kingdom by the community. The aim of our quest to understand worldview, then, should not simply be to understand, but to put into action for Christ the witness and warfare activity that we see Him model. The title of our book is "Worldview for Christian Witness" and of this chapter, "What Are We Taking to the World?" It is my hope that we will understand both what worldview is about and to adjust our worldviews (if needed) so that what we take to the world is characterized by the balance I have been presenting in this chapter—a balance that does not neglect any of the three crucial dimensions but that moves in all three with our primary concern for the relational features of our faith.

Chapter 15

How Are Worldviews Changed?

Having considered what it is that we want to communicate concerning the gospel, we turn to the question of the relationship of the communication to the changing of a people's worldview. So we ask:

1. Under what circumstances do people change their worldview assumptions? And when, why and by whom?
2. Under what circumstances should we appeal to them?
3. Where does what we've been learning about worldview fit into the scheme?

We need to ask and try to answer challenging questions such as these, in hopes that we may be better suited to relate the gospel to the deep worldview issues of our receptors.

People, Paradigms and Change

As we have continually pointed out, it is *people* that do whatever is done, whether by following the worldview patterns they have learned or by changing them. All of us are taught how to picture the various aspects of the reality around us and how to follow our society's cultural maps for getting around in the reality as we picture it. As we learn the pictures and the maps, then, we habituate our responses to them, "empowering" the themes and paradigms, as it were, with our habits.

The themes and paradigms in our minds enable us to make sense out of what we experience and to move around within our "life space" in ways that meet with our own approval and that of the society around us. The circumstances of life are not, however, stable over time. That is, the situations in which we in our generation find ourselves are not always the same as those our predecessors encountered and to which they adapted the cultural structures. When we find ourselves in situations for which we were not prepared, we are forced to be creative, either to adapt our habitual assumptions to the new contexts or to switch themes and paradigms altogether. Probably our larger assumptions, the themes are seldom changed. It is at the paradigm and subparadigm levels that the changes usually take place. Some of the principles for such change follow.

1. *A change is initiated whenever a person or group adopts a new perspective to which a commitment is made.* If an advertiser analyzes bath soaps in such a way that viewers become convinced that the kind of soap they have been using is inferior to the kind being advertised, a new perspective is developed. The viewers may (or may not) commit themselves to using the new brand. I once made such a change in commitment, from one kind of cold medicine to another after reading an article in a publication I trusted. The author contended that the only valuable medicine in the product I had placed my faith in was aspirin. And since, the article contended, the price of aspirin was considerably less than the price of the medicine I had been using, I could both save money and have just as good medical results if I simply used aspirin. I, therefore, changed my perspective and my allegiance from my previous medicine to aspirin.

2. *The new information I received led me to reinterpret* both my behavior and the faith I had placed in my original medicine. I took a new view of my situation and ultimately decided to develop a new habit. The process I went through seemed to involve first (a) becoming aware of a new perspective, then (b) a reinterpretation of the old perspective, followed by (c) experimentation leading to a new commitment that when acted on led me to develop (d) a new habit. This, I believe, is a typical sequence in the change process. It is preceded by new information leading receptors to analyze a belief or behavior that they may or may not have been conscious of previously.

3. A very important factor to consider in advocating change is the *strength of the commitment to the previous assumption or behavior.* In general, it is much easier to convince people that they should make changes in those things that they are not strongly committed to than to things they are strongly committed to. It is much easier, for example, to convince people that they should switch to another brand of toothpaste or soap than to get them to relinquish their commitment to family, religion or some precious aspect of doctrine.

Such depth of commitment, then, needs to be assessed when deciding which assumptions to attempt to get changed. Disturbingly, western evangelical Christians seem to have a deep commitment to secular worldview assumptions concerning supernatural beings and powers in spite of the fact that scripture is full of references to them. People with deep commitments to their gods and spirits can also be very difficult to budge, though power demonstrations have been effective in many mission areas. It is likewise usually very difficult to induce someone who has a strong commitment to him/herself to replace that commitment with a faith allegiance to God.

If, then, we can find aspects of a person's or group's worldview that they are not highly committed to, there is usually greater hope for change. The exercise at the end of this chapter is aimed at helping us to think about this area.

4. Jacob Loewen provides helpful insight into the nature of the change process in three excellent articles published in 1968 and 1969. He refers to the process of Christian growth as "resocialization," comparing and contrasting that process with the normal process of socialization that we all go through as we grow up. He points to the great importance of the supporting group to the process a person goes through in making changes at the worldview level. According to his analysis, persons making such changes go through a three-step process in which they successively seek (a) gratification or satisfaction, (b) social approval, and (c) self-approval (1968a:147). Appealing to persons and groups in terms of their search for both personal and relational satisfaction is, thus, crucial to guiding them into the change process.

Much of what I've been saying about felt needs may too easily lead to the assumption that we are speaking about individuals apart from their groups. Such is not the case. Persons function in groups and routinely consider the opinions of their group members when considering change. It is group disapproval (and its extension self-disapproval) that can most hinder worldview change and group approval that can lead to the making and confirmation of changes made. The opinion of the group advocating or hindering conversion to the new perspectives and allegiances is, then, crucial to the change process. Such a fact speaks to the great importance of a supportive church in the process of change from non-Christian to Christian and in the continuing process of growth toward maturity.

A Personal Change

As mentioned, in my book, *Christianity With Power* I attempt to document a rather dramatic series of changes that took place in my life, starting in January of 1982. At that time I had been a committed evangelical (non-charismatic) Christian for 38 years. My Christian commitment had already required me to modify many of the secular paradigms I had been taught early in life by replacing and/or modifying the subparadigms of which they were made up. Though the part of American society I grew up in believed in God, few of those around me took Him as seriously as I did. My assumptions in this regard, including my overall picture (paradigm) of who God is, my relationship with Him and the life-changing implications of these facts had been undergoing continuous modification for years.

Thus, I was already some distance from normal American secularism when the events of 1982 and following began to challenge my spiritual understandings.

Just as the process of growing up involves expected changes in our paradigms, so those of us who are serious about our Christian commitment expect changes of understandings and perspectives in the process of Christian maturation. Even with the expectation of growth as a part of a very gratifying Christian experience, however, I did not expect the radical shift in my understanding and experience that came with my being introduced to praying for healing in 1982.

It was as if I had been walking along in a steady but gradual climb in my Christian experience to this point when all of a sudden I was allowed to jump up or over to a new paradigm. I moved, then, to a completely new and higher level on which to continue my journey. In many ways this was like entering another world, what I like to call "the world of Christian normalcy." As I came to see others, and eventually myself, praying with authority and seeing people get healed from physical and emotional problems and delivered from demons, my whole view of God, the scriptures and ourselves as Christians changed radically.

I was faced with data that my teachers in the faith had either not seen or, if they had seen it, not taken seriously. I had basically two options: take the evidence seriously and change my paradigm(s) or, as some of my colleagues did, dismiss or ignore the evidence and go on with life as usual. I chose the former course and have, to date, seen no reason to go back on that choice. That choice has, however, meant a lot of hard work for me. I have had to change a lot of habits, revise a lot of what I had been taught to believe and cultivate several new relationships to replace some of those with people who now hold me at arm's length.

Thus it is that people have to make creative choices as a result of experiences that force them to consider approaches other than the ones they have learned to follow. The whole of American society, for example, has to create approaches not envisioned by previous generations when faced with the fact that our air and water are polluted, our oil and other resources are running out, we could not win in Vietnam, our school system is failing, we don't know what to do about illegal immigration, our cities are crime-ridden, our governmental structures don't seem to be working very well, the threat of atomic disaster looms large and, what may be an even bigger problem, the external enemy (Islamist terrorism) does not play by our rules. Each of these factors has created new challenges that will require radical shifts in the paradigms of nearly all Americans if such problems are to be fixed.

If we or any others are to survive in the face of challenges we have not been trained to deal with, we will have to learn how to shift perspectives, not just behavior. And shifts in perspectives require humans to make choices. For it is people who change systems. In this and the following chapters we discuss the principles and processes engaged in by people as they either move toward or resist worldview change.

What Chance is There for Major Change in Worldview?

A worldview is such a complex thing and so deeply engrained in its adherents that I strongly doubt the possibility that a person can completely escape from the one he/she learned as a child. If a person could escape from one worldview, he/she would simply be exchanging that worldview for another. Perhaps those who grew up with two languages and worldviews would have the possibility of escaping from each worldview as they moved back and forth between them.

Failing total escape or exchange at the worldview level, though, what kind of substitution is possible at theme, subtheme or paradigm levels? Taking as an illustration the possibility of moving to supernaturalism from secularism of vice-versa, we may ask questions such as the following:

- Can a secularist become a supernaturalist?
- For those brought up with a keen sense of the supernatural world, can they become truly secular?
- Will those brought up secularist always retain at least some secularist assumptions?
- And will those brought up supernaturalistic always retain at least some supernaturalistic assumptions?

In my own case, I am often disturbed at the tenacity of my non-supernaturalism. By now I've participated in well over two thousand experiences in which someone was healed and/or delivered from demons. Yet, over and over again when something marvelous happens, I find myself wondering if what I saw was really of God. Fortunately, I am not inclined to dwell on these doubts. But the fact that they are there tells me that my secularistic worldview has deep roots.

I wonder if those moving from supernaturalism to secularism experience the same kind of tenacity of the perspective they were first taught? The widespread presence of animistic ideas and practices in converts to Christianity would point in that direction.

But I believe there is hope. For, even with this nagging skepticism in myself, there has been dramatic change in many of the paradigms and subparadigms in my worldview, and perhaps even in some subthemes and themes. As I see it, the keys are will, knowledge, experience, and the abiding grace and encouragement of God. Let's look at these factors. And note that they are all person factors, not structure factors. In advocating change, then, our appeal is always to be to persons.

1. **Will** is undoubtedly the most important factor in a change of perspective. As Rom. 12:2 implies, we are to choose to not conform to the "standards of this world." Rather, we are to choose to "let God transform [us] inwardly" through choosing to completely change our perspective. I believe the Greek word *nomos*, usually translated "mind" (e.g., "a complete change of your mind" is the GNB translation of this verse) should regularly be translated "perspective" as I have done here. In this verse the Apostle Paul is appealing for worldview change, not simply a change of thinking.

There are at least three points in the process where the way people exercise their wills is crucial.

1. People choose either to be open to a change or to be closed to it. Then, even if they open up to the possibility,
2. They will choose either to make the change or not. If they decide to make or at least try the change, then,
3. They will choose either to continue with their decision to change or to eventually give up the change.

Whether or not a person or group is open to change in a given area is, of course, a major consideration. Social as well as personal factors will be of great importance. In some societies, there is traditionally little allowance for an individual, especially if the person is young or female, to openly change any perspective at as high a level as theme or subtheme. Indeed, it is unlikely that one would be allowed to change a paradigm unless the change is sponsored or at least allowed by an older, highly respected male.

With the rapid changes that are occurring in traditional societies today, however, there is often much more leeway for individuals to be open to considering even deep-level change. We who advocate change, though, need to be careful we don't assume too much concerning the staying power of decisions for change that might be made, especially by youth and women. Often, if people in societies with tight relationships open themselves up to change and experiment with the changes, they will come under extreme social pressure to return to their old ideas and ways. This pushes some to make secret changes in their worldviews that do not appear on the surface even to their closest relatives and friends. Others declare their change openly and are pressured unmercifully to revert, even to the point of being ostracized from their families.

A typical pattern in Japan, for instance, is for young people to come to Christ but, under intense social pressure, to revert to traditional ways after they get married (often in a western wedding ceremony performed in a Japanese hotel). It is proverbial in Japan that there is a constant influx of converts through the "front door" that then leave through the "back door" at some later point in their lives due to the social pressure applied to them by their families.

Nevertheless, current social change has loosened the grip of society on many of the world's peoples. There is, therefore, more ability even for young people (and sometimes women, too) to choose alternative values and commitments. Many who leave their home countries for study abroad open themselves up to new understandings and new allegiances while they are out of their home situations. Though the social pressure when they return to their home countries results in some returning to their old ways, many continue in the new ways, whether the changes be simply in clothing and living styles or whether they involve a commitment to Christ.

Many young people in western countries choose to change their perspectives fairly radically when they go away from home to attend a secular university. They are exposed there to much irresponsible thinking on the part of professors and classmates without the steadying influence of home to keep them balanced. It is impossible to overestimate the corrupting influence of our universities on the worldviews of our youth.

However, even in individualistic America, many refuse changes in perspective and/or behavior because they anticipate a negative reaction of their peers. A primary question in even American minds as we consider a major change is, "What would my peers think if I made this change?" I raised this question with myself many times as I contemplated the possibility/probability that I would be regarded by my peers as having "gone charismatic" (i.e., lost my balance). The thing that pushed me over the edge, however, was the fact that I was "hungry" for something more than what I was experiencing in my Christian life.

A crucial factor, then, in how people use their wills in the change process is the relative satisfaction or dissatisfaction they feel with a present perspective in this area. Many Christians have the feeling, "There must be more to Christianity (or to life) than this." They read the scriptures and see all kinds of things happening that don't seem to happen in their experience today. They believe in their heads that Jesus is "the same yesterday, today and forever" (Heb. 13:8), but what He seems to be doing today doesn't come close to what they read about Him doing in the past. So they feel let down by Christianity, even though they are frequently quite committed to it.

People who are either openly or secretly dissatisfied with their present Christian experience are often open, as I was, to investigating new approaches. Their feeling that they have an important unmet *felt need* opens them up to alternative suggestions. In the area of spiritual power in the Anglo-American context, often non-Christians who have been affected by New Age thinking are more open to a Christianity with power than most of those who already have a Christian commitment. They have already felt the powerlessness of western life and have sought to overcome that lack through a counterfeit system that they eventually came to question. If, then, they are exposed to a live, powerful Christianity, they will often take the risky step to investigate it.

A feeling of need (conscious or unconscious) is, then, a powerful motivator in opening people's wills to the possibility of change. The specific need among Americans or among the many power-oriented peoples of the world for a Christianity with power is heightened greatly if someone in their group is in need of healing. Desperation tends to make people more open to displays of God's power. Desperate people (e.g., the woman with the severe bleeding in Luke 8:43-48) will often even risk social disapproval to get the help they sense they need.

Often in open societies and sometimes in more closed societies as well, we find that people who feel personally secure are more likely than others to be venturesome. This is in contrast with those who feel insecure in their position in society and, therefore, live with the fear that they might make some choices that would reduce their social standing. Those who by virtue of wealth, education or other indicators of high status are secure in their positions in society, however, don't need to fear that social missteps may deprive them of their prestige. They often feel free to make risky choices.

Among the things that encourage people to choose change is the knowledge that there are others whom they respect who are "in this with them." Whether this is a person who moves along with us or "a credible witness," a person whom we trust who recommends a change, it is good to know we are not alone. My own change of perspective was "midwifed" by just such a credible witness, a person we knew and respected. And others around him were also credible. So there was a respectable community to fit into if our own rejected us (which it largely did).

In choosing such change, it is hard to overestimate the importance of knowing and getting frequent support from at least one other person within one's own reference group who embarks on the same journey into uncharted territory. I am thankful for such a person in my life as I began this uncertain pilgrimage. We have had each other for support in all kinds of tangible and intangible ways, as we have moved into an area not ordinarily thought of as academically "safe." Though we have had others who supported us at a distance, the fact that two—rather than one of us—have been following the same new path has at every point strengthened our wills to continue.

The openness of one's reference group to the change is another important will strengthener. The fact that in many societies, the reference group is pretty closed, at least to major changes, is a big impediment to people turning to Christ. As mentioned, many groups, even in open societies like Anglo-American, will exert extreme pressure to keep a person from "getting out of line." Even groups that seem open to new ideas—such as the academic community of which I am a part—will often turn negative when it comes to changing perspectives on spiritual power. They might be charitable if you simply change your belief, since religion is usually regarded as a private matter. The rub comes if you begin to practice ministering in power as Jesus did. Those among my academic colleagues who objected to our *Signs and Wonders* course, for example, made it clear that they would not complain much if we simply offered a course that discussed healing ministries. It is when we insist on practicing what we preach that they get upset. Westerners, especially academics, are typically a good bit more open to "talking about" than to "doing the works."

2. If the will is there to change a perspective, is there enough **knowledge** for people to understand what the implications are? Every shift of perspective requires, at the very least, that a person know that a shift is possible and enough understanding about what lies on the other side to have an inkling of what to expect. One of the biggest hindrances to change is the lack of knowledge that there is an alternative.

As mentioned, there are at least three kinds of knowledge: intellectual, observational, and experiential. In western societies, it is information at the purely intellectual level that we are most aware of when we think of knowledge. Such knowledge is valuable but seldom life-changing in and of itself. Unless a person goes on to observational and experiential knowledge, a change of perspective is not very likely. That is where the will needs to be involved.

There is a close interaction between knowledge and will. People often allow purely intellectual knowledge to keep them from deciding to investigate a new idea. For instance, what the Pharisees thought they knew intellectually they used to reinforce their willful rejection of Jesus (see John 9). Yet one Pharisee came to Jesus by night to check out his claims because he had observed and come to "know that [Jesus is] a teacher sent by God" (John 3:2).

Even the intellectual knowledge that God is doing mighty works somewhere can provide a powerful impetus for a person to open him or herself up to investigating spiritual power. As a missiologist, I became intellectually aware that Pentecostal and charismatic Christianity was and still is by far the most rapidly growing kind of Christianity. When I came to understand that the major reason for this was that signs and wonders are a prominent dimension of charismatic Christianity, I began to open up to people from these traditions. However, I had very little idea of how one went about such a ministry.

For me it wasn't until I attended the class on signs and wonders, that my intellectual knowledge became observational knowledge. I began to "know" at quite a different level when I was able—like Nicodemus—to observe others ministering in supernatural power and then see tangible results. It was only at this point that my openness was transformed into a genuine shift in perspective.

Yet many people are quite capable of observing and rejecting something. Because of a strong will or some lack of ability or imagination on their part, they may not be able to see in a new way. I've interacted with several people who just could not move into spiritual power even when they saw the results. Like the Jews who could "listen and listen, but not understand; … look and look, but not see" (Acts 28.26; Is 6;9), their intellectual "knowledge" that such things don't happen anymore may keep them from even exposing themselves to seeing (observing) what was happening, since such knowledge affects imagination. And one's inability to imagine a new perspective can provide a powerful barrier to keep one from moving toward that perspective.

On the other hand, an ability to imagine something different can aid one greatly in an attempt to move into a new perspective. Indeed, even among rationalistic scientists I have heard it said that "the difference between a good scientist and a great one is imagination." Certainly the greatness of Einstein lay largely in his ability to imagine new possibilities

3. ***Experience*** The thing that really changes one's perspective, though, is new *experience*. Whether this is experience forced on a person or that that one moves into voluntarily, there is no substitute for experience in the process of worldview change. When a farmer tries out new seed and it yields a crop many times more than the old one, this experience is likely to propel him into a new habit. When a volcano erupts or a war is lost among a people who believe no misfortune could come upon them, it is likely that

some paradigms will be at least weakened if not replaced.

When I began to experience God healing people through me, changes in themes, subthemes, paradigms, subparadigms and all the rest began to take root. Changes in head knowledge can loosen things up and bring some changes, but there is nothing like experience to really confirm the changes. I like to refer to my own change as involving first a paradigm shift and then a "practice shift."

The practice shift, then, no matter how tentatively one might move into it, will issue in new habits if one continues to pursue it. These will be new habits of assuming and of doing. For some, the new assumptions come first, followed by the development of the ew habits. For others, they begin to practice something new first and only later go into their worldview to adjust their assumptions.

We might picture the process of moving from openness to a change through a paradigm shift and on to a practice shift (new habit) as follows:

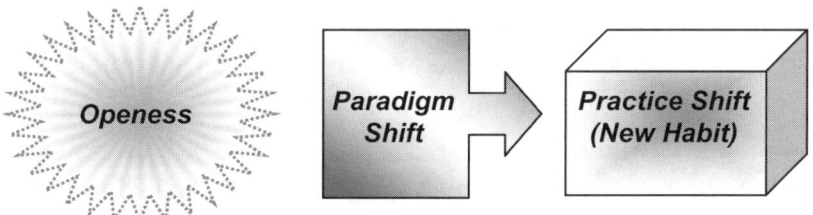

Figure 15.1. From Openness to Practice Shift

With enough effort put into changing will, knowledge and practice, then, it is possible to "escape" from and exchange at least certain of our worldview perspectives. I am skeptical about the possibility of exchanging one whole worldview for another. I just don't believe that can happen. But it has been demonstrated over and over again that parts of one's worldview can be altered or even replaced, whether at the level of themes, subthemes, paradigms, and subparadigms or at some even smaller level.

What Needs to be Changed?

If not everything in a worldview can be changed or needs to be changed, what should we focus on? Trying to keep the whole enormous task in mind will just confuse us. So we need to identify certain crucial areas to focus on.

1. The most important area in dealing with non-believers is, of course, the need for ***change in allegiance***. This change and growth in the relationship with God that issues from it is our primary concern. Though we often focus mainly on the initial commitment to Christ that signals the start of

the Christian life, growth in this commitment is still an important area throughout the Christian experience. For Jesus demands complete and continual commitment to Himself with all other allegiances to be secondary to that commitment. And such continual and complete commitment is often challenged by the necessity of directing our attention to other concerns throughout our lifetime.

The Bible is clear that it is only with commitment that the saving relationship with Christ can begin. However, judging from Jesus' interchange with the thief on the cross (Luke 23:39-43), the start of the allegiance He requires may be understood as a very basic turning toward Him, with or without much understanding of what makes salvation possible or of the implications of such a turning.

Commitment, then, is a directional thing, not merely a positional thing (see Kraft 1979, 2005). That is, even though through commitment to Christ one attains a position of "saved" rather than "lost," the crucial thing is not one's standing in a kind of box labeled "saved," but the direction in which one is headed—toward Christ or away from Him. The Pharisees, for example, showed all the marks of being in what we might label the "saved" box but, due to their motivation, they were pointed in the wrong direction—away from Christ.

I have attempted to diagram this concept of directional versus positional understanding of conversion in *Christianity in Culture* as follows:

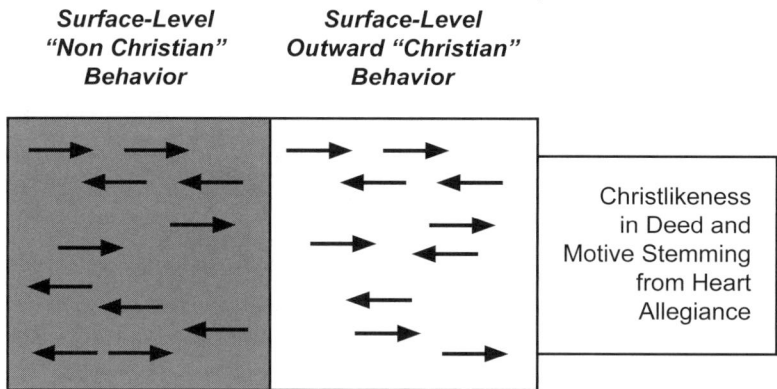

Figure 15.2. Directional Versus Positional Understandings of Those "In" Christ and Those "Outside" of Christ (from Kraft 1979, 2005)

The *positional* understanding of Christianness sees all those in the compartment on the left as positioned outside Christ and those in the compartment on the right as in Christ. Those whose behavior seems "Christian" are assumed to be Christians and those whose behavior is ungodly are considered lost. This is perhaps the most common way of evaluating the "saved" and the "lost" in evangelical circles. It fails to take into account, however, how close a person may be to a starting point far from Christian ideas. A person just converted out of a life of deep sinfulness who has not yet learned to behave as a Christian is just as saved as a saint who has been on the Christian path for forty years and exhibits exemplary Christ-like behavior. The thief on the cross, for example, had no chance to change his behavior after committing himself to Christ in the last moments of his life. But he was saved. Large numbers of the Pharisees, on the other hand, behaved admirably but refused to commit themselves to Jesus and were lost.

The *directional* understanding of conversion sees all those who are moving toward greater Christ-likeness (the arrows pointing to the right in Figure 15.2) as saved, no matter what position they may occupy in the above-pictured, behaviorally-defined compartments or how distant they may be in their movement toward Christ-likeness. Those people who are headed away from Christ, then, signified by the arrows pointing to the left, are lost, even if behaviorally they exhibit what would be regarded as "Christ-like" behavior. Thus salvation belonged not only to Peter and the other apostles who were close to Jesus and becoming more Christ-like but also to the thief on the cross who, though still distant from Jesus, turned and headed in the right direction. The disciples had time and opportunity to change their behavior and beliefs and to develop their commitment to Christ. The thief on the cross had no such opportunity. But both were saved by heading in the right direction, having committed themselves to Jesus. It was the direction in which they were going, not the perfection of their behavior that saved them.

I once met a Thai man who started his life with Christ in the well of a Buddhist monastery. As a youngster in the employ of the monastery he fell in the well and, after appealing to many gods, came up with the name Jesus. As he appealed to Jesus (without even knowing how he knew that name), a monk appeared and rescued him. He pledged at that time to follow Jesus for the rest of his life. But it was not until more that a year later that he found someone to tell him who Jesus was. I believe the fact that he was headed in the right direction, even without knowledge about Jesus, would have resulted in heaven for him had he died in the interim before learning more about the God he had in ignorance pledged himself to.

2. Given the primacy of change of allegiance and the apparently small amount of knowledge one needs to be saved, does there need to be **change in the knowledge** the receptors have? Though as westerners we may

recognize a proneness to inundate people with knowledge, we dare not go to the opposite extreme and assume that they may not need any additional knowledge. What they need is usually *stimulus* even more than knowledge for its own sake. But new knowledge can be a very powerful stimulus.

Often correct knowledge is needed to remedy incorrect understandings. The lies many people believe about Christ and Christianity are powerful hindrances to people opening up to the truth and turning to Jesus. Though, as we have said, people may not need much knowledge, they do need enough accurate understanding to make the decisions they have to make if they are to come to saving faith.

As with all other areas, converts are expected to grow in their knowledge, especially in their experiential knowledge of Christ as they grow in their relationship to Him. The changes in knowledge, then, are to be a continuous thing in Christian experience.

3. A major issue for most of the peoples of the world is to **change the source of the power** they seek. For many peoples, any power is acceptable power. They may make no clear distinction between the power of God and that of spirits or gods that represent Satan. When they seek healing, they usually are willing to accept it from any source with no understanding that accepting power from the wrong source incurs bondages they will regret later. The need to be in a relationship with the source of the power they seek is foreign to their worldview assumptions.

One of our greatest problems, then, in witnessing for Christ is to help people to understand the important distinction between God as Source of power and Satan as source. Often deliverance from demons that represent the wrong source can be the catalyst to open people up to this recognition. Healing often is not convincing. There have been very successful healing campaigns among power-oriented people that resulted in many people healed but few who saw any need to seek their next healings from the true God. Having received blessing from the true Source, they returned the next time they needed power to whatever source was at hand (e.g., their spirits and gods).

When people catch onto the need to change power sources, though, they find that much of what they were able to experience before can continue as a part of their new relationship with Jesus. It is as if they have unplugged themselves from satanic power and plugged their plug into the true God for the same kinds of blessing, guidance, healing and the like for which they depended on their old gods and spirits. Unfortunately, many in power-oriented societies who have become Christians have been secularized in the process of coming to Christ. Though this may have broken much of the hold of the old sources of power, it has often left them with a powerless Christianity and a strong temptation to return to their old power sources when they are in trouble.

4. In all of this, the crucial change and the most difficult one is in the area of the ***change of meanings***. The fact that meanings are in people rather than in any of the vehicles we use to communicate means that the receptors will construct the meanings they understand from the materials within their own heads. Thus, when we seek to appeal for allegiance on the basis of our understandings of Christian messages or even our demonstrations of God's power, we can be sure they are interpreting what we say and do from their own perspective.

Monitoring the meanings they are constructing is, therefore, an important activity for the one who would like to see change in the right direction. Advocates of Christianity, especially in cross-cultural situations, need to be aware of the great likelihood that a meaning problem exists between them and their receptors. In the area of power, for example, it is the meaning problem that results in the tendency of most people to interpret a demonstration of God's power as just another example of spiritual power without seeing it as distinctive. Likewise, it is the meaning problem that for many traditional people results in an interpretation of acts of love expressed through institutions (e.g., hospitals, schools) as relating more to money or cultural imperialism than to love.

If people are to change the meanings of the words and techniques we use in our attempts to win them, they usually will need help. As a first step, we need to regularly ask them how they are interpreting what we are doing and recommending. Then, as a second step, we need to find out from them what we will have to do to communicate the meanings we intend. We can ask such things as, "If we wanted to communicate love in your way, how would we do it?" And, "If this thing we are doing is to be interpreted as loving, what modifications must we make?"

Some Basic Principles to Follow

Recognizing what needs to be changed, then, needs to be accompanied with a statement of some of the basic principles for the Christian witness to follow. I will point to three of these as probably the most important.

1. The most important principle is to discover the answer to the question, ***what is the Holy Spirit already doing*** in the area in which we are working? Unfortunately, this is a very neglected principle. Most of us are prone to going at things as best we know how, as if the ministry was ours rather

than God's. But remembering whose ministry it is should be the guiding principle of our whole endeavor. So, consulting the Holy Spirit before we initiate anything should be our first move.

As Paul said to the Athenians, "God is actually not far from any of us" (Acts 17:27). Probably all of us believe that God has not left Himself without a witness in any time or place, but do we look for that witness before we begin to proclaim our own witness? At the very least, there is the witness spoken of in Rom. 1:20-21:

> Ever since God created the world, his invisible qualities, both his eternal power and his divine nature, have been clearly seen; they are perceived in the things that God has made. So those people have no excuse at all! They know God, but they do not give him the honor that belongs to him, nor do they thank him.

We should be looking for evidence of that witness, plus the possibility of even more things that God has been doing in the context to which He has called us. We could start by trying to discover just how the people to whom we go are interpreting the things about God that these verses point to. As one Nigerian said to me, the missionaries could have been at least one generation ahead in their efforts to win our people if they had started where we were rather than where they were in helping us to understand God.

2. A second important principle is that ***our appeal should always be to people***. This may seem like an obvious principle. But it is very easy to get tangled up in our concern for the change of customs and forget that it is change in people much more than change in culture that God is interested in. It has been one of the major aims of this book to focus our attention on *people* and the choices they make, especially those choices that manifest their God-given creativity in choosing something other than that indicated by their worldview.

Our questions should concern what needs the people are feeling and how to present Christian messages so that they will be connected by the people with the concerns already in their minds and hearts. We should be researching the things people talk about. These things will probably help us to focus attention on their felt needs. Our concern for a people's needs should not, though, simply relate to their need for salvation. Though that concern is primary, people also need to grow in their faith, their commitment, their understandings and their service for Jesus. Our Christian aim for people goes far beyond a concern for their salvation. Jesus wants them to experience freedom and to grow into maturity.

A people's culture and worldview do not provide for all of the needs of a people. There are always things that are not adequately addressed even by the most intact cultural systems—and most are not very much intact these days. Looking for latent concerns that lie beneath the surface should be a major focus of our research as we seek to develop our strategies. These concerns, then, may or may not be at the level of the people's consciousness. If, however, we participate in their discussions, we may find that they are more aware of such concerns than might be apparent to an outsider who is just observing and listening rather than participating with them.

Our primary concern with people should be, of course, the matter of their allegiance. Are they happy with the allegiances they now have? Or is there some underlying quest for something more satisfying? Many people of our day are looking for something worth committing themselves to. They are often subconsciously quite dissatisfied with the primacy in their lives of their commitment to reaching material ends. And many are very concerned with the breakdown of cultural structures and looking for the kind of peace that Jesus offers as an antidote to the worry such cultural breakdown fosters.

The question often is, however, just what will be the most effective paths to follow to help people to become aware of their need for a new allegiance. For some it will be new understandings. For most of the peoples of the world, however, the awareness we seek will probably be most effectively brought to their attention through demonstrations of the power of God. All peoples struggle with concerns over adequate food and shelter, good health, prevention of accidents, protection from harm and the like. A major problem of which many are aware, then, is their feelings of powerlessness in the face of life's circumstances. It is probable that God allows the negative things into our lives so that we will reach out for Him. When Jesus was on earth, He showed God's concern for such problems and His answer through the use of spiritual power.

3. The third of these principles is to **look at the characteristics of a people's worldview** to discover possible avenues for the communication of Christian messages. The exercise below is designed to help us to see how valuable this strategy is. As we look at the themes, subthemes, paradigms of a worldview and at the ways in which these deep-level assumptions are played out at surface level, the ways in which a group's worldview does not adequately fulfill the expectations of a people can become much clearer.

Though our focus is always to be on people rather than simply on the cultural structures in which they are immersed, we can look to the structures for clues as to how the people are seeking to meet their needs. That's why a study of worldview assumptions is so important for Christian witnesses. A study of the underlying paradigms enables us to gain insight to help us reach the people.

Basic Underlying Factors in Worldview Change

In spite of the fact that the depth of our worldview conditioning assures that it is unlikely that we will change most of what we have learned, we seem always to be in the process of modifying the perspectives we are taught. Change at both surface and deep levels seems to be a continual part of our lives, though much more change seems to happen at the surface level. There are at least five reasons for this constant process:

1. ***We always seem to learn imperfectly***. Though each generation tends to rather fully adopt the perspectives of the previous generation, there always seems to be some slippage from generation to generation. This is at least partly due to imperfect understanding and/or lack of complete acceptance on the part of the learners.

Often parents, due to experiences in their own lives that raise questions about certain worldview perspectives, become less convinced of a given assumption than their parents were. They, therefore, pass the assumption on to their children in such a tentative way that their children will alter or reject it. They may not have gotten to the point where they rejected what they had been taught but perhaps could not think of a better alternative, so they passed on what they had learned but without conviction.

This kind of thing probably happens when parents who are faithful in church, are let down by the pastor or other members of the church and share their disappointment with their children. It happens often in pastors' families where the children regularly hear criticism of members of the congregation who cause the pastor problems. Though the assumption that a commitment to church membership and attendance are important may still be strong for the parents, that conviction is very much weakened in the children. This may lead to the children replacing their parents' strongly held assumption with another—that church is a place where people hurt each other so who needs it?

2. A second reason for change is that ***our teachers have not taught us well***. The slippage between generations is not solely the children's fault. Often parents and teachers are not very good at getting across what they know to the next generation. Even when they are convinced of the rightness of the ways they have been taught, parents and teachers differ in their skill at getting their perspectives across. In addition, there often are conflicting

expectations between parents, school teachers, Sunday School teachers and other significant others concerning who has what responsibility for which areas of teaching.

Due to such conflict, certain aspects of what children are expected to understand often fall through the cracks. For example, parents often expect public school teachers to provide more moral instruction and discipline than the teachers consider appropriate (or are allowed to do). The teachers, for their part, often fail to see that what they teach is much more highly regarded by the students than what they learn from their parents. So, the example of the teachers in avoiding moral instruction or, worse, in questioning the perspectives of the parents, is what carries the most weight with the children. The high prestige of school teachers coupled with their "neutral" or negative stance on moral issues, then, often leads to the children of even highly committed Christian parents going astray.

For example, even when parents are strong on the assumption that what is taught in church is very important and they set a good example by being faithful in attendance, this value may not get across strongly to the children. The negative influence of secular teachers and peers may be too strong and the parents may just not be good at articulating their convictions in meaningful ways so that the children genuinely internalize their parents' value in this area. Peer and teacher pressure, then, may result in quite a different perspective on the part of the children.

3. A third reason for changes in our mental maps is the fact that, *as we experience life we seem to constantly test our perspectives in relation to that experience*. And, since the perspectives we were taught had been developed to fit the experiences of those of previous generations, there is likely to be some lack of fit, at least in certain areas, with our own experience. This fact faces us with the choice between ignoring the lack of fit, altering the perspective, or denying any interpretation of our experience that does not conform to the perspective. People seem to choose each of these options fairly frequently. When, however, we choose to alter our mental map, change takes place, at least in the way we use the patterns of our own culture.

Say, for example, we were brought up in a pagan home and as children assimilated well a perspective on life that views Christianity and Christians very negatively. Then, through a credible witness and encouragement from Christians we turned to Christ and as we tested our pre-conversion perspectives we found them wanting. Life experience, then, based on the new commitment is such a positive change that a lot of the old pagan paradigms are changed completely. These perspectives have been tested, found wanting and replaced or greatly altered.

4. A fourth pressure for change in our mental grid occurs when *we are faced with a conflicting model of or approach to some aspect of reality*. In traditional societies (at least in the past) and in more isolated segments of western societies (e.g., the Amish), exposure to other options tends to be minimal. But in the mainstreams of both western and non-western societies today people are being faced in an unprecedented way with models of reality that often conflict in whole or in part with what they have been taught. There are at least three frequent results of such pressure.

a. Not infrequently, people simply refuse to deal with the new perception. They kind of "sweep it under the rug" and act like they never experienced whatever it was that challenged their present model. This was the approach taken by a student who asked if he could watch while a colleague of mine and I were working with a demonized woman. As we challenged the demons, they replied to us, put up their resistance and finally had to leave. But the student left before the demons did! He told me later that he felt he had to leave because he "had no categories in his mind to put what we were doing in." He tried to explain what was happening naturalistically and psychologically but couldn't. So he gave up, preferring to act as if the event had not happened rather than attempting to develop a new "compartment" to his worldview.

b. Frequently a person or group will be so convinced of the greater validity of the new understanding of Reality that they make a *paradigm shift*, converting to a new perspective (see Kuhn 1970; Barbour 1974; Kraft 1979a, 1989, 1996). In our day, many non-westerners are becoming convinced of a new perspective on Reality and converting from a spirit-centered view of Reality to a materialistic "scientific" perspective. They are often so impressed by western technological superiority that they uncritically adopt major portions of the naturalistic interpretation of life in general.

Such shifts also occur when a non-Christian converts to Christianity or when a westerner brought up in a Christian paradigm converts to a secularistic perspective or (in a more restricted context) when a scientist who has learned to understand his/her science (or some part of it) in one way abandons that picture of Reality for a different understanding (e.g., flat earth to round earth or earth-centered universe to sun-centered universe or naturalistic to creationistic understanding of the origin of the universe).

c. Perhaps as frequently as people convert from one perspective to another, they retain at least a major portion of the old view while adding a new understanding of Reality. They may, then, switch back and forth between the two as they move from situation to situation. It is not uncommon, for example, for people of non-western societies who have been taught secularism in western schools (often mission schools) to employ that secularistic perspective when involved in activities associated with western culture (e.g., business, school, politics, church). They may then switch to a spirit-centered perspective learned within their home society when faced with life experiences not (from their point of view) adequately handled by the western paradigm (e.g., illness, breakdown of interpersonal relationships, oppression by spirits, personal or group misfortune).

Similarly, western Christians often find two separate views of many aspects of Reality in conflict within them. We westerners may, for example, hold within us two separate interpretations of given events and switch back and forth between them at different times. We may interpret an event either as luck or as the blessing of God, either as misfortune (bad luck) or as the activity of Satan. We may see something as permitted by God to challenge us to growth or as chance, as the result of specific activity on God's part (i.e., a miracle) or as chance. A healing may be interpreted as either brought about by doctors and/or medicine or as brought about by God using doctors and/or medicine.

5. A fifth reason for change is the ***recognition of the fact that there is often a larger or smaller difference between what we believe and what we practice***. This inconsistency, when we notice it (or someone calls it to our attention), may stimulate us to make adjustments either in what we are doing or in what we are assuming. Or we may simply decide to live with the inconsistency. If we decide to continue the new behavior and adjust some portion of our worldview to the behavior, this becomes a basis for change.

Some years ago, we had a Nigerian living with us. On one occasion, we took him with us to a family party near a lake. One of the events was to be swimming but it became known to some of us that a Black man would not be welcome on the beach we were planning on using. Now, I knew and loved this man and saw no problem with him swimming with us—in the abstract. In the actual situation, however, I found myself planning with some of the relatives to work out something else for him to do so that none of us would be embarrassed by his presence on the beach. The inconsistency between what I claimed to believe and my behavior didn't come to light, though, until one of the relatives who had not been in on the conversation, upon hearing what we were discussing, simply said, "If so-and-so is not welcome on this beach, I'm not going swimming." At that, I felt convicted and, I believe, got rid of the conflict between what I claimed to assume in this area and what I actually did assume. None of us went swimming.

The Steps to Take

Though there are sure to be variations, there are some common steps that a person will need to take to change worldview paradigms (and higher and lower perspectives). We will assume that the person making the change is moving either into Christianity from a non-Christian background or, within Christianity, from a powerless Christianity into one with power. I make no apology for including this latter paradigm shift because I believe a Christianity that includes the spiritual power dimension is the only one that is truly Biblical. This is what I call "Kingdom Christianity."

So, the following steps can apply either to the ones we seek to reach or, perhaps, to ourselves if we have been practicing a Christianity without the power dimension. For many of us, the Christianity we have been practicing has been the rationalistic, secular type spoken of in the previous chapter. If so, let's follow these steps into Kingdom Christianity.

1. The first step toward any worldview change is to **make sure there is no will problem**. The person making the change needs to be willing to reexamine and reconsider previous understandings and to choose a new option. For those of us attempting to lead a person into such a change, we need to be very conscious of the place of the receptor's will and the need to win the right to appeal for that person to make a choice. This may not be easy. We will need to be practicing the communication principles spoken of in the next few chapters and in my *Communication Theory for Christian Witness* (1991).

In the New Testament, the Pharisees are the prime example of people who had a will problem. They would not follow Jesus because they *chose* not to. Nothing He did would convince them to change their minds. It is, in fact, rather ludicrous to see in passages such as John 9 the lengths to which they would go to keep from accepting the plain fact that it was Jesus who had healed a man born blind. To ourselves or our hearers to open up for change we/they must reject such things as vested interests, rebellion against God, unwillingness to risk prestige for truth and fear of becoming odd. To will to be open to change is the first step.

2. As a second step, we will return to the above discussion of **what we do with our intellect**. People (whether they or we) will need to study their options. They will need to let their minds and imaginations accept, at least tentatively, what God is offering in and through Jesus Christ— whether salvation or movement into the three dimensional Christianity discussed in the previous chapter. One approach to evangelism that I once read in a tract by Billy Graham was to invite people to "act as if" what they were

hearing was true and to experiment with living that way for a period of time to see if one would prefer the new way or not.

Curiosity is an important aspect of this step. Wondering what it might be like to make the recommended changes and observing those who have made them can be crucial. In witnessing to others, we gain ground quickly once the person's curiosity is engaged. This is a good prelude to the next step.

3. ***Exposing oneself*** to observing and, if possible, experiencing the new assumptions and behavior makes an important third step. People need to risk old perspectives by testing the new experientially. This is, in fact, what we do as we grow up and experience new things—we continually test our perspectives in new situations to see if they hold up as is or if they need to be modified. Our lives go in a kind of "perspective-experience circle" as we test each new idea in experience, and each new experience in relation to our ideas and assumptions.

To expose ourselves to possible new insight, we need to get in on a variety of experiences that challenge previous understandings. A pastor in Nigeria who wanted his people to change from a very western form of worship to a more African style took several of his leaders with him to visit a church that had the kind of worship he was recommending. Upon returning, the leaders arranged for several others from the congregation to visit that church. Eventually, then, enough of the congregation had visited the other church and had a positive experience with its African-type worship that there was no problem bringing about the change in their church.

Introducing others to potentially paradigm-challenging experiences, then, can be a part of our strategy to bring about worldview change and, when the issue is conversion, leading them to Christ. We should ourselves bring about and encourage others to bring about occasions in which newfound observational knowledge challenges our/their previous knowledge and imagination.

Exposing oneself or another to books, tapes and other media is another way to encourage worldview change. In this area, though, we need to be careful to recommend reading and listening to practitioners, not simply to academics who may specialize in theory but not in practice. One advantage we have, of course, is that the Bible is a record of and by practitioners who knew what they were talking about because they lived it.

4. ***Timing*** is important in worldview change. Change is a process and not everything can (or should) be changed at once. Nor should a lot of things be introduced at the same time. Under most circumstances, people have to consider a suggestion for change for a while even if they are positive

toward it. And it takes much longer if they are not at first positive toward a suggested change in perspective.

5. A further important step is for people to *practice the behavior* built on the worldview changes they are trying to make. When agriculturalists seek to introduce new crops they regularly start what are called "demonstration farms." The aim of these farms is to provide a place in which to practice innovations and to demonstrate that newly introduced crops can make it in the new setting. Jesus' ministry was a kind of demonstration farm concerning what God is like and how He wants to use His love and power.

Experimenting with and practicing new behavior based on new understandings is what confirms or disconfirms the validity of the new assumptions. Only in practice do we learn how to venture forth in faith, how to hear God, how to take authority, and whatever else is appropriate to the new perspectives. We can't learn to swim by simply swinging our arms on the beach! We need to jump in and swim!

6. In working with God to change paradigms, we need to help people to *give Him permission* to do anything He wants with them. Sometimes this will involve embarrassment or social ostracization. The determination to follow God even when it is not easy is crucial in the face of opposition. But we who advocate the changes need to help those we seek to guide to listen to God directly (i.e., not just through us) and to follow what He says, no matter what the cost. Often non-westerners will more easily hear God than those of us who are westerners can. We should set them free to work directly with God even when His leading as perceived by them does not follow our expectations. God should be in control, not ourselves.

7. In all matters of change, we need to *be patient* with the process and with God, whether the changes are in ourselves or in others. Any learning process takes time. There may be a few people who make changes quickly. But most people don't, especially if they are major changes. People try something and fail. Then they pick themselves up and try again. They and we can get discouraged and even consider quitting. But they (and we) shouldn't quit until, like Jacob (Gen. 32:26), the blessing God intends is received.

We shouldn't even be overly concerned about people's doubts. Jesus honored the faith of Thomas and also of the man who had changed his worldview enough to say, "I do have faith, but not enough. Help me have more!" (Mark 9:24). Jesus knows how hard it is for us and honors our attempts even though they are feeble. I once heard someone say, "Little faith is not necessarily weak faith." Thank God for that!

An Exercise

At this point I would like us to return to the outlines of worldviews presented in chapter 12 and to ask a series of questions concerning the various themes, subthemes, paradigms and subparadigms presented there. I would like us to choose one of the worldviews outlined in chapter 12 and ask such things as:

- What potential for evangelistic engagement is represented by each of the fundamental assumptions (the themes, subthemes, etc.) that make up the worldview in question?
- Which assumptions can converts continue to follow with little or no change?
- Which will require eventual change but can be accepted at the start?
- Which will require immediate change if people are to be fully Christian?

The majority of worldview assumptions will fall into the first category. Almost all of the rest, then, will fall into the second category as candidates for eventual, gradual change. The only ones that require immediate change are those that conflict with a primary allegiance to Christ, and even then God is usually patient with those who move slowly. God starts with people at a point of faith and works with people from there in a process toward His ideas.

Ask yourself which category each of the assumptions in the worldview analyses fits into.

- Next, given the fact that these analyses are very brief, generate suggestions concerning what additional information would need to be gathered to enable us to develop more effective strategies.
- Are there more things we need to know concerning those areas where it looks like there does not need to be change?
- What about those areas that look like they need slow or immediate change?
- Next, try to assess as best you can the strength of commitment of the people to various worldview values.
- Are there some subthemes or paradigms that you judge the people might be less committed to than others?
- If so, what strategy might be effective in advocating change in those areas?

On the basis of your answers to these questions, suggest a strategy for witness to the people you have chosen.

PART III:

WORLDVIEW CHANGE

Chapter 16

Obstacles & Opportunities in Worldview Change: Person/Group

There are a number of factors that can hinder or facilitate worldview change. We have come upon many of them as we have been working through the material in the previous chapters. In this chapter, then, we want to look more closely at some of these factors with the question in mind, what are the things that tend to hinder or help worldview change?

Since most of these factors relate directly to people, we will look at those that fall under the Person/Group universal first. In the following chapter, then, we will take up those factors that fall under the other universals.

Person/Group: Five Dimensions

In dealing with obstacles to and opportunities for worldview change within the person/group universal, there are at least five major dimensions to reckon with. The most important of these is will (choice). Whether we are considering the worldview assumptions of the advocates (e.g., missionaries) and the choices they make, or the assumptions of the receptors and the choices they make, it is the ***will*** of persons that we are dealing with. We then need to ask what are the factors in the lives of the advocates and the receptors that hinder certain choices and facilitate others?

I suggest that these are their internal habits and their external relationships. Choices are made by both advocates and receptors, often quite unconsciously under internal pressure from their habitual following of worldview guidelines and under external pressure from their relationships with the members of their society. We may diagram these five dimensions as follows and note that each of the participating persons/groups (the advocates and receptors) needs to deal with the effects on their wills of the pressure coming from internalized habits and the external pressures coming from their relatives and other significant others with whom they have relationships.

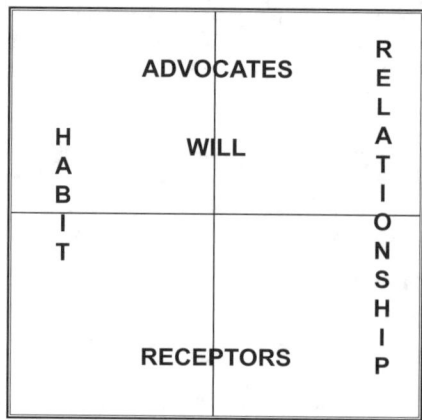

Figure 16.1. Five Dimensions to Consider

The primacy of the will is the first of these dimensions to consider. All change requires choices. But the choices are never made in a vacuum. It is fairly easy for those of us brought up in individualistic, personal freedom-oriented societies to assume a greater freedom of will than is ordinarily the case, even in our own societies. There are pressures on the will. The pressure of habit is incredibly powerful, especially since it operates subconsciously. Though in individualistic societies, many people are able to feel only minimal social pressure coming from their relatives, in group-oriented societies that pressure can be nearly as powerful as habit. And strong social control mechanisms (see below) are the vehicles that enforce the worldview guidelines underlying the relational dynamics.

There are habits and relationships relating to their home society and culture that advocates have to deal with. There are also habits and relationships related to their society and culture that receptors have to deal with. Both sets of habits and relationships are designed to keep people from straying from their worldview guidelines. Habits produce a kind of internal pressure to conform. That is, internal to both the advocates and the receptors are certain habits that tie them tightly to their home-culture worldview assumptions. If, as is normal in cross-cultural witness, the advocates and the receptors come from different societies, then, the assumptions will be different and so will the habits. And habit is a powerful mechanism for keeping people on the same tracks they were taught as children. So are the relationships persons have with their significant others. These are important mechanisms of social control.

With the differences in assumptions, there are obstacles on either side of the communicational gap. But usually there are assumptions on either side that provide opportunity as well. Often the worldview obstacles we are most aware of are those of the receiving people. But often the things that prevent a receiving people from accepting the gospel are worldview assumptions the witnesses are unaware of in their approach. For the approach of the witnesses is based on assumptions that the receiving people (and often the advocates) are unaware of. Unfortunately, then, we who advocate Christianity are often also unaware of those worldview assumptions that provide opportunity for the gospel.

Suppose, for example, that in the advocates' worldview time is considered such an important factor that they tend to rush and be impatient for decisions to be made. But in the receptors' worldview, there is always a tomorrow to make the decision. And, the receptors assume, everybody in the social circle must agree before the decision can be made. But this takes time. Or suppose, as is frequently the case, anger is a cardinal sin for the receiving people. But the missionaries, though they recommend a gospel that features peacefulness, tend to get angry (and show it) at least in mild forms as allowed by their worldview. Each group may be quite unaware that such "little" things produce large obstacles to the willingness of the receptors to adopt the recommended changes. On the other hand, many missionaries have developed close friendships (relationships) within the receiving people group and found that the people were wide open to many of the changes they suggested. The pleasantness of the friendships opened up the people to changes, even large changes.

A basic picture of what goes on in people's minds when they consider a change is as follows: benefits minus cost = ?? That is, when persons or groups are considering whether or not to make a given change, they ask themselves about the benefits of such a change. Whatever the perceived benefits, the next concern is what the change might cost them socially, economically, politically, etc. If the benefits are seen to be high and the cost low, it is likely that they will accept. If, however, the social, economic or political cost is high, rejection is likely even if the benefits are also high.

What I mean by cost is usually a social cost. In terms of the above diagram, this is usually in the receptors' relationship category. Most of the societies of the world are characterized by much tighter family relationships than we see in American society. And the usual family in their society is what we call the "extended family" (though it would be more accurate to consider the extended family a normal family and American families "truncated"). It is in such tight family relationships that the people of most societies find their social security. To ask them to give up that security just because we say it would be better is very presumptuous on our part.

For example, if a given man is approached with the gospel and sees great value in accepting Christ but the cost will be ostracization from his family, he is not likely to accept. In many situations today, however, that man may gain permission from the elders of his society to make that change, even though those elders themselves will stay traditional. In such a case, the cost may not be high enough for the person to consider it to outweigh the benefits. So he/she might make the change with little or no social cost. Or that man's family relationships may have broken down under the pressures of contemporary sociocultural change so that he feels free to make such a decision without consulting anyone. The cost for him, under those conditions is not very high either.

I have seen all three of these situations in Nigeria. On several occasions I heard of older men who admitted that the Christian message was very attractive to them but refused to convert. One of them said to me, "I would convert but I am too old." My guess is that he was thinking he could not have a proper funeral if he converted. On other occasions, older men would not themselves convert but gave permission for their wives, their children and grandchildren to convert if they so chose. William Reyburn tells of a case in Cameroon in which older men who had several wives and, therefore, were prevented from joining the church, ordered their first wives to join the church, reasoning that "God will not reject a man who gives Him his first wife" (Reyburn 1958). In the growing number of situations where sociocultural breakdown is the norm, people regularly choose Christ without permission.

As mentioned in chapter 15, a good example of the great power of family relationships comes from Japan. Japanese youth are allowed a good bit of freedom to choose allegiances that their parents are not a part of. So, many Japanese youth experiment with a variety of associations and causes while they are young (e.g., environmental groups, student strikes, Christianity), some of which are not positive (e.g., gangs). But when they marry, they are expected to abandon such associations and to settle down to work to support their families. Thus, for years now Japanese churches have been taking in fair numbers of young people who, when they marry, drop out of the churches. Their social security, as defined traditionally in terms of their family relationships, becomes their primary concern, and their association with the church merely a youthful detour.

Person/Group: Social Control

The first set of factors to look at in this regard are those that constitute the social control subsystem of a sociocultural entity. Note that it is specifically *social* control, not cultural control, even though the mechanisms are a part of cultural structuring. It is social because the control factors are operated by *people*. They are not simply parts of the structure. As always, the cultural structuring provides the patterns by means of which people protect their worldview, but it is *people* who decide whether or not to implement those structural safeguards.

When people attempt to change a cultural practice, they are likely to become subjects of the society's attempt to "get them back into line." Underlying such techniques, however, are certain worldview assumptions and certain social habits that people are reluctant to see flaunted. The worldview assumptions, of course, underlie all sociocultural behavior. These are the basic principles, the foundation for the rules and regulations from which the social control techniques flow. Since people tend to be quite protective of their worldview assumptions, then, these provide the primary obstacles to change. These hindrances are in the patterning, the script that people follow.

What we call social control involves the pressure put on by the reference group. For most of the peoples of this world, their security is provided by their family, clan and broader group relationships. Whereas in America we think of "social security" in monetary terms, for traditional societies this is an intensely person-oriented factor. It is the extended family that provides a secure base from which to operate in life. Security is provided by one's close relatives. So one must keep on good terms with them or sacrifice what might be considered life's most valued "possession."

This group factor, however, also has a major individual component—*habit*. It is habit that empowers worldview and culture in general. We learn our worldview assumptions and habituate them, usually quite unconsciously, as we grow up. As in most other areas of life, it is habit that keeps people following their cultural guidelines. Habit, therefore, is what makes social control at the group level work. More on this below.

The effectiveness of social control is an important element in the potential for worldview change. When social control mechanisms are strongest, the possibility of change is usually lessened, especially at the deep level. Those who change even peripheral paradigms and assumptions will often be treated harshly when social controls are at full strength. Many in traditional societies have experienced the full brunt of the society's attempts to keep them from changing when they accepted Christ or sent their children, especially their girls, to school or in other ways pioneered changes of practice that often later became commonplace. When, though, there is a lessening of the effectiveness of social controls, there is more of an openness to change, for better or worse. Even when social controls are loosened in certain areas of cultural practice, though, they may still be tight in other areas so that worldview change will happen at different rates in different sectors of the culture.

1. In a longer presentation on social control (Kraft 1996:343-57), I pointed out that perhaps the most important mechanism of social control is public opinion wielded through *gossip*. The fear that most people seem to have that any change in cultural behavior might get them criticized is a powerful anti-change mechanism at both surface and deep (worldview) levels of culture. Gossip is intended to shame people into conforming. Fear of being shamed or made to feel guilty, therefore, are usually quite effective in keeping people in line. Though these are surface-level mechanisms, the worldview assumptions underlying them justify the pressing or pulling of people through such social control mechanisms toward conformity in behavior with the other members of the society.

Suppose, for example, that a Buddhist man in Thailand hears the Christian message and is attracted to it. Thoughts quickly come to him concerning how he would be regarded by the members of his extended family if he converted. Perhaps they would ostracize him and cut him off from his inheritance. Or perhaps he would be laughed at or not invited to family functions. And what would he do when Buddhist festivals come around? If he participated, he might be untrue to his Christian allegiance. If he refuses to participate, he would be untrue to his family relationships. Many reject Christ because they consider such social confusion too hard to handle and/or the social price too high.

2. *Law and punishment* can be very effective mechanisms of social control if the change advocated is considered illegal. In many Islamic countries, for example, it is illegal to convert to another "religion." And even when not officially illegal, conversion may be informally illegal. In either case the punishments may be severe for those who disobey. Such practices are based on deeply held worldview assumptions that link nationality and/or ethnicity with religion.

3. One of the most effective mechanisms of social control is the use of *spiritual power*. In many societies, those who are bold enough to convert to Christianity or to make certain other changes are likely to be cursed by those upset by their choice, even by family members. The assumption is that there are spiritual beings that will participate in bringing people back in line and that these beings can be accessed through certain rituals. See the following chapter under Causality for more on this.

4. Another important social control mechanism is *logic*. This will be dealt with in the next chapter under categorization. This mechanism works according to compatibility or incompatibility between assumptions.

Person/Group: Receptor Conservatism or Openness

It is obvious that people will be more likely to change if they are open to changing and less likely if they are closed. In every society, even the most closed, there are those individuals who seem to be more open to change than most of their compatriots. Usually the implementation of that openness is conditioned on such questions as when, how and by whom the change is suggested. The answers to these questions, then, depend on such factors as interest, curiosity, presence or lack of an inclination to experiment and whether or not there is a friendly relationship with a person who can suggest change.

1. ***The Social Climate***. There are differences in the social climate of a society that strongly influence whether or not they are open to changes in basic assumptions and values. The tendency of western societies, and now many others under western influence, to open themselves up to rapid surface-level change has an important effect on people's openness to deep-level change. This effect should not be overestimated, though. A society such as American whose worldview value is to be open to material and technological change will change rapidly on the surface in those areas precisely because of that value. And many societies without that value but faced with the glitter of such change have in our day changed that value. In observing their opening up to such surface changes, however, we must be careful not to assume that they have opened up to the same degree at the deep level. Nor can we assume that the changes they are now accepting are motivated by the same values as are such changes in western societies.

For example, the surface-level materialism of many peoples is based on traditional assumptions concerning a close connection between material goods and the favor of God. And the acceptance of western medical techniques is often based not on acceptance of western worldview assumptions concerning healing but, rather, on more traditional assumptions concerning willingness to accept and use any technique that works. Thus, they add assumptions concerning western techniques while retaining their traditional assumptions concerning the efficacy of their own techniques.

Furthermore, many peoples interpret the way western medicine works in accord with their previous theories rather than according to western understandings. Even when people are quite open to surface-level changes in material areas and have changed a bit in their worldview assumptions and paradigms, however, they may remain very closed in other areas. The Japanese, for example, have borrowed freely in technological matters but changed little in social custom and religion.

2. ***Belief in the Possibility of a Given Change***. It is very unlikely that people will choose to make a change if they don't believe in the possibility of the change. If people are to get involved in changing a concept, they must first be conscious of that concept and then believe the change is possible for *them*. Something believed to be impossible, either in general or for a given individual or group, is likely to be dismissed even it is recognized that the change is advisable. The human ability to interpret in terms of what is believed is incredible. Often people will reject a solution to their problem because they don't believe there could be any solution to it or because they see the change as too difficult.

One kind of example is provided by societies that consider certain areas of life virtually sacred or untouchable. There are societies, for example, who traditionally have seen the earth as analogous to a pregnant woman and, therefore, consider it unthinkable to cut into it for agricultural purposes. Something akin to a belief that the English spelling system is sacred seems to relegate the idea of spelling reform to the area of the impossible in English-speaking countries.

To turn to another example, I have talked to several older Nigerian men who refused to accept Christ simply because they believed such a step to be impossible for a person of their age. Perhaps because we presented the gospel in a way that seemed to them to demand too much, they turned sadly away, saying the new message was only "acceptance-possible" for younger people.

In looking for opportunities, then, we need to reckon with this basic factor and help people to believe they can change and that such a change will be good for them. To do this, there is hardly any better way than to demonstrate the differences. Agriculturalists often set up demonstration farms to prove that new methods can yield more than traditional methods. Jesus demonstrated God's love and power in His ministry by healing and freeing people as signs that the Kingdom of God had truly come.

3. ***Cultural Pride***. People who are proud of their way of life tend to be fairly closed to at least certain of the ideas and perspectives that come from outside. Those with great pride but great security will, however, often adopt certain perspectives from other peoples. Japan is a prime example of a proud people who have rejected western religious, philosophical and social perspectives but accepted, though with considerable adaptation, many technological assumptions. Muslim peoples, proud of their own religious perspectives have, likewise, been largely unreceptive to Christian witness, though there are now significant breakthroughs in certain areas of the world. They have, however, also rejected much more of the rest of western worldview perspectives than have the Japanese.

When things are going well for a people, the social climate for even considering the possibility of making changes in deep-level paradigms is not a good one. On the other hand, when a people is desperate, when their traditional perspectives and strategies are not working, the climate is often right for at least certain types of changes.

After the Japanese were defeated by America in World War II, reportedly the climate was right for widespread acceptance of Christianity. Things were not going well for them at that time and it was clear to them that the United States, a "Christian" country, was "on top" in the world for religious reasons. Within a few years, however, that social climate passed and they became resistant. In Korea, meanwhile, due to some extent to their gratefulness to America for liberating them from Japan, people began to open up to the Christian message coming largely from America.

Many smaller scale societies with a good bit of pride have found themselves unable to protect themselves in the present worldwide climate of rapid change. In their traditional state they have been extremely resistant to change at the worldview level, depending on this conservatism for their existence. Unfortunately, such societies tend to be "brittle." That is, under pressure from outside they break rather than bending. The extreme pressure for change that many such societies, especially small-scale societies, are now under is destroying much of their traditional pride and creating an enormous amount of human wreckage. Many of those within these societies are, however, finding they are able to some extent to adopt enough of the assumptions of western worldviews to survive.

The opportunity that such breakdown affords, however, should not be ignored. Often the communication of constructive new approaches to life can save people at risk from the worst effects of contemporary sociocultural contact.

4. ***Freedom to Pursue Change***. The amount of freedom of inquiry and action allowed by a society is an important person/group characteristic. Though no society allows total freedom to change, some societies are more free than others in encouraging their people to question, to inquire, and to act. Even when quite open, however, a society exerts some control over the process. We who seek to introduce change need to look for areas of life in which people are free to investigate and to change. Once again it should be noted that many of the peoples of the world are more open in the area of spiritual power than they may be in other religious or even technological areas.

If people are to invent and discover, they need a certain amount of leisure. When all of one's time and energy is expended in merely surviving, creativity tends to be squelched. If, however, there is a measure of freedom and leisure to go along with the pressure of problems that need solving, much innovation can come about. Yet leisure without pressure does not always lead to innovation. It may simply lead to laziness or to simple enjoyment of life without the feeling of pressure to innovate.

Openness often depends on interest. Many will admit they have a need for something, say, better housing or greater spiritual power, but will not pursue it for lack of interest or a feeling that it will take too much energy to bring it about. They may be devoting so much of their time and energy to other things that this area of life simply doesn't interest them at this time.

Curiosity, too, can be a powerful motivator in the direction of change. Often information concerning some aspect of life not completely understood can stimulate such curiosity. And curiosity in one area may well lead to openness in other areas. Those inclined to experiment or even to play with new ideas are more likely to innovate than those not so inclined.

The power of personal relationships is demonstrated in the fact that often people are opened up to change through the development of friendship with and respect for outsiders who have come as change agents. Whether it is a material object or a spiritual relationship that is being advocated, people respond to friendship. The importance and effectiveness of friendship in incarnational Christian ministry cannot be overemphasized. More on this below.

When people are in a period of social disorganization or confusion, they are usually more open to change than when things are going well for them. Many contemporary societies are, therefore, very open to at least certain changes.

5. **Change Begets Change**. A further element of the climate for change that needs to be recognized is the fact that change itself easily becomes a factor in encouraging and facilitating change. Though the well-known principle, "Change begets change" is much more true at the surface level than deeper, we can still point to it as a factor, especially in areas of life where our loyalties are not strong. People used to frequently changing surface-level things such as cars, toothpaste, clothing, even careers are more likely to change the allegiances and other assumptions underlying those things than those who are not used to changing. In addition, each change of idea or material objects will usually require additional changes. Those who do not change residence, career and material accouterments very often, however, can be very conservative in their assumptions, even in the United States.

6. **The Literacy Factor**. People who read tend to be more open to change than those who don't. Though not all of the changes that come through

literacy are to be recommended, reading is still a potent force for change. Part of this is due to the fact that literacy itself is an innovation and those who accept one innovation are more open to others. In addition, reading puts people in touch with a world outside their own, frequently introducing them to new ideas that stimulate them to change. The simple acceptance of reading involves the adding or adjusting of a whole series of worldview-level assumptions and values relating to such things as books, information, the world outside one's society, history and writing.

Person/Group: Conversion

Conversion is an area in which worldview provides a major obstacle in many societies—an obstacle that most western missionaries down through the years have not taken adequate note of. Our western freedom-orientation enables us to appeal for conversion to any member of our society (except, perhaps, very small children), on the assumption that any person has the "right" to make an individual decision to follow Christ. Indeed, we don't feel that a person is genuinely converted until he or she has made that individual decision. Many of us go, then, to group-oriented societies assuming that individual decision-making is the only way there is to enter the Kingdom of God.

In many group-oriented societies, however, unless the whole group decides to make a change (such as conversion to Christ or adoption of some new agricultural technique) at the same time, no individual is allowed to. Such important, life-impacting decisions can only be made in cooperation with those who, by reason of their status in the society, have the society's permission to strongly influence such decisions and, later, once the decisions have been made, to announce them. Typically, these will be the older men in positions of family, clan and tribal leadership.

The worldview assumption such societies work on is usually that the possibility for any such major decision has to be presented to the elders, talked over thoroughly between the elders and between them and their extended families, resulting over time in a decision as to whether the whole group moves in the new direction or stays as is. In some societies, though, if permission is obtained from the leaders, some will be allowed to make such changes even if the whole group does not go along with it.

Great opportunity exists to introduce new ideas in such societies if we know a bit about the dynamics of decision-making and can be patient in building relationships with those we seek to win and waiting for the process to come to fruition. Contrary to the approach of many western missions, though, the opportunity afforded to win such people groups to Christ is squandered if our appeal is primarily to the young. Working for such group ingatherings (whether a whole tribe or a single family) usually requires that we win the older leaders to either accept Christ themselves or give permission for those under their authority to move in that direction. Once a group has chosen to turn to Christ, it will be necessary for someone to lead each person in the group to make individual decisions at their own pace within the context of the broader acceptance of the gospel. In a sense, the group turning is the first step and individual evangelism is a second step in the conversion process.

Tippett (1971) documents the fact that many of the peoples of the South Pacific made decisions for Christ in just such a fashion. He called these ingatherings, sometimes of thousands of people, "people movements." Tippett's discussion of the Batak response showed how such a movement happened among an Indonesian people group. And these group movements into Christianity were usually preceded by a "power encounter" in which the power of Christ was demonstrated to be greater than the power of the traditional gods. These power encounters were sometimes as spectacular as the great power encounters of scripture—between Elijah and the prophets of Baal (1 Kings 18) and between Moses and Pharaoh (Exod. 3-14).

Person/Group: Needs

The place of needs in considerations of change is of major importance. People have needs, both as individuals and as groups. Many needs are, however, denied or unrecognized and, therefore, not felt, leading some to suggest a distinction between "real" needs and "felt" needs. Though I agree with the point being made, I will not focus on whether a need is real or unreal, felt or unfelt. Needs are needs whether or not they are felt and if they are felt, they are real whether or not they seem important to outsiders.

1. **Feeling of need**. A major obstacle to worldview change is the lack of feeling the need for change. People may be feeling relatively comfortable in their present situation, with their present worldview assumptions and allegiances. If they have complaints, they only share them with the members of their ingroup (see below). They are usually reluctant to share them with outsiders and, in fact, they may get quite defensive if we appear to be raising criticisms of their present situation.

Nevertheless, there may be opportunity to reach them if we will patiently watch and listen to discover what needs the people *feel*. Usually, witnesses will not be given permission by receptors to focus on deep-level needs, especially those of which the receptors are not very conscious, unless the witnesses first address themselves to needs that the people feel at a conscious level. Communication involves negotiation and messages only get across the communication gap by permission of the receptors (Kraft 1991). If, then, communicators do not show interest in meeting needs that the respondents are already concerned about, they are very unlikely to be given permission to deal with deeper needs—with at least one exception. That is, if there is an unrecognized need that the witness is able to bring to the attention of the receptor, to which he/she agrees, the receptor may be open to dealing with it.

Christian witnesses working in India, for example, tell me that many have responded to the gospel when they learned that it offered forgiveness. Christian witnesses have offered many other things but not gotten through nearly as well as when they discovered the attractiveness to Indians of the possibility of forgiveness. It appears that this is a very deep-seated need of many Indians of which they are often unaware until they hear it offered to them. The uncovering of such a need that has been there in a kind of dormant state is quite different from the conscious aim of much advertising—to create a need that has not been there previously. As Christian witnesses, we would take a dim view of *creating* a need. We would not, however, hesitate to uncover a need for Christ already there but not consciously felt. This could involve us in attempting to *create a feeling of need*. People have to come to both acknowledge the need and reach out for the solution if they are to change.

2. ***Motivation***. A high level of need is likely to be accompanied by a high motivation to change. Low motivation, of course, mitigates against change. Among the conscious or unconscious attitudes underlying high motivation are such things as

- A desire for change.
- A need to "improve."
- A need to reconcile present experience with traditional understandings.
- A need to bring old ideas into harmony with new ideas already adopted.
- A need to overcome obstacles.
- A need to "outdo" some other person or group.
- A desire to gain relief from discomfort.
- A desire for greater efficiency.
- A just plain creative bent.

3. ***Deprivation***. Feelings of deprivation may figure in important ways in opening people up to consider a change. This is particularly true in the

West where we have learned to assume that we are "entitled" to such things as ease and comfort. We dare not assume, however, that other peoples are as motivated as westerners are by feelings of material deprivation. Though non-westerners, especially in the cities, are increasingly motivated by such things, many are quite fatalistic about their lot in life. Fatalism, then, is a major obstacle to Christian witness.

4. ***Dissatisfaction*** or disaffection with the way things are, coupled with the belief that things could be better, can provide a powerful impetus toward change as can the desire to improve one's situation in life, whether economically, socially or spiritually. Again, fatalism in such areas can provide a formidable obstacle to change. A keenly felt need, generated by dissatisfaction, may propel at least the more venturesome to seek new answers even if such behavior is contrary to their tradition.

5. ***Power***. Perhaps the most widespread felt need among most of the peoples of the world is that for greater power and control over material, relational and especially the spiritual aspects of their lives. Though many, often under the influence of westernization, have learned to focus on technological and political power, the quest for greater ability to handle illness, fertility and the many other vagaries of life keeps the desire for more spiritual power in the forefront of their thinking, often in spite of the fact that they have become secularized in most aspects of their life.

This desire for greater spiritual power is certainly one of the most potent motivators to change. Perhaps the majority of the peoples of the world feel themselves oppressed by evil spiritual powers and/or forces. Their question, then, is, How can I cope with or even gain an advantage over these powers/forces? Contrary to the religious conservatism of most westerners, many peoples are quite ready to change religious ideas and practices if there is some demonstration of greater power.

When missionaries first arrived in East Africa, the people asked, "What are these people all about? Can we get any help from them?" They were impressed by the amount of power wielded by the westerners in material ways. They interpreted this control of the material world as spiritual power since it seemed to benefit westerners materially and health-wise (two ways East Africans expected greater spiritual power to manifest itself). In addition, of course, the missionaries talked a lot about God. So the people observed and listened to discover what was the source of this power, concluding that it was in the westerners' ability to read. This led them to desire reading very much. While the missionaries applauded this desire greatly, it is doubtful that many of them fully understood the reasons for it (Welbourn 1961).

With spiritual power so high on people's list of felt needs, it is a shame that so much of western Christianity has ignored this very natural bridge to the peoples of the world. There are, however, dangers. Stemming from worldview assumptions, Christian objects such as Bibles, crosses, anointing oil and other things introduced for Christian purposes are often accepted as fetishes with greater power than traditional fetishes. Likewise with Christian rituals. To be unaware of the likelihood of such misuse of these things produces obstacles on the witnesses' side of the fence. And it points up the need for helping people to understand that the power is in the relationship with Jesus, not in the objects or rituals that are used in connection with that relationship.

6. **Demonstration**. When dealing with needs and the ability to work through them to effect worldview change, it is important to recognize the major role demonstration can have. It is definitely an obstacle to worldview change if all we do is talk without demonstrating the value of what we recommend. Interest in something new is often only stimulated when the practical value of the suggestion is demonstrated. In our ministries, as in that of Jesus, it is the *demonstration*, not simply the theoretical explanation, of the betterness of the Christian way that will lead people to be interested in it.

In dealing with the Christian message, we have several ways in which its benefits can be demonstrated. Living incarnationally among the people we seek to reach provides great opportunity to demonstrate such things as love, trustworthiness, righteousness and other indications of transformed life. The difficult part is to discover how our receptors define these things and how they expect them to be demonstrated in life. Demonstrations of spiritual power, of course, are often the easiest way to attract attention. People are impressed when Jesus heals them, blesses their farms and families with tangible things or delivers them from demons. In power-orientated societies, however, their needs to be a good bit of explanation of the connection between the power and the relationship with Jesus Christ. For power-oriented peoples are often willing to gladly accept power from Jesus today and from other spirits tomorrow without feeling the need for allegiance to either.

Person/Group: Ingroup-Outgroup

Another set of obstacles and opportunities in the Person/Group area of worldview lie in worldview-based assumptions concerning ingroup and outgroup. Every people has those considered "us" and those considered "them." If a "them" group accepts Christianity, the openness to the gospel in another group will probably depend on how this second group views the first. If the first group is considered "not us but prestigious," the second group may have a worldview-level assumption that prods them in the direction of accepting whatever the prestigious group accepts. Often, though, the "them" group is considered untrustworthy or to be enemies. Whatever they accept, therefore, is to be rejected.

I have been told that in some parts of Latin America the competition between families is so great that if one family chooses to convert to evangelical Christianity (as opposed to Roman Catholic Christianity), the other families will automatically reject it. Likewise, in India the widespread acceptance of Christianity by the outcastes has been an obstacle to the acceptance of upper caste people (see below).

The fact that God accepts people where they are leads Christian strategists to endorse the practice of *appealing to people in terms of the interests of their own people group*. This is the approach sometimes called the "Homogeneous Unit Principle" (see McGavran and Wagner 1990). It takes advantage of the groupness and ingroup cohesiveness felt by a people whose way of life derives from the same worldview. To take advantage of such a factor can be an effective and, I believe, scriptural strategy for reaching the lost (see Kraft 1978).

Christians are, however, commanded to love outsiders, even enemies. In the process of Christian growth, therefore, such natural ingroup/outgroup barriers are to be weakened and abandoned in favor of the Christian principle of oneness in Christ. But this seems to happen infrequently. The presence of such a person/group assumption and the strong allegiance people pledge to it provide a formidable obstacle to change in this area. And such blatant resistance to replacing the traditional worldview assumption with a Christian perspective are an embarrassment to us all—as the racism, nationalism and "classism" that spawned such ideologies as South African apartheid and the numerous attempts at "ethnic cleansing" in our world have shown.

Person/Group: Status and Role

A person's position in a society often has a lot to do with whether or not that person is open to change. Those in official positions, for example, are seldom interested in changing very much lest some change deprive them of their position. Their job is to protect the status quo. Leaders of opposition parties, however, are often open to considering new concepts. They have a lot to gain if they can make use of new ideas to attain positions of leadership.

The desire for prestige, though an individual thing, is also a group concern. Worldview assumptions concerning where the group or individual belongs on the social ladder and if any change is possible have a powerful effect on whether a person or group pursues their desire ("need") for higher prestige. Within a group, those who feel most secure and those who feel most desperate are likely to be more receptive to new ideas than others. This is true of families, occupation groups, associations of like-minded people and other subgroups within a society. Those who feel their position or wealth gives them security are often (not always) more likely than others to experiment with new ideas, items and practices.

At the other end of the spectrum, then, are the desperate and the marginal ones, those for whom the answers provided by their society don't seem to be working at all. These often (not always) have a high motivation for change based on assumptions such as, "We can't drop any lower on the social ladder so let's go for it and try something different." Something that has occurred in India and elsewhere is that desperate and marginal people are often those most easily won to Christ. This is opportune for Christian witnesses in terms of gaining adherents but an obstacle to any desire to convert on the part of the ordinary people and, especially, those of status in the society. When the churches are full of people to whom others are not attracted church growth is usually stifled.

The fatalistic assumption that any attempt to climb higher socially may make things worse often cripples those just above the desperation level. These may be the most conservative people in the society. They fear that any experimentation may result in their dropping to a worse position than they already occupy. So they tend to resist new ideas and practices. Others in the middle who are not desperate enough to grab anything but not secure enough to play around with whatever comes along will also tend to be more resistant to change. But for the genuinely desperate, the idea that God and His people will love such a person often has great appeal. Likewise with anything that promises economic gain and/or social advancement.

Understandings of status and role that do not coincide between the agents of change and the potential adopters of change can provide significant blockage to acceptance. Westerners often simply assume that the way we in the West have chosen to work out men's and women's roles would be good for the rest of the world. Western roles for women, for example, often provide models that the men of the receptor society are afraid will be imitated by their women.

Likewise with children. Traditional men may, therefore, be quite resistant to Christianity lest their women and children become like those of the advocates. The individual freedom orientation of westerners is based on quite a different set of assumptions from those underlying security-oriented societies. Unfortunately, the latter, though feeling threatened by the incursion of behavior imitating that of westerners, have often been unable to block its adoption and are seeing their social systems greatly damaged because of this inability.

As for status, western concepts of egalitarianism are in radical conflict with assumptions that people are to relate to each other hierarchically. In India, for example, it is crucial that one know whether to look up to or down on whatever person one is dealing with. In Korea, Japan and China one's family and one's age provide status identification without which people find it difficult to interact. I remember being on a train in Korea, unable to speak the language and finding no one with whom to interact in English. A man across the isle, however, went to quite some trouble to find someone in our car who could ask me one question, in broken English. It was, "How old are you?" Even though we couldn't converse, he needed to know whether to regard me as his senior or his junior!

In many societies a westerner is automatically assigned a high status. We experienced this in northern Nigeria and found that it created many opportunities but also many obstacles. The obstacles sprang from worldview assumptions such as, that whatever we westerners suggested was the right thing to do. Or that they should try their best to never say or do anything that would offend us. When I asked a question, therefore, I could count on getting a polite, non-offensive answer, whether or not it was a true answer. And when I suggested a plan or a program or a Bible interpretation, I could count on them accepting it, whether or not they felt it a good idea. I learned, however, to lean over backwards to compensate for this problem by replying to their questions for advice with questions rather than answers—questions designed to push them to think things through and come up with their own plan, program or Bible interpretation.

In many societies a person of high status is expected to flaunt it by ostentatious display of material possessions. When, in such a society, we are perceived to be very rich but attempt to live among them incarnationally, it raises major questions in their minds. These questions can be obstacles if the people suspect we are doing something subversive or are mocking them. Their questions concerning our attempts to identify with them can, however, be helpful if they give us opportunity to explain that this is the way Jesus worked.

People often feel restricted in their attempts to pursue change because of their social position. Social position is accompanied by authority and power that one who possesses them is loathe to risk. "Will the change support or detract from my present social position and/or my authority?" is an important question to those who feel neither totally secure nor desperate.

The quest for meaning through attaining social prestige has been around for a long time. Though the definitions differ as to what is prestigious, the desire to attain it often leads people to adopt new strategies. Again, the prestige of the advocates of Christianity has often resulted in acceptance of the gospel for the purpose of attaining greater prestige. Often, however, this "religious" motivation leads to attitudes and practices not expected nor wanted by Christian advocates.

In many societies there are those who are allowed the privilege to innovate by accepting new ideas and implementing them and then advocating that others follow their example. Often these are older men who have earned the right to make changes. Or it may be there are persons who possess personality characteristics that seem to propel them into the position of being among the first to identify and adopt new things. Though they may have this right, however, those with the privilege and/or the compulsion to innovate are not always opinion leaders or good at innovating. It is, therefore, not a sure thing that others will follow them. They may be regarded as oddballs. If they are followed, though, substantial change may occur.

Person/Group: Class and Caste

A major set of obstacles flows from the social status of the converts. If those who turn to Christ are largely from lower classes or castes, those who see themselves as higher on the social ladder are likely to be reluctant to convert.

In India, if the members of one caste accept Christianity, very often they will have little or no ability to communicate their faith to members of other castes. The fact that it is the outcastes, the "dalits," who make up the membership of most Indian churches automatically means that high caste people are not interested, unless they can be approached separately and have their own churches. Indeed, the dalits often do not want upper caste people to become Christians because 1) if they do and join the outcaste churches, they may well take them over and 2) if upper caste groups have their own upper caste churches, those will have more prestige than the outcaste churches.

An innovation such as Christianity must, therefore, be introduced at each social level separately, if it is to be acceptable to all of the peoples of India. We can't ordinarily expect the message to flow from one caste to another. A similar blockage occurs between blacks and whites in the United States. Such caste barriers tend to block movement of ideas from upper to lower as well as from lower to upper.

Class barriers, though not as difficult to permeate as caste barriers, also provide significant blockage to change. As with castes, ideas tend to flow from person to person and group to group horizontally within classes rather than from members of one class to those of another. There is, however, some flow of ideas from upper to lower classes and a much lower flow from lower to upper, usually between contiguous classes. We must, however, be aware that God sometimes breaks the normal social and communicational rules. He did this in Acts 2 when He brought about a revival in Jerusalem through despised Galileans.

All such class and caste obstacles are rooted in the deep underlying worldview assumptions held tenaciously by people. If we come from the West where we think we have no classes, we can be quite naïve both about the situation in the receptor society and about the way class differences play out in our own society. It has been reported, for example, that certain American missionaries to the Philippines were quite frustrated in their attempts to reach middle and lower class Philippinos. They saw themselves as lower middle class in the States and assumed they would most easily relate to lower middle class Philippinos. Not so, since the classes didn't match cross-culturally. Middle class Americans matched most easily with upper class Philippinos, resulting in reasonably good contacts with upper class people but rather complete isolation from the people the missionaries most wanted to reach.

Person/Group: Competitiveness

When there is heterogeneity within a society, there is inevitably competition. Competition, then, is one of the greatest encouragers of the seeking of new ideas. The competitiveness may center around personal goals (e.g., prestige), economic goals, political goals, religious goals (e.g., for more power) and the like.

Though most societies attempt to strictly limit potential competitiveness between their various segments, the desire of one person or group to attain an advantage over another is powerful. This desire strongly motivates some to seek new ideas and material prosperity. Again, though, the marginal people of a society, those who have most to gain by obtaining an advantage and the least to lose if their attempt doesn't work, are usually the most ready to respond positively to new things on the basis of this motivation

Advocates coming from individualistic societies where individual and group competitiveness is assumed and valued, often inculcate divisiveness in our attitudes toward other Christian groups. This can result in obstacles caused by divisions within families if some members of a family go to one church and others to another. We advocate Christian brotherhood but often practice western competition. Such inconsistency often leads to such things as unchristian competition between churches or individuals who are supposed to be brothers and sisters, inability of fellow Christians to function as parts of the same body and severe weaknesses in relationships and behavior among members of the same church.

Factionalism, however, can often enhance attempts to introduce worldview change, at least with one of the groups. When a group perceives that they can gain an advantage over another group by adopting new perspectives and understandings, they are usually open to it. Adopting assumptions that lead to higher prestige and/or more material goods frequently results from such a desire. Even Christianity has often been adopted with this motivation. Many non-western young people see in Christianity the opportunity to escape from such things as the control of the traditional leaders, having to work on the farm, having to live in a rural area and the like by going to school and gaining prestige based on western criteria.

Notice that the New Testament shows Paul using the factionalism of his opponents on at least three occasions: Acts 13:46, 18:6, 23:6,7. In the first two, Paul rebuked the Jews and turned to the Gentiles. In the third, he fomented a dispute between the Pharisees and the Sadducees over the doctrine of the resurrection. Sometimes factionalism can be used for constructive purposes. In Christian witness, we may find a given group open to the gospel just because their enemies are resistant. I think we would do well to follow Paul's example, however, and to make use of factionalism only as a last resort.

Collaboration and cooperation stimulate innovation. When people and groups work together, challenging, stimulating, perhaps even goading each other on, more happens. This has been a primary factor in scientific developments. But willingness to share what one knows with others is crucial. Many people in traditional societies possess good and original ideas that are not shared with those outside their immediate family or kin group. Often, for example, effective medical treatments are owned by particular individuals or families and not shared with those who would have the potential of combining such ideas with other good ideas to come up with something better. In addition, learning from outside sources is usually productive. People in a society who, often through reading, become aware of the ideas of others in areas relatable to their own often become very creative.

Person/Group: Ideal Person

Assumptions concerning what is ideal in personal characteristics and behavior can also provide either obstacles or opportunities for change. Richardson (1974) documents some of the difficulties experienced by Sawi Christians with respect to the high value they have traditionally placed on treachery toward outsiders. When an idealized personal characteristic turns out to be diametrically opposed to what Christianity recommends, a high barrier is produced. Fortunately, this does not seem to occur very often, at least with idealized characteristics. The actual personal characteristics, however, may be a different story.

As mentioned above, in many societies overt expression of anger is considered a major sin. Missionaries in such societies who preach against bad behavior, then, are often felt by the people to be hypocritical if they show anger occasionally. Incompatibility between concepts of "manliness" and Christ-like ideas in America and many other societies have proven to be obstacles to the conversion of men. Western ideas for men, such as strong individualism and self-reliance, aggressiveness, competitiveness, fear of weakness and self-revelation, can be strong hindrances to worldview change toward scriptural concepts of manliness.

The fact that ideal Christian behavior embodies many of what a society may see as female characteristics, then, may make the Christian message more attractive to women. The preponderance of women in churches may then become an obstacle to male acceptance.

As we have seen in chapter 12, most of the items on the Kamwe list of personal characteristics line up well with scripture. For them, the most important personal qualities are kindness, good character, generosity, possession of riches, hard work, discipline, showing honor/respect, good health, living in harmony, peace and unity. We found this set of ideas to provide great opportunity for witness, especially since many found in their Christian commitment both incentive and power to live closer to these ideas.

Person/Group: Language

The worldview valuing of the means of communication employed is another person/group factor that needs to be assessed to see where help or hindrance lies. Many of the world's societies show a high proportion of their people who are bilingual. Frequently, they will speak both a home language and one or more languages of commerce and/or government. In our area, for example, in the weekly market one could hear English, Hausa, Fulani, Margi and at least three quite different dialects of Kamwe, plus, often, one or more languages of the traders who had come from over a hundred miles away to sell their goods. And it was common for some of our men to be able to handle at least four or five of these languages.

Our people would speak their dialect of Kamwe at home, a regional (trade) language (either Hausa or Fulani) in the market, and, if they knew it, a national/world language (English) in school and in their broader contacts with the outside world. For most, the use of English was quite restricted. Hausa or Fulani (or, perhaps, Margi, a nearby tribal language) would be used anytime one was interacting with a member of another tribal group. In those languages one ordinarily discussed subjects such as buying and selling, politics, government, travel, schooling and the like.

They very seldom used Hausa or Fulani to talk about deep things inside their hearts and minds, since they seldom used these languages with anybody except outsiders. There was, however, a different "feel" to the two trade languages. Hausa was regarded positively while, for historical reasons, Fulani was regarded negatively. When insiders converse, though, only the home language is used, and for most people only this language is adequate for discussing deep things such as a person's relationship with God.

We see, then, that different languages are valued differently. There are deeply held worldview values attached to the vehicle through which any suggestion of change comes. Since meanings are primarily *felt* rather than reasoned, the attitude of receptors to whatever is discussed is greatly affected by what language is used. If a heart thing like Christianity comes through an outsider language, it is likely that people will regard it as foreign, not really theirs, at least at first. This fact means that working through a trade, national or world language can provide a major obstacle to the people's understanding of God's desire to get really close to them.

On the other hand, Bible translators often speak of the excitement in the voices of people when they first hear God speaking in their heart language. "Now I know God really cares for me, really loves me," they often say. The climate for worldview change is greatly increased when the messages come in the people's heart language. Changes advocated are associated with the values placed upon the vehicle through which they are presented.

The same is true of the art and music used in association with the Christian message. Foreign hymns and European pictures can prove to be major obstacles to understanding and acceptance of the Christian message.

The message is received with very different connotations when in foreign art forms than when in familiar forms. I'm convinced that the rapid church growth we experienced in our area was in no small part due to the fact that we used traditional music forms rather than translated hymns.

Person/Group: Displacement

When people move from a rural area to an urban area or from one part of the world to another, whether voluntarily or under pressure, they are usually more open to change than they might have been in their home area. Perhaps they feel they have left their traditions behind, so they might as well open up to other changes. Or perhaps they see a new habitat requiring new strategies or allowing new freedoms. In any event, we find people more open to Christianity when not living in their own home territory.

For example, there is great resistance to Christianity among the Japanese who live in Japan. Those living in Brazil, however, are much more receptive. Likewise, with people who move from a rural area into an urban one. In this case, though, people in urban settings often will not make major decisions without consulting with their family members back in the rural area. The witness, therefore, needs to be two-pronged—both to those in the urban area and to their relatives in the rural area.

Person/Group: Advocates

It is often assumed by advocates that the major obstacles to the receptors' accepting the suggested changes are on the receptors' side of the gap. When, however, the conditions required for acceptance are perceived to be too costly, especially in terms of social relationships, we might argue that the hindrances are primarily on the side of the advocates. It is incumbent upon us as advocates, therefore, to strongly consider what we may be assuming, doing or saying that might be producing obstacles. Rejection of the gospel message is often less the fault of the receptors than of the advocates. I have written more on this factor in *Anthropology for Christian Witness* (1996), chapter 25.

A major problem arises when individualistic missionaries attempt to take the gospel to group-oriented societies. This has, of course, happened countless times as the gospel message is taken by westerners to African, Asian and Latin American societies that are strongly dependent on family, clan and tribe for their security. As noted above, most of the societies of the world assume that a primary function of such institutions as family, clan and tribe is to provide people with security. In western societies, however, the focus is on providing as much freedom as possible for as many people as possible. Such nearly opposite values, living quite unconsciously within advocates and receptors, often result in major misunderstandings at the worldview level.

It has often happened, however, that advocates of new paradigms and assumptions coming from individualistic societies have been able to make good friends of insiders and to establish good rapport with them. In such cases, their advocacy can be powerful. Failing such good rapport, though, any cause can be a failure even if the ideas are good and helpful. When agents of change come from outside a society, it is crucial that their rapport be established with the right insiders if the response is to be widespread.

One problem often faced by cross-cultural Christian witnesses is that our appeal, either by design or default, is often to people who will not be followed if they adopt our perspectives. They are not in the category of people allowed by the society to accept and implement change. They may, in fact be marginal persons or be marginalized by the society when they have made the changes we recommend. When they adopt changes, their people do not imitate them and may even turn against them.

It is important, therefore, to consider the characteristics of the advocating groups and individuals that either hinder or facilitate changes in worldview. Any given social group will have varying degrees of openness depending on their attitude toward the group who seeks to bring them something new. Among the things to evaluate are the following:

1. ***Prestige of the donor group***. The perceived prestige of the group from which the change comes is of great importance. Though people do regularly borrow a few things from groups they don't respect (e.g., Americans have borrowed corn, tomatoes, moccasins and several other things from the Indians), they tend to borrow much more heavily from those groups they consider more prestigious. The openness of people to new ideas from societies and subgroups they respect usually differs greatly from their openness to ideas from other sources. If there is a coolness or animosity toward the source of a potential new idea, the chances that the ideas will be accepted are slim.

The response is emotional rather than rational, and may be quite subconscious. People who are prejudiced against a given people are likely to be reluctant to accept ideas coming from them. On the other hand, a positive bias toward the donor group can result in the acceptance of harmful things as well as helpful ones.

2. ***Perception of motivation***. The perception of the motivation of the outside group by the receptors is crucial. If the relationship between the two

groups is unfriendly, you find less interest, less likelihood of change than if the contact is friendly. Communicationally, all messages are interpreted according to the relationship between the participants. People respond to loving concern. But it is the receptors who will decide whether our behavior is loving or not. we need to remember that friendliness, love, concern and all other attitudes are interpreted by the receptors in terms of their worldview assumptions.

It has often happened that what the advocates intended as love, was interpreted by the receptors as manipulation or some other negative attitude or motive. We found in northeastern Nigeria, for example, that our mission institutions (e.g., hospitals, schools) were regularly understood by the Kamwe and the other tribal groups in the area as intended to earn money and/or to produce workers to serve us. One of the challenges we faced, therefore, was to so relate to the people that we were able to overcome that perception.

3. ***Ability to influence opinion leaders***. When we go to another society to witness for Jesus Christ, or even to introduce agricultural or other innovations, we hope for widespread acceptance. We are not content to simply win one or two people. We want many. It is crucial, therefore, for those introducing a change, whether from outside or from inside a society, to be able to influence the opinion leaders. This ability, of course, often depends on such criteria as those listed above.

As mentioned, frequently it is the marginal people in a society who are most anxious to adopt changes. They usually have everything to gain if the innovation works well and not much to lose if it doesn't. They, therefore, are the ones most likely to be attracted to outsiders. When marginals adopt, however, the opinion leaders will often reject, simply because of the reputation of the adopters. The result is that the marginal adopters form the core of the receiving group (e.g., a church) and ordinary and prestigious people reject the message because they don't want their reputations to be affected by being associated with that group. If, however, a prestigious group makes a change, their acceptance can provide a valuable springboard from which the innovation spreads throughout the whole society.

4. ***Duration and intensity of contact***. The nature and intensity of the contact between those advocating change and the potential receptors is critical. This is especially important if the changes being advocated are at the worldview level, since deep-level concepts usually need more explanation and demonstration than do surface-level innovations. Less intense, unfriendly and short contacts are less likely to produce the spread of new ideas than are those that are more intense (in a positive sense), friendly

and extend over a longer period of time. Even a very intense relationship, though, if it is of short duration may not produce much change while sometimes, reasonably unfriendly contacts if intense and long lasting will result in a great amount of change.

For example, the greatest amount of westernization has occurred in those countries dominated by the West in colonial situations, even though there was much unfriendliness. Christian witnesses living among the people they seek to reach are likely to have a greater influence than those who simply visit from time to time, especially if the contact is friendly.

5. ***Enthusiasm***. The activeness and enthusiasm of the introducing group is frequently a factor in stimulating change. Those so sold on their ideas that they would die for them (e.g., Communists, sometimes Christians) are often much more likely to get their ideas accepted, especially if they express themselves in culturally appropriate ways. Enthusiasm that is culturally inappropriate can, of course, greatly hinder acceptance. The enthusiasm of the group that accepts the new ideas within the society is also important. If the adopted idea is to spread, the advocating group must also be aggressive. The size of either the introducing or the accepting group is often quite secondary to their enthusiasm and the commitment demonstrated by aggressiveness.

Person/Group: Impression of Innovations

In addition to the importance of the above people characteristics, there are characteristics of the worldview assumptions, values and allegiances themselves that need to be taken into consideration.

1. ***The Assumption or Idea Fills a Gap***. If an introduced assumption seems to answer questions that people perceive as not being answered or not answered well, it has a fairly good chance of being accepted. One reason many people reject (at least initially) the germ theory of disease is that it doesn't seem to explain very well why some people get sick while others don't. Their theory that disease is caused by personal spirits seems to explain more of what they feel they observe. Surgery seems to make more sense than believing in germs since the assumption that repairing or removing defective internal organs fits better into a cognitive space that many prewesternized systems could not fill. The germ theory gains ground, however, when they see fewer of their babies dying if they work on the basis of that assumption.

With the increase in crime in American urban settings, our countrymen easily develop the assumption that installing an alarm system is the right thing to do to protect their homes from being broken into. This assumption may not have existed in the worldview of those who lived in rural areas, but it makes sense to add it when they move to the city. It fills a gap for urban dwellers. The assumptions underlying ecological innovations related to basic survival are not, however, being well received by Americans because they conflict with the deep seated worldview assumption that such things as air, water, forests and land are inexhaustible. Instead of fitting into our system in a place not previously occupied, they bump against assumptions that are firmly entrenched.

Assumptions that are complementary to what is already in the culture are more likely to be accepted than those that contradict assumptions already there. The principle of felt need is based on this fact. If something felt (consciously or unconsciously) to be missing in the cultural system is provided by what is introduced, the new idea is likely to be accepted—provided it does not contradict some other value in the culture. Often, however, the assumption comes after the people see an implement or a technique. Such was probably the case with the Yir Yoront (Sharp 1952) who most likely couldn't imagine either that there could be a more efficient cutting implement than the stone axes they used nor that any cutting implement could be obtained without going through the clan leaders. When, however, ordinary Yir Yoront not only saw steel axes but were able to obtain them for themselves, new assumptions were developed, most of which were complementary to assumptions already in their worldview.

When attempting to communicate Christian messages, then, it is important for us to look for those things that fill a gap to focus on first. In every society there are questions in people's minds that are not answered by their culture. I have mentioned the attractiveness of forgiveness to at least certain of the peoples of India. This sort of concern may lie just beneath the surface of people's consciousness, waiting for Christian witnesses under the guidance of the Holy Spirit to lift the lid to find it.

A similar kind of gap to be filled occurs when people are aware of problems but don't know how to solve them. Individuals and groups who have regular outbursts of anger, for example, may recognize this as a problem but feel powerless to control it. They continually try in their human power but need supernatural power if they are to succeed.

One approach to Christian witness that I would recommend is to present the gospel as embodying the power of Jesus to assist us in living closer to our own ideas than we have been able to under our own power. I believe this is one of the first things Jesus offers us. His ideas are, of course, much higher than our own. And those who in the early stages of their Christian life focus on living up to Jesus' ideas can get pretty discouraged. But if we suggest that the first step is to claim Jesus' power to live up to our own ideas, people will often find this doable. Later, then, when converts have experienced Jesus' power enabling them to take this first step, they can give attention to dealing with higher ideas.

2. ***Compatibility and Fit***. It is important that the new idea or assumption relate well to what is already there or it is likely to be rejected completely. Assumptions, values and allegiances compatible with what is already there are more likely to be accepted than those that contradict what is there, especially if they connect with what the Holy Spirit is already doing in the society. Something related to a basic need such as survival is more likely to be accepted than something that relates to some less pressing area of life. Something related to their cultural focus, that fits in with their primary values, is more likely to be accepted than something that contradicts those values.

People are often quite ready to adopt something that clearly assists them in an area of cultural focus. If, as it appears, most of the peoples of the world are greatly concerned to gain more spiritual power to fend off the evil powers that plague them, they are likely to be open to gospel presentations that emphasize and demonstrate this feature. They already believe that the spirit world is very real and malevolent but assume that the only thing they can do about it is to appease the evil spirits.

A message that presents them with a better alternative assumption in line with their concern—i.e., that a more powerful God will tend to the spirits if we get into a relationship with Him—is very appealing. Such an assumption both fits into the "cognitive space" covered by their traditional belief and improves upon it. The greater effectiveness of those churches with this focus testifies to the appeal of this message. Two important cautions need to be registered, however: 1) Many people will gladly seek to avail themselves of the greater power of God without making any commitment to be faithful to Him and 2) Christian experience based on power without knowledge and wisdom (see I Cor. 1:22, 24) is unbalanced and easily moves into syncretism.

The point is that new or modified worldview assumptions that fit in with or can be built upon unconsciously held attitudes and/or deeply ingrained habits stand a better chance of acceptance than those that go against such attitudes and habits. Things that don't fit are generally either rejected or adapted. This is why democratically governed missionary churches were more readily accepted by the democratically governed Samoans than those churches with more authoritarian polities. The latter, however, fit better in more authoritarian societies. Attitudes and habits developed in early youth are especially difficult to break (e.g., areas such as nutrition, sanitation, toilet). When, however, ways can be found to work with such early conditioning to promote betterment, these attitudes and habits become solid foundations for constructive change.

An experiment in northeastern Nigeria provides an example. These are people with minimal literacy at best but a strong attachment to storytelling. In an attempt to change deeply ingrained attitudes toward health and sanitation, a missionary launched a program to teach basic truths through fables. He taught Nigerians the kinds of things he wanted to get across and set them to producing fables after indigenous patterns that gently prodded the people in the direction of reconsidering and changing some of their basic assumptions concerning health and sanitation. The technique was very successful in changing some basic worldview assumptions.

Another aspect of the matter of fit stems from the fact that all human structures are imperfect and often ill-suited to contemporary situations. The cultural structures have been created long ago and continually adapted to contemporary situations. The customs any generation is taught, therefore, are those adapted by the previous generation to the problems they faced. To the extent that the present differs from previous times, then, those structures will not fit. This fact produces a situation in which there is a certain amount of "lag" to the cultural structures, including worldview assumptions. This lag makes those structures to some extent inadequate to present situations, especially in contemporary situations of rapid sociocultural change.

For this reason many societies are not able to carry out the promises made to new generations because their structures are not capable of handling all of the situations their people face. This leaves many of them seeking for better assumptions, values and commitments to embrace. A society seems to "promise" each new generation a certain number of things. Youth, for example, tend to assume that they will be provided with physical, social and spiritual security. They usually expect health, marriage, family, meaningfulness in life and the like. These expectations are, however, often frustrated, especially in situations of rapid culture change, raising felt needs at points where the system doesn't work as promised. These gaps provide places into which new ideas and practices can be fit. Looking for such inadequacies in a cultural system is an important activity for the would-be agent of change to engage in.

Often the people of a society are themselves already aware of such gaps in their system. A desire for greater spiritual power, for example, often stems from the fact that the religious structures provided by the society do not work as well as the people expect them to. The desire for greater control over the material universe, likewise, often stems from dissatisfaction with the ability of the existing technology to provide for a people's felt needs in the material area. Health needs, too, provide opportunity for the introduction of new answers to pressing questions based on different assumptions. These answers, though, need to be fit to *their* understandings of what they need, not *ours*.

These assumptions are unlikely to be accepted, however, unless they fit in with those that are already in the system and in the minds of the people. The introduction of white chickens into a part of China where the people had a taboo against raising and eating white birds, for example, met with rejection. If red chickens had been introduced, the project might have been successful (Foster 1973:165). In many areas, however, attempts to introduce large European chickens of any kind are frustrated by the fact that deep-seated worldview assumptions keep the people from understanding that such animals need to be fed and protected. The European chickens are, therefore, like their native chickens, allowed to run free and forced to find their own food with consequent high mortality and small size.

Most societies have a place for health practitioners. Most people assume that these practitioners can work both with medicine and with spirits. It is often puzzling to a people, then, when a western health practitioner can manipulate medicine but does nothing with spirits. A better fit between what the West has to offer in the realm of medicine can be attained if those who go out with this specialty are also trained to deal with the spirit world. Similarly with those who talk (preach) about spiritual things. It is usually assumed by non-secularized people that those who can deal with spiritual things can also deal with illness caused by demons. Cross-cultural workers in traditional societies would fit better and bring about a better response to the gospel if they, like Jesus, were "into" this aspect of reality as well as the other important aspects of the gospel message.

3. **Complexity**. As is true with surface-level culture, less complex assumptions are more easily borrowed than more complex ones. Advocates of Islam have capitalized on this principle by reducing what converts are required to believe to two items: No God but Allah and Muhammad His prophet. I'm afraid our western rationalistic approach to Christianity has required too complex a belief system to be easily accepted. This is, I believe, especially unfortunate since, contrary to the impression we often give, it is the relationship with God, not the doctrines about God, that is saving.

One major problem with worldview change is that by definition, paradigms are complex. When a totally new paradigm is demanded to undergird a new approach to some aspect of life, change agents don't have the option of introducing something that is not complex. They may, however, be reasonably successful if they can introduce parts of the paradigm without getting too far into the complexities of it. Some have suggested, for example, that Christianity would do well to develop a creed as simple as that of the Muslims. The Early Church, of course, did have something like such a creed in "Jesus is Lord." This worked well in a context in which calling Jesus Lord contrasted with calling Caesar Lord.

The difficulty presented by this complexity factor is well illustrated by the fact that, though many of the peoples of the world have adopted great numbers of the products produced by western societies, only a few of them (e.g., Japan, Taiwan, Korea) have exerted the great effort to learn the assumptions underlying these technological achievements. This lack has resulted in the fact that in many places in the world western machinery is only useful until it breaks down. Once there is difficulty with the machinery, it becomes useless since few or none of the people in the society have learned the assumptions underlying the technology needed to be able to fix it.

4. ***Observability***. Though assumptions are not directly observable, it facilitates worldview change if their effects are easy to see, as long as what is seen is not interpreted as the result of a different cause. This is a major problem with regard to acceptance of the assumptions underlying western medicine. Much of what western medics do and the results they achieve are interpretable, in keeping with traditional assumptions, as clever manipulation of spirit beings. Though the results may be impressive, then, change agents dare not assume that the people are interpreting what they observe in the same way as they are.

Nevertheless, it is much easier to help people change their assumptions concerning medicine that almost immediately cures a headache, a fever or some other obvious malady than to get them to make a similar change in assumptions concerning preventive medicine. The latter is much more difficult since such observations as those necessary to prove the value of sanitation usually require quite a long time.

5. ***Timing***. The timing of the introduction of a change can be crucial. Helpful things introduced at the wrong time are usually rejected. The question is, Does this change fit at this point in a sequence of new things coming into the society? Innovations frequently require what might be called "supporting circumstances" (Foster 1973:167). In American car manufacturing, for example, compact cars did not fit well into the American mindset until the supporting circumstance of higher prices for gasoline came

about. Only then did people begin to assume that small can be better.

In many previously non-literate societies, literacy is not readily accepted or maintained until the supporting circumstance of Christian allegiance, accompanied by a desire to read the Bible, come about. Reading is hard work for most people and is often felt to bring little reward as a mechanism of communication between humans. But when people begin to assume that they can learn about and hear from God through reading, they often become motivated to read scripture and their felt need for reading increases considerably.

One aspect of timing that is important to Christian witnesses is to recognize that the Holy Spirit seems to bring people to greater openness to the gospel at times that seem unpredictable to us. We need, then, to be observant, looking for such times and to employ the scarce resources of the Church in such a way as to maximize their effectiveness during times of openness, times when the fit between felt needs and the gospel message will be greatest.

Chapter 17

Obstacles & Opportunities in Worldview Change II: Categorization, Causality, Time, Space, Relationship

Categorization and Logic

The next worldview universal we will deal with is that of categorization, classification, logic and picturing. As we have pointed out, this universal provides a people with their basic conceptions concerning how the various components of their universe are to be compartmentalized and related to each other. In much of the "territory" covered by this universal we would not expect to find a large number of changes required in the basic structuring of worldview categories when people come to Christ. In certain areas, however, usually because of a change in another area, a major change has to be made in categorization or logic.

1. ***Naturalistic to Supernaturalistic***. When people move from a naturalistic view of the universe to a supernaturalistic view, their picturing of Reality has to undergo a major change. The habits of seeing the world naturalistically, however, are hard to break. The habit of understanding events as being caused by chance gives way slowly, if at all, to a supernaturalistic perspective. For many American Christians, it is very difficult to come to the point where, after nearly missing an accident, they say, "Thank you Jesus," rather than, "Boy, was I lucky!" Indeed, the fact that we may immediately say something about being lucky before we thank God points to the fact that frequently we seem to hold to at least parts of more than one worldview paradigm at the same time.

In the same cognitive category, the challenge of moving demons and angels from the "fairytale" part of a person's classification (where Anglo-American society has put them) into the Real part may be more than a person can handle. For this reason, many committed western Christians are very resistant to perspectives on the Bible that focus on the reality of spirits and spiritual warfare. Likewise, with understanding prayer as warfare rather than merely a matter of asking or of seeing temptation and disease as involving satanic activity, rather than simply being natural happenings.

An opportunity to help people to make the change in their assumptions is provided by the possibility of demonstrating the reality of spiritual warfare through taking the authority Jesus gave us to heal people and to deliver them from demons. Jesus challenged the people of His day through such demonstrations and this is the way God worked in my own life. When I put myself in a position to observe healing and deliverance, I found my skepticism being drained away. Then, when I ventured out and began to experience the willingness of God to heal and deliver through me, the change became permanent. See Kraft 1989 for more on this paradigm shift leading to a "practice shift" in my own life.

2. ***Popular Classification***. An interesting hindrance to worldview change is illustrated by the fact that with all the honor accorded to science in the English-speaking world, the popular classification of several natural phenomena remains the same. Such is the case in American worldview with animals such as the whale and the bat. Scientists tell us that the whale is not a fish and the bat is not a bird. But at the popular level we are tempted to say, "So what?" Most of us still consider swimming in water and flying in the air as the primary criteria for classifying these animals and so think of whales as fish and bats as birds. We also know that technically the Sun does not "rise" and "set." But popularly we continue to talk as if they do. Our real classification system has remained the same, in spite of our knowledge of scientific accuracy.

Nor is the scientific understanding of radio and TV waves able to become real to most Americans. The worldview assumption that if we can't see something, it doesn't exist, seems to overpower the scientific understanding to such an extent that we don't seem to be able to make ourselves conscious of their existence in the air. A similar challenge to our view of physical invisibility comes from such things as gasoline fumes in containers designed to hold liquid gasoline. Our automatic perception is that the container is empty when there is no liquid in it when, in fact, far from being empty, the container is filled with invisible and dangerous gas fumes as many have found out by lighting a match too close to the "empty" container.

When we classify things at the popular level as invisible, or as the wrong kind of animal or in terms of the way celestial bodies look from earth in opposition to how they are classified scientifically, we show the tenacity of popular worldview classification. If there is such tenacity in western societies with our high regard for science, is it surprising that animistic peoples who embrace westernization typically find it nearly impossible to jettison their way of categorizing and reasoning about spiritual Reality even under intense pressure from naturalistic western perceptions taught in western schools?

Such a deeply-engrained reluctance (inability?) to completely replace such spiritistic assumptions can be turned to the advantage of cross-cultural Christian witnesses if we are able to connect biblical concepts of the spirit world with their animistic spirit-world perceptions. Animism, in fact, generally provides a number of effective points of contact that can be utilized by a supernaturalistic Christianity (as opposed to the secular kind of Christianity that I've been decrying).

3. *Logical Incompatibility*. The logical incompatibility between something introduced into a society and what is already there can be an obstacle to acceptance. In the governmental area, for example, a dictatorship would most likely be rejected by a people accustomed to assume that democracy is the right way to govern, for it is incompatible with the worldview picture in their minds of what should be. It wouldn't fit into the people's definition of the category "government." Nor would an elected approach to leadership (say, in the church) when the custom is for leadership to be passed on from one generation to another within given families. We had difficulty in this regard among the Kamwe and neighboring peoples who belonged to our "democratically governed" churches. The fact that we elected the leadership of the churches in a very western way strongly supported the impression they had from many of the things we did that this thing we called God's church really is a western entity. As such, then, it either attracted or repelled people as much or more on the basis of its westernness as on the basis of its message about Christ.

If people are free to accept or reject, traditional patterns are more likely to be attractive unless the imported patterns are more prestigious. We found among the Kamwe that a western approach to Christianity was attractive to the younger men, at least partly because of its prestige. The fact that the worship style followed a fairly traditional pattern, then, was probably a motivating factor for the women (both young and old) and at least some of the younger men. With the exception of a few of the younger men, most of the adherents did not seem to care much how the church was governed. The older men, however, the ones who would traditionally be in charge, were largely alienated by this western governmental style and a number of other anti-traditional practices in the church (e.g., the condemnation of polygamy and the monologue style of communication in church).

Another instance of logical incompatibility occurs in societies in which we attempt to introduce Christian monotheism to a polytheistic people. To the person who believes in many gods it often seems arrogant and irreligious to claim there is but one God. the early Christians faced this problem and were called "atheists" by the peoples of the Greco-Roman world whose worldview held that there were thousands of gods running the universe. A similar obstacle occurs when we attempt to get people whose focus has been on appeasing evil spirits to focus on God, appealing to Him to protect them from the spirits, rather than seeking the good will of the spirits themselves.

A serious obstacle for cross-cultural communicators of the gospel is raised, for many of the peoples of the world (including first century Jews), by the fact that their logic puts such things as material prosperity and physical health in the same category as spiritual blessing. Though there is also a causal dimension to this (see below), it is the classification that is in focus here. From the point of view of their logic, the category "wealthy" automatically implies "spiritual." These peoples, therefore, tend to see wealthy westerners as close to God (or other good spiritual powers) and assume that if they themselves get close to God, westerners or other blessed beings, they will become wealthy also. Even after people in these societies have observed the excesses of wealthy non-Christians and become Christian themselves, such a worldview classification is hard to overcome.

Causality and Power

We now turn to an area that has already come up several times: causality. As mentioned, the areas of person/group and causality are probably going to need the most attention in our attempts to witness to Christian messages. Since, however, there is a tight relationship between each of the areas of worldview, we have found it impossible to deal with the universals in isolation from each other. Thus it is that certain of the things we have already dealt with could have been saved for this section.

Those who believe in no god or many gods find their assumptions hindering any desire to accept the Christian God. And, should they accept Him, they find constant interference from their old belief as they seek to understand and relate to the true God. But such beliefs also provide opportunities. The fact that most of the peoples of the world are supernaturalistic opens them up to a supernaturalistic approach to Christianity.

Many of the major obstacles and opportunities to the effective communication of the gospel lie in the area of *Causality and Power*. The question of who is in charge of the universe (e.g., God, spirits, humans) and what should be our relationship to Him/them is, of course, a major item. But the existence of and attitude toward the power of humans over other humans (in relation to e.g., family, social position, politics) is also a crucial issue in both the communicating of Christianity and in the personal growth of

Christians. In addition, there is the matter of what kind of power Christians have been given by God in material, human and spiritual spheres.

1. ***Material World Causality***. All peoples have to deal with physical occurrences that show the ability of the natural world to influence life. In the West, of course, we interpret such things as volcanic eruptions, earthquakes, droughts, floods, hurricanes, tornadoes and the like as "natural world" occurrences, though most of the world would see spirits behind them. These events, however, show power and causality in the material world, giving rise to worldview assumptions that provide obstacles and opportunities for Christian witness.

When a hurricane hits, people will interpret it and the destruction it causes according to their worldview assumptions and respond to it accordingly. Some might blame God or the gods or spirits for it. (Interestingly, western insurance companies refer to such occurrences as "acts of God.") Or they might blame themselves for displeasing the God or spirits. In the West, most people will tend to assume that it was a chance occurrence caused by certain weather patterns, without reference to spirit influences. If people blame supernatural beings, they may be closed to Christian messages, assuming that since God allowed the tragedy, He is evil or at least negative toward humans. Or, they may assume that the tragedy was because they did something to anger God or the spirits. In this case, there are probably assumptions concerning what to do to prevent such a thing from happening again.

Such reactions, if we think about them, raise some questions for us as Christians. Is God behind such events? Are Satan and demons? If, as we believe, God is in charge and allowed the tragedy, is it because He gave Satan freedom or, perhaps because Adam gave Satan rights to the creation (see Gen. 3 and Luke 4:6)? And if we pray against such things, does God hear and prevent them? Such important questions concerning causality need to be pondered by us western Christians. For it is likely that if we can figure such things out, they will provide opportunities for witness among animistic peoples.

If, for example, when a major hurricane was coming toward Virginia Beach, Virginia, and Pat Robertson and many other Christians in that area were mobilized to pray against it, could their prayers be the reason the hurricane turned out to sea and did no damage to Virginia Beach? Or, when the flooding of a river in Bangladesh several years ago threatened to wipe away a whole village and the Christians prayed against the tragedy, were their prayers the reason the tragedy was averted? Or in the same country when rain came after a severe drought after the Christians, in response to a request by some Muslims, prayed for rain, was it their prayers that changed things? Whether it is God or Satan who causes "natural" tragedies, the ability of Christians to change things through prayer can be a powerful witness if we learn to use it.

There is a remarkable demonstration of the ability of Christians to effect change in natural causality in a small agricultural, town named Almolonga in Guatemala. In 1974, an evangelical pastor named, Mariano Riscajche and other Christians began to pray authoritatively against the demon gods Maximon and Pascual Bailon (the patron of death) they believed to be over their city of about 20,000. As the Christian group grew, often in response to miraculous healings, the people noticed a change happening in their agricultural production as well. Without going into other details such as the fact that drunkenness that had been a major problem in the town and crime have just about disappeared (the last of their four jails was closed in 1994), we can note a major change in the town's agricultural output. 30 years ago, one truck per week was enough to handle the agricultural surplus they exported to other communities. In 1999, however, they were sending out up to 40 trucks per week! And the size and quality of their produce is phenomenal. Furthermore, the land, once considered largely infertile, is now allowing three growing seasons! George Otis Jr.'s 1999 book entitled *Informed Intercession* documents this and several other examples of city transformation through prayer. And his 1999 video entitled *Transformations*, records impressions of the Almalonga transformation plus that of three other cities.

In this area of material world causality obstacles to Christian witness are often greatest in times of ease and plenty while opportunities are often greatest when tragedy strikes.

2. **Human World Causality**. Humans also can cause many things. In dealing with such human characteristics as status and role in chapter 15, we pointed to many of the things that could have been saved for this chapter. Here, though, we can point to quite a number of additional characteristics that can help or hinder. Among them are

- Fatalism.
- A concept of God as distant and uncaring (e.g., Deism).
- Seeing God as judgmental and harsh.
- Taboos generated by such concepts of God.
- The belief that humans are (through science and education) potentially all powerful.
- The nearly opposite belief that capricious spirits control the universe and human destiny, etc.

To give an example of the blockage caused by *fatalism*, I had the following conversation with a Nigerian whose relative was dying. His attitude was that God wills such things and that, therefore, we cannot interfere. He told me his relative was dying because "God wants him to die." "How do you know?," I asked. "Because he's sick." "Why don't you take him to the hospital?" "Because God wants him to die." "If you took him to the hospital, perhaps he would live. Then what?" "Then I would know that God doesn't want him to die." "Well, why don't you take him to the hospital and try to find out?" "Because God wants him to die." "How do you know God wants him to die?" "Because he's sick?"

And the conversation never got beyond that point. It was hard for me as a westerner to deal with such fatalism since my worldview sees humans as virtually all powerful, and human life as something close to the most valuable thing on earth. I, therefore, saw no conflict between believing that God is in charge and believing that we are both allowed and encouraged by God Himself to make every attempt to save a human life.

The opportunity for witness presented by fatalism may be quite small. In the case of a relative that is dearly loved by a person such as the above, however, the person's desperation may offer opportunity either to take the person to a hospital or to pray for healing. If either is successful, the fatalist may become open to changing his/her worldview assumption.

When people conceive of God as distant and uncaring and/or as judgmental and harsh, the concept of God as close and caring may be difficult to get across. Jesus faced this problem in a society that believed that if God gets close, we die (see Isa. 6:5). His approach was to live among humans to demonstrate that when God is close it is good news rather than bad. And His constant references to God as Father were transformational to those who were willing to see Him as loving rather than as fearful. We can learn from that approach. Within it, he behaved lovingly and helpfully, using words and God's power to heal and to free to back up His claims to represent a God of love and concern.

In dealing with the taboos generated by such a concept of God, Jesus made statements such as, "the Law [i.e., traditions] was made for humans, not humans for the Law" (Mark 2:27). The taboos that support tradition can indeed hinder change, especially if, as with the Jews and many other peoples, tradition is highly valued. It may be, though, that a people is tired of their taboos, or at least some of them, and looking for the freedom Christ seeks to bring them. If so, the opportunity may be there to bring release from their bondage to the taboos.

We need to be warned, however, that too much freedom too quickly can lead to a very unscriptural kind of Christianity. John Messenger writes of just such an occurrence in an article on the Anang Ibibio of southeastern Nigeria. Reportedly, these people took to Christianity quite readily with the understanding that the Christian God is an easy God to follow since He is very lenient and forgiving. The Anang concluded that they could do whatever they pleased without penalty since God would always forgive them (Messenger 1959).

A western causality problem that is infecting much of the rest of the world is the belief, conscious or unconscious, that humans are through science and education potentially capable of just about anything. We have seen science develop so many answers to so many difficult problems that many assume that it is just a matter of time before humans have the answers to all of life's problems. If this is true, who needs God? This is an obstacle of major proportions for some, even if they believe there is a God, since it focuses one's attention of what humans are doing rather than on what God is doing.

Nevertheless, as Pennoyer points out in his chapter in the book *Wrestling With Dark Angels*, among animistic peoples secularization can be a step in the right direction. For it can lead to the death of a people's confidence in their gods and thus pave the way for the effective introduction of Christianity (Pennoyer 1990).

Among animists the nearly opposite belief that capricious spirits control the universe and human destiny can be both obstacle and opportunity. The obstacles in this area have been great for many western Christian witnesses who have gone to peoples around the world with very little understanding of animism. They have, therefore, missed the opportunity to affirm the animistic assumption that the world is full of malevolent spirits and, working from those assumptions, to present Christ as the One who can control them. This, however, will require demonstration and a higher level of participation with God in such Christ-like events as healing and deliverance than most missionaries have been wont to do.

3. ***Habit***. Another aspect of causality is raised when we consider the *power of human habit* in the perpetuation of traditions. Many peoples value tradition so highly that when ideas are introduced that conflict with previous ideas, the people resist fiercely, at least at the start. To such tradition-oriented societies, what has been done in the past is automatically regarded as good and any change is automatically bad. In the West, of course, the tradition in many areas of life is to change, even if the influences of such change on other parts of our life turn out to be detrimental (e.g., mobility based on occupation, urbanization, free speech, new media). We regard change as good, even as "progress."

We can talk of barriers produced by the power of habit in other attitudes as well:

- *Ethnocentrism* often breeds the attitude that a people's approach in any given area is already the best approach. Why do they need to change?
- *Pride and dignity* in their present way of life can result in the same resistance.
- *A fear of losing "face"* is often associated with such pride at the individual level.
- *Insecurity*, both individually and on a group level usually shows up in a fear to risk.
- *Habits of modesty* can be particularly troublesome when changes in such things as clothing, housing and toilet customs are suggested. For some, modesty demands that they wear clothes, but for others it is modesty that keeps them virtually naked, as with many of the peoples of Papua New Guinea and formerly some of the groups along the border between Cameroon and northern Nigeria.

The power of habit is indeed formidable and a constant hindrance to change. Yet, if constructive habits can be encouraged, there may be opportunity here as well. We may think of the habits that keep relationships between relatives intact or those that produce good behavior on the basis of worthy values such as those discussed in chapter 15 concerning Kamwe ideal persons.

One problem not yet addressed in the causality area is the fact that power-oriented people will tend to accept any power that gives them what they want. They will, for example, gladly receive healing from the true God today and from a different spirit tomorrow. They may not, therefore, be as impressed with Christian healing as we would like them to be. We might reason that if they see God really heal someone as a result of prayer, they will automatically want to get into a relationship with God. They, however, may have seen healings performed by what we know to be evil spirits who counterfeit God's healing activity. And, from their point of view, one healing is just as good as another and does not imply that they need to get into a relationship with the Healer. They, therefore, do not get the message intended to flow through such power demonstrations.

The opportunity in this area lies in the fact that often Christian healings are obviously more spectacular than satanic healings. And the Christian ability to cast out demons is usually beyond anything that the servants of Satan can offer. Our example is, of course, Jesus who, in working among a power-oriented people, took the risk of doing power demonstrations but spent a good bit of time explaining, at least to the disciples, that it is their relationship with God that gives them the authority to do mighty works.

4. ***Spirit World Causality***. For many of the peoples of the world, just about everything is understood to be caused by spirits. Animism holds that the world is populated by spirits that can help or hurt human life. Weather, health, material prosperity or poverty, fertility, accidents, death and just about all else that we consider "natural" causation is interpreted as under the influence of spirits. This being so, a concern for spirits and their influences are for many of the peoples of the world today including more and more westerners, as they were for the people of Jesus' day, a central focus of their individual and corporate lives.

Biblical examples of cause attributed to spirits are many. In the Gospels we see many examples of the activity of demons causing strange behavior. In the Old Testament, then, the Assyrians' interpretation of the reason that the lions were killing their people in Samaria is a case in point (2 Kings 17:24-28). So is the interpretation of King Ben-Hadad and his officials who decided their gods would bring them victory over Israel if they fought on the plains rather than in the mountains because, they believed, the God of Israel was a god of the mountains (1 Kings 20:23-25). Throughout the Old Testament, the enemies of Israel interpreted the military successes of Israel as the triumph of Israel's God over their gods. And the fact that the authors of Old Testament scripture attributed the ups and downs of the people of Israel and Judah as related to their obedience or disobedience of God is a further instance of a belief in spirit world causality.

It should be obvious by now that I believe Christian cross-cultural witnesses need to become as knowledgeable as possible in this area so that we can imitate Jesus' approach to witness. His was a Christianity with power. Ours often is not. Power-oriented people, therefore, often find little to attract them spiritually in the gospel we bring, though they may be attracted by the material aspects of the cultural package we present them with and respond to the love of the witnesses and the peace and joy Jesus gives. But that is only a partial gospel, representing poorly the major emphasis Jesus put on using the power God gives us to heal and deliver from demons.

Time/Event

A people's concept of *Time/Event* can hinder or facilitate change as well. Though there may not be as much to discuss under this universal as under some of the others, the way time is regarded can influence the communication of the gospel in various ways.

1. ***Lateness***. Such things as assumptions concerning lateness can be a factor if one or the other participant is uptight about lateness. If, for example, westerners working in Africa find the people very casual about getting to meetings on time, they can show impatience and even anger. If, then, they are working in a society in which these emotions are considered sin, the result can be a very negative impression of Christianity. Likewise, if a westerner is impatient to get meetings over with, while the people are content to continue for hours if what's going on is meaningful to them.

2. ***Efficiency***. A whole set of assumptions we westerners have concerning efficiency in the use of time and the need to schedule events are often very damaging to our cause if we let them intrude into interpersonal relationships. As pointed out in earlier chapters, most of the peoples of the world are "event-oriented" rather than "time-oriented." This means they are much more concerned with the *quality* of an event than with its timing. The time-oriented Christian witness who learns to "go with the flow" in an event-oriented society will not only endear him/herself to the people but will probably learn something valuable about the fact that participation with people is more important than compressing events into short periods of time.

The tendency of westerners to structure even interpersonal interactions by the clock is not conducive to healthy relationships between people. The way we in the West schedule appointments with people, for example, can be a great obstacle to our relationships with them. Our technological assumptions concerning the efficient use of time, lest we waste it, often hurt us in our attempts to develop solid relationships with the people we seek to help grow in Christ. Efficiency is a good principle for working with machines but a poor one in working with people. People need to be treated as important enough for us to spend as much time as necessary on a given topic without having to turn to another activity before that topic is adequately dealt with.

I had this truth driven home to me one day when I was interacting with a Kamwe village leader. He had come to my home to ask a question and I had met him on the porch. We sat there for nearly an hour talking about one thing and another when he suddenly looked up asking, "How long have we been here?" I calculated the time on my watch and replied, "About three quarters of an hour." Then he asked, "Do you know how long we'd have been here if your predecessor was still living here?" I lied and said, "No" (since I knew very well how long that would have been). He replied, "About five minutes! He would have come to the door and asked, 'What do you want?' Then I would have stated my business and been on my way."

I knew that in that society there is hardly anything more rude than for someone to ask, "What do you want?" And the fact that my predecessor was rude meant that the village leader would not stay any longer than absolutely necessary. As it was with me, however, he remarked, "Now we've been here nearly an hour and I didn't even notice the time passing!" The quantity of time spent in such societies contributes greatly to the quality of the relationships. I believe the fact that I had learned this and regularly spent this kind of time with the people, especially with the leaders, had a lot to do with the people's receptivity to the gospel. And I learned a lot about the connection between the use of time and the quality of relationships with people.

Any attempt to introduce greater community and intimacy into western church structures has to overcome the barrier erected by western values with respect to time. Westerners frequently feel uncomfortable when church meetings or other formal meetings go long. Though we can sometimes spend long times in informal visits to the homes of friends, we do not easily tolerate long formal meetings.

I believe the Holy Spirit is event-oriented rather than time-oriented. If so, even though we westerners are used to the scheduling of church services with beginning and ending times, I believe we often stifle the Holy Spirit thereby. I have been in a couple of meetings in America in which the Holy Spirit took over and they just kept going and going. One of those meetings continued for two full days and nights and was the most awesome experience most of us have ever had! We called it "revival." If we were to regularly give the Holy Spirit opportunity to work without time limits, there's no telling what He would be able to do in our midst. Fortunately, some churches are learning to spend long periods of time in worship and by doing so are finding that His presence is often more tangible than it was when worship time was more truncated.

3. ***Now Versus Not Now***. Another type of time problem occurs in societies like many in Papua New Guinea that have a basic "Now" and "Not now" division of history. As pointed out in the discussion of time in chapter 10, both past and future fall into the "not now" part of time with not much known about them. Since the missionaries spoke very knowingly about Jesus, this concept led to the people assuming that the missionaries knew Jesus when He was alive. With this perspective on time, then, combined with a fragmentary understanding both of the western world and of the gospel story, certain groups came to assume that the reason for Jesus' coming was to bring material goods to humans.

Since Jesus had come first to whites, the New Guineans believed, they were the first to learn the secret that allowed them to obtain material goods. The whites then decided to kill Jesus and to keep that secret for themselves. Indeed, some assumed that it was in this present generation that Jesus was crucified. The New Guineans reasoned, then, that if they joined the whites and listened carefully to them, sooner or later the whites would reveal the secret. And, by using that secret, the New Guineans could assure that the material goods that came on ships and planes would be addressed to them.

Though this understanding of Christianity is far off the mark, it or similar understandings are taken quite seriously by many of the inhabitants of Papua New Guinea. To attempt to bring about change in this area of worldview, Wycliffe Bible Translator, Wayne Dye began to line up the events of the Bible along a time line drawn on a blackboard with each generation indicated by a vertical line, something like the following:

|---|---|---|---|---|---|---|---|---|---|---|---|---|---|---|---|---|---|---|---

Each vertical line stood for a generation (about 30 years) and the names attached to each vertical line, starting from the left end were the names in the biblical genealogies. Starting from the right end, then, the lines represented known people (e.g., those of the present generation and their deceased ancestors) and events (e.g., the first coming of whites, ships, invention of automobiles, planes). By starting at the present and working back, 30 years by 30 years from these known people and events, Dye and later, an Australian Assemblies of God missionary, Kevin Hovey were able to help the New Guineans to "expand" their concept of time. Hovey was able to take this approach to many villages where there were no blackboards by using a palm frond, stripped of its leaves into which small sticks were stuck vertically to represent the generations. This approach resulted in comments such as, "Then you didn't know Jesus personally, did you?"

A major part of the problem in the New Guineans' minds had arisen because the missionaries were so certain about the events of the Bible. With no understanding of the ability of westerners to record history and to pass down those records through literacy, the only conclusion the New Guineans could come to was that the missionaries were speaking of first-hand, person to person experiences with Jesus and even the more ancient heroes of the Old Testament.

In the transformations of worldview values required by Christian commitment, necessary changes in the concepts of time held by most of the peoples of the world are usually not among the most important changes that need to take place. In societies such as those of Papua New Guinea, however, the required changes can be earth-shaking. Yet even for westerners who have practiced a mechanistic, efficiency-oriented approach to time, a change in the direction of a greater event-orientation with a focus on people rather than time can provide a great challenge. Neither we nor they are likely to change our understanding and use of time quickly unless we are highly motivated to do so.

Space/Material World

1. **Land Ownership**. Concepts of *Space* can also provide obstacles and opportunities in the processes of culture change. One major area of difficulty has been the assumption of westerners that land is a material commodity that can be bought and sold. On many occasions missionaries have aroused the ill will of the people they sought to win by engaging in what the missionaries assumed was purchase of land in a society that, like probably most of the peoples of the world, assumed that land cannot be "alienated" (i.e., bought and sold). Often the worldview assumption is that the land belongs to the ancestors and is to be tended and protected by each succeeding generation on behalf of the ancestors. To such people, land is not owned, only used. When practices are introduced from the West that require individual ownership of land (e.g., to build buildings on), there can be considerable misunderstanding.

In the early days of the United States, the European settlers often "bought" (from their point of view) land from Indians who, from their point of view could not sell land, though their worldview allowed them to rent it to others. On occasion, then, when Indians demanded that land be returned that, from their point of view had been rented to whites, conflict arose. For, from the settlers point of view, the land had been bought and paid for "fair and square." A proverbial expression was added to our language based on this experience: people who gave things but later wanted them back were labeled "Indian givers." As I was growing up in New England, we frequently labeled other children "Indian givers" who wanted their marbles back after we had won them fair and square!

2. **Where to Meet**. Wayne Dye tells me that for at least some of the aborigine peoples of Australia, important meetings take place outdoors and in the evening to avoid the extreme heat. Church meetings that are scheduled for midday and indoors (e.g., Sunday church) are, therefore, considered to be unimportant and are poorly attended. On Wayne's advice, some of the missionaries in that area began to schedule their church worship times for evenings and out of doors. This change raised the attendance considerably. Other missionaries continued to hold to the "sacred" Sunday morning time for their meetings. Their meetings continue to be poorly attended.

3. ***Separate Rooms for Children***. For many people (including traditional Japanese), the western custom of providing separate rooms for our children is considered cruel. Their assumption is that children should sleep in close proximity to their mothers. For cross-cultural witnesses to seek to change this Asian practice among converts (as some have), on the assumption that it is more "Christian" for children to have their own space is, therefore, ill advised. Indeed, we westerners might learn that their practice is more in line with what God must have intended than ours.

4. ***Clean Space***. For Asians and some westerners (e.g., Dutch), the floor of a private building such as a home or a church is defined as "clean space" whereas in Anglo-America it is defined as "dirty space." Anglos, therefore, keep their shoes on in houses and churches, while Asians take them off. Though this doesn't look like it ought to be a big deal in cross-cultural witness, the aggravation resulting from the ignoring of such a value can block Christian witness. On the other hand, there is no estimating the positive value put on the observing of such a custom.

5. ***Interpretation of Pictures***. The size of material objects is also a matter of space. A fascinating story of blockage based on size perception comes from the South Pacific where a group of health specialists from the West were trying to instruct people concerning the dangers of houseflies. They made a poster with a foot-long picture of a house fly on it. Under it was a caption something like, "Kill the housefly because it causes disease." The people, however, though they were fascinated by the fly in the picture, came to a conclusion quite different from that intended by the outsiders. They agreed that such flies looked like an enormous threat to life and health. They also agreed to kill them if they saw them. But their interpretation, based on worldview assumptions concerning how to interpret such pictures, was that there was no real problem in their area of the world. "If we had flies that large around here," they concluded, "we'd see that they were dangerous and kill them also. But our flies are just tiny things. We're not concerned about them because they're not big enough to hurt anybody" (Foster 1973).

The possibility of such misperception applies, of course, to any kind of picture. Learning to interpret pictures the way westerners do takes a lot of teaching. Often people, especially traditional peoples, interpret pictures, including photographs, quite differently from what westerners expect. Depth perception is particularly troublesome for some, leading them to ask why some of the people, buildings or other objects in the picture are so large while others are very small.

On the other hand, with the spread of literacy and electronic media, many of the traditional peoples of the world have learned to interpret pictures quite accurately. This fact can result in effective evangelistic use of pictures in places such as New Guinea and Africa. The United Bible Societies found, however, that frequent misunderstanding of the (for westerners, very meaningful) line drawings in the Good News Bible made it unwise to include them in editions marketed in non-western areas of the world.

Relationship

Major obstacles and opportunities for Christian witness stem from the relationships people have with each other. In most parts of the world, kinship relationships will exert a major influence on whatever people may be tempted to change in their cultural behavior. Friendship relationships across kinship lines will also be strongly considered, especially in societies such as western in which extra-familial associations are often more important to people than many of their family relationships.

1. ***Family***. In societies where the family is strong, decisions for change will ordinarily need to be made by the family or larger kinship group, especially for younger or female members of the family. That is, for those under the authority of others, the decision-making process in major areas of life may be totally out of their hands. We often found in Nigeria that a recommendation that an ill person go to the hospital was met with the statement, "I have to ask my family." Quite often, then, the authority in the family would not let the sick person go to get the medical attention we thought he/she needed. The authority to make such a decision was in the family, and the individual did not have the right to make that decision on an individual basis.

On the other hand, if the family leaders are impressed with the suggestions for change, they may lead in making the change within the whole family. Or they may decide not to change themselves but allow others in the family to make the change. In my Nigeria days it was not uncommon to hear an older family leader recognize that times had changed. He, therefore, though declining to turn to Christ himself, would suggest that if the younger members of his family wanted to change, he would not stand in their way.

Whatever the cultural patterns, though, good relationships are crucial between the advocates of change and the recipients. Poor relationships bode ill for effective advocacy, while good relationships can often overcome even well-entrenched sociocultural conservatism.

2. ***Authority Structures***. A major relational factor is the nature and relational characteristics of the authority structures. In all societies there

are several levels of authority. When *personal authority is high*, as in individualistic societies, whatever barriers to change appear may often be dealt with at that level. Conversion to Christ, for example, can usually be expected on the basis of an individual decision. Though the individual considers the opinions of others in the decision-making process, any blockage occasioned by such influence is ultimately evaluated and processed at the individual level.

A crucial question when change is introduced is, "Where is the authority and for what kinds of issues?" Even in tightly-structured, highly group-oriented societies, many small decisions not considered to be important for the ongoing stability of the society can be individually made. Larger decisions such as changes in "religious" practices or decisions concerning schooling or medical attention, however, are often considered to be group affairs.

When appealing for such major changes, it is important for outsiders to look for *opinion leaders*. These will often be less obvious to outsiders than the *political leaders*. And the latter, since they are expected to keep on an even keel the system that gives them their authority, are seldom the kind of opinion leaders that are interested in introducing social change. They often interpret their job as maintaining the status quo and, therefore, often feel threatened by changes. This fact provides a caution against too easily assuming that the political leaders are the kind of opinion leaders needed to bring about changes.

Unusual individuals wield authority in some societies, even those that are quite group-oriented. Such individuals, therefore, can hinder or facilitate change. Often, however, the unusual ones are merely deviants or dissenters, without prestige or authority. They may readily accept change. But their poor relationships with others and the lack of respect others have for them usually will block any possibility that their acceptance of an innovation will spread to other members of the society. The fact that these marginal people have accepted a change means that others automatically reject it.

Unfortunately, in many parts of the world, the churches are largely made up of marginal people. The early advocates of Christianity found a ready acceptance among those who were not "making it" in their societies and, following western egalitarian principles, went ahead and baptized them without considering the potential impact on their desire to win the whole people group. Now, years later, churches are often known as collections of marginals.

3. **Group Solidarity**. The existence and nature of a group's solidarity, then, needs to be continually recognized by those who would advocate

change, whether in traditional societies or even in the West. People behave in groups even when they highly value individualism. Public opinion seems to be extremely important to all peoples. A powerful hindrance to change is the fact that people always ask themselves the question, "What would those in my group (my 'significant others') say if I broke from the accepted patterns and changed in the way you're suggesting?" There is often an "all for one, one for all" mentality in groups that becomes especially evident when they feel threatened or insecure. This mentality can be a strong barrier to change, even if logic would seem to indicate that the change would be helpful.

Such a mentality can, however, work for change when the leaders of the group become convinced that what is being advocated would be a good idea. The *attitude of the group toward those introducing the change* is important in this regard. If they respect the advocates in the area in question, they are much more likely to accept the innovation. Many Japanese seemed willing to accept most ideas coming from Americans immediately after World War II. Soon, however, they seem to have made a distinction between technological ideas that they accepted and religious and social (e.g., family organization) ideas that they largely rejected. Perhaps they decided we knew what we were talking about in the one area but not in the others. In Korea, on the other hand, the pro-American attitude carried over in a big way to the acceptance of Christianity.

Internal factors that crosscut the overall solidarity often play a part also. Often there is *conflict between subgroups* producing various factions. If one faction accepts something, the other will automatically reject it. As mentioned, in many parts of Latin America, if one extended family accepts evangelical Christianity, other families will automatically reject it due to animosity between the families. The groups work in solidarity, but against other groups within the same society.

Conclusion

These, then, are some of the obstacles and opportunities presented by the various peoples of the world relating to their distinct worldviews. However, we need to keep ourselves constantly aware of the fact that though the worldview provides the basic assumptions, it is *people* who actually follow through on those assumptions. The worldview does not block or encourage change. It is *people following the guidelines of the worldview* who throw up the barriers or lower them. It is people who will, emote, think, interpret, evaluate, make commitments, explain, relate and adapt on the basis either of the traditional assumptions or on the basis of changed assumptions. And people tend to do this habitually, without thinking, often strongly influenced by the quality of the relationship between the advocates of change and themselves.

As we conclude this section, I would like to raise one caution: that we attempt to look deeper than either the worldview or its surface-level outworking to discover if there may be areas of dissatisfaction with existing patterns. Often there are latent tensions caused by the lack of fit between a people's present worldview assumptions and the needs of the present generation. For the structuring of a culture always comes from the past and is, therefore, often ill-suited to the present or the future. We must learn to look for the felt needs that are not now being met by the structuring as it is. And felt needs are a personal, not a structural thing. Therefore, things that seem to be incompatible with the society as it is are often appealing to a people in relation to a felt need to get out from under the tight control of some aspect of the society as it is.

For example, people are often tired of the tyranny of the spirit world as represented to them by the traditional religious leaders. They may also be tired of social pressure to marry only in certain ways, (e.g., sometimes fathers of potential brides can get very greedy and set the brideprice unreasonably high) or of political structures controlled by a small handful of people whose power comes from birth, not achievement. Such dissatisfactions can often be discovered and tapped as facilitators of change.

Chapter 18

Patterns of Worldview Change

As we have seen, when people change their worldviews, they usually change only parts of them. Certain paradigms within their worldviews undergo change while other paradigms, though affected by the ramifications of the changed ones, undergo but slight if any change. And not all such change is positive. Indeed, in today's climate of intensive sociocultural interaction, it is more likely that the changes will be disruptive than that they be constructive, at least in the first generation or two.

Internal Worldview Change

Types of Internal Worldview Change

There are several types of change that result in greater or lesser transformation of worldview. The two basic kinds involve *replacement* and *modification*. Replacement is what we have called *paradigm shifting*. To keep from having to repeat the whole list of worldview components, I will use the term "paradigm shift" to refer to replacement at any level—theme, subtheme, paradigm, subparadigm or lower. Such a "shift" is where a person replaces one paradigm (or other higher or lower component) with another. What I am calling paradigm modification, then, may be of two kinds. One kind may be a modification of a higher level component, say, a subtheme, due to the replacement of a lower level component, say, a subparadigm. Another type of modification may be *additive* or *subtractive*. Let's look at each of these types in detail.

1. **Paradigm shifting/replacement**. This is a radical kind of change in one or more of the major components of the worldview. Though Kuhn (1972) spoke of such replacement as if it always happens quickly, I believe such shifts can also take place at a slower rate. The key characteristic, though, is the completeness of the change from one picture of some portion of reality to another.

Illustrations of shifts at one or more of our levels abound in the history of western societies. The so-called "Copernican Revolution," is one of the more famous. This change came about over a period of time and involved, first scientists and later laypeople, in replacing their view of the universe as earth-centered ("geocentric") with a sun-centered ("heliocentric") understanding. Others in western societies include, under the influence of science, the replacement of supernaturalism with naturalism, paralleled by the change from a personalistic to a mechanistic view of the universe. Certain aspects of the Protestant Reformation would also qualify. Paradigms were shifted, for example, when Luther and others moved from assuming that only the Latin language was adequate to convey scripture and only highly trained priests were adequate to interpret it to seeing that scripture could and should be translated into German and that common people could be allowed to read and interpret Holy Writ. Likewise, when Luther's eyes opened to the truth that salvation is obtained through faith, not works.

Whenever non-western peoples accept western scientific understandings of parts of the universe in replacement of their former understandings, there is paradigm shifting. Such is the case when germs are accepted as the cause of illness rather than spirits, when the universe comes to be seen as a machine rather than in personal terms and when people begin to picture themselves as disconnected individuals capable of making important decisions on their own rather than simply as parts of families with all major decisions made by the elders of those families.

Jesus' disciples were led by Jesus into quite a number of paradigm replacements. They, along with the Jews of their day, believed that if God got close it meant death for anyone around. Thus, Peter told Jesus to leave them when, because of the incredible intake of fish, he perceived that Jesus had done a miracle in the power of God (Luke 5:8). An important part of Jesus' activity, then, was designed to help people understand that when God is close, it is good news rather than bad. In John 9, we see Jesus attacking the disciples' paradigm that blindness is the direct result of the sin of a person or of that person's parents (John 9:2). Throughout Jesus' ministry, then, we see Him advocating a "faithful people suffer" paradigm in place of their "faithful people are blessed with material wealth and ease" paradigm. Perhaps, though, Jesus' strongest pressure for a change of paradigm was in His replacement of "God as King" with "God as Father."

Christian conversion usually involves the replacement of a major unbelief paradigm with a belief paradigm, at least for those not brought up in the church. For those who do not believe in God, the "no God" paradigm needs to be replaced by the "there is a God" paradigm. For those who do believe in a god or spirit other than the true God, that paradigm will need to be replaced by the correct one. Such a change, then, needs to be accompanied by lower-level changes concerning just what kind of a God He is—e.g., loving rather than unconcerned, positive toward humans rather than totally judgmental and the like. These replacements/changes may take place over a period of time as the person matures in the faith or they may take place rather quickly.

Often major paradigms and subparadigms concerning the nature of humans also need to be replaced and/or modified. The change from seeing humans as animals, the product of evolutionary processes yet basically good and perfectible to seeing ourselves as in the image of God yet fallen and now redeemed can be a major paradigm replacement. This can involve subparadigm replacements such as from "I'm alright" to "I'm a sinner," from "we can't know what happens after death" to "I go to be with God at death," from "it doesn't matter what I do" to "I live to please God" and the like.

For those brought up in the church, conversion may simply mean the replacement of smaller subparadigms. See below for more on this.

2. ***Subtheme, paradigm and subparadigm*** replacement is a second type of alteration that can occur. This happens to pieces of subthemes, paradigms and subparadigms, often as a result of a new experience that challenges a paradigm already believed in. For example, my belief structure may include a paradigm that holds that God loves everyone. But not until I have experienced the kind of inner healing that confirms this experientially will it really be driven home to me that the "everyone" of this paradigm I already believe in includes me. In such a case, I have not changed a whole paradigm. I have modified (and corrected) a part of the paradigm I wasn't quite into by exchanging an "except me" subparadigm of the "God loves everyone" paradigm with an "including me" model.

In conversion to Christ, those brought up in Christian homes may simply have to change subparadigms such as "I think I'm alright because I've been brought up in church" to "I know I'm saved because I've made a conscious commitment to Christ." Unless such persons have rebelled against their upbringing and denied what they have learned as children, more radical total paradigm shifts would likely not be required. That is, unlike many without a Christian background, they would not likely have to shift from a non-belief in God to a belief in God or from not understanding and accepting various crucial doctrines to acceptance of them.

3. ***Growing new subthemes, paradigms, subparadigms, etc***. A part of this whole subject that I find fascinating is the fact that we can create new components—new subthemes, paradigms, subparadigms and, perhaps, even new themes—that become parts of our worldview. I suspect that this is a major activity of babies and young children as they "format" their minds in response to one new experience after another. As babies discover

their fingers and toes, for example, they probably begin or continue the process of creating a worldview component relating to their bodies. This component has, of course, many other aspects or parts to it, created in response to eating, potty training, tickling, touch, taste and a multitude of other activities relating to the babies' bodies.

As we grow up, then, and go to school, we have to grow paradigms concerning such things as the world (moving from understanding the world to be limited to our home and environs to seeing it as global), the various sciences (from perceiving naively to understanding more knowledgeably), a new language (from monolingualism to bilingualism), cross-cultural reality (from understanding from a single cultural perspective to seeing things from a cross-cultural perspective) and the like.

In the realm of spiritual reality, many westerners just don't seem to be able to grow a place in their mental "space" for the existence and activity of spirits. Perhaps their naturalistic theme is just too rigid to admit a new category or subcategory. Or perhaps they just don't want to be bothered. So it doesn't happen and they are left to interpret spiritual things naturalistically. Some, however, do create a new compartment, accepting the existence of invisible spirit beings that previously had no place in their worldview. The creation of such a paradigm, then, results in ramifications throughout their worldview.

4. ***Modification of worldview components***. Modification of components is probably the most frequent type of change. Indeed, some of the above-mentioned changes may actually be modification rather than replacement changes. Whether the change is a replacement or a modification would depend on how great the change might be for any given person.

Modifications may involve either or both additions or subtractions of smaller units. These may be seen as matters of "fine tuning." As we grow up and learn more about the realities of life, we continually fine-tune our perceptions and the assumptions that underlie them. "My mommy has a baby in her tummy" gets modified by our learning that the womb where the baby is carried is a different part of the anatomy than the stomach.

Modifications may involve additions or subtractions. Suppose a person believes that God can heal directly if He chooses to but that He no longer heals as we see in scripture at a human's command. I have heard such a position articulated by some who believe that the kind of healing we see in the New Testament no longer happens today. But then he/she sees someone speak healing as the Apostles did in the New Testament and the healing happens at once. It is likely that that person will modify her/his paradigm by adding to the assumption that God can heal directly the belief that He can heal in response to a person boldly speaking the healing. This person already assumed that God could heal but added to that assumption the fact that God still empowers people to speak the healing.

Or suppose someone believed that, though others might make mistakes while driving that result in accidents, such a thing could not happen to him/her. Then, this person makes a bad judgment in traffic and actually causes an accident. His/her paradigm gets modified by subtraction.

A Basic Model of Worldview Change

As we have seen, it is on the basis of worldview that people interpret and understand the world that surrounds them, and learn to operate effectively within that world. The people of a society use their worldview to *interpret* and *evaluate* the items and events of the world around them. On the basis of these interpretations and evaluations, then, people *explain, pledge allegiance, relate and adapt*. The worldview also provides people with patterns for *willing, emoting, reasoning and structuring motivation and predispositions*.

These are the functions of worldview. If the society is operating in a healthy manner, these functions are carried out well and the entire society is pervaded with a sense of equilibrium and cohesiveness. When healthy, the worldview and the cultural subsystems "fit" together in a satisfying and pervasive gestalt. The people have a sense of security and perceive their sociocultural life to be uniquely "real," and destined to endure.

But people are faced with options. Alternatives are presented to them and they make changes. And in our day, such changes are often taking place too rapidly and on too large a scale for people to keep their social and psychological balance. The changes are, therefore, disruptive to a people's sense of security and satisfaction in their way of life. This frequently leads to sociocultural crisis followed by breakdown, plus or minus a regrouping and return to relative equilibrium. It is this process that we will focus on in what follows.

We will borrow from Anthony Wallace (1956) a basic model of the process of worldview transformation. It consists, simply, of three consecutive stages:

Figure 18.1. From Old to New in Worldview Change

The first stage represents the equilibrium we have been describing above. All systems are "go." An integrated worldview functions normally. It represents a society in a "steady state," stable and enduring.

The second stage represents the entry into a people's experience of a radical challenge to their "steady state." A crisis has come: war, perhaps, or natural calamity, or the imposition of one society's customs on another. An increasing number of traditional valuations and allegiances are called into question by the new circumstances. Many of the familiar rules and guidelines, especially in the area of social control, no longer work and many traditional assumptions no longer satisfy.

The worldview, the perceptual paradigms that "steadied" the "steady state" no longer enable people to understand major portions of the reality around them. Nor do the worldview assumptions enable the people to adequately deal with the "crisis situation" that now has intruded. People become confused and discouraged, often feeling that life is no longer meaningful. Anomie and demoralization are typical products of the second stage of our model. The people no longer experience "equilibrium", life according to cultural guidelines that are predictable, effective and in relative balance. Rather, they experience dissonance and imbalance with regard to traditional expectations and cultural guidelines in process of transformation, whether for good or for ill.

Our third stage represents the ideal resolution of the crisis: the survival of the society living within the formulation of a new "steady state." Though such a steady state is usually a long time in coming, if at all, we present it as the goal toward which a society strives. As we will see below, there are several possible directions a society can move in dealing with the crises represented by the second step above.

Worldviews are changed because of pressure, pressure that comes from inside the society but that is frequently stimulated by something coming from outside. That is, though it is the inside implementers who feel the pressure and make the changes, it is often the case that they were influenced primarily by their contact with outside factors and advocates. Such influences, especially those coming from contemporary western sources, tend to breed dissatisfaction with traditional assumptions and approaches to life. This, in turn, pressures people to develop new ways of understanding and coping with the new circumstances. New assumptions about the world, what is possible and appropriate and what is not, and new strategies to deal with it are generated. New valuations and allegiances are formulated. People press toward what they hope will soon issue in a new steady state.

The generation of new suppositions, valuations and allegiances implies the concomitant rejection of old suppositions, valuations and allegiances. Yet the new assumptions and strategies, whether those that characterize the transitional period or those of the new steady state, are not entirely discontinuous with the old assumptions and strategies. Even radical paradigm shifts, such as accompany, for example, the introduction of Christianity into unevangelized societies, permit a large measure of continuity with antecedent worldview assumptions and the strategies built on them. New experiences, to be sure, will have impinged upon traditional understandings. New conceptions and perceptual models will have influenced the old strategies and precipitated change at important junctures. Especially significant, new allegiances will have emerged. But many features of the old will continue on, often in modified form, into the new.

A model of culture will elucidate the matter further.

Change at Many Levels: A Basic Model of Culture

Following Alan Tippett (1987:157-82), though substituting *worldview* for what he labels *religion* at the core and adding some subsystems, we can picture culture as follows:

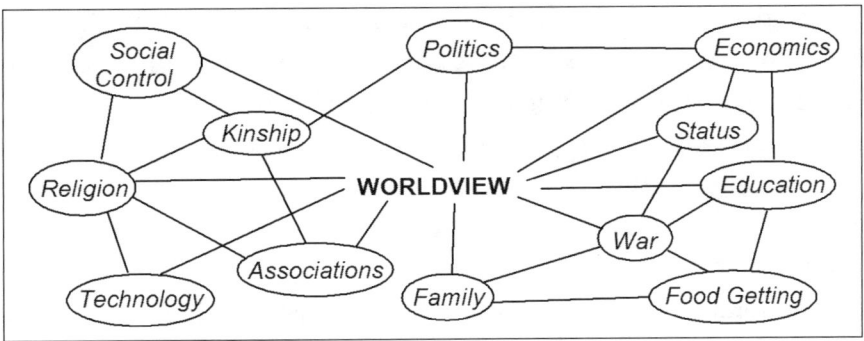

**Figure 18.2. A Model of Culture
(Tippett 1987:162, modified)**

What this picturing of culture enables us to show are the many and varied interrelations between subsystems, and between each subsystem and the core assumptions of worldview. Arranged about the core, each circle represents an integral cultural subsystem: economics, social control, religion, war, kinship, etc. But subsystems interrelate with more than the "core". Each one interfaces with every other. The model attempts to portray culture as a living organism, with muscle and ligament, tendon and sinew connecting an entire array of parts and members into a living, functioning whole.

As with a human body, then, what affects one part affects the whole. Even if the change is in a peripheral subsystem, the lines of connection between that subsystem and the worldview will see to it that change also happens at the core. We have spoken of the fact that pressure for change at the worldview level is what precipitates the crisis situation discussed above. We have also made it clear that it is at the level of worldview that the cross-cultural Christian witness seeks to bring change as a result of the entrance of the gospel of Jesus Christ.

Often threats to worldview come via one of the lines from a subsystem. Frequently such threats have resulted from the people's response to Christian witnesses who have pressured for changes in peripheral matters. Pressure for change of customs, even whole cultural subsystems, without corresponding transformation of worldview assumptions is one of the surest roads to syncretism, for it frequently results in the adoption of foreign *cultural forms* to which are attached meanings that derive from the traditional background.

For example, among the Kamwe, the traditional funeral custom included a three-day ritual, involving day and night drumming and dancing before interment. The deceased was propped in a chair, permitting him/her to "observe" the activity. On the third day, the funeral director would hoist the body up on his shoulders and dance around the house of the deceased, before finally carrying the body off to be buried.

Western missionaries vigorously objected to the custom and taught the Nigerian pastors against it. They considered it dreadfully unhygienic—especially in the tropics! Mainly through teaching the pastors, they tried to put a stop to the custom, recommending instead an immediate, simple and quick (and totally unsatisfying) burial. Public display of the deceased was not only unhygienic, but pagan, they felt. The deceased were to be buried immediately. It was the only "Christian" thing to do!

What the missionaries failed to appreciate, however, was the significant interrelation between this "peripheral" custom—funeral ritual—and the entire fabric of the culture, including its worldview. The funeral custom reflected important assumptions concerning the importance of human life, the significance of its passing, the transition to ancestorhood and the grieving process appropriate for bereaved family and community.

The excision of the traditional funeral custom that enabled them to "work out" their grief and the imposition of a western custom that allowed no such working out of grief issued in a tremendous void in heart and spirit among "westernized" Nigerians. Furthermore, they felt guilty themselves. And they were ridiculed by non-Christian neighbors for treating their dead so crudely. How could they treat their own dead with such unfeeling indifference? The issue became an important obstacle to evangelization, especially among the aged. For who would want to convert to Christianity, if the pastors would not conduct a proper funeral for them when they died?

One potential convert, an old lady, refused to become a Christian unless the church leaders promised she would be buried in traditional fashion. Fortunately, the leader she talked to was willing and able to guarantee her what she asked, so she converted. Unfortunately, many of the other leaders have been so indoctrinated against the traditional custom that they would not have made such a promise. They would, then, lose converts for a wrong reason.

In response to Christian banning of this custom among the Kamwe and other customs among other peoples, people draw some very improper conclusions at the worldview level concerning God and his desires. In many African societies the banning without providing functional substitutes that are equivalently meaningful of numerous "peripheral" customs has constituted an enormous attack on traditional ways in the name of Christ. Among the practices attacked in this way have been initiation ceremonies, weddings, traditional healing, divination and polygamy. *The response to such attacks has been disastrous misinterpretation at the worldview level of the aims and motives of Christian witnesses and of God himself.* Many African peoples, Christians and non-Christians alike, have come to assume that God is against anything that comes from their traditional way of life. He only endorses customs that come from the West. I call such impressions both unethical and heretical. This approach in Africa and elsewhere has provided fertile ground for Satan to do his work within Christian communities.

The Kamwe funeral example illustrates the delicateness of the relationship between surface change and worldview transformation. The missionaries intended well. They were genuinely concerned about the hygienic implications of Nigerian funeral ritual. But their efforts had unintended consequences at the worldview level, in spite of the fact that on the level of external custom they were successful with most of the church leaders in getting the custom changed. The unintended worldview conclusion was, however, that God stood against traditional propriety and in favor of imposing strange western customs.

Worldview transformation, however, need not result in such misunderstanding. Human beings and human cultures are remarkably adaptable. Even very significant cultural change in worldview, *need not* result in disequilibrium if guided properly. Cultural patterns are always being changed in major and minor ways. And, as with individuals, whole societies may experience significant change and come out the stronger for it. The missionaries could have patiently worked with the Nigerian church leaders to develop a modification of the funeral custom that would have been acceptable to both Christians and non-Christians and satisfied the felt needs of the society. Such an approach would have conveyed to both Christians and non-Christians the very important scriptural principle that God desires to work with a society and its felt needs rather than against it even when He desires change.

Four Patterns of Worldview Change

Tippett (1987:157-82) suggests *four fundamental responses* to change in worldview (though he, following the older anthropological tradition, refers to it as religious change):

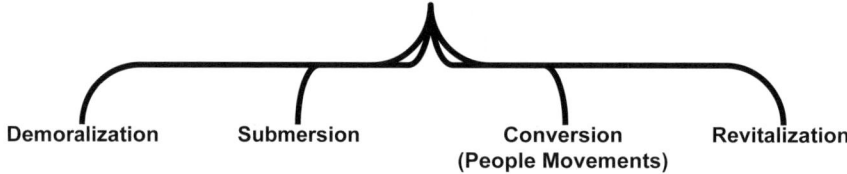

Figure 18.3. Four Responses to Worldview Change

Combining these four responses with the steps pictured in Figure 18.1, we come up with the following possibilities for the process of worldview change and its results:

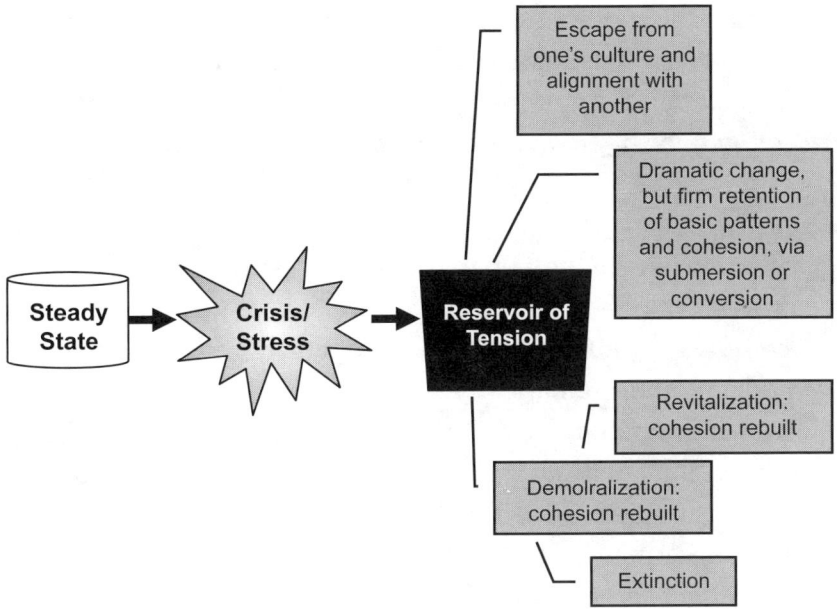

Figure 18.4. The Process of Worldview Change and Its Results

As in Figure 18.1, we begin with the ideal of a steady state. Then comes something from inside or from outside the society, that produces significant cultural stress. This stress builds and produces what Tippett calls "a reservoir of tension." This is "a built-up communal experience which only requires a spark to explode it" (Tippett 1987:287). The society, though experiencing this buildup of tension with its explosive potential for dramatic cultural change, yet preserves what Tippett labels "ethnic cohesion"—the fundamental cultural glue that makes and keeps a people a people. At some point, however, something may happen to "ignite" the reservoir, precipitating dramatic change and innovation, issuing in *conversion*, or *submersion*, yet without disrupting the fundamental configurational patterns that hold a people together, providing them with security and an identity. Tippett explains:

> Over a period of time an ethnic group interacts within itself and in relationship with its environment. From time to time would-be dominant factors are imposed on it, it encounters conflicting and sympathetic forces, it may even be confronted by advocates of change, but it goes on its own sweet way oblivious of all these forces around it. Yet it is not unaffected. In reality the ethnic group is testing, watching, being impressed or unimpressed, as the case may be. Even though it vigorously rejects these new ideas, it is building up an attitude, an ethnic group attitude, fixing its reference points.

There may be gradual approval, or increasing hostility, desire, resentment, and sense of need. It may be an intellectual, emotional, or spiritual build-up, or a complex of them all. *This reservoir of tension may be a feeling of expectancy or an intense passion for emancipation* (1987:287-88, emphasis mine).

This tension having built up in the society, people may respond in one of three ways. First, they may *seek to escape* from their parent society to *align themselves with another society* altogether. This first response may occur suddenly and dramatically, as by cultural conversion, or unfold gradually over generations, as by intermarriage, for example, or the natural processes of assimilation that accompany invasion and colonization or large-scale emigration. In the United States we have seen an entire spectrum of ethnically distinct immigrants "escape" their cultural distinctiveness—their language, their customs and traditions—in favor of "Americanizing."

The second response that society may choose is that of *demoralization*. The demoralized society experiences a significant *break* in its ability to hold itself together. Traditional conceptions of the world, traditional values, and allegiances "fall apart." And the result can issue in one of two directions: *extinction*, as nearly happened with the Yir Yoront, discussed below, or *revitalization*, discussed at the end of this chapter. Extinction, of course, represents an abandonment of the search for security and cohesion altogether.

Revitalization, however, represents a conscious effort to rebuild a workable sense of cohesion once again. With regard to the movement from the reservoir of tension stage into revitalization, Tippett says,

> Then suddenly into this ethnic group is injected *a new factor that releases the tension*. It may be a person—a mad prophet, an idealist poet, a political agitator—or it may be an invention—writing, firearms—or the Koran or the Bible. From this new factor flows a whole flood of new innovations. A whole culture pattern seems to turn over and find a new level. The innovations are spontaneous, unpremeditated, but when the ethnic group recovers from its initial shock and finds its equilibrium again in a new direction, we are amazed to find the ethnic cohesion still applies and the intra-configurational involvements are still the same. There has been terrific change but something lives on—at least as far as we can test it in historic periods (1987:287-8).

The third reaction to this reservoir of tension is for a society to move into *either submersion or conversion*. Either of these retains the basic patterns of the sociocultural structuring of a people, but in different ways. As discussed below, the submersion approach involves covering what remains of the traditional way of life with a veneer of cultural forms adopted from another culture. Such a response has frequently occurred in reaction to colonialism and, within Christianity, in response to the requirement that converts Europeanize in order to be acceptable to those in power.

Conversion, then, is the approach of those who convert to a new worldview allegiance, keeping the rest of the social structure pretty much intact. Though this change at the worldview core is not always in response to Christian witness, it is what happens when entire sociocultural groups choose to come into Christianity together. When this happens, far from westernizing to become Christian, they bring their social structures with them.

These four responses are discussed and exemplified below.

1. Demoralization

The first of the four responses to worldview change is the most desperate. When the worldview of a society is so damaged that no one can mount a movement to rescue it, the entire society may break down. At this point extreme anomie dominates the individual consciousness and incapacitates the collective will. Neither traditional nor novel adaptations to life and answers to problems and challenges are perceived as effective. The people lose their will to survive, and couples refuse even to reproduce new members. When a society gets to such a point we refer to its condition as *demoralization*. This is a radical response to pressure on a worldview.

Scores of islands in the South Pacific have been depopulated, whole groups of people have died out, because of extreme sociocultural demoralization. The precipitating crisis, in many instances, has been westernization. Yet it is not encounter with the West, in and of itself, that provokes so radical a result. Many societies survive such an encounter (see below). It is, rather, the fact that people allow themselves to become demoralized that undermines the last vestiges of security and saps their will to survive. "We are lost," people reason. "We cannot do right. Everything we do is wrong. Whatever is good anymore comes from somewhere else." And it is this demoralized reasoning that is most damaging, most pathological, both psychologically and culturally.

Physical circumstances may contribute to a people's demoralization. An unstoppable epidemic may sweep through the society, as measles did in the South Pacific on more than one occasion. Or an untimely war or a volcanic eruption may decimate their numbers or ruin their land. Or, as with the Ik of Uganda, a whole people group may be moved to make way for a dam (Turnbull 1972). Such factors often put in motion psychological reactions of hopelessness that initiate a movement toward demoralization. It is not the epidemic itself that is crucial, but the reaction to the epidemic, "Our god no longer protects us, he must have died!" It is not so much the war, but the reaction to the war, "We thought we could not be defeated, but we have believed a lie. We are weaklings and fools, what is there now to live for?" Psychological attitudes such as these quickly ramify through an entire society, calling into question its will to persevere.

A Case of Demoralization: The Yir Yoront

Anthropologist Lauriston Sharp (1952) has described a classic example of cultural demoralization among a people called Yir Yoront. They were once a thriving aboriginal people of the Australian outback who, under pressure from outside influences, largely missionary, became utterly *demoralized* and nearly extinct! Indeed, we thought they were gone forever until John Taylor (1988) found and described a group of them who have survived through adapting to the outside world.

The Yir Yoront had no knowledge of metals. Technologically, they were a stone-age people: stone crafting and the use and trade of stone items were fundamental to Yir Yoront society. An important part of their life was the crafting and polishing of *stone axes*, a useful implement, hafted in a short handle.

But the stone axe was more than a useful implement. Indeed, the axe of polished stone was, among other things, a symbol of the status relationships between older males and women, on the one hand, and the younger males, on the other. These axes were made by traditional Yir Yoront technology and controlled and distributed by the revered old men of Yir Yoront society. They were also central to Yir Yoront trade and economy and had become a symbol of Yir Yoront identity.

The manufacture and trade of the stone axe required the Yir Yoront to maintain and nurture positive relationships between themselves and trading partners from neighboring tribes. The Yir Yoront traded for raw material to fashion their prized axes, and traded the finished product too. The stone axe, therefore, represented well-functioning interpersonal relationships with their neighbors! Owned by the older men and only loaned to others, the movements of any given axe presupposed the entire pattern of Yir Yoront kinship structuring. The stone axe represented established patterns of sex, age, and kinship roles and authority! The entire configuration of cultural traits surrounding its ownership and use presupposed the predominance of the Yir Yoront male. The stone axe represented Yir Yoront masculinity, providing the Yir Yoront male with a sense of meaningfulness.

And then steel axes were introduced. Missionaries, in particular, were responsible for introducing the steel axe. As is typical of westerners, the possible social consequences of the introduction of a new technology were not considered. The westerners might have noticed that only certain people in the society owned axes and given them only to those people. Instead, they gave steel axes to anyone who pleased them, even females and young men, thus threatening all of the internal social relationships and values, plus the external trading arrangements that surrounded the stone axes.

> The white man believed that a shift from steel to stone axe on his part would be a definite regression. He was convinced that his axe was much more efficient, that its use would save time, and that it therefore represented technical "progress" towards goals which he had set up for the native. But this assumption was hardly borne out in aboriginal practice (Sharp 1952:20).

Doubtless the missionaries' motivation was proper. But the practical outcome of this unnatural replacement of the Yir Yoront stone axe by a technologically "superior" steel axe was disastrous. Suddenly, a major symbolic focus of Yir Yoront society was removed. And nothing put in its place.

We may diagram what occurred as follows:

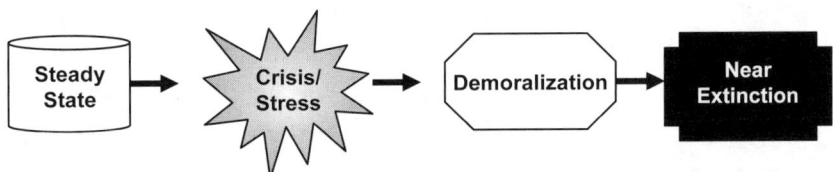

Figure 18.5. The Process of Demoralization Among the Yir Yoront

Yir Yoront society had functioned in a more or less steady state though, as we have pointed out, no culture is completely stable. Even in the most stable times all sociocultural systems are being changed. But, if not interfered with too much, a society can achieve a relatively steady state and function well. So it was with the Yir Yoront. They may have had only Stone Age technology. But their customs worked!

Enter crisis. The effects of the introduction of the steel axe ramified negatively throughout the basic configurations of Yir Yoront life. Well-structured situations centering around the manufacture, distribution, and use of the stone axe were superseded by ill-defined and stressful new situations. The revered old men were once independent, and their special role vis-à-vis the stone axe reinforced their independence. Now, however, the steel axe represented and reinforced a new relationship—dependence upon the White Man. Being dependent didn't bother the women and young men so much. They had always been dependent on the old men of their own society. But now, if the old men wanted the new technology, they had to curry the favor of the whites or, worse, ask the women and young men to borrow their axes.

In the past, interpersonal relationships were oiled, as it were, by the continual trading surrounding the manufacture and distribution of the stone axes. Now, the steel axe could be owned by anyone and, therefore, represented no such strength. In the past, sex, age, and kinship roles were clearly represented in the use and distribution patterns of the stone axe. Now, the steel axe was distributed indiscriminately, even to young men and certain women, with the result that traditional roles were confused and insubordination became common. The Yir Yoront had once governed themselves without the intervention of a "chief." Now, the individuals, even younger men, who most directly interfaced with the mission became leaders, tacitly endorsed by the White Man.

The result: Yir Yoront society became *demoralized*. Sharp summarizes:

> From what has been said it should be clear how changes in overt behavior, in technology and conduct, weakened the values inherent in a reliance on nature, in the prestige of masculinity and of age, and in the various kinship relations. A scene was set in which a wife, or a young son whose initiation may not yet have been completed, need no longer defer to the husband or the father who, in turn, became confused and insecure as he was forced to borrow a steel axe from them. For the woman and boy the steel axe helped to establish a new degree of freedom which they accepted readily as an escape from the unconscious stress of the old patterns—but they, too, were left confused and insecure. Ownership became less well defined, with the result that stealing and trespassing were introduced into

technology and conduct. Some of the excitement surrounding the great ceremonies evaporated and they lost their previous gaiety and interest. Indeed, life itself became less interesting, although this did not lead the Yir Yoront to discover suicide, a concept foreign to them (Sharp 1952:21).

The response of the Yir Yoront to such a challenge was to lose interest in their own way of life. And, as pointed out above, they nearly died out.

Would We Have Done Differently?

We'd like to think we would have handled such a difficult situation much differently. I am not so sure. It's easy to look back and see what went wrong. I wonder, though, if anyone, even those with anthropological training, could have foreseen the extent of the consequences in time to prevent the worst of them. Hopefully, though, we might have been able either to stem the tide at some point or, at least, to be more understanding and helpful to those caught in the situation.

Without being unduly critical of those missionaries, we may learn from an analysis of what went wrong for the Yir Yoront something of what to look for in contemporary situations. We may, then, realistically hope to understand the basic dynamics of worldview and culture change so as to *recognize* situations of pending demoralization when they occur. Had the missionaries first respected and tried to understand Yir Yoront society, they would have recognized that radical demoralization was undoing it and they might have responded differently. They might have tried to support the status system rather than to do what would destroy it.

Furthermore, they might have undertaken to promote a *new mythology* capable of explaining the crisis precipitated by the coming of the steel axe. For example, they might have pointed out that it was the Yir Yoront's traditional deity who had brought the whites and the new technology. In this way they might have maintained some semblance of continuity with the traditional Yir Yoront way of life. They might have taken care not to disrupt the interpersonal relationships and the authority patterns that had functioned for the Yir Yoront for generations.

For the Yir Yoront still in the bush, a time could be predicted when personal deprivation and frustration in a confused culture would produce an overload of anxiety. The mythical past of the totemic ancestors would disappear as a guarantee of a present of which the future was supposed to be a stable continuation. Without the past, the present could be meaningless and the future unstructured and uncertain. Insecurities would be inevitable. Reaction to this stress might be some form of symbolic aggression, or withdrawal and apathy, or some more realistic approach. *In such a situation the missionary with understanding of the processes going on about him would find his opportunity to introduce his forms of religion and to help create a new cultural universe* (Sharp 1952:22, emphasis added).

Demoralized Churches?

Cross-cultural witnesses should be aware of the processes of demoralization, and structure their witness in such a way that it does not contribute to this kind of insidious dynamic. Rather, we should try to help people move into cultural *conversion* if they are not already in some stage of demoralization or into *revitalization* if they are experiencing some form of demoralization (see below). In addition, if Christians are to survive culturally, it is important that they be helped to develop an intimate relationship with God, over and above the relationship that will naturally develop between national converts and the outside advocate.

A national church that looks to the missionary, or the mission agency, for the "final word" on every important issue is headed for demoralization. Its leaders do not trust that God deals directly with them and their members and that they themselves are able to address important issues under the leading and power of God. Rather, they ask perpetually, whether consciously or unconsciously, "What would the missionary do?" or worse, "How will our decisions be perceived at Mission headquarters in New York or Wheaton?" Demoralized thinking such as this does not result in strong and mature Christian disciples.

Affirmation of our national colleagues as equal and full partners, however, with the expectation that God is quite able to direct and illumine them directly, leads to their genuine development into mature and responsible disciples of Jesus Christ.

2. Submersion

A second fundamental variety of worldview change is *submersion*. Like demoralization, submersion represents a radical response to external pressures, impinging upon a society from without. Again, basic worldview assumptions are challenged. Traditional perceptions of the universe are threatened by the advent of powerful new models. New behaviors and behavior patterns are promulgated. New perceptions, new thinking patterns are promoted. But the result is not the anomie of demoralization issuing, finally, in the total eclipse of traditional worldview parameters. Rather, traditional worldview configurations survive, though submerged under a veneer of the new.

Submersion is a defense and coping mechanism on a sociocultural scale. When traditional worldviews are threatened with sweeping external changes, their only hope for survival may be to submerge, to hide "behind" the changes, to adopt the external form of change while maintaining largely the self-same worldview within.

Throughout the centuries, military conquest has resulted in many examples of cultural submersion as a survival mechanism. An oft-cited example is what has developed from the Spanish and Portuguese conquests in Latin America. By military might, large indigenous populations were made into a "New World," conceived and administered by Europeans for European profit. Through military might and other pressures, tens of thousands of Aztec, Mayan and Incan peoples were baptized into the Roman Catholic faith, signaling thereby their capitulation to European political and religious authority, and their deference to a European conception of the world. But this submission took place only on the surface. Underneath the surface, an indigenous worldview prevailed still. Entire indigenous societies were baptized, made to conform externally and forcefully incorporated into European and Roman Catholic systems. But at their heart they remained largely Aztec, Mayan and Incan.

The survival mechanism worked. By submerging the presuppositions, values and allegiances of their own, traditional worldview under a "European" or "Roman Catholic" veneer, indigenous peoples were in many cases able to maintain some identity as a people. There are many examples that can be cited. Among the Mazateco people of Mexico an indigenous mushroom cult springs up (Pike and Cowan 1959). Superficially, the cult deals in "Roman Catholic" categories: Jesus Christ, the Virgin Mary, prayers, the mass, etc. These same *"Christian" forms* have been imposed across all of Latin America since the time of the conquest itself. But the *meanings* that operate beneath the surface are another matter altogether. The Mazateco will tell of drops of blood issuing from the sacred veins of Christ, having somehow reached the Mexican highlands. And wherever they fell, drop-by-drop, a sacred mushroom grew. Now the mushrooms, containing as they do a psychotropic chemical substance, are said to effect communion with God or with Jesus Christ. Is this "Christian?" Not at all. It represents, rather, a *survival* of traditional Mazateco worldview and culture, dressed in a veneer of respectable, "Christian" categories.

A Case of Submersion: Juan the Chamula

Ricardo Pozas documents for us the case of Juan, a member of the Chamula people of southern Mexico. Juan claims he is a Christian. His Christianity is, however, distinctly unorthodox by biblical standards. Pozas describes Juan's Christianity as

> A religion that mingles the worship of pagan deities and Roman Catholic saints, whose attributes are associated with the economic life of the community and the forces of nature, especially the sun (1962:5).

Though Juan's faith is basically animistic, he and his people have taken from Roman Catholicism such elements as the Virgin, the symbol of the Cross and the taking of oaths at the Cross, the Trinitarian formula and patronage of the saints. Combined with these, however, are purely animistic features such as worship of the sun, communion with ancestors, their attitude toward the spirits of the dead, their burial ritual and their attitude toward sickness and healing. The mixture has produced a cult of San Juan, several myths and festival performances and a syncretistic approach to disease and healing. These features come out plainly in quotes such as the following. The first is a summary of what he believes about Jesus, Mary and Joseph:

> San Manuel (or San Salvador or San Mateo) watches over people on the road. He died on the cross to teach respect. The Jews (devils) were eating people, and he gave his life to save them.

> Before he was born the sun was as cold as the moon. The devils (Jews) lived on the earth—eating people. The sun grew warmer when the Holy Child was born. This is the Savior, son of the Virgin. Her relatives were Jews. When she knew she was pregnant she told St. Joseph. Her relatives knew the Child would bring light and they made the Virgin go away. St. Joseph took her to Bethlehem and the Christ Child was born there in a manger. When he was born the sun grew warmer and the day brighter. The demons ran away and hid in the mountains and ravines.

If a devil (Jew) comes out by day when the sun is shining, he cannot eat anybody because Saint Savior is watching; for the sun is the eyes of God.

The holy family had nothing to eat and after three days the child determined to start work. He began making a door from a log. The log was too short, as Joseph pointed out, but the child stretched it like a rope until it was the required length. When the people heard of this they determined to kill him, and the family had to cross the mountains from village to village to save themselves.

In one village he planted a cornfield. There were many flies, and they bit. Joseph had a carpenter make a cross and he took it to the Savior. The Savior said to the Jews, "Don't eat my children. That is why I am here. Eat me instead." He was nailed to the cross.

Before that he went to see what the afterworld (Olontic) was like, and after that he returned to be nailed to the cross, so the people would remember that the demons, the Jews, would be punished and wouldn't go on eating people (pp 94-96).

Concerning Saint John, Juan says:

He was the first person to plant a cornfield. He was the first man in the world. He was born before Jesus Christ. He cleared the scrub off the mountains and taught the people to live the way they do today. At each fiesta the people ask him for good health so they can get their work done (p 96).

This account contains a series of syncretistic features that are quite typical of a submersion reaction to worldview change. The story is a completely confused account of Christian (Roman Catholic) teaching mixed with traditional myth. Coming from the New Testament is a confused version of the life of Jesus, including the journey to Bethlehem, the nativity, the flight into Egypt and his death on the cross. But Jesus is a fully mature person and does a miracle only three days after his birth. Jesus (San Salvador) is confused with Matthew and Manuel. His descent into Hell precedes his death on the cross. Coming from the pagan mythology of Juan's Mayan society are such things as the role of sun and moon, the demons (confused with the Jews), that the demons (Jews) eat (kill) people, legends of the cornfield and the biting flies.

There is no coherent relation between all the factors, but there are clear attempts at equating traditional items with biblical ones. The demons, the Jews and the biting flies are equated. The light and warmth of the sun are equated with the light of Christ. There is a conflict between light and darkness. And Jesus' vicarious and voluntary offering of himself is both to be bitten by flies and to die on the cross. (I am indebted to some unpublished notes of Alan Tippett for much of the above).

That such a myth could be believed by Mexicans today demonstrates the tenacity of a submerged explanation system that still has not been challenged by proper teaching of Christianity.

Another part of Juan's belief system follows:

How lonely Chultotic [the sun] is! He still has his mother, Chulmetic [the moon], but his father is dead and never comes back to this world, not even his soul. He died a long time ago. The Virgin Chulmetic wept and wept when her lord died, and her son Chultotic said: "Don't weep ...father will return in three days, but if you keep mourning him, he'll never come back."

Chulmetic wept and wept without listening to what her son told her, and the father of the sun never came back. If our mother Chulmetic hadn't wept so much, everybody who dies would return to this world in three days. That's why Chultotic goes to the Olontic every day, to see his father and to visit those who have died ... Today is the only day their souls can come out to visit us.

It's Chultotic's father who punishes the dead. If you used to steal or fight, he burns your hands. If you used to deceive your husband or wife and have a lover, he burns your sins with a hot iron. If you murdered somebody, you're punished for your own sins and also for those of the man or woman you killed ... (pp 48-51).

As a final example, I quote a prayer Juan prayed during a sacrifice ordered by the shaman when Juan fell sick after his father's death:

Holy Earth, holy Heaven; Lord God, God the Son, Holy Earth, holy Heaven, Holy Glory, take charge of me and represent me; see my work, see my struggles, see my sufferings. I place the tribute in your hands. In return for my incense and my candles, spirit of the Moon, virgin mother of Heaven, virgin mother of the Earth, and in the name of your first Son, or your first Glory, see your child oppressed in his spirit (p 91).

These statements of what Juan believed show conclusively that what we have here is not really Christianity, though some of the forms of Christianity are used. This is animism with a veneer of Christian symbols on it. The meanings show very little resemblance to orthodox Christianity, however. The traditional culture is submerged with the traditional meanings "calling the shots," as it were. The sad thing is that most of the millions of people who believe and practice such things as these don't know they aren't practicing Christianity.

Submerged Churches?

Unfortunately, the problem of submersion is not limited to Roman Catholicism and Latin America. We need look no further than contemporary North American Protestantism to discover churches in which Christian symbols are grafted to secular worldview assumptions. Whether it is the rationalism of much evangelicalism that has its roots in the eighteenth century philosophical movement called "The Enlightenment" or the unconsciously deistic concept of God that evangelicalism shares with mainline Protestantism, our basis is not scripture but the assumptions we share with the society around us (see Kraft 1989). Even more obvious in North America are the syncretisms of the "Prosperity Gospel" and "America First" Christianity.

Our myths are often a combination of our secularisms and pop Christianity, just as Juan's are. For example, we assume religion to be a private thing. Is this a Christian assumption? We assume individualism, the need for fancy church buildings and full-time church workers (materialistic), the need for pastors to be trained in schools (secularism) and the separation of people into three distinct parts: physical (for medical doctors to deal with), psychological (for psychologists) and spiritual (for pastors). Are these assumptions even compatible with biblical verities? Or are we, like Juan, practicing what we call Christianity in a submersion-type combination with our secular American worldview?

In most of the rest of the world, then, both Protestant and Roman Catholic Christianity is characterized by what may be called "dual allegiance." Since western Christianity seldom provided any substitute for the spiritual power sources to which people traditionally appealed for assistance, most non-western Christians continued to seek power from their traditional spirits and gods even after becoming Christian. Thus, as a demon once told a Tanzanian priest, "Man of God, you cannot win. Your people ride two horses!" That is, they follow Christ some of the time but give themselves to evil spirits whenever they need help. Their allegiance to Christ is compromised by their continued allegiance to the spirit powers they have always served. Though not technically submersion, the lack of spiritual power in western churches has led many westerners to also move into the syncretism of dual allegiance through movements such as New Age.

3. Conversion

We have considered two responses to severe, external pressure for worldview change: demoralization, and submersion. The first is a "defeatist" response that may eventually lead to cultural extinction. The second is a "survivalist" response that leads, often, to syncretistic melding of worldview characteristics. We shall now consider a third response that is altogether different—the response of *conversion*.

Once again, the pressure for change usually comes from without—typically, in the form of perspectives that represent a radically new perception of the universe, at once challenging traditional perceptions and precipitating the formation of new perceptual paradigms. Such perceptions touch the very core of a culture—at the level of its fundamental presuppositions, valuations and allegiances. It issues in a more radical change in worldview than either of the previous two reactions.

Though we use the term "conversion" for this type of reaction, it should not be concluded that we are talking only of a movement toward Christ. *What is in view is any conversion of the worldview of a society*, whether toward Christ, away from Christ or without reference to Christianity at all. For example, several years ago it was reported that 40,000 members of the Borana tribe of Ethiopia had turned from animism to Islam. And in 1956 Margaret Mead wrote a book entitled *New Lives for Old* in which she reported that the Manus people of Papua New Guinea had converted from their traditional ways of life to western practices and assumptions in one generation. Her analysis is, however, strongly disputed by missionaries who know the Manus better than she did.

Another thing to note is that when we speak of the conversion of a worldview, we are not talking of a complete conversion. A complete exchange of one worldview for another is as far as we know totally impossible. We are, rather, looking at partial conversion in terms of the number of assumptions (subparadigms, paradigms, subthemes, etc.) that are changed, though speaking of significant conversion in terms of the importance of the changes and the significance of the people's new commitment.

In spite of what we have said concerning the fact that worldview conversion is not necessarily Christian conversion, Christian "people movements" provide good examples of the radical change involved in this reaction. For, as we shall see, the primary focus of the entire process is the conversion of allegiances relating to the deepest level of worldview. A "power encounter" such as that between Elijah and the prophets of Baal (1 Kings 18) often precipitates the process. By direct confrontation, the gods or forces that once claimed a people's fundamental allegiance are shown to be less powerful than the Christian God, demonstrating the truth of the Christian message in a way power-oriented people understand (see Tippett 1987). People then shift their allegiances to ally themselves with the new Source of power. Thus, with the allegiance changed (a people thing), the process is started that issues in the people changing major portions of the rest of the culture, including the worldview, to conform to the change in allegiance.

That process, then, soon ramifies throughout the entire sociocultural context. What has happened is a kind of cultural *heart transplant* springing from the allegiance changes. And these new allegiances, affecting the worldview heart of a culture, are soon connected by the existing "veins" and "arteries" of the culture to the entire "body" of the culture with all of its varied subsystems. Power encounter conversions usually issue in what have been called "people movements," the rapid turning of large groups of people who, in keeping with traditional decision making patterns, decide for Christ all at the same time. Following such turnings, the people themselves soon begin to adapt existing customs and develop Christian functional substitutes to express the new allegiance more adequately than the old usages would. A worldview is changed and eventually the entire culture is affected and changed in accordance with the new commitment.

This is a response to pressure for change that is neither "defeatist" nor "survivalist", but fundamentally positive and constructive. The following case, though not the result of a single power encounter did include several small power encounters over the many years before the conversion took place.

A Case of Conversion: The Batak

Tippett (1987:285-301) has described a moving example of radical worldview change—change that ramifies throughout an entire sociocultural system, yet preserves intact the society's ethnic cohesion, that fundamental identity and cultural glue, that makes a people a people. He refers to the radical worldview change implicit in the experience of *Christian conversion*, in this case a people movement. And the example he describes is the conversion of the *Batak people* of Indonesia.

In 1881 there were no Christians among the Batak. The people were quite resistant to the Christian message. But the persistence of the advocates of Christianity eventually began to pay off. The Batak began to listen and then to convert. Within three decades of the original introduction of Christianity, then, a veritable wave of Christian conversion swept through the group. And by 1911 there were more than 100,000 Christian Bataks. At the time of the writing of Tippett's article (early 1960s) they numbered more than 1,000,000.

Yet the Batak remained Batak! The people, in commitment Jesus Christ, substantially transformed their worldview. And distinctively Christian assumptions and their implications ramified throughout Batak culture. The Batak underwent changes as substantial as the Yir Yoront. Yet the Batak did not allow their internal cultural glue, their ethnic cohesion, to fail as the Yir Yoront had. So, rather than falling into demoralization and extinction, the Batak engaged in the process of conversion of their whole cultural system around a power replacement (spirits to God) stemming from their new allegiance to Jesus Christ.

German Lutheran missionaries had labored among the Batak for twenty years before observing any appreciable sign of the mighty wave of conversion that was to engulf the Batak people. These were twenty years of cross-cultural *advocacy*. But very little *adoption and implementation* followed. These were years of intense resistance to the Christian message. A handful of Batak experienced conversion, but the majority united in their opposition to the message and its messengers.

What was it that occasioned the profound change of attitude that was later to make a resistant population exceptionally receptive?

Tippett surmises that "change is acceptable as long as it fits the pattern, but if it upsets the ... balance there is resistance" (1987: 286). What "sparked" the reservoir of tension and unleashed a great wave of conversion, was in large part the perception that Christianity "fit" the Batak pattern, that Christianity served Batak cohesion, that by conversion to Christianity one could in fact become a *better Batak*! "Society is disposed to accept new ideas if they are in alignment with ethnic cohesion, but disposed to reject when they threaten it" (ibid: 287).

> In the absence of any change of advocacy we are here confronted with one of our basic problems in this investigation—what broke down the 20 years resistance and achieved widespread acceptance?

Tentatively we suggest that a reservoir of tension had been created, possibly because the demonstration of Christianity by a few families revealed that the family structure did not disintegrate, that the Christians were good members of society, that their "atheism" did not injure the group, that *adat* (the core values and prescriptions of Batak tradition) still meant something to them, and that there were some superior points about the Christian way of life, and that it was [supernaturalistic]. To the Batak, custom, law, morals, social and family life was built on a foundation of [supernaturalism]. ...The probability is that the animistic Bataks came to see the Christian Bataks were also deeply [supernaturalistic] and came to set the two [approaches] beside each other of their own accord. The reservoir of tension, then, would include the growing conviction that the new ...was better (ibid: 291-2. My bracketed substitutions are for Tippett's word "religion ").

Out of Control

What now ensued, in effect, guaranteed the lasting success of the Batak movement to Christianity: the movement got out of the control of the expatriate missionaries!

The advocates did not achieve all they desired, they had themselves to accept modifications of their proposals. The Church as they would have had it was Patriarchal—the missionary being the "father." For the first twenty years this had been practical. However the sudden influx of 20,000 "children" in a few months rather dislocated the role of "fatherhood." This led to a reduction of the time demanded for catechetical instruction prior to baptism, a leaning far more on indigenous workers, with the result that the Church became far more indigenous than it might otherwise have been.
To meet, what seemed to be the shortcomings of the new converts the missionaries were forced into policy changes. A special place had to be given to missionary linguists, who worked on scripture translation, the preparation of pre- and post-baptismal tracts, etc. The vernacular language was quickly and effectively accepted and absorbed into the indigenous pattern, without any need of advocacy, the need itself being adequate and as a result the Christians from this movement were far more thoroughly Christians than the Moslems (sic) were Moslem. The pattern of Christian learning inter-related

with the school organization and with educational literature, and thus the Batak Christians were oriented for an educational program and for independent thinking which was to be significant later on in the history of their race.

Thus it will be seen that the roles of indigenous worker and missionary changed considerably between 1881 and 1911—three significant decades when the Christian movement grew from nothing to 103,528. The missionary became, not the "father" of the congregation he knew personally, but a director of a large area, a supplier of advice for leaders, and a producer of vernacular literature; and the pastoral role was assumed by an indigene, who was himself very much nearer the popular level in intellectual outlook and not foreign.

I have attempted to schematize this situation. Missionaries were wise enough to see their dependence on indigenous agents on the popular level and modified their own role to suit the needs. They restructuralized (sic) the situation to make themselves trainers of indigenous leaders. This demonstrates an interesting factor in advocacy and acceptance. An advocacy can itself be deflected from its course by striking a non-responsive or an obstructive situational matrix. To have pressed advocacy at this point would have meant to confine themselves to a single small mission station, and the flood of released energy would possibly have turned to a nativistic cult or movement; which is exactly what happened in Papua when a mission, unwilling to restructuralize its own role to absorb a movement, left it to pass through and beyond its area in the form of a Taro Cult (Ibid: 294-5).

We have quoted Tippett at considerable length in order to emphasize the fundamental importance of the local leadership role vis-à-vis the expatriate missionary. In case after case, in diverse societies and missionary situations around the world, the relative strength of the local church seems to bear an inverse relationship to the level of direct expatriate influence and control. Very often, the weakest church in an area will be the church on or nearest the mission station. But farther away, where well-intentioned but culturally distanced expatriate personnel cannot "check up" so often, the church is forced to depend upon itself, its own leadership resources, its own relationship with Jesus Christ. And the church often prospers.

Are we willing to allow an emerging Christian movement to escape *our* control? Are we willing to trust that the same Lord who led us will direct and lead local converts? Most importantly: Are we willing to assume those roles vis-à-vis an emerging local church that will facilitate the emergence of contextually appropriate patterns based on local resources? Most likely we will prefer different patterns and resources, patterns and resources more natural to us. But if the local church is to endure and mature, it must discover what patterns are natural to its own people.

The Conversion of (Western) Christianity

The Batak people were converted to Christianity—but they, in turn, "converted" the western Christianity of the expatriate German Lutheran missionary! The Batak became Christian—and Christianity became Batak!

The following represents, in somewhat oversimplified fashion, an ethnocentric conception of Christian advocacy in non-Christian societies (ibid: 297):

Figure 18.6. Ethnocentric Conception of Christian Advocacy

This is a nice, simple diagram. It moves in straight, neat lines, as if it were a mathematical equation, or perhaps an experiment describing the modification of behavior in colonies of laboratory mice. Input stimulus, output predictable response. But as a model of Christian advocacy, the diagram is hopelessly inadequate.

Tippett's diagram below, on the other hand, represents far more realistically the process of cultural and Christian conversion experienced by the Batak people. The process they went through was not a simple, straightforward matter of substitution—if, indeed, true Christian conversion ever is. It was rather a multifaceted process unleashing many levels of response: acceptance, modification, new innovations, differentiation, rejection, and discarding (ibid: 299).

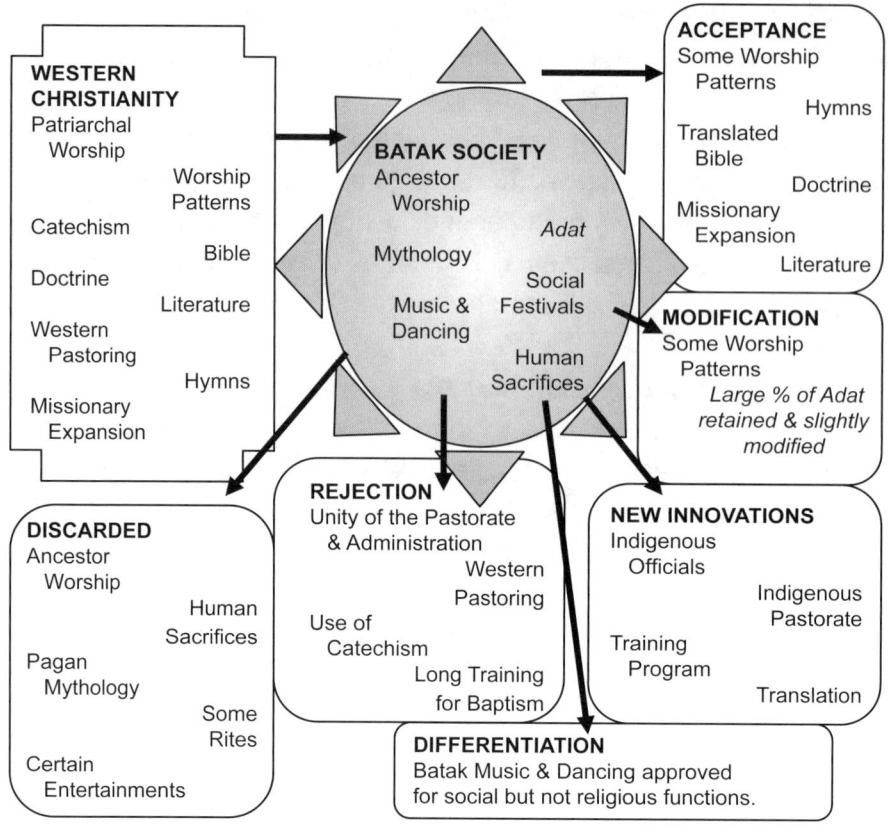

Figure 18.7. Batak Reorientation After Accepting Christianity
(Tippett 1987:299)

The stimulus of German Lutheranism is represented by the upper-left square. What was characteristic of pre-Christian Batak society is represented by the top-center square. But what fills out the diagram are *many and varied responses*. The Batak accepted certain characteristics of German Lutheranism outrightly. Other characteristics—both Lutheran and pre-Christian Batak—were modified and retained. The Batak *innovated* as well, evolving their own new and distinctive patterns of leadership and organization. They *differentiated* other characteristics, retaining, for example, traditional Batak music for social occasions but not for religious functions.

Certain characteristics of German Lutheranism were *rejected*, such as the use of the catechism and western patterns of administration. And finally, certain characteristics of pre-Christian Batak society were *discarded* as well, including human sacrifice and other rites and mythology. What eventually emerged from the cultural soil of Batak society was both alike and very much different from the Christianity rooted in the soil of German Lutheranism.

It was alike at the point of essential allegiance: both pledge their ultimate allegiance to Jesus Christ. But at every other point they are *free to be different*. The Batak became Christian—and Christianity became Batak!

4. Revitalization

Finally, we consider a fourth variety of worldview change—*revitalization*. Whereas demoralization, submersion and conversion each represent an initial response to external pressures for change, revitalization is a secondary response. That is, the processes that lead to revitalization are a kind of rebound from the pressures that appear to be leading a people toward demoralization. Revitalization, even more than the other responses, results from the attitude of the people, not merely from the external pressures themselves.

We may speculate that every human being, and every human society, has experienced at one time or another, to one degree or another, the processes of stress and crisis. Often, then, such stress and crisis lead to some degree of demoralization. But not every society moves, as the Yir Yoront almost did, from demoralization into cultural extinction. Happily, many peoples will respond with what Sharp refers to as a "more realistic approach," an approach born from an attitude that says, "This can't happen to us. We will not allow our way of life to disintegrate!" So they take steps to restructure and reorganize.

Such determination produces an opposite pressure, the pressure to steady and stabilize themselves in spite of the fact that they are caught in the throes of crisis. This is the pressure from within to revive, to re-vitalize a society that is conscious of having lost or nearly lost its accustomed equilibrium and cohesion. A people's determination pushes them to seek something around which to reformulate their way of life. The stage is set for revitalization, then, when a people are able to discover a new paradigm and a new allegiance, around which to reorganize themselves and their culture. Very often the new paradigm, the impetus and pattern for reorganization, will be supernaturalistic in nature.

Anthony Wallace (1956) has described in detail the concept and fundamental processes of what he calls *"revitalization movements."* He points to societies such as the Yir Yoront, in the throes of individual and collective stress and cultural distortion and heading toward extinction that then return to more or less equilibrium and cohesion. Wallace sees this as embodying a "deliberate, organized, conscious effort by members of a society to construct a more satisfying culture" (1956:265). Such a society "revitalizes" by reformulating its worldview and effectively reconstructing its cultural structures to reduce stress, thereby permitting survival.

We may diagram the processes of revitalization as follows:

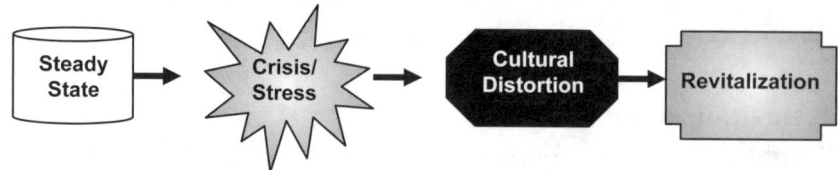

Figure 18.8. The Process of Revitalization

As in our earlier diagram, we begin with a "steady state"—a relatively functional and satisfying cultural *gestalt*, including the presuppositions of a worldview core and the societal organization and behavior that derive from them. As in our earlier diagram, something happens that results in crisis, issuing in greatly increased individual stress and, eventually, in the distortion of cultural patterns. Alcoholism, intra-group violence, disregard of kinship and sexual mores, and psychological states of depression, self-reproach and other dysfunctional emotional reactions occur increasingly, as the inadequacy of existing ways of coping with stressful situations becomes more and more evident.

Widespread disillusionment may ensue, issuing eventually in cultural extinction. Or the society in crisis may *revitalize*.

> A society will work, by means of coordinated actions (including "cultural" actions) by all or some of its parts, to preserve its own integrity by maintaining a minimally fluctuating, life-supporting matrix for its individual members, and will, under stress, take emergency measures to preserve the constancy of the matrix (Wallace 1956:265).

The Characteristics of Revitalization

A revitalization movement is *born from within* a society. As we have pointed out in earlier chapters, genuine cultural *implementation* issues from within. Implementers are insiders. Implementation of any sort—and this is especially true of the radical innovation characteristic of revitalization movements—cannot be imposed upon a society from without. Though it may be catalyzed or advocated from outside, it must be a process "captured" and *owned from within*.

A revitalization movement begins with generalized and profound dissatisfaction with the present sociocultural situation. Dissatisfaction may be precipitated by any number or combination of stressful agents: military defeat, political subordination, extreme economic distress, governmental or social breakdown, volcanic eruption or other natural disasters, epidemics, etc. When people conclude that existing patterns are inadequate for coping with situations such as these, a society may be ripe for a revitalization movement.

A revitalization movement occurs when a society deliberately reformulates a more satisfying cultural system. Its members must recognize the inadequacy of their traditional cultural system—for it has become inoperable. "The world is falling apart" may characterize their thinking. But thinking such as this will not automatically issue in revitalization unless a society wills to survive, and proceeds to define and reformulate a new cultural system capable of integrating within some new *gestalt* the stressful experiences that precipitated the crisis. Their thinking must be,

> Things are falling apart, yes. But we will not let this drive us to extinction. We will reformulate. We will rework our assumptions, our culture, and our thinking. We will survive.

Wallace describes six stages apparent in the reformulation of a new, more satisfying cultural system:

---

1. Individual worldviews (Wallace calls them *mazeways*) are reformulated. New ideas, new presuppositions will be formulated. New perceptions of the world, the meaningful, and the possible will be introduced.
2. This reformulation will be *communicated* from one member of a society to another, with a view towards the "conversion" of as many individuals as possible.
3. The converts are *organized*. A movement is born.
4. The movement *adapts* to the population's cultural and personality patterns in order to minimize opposition and to ensure further expansion.
5. This movement of revitalized individuals precipitates cultural transformation. Programs of social, political, or economic reform may result.
6. *Routinization* of the movement's successful programs ensues. With respect to religious movements, the organized "church" is born.

Figure 18.9. Stages in the Reformulation of a More Satisfying Culture

Finally, we note with interest that Wallace found that *most revitalization movements reformulate around a supernaturalistic idea or core* (Wallace calls it a "religious" core). Thus, the revitalization phenomenon and the fact that so many societies are in some stage of demoralization should be of great interest to cross-cultural witnesses of Christianity. For they provide opportunity for inside Christians to light a gospel "spark" around which a people may formulate a new conception of the world and humankind and bring about the revitalization of a society and its culture.

Examples of Revitalization Movements

Following Wallace's description of revitalization, we find that thousands of such movements have occurred in human history. Major religions such as Islam, Buddhism, Judaism and, yes, Christianity, at the beginning and at the Reformation, are labeled revitalization movements by Wallace, since each sprang up out of situations of social demoralization and resulted in substantial reformulation of individual and group worldviews. Communism would also qualify. In Japan, someone has estimated that more than 23,000 so-called "New Religions" have come into being in the twentieth century alone, "attracting more than 57 million followers" (Hiebert, Shaw and Tienou 1999:357). And the number of such movements in smaller scale societies over the centuries is also large.

In Japan, many of these religions sprang up "after World War I during a period of severe economic deprivation and military totalitarianism," others after the defeat of Japan in World War II. "An estimated ten or twenty new religions are now founded in Tokyo alone each year" (Hiebert, et al. 1999). The background reasons for such an explosion of "New" and "New New" religions are described by Hiebert, Shaw and Tienou as follows:

> [F]ollowing World War I Japan faced an invasion of modernity, a severe economic depression, and a major earthquake in 1923—all of which contributed to a cultural identity crisis. The defeat in World War II, the public declaration by the emperor that he was not a god, the desperate social, economic, and spiritual conditions from 1945 to 1955, and the ongoing invasion of modernity with its secularism and materialism compounded the identity crisis. Buddhism and State Shintoism failed to provide meaningful understandings of life, so the people are presently turning to new religions that combine Buddhist, Shintoism, Christian, and modern themes in new ways. These promise the people hope in a confusing and changing world—health, wealth, success and happiness, and a restoration of good family life by affirming ancestor veneration. The appeal of these religions is that they offer answers to the central questions of folk religion. Moreover, they offer a strong sense of community in small intimate groups (hoza circles) in which people can share their troubles and blessings and in mass ceremonies which affirm their new corporate identity (1999:357-8).

In traditional societies, the many "Cargo Cults" of Melanesia, the Ghost Dance movements of the late nineteenth century in America, the spiritist movements in Brazil and the African Independent Churches are among the best known. More than 10,000 African Independent Churches have been counted, over 3,000 of them with more than three million members in South Africa alone. Most of these have sprung out of African reactions to the perceived threat from missionary Christianity to their traditional worldview values and assumptions.

The Dynamics of Revitalization Movements

Students of revitalization movements point to many similarities between the movements in the various places in which they occur. We have focused on the fact that such movements tend to develop out of conditions of demoralization. But there are many positive factors that need to be present if a movement is to survive—and many of them do not survive. Hiebert et al state that

> Revitalization often begins with a prophet who, in a vision, sees a new world that provides a fresh explanation to life and its possibilities. The prophet has often experienced an abrupt and dramatic change of personality, leading to significant changes in lifestyle, such as the dropping of deep-seated habits like alcoholism. The leader's message of a new worldview generally calls for the destruction of the old world and the emergence of a new utopian society. The prophet is the final authority in defining the message. People are converted and join the movement as followers. A few cluster around the prophet as disciples, and later become leaders who interpret the message and institutionalize the movement. Generally there is opposition from outside, and the leader must devise strategies to face the resistance.
>
> For individuals, revitalization leads to a more active and purposeful life. As increasing numbers of people join the movement, a social revitalization takes place. Relationships are renewed and group action enthusiastically pursued. If the new activities help to reduce stress and restore meaning to the society, they soon become part of the social order (1999:350).

We can see in this description of the rise of a prophet and the start of a movement how closely it parallels the way Christianity started. I would also like us to see the possibility of planting a movement in our day that will develop along these same lines. The continuing success of a movement, however, will require the following five characteristics pointed to by David Burnett. These are unlikely to all be present at the very beginning of a revitalization movement. But they need to be developed over time if the movement is to continue.

> There needs to be a "formulation of a new pattern for the future that will provide the basis of a new worldview." And, as pointed out by Wallace, this is most likely to fit into what we in the West label "religious." The revitalizations brought about by Marxism and Nazism are two notable exceptions.

> "Secondly, the new vision must be communicated to others" in such a way that converts are made. The new vision for the future is proclaimed in contrast to the present situation. Often a new symbol is presented such as a white robe or a staff. "In small-scale societies, the message of the prophet is directed to the entire community." In larger societies the leaders may target only certain people or groups "deemed eligible for the new society."

> Thirdly, the movement needs to "develop patterns of leaders and organization." Many movements die out because they have not developed the necessary organization to continue and grow. If the necessary organizational patterns are developed, however, the movement grows and "tends to divide into two parts: the committed disciples and the followers." The disciples devote themselves to full-time activities such as recruitment, training, developing doctrine, organizing rituals and raising the necessary financial and/or other support. The followers are part-time supporters.

> A fourth necessary activity is to make whatever adjustments are found to be necessary in the original vision(s) and promises, often in response to critics who have pointed out deficiencies. "The teaching of the movement therefore is gradually reworked until it provides a satisfactory answer to a wide variety of issues."
> "Finally, the movement needs to generate a new lifestyle that can provide for the basic needs of the people." In small-scale societies, this lifestyle is taken on by the whole group. In the beginnings of Islam, though Muhammad and his early followers were at first rejected, before long all of the Arab tribes accepted the new religion. "This not only united the various factions, but also revitalized them

into a community with a new religion, mission and lifestyle." Islam, then, like Christianity and Buddhism "broke out" of its original culture (Burnett 2002:147-9).

Renewal

Before we leave this topic, I'd like to point out another application of the revitalization concept. The term revitalization may also be used to refer to the cultural dimension of a spiritual revival. In Christian conversion, for example, the first generation experience typically involves a radical change in worldview and behavior. But the children, grandchildren and great-grandchildren of the pioneers seldom experience the same kind of worldview transformation so meaningful to their predecessors. They inherit the forms, the external accoutrements, of their parents' expression of their faith, but often not enough of its meaning for those cultural expressions to be vital to them.

What was satisfying and integrative for their (grand) fathers and (grand) mothers no longer serves the same function for them. Their cultural experience as a part of that movement, then, usually slides toward disintegration, leading some to remain in the movement but become nominal (=submersion), others to convert to other, often legitimate, expressions of the faith and still others to become disaffected (demoralized) and to abandon spiritual things altogether.

Some, however, discover a spark around which to reformulate their faith and their practice. They may have been brought up "standard" evangelical as I was and come to renewal through charismatic experience. Or, they may simply have moved from a Presbyterian Christianity to a Baptist experience. Or, from Baptist to Episcopalian or even Roman Catholic. At Fuller Seminary we see these changes taking place all the time and students being renewed simply by making such changes. For some, simply experiencing "contemporary worship" regularly or experiencing a new approach to Bible study has brought them into a more vital relationship with God. Such changes may usher people into spiritual renewal/revival from which springs the kind of vital, meaningful experience that led their ancestors to start a movement. Centered around this experience, then, they reformulate much of their behavior and enter into cultural revitalization as well.

Chapter 19

Strategies for Constructive Change

As Christian witnesses, we are deeply concerned that the changes that result from our efforts are the right kind of changes. By "right kind of changes" we mean changes that make it easier to believe and live according to biblical Christian principles.

As we have seen from many examples, not all change is constructive change. Indeed, in our world of rapid culture change, there is much damage done through worldview and culture change.

Change and Choice

We have attempted to present an approach to worldview that recognizes the importance of persons/groups in relation to cultural structures. An important implication of this approach is that *people* change structures, the structures do not change by themselves. Structures change, then, when people choose to change them.

It is, then, personal and group choice that brings about change at the worldview level as well as at the surface level of culture. However, the choices to change at worldview level are often subconscious.

Our Aim—Transformational Change

Our aim is what I will call transformational change at worldview level in directions that will facilitate Christian belief and behavior. Our problem is, on the one hand, how to bring that about within our own worldview and, on the other, how to assist others in effecting such change in the worldviews of others.

We are concerned both that change take place and that such change will facilitate Christian belief and behavior. For we know that worldview change will take place, especially in our rapidly changing world, but that not all change is compatible with Christianity. Nor is all change transformational change.

Though our aim may be fairly clear, however, we need to recognize that there do not seem to be any surefire techniques that will work for every change agent in every cross-cultural situation to effect transformational worldview change. Since transformational change issues from within a society and depends on choices of people, we must be very careful about anything we as outsiders do to attempt to bring it about. Though manipulation of cultural behavior, whether surface or worldview, may bring apparent success in getting people to believe and behave as we want them to, there is often a reaction against such changes at a later time. Such reactions, then, tend to undo or destroy whatever temporary benefits may have been gained.

We found in Nigeria, for example, that when Christian teachers came under government management rather than mission management, several of them took second wives. The mission had prohibited its teachers from having more than one wife, believing that making such a rule was the proper way to assure that the teachers lived in accord with Christian principles. Apparently, however, the forced change of surface-level behavior did not lead to a choice on the part of the teachers to change their worldview in this (and, for that matter, in many other areas mandated by the mission).

Having noted the warnings, however, it is possible to point to principles that can be helpful if followed. Cross-cultural witnesses can learn an *attitude*, or better, an approach, if not a technique. Such an approach can inform and enlighten our ministries and, hopefully, protect those we work with from most of the kinds of mistakes that have characterized cross-cultural witness in the past.

1. An important part of a constructive approach to transformational worldview change can be developed from recognition of the **advocate-implementor** distinction presented in my 1996 introduction to anthropology (chapter 25). This distinction is based on the excellent work of Homer Barnett who used the term *advocate-innovator* (Barnett 1953).

This important distinction enables us to understand that outsiders and insiders play different parts in the process of worldview transformation. Cultural outsiders can participate in the process but need to recognize that the part they play is as recommenders, as advocates, never as those who put changes into practice or implement them. As outsiders, it is not our place to actually introduce and put into effect a change in someone else's culture. Something in the very nature of cross-cultural dynamics makes it that only cultural insiders, those who "own" the culture, are able to genuinely implement change. Those working from outside to bring about transformational worldview change need to be constantly aware of this fact.

Though we as outside advocates can and often do play important parts in the introduction of ideas, we must not overstep our boundaries by trying to do something we do not have the right to do. This means that outsiders (and cross-cultural agents of change will always be outsiders) can only *advocate* change, *witness* to alternative assumptions, values, and allegiances, and *commend* their acceptance.

It can be very destructive when outsiders, no matter how wise they are, attempt to impose even desirable changes on a society not their own. This is especially destructive when the changes imposed by outsiders are in surface-level areas. This, then, leaves people on their own to decide what worldview-level assumptions they will make, usually without the help and outside of the awareness of the outsider(s).

Even if the outsider is aware of what is going on at worldview level, however, the cross-cultural advocate should not expect to control the natural processes of the spread and implementation of a change in another society. Again, we can advocate such spread and innovation. But most aspects of the process are for us to watch and encourage, not to control. In a very real sense, gospel-influenced changes within a sociocultural context that is in the process of being transformed is a matter to be decided between the people themselves and God. The outside advocate should claim no inherent veto power over the process.

2. Another important part of our approach to transformational worldview change is something that should by now be very obvious—that such change consists fundamentally in ***a change of ideas*** (Barnett 1953). Worldview is a mental thing, an idea thing. Transformational worldview change is the changing of "socially acquired sets of ideas [that] exist only in the mind, not on streets, farms, or in places of worship" (Luzbetak 1963:196).

Our strategy, then, needs to be aimed at idea change. Our concern is a concern for what happens in people's minds. *Truly transformational change issues from transformed ideas at the level of worldview.* It is the transformation of worldview assumptions, values, and allegiances, either before or after changes in surface-level behavior, that provide an adequate and lasting foundation for both surface and deep culture change.

3. The ***principles of effective cross-cultural communication*** make a third important facet of our approach. Given the fact that it is the receivers of the messages that determine what those messages mean, it is crucial that we approach the communication of the ideas we seek to get across in a receptor-oriented manner. Though the changes need to be made by insiders, we as outsiders are not to be passive. Nothing said here is intended to keep us from participating in transformational change in other societies. It is only intended to help us to participate in proper ways.

For a start, what we say and do needs to be perceived by our receptors as relevant to their way of life. If we are to communicate effectively for deep level change, it is not enough that our messages be true and important to us. They should be both. But they also will need to be relevant to those who watch and hear us. It is crucially important that the receptors be able to make sense of what we recommend from *within their way of life* and be able to apply it there.

Our aim is to present the truths of Christianity in such a way that our receptors perceive their relevance and applicability to their real, day-to-day life. In order to do this, we will need to investigate thoroughly and experience for ourselves the sociocultural milieu in which we are to labor. We need to ask ourselves, What are these people's felt needs? What are their unfulfilled desires? As these questions are answered, we discover strategic bridges, points of engagement, for the communication of the messages we seek to get across—one of which is that the people we work with are free to make their own choices.

Once we have at least begun to discover such bridges, Jesus Himself provides us with our best model for ministering cross-culturally. Just as He moved from *above* culture to *in* culture, so we are to move from one cultural context into another. The way He operated on this side of the gap He crossed, then, is instructive for us. Following are ten of the points concerning Jesus' communication that I treat in more detail in my book, *Communication Theory for Christian Witness* (1991a).

In presenting these points, I am suggesting that Jesus has showed us not only *what* to communicate but *how* to go about communicating it. If we are to see Jesus' work done properly, we need to do it in His way— incarnationally. The concepts for which He gave His life need to be understood and He has commissioned us to continue to do what He initiated (John 20:21). If we can do our part according to these principles, we will find much greater effectiveness in the carrying out of our aim to assist people toward worldview transformation.

a. Jesus started by becoming a Man and **identifying with** His receptors. In His case, He was incarnated in the receiving society. We cannot become incarnate, but should do our best to enter sympathetically into our receptors' way of life with understanding and empathy, even learning to participate with them to some extent and to share ourselves with them in person-to-person self-disclosure. Our messages are *relational-life messages*, not simply cognitive word-messages and can only really be communicated through close contact over a prolonged period of time between communicators and receptors.

b. While participating in the society around Him, Jesus was **receptor-oriented**. He knew what communication specialists have pointed out—that it is the receptors who decide the meanings of whatever we do in our attempts to communicate with them. His primary concern was that those who heard and watched Him have a decent chance to understand and do something about His messages. To that end He both lived as they lived and spoke a language (indeed, the disrespected Galilean language of His receptors) that they could understand. Furthermore, He used cultural forms (e.g., parables, healings) that would be familiar and attractive to His audiences.

c. An important part of the impact of Jesus' messages lay in the fact that *He gave Himself to His hearers in **two-way communication***. He was out with the people constantly, seldom putting Himself in formalized, monologue situations. His hearers, then, could ask Him questions, challenge Him and interact with Him over every issue. He especially gave Himself to the twelve, training a group who would carry on the ministry after Jesus was gone. He knew what we often don't seem to know—that it is through personal interaction that people are changed, not through monologue lectures.

d. He didn't settle for simply communicating verbally, however. Jesus ***demonstrated the Father***. As He said to Phillip, "If you have seen me, you have seen the Father" (John 14:9). Through healing and deliverance from demons, He employed the power of God to demonstrate the love of God. Through forgiveness and acceptance He demonstrated God's mercy toward people, not sacrificing God's righteousness or going soft on God's right to judge us but showing in human life what God is really like to people who had a wrong understanding of Him. Just as Jesus demonstrated God, then, so it is our task to demonstrate (not just talk about) God in carrying out His purposes on earth.

e. As Jesus communicated, *He **earned, rather than demanded**, the respect He received.* He did not depend on His position or reputation to establish His standing with the people around Him. He spoke and did things that led people to accept or reject Him on the basis of their real-life experiences with Him. For those open to Him, He earned the right to lead them into major paradigm shifts, new understandings of what God is like and what He requires of us. He did not force change, but for those of us who choose to follow Him He earned through life participation with us the right to set for us an example we cannot ignore. We are to do likewise in our ministries on behalf of Jesus—earning the right to recommend and demonstrate changes in the worldview of those we minister to and with.

f. Jesus did not simply approach people in general, *He dealt with **specific people**.* Though His messages were for all mankind, He treated each individual, even outcasts, as important, loved by and acceptable to God.

There is no denying the communicational power of life-specific messages. Again, it is through personal contact that worldview change is effected.

g. Jesus was also specific with His messages. *He spoke to **specific situations***, contextualizing His messages in appropriate and specific ways to meet concrete situations. He spoke in pictures but not in abstractions, focusing more on applications than on generalities. If people are to be led into worldview change, they will often need to see just how the recommended change will work out in their situations. Even when, as in scripture, the applications are to specific life in another sociocultural context, it is easier for receptors to apply the insights in their lives than if the recommendations are given in general, non-specific terms.

h. ***Jesus refrained from information overload***. Unlike our usual approaches to teaching, Jesus regularly gave people enough to chew on but not so much that they were inundated with information, much of which they would forget before they could make use of it. He taught through "life involvement" in a discipleship format. In contrast to monologue presentations of information, this non-formal approach, like learning in families, presents comparatively small amounts of information over comparatively long periods of time with maximum opportunity for practicing the new approaches. Jesus' disciples spent 24 hours a day with Him, observing, listening and practicing their new paradigms. Such an approach maximizes the possibility of transformational worldview change.

i. Jesus' non-formal, discipleship teaching method, with maximum use of stories specialized in ***inviting people to discovery***. Much of what Jesus said and did was difficult to interpret until a person pondered it awhile and figured out what He was driving at. Our tendency is to predigest our messages and to present them in terms of generalizations and implications, leaving the hearers little to discover. Yet meanings discovered have much greater impact than meanings prepackaged and simply delivered, and greater possibility of influencing people's worldviews.

j. *Jesus put great **trust in His receptors***. In spite of the continual ups and downs of His followers, Jesus trusted them, first to understand and then to go out into the whole world to continue the job He had started. He simply said, "As the Father sent me, so I send you" (John 20:21). This trust made men of them. And, functioning in this trust, they continued to learn and change in the directions toward which Jesus had been pointing them.

Biblical Analogies and Examples

The Bible provides us with quite a number of the kinds of worldview change we need to recommend. As we strategize for such change, we do well to focus on the kinds of things our Bible presents as important for the people of biblical times, many of which need just as much emphasis today in our attempts to see transformational change in contemporary people and societies.

Jesus described the "touch" of the Kingdom of God to be like the touch of yeast in a lump of dough (Luke 13:21). This is an image of how transformational change works. It affects the most fundamental level of things, the internal "chemistry" of things, and eventually pervades the entire "lump." Transformational change is change that works from *within*. Transformation seldom comes rapidly or by revolution. It changes the loaf by "leavening," rather than by "blowing it up."

Another analogy Jesus used was to liken the radical changes attending the Kingdom of God to the planting and growth of a seed (Mark 4:26-32). As with yeast, the change in a seed comes *from within*. But notice this further point of analogy: just as a mustard seed, "the smallest seed in the world," can eventually produce "the biggest of all plants" (Mark 4:31-32), so "small" changes in worldview can transform both worldview and eventually the entire culture. The analogy suggests, as well, that for the growth of great shrubs and the transformational change of cultures everything depends upon the selection and placement of the appropriate *seed*.

The Apostle Paul commanded the church at Rome to let God transform them. He also showed us some of the steps we need to take and to recommend to others plus one of the results when he said,

> So, then, my brothers, because of God's great mercy to us I appeal to you: Offer yourselves as a living sacrifice to God, dedicated to his service and pleasing to him. This is the true worship that you should offer. Do not conform yourselves to the standards of this world, but *let God transform you inwardly by a complete change of your mind*. Then you will be able to know the will of God—what is good and is pleasing to him and is perfect (Rom 12:1-2).

The aim for the Christian is nothing short of transformation at the deepest levels. For this to happen, though, we need to "offer" ourselves completely to the only One who has the power to do the job—God. This offer of ourselves is to be like that of a lamb about to be sacrificed, holding nothing back. As that lamb was committed without the ability to turn back, so we are to totally dedicate ourselves to Him and His plan for us. Such dedication, however, requires the choice to refuse to conform any longer to the standards of the world.

As Phillips translates verse 2, we should not let the society around us ("the world") press us into its mold. Building from this commitment and refusal, then, we submit to God for transformation through a complete change of mind (= perspective) that leads to a knowing (= experiencing) of His will in continuous operation in our lives. (The Greek words for mind and knowing are better translated "perspective" and "experiencing," respectively.)

This is, of course, a tall order for mere human beings. And when thought of as recommended for a whole society, we can imagine an incredible number of complications. But this is God's way and must, therefore, be our practice and our teaching. Perhaps the real reason why transformation, either on the individual level or with groups, is so uncommon is because so few do it God's way and with His empowerment.

Our analogies illustrate change. They do not suggest the wholesale transplantation of entire shrubs, but the introduction of seeds. Fully developed, transplanted shrubs are likely to die anyway. Nor do the analogies recommend the blowing up of dough masses with the power of dynamite, but the transformation of the mass with the slower and more penetrating power of yeast.

Let's look a several scriptural examples of teaching aimed at transformation of worldview.

1. *Neighborliness*. Jesus intends the Kingdom of God to be inclusive. There is no room for ingroup-outgroup distinctions that exclude people just because they fall into a certain category. Paul teaches this in Gal. 3:28 where he disclaims distinctions in the Kingdom between Jew and Greek, slave and free, male and female. But how should a society like that of the first century Jews, a society deeply flawed by such biases be challenged to deal with this flaw? Jesus attempted to evoke this radical change by planting a "seed." He took a concept that was very important in first-century Jewish thinking and redefined it, a concept very carefully defined, delimited and protected—the concept of *neighbor*.

"Who is my neighbor?" someone asked. Who comprises the ingroup? Jesus answers by telling the story we know as The Parable of The Good Samaritan (Luke 10:29-37), concluding with the question, "In your opinion, which one of these three acted like a neighbor towards the man attacked by the robbers?" (v 36).

Jesus was, of course, always extremely clever when He answered His critics. In this case, however, He seems even more clever than usual. For He makes two important and unpredictable changes in the presentation, each of which is intended to jolt His listeners at the worldview level.

First, the way the story was going, it looked as though Jesus was going to make a common Jew the hero. This would have made the point He seemed to be driving at quite well. But it was unthinkable to make the hero a lowly Samaritan, one considered an outcast and heretic. This jolted the hearers' sensibilities and drove them to consider what was being taught from a new angle. "Could it be that even an outcast was capable of behaving in a way acceptable to God?" the hearers were forced to ask. We would have to ask such a question concerning those we despise—Liberals, Mormons, Jehovah's Witnesses. The Jews' worldview would have allowed for no possibility of Samaritans gaining God's approval. Would ours? Because their judgment of such people was harsh, they assumed that God's judgment was the same.

Allow such a seed to germinate and the human landscape looks different. So does God's working. Classifying who is "in" and who is "out" no longer seems as important as discovering which people in either category are doing the Father's will and which are not. For, as Peter came to realize,

> God treats everyone on the same basis. Whoever worships him and does what is right is acceptable to him, no matter what race he belongs to (Acts 10:34-35).

But the biggest jolt was yet to come. The original question was a simple one. It was an inquiry about *being*—who is my neighbor? The problem raised in such a question is one of definition, of the categories into which people are classified. It was, furthermore, a question about other people. "As we look over the human universe," the questioner asks, "which of these other people fall into the 'neighbor' category, and are, therefore, to be treated as members of my ingroup?"

But Jesus, in apparently answering the question, plants another transforming seed by changing both the essence of the question and the focus of the classification! For His answer is about *doing*, not being, about how one is to behave in relation to outcasts, not about how one classifies them. His focus is on the worldview category into which the *doer* fits, not on that of the receiver! He does not answer, as expected, the question, Who is the neighbor?, but a quite different question, *Who is behaving in a neighborly manner?* The teaching is not, therefore, concerning the class of people we should treat as neighbors, but concerning the class of people who behave in a neighborly manner.

These are seeds that possess worldview transforming potential. All who heard Jesus that day, and all who hear Him now have to wrestle with the implications of these seeds for our own lives. In the way Jesus handled this (and many other) stories, He planted transformational seeds intended to germinate in individuals and the society as a whole to bring deep level change both in belief and in behavior.

2. *God as Father*. It is impossible for us at our distance in culture and time from New Testament concepts to even imagine the pressure toward transformation of Jesus' use of the term "Father" for God. The Jews honored God at a distance, probably not unlike Muslims honor God today. He was seen good but related to humans only as a king to his subjects—distant, powerful, to be feared, admired and worshiped. But not close, except when He comes to judge and punish. The concept of God as Father is not unknown in OT times but it was certainly rare among the people of Jesus' day.

Jesus deliberately used the term over and over, however, planting the seed of God in a family relationship with us, powerful and secure, to be sure, but on our side. Though the picture is of a Jewish father, not an American one, and thus not quite as close as our ideal of an American father might be, God is still portrayed as One who favors us, loves us, cares for us and can be approached directly. And this was a transformational concept for first century Jews.

3. *When God gets close* ... The Jews of Jesus' day firmly believed that if God got close, it meant sure death. Note the lament of Isaiah in response to his vision of God, "There is no hope for me! I am doomed" (Isa. 6:5). And when, after pulling in two boatloads of fish, it became clear to Peter and his partners that Jesus had power from God, Peter, filled with fear, "fell on his knees before Jesus and said, 'Go away from me, Lord! I am a sinful man!'" (Luke 5:8).

The seed that Jesus sowed with the disciples and the other common people of first century Palestine was to the effect, however, that when God gets close, good things happen. For God is on our side. Only the Pharisees and others who were rebellious and victimizers need fear the closeness of God.

4. *Polytheism*. The early descendents of Abraham believed in many gods. This was, of course, a problem that God had to deal with. He did not, however, attempt to change the belief quickly. Instead, He was patient with His people, carefully but consistently inviting them to focus totally on Him and to change their assumption concerning the existence of many gods to the recognition that there is only one God.

God's patience is such that it is not until Moses' time that we have the command to "Worship no god but me" (Exod. 20:3). And even in that command, God allows the implication that other gods are real. In the commandment, He neither condemns nor approves their belief in other gods. He simply directs their attention to Himself above others. Later in the OT, of course, the very existence of other gods was denied (e.g., Jer 14:3-5, 14-16). But the worldview change occurred slowly over an extended period of time with God applying pressure for change but patient until the people themselves got around to making it.

The real problem, of course, was not that the Jews *believed* in many gods but that they continually fell into the animistic practice of worshiping them. Like animists throughout the world and throughout history, the Jews kept treating the gods of the nations around them as if these gods owned the territory they claimed and, therefore, deserved to be consulted and honored in "their" territory. The true God, of course, allows no rivals. Primary allegiance to other gods, therefore, is not allowed. Thus, God allowed difficulties into the lives of the Israelites when they followed these other gods. But still He blessed them when they were faithful to Him.

Though Yahweh never approved of Jewish animism, He was amazingly patient with His people when they went astray and very merciful to them when they turned back to Him. Israel had a kind of "bungee-cord" relationship with God—close to Him, moving away from Him, snapping back, moving away, snapping back and so on. Their worldview straddled the fence, holding on the one hand to a radical monotheism but on the other to a belief in many lesser gods, to which they continually appealed.

This flip-flopping, however, eventually exhausted God's patience and He allowed them to be taken captive. Yet we learn from scripture that God still has a place in His heart for the Jews and will bring them back into the picture in the last days.

5. **Polygamy**. In the early history of the various Semitic tribes, including Israel, this custom was widely practiced, at least by those in prestigious positions. The Jewish patriarchs, then, continued the custom of marrying more than one wife, a custom that had come down to them from their predecessors. Later, we see kings Saul, David and Solomon following the custom without condemnation from God. Indeed, in 2 Sam. 12:8 where God says, "I gave you [Saul's] kingdom and his wives," God comes very close to endorsing the custom. But by NT times, the custom was virtually dead in Jewish society and is not a factor in the NT, since it never occurred in Greco-Roman society. I believe we can point to the yeast-like influence of God's Spirit over a long period of time as the reason for this dying out of polygamy in Jewish society.

6. ***Judging people in the Kingdom***. In the Parable of the Wheat and the Tares, Jesus has the master refusing to allow his servants to try to distinguish between the wheat and the weeds (Matt. 13:24-30). Kingdom seeds are to grow quietly, as ordinary seeds and plants grow, even while the Enemy's plants are growing—and in the same places. And Kingdom transformation takes place, like bread rises, so slowly it amazes the observers.

We are not, therefore, to try to judge or to sort out the true followers from the false. The apostles were forbidden to use their power even to punish a Samaritan village that openly rejected them (Luke 9:51-56). Likewise, when Peter wanted to use his sword to try to protect Jesus Himself (Matt. 26:51-2). Be patient, He says, even with opponents. Use your power to help, never to hurt—even if they deserve it.

7. ***Slavery***. In the event dealt with in the book of Philemon, Paul had an opportunity to fight slavery head-on but worked more gently. He didn't avoid the issue, but contented himself with sowing a tiny "seed." This he did by counseling Philemon to accept and forgive Onesimus, his runaway slave *as if he were a full-fledged person and with the right to be forgiven*. Philemon had the legal right to treat Onesimus both as a piece of property and as a criminal, exacting on him the harshest kind of punishment, even death. The slave had no rights.

It was into this situation that Paul speaks. He calls the criminal slave "my own son in Christ" (v 10) and, risking everything, sends Onesimus back to his master saying, "with him goes my heart" (v 12). Then he says, "And now he is not just a slave, but much more than a slave: he is a dear brother in Christ" (v 16). Paul sees Onesimus as much more than a slave, and invites Philemon to transform his attitude toward him as well. If, then, the slave is now a beloved brother, Paul could exhort Philemon to *"welcome him back just as you would welcome me"* (v 17)! It is a matter again of planting a "seed," a seed that would germinate in Philemon's heart (and the hearts of countless others who would read the account) and eventually bring about the transformation of the institution from within—by redefining the worldview assumptions at their core.

8. ***Marriage relationships***. First century Greek patterns of marriage and family relationships did not easily square with the inclusive and egalitarian nature of the emerging Kingdom of God. Though contemporary westerners, in keeping with their own values, frequently go to unwarranted extremes in describing what they believe to be the inferior position of women in Greco-Roman and Hebrew societies, it is true that love was not necessarily expected between spouses. So when Paul says "husbands love your wives" and even goes to the extent of advocating that husbands give themselves for

their wives "just as Christ loved the church and gave his life for it" (Eph 5:25), he was planting a transformational "seed" of great significance.

Wives were equally *persons*. From the Christian perspective both were created in the image of God, created equally responsible before Him and equally dignified. From the perspective of either Greco-Roman or Jewish society, the personhood of women was likely to be ignored. For the ideal, at least in Greek society, was for a woman to carry out her duties in such a way as to attract as little attention as possible. Large numbers of women were, of course, treated reasonably well, some very well. But whenever there is potential competition between segments of society and one segment has the opportunity to gain an advantage over the other, there are plenty of the privileged ones who make unloving use of their advantage. So many husbands did, in fact, rule their households with despotic abandon.

How should the situation be challenged and changed? Again, by speaking to the core of the problem, the worldview assumptions people hold, assumptions that lie beneath the unChristian behavior and permit it. This was Paul's intention when he exhorted husbands as well as wives to "be subject to one another out of reverence for Christ" (Eph 4:21). Paul went right to the heart, recommending not only fair treatment, but love, and the kind of love that patterns itself after the love of Christ. As mentioned, to twentieth century ears the command to love one's wife may have little impact (not that we do it well, but we know we should). But to first century ears the command must have startled many. For it flew in the face of much of the practice of the time, the practice of ignoring the personhood of women. The command was a seed, yeast, designed to take root and grow in the soil of worldview, and eventuate in radically transformed societal patterns and relationships affecting entire cultures.

9. **Other examples**. We could point, further, to Jesus' attack on the assumption that the blindness of the man born blind was a payment for his or his parents' sin (John 9), His choice of people to call "blessed" in the Beatitudes (Matt. 5:3-11), His teaching concerning loving enemies (Matt. 6:43-47) and literally hundreds of other seeds Jesus and other biblical personages sowed. The New Testament is full of such seeds, new conceptions, new paradigms and definitions of reality, new understandings of what is possible and what is not, of what is vitally important and what in the end is of little importance at all, "seeds" that when fully grown produce radical transformations.

But these few examples suffice for our purposes. They illustrate the fundamental principle of transformational worldview change: the process of cultural transformation is best pursued through the planting of new worldview assumptions in peoples' minds. The Christian agent of change should concentrate on planting a few crucial seeds, worldview seeds, rather than attempting vainly to replace or transform surface level behaviors. *Both people and cultures are transformed from within!*

Some Important Concerns

As we strategize to bring about transformational worldview change, we must remember that our primary concern needs to be for what happens to the *people*, not simply what happens to the cultural and worldview structures we are seeking to change. It is people that God loves and it is people who are likely to get damaged if the changes in which they are involved do not go right. Whether, then, we focus on what happens to individual people or on groups of people, we need to concern ourselves with several conditions that can either enhance or disturb the process of worldview change.

1. People in our day are under a great deal of **stress**. The rapidity of culture change forces a certain amount of accommodation of worldview assumptions whether or not these are chosen or even wanted by the people involved. This factor, added to the changes at the surface-level, results in the unpredictability of cultural activity that pushes people into the condition known as *culture stress* (also known as culture shock) even within their own culture (see Toffler 1970).

People suffering from culture stress, then, often tend to gravitate toward the culturally familiar, becoming very conservative in order to keep their balance. This can happen either to the receiving persons or to the advocates of change or to both. Receptors under culture stress will often resist any further suggestion of change. Advocates under culture stress often find themselves recommending approaches they are familiar with in their home country, whether or not these are appropriate for the receiving people.

Sufficient stress impinging upon a society at the level of its worldview, will result in what Wallace (1956) calls a "crisis situation." How much stress it takes to produce such a worldview crisis we don't know. It is a sad state of affairs, however, when it is Christian witnesses who are responsible for the development of such stress and its contribution to social breakdown.

Yet, such stress can also be a major factor in opening people to new answers to their worldview questions. People who, under great stress due to conditions in our day, have moved far down the demoralization road toward extinction, may be wide open for new approaches. Thus Sharp has suggested with regard to the demoralized Yir Yoront,

> In such a situation the missionary with understanding of the processes going on about him would find his opportunity to introduce his forms of religion and to help create a new cultural universe (1952:22).

A gospel "seed", properly placed at the right time might be most effective in providing the "spark" around which a demoralized people might revitalize.

2. A second characteristic that needs to be taken into account is ***the interrelatedness of the parts of a culture and its worldview***. Changes in core worldview presuppositions will ramify throughout an entire culture and all of its subsystems. This is true because each part of the system interrelates with each other part throughout the system. Even apparently "superficial" changes produce a "ripple effect" throughout a culture, affecting both surface and deep level structures. Extreme damage has been done by cross-cultural agents of change who, whether through ignorance or neglect, have not considered the interrelatedness of the many parts and aspects of a cultural configuration.

3. Such interrelatedness of the parts of culture with each other and of surface-culture with deep-culture worldview results in cohesion of the total configuration. If a society is to survive in spite of the stress, it will be because it is able to maintain what Tippett has labeled its ***ethnic cohesion***. Though difficult to define and identify, it is this cultural glue that keeps a way of life together. As we have seen, the Batak were able to maintain their cohesiveness even during radical change while the Yir Yoront were not. Societies that revitalize, then, are able to do so because they are able to regain whatever cohesiveness they may have lost. Under pressure, the more cohesive a culture is, the more able it will be to hold together, or at least to retain enough of its "sociocultural glue" to provide the basis for revitalization.

In spite of the intangibleness of this factor, we who witness cross-culturally should do our best to assure that what we recommend contributes to the maintaining or rebuilding of ethnic cohesion. Where that cohesiveness has been damaged, we should seek to introduce things that will repair and build it. Where the culture is still functioning well, we should do our best to refrain from threatening that functioning. God wants every people to be a people of God, supported by their cultural structuring and secure both in their relationship to Him and in their relationships with each other.

4. People need, then, to ***maintain a sense of balance***. Some degree of equilibrium, some sense of stability, is essential for the normal operation of human societies. It is easy under stressful conditions for a people to become

unbalanced. In our day, the lure of material goods is often combined by a people with their spiritualistic assumptions to produce a caricatured way of life that is neither satisfying nor even intelligible to those who seek to live by it. When change comes too rapidly, people have no opportunity to properly absorb and integrate the changes with what they retain of the old ways.

As we work with people in the throes of such destabilizing factors, we should be concerned that our efforts contribute to balance rather than pushing people to greater imbalance. Even good change, coming either in wrong ways or too rapidly, becomes bad change. In many cases, we are in a position to help people rebuild a balance they have lost.

Strategy for Cross-cultural Workers

In strategizing to reach people with Christian messages, here are several general suggestions. We will discuss more specific suggestions in the following chapter.

1. It is important to **study the receptor group** to discover what things in their sociocultural context might provide possibilities for worldview change and what things will likely be hindrances. A detailed discussion of hindrances and facilitators of change can be found in chapters 16 and 17 and in Kraft 1996. The following guidelines and questions may be helpful.

- Observe.
- Ask questions.
- Attempt to discover what is changing, what is not and why.
- Look for felt needs and areas of dissatisfaction.
- Look for opinion leaders and discuss with them what they think can be done.
- Seek to discover if the people are open to change or closed to it.
- If they're open, are they open in all areas or just in certain areas?
- Or have they been swept off their feet by changes they feel powerless to control?
- If so, has this made them less open to change in spiritual areas for fear they will lose out there as they feel they have in other areas?

Questions of this sort need to be raised. An important purpose for a chapter like this is to enable us to ask them more intelligently. Another set of important questions relates to what part we can play in the situation. Often we can help most by helping people evaluate the changes they are making and sometimes encouraging them to reject certain things or to slow down the process. Often the changes being made are not so bad, but the process is going too fast. The people are off balance, not because the changes are necessarily bad ones, but because they are happening too rapidly. Our primary task often is to support them by helping them to recognize what's going on.

To do this, we need to develop informed policies designed to enable us to help rather than to hurt the people God has called us to minister to. Love must undergird all we do. But love without understanding them and their situation and of the possibilities and limitations of our position is deeply flawed. We need to recognize and work with suitable innovators (opinion leaders), to win their confidence and support, to deal with felt needs and, in short, to apply all the insight and principles we have been learning to the tasks God leads us into.

2. In line with such insight, we need to **assign ministry personnel strategically** with the aim of applying a maximum amount of helpful influence in spite of the limitations of our resources. Placing personnel where things are happening rather than where things are not happening is ordinarily the reasonable thing to do. Strategy considerations should include such questions as

- How does change take place?
- Who is receptive?
- To what approaches are they receptive?
- What hindrances and helps exist in the present personnel and strategy?
- Who are the opinion leaders?
- How can they be reached?
- What are the implications of the answers to such questions for the assignment of personnel and resources?

A realistic appraisal in these terms of the actual situation needs to replace any tendency to simply assume that God will bless whatever we do if we are sincere enough. This, then, needs to be followed by what McGavran calls "hard, bold plans" to correct and improve the ministry.

To illustrate, McGavran cites an example from Zaire (now Congo) in which a mission worked in two different tribal groups, one on either side of a river. The mission wanted to make sure they were treating each of these groups equally, so they assigned an equal number of staff to each group. Over a given period of time, however, the church membership in one of the groups grew from 3,000 to about 30,000 members, seriously overtaxing the personnel and resources allocated to that group. On the other side of the river, though the church there also started with about 3,000 members, it only grew modestly over the same period of time.

McGavran raises such questions as, Did the mission do the right thing to treat the two groups equally? Should they not have recognized that the timing was right for one group and have used most of their forces with the group where the results were happening, rather than trying to keep equal influence in both groups? (McGavran and Wagner 1990).

3. Our strategy should include the ***study and use the social mechanisms by means of which information and influence flows***. Reading and courses in the area of communication can be very helpful for this purpose (e.g., Kraft 1991). What kinds of mechanisms are there and how can they be used? In some situations the gospel has been propagated effectively because Christians have used gossip as the main mechanism. They are "gossiping the gospel."

One communication study sought to discover who in a housing project talked to whom and when. It was found that people talked to others in their same building and to those in the next building on the same side of the street but seldom, if ever, to anyone across the street. The main vehicle for the flow of information was the talking that took place between the ladies as they hung their clothes out on lines hung between the buildings. Getting the Christian message into this channel could be very important to its spread. The planting of the message would, however, have to be done separately on either side of the street.

On one of my visits to Japan I was told of a strategy some of the Christian ladies employed to bring their husbands to Christ. They found it very difficult to communicate the gospel directly to their husbands and judged that such an appeal would have to come from another man. One of the ladies with her husband who was a Christian, however, ran a small grocery store. So they worked out a clever strategy. When the non-Christian husband of one of the women was at home, she would find some reason to send him to the shop to buy something. Once he had gone, then, she would telephone her friend at the shop, alerting her to the fact that her non-Christian husband was coming. The lady at the shop would then make sure her husband would be at the counter, in hopes that he would be able to engage the non-Christian husband in a conversation about spiritual things.

These and similar strategic considerations need to be at the forefront of our minds as we engage in presenting Christian messages with a view toward transformational worldview change. To continue our discussion of strategy considerations, we now turn to more specific approaches to each of our three worldview types.

Chapter 20

Reaching Peoples of Three Types

In chapter 11 we opted for a broad classification of worldviews into three types in terms of their orientation in the causality dimension. The reader will remember that these three types are Theistic, Animistic and Naturalistic.

What I seek to do in this chapter is to suggest ways that might be productive in reaching people in each of the types. As we look at these suggestions, though, let's not forget that the basic requirement is prayer. Prayer plus insight can effect wonders. Sometimes God uses insight without prayer but it is much more effective with prayer. Don't forget.

Since animistic causality is the most common, we will deal with that first.

Animistic Causality

As we have indicated in chapter 11, the essence of animistic causality is their focus on the realm of spirits. Most animists believe in a High God who is conceived of as good and positive toward humans. Often He is regarded as the Creator of the universe but not actively involved at the present time. But His position as Creator is not the attribute in focus for animists. Rather, He is most notable as the Source of spiritual power.

On one of my trips to Papua New Guinea, I was assured by the missionaries in a given area that the group of people they worked with had no concept of a High God. Not believing this, I requested the opportunity to meet with some of their people to ask them about this. When we met, I asked where their father had gotten his power. They answered, "From his father." "Where, then, did his father get his power?," I asked. "From his father," they answered. "Where did your great-great, ever so great grandfather get his power?," I asked. After a long pause, one of the ladies said, "I heard once that when my ancestor wanted more power, he climbed the highest tree in the forest and talked to someone up above him and came down with more power." "Could it be that this was God that he talked to?," I asked. "Of course," they answered.

They did indeed have a concept of God, but the missionaries had asked the wrong question. They had asked, "Who created the universe?" and gotten no help in their quest to discover their people's concept of God. Many of the world's peoples aren't much concerned with who created the universe but are very concerned with who gives power. To learn about an animistic group's concept of God, then, we need to ask power questions, not creation questions.

Regardless of how they see God, though, it is the spirits that exist between the High God and humans that are believed to be able to cause great inconvenience and harm. Many of these spirits are believed to control the areas they inhabit and need to be treated with the kind of respect granted at the human level to the kings and chiefs in authority over the people and places they control. Other spirits roam more freely. Some of these are believed to be the spirits of dead ancestors. To counter the potential harm these spirits could cause, animists seek to honor them and appease them through sacrifices and other rituals designed to keep them happy. This is a reasonable approach, given their worldview presuppositions.

Given such worldview presuppositions, I believe we do well to respect the logic of animists, whether or not we agree with how they behave. They live in a world of spirits and it should not surprise us if they know a lot about how the spirits behave. Though the way animists respond to what they understand is in many ways inaccurate, their understandings are often very instructive.

We also need to note the fact that there are many similarities between animism and Christianity. Animism is, I believe, one of Satan's most clever counterfeits. Among the major similarities is that their inventory of spiritual beings and techniques is very similar to ours. Biblical Christians, too, believe in a High God with an intermediate spirit world between us and God, populated by spirits that may be positive or negative toward us. They usually see such spirits as powerful, below God but, like God, able to be in relationship with humans. They also usually see, as does scripture (e.g., Dan. 10:13, 20), that some spirits are in charge of territories. We and animists also agree that spirits can inhabit humans.

A major difference exists, however, in the way we approach spirit reality. Though animists are primarily concerned with and in fear of the activities of the spirits, we Christians know that we can appeal directly to God, through Jesus Christ, to engage His power to protect us and to control the activities of evil spirits. This difference in our presupposition in this area and theirs, then, points to the major change that needs to be made in animist thinking and the primary focus of a strategy to win them.

Following is more on these subjects plus a list of concerns and techniques designed specifically to assist us in witnessing to animists:

1. As mentioned, ***helping converts from animism to look to God rather than to the spirits*** both for guidance and for protection is the big challenge. We see in the OT that Israel continually returns to appeasing and relying on the spirits rather than on God. Perhaps they think God is too slow in answering their petitions. Or maybe they don't realize that honoring the spirits means sacrificing their relationship with the true God to whom they return when things really get tough. The OT is a veritable gold mine of insight into the struggle the Jewish people experienced between the allegiance they purported to have to the true God and their constant tendency to fall back into animism.

It was the slowness of God to answer that the ladies (pastors' wives) of Truk gave as their excuse for consulting the spirits when my wife asked them why they continued the practice. They knew that God is more powerful than the spirits but when there was an emergency, they felt they couldn't wait for Him to answer. So they would appeal to the spirits. And they didn't seem to realize that receiving favors from satanic spirits hurt their relationship with God. But the missionaries who had brought the gospel to them considered Trukese understandings of the spirit world to be mere superstition, not to be taken seriously. So the people, though pledged to Christ, continue to practice their traditional divination and other animistic practices away from the gaze of the westerners.

Where animistic people experience God as a God of power, however, able to control the enemy spirits and their disruptions, things are quite different. There are frequent power demonstrations, with people getting healed and freed from demonic infestation. People learn in experience that God is a God of power as well as a God of love. They learn by experience that God is the true healer, whether or not He chooses to use medicine. The animistic worldviews of converts to Christianity get transformed through experiencing God's power, however, not just by hearing about it. Missionary advocates need to learn this lesson and be in the forefront of leading converts to work in God's blessing, healing and delivering power to demonstrate the greater power of God.

2. To begin to deal with the transformations that need to take place, a first step for Christian witnesses should be to ***discover what God is already doing in their midst***. God started His major thrust for winning humans back to Himself by reaching into animism to approach Abraham. We are told that Abraham's father, Terah, was a worshiper of other gods (Josh. 24:2). We might guess, however, that Terah was on a quest to discover the true God and that he passed this desire on to Abraham. We don't know how many other animists God has been able to bring into the fold either in early times

or more recently. I would guess there have been many.

We read of Melchizedek (Gen. 14:18-20; Heb. 5-7) and Jethro, Moses' father in law (Exod. 18) and others in the OT. Indeed, the OT is written with the problem of animism constantly in view. Israel was continually lapsing back into animism, in spite of all that God had done with them. The Baal gods were animistic gods inhabiting much of the territory God had given to Israel.

But, as Henri Maurier has pointed out, paganism (=animism) can and should be utilized today, as it has been in the past, as the context within which God draws people to Himself. Maurier writes, "the grace of God has never deserted mankind and ... even among the pagans, some men have responded to it" (1968: xii). He holds that

> men are able to reach a certain knowledge of God (Rom. 1:19-20). They carry within themselves the lights of the natural law (Rom. 2:14-15). They are judged according to their consciences and what they have been able to know (1968:5).

If this is true, animism provides pointers toward the truth, the places at which God starts His saving process for those who pay attention to those pointers. If Maurier is right, then, there is enough information in animism to alert people to their need for a relationship with the true God. As I have said elsewhere:

> We have usually assumed discontinuity and antagonism between Christianity and paganism. Yet it is *within* paganism that God stimulated Abraham (and countless others whose stories are not recorded in the Bible) to faith based largely on the knowledge they already possessed. In the Old Testament mention is made of a few of those outside Israel who apparently came to saving faith without contact with the people of God. Among them were Melchizedek (Gen. 14:18; cf. Ps. 110:4; Heb. 7), Abimelech (Gen. 20), Jethro (Exod. 3), Balaam (Num. 22-24), Job, and Naaman (2 Kings 5). These came within paganism rather than within Israel to the same faith-allegiance to the true God that those saved within Israel experienced. In the New Testament, too, we get a glimpse of such a possibility when, in Acts 18:24-19:7, we see that there were roving bands of John the Baptist's disciples making converts without, apparently, even having heard of Jesus (1979:254, 2005a:198).

An example I omitted in the above quote would be the Magi who came to worship the baby Jesus (Matt. 2:1-12).

3. Another strategic consideration would be to **take seriously what animists have learned about the spirit world**. Though some, perhaps many, of their strategies may be wrong, their insights can be very helpful to us. For this is the world they live in—a world of real spirits. And we westerners, who are very ignorant of this part of reality, have a lot to learn from them.

Animists' understandings of the territoriality of Satan's kingdom, for example, should be taken seriously. Their belief that there are spirit entities governing the territories in which they live seems to correspond with what we've been learning about territorial spirits, what Daniel 10 suggests and what Eph. 2:2 and 6:12 seem to be pointing to. Animists can also give us a great deal of insight into the ways in which shamans interact with the spirit world. Such insight tends to confirm the theory that rules that God has made for His interaction with humans apply to Satan's interactions as well (see Kraft and DeBord 2000).

As mentioned in chapter 11, it is the territorial understanding of the rights of spirits that enabled the Assyrians to stop lions from killing their people who had settled in Israel (2 Kings 17:24-28). When the Assyrian king took the Israelites into captivity, he resettled the land with people from several areas he had conquered but they were attacked and some of them killed by lions. The Assyrian analysis of the situation was that, because they had all been deported, there were no longer any Israelite priests in the land to teach the newcomers how to worship "the God of the land." When, then, one of the priests who had been deported to Assyria was sent back to teach the people how to worship the Lord, the lion attacks ceased.

Sacrifices, rituals and other expressions of allegiance to spirits appear to empower them to do more of what they are called on to do. Blood sacrifices especially seem to give great satanic power to evil spirits. This fact seems to suggest that the blood sacrifices God ordered the Israelites to offer in His name were vehicles both of obedience to God and of empowerment of God. Jesus' sacrifice, of course, was the blood sacrifice to end all blood sacrifices empowering God to defeat Satan once and for all.

A fascinating example of satanic empowerment in response to a blood sacrifice occurs in 2 Kings 3 where Israel is at war with the Moabites. The war is going well for Israel and its allies Judah and Edom. God is on their side and they push the Moabites all the way back into their walled city. Not even the attempt by the Moabite king and 700 of his best swordsmen to break through Israel's lines to get help from Syria was successful. At that point, though, the Moabite king decides to sacrifice his oldest son, the heir to his throne, on the wall of the city, unleashing an incredible amount of spiritual power on Israel. Israel then runs home, thoroughly defeated. What they had all but won on the ground, they completely lost when they were hit by the spiritual power produced by a blood sacrifice to the Moabite god Chemosh (2 Kings 3:27). Unfortunately, Israel did not remember they had the right to call on the power of the true God to defeat even the high level of spiritual power that came at them through the blood sacrifice of the second most important person in the Moabite kingdom.

Though such examples as these may seem strange to us, animists understand at least certain of the rules behind them. We can, then, learn some things from them if we are careful not to imitate their mistakes, especially their mistakes in strategy for dealing with the spirit world by focusing on the spirits rather than on God. With the direct access to God given us through Jesus, we need not be focused on keeping spirits happy.

4. ***Animists are spirit power-oriented***. It is incumbent upon us, therefore, to learn how to understand and work in spiritual power. We western Evangelicals have been strong on reasoning with people to bring them to Christ. Reasoning, however, seldom is convincing to animists, though, through western schools and other western influences a westernized Christianity has come to flourish in many animistic areas among those who choose to westernize. Such Christianity, however, leaves the majority of the traditional peoples of these areas completely untouched. In South Korea, for example, though the Christian population in westernized churches has grown large, approximately 75 percent of the population is still animist.

In many parts of the animistic world (e.g., Africa, Latin America, Melanesia) it may appear that our rationalistic approach has been effective even among the non-schooled. If we investigate, though, it becomes apparent that it is usually more the impression made by western technological achievements than our reason-oriented witnessing that has led to conversions in these areas. And behind this impression lies their worldview interpretation that people who can do such miraculous things with technology must have command of great spiritual power. Animistic peoples with very little understanding of the human inventive processes by means of which the technological achievements came about easily attribute them to insight gained spiritually.

It is spiritual power to heal, bless and to overcome the power of demonic spirits that have held animists captive for generations, that really speaks to them. As in the early days of the introduction of Christianity into the Polynesian islands, it is the demonstration of the superior spiritual power of

Christ that attracts animists. In an excellent book entitled *People Movements in Southern Polynesia* (1971), Alan Tippett records many instances of such power encounters that resulted in the conversion of large numbers of Polynesians. Tippett notes that "the Samoans believed that the only real and effective way of proving the power of their new faith was to demonstrate that the old religion had lost its powers and fears" (1971:164).

Typical of such power encounters was the case of a Samoan chief named Malietoa. He listened to the missionaries over a period of time, decided to convert and eventually announced his intentions to his people. But "in a power-oriented society, change of faith had to be power-demonstrated" (1971:81). Malietoa's conversion would not have had any impact on his people if he could not demonstrate that Jesus is more powerful than the gods he and his people had been worshiping. In order to prove the validity of his conversion, then, he arranged for a public act of desecrating the symbol of the god they had been worshiping. The symbol was a kind of fish, so:

> On the appointed day the forbidden food was set before Malietoa. The incident created tremendous excitement. Friends and distant relatives had come from afar to witness the daring spectacle. Many expected all who ate to drop dead there and then. Those of the family who were to share the experiment were in some cases so frightened that they doused themselves with oil and salt water as possible antidotes to the [power] of the [sacred fish]. But Malietoa and a few others with him took no precautions. As a power encounter it had to succeed or fail on its own merits. ... They ate. The excitement subsided. No evil befell them. Thereafter for many the [Christian message] was true and the [god of the sacred fish] was false. ...
>
> This incident led many to dispense with their personal [gods] or break the taboos, and to put themselves under the instruction of the Christian teachers. ... Their gods had been discarded, evil spirits had been cast out, and the houses swept—and were empty (1971:164-5).

Such nineteenth century examples point to the kind of thinking we are dealing with in animistic, power-oriented societies today. There may or may not be large numbers of people coming into the Kingdom at one time as there were during this time in Polynesia. But it is still true that the most effective way to bring about a change of faith among animists is to demonstrate that Jesus is more powerful than their gods and spirits.

5. Something to note about animists is that they frequently are ***beset by fear***. There are a variety of fears to recognize, most of which are felt to involve the activities of malevolent spirits. These spirits, however, may have been sent by humans seeking revenge for acts perceived to be antagonistic by the people who sent them. Or they may be understood to be ancestral spirits who have been hurt either while still alive or after death.

In addition to their fears related to spirits are the fears concerning health, safety and relational amity just as likely to be important to Euro-Americans as to non-westerners. Whether the fears are spirit related or not, though, they are often very intense.

Presentation of the Christian message in relation to the fears of animists can be very effective. The Christ who is the remedy for their fears will often be more attractive than the Christ who saves them from their sins.

6. One of the things that becomes clear when we begin to understand spiritual power is that we ***cannot fight Satan with knowledge alone***. Power cannot effectively be countered by knowledge or even by truth. It must be countered by power. Our western evangelical Christianity has been strong on knowledge of the parts of biblical truth we have focused on. We have felt, therefore, that we are being effective when we simply point out the errors of other religions, cults and occult organizations such as New Age, Freemasonry, Mormonism, Jehovah's Witnesses and the like. If we don't deal with the spiritual power behind these faiths, however, we have only done part of our job.

Because western missionaries have brought a knowledge-based Christianity without providing a substitute for animistic power, a large percentage of the Christians of the world are practicing what I call "dual allegiance" Christianity. They may attend church regularly, but when they need spiritual power, they go to the traditional practitioners (shamans, priests, healers) because they do not find in Christianity the power they feel they need. They, thus, are maintaining their allegiance to the traditional animistic power sources as well as to Christ. This is the kind of syncretism God most strongly condemned in the OT. I don't know how God will judge those affected by this perversion, brought about innocently by well-meaning but power ignorant missionaries.

When we come to understand and know how to deal with spiritual power, it becomes clear to us that converts from the religions or from cults or occult organizations, are carrying demons. They need, then, to be set free if they are to be able to grow in their new faith. Typically, we teach them a bit of knowledge as they join our churches, but do not deal with the power conflict inside them. That conflict can only be dealt with by working in the power of Jesus to set them completely free from satanic captivity. We must fight satanic power with the power of Christ if animists are to be converted and freed.

7. Among the most difficult problems in working with animists is dealing with assumptions and practices that God has condemned such as the ***assumptions underlying the magical practices*** of animists. The essence of magic is the expectation that when certain things are done, spiritual power results are automatic. Thus, certain rituals, certain phrases, certain ways in which the Bible is used are all considered to assure protection and/or bring blessing. Many are the converts who regard even so-called Christian practices as magical. The Bible and Bible verses are frequently used with magical expectations (even as they often are by Christian conservatives in the West).

Our aim should be to help people to focus on God as the Source of power rather than leaving unchallenged their assumption that power inheres in rituals and/or the Bible. The habit of western Evangelicals of making statements concerning "the power of the Word" leads both themselves and their converts from animism to regard the Bible as magic. In reality, there is no power in the Word, only in the God who stands behind and powerfully uses the Word.

8. ***Animists commonly practice divination***. This is the practice of claiming spiritual power to discern the future or the will of God/gods. The enemy, though he doesn't know the future, is very ready to deceive people into thinking they are getting a true revelation. Various techniques are used in divination such as throwing bones or marked stones to see how they land or interpreting the liver or entrails of animals. In our area of Nigeria, the shamans interpreted the marks made by tiny crabs walking in sand.

God is totally against divination and necromancy, a form of divination that involves seeking information concerning the future by consulting the dead. The OT scriptures are full of condemnation of divination (e.g., Lev. 19:26-28, 31; 20:6; Deut. 18:9-14; Is. 8:19; Mal. 3:5) and necromancy (e.g., Deut. 18:11; 26:14; Is. 8:19; 29:4).

Again, our approach should be to help people focus on God, the Giver of insight, rather than on techniques designed to control and automatically bring supernatural insight. It is out of a relationship with God that true insight comes. God gives spiritual gifts to certain people, enabling them to see or hear what He wants to reveal but He does not allow us to control Him. Those who have these gifts, then, are often the same people who had such gifts under satanic control but were deceived into thinking that they controlled the spirits rather than vice-versa. Gifts of prophecy, word of knowledge and wisdom plus the scriptures are God's ways of providing insight and leading. Converts from animism need to learn, though, that it is God who is to be in control, not us and that divination is satanic deceit and, therefore, needs to be abandoned.

Hinduism

Hinduism is a special form of animism of great significance both because so many people practice it and because so many of its tenets are gaining acceptance in the West.

As pointed out in chapter 4, Hinduism is centered in belief in one indescribable force, Brahman, that is impersonal and without any attributes. They hold that all life is of the same essence (monism) and that people go through endless reincarnations, determined by karma, that can end through enlightenment. The world is seen as illusion (maya), though earthly reality includes nature, spirits and demons and is unpredictable. Since all is relative, Hinduism tolerates almost any views and there is no absolute morality. The highest good is detachment from material and sensual pleasure, moving into oneness with the cosmos.

There are so many differences between Hinduism and Christianity that one is tempted to see no bridges. However, beneath the doctrines are people searching for something solid to attach themselves to. Some would like to escape from the endless reincarnations and the relentless force of karma. I have heard also that a message of forgiveness stirs many. We should search for felt needs among Hindus. They need freedom from a desperately harsh system and may be open to ministries that work in the power of God to bring such freedom.

New Age

As pointed out in chapter 4, New Age has its roots in animism, naturalism and pantheism. As Sire says, New Age reflects every aspect of animism, though often giving it a naturalistic twist—or demythologizing it by psychology. One important facet of animism that should give us clues as to how to reach those into New Age is their quest for spiritual power.

Though there are several varieties in this emerging perspective, several generalizations can be made. For one, the Self is the prime reality. Yet, the cosmos, while unified in the Self, is also manifested in the visible universe, accessible through ordinary consciousness, and the invisible universe of the Mind, accessible through altered states of consciousness. "Cosmic consciousness" is the core experience. In it, ordinary categories of space, time and morality tend to disappear. Reincarnation is also commonly believed.

New Age seems to be more a quest than a settled system of beliefs and practices. And people on a quest are often open to seeking in new places. An approach to Christianity that is new—not the same old thing they have been reacting against—could possible interest New Agers. Like most people, they are probably looking for something solid. We have what they need if we could put it in the right clothing. Again, as with all animists, spiritual power, especially power greater than their own, can be impressive to them.

Theistic Causality

As mentioned, though most animists believe in a High God as well as in intermediate spirits, there is a defining difference of focus. The focus of Theistic Causality is on the High God, with or without a focus on intermediate spirits. The focus of Animistic Causality, by contrast, is on the intermediate spirits, with or without a belief in and attention to a High God.

The "book" or orthodox versions of Christianity, Judaism and Islam provide the major examples of this theistic understanding of causality. Orthodox Christians and Jews who obey the Bible and Muslims who obey the Koran appeal directly to God/Allah when in need. Though they may acknowledge the presence of intermediate spirits, their approach is to seek God/Allah's assistance rather than, like animists, to appease the spirits.

Unfortunately, most of the adherents of these monotheistic faiths are theists in name only. We often refer to them as "folk Muslims," "folk Jews" or "Christopagans." These are really animists, choosing to focus more on the intermediate spirits than on the God that their book points to.

On one occasion, I visited a Roman Catholic cathedral in southern Mexico on a weekday. On entering, I became aware of five or six small groups of people sitting in circles on the floor of the cathedral. There were candles, pictures and other paraphernalia used in divination and a leader in each group working with these items to appeal to the spirits for assistance. Though the pictures were of Christian saints and holy water and other items were of obvious Roman Catholic origin, what was going on was definitely not Christian. And similar kinds of animistic practices are to be found in folk Islam and folk Judaism.

Any Christian witness to people such as these who claim to be theists but are really animists needs to take account of both their animistic worldview and of the fact that they see themselves as theists. For example, though folk Muslims are really animists, they have an often fierce loyalty to Islam and to the prejudices Muslims have against Christianity. They are, however, often open to witness through the exercise of spiritual power in Jesus' name and may even convert if they don't have to be labeled by that hated name "Christian."

The following points can be made concerning a witness to theists:

1. We can assume they are *focused on the High God*. Though the God of Judaism tends to be perceived as judgmental and the God of Islam as radically distinct and distant from his creation, fatalistically determining everything—good or bad—according to His will, we do have this as a starting point. And both Jews and Muslims consider their God to be the same as that of Christians.

2. And each of the great monotheistic faiths believes God's highest revelation is in a book with **some overlap in the books they hold to**. Both Jews and Christians, for example, hold to the inspiration of the Old Testament, though their interpretations often differ. And the Koran advises its readers to read the Christian scriptures. Furthermore, the Koran gives a higher position to Jesus than to Muhammad in at least five areas: Jesus is virgin born, He's sinless, He's a miracle worker, He will come again and He will judge at the Last Day. None of these things are claimed for Muhammad.

3. The rigidity of orthodox Jewish and Muslim understandings of law can leave their adherents with *a large void* when it comes to satisfying the inner needs of the heart. And even evangelical and especially liberal Christianity can be deficient in satisfying hopes raised by Bible study and/or preaching for a close relationship with God. When there is a consciousness of the need for a more meaningful relationship with God than that provided by merely practicing the rituals of these faiths, there is often opportunity for effective Christian witness. The discovery of renewal movements within these traditions or a mystic movement such as Sufism within Islam might provide valuable points of contact with the adherents of such movements.

4. The *belief in angels and demons* within these traditions can serve as a springboard if Christian witnesses are able to work in spiritual power. The books of each of these monotheistic traditions present a God who is at war with the forces of evil. Unfortunately, the traditional forms of these faiths usually act as if that war does not exist, leaving them open to all kinds of satanic activity. Where the adherents of these faiths become aware of demonic activity in their midst, however, those who know what to do

about it have great opportunity for witness. Power demonstrations usually speak powerfully to those aware of spiritual warfare.

5. God reaches many Muslims through **dreams, visions, healings and deliverances**. Each year, after the Muslim pilgrimage, as well as at other times we hear reports that some have had dreams and/or visions of Jesus beckoning them to come to Him. We can pray that God will continue to do this. When people are looking for healing and/or deliverance, then, even Muslims sometimes direct them to Christians, since Jesus is presented in the Koran as a healer and miracle worker.

6. An important thing to remember when witnessing to Muslims or Jews is that **the name "Christian" is often a very bad word**. Current associations with that name suffer from memory of a regrettable past history. Muslims see those called Christians as the supporters of Israel and the Crusades. They also tend to assume that Hollywood decadence is a function of Christianity. We are finding today that many Muslims in Bangladesh and other places are open to Christ as long as they don't have to be called Christians. Names such as "Messianic Muslim," "Jesus Muslim" or even "Jesus follower" seem to work fine, though. Similarly, Jews who follow Jesus like to be called "Messianic Jews" rather than Christians.

7. A large-sized **problem** arises in witnessing to non-Christian theists when the best we can offer is a kind of **secular Christianity**. According to 1 Cor. 1:22, Jews are looking for miraculous signs. So are Muslims. When, then, the Christianity we offer is powerless, dependent in witness on reason, and offering only secular forms of healing, agriculture, education and everything else, power-oriented people are not impressed with our faith in spite of the good impression made by our technology. It is true we can offer love, peace and perhaps other personal characteristics and that these have attracted some. But without the ability to work in the power of God, what we offer is far less than Jesus and His early followers offered and far less attractive to those looking for manifestations of a powerful God.

8. Among theists who need to be won to Christ are multitudes of **nominal Christians** who think they are Christians but have no real relationship with Christ. Whether these be those brought up in Liberal Christianity or those who have misunderstood Evangelicalism, they are often tangled up in the misconception that Christianity is a set of rules and standards and that God will accept anyone who is trying to live close to those standards. They may have no concept of Christianity as the relationship with God that Jesus modeled and offered to us.

In presenting the true gospel, it may help to recognize and take advantage of the fact that many today are hungry for a meaningful relationship. By relating to them ourselves and then pointing to Jesus we may be able to help them meet this deeply experienced felt need.

9. Another felt need that connects with many is the ***need for peace***. Many have been opened up to seeking Christ by a question such as, "Do you have real peace inside?" or "Are you experiencing the kind of peace deep inside that you expected in life?" People today in a wide range of societies are remarkably unpeaceful and, often, quite aware of this fact.

In working with demonized people I have discovered that our enemy, Satan, though good at counterfeiting such godly characteristics as love, joy and even faith, cannot counterfeit the kind of peace that God gives. Recognizing this fact should give us one more way of approaching people, whether they claim to be Christian or not. For those who claim to be Christians but have no real relationship with Jesus, the fact that the promise of peace has not been fulfilled can provide a powerful incentive to listen to an offer of real, deep peace.

10. In considering the possibility of witnessing to nominal Christians, we might look at ***the contrasts Sire draws between dead orthodoxy and the approach he labels "theistic existentialism."*** I repeat a part of the chart in chapter 4 to point to some of the contrasts between a Christianity that is oriented toward obeying rules and a faith that is "relationship-oriented":

Concept	Oriented Toward Obeying Rules	Relationship-Oriented
Doctrine	Depersonalized	Personalized
Sin	Breaking a Rule	Betraying a Relationship
Repentance	Admitting Guilt	Sorrowing over Personal Betrayal
Forgiveness	Canceling a Penalty	Renewing Fellowship
Faith	Believing a Set of Propositions	Committing Oneself to a Person
Christian Life	Obeying Rules	Pleasing the Lord, a Person

Figure 20.1. Rules /Relationships

Though there is great truth in each of the columns above, I believe the relationship column is both more in line with the true intent of scripture and closer to what most of the peoples of the world, including nominal Christians, are really looking for. To the extent that this is true, a presentation of Christianity with a primary focus on the relational aspects is likely to be more effective than a focus on the obeying-rules orientation.

Naturalistic Causality

As we all know, the commitment to naturalistic science as virtually the only path to truth has for several generations thrown western societies into a morass of non- and anti-supernaturalistic interpretations of every aspect of human experience. This makes what we may call "secular humanism" the real faith of most westerners, even of many who claim to believe in God and may call themselves Christians. Naturalistic cause and effect with a focus on human achievement and an incredible faith in chance serve, then, as the rule of life.

Finding the weaknesses in this worldview orientation is less difficult than breaking through the very deep commitment of people to this faith, especially since most have been taught that science is fact rather than faith. The lack of satisfaction many recognize within themselves, however, often opens opportunities for discussion of a more meaningful option. Such discussions are most likely at times when life caves in on secularists or when such things as weird dreams or the experience of demonic presences begin to convince the person that there is a reality beyond what science can deal with.

1. The first thing to consider, then, in seeking to witness to naturalists is whether there may be ***unexplainable occurrences*** or happenings that a naturalistic approach cannot deal with satisfactorily. Accidents and deaths, dreams and other events that cannot be explained naturalistically can provide opportunities for witness to meanings that cannot be derived from mere chance cause and effect.

Many are beginning to doubt that we only know what we can learn through the physical senses. They are even doubting that reason is the only way or even the primary way to truth. These doubts are pushing many into skepticism. But many are searching. And those who have the will to consider Christianity, an area written off by many as obscurantist, outdated, over-ritualized, even irrational, can often be reached with new forms of Christianity.

2. One of the characteristics of our day that can often be helpful is that there are ***forms of Christianity today that do not fit into the stereotypes*** mentioned above. There are Christian groups that are doing things that are relevant to the life of contemporaries. I have recently been working with an organization that ministers on university campuses. The titles of various meetings scheduled by this group show a concern for relevance that many have not found in traditional churches. Such topics as evolution, sex and dating, handling money, relating to roommates and the like, all related to Christian themes, encourage students to see Jesus as up-to-date and His teaching as valid for today.

Contemporary music with Christian lyrics is a major draw for some, though many secularists are still suspicious of anything that gets too emotional (unless it is a football game). Churches that meet on Saturday evening or Friday evening rather than on Sunday morning may also attract some. And casual dress, rather than dress up, also helps.

3. As with most ways of looking at causality, an approach to secularists can be very effective if it involves **demonstrations of spiritual power**. Science has been looked to as the way to explain things for so long, it shakes naturalists out of their comfort zone when things happen that they cannot explain. It is exciting to see the looks on the faces and to hear the exclamations of unbelief of Christians who are basically secular when they experience or observe a genuine healing. I remember clearly the shock expressed in several ways by an evangelical pastor whom God had relieved of a demon of fear one noon as we waited for our food in a restaurant. "It's gone!" he said, over and over, incredulous at what God had done, and betraying his lack of faith that there was any hope of gaining freedom from the lifelong problem he had been experiencing.

Such hopelessness in the face of deep-level problems is characteristic of large numbers of people in this category. Secular answers, even those based on medical or psychological insight often do not work. Neither do many of the answers given in church. Prayer often does, though.

Recognition that there is a spiritual world beyond the physical, however, is not limited to Christians. Many are abandoning at least some of their naturalistic assumptions in favor of New Age assumptions. There now are doctors and psychologists (not to mention a fair few pastors) who have moved into New Age supernaturalism in their quest for more power than science can provide. These, of course, can be approached as recommended above for those in New Age.

4. Weaning secularists from their faith in chance can be either difficult or fairly easy. *Many are questioning that things happen only by chance*. This aspect of a naturalistic worldview dies hard, however, even for those who have committed themselves to a Christian position. The difficulty of overcoming chance as the explanation of choice may not be a major deterrent, though, at least at first. Many western Christians get along fairly well with a good bit of internal contradiction in this area.

Moving from belief in a God-created but basically mechanical universe to a God-created and God-sustained universe may be more difficult. I like to ask people, Who keeps the Law of Gravity working? Often, people have not thought of the fact that God is actively, rather than passively, involved in keeping the universe going. In addition, then, and probably more difficult for converted naturalists to handle, is the fact that there are an incredibly large number of invisible personal beings, both good (angels) and evil (demons) populating and affecting the universe. So there is more than simple machine-like activity in the universe and in our bodies as well. That these invisible creatures can cause things not explainable from a view that sees the universe and our physical bodies as machines can be a stretch for people brought up in secular humanism. But this is an important area for witness.

It can be important for Christian witnesses to look for doubt on the part of secularists that everything takes place by chance. As mentioned, many are beginning to question this assumption. Yet many refuse to go to church or to pastors to deal with their questions since Christians often seem just about as secular as those who openly espouse secular humanism. A vital faith, as opposed to "normal" Christianity, can, however, make a lasting impression on those who have learned to ignore supernatural activity and explanations.

5. Similarly, it *may be difficult for secularists to move from the closed universe mentality to seeing the universe as open*, with God at the top, always ready to move in to do miraculous things. Even many Christians and Christian denominations have been infected with a closed universe assumption to the point that they deny that miracles happen today. The way to work on getting such an assumption changed is, of course, to demonstrate that God is still in the miracle-working business.

Some of the findings of astronomers may help also. It is my understanding that astronomers are saying that the universe is expanding, that its size is not fixed. Perhaps this is another indication that God is there and still at work.

6. **Relativism** is frequently a part of a naturalistic perspective. Indeed, it is not uncommon for relativists to make absolute statements concerning the existence and spread of relativism. We need to admit the validity of relativism at a certain level but to advocate the parallel existence of an absolute God. The "big R" REALITY, "small r" critical realism approach is my favorite way of dealing with this understanding. Though we cannot force people into believing in both kinds of reality, such an approach makes sense to many. It certainly has a better chance of being accepted than the denial of relativity some Christians flaunt.

For those who have heard of cultural relativity, it can be important to help them to make a distinction between cultural relativity and ethical relativity. The former is taking everyone's cultural practices and values seriously, though not necessarily approving of them. This means that we accept other people's customs as valid for them, though we are responsible to live according to our customs. Ethical relativity suggests that since other people in other societies have a certain practice, we are allowed to do that same thing, even though we are in a different culture. This is just the opposite of cultural relativity and is unethical.

Recognizing that there are two realities enables us to recognize the validity of cultural relativity or, better, "sociocultural validity," but to deny the irresponsibility of ethical relativity. Sociocultural validity takes seriously and respects a people and their customs, whether or not we approve of them. This respect for a people and their way of life, then, forms the basis from which any recommendations for change are to begin. Ethical relativity holds that "anything goes" in any culture, no matter what the "home culture" cultural rules may be. This is a totally irresponsible approach to life based on a faulty understanding of how to use our knowledge of cultural data.

7. A problem many naturalists have with Christianity is that **they perceive us as being unfriendly to the universe**. This is not necessarily so. We can be just as concerned about the excesses we and others have perpetrated against the physical environment as non-Christians can. We, however, can see this as stewardship, motivated by our relationship with God, not a concern for the environment simply for its own sake or the sake of our children, and certainly not stemming from a worship of nature.

8. Many naturalists have been **infected with Communism**. Though the fall of Communist governments in recent years helps our position, many with Marxist ideas are still not convinced that their perspectives are wrong, especially their belief in economic determinism. Though there are, I think, good arguments against economic determinism, I would suggest not arguing the point. Indeed, I would allow for the possibility that one might be a committed Christian and a Marxist (though not an atheistic Marxist) when it comes to economics and culture in general. I would seek, rather, to deal with the person's relationship with God, if he/she is at all open to that subject.

9. Whatever the specifics of a naturalist's problems with Christianity, a key to all witness is *positive relationships*. People respond to personal interest and friendly relationships. Caring for those to whom we seek to witness and extending to them help when they need help and friendship at all times can result in great attractiveness for a Christian perspective. When, then, personal interest is combined with spiritual power for healing, blessing, deliverance and the meeting of other felt needs, the results can be truly gratifying.

People are looking for love. Often it is the spending of time with people that conveys love and concern. These attract people, especially if there is no ulterior motive involved. An atmosphere of love and personal concern provides the best context within which to witness to naturalists or anyone else.

Postmodernism

As with these other positions, a review of my summary of Sire's presentation in chapter 4 will be helpful. Postmodernism, the latest form of naturalism, seems to be a retreat from any position that claims to know anything for sure. As Sire points out, Postmodernists question what has been regarded as reality. They deny any connection between what we think and say and whatever is actually there. We can tell stories and construct truth as we go along but any meaning is simply a construction, not something we discover.

The relativism and nihilism of this perspective makes it especially difficult to deal with. Again, though, there is nothing like a demonstration of the breaking into our world of a good God who heals and frees to alert people to the existence of a Reality beyond our stories. Reason often will not get far with those immersed in this deceit. Power might. Love and personal concern also might. I believe it to be a universal that people down deep are looking for a relationship with God. Postmoderns are undoubtedly looking for this relationship as well in spite of this intellectual smokescreen.

Conclusion

I have tried in this chapter to assist us in learning how to witness to people caught in each of these three broad categories of worldview causality. Whether or not any of these suggestions will be effective, of course, depends on the will of the person(s) approached. Some are open, some seem closed. Not even the best techniques will work with someone who is closed. Yet, even the worst techniques can be successful with those who are open. I hope that prayer plus these and other insights throughout this book will bring success. Without the prayer, don't count on the technique alone.

Chapter 21

Wrapping Things Up

We have now completed this study of worldview for Christian witness. By now I trust you readers have agreed with me that this is a vital study for those who seek to bring people to change their worldview and allegiances in the process of embracing Jesus Christ as Lord and Savior.

I expect the reader has come to agree that the most difficult problems to deal with in Christian witness are worldview problems, both in the witnessing process and in the growth process intended to proceed from the initial pledge of allegiance to Jesus. This being true, I pray that the results of our study will contribute to greater effectiveness in recognizing and dealing with worldview-related problems.

In this concluding chapter, I want to highlight several of the findings I feel to be the most important. These summarize the implications of worldview study for missiology.

People and Culture/Worldview

It has been a major concern of mine that we distinguish carefully between people and the cultural structures in which we exist. It is *people* who do cultural things, not culture itself. And it is *people* that God loves and wants to come into a relationship with Himself. It is *people*, then, that we seek to reach and *people* who need to change.

All other considerations, including our concern for worldview, need to take a back seat to our concern for *people*. It is to *people* that we appeal. It is people that we seek to help in the process of their movement to maturity.

We have noted, however, that people live in culture, behaving largely in habitual ways in terms of the cultural script they have been taught. We are like actors in a drama, usually following that script but for various reasons deviating from it. When the script for some reason isn't adequate to handle some circumstance, we improvise and may make the changes permanent. New things may come into our lives that the old script wasn't designed to deal with, so we make changes. Or someone else may have changed something in his/her script necessitating an adjustment on our part.

Part of this book involves an analysis of part of my own story. In order to deal with unexpected experiences in my Christian life, I was faced with the need to make changes in my basic assumptions concerning God and His activities in the human realm. Much of the book involves making us aware of the structuring of worldviews and how to use the insights into that structuring to reach the people God wants us to reach.

But whether the focus is on my or someone else's experience as an individual or whether it is on the more technical aspects of our subject, the aim has consistently been to enable us to get beyond the cultural structuring to the people God wants us to reach.

Critical Realism

We have taken a critical realist perspective in this book, asserting that there are two realities labeled REALITY and reality. So much of our world has moved toward absolutizing relativity that it is important that we work from a balanced view. We must not deny that there is a lot of truth in relativistic understandings of much of reality. But we must not give up the fact that where there is relativity, there must be something absolute for the rest to relate to.

We lose nothing in our discussions with those who have gone overboard with relativity if we admit that cultural life is relative. But we give away the store if we submit to their contention that we create our own gods and that one god is as good as another. A universe like ours peopled by complex creatures like humans cannot have gotten here by chance, generated from nothing by forces that themselves came from nothing. As a current roadside billboard puts it, "Big Bang? You've got to be kidding!!" signed, GOD. There has to be a God beyond any human concept of Him. He exists, whether or not our concept of Him is accurate. It is to Him that the world is relative.

Yet perception is reality here on planet earth. And worldview is the major factor in individual and group perception. So it is this reality in which we live and which we have to deal with in Christian witness. We must, then, take seriously both "capital R" and "small r" realities.

Learning About Worldview

We attempted to learn what we could about this thing called worldview.

- We learned that worldview is made up of assumptions concerning reality, including assumptions concerning what to value and what to commit ourselves to.

- We learned that worldview is structured as the deep level of culture—not separate from culture but a part of it.
- We learned that most of worldview is subconscious for most of the people influenced by it.
- We learned that worldview may be seen as a lens or model, or as a script on the basis of which people interpret and respond to the reality they perceive.
- We surveyed two non-anthropological and four anthropological approaches to worldview and found Sire's and Naugle's non-anthropological approaches and each of the four anthropological approaches helpful.
- We learned the differences between worldview and religion and that communicating Christianity should be a worldview matter, not a religion matter.
- We learned, though, that the major complications in cross-cultural communication lie in differences of worldview assumptions.
- We learned something about the functions of worldview.
- We learned something about worldview universals, those areas of life represented by worldview assumptions in all of the world's societies.
- We learned that the most important worldview universals to understand in the communicating of Christianity are the causality universal and the person/group universal.
- We learned that a people owns its worldview as one of its most precious possessions.
- We learned (I hope) that there is no such thing as a thoroughly "Christian worldview" but that there are "Kingdom Principles" that God expects us to make a part of the worldviews of every Christian.
- We learned that it is important to understand not only the worldview of the people we go to but also our own worldview and the worldviews underlying the biblical passages we work from.

A Focus On Causality

We chose the area of causality to focus our attention on and produced a typology that divides worldviews into three categories according to their predominant view of supernatural beings and powers. We noted that most of the world fits into a very broad category called "animism," while other portions of the world may be labeled "theistic" or "naturalistic."

Animism, with many varieties, may or may not hold to a High God but when there is a High God, he is usually seen as distant and relatively inactive and uninvolved with his creation. It is the spirits between that High God and humans that must be watched. They are usually seen as capricious and ready to cause problems if not treated right. The primary aim of animists, therefore, is to keep these spirits happy. In this category, we find Hinduism, Shinto and most of the people who call themselves by the names of world religions but who practice what we sometimes call "folk Islam," "folk Buddhism," "folk Christianity," "folk Judaism" and the like. New Age and Eastern Mysticism also fit largely into this category.

Theism, on the other hand, is seen as an approach to causality that focuses on the High God. There is usually a belief in spirits, but God is seen as in control of them as well as of the material and human worlds. Under this category we lump the "book" or orthodox versions of Judaism, Christianity and Islam including many liberal and conservative varieties of each. Biblical Christianity is one of these varieties.

Naturalistic causality, then, treats supernatural beings and powers as mythic and ignores or denies them. The focus of naturalists, often called "secular humanists," is on the material world as if this is the only world we need to be concerned with. Various varieties of materialism, socialism and communism fit here as do atheism, agnosticism and not a few liberal and even evangelical Christians as well as orthodox Buddhism and Confucianism.

At various points in our treatment, I have suggested that the major concern of most of the peoples of the world is spiritual power. A powerless Christianity, then, is unlikely to be attractive to most, especially if they get to read the Bible and discover that following Christ wasn't meant to be a powerless experience. The incursion of secularism into western Christianity, however, has reduced much of the Christianity we in the West have experienced to logic and reason plus some love and compassion but minus the spiritual power Jesus modeled and said we would continue (John 14:12).

If we are to be as effective as the New Testament witnesses were, then, we need to practice and advocate a powerful Christianity that shows Jesus' love through acts of power as well as through caring relationships. Jesus said that if we have faith in Him, we will do the works that He did (John 14:12). Most of western Christianity has, however, allowed secular paradigms to govern their approach to spiritual power and ceased to do the works of Jesus. If we can get back to the powerful Christianity Jesus modeled, we will both become more Biblical and more attractive to the majority of the societies of the world whose primary concern is to achieve more power to handle life.

Strategy

We spent several chapters on strategy. We first asked, "What are we taking?" Hopefully we learned from that chapter that, beyond our concern for knowledge and truth, two additional crucial dimensions of Christianity are relationship and spiritual power. I tried to point out the overbalance on knowledge and our understandings of truth that we in the West have engaged in and propagated. This has had disastrous effects on the understanding and practice of Christianity both in the West and cross-culturally.

Relationship, the most important of these dimensions, has often been relegated to being merely a byproduct of knowledge, resulting in spiritual starvation for many. And the power dimension that was so prominent in Jesus' life and ministry is often lacking altogether. It is incumbent upon us, then, that we experience and seek to communicate the whole biblical message, rooted in the experiencing of a close relationship with God and the freedom that comes through the application of the power of the Holy Spirit. "Knowledge-about" Christianity is neither fully biblical nor transforming, resulting in widespread nominalism both at home and abroad.

An important part of our strategy, then, must be the assessment of the obstacles and opportunities resident in the worldviews of the people we seek to reach. These I have related to the universals.

We have also dealt with principles for change, including scriptural examples, and suggestions for approaches to each of the types of assumptions concerning causality.

What Now?

This is the end of what I have to say here except to express my hope and prayer that whatever insight you may have gleaned here may be of great help to you in following the lead of the Holy Spirit in whatever ministry He has called you to.

The purpose of this book, as I hope you have discovered by now, is not simply academic. We do academics for a greater purpose—that God may use such insights as these in the hearts and minds of you, His chosen servants, to enable you to make of your ministries much more than you and He could have made of them without what He has been teaching me over the past several years.

I see my task as an attempt to participate in God's ministry through you. He alone can connect the things discussed here with wherever you are and my prayer is that He will do just that. Each of you have come to this study from a different place, with different backgrounds and different needs. May God connect at least some of this with wherever you are so that you can be more of what He intended for you to be in the ministry to which He has called you.

I leave you, then, with a very familiar verse in what for many of you will be a new and fresh translation. The verse is Prov. 3:5 rendered in the Good News Bible:

Trust in the Lord with all your heart. Never rely on what you think you know.

The point I want to make from that verse is that you should trust the Lord, not your knowledge. If there is anything to learn from this book it is to ask a lot of questions because there is a lot that we need to know that we don't in working with people that God wants to draw to Himself. So, trust Him, not me, not this book, not your present knowledge. But with your trust in Him GO FOR IT. And may this book help.

I launch the book into your life with my prayer that God will bless you richly and, through you, that He will bless many others.

Appendix A

History of the Concept of Worldview in American Anthropology

Introduction

Serious students of human behavior have long recognized the fact that there are basic, largely unexamined, assumptions underlying that behavior. Though these assumptions have only recently been labeled "worldview," their existence has been pointed to in various ways for centuries and are now spoken of in popular circles as well as among academics. Philosophers have often indicated such a recognition, some in Germany even labeling it "view of the world" (German: *Weltanschauung*).

Michael Kearney, in his excellent text entitled *World View* (1984), to which we will refer repeatedly, speaks of two German culture historians as examples of those who have dealt with antecedents of our present concept of worldview. The first is Jacob Burckhardt who in 1860 in a book entitled *The Civilization of the Renaissance in Italy* attempted to write a new kind of culture history in which he explained such diverse things as the festivals, dress styles, etiquette, folk beliefs and science of Renaissance Italy in terms of one paramount theme--individualism. As Barnouw has said, "To find an index of 'individualism' in such disparate areas as fashion, crime, and the writing of biography was a brilliant departure" (1963:30) (Kearney 1984:24).

Though this analysis of medieval Italy was probably in many ways oversimplified, it was an attempt to find a worldview-level unifying theme. We find Benedict and others attempting a similar type of analysis in the 1920s and 30s.

Another early advocate of a kind of worldview approach was Oswald Spengler who attempted to find a single unifying theme in any given culture in terms of which the people of that society would deal with borrowings from other cultures. He believed that "The way in which a people reject alien cultural traits or borrow and transform them tells us something about their basic values. ... [He] saw an underlying world view as responsible for such transformations and rejections" (Kearney 1984:24). In a way similar to the approach of Ruth Benedict, Spengler characterized modern western culture as "Faustian,"

> concerned with planning and history, and by a desire to dominate space and seek mastery. Spengler pointed to the invention and widespread use of clocks and chimes in bell towers as reflecting a concern with the passage of time. Western musical instruments such as the organ, a "space-commanding giant," were expressive of a desire to fill infinite space with sound. Western mathematics similarly revealed this Faustian tendency with its irrational numbers, decimal fractions, negative numbers, all unrealized by the Greeks. ... He also drew similar conclusions from drama, art, and even language. ... In architecture the Faustian feeling for depth and the infinite was expressed in soaring Gothic cathedrals which contrast with low, flat Greek temples (Kearney 1984:25).

Given these early European attempts to deal with what we are calling worldview, by far the deepest penetration into an understanding of worldview has come from American anthropologists. Kearney sees a connection, saying,

> The tradition of Germanic idealist scholarship that produced Burckhardt and Spengler (and against which the young Marx and Engels reacted ...) was carried into American anthropology by the immigrant ethnographer Franz Boas ... where it culminated in the concept of culture (Kearney 1984:25).

Though European and British anthropologists tended to go in a different direction, with Boas, the "Father of American Anthropology," there was a concern from the start to discover the "underlying patterns" or "configurations" that are hidden under what we see on the surface of culture (see below). Our primary attention is, therefore, focused on the development of insight into worldview within American anthropology.

There are within American anthropology, several "streams" that have contributed to the perspective here presented. Present worldview theory grows out of the work of the various contributors to these streams. Their contributions are briefly described below to provide a backdrop for the materials in these chapters. These theorists have greatly influenced the concept of worldview as it is presently applied in missiology. Their impact on missiology has been direct, largely through the influence of Paul Hiebert and myself.

General Anthropology

Several anthropologists can be listed in the "general" category, as opposed to the more specific streams that follow. These made important contributions to our subject matter, largely either by providing foundational insight for those who were more focused in on worldview study or by identifying some area that was later dealt with more specifically by someone else.

Franz Boas

Franz Boas (1858-1942), though born in Germany and trained in physics, was in most respects the founder of a distinctively American anthropology. As founder and chairman of the nation's first anthropology department, at Columbia University, Boas both established his own approach to the study of the peoples of the world (mostly for him American Indians) and got to train the first and second generations of professional anthropologists in this country.

Breaking away from the evolutionary and "armchair" approach to the study of non-western peoples prevalent among continental European and British anthropologists, Boas studied people in their own contexts and with a concern to describe them in their own terms rather than in terms of some grand scheme such as the supposed evolutionary development of mankind. The concern of the armchair anthropologists was the study of the development of *culture* (in the singular). Boas' led American anthropology into a concern for specific *cultures* (in the plural).

This concern led him and his students first to study the surface level phenomena of cultures and then to seek to find underlying, unifying principles, what he called the "underlying patterns" in terms of which people lived. It was this latter quest that led to an interest in what we call worldview.

Beginning as an ethnographer, he believed situational conditions influenced the mental state. Out of Boas' work grew the conditions that led to the study of worldviews. Boas and his disciples attempted to reconstruct the cultural history by compiling elements of a worldview, though they didn't use this term. The Boasians demonstrated that each cultural area had distinctive elements that made it unique and at the same time provided an integration within the culture for that group of people.

Edward Sapir

Edward Sapir (1894-1939) was probably Boas' brightest student and certainly the most creative of the early American anthropologists. At least three current anthropological specialties trace their beginnings to his seminal thinking and writing: anthropological linguistics, ethnopsychology (including the culture and personality school treated below) and ethnohistory. The first two of these figure in the development of worldview study.

Sapir helped move early twentieth-century American anthropology away from its fascination with the forms of various customs to a look at the deeper level of ideas and assumptions underlying those forms. His concern was to discover "those general attitudes, views of life, and specific manifestations of civilization that give a particular people its distinctive place in the world" (Sapir 1924, in Mandelbaum 1949:311). We would say that Sapir's interest in "general attitudes" and especially in people's "views of life" was an interest in what we call worldview. He sometimes referred to this as a "world outlook."

Sapir has been accused of an overly deterministic view of the influence of language on culture. In one of his most famous quotes, he said,

> Human beings do not live in the objective world alone, nor alone in the world of social activity as ordinarily understood, but are very much at the mercy of the particular language which has become the medium of expression for their society. It is quite an illusion to imagine that one adjusts to reality essentially without the use of language and that language is merely an incidental means of solving specific problems of communication or reflection. *The fact of the matter is that the "real world" is to a large extent unconsciously built up on the language habits of the group. No two languages are ever sufficiently similar to be considered as representing the same social reality. The worlds in which different societies live are distinct worlds, not merely the same world with different labels attached* (Sapir 1929, in Mandelbaum 1949:162, emphasis mine).

Sapir was not simplistic in his understanding of the relationship between language and culture, however. As Nigel Lemon says,

> In spite of the tone of this passage, Sapir was not arguing for the complete determination of thought by language, and in other sections of his writings he emphasizes the interactive relationship between

language and culture. Language is not only a potential determinant of such worldviews but is also a reflection of them (1981:202).

Alfred L. Kroeber

Another of Boas' students was Alfred Kroeber (1876-1960). As a long time professor of anthropology at the University of California, Berkeley and the author of a major anthropology textbook, Kroeber made important contributions to anthropological theory and to the training of a generation of anthropologists. One of Kroeber's major concerns was the study of the ideas underlying certain customs and the ways in which these ideas changed throughout the course of history. His study of the changes in clothing styles and his search for what he called "super-styles" are classic.

Kroeber departed from Boas and mainstream American anthropology by embracing and developing what we call a "superorganic" view of culture. He felt that culture was more than simply structure (my position) but that it is like an organism, with a life of its own. Such a position implies that human behavior and the assumptions underlying it are largely determined by this force called culture.

In articulating his position, in a major article entitled, "The Superorganic," Kroeber said,

> The mind and the body are but facets of the same organic material or activity; the social substance--or unsubstantial fabric, if one prefers the phrase,--the existence that we call civilization [culture], transcends them utterly for all its being forever rooted in life (1917:212).

Note our discussion of this view that culture is superorganic in chapter 5 where we deal with Paul Hiebert's approach to worldview.

Adamson Hoebel

Hoebel (1906-1993) still another of Boas' students, taught for many years at the University of Minnesota. Paul Hiebert studied under him there. Hoebel's view of worldview focuses on what he calls "postulates." These are largely implicit basic propositions, much like Opler's themes (see below). Postulates are of two kinds: existential and normative. He says, cultures are not simply ways of doing, or of organizing societies. They also define the nature of the world, of man (existential postulates), and of what is to be sought after and what is to be avoided (normative postulates or values) (Hoebel 1972:557).

In general, however, worldview is

the life scene as people look out upon it. It is the human being's inside view of the way things are, colored, shaped, and arranged according to his cultural preconceptions. The planet we live on, a world of physical objects and living things, is by no means the same world to all peoples. Indeed, a simple description of the most basic observable components of this world (the sky, the land, water, trees) by a member of one culture might prove totally unintelligible to a member of another (Hoebel 1972:542).

The Linguistic Tradition

The linguistic tradition grew out of the work of Edward Sapir who early became concerned about the interaction between linguistic variables and psychological reality. I believe he was actually noticing worldview but attributing the things he saw to language. Though my perspective on worldview is broader than that of any of these linguists, they have heavily influenced me and a key to understanding my approach is a clear understanding of the linguistic input.

Benjamin Lee Whorf

Whorf (1897-1941) was an insurance adjuster whose interest in the influence of language on cognition (and thus in what we call worldview) was, it is said, at least partly influenced by the fact that as an insurance adjuster he sometimes had to dole out insurance money to the relatives of people who accidentally blew themselves up by lighting matches too close to "empty" gasoline drums. The fact that they defined something as dangerous as a drum full of gasoline fumes as "empty" and, therefore, safe, intrigued Whorf and started him on a career of studying what he, following Sapir, considered the influence of language on thought. Specifically, Whorf concluded that it was the influence of the English language that misled people by classifying these drums as "empty" because we English speakers focus on visible things when in fact they were full of dangerous fumes that we ignore because they are invisible.

From this beginning, Whorf became fascinated with the study of linguistics, took courses with Sapir and began to apply his brilliance to discerning the conceptual contrasts between what he called "Standard Average European" (SAE) languages and Hopi, an American Indian language spoken by a small group of people living in the southwest United States. The Hopi have a radically different way of conceptualizing reality and Whorf wrote extensively about the contrasts between their linguistic categories and those of SAE.

With regard to time, for example, the segmenting of time into units as if it could be measured like a stick in such expressions as "a long/short time ago," (compare a long/short stick) or treating it as if it were like food or money that can be wasted ("waste time"), saved ("saved time"), or spent ("spend time") are concepts that would be virtually unintelligible to the "Standard Average Hopi" of Whorf's time and to many other traditional people with concepts of time similar to that of the Hopi. For, according to Whorf, Hopi has no words, grammatical forms, constructions or expressions that refer directly to what we call "time," or to past, present, or future, or to enduring or lasting (Whorf 1936, in Carroll 1956:57).

In contrast to our way of thinking of time as something moving over a space, for the Hopi, "time is not a motion, but a 'getting later' of everything that has ever been done" resulting in the "storing up [of] an invisible charge that holds over into later events" (Whorf 1941, in Carroll 1956:151). Thus, the repetitiveness of Hopi religious rituals such as dancing or praying is to be seen as storing up this "invisible charge" that will have its effects on later events (Barnouw 1973:83).

Such statements indicate that there are between SAE and Hopi worldview differences of a high order mirrored in the differences in our languages.

Kenneth Pike

The contribution of Kenneth Pike (1912-2000) is of quite a different order. Though a linguist, Pike wrote a groundbreaking article in 1954 entitled "Etic and Emic Standpoints for the Description of Behavior" (reprinted in Smith, 1966), followed by a large book entitled *Language in Relation to a Unified Theory of the Structure of Human Behavior* (1959 rev ed 1967) in which he proposed the use of the terms "emic" and "etic" as descriptors for two views of human behavior. An informed outsider can study the whole range of phonetic or cultural phenomena that occur in any language or culture. In terms, then, of a cultural outsider's organization of those phenomena, he or she can describe individual languages and/

or cultures and also compare and contrast them. The informed outsider's point of view, Pike called "etic." When, therefore, we set up linguistic or worldview universals and functions, we are setting up an etic scheme in terms of which to talk in general terms about the characteristics of worldviews.

Each individual language and culture, however, is structured in a particular way, making its own use of phonetic and/or cultural items functioning in relation to each other in ways specific to that language or culture. Understanding how such items function internally, then, is an emic perspective, an insider's view. When we try to understand any given worldview from the perspective of insiders, we are engaging in an emic pursuit.

Both etic and emic perspectives are valid but they serve different functions. An analyst who is attempting to understand worldview or culture or language broadly, of necessity thinks in terms of etic categories such as time, space and causality for worldview or religion, politics and economics for culture or sounds, morphology (word structure) and syntax (sentence structure) for language. But when that analyst seeks to understand the way of thinking, behaving or speaking of a single group of people, he or she will give attention specifically to their emic, insiders' concepts of time, space, causality, religion, politics and the like.

These insiders' concepts are a selection from the large number of possible concepts that constitute the etic inventory. For example, the etic phonetic inventory for languages would consist of all the possible sounds that are used in any language. But any given language only uses a select few of these sounds to make up its emic inventory, its alphabet. Likewise, the etic inventory of possible concepts of time, space, cause, and other worldview universals would be very large. But each people "selects" one concept of each universal to fit into its emic worldview inventory.

Noam Chomsky

Chomsky (1928-) theorized that language events need to be analyzed at two levels: surface and deep. The sounds we hear are surface level phenomena, as is the grammar we have traditionally described. Underlying surface level phenomena, however, is a deep level of linguistic and semantic (meaning) phenomena that is just as structured as the surface level but of which speakers are largely unconscious. Furthermore, there are far less differences between deep level structuring from language to language than there are between surface level structures.

We are able to make use of this surface-deep concept in our discussion of the relationships between worldview and the rest of culture. We see worldview as the deep structuring of culture, made up of the basic assumptions, beliefs, philosophies, values and the like on the basis of which people give meaning to verbal and cultural behavior. But, though Chomskian linguistics is not clear on the issue, we must maintain that meaning is in people, not structures.

James Spradley

Spradley (1933-1982) devoted much of his professional life to developing an approach to the study of culture called "ethnosemantics." For him culture is *knowledge* and the best way to analyze it is patterned after the way linguists analyze language. His view of culture as knowledge leads him to see culture much like we see worldview. In our categories, his system would suggest that culture/knowledge = worldview (deep level culture), while what I call surface-level culture = "products of culture."

In two books, The *Ethnographic Interview* (1979) and *Participant Observation* (1980), Spradley details how to go about obtaining and organizing cultural data with a primary focus on how to classify the various parts of that data. He then incorporates the concepts of themes and worldview into his system. From this perspective, Spradley's approach is very helpful in dealing with the area of worldview called classification or categorization. This universal, however, touches all of the other universals. Spradley's helpfulness is, therefore, not limited to that single aspect of worldview, though his approach to themes and to worldview as a whole is not as comprehensive as we might have wished.

In the introductory textbook he produced with David McCurdy, Spradley defines worldview helpfully as follows,

> Every culture involves a way of viewing the world, a perspective for interpreting the universe of human experience. Worldview is the way a people characteristically looks out on the universe. It consists of the most general and comprehensive concepts and unstated assumptions about life. Worldview, in part, helps to integrate the bits and pieces of culture, the customs that seem unrelated or contradictory; worldview permeates the hundreds of named categories and domains. A particular worldview cannot usually be stated or formulated with precision by the people. You will have to discover [a people's] worldview by searching for the unstated

ways of looking at life, by putting together the pieces of this puzzle and making inferences about the perspective that gives it overall meaning (1980:280).

Note in the first line of the above quote that Spradley sees worldview as a "way of viewing the world." It would have been helpful if he had discussed any similarities and/or distinctions between culture as "knowledge" and worldview as "viewing." Are knowing and viewing the same or different?

The Culture and Personality Tradition

Edward Sapir is considered the father of this tradition. It was, however, when a group of anthropologists began to meet regularly with a group of psychologists at Columbia University from the late 1920s through the 30s that the emphasis really got launched. Whereas other schools of anthropology focused almost entirely on people in groups, this school asked questions concerning the influences of culture on individual personality. Prominent in this Columbia group were Ruth Benedict (see below), Margaret Mead and the psychologist Abram Kardiner. The major concern was an interest in the individual in relation to culture.

With that concern, the scholars in this school noted that each culture seemed to have a kind of personality of its own, one that differed from the "personalities" of other cultures in much the same ways that individual personalities differ from each other. They, therefore, became fond of discussing the "basic" or "modal personality" or the "national character" of the peoples they studied. Another major interest was/is child rearing and the cultural results of differences in child rearing practices.

If there should be such unifying traits in a culture, there are likely to be implications for a concept such as worldview. Thus, the scholars belonging to this school have generated concepts such as "core values," "themes," "value orientations" and the like that we find useful in our treatment of our subject.

Again, I have been influenced greatly by this school, so that an understanding of where I'm coming from can be helped by a look at the following contributors.

Ruth Benedict

Benedict (1887-1948), another of Boas' students developed an approach implicit in Boas' work. We call this "configurationalism." This approach holds that each society has over time crystallized specific traits into characteristic cultural patterns that can be seen as a kind of personality, a configuration, a "psychological attitude" that can be described and labeled.

She illustrates this approach in her most famous book, *Patterns of Culture* (1934) in which she described three different cultures, labeling them with names intended to signify the basic characteristic of each. She called the Pueblo peoples "Apollonian" because of an impressive list of traits pointing to a preference for an orderly and routine way of life. By way of contrast, she portrayed the Kwakiutl of the northwest coast of the U.S. as "Dionysian," a people who seek "to escape from the humdrum round of daily life and to achieve excess, ecstasy, or unusual psychic states" (Barnouw 1979:61). She found a further contrasting configuration in the Dobu of Papua New Guinea whom she characterizes as "paranoid" and of whom she said, "Life in Dobu fosters the extreme forms of animosity and malignancy which most societies have minimized by their institutions"(1934:172).

What we call worldview, then, was seen by Benedict as a kind of single overriding theme describable in psychological terms. Such an approach stimulated for a time quite a number of studies highlighting concepts such as "basic personality," "modal personality" and "national character." Another example of a configurationist approach can be seen in the title of an article by Francis Hsu, "Self Reliance, The American Core Value." Note the use of the word "the" in that title.

The idea that each culture could be characterized so neatly in terms of a single characteristic or core value, however, came under rather intense criticism, leading to a more complex but more satisfying approach by people such as Opler and Hsu (below).

Morris Opler

Opler (1907-1996) was the first to provide a widely accepted alternative to configurationalism. He argued that seldom, if ever, do we find cultures characterized by a single, dominant integrative principle. He proposed instead that what we find is a series of a half dozen to a dozen "dynamic affirmations" that he calls "themes." The term theme "denote[s] a postulate or position, declared or implied, and usually controlling behavior or stimulating activity, which is tacitly approved or openly promoted in a society" (Opler 1945:198). Themes "are found, in limited number, in every culture and ... structure the nature of reality for its members" (Barnouw 1979:73).

These affirmations both highlight the significant characteristics of what we call worldview and interact with each other, limiting each other and providing cultural and worldview balance. As an example, both of themes and of the way they limit each other, Opler points to the fact that in Chiricahua Apache it is a theme that long life and old age are highly valued but there is another theme that limits and balances the old age theme. This theme, which he calls "validation by participation" says that "an old man is admired and respected as long as he is active and fit, but when he can't keep pace with younger men, his years and knowledge do not prevent his retirement" (Barnouw 1979:73).

Francis Hsu

Francis Hsu (1909-1999) worked within the configurationist paradigm for years. But by 1969 we see him adopting a "postulates" approach that is much like Opler's in comparing Chinese society with that of the United States. To quote Barnouw's summary of Hsu's approach,

> The postulates would be underlying assumptions about the nature of things which carry with them various associated corollaries. The postulates and corollaries of a particular society may be inferred from a study of the society's literature, philosophies, ethical systems, laws, mores, and from studies on abnormality, crime, and other forms of breakdown.

To give an idea of Hsu's suggested approach, here is Hsu's Postulate 1 on China: "An individual's most important duty and responsibility are toward his parents, which take precedence over any other interest, including self-interest. The essential expression of this is filial piety. Filial piety is the individual's way of repaying parents for giving him life and raising him" (Hsu 1969:65). Associated with this postulate are 15 corollaries. There are 14 postulates in all (Barnouw 1979:73-74).

Hsu, then, uses the term "postulates" to label essentially the same components of worldviews that I and Opler refer to as themes.

Clyde Kluckhohn

Clyde Kluckhohn (1905-1960) taught for years at Harvard and did a good bit of fieldwork among the Navaho. He and his wife, Florence (see below) became very interested in values and what they called "dominant values" and "value orientations." Significant among Clyde's publications was "Values and Value Orientations in the Theory of Action" (1952). He also played a major role in the study authored by Florence and F. Strodtbeck (see below). His recognition of worldview is summarized nicely in the following quote:

> Cultures or group life-ways do not manifest themselves solely in observable customs and artifacts. There is much more to social and cultural phenomena than immediately meets the ear and eye. If the behavioral facts are to be correctly understood, certain presuppositions constituting what might be termed a philosophy or ideology must also be known. ... Each different way of life makes its own assumptions about the ends and purposes of human existence, about ways by which knowledge may be obtained, about the organization of the pigeonholes in which each sense datum is filed, about what human beings have a right to expect from each other and the gods, about what constitutes fulfillment or frustration. Some of these assumptions are made explicit in the lore of the folk; others are tacit premises which the observer must infer by finding consistent trends in word and deed (C. Kluckhohn 1949b:357-59).

See more on Clyde Kluckhohn's approach below.

Florence Kluckhohn and Fred Strodtbeck

Florence (Mrs. Clyde) Kluckhohn (died 1986) and Fred Strodtbeck are the authors of a book *Variations in Value Orientations* (1961), a report of research done with five societies in the U.S. southwest from 1949 to 1953 by the authors and several others with major input from Clyde Kluckhohn. These societies--Navaho (off reservation), Zuni, Mormons, Spanish-Americans, Texas Homesteaders--were all located in a single area, no more than fifty miles from each other.

Among the findings of this ambitious project was the fact that variation existed not only between the societies but within them. It was concluded, therefore, that, contrary to configurationist theories (like that of Benedict and the early Hsu), "societies were not integrated by monolithic value orientations but required a degree of controlled variability for a healthy existence" (Voget 1975:415).

The concept of "value orientation" is one that Clyde Kluckhohn had been working on for awhile. It is not greatly dissimilar from the concepts of postulates and themes spoken of above. Voget says of this concept,

A value orientation constituted a value complex; that is, value orientations had an element of organization, enunciated a general value base, and included postulates about the nature of the world (Kluckhohn 1952:409). Kluckhohn's value orientations, as a complex of values and existential postulates which applied to broad segments of life, converged on the broad context of cultural meaning that Redfield and others had attempted to master through the concept of world view (1975:416).

George Foster

One of America's foremost experts on applied anthropology, George Foster (1914-2006) has contributed a valuable insight concerning peasant worldviews in the development of the concept of "the image of limited good." By this he means that peasants, and probably many others in the world, live with the assumption that there are in the universe finite quantities and scarce amounts of anything considered good.

Whether it is land or water or love or prestige, if one person or group gains more, the assumption is that it can only be at the expense of another person or group. Thus, if any given person becomes famous or wealthy in such societies, he or she is likely to be the subject of envy at the least and perhaps attack or other forms of revenge (often by spiritual means) by those who feel they have been cheated out of their due. Since there is always the threat of being deprived through someone else's good fortune, "Preferred behavior ... will be that which is seen by the peasant as maximizing his security, by preserving his relative position in the traditional order of things" (Foster 1965:301).

Barnouw says,

> The notion of "limited good" has some basis in the realities of peasant life; most peasants are poor, land is in limited supply, and so are other goods. This state of affairs could easily be projected onto the world at large. Thus, Foster considers sibling rivalry to be influenced by the conception of a mother's love as being finite and directed mainly to the youngest child; hence the jealousy of older siblings (1979:43).

The assumption that some "good" is limited is quite common both in peasant societies and, at least with respect to some life experiences, even in developed societies. Grading "on a curve" where a given number of high grades requires that there be a similar number of low grades, for example, is a limited good approach to grading.

Oscar Lewis

Oscar Lewis (1914-1970) in his book *The Children of Sanchez* (1961) has introduced another concept that helps us to understand certain worldviews. This is called "culture of poverty."

> By using the term "culture of poverty," Lewis ... made the point that living in poverty was not just a condition of economic deprivation and personal and social disorganization. As a way of life, the culture of poverty possessed strategies and defense mechanisms by which the poor rationalized their existence. The culture of poverty exhibited considerable stability and was passed down through family lines from one generation to the next (Voget 1975:750-51).

Again, such a concept helps us to understand what a segment of the world's peoples may be assuming as a part of their worldview.

Anthony F. C. Wallace

Wallace (1923-), in his "Revitalization Movements" (1956) introduces a concept he calls "Mazeway Reformulation." The term "mazeway" is Wallace's label for what I would call an individual worldview. Mazeway reformulation, then, refers to the reworking of an individual's worldview in the process of rebounding from cultural demoralization into a reconstituted cultural structuring.

The Redfield Tradition

The most straightforward early approach to worldview was that of Robert Redfield. And it is his approach that is foundational to ours. Though each of the other contributions plays its part, most of what we do here is elaboration of Redfield's early work as built on by Michael Kearney (see chapter 3).

Bronislaw Malinowski

Malinowski (1884-1942), though born in what is now Poland, became one of England's greatest anthropologists. His concern was for the integration and functioning of cultures. As such, he postulated an underlying mental structuring that he referred to by the German term *Weltanshauung,* and conceived of in a way that approximates our concept of worldview.

Though it is doubtful that Malinowski directly influenced Redfield, in some ways he can be seen as a predecessor, at least conceptually.

Robert Redfield

Redfield (1897-1958) may be thought of as "the father of the concept of worldview." Though an American, he worked to some extent independent of the Boas tradition. He taught at the University of Chicago where he developed many ties to American sociology and British social anthropology. He was influenced by the great British social anthropologist A. R. Radcliffe-Brown who was on the Chicago faculty near the end of his career (1931-37). Redfield was concerned with the influences of more powerful peoples on smaller cultural groups, especially in the area of worldview, a term that he was the first to use. His *The Primitive World and its Transformations* (1953) outlines much of the approach to worldview that we still use.

Redfield started with a single question, How do a people characteristically look outward upon the universe? He followed roughly the total culture approach, called configurationism, developed by Benedict but avoided her reductionism by breaking a worldview down into several universals. He identified three basic needs. Humans need to know and understand 1) what they see: the cognitive dimension, 2) How they feel about what they see: the affective dimension, and 3) what they will do about it: the normative or moral dimension.

Redfield believed that all persons are conscious of a Self that looks out on reality, which he called Other. This interaction between Self and Other, then, is the axis of worldview. Within Other, there are human and non-human dimensions. Within the non-human realm he saw a major cleavage between God and Nature. He also reasoned that all people must take into account extension in space, and duration of time. From such observations, Redfield developed what he called world view (he wrote worldview as two words) universals.

According to Spradley and McCurdy (1980:280),

> Robert Redfield maintained that the ground plan for every worldview is similar. Each human culture, he argued, is like a stage set; it provides people at the center of the stage with a view, a perspective. Every such stage set includes very general conceptions of the following.

1. The self as a kind of actor on the stage.
2. Others as generalized kinds of people.
3. Groups of people.
4. Ways in which men and women differ.
5. A distinction between "we" and "they," between one's own people and other people.
6. A distinction between that which is human and that which is non-human.
7. Invisible beings, forces, or principles.
8. Animals.
9. Concepts of human nature.
10. A spatial orientation.
11. A temporal orientation.
12. Ideas about birth and death.

Redfield's approach was fairly descriptive. He didn't spend much time discussing causes for differing worldviews. He did, however, divide worldviews into two basic types that are related by historical processes 1) primitive or folk worldviews characteristic of what he (in keeping with his time) called "primitive," non-literate societies, and 2) urbanized or complex worldviews that characterize so-called "developed" societies. He believed that primitive worldviews get transformed gradually into urban ones under conditions of continual contact.

Redfield defined worldview as follows:

World view is one attempt to characterize the way of life of a people. ... It is one of those terms which are useful in asserting something of what is most general and persistent about a people. ... It has to do with the structuring of what man perceives and which clarifies how man sees himself in relation to all else. World view differs from culture, ethos and national character traits, in that it is a structure, an arrangement of those things—what are legitimate/illegitimate ways of knowing them, and the ensuing consequences for man the perceiver (Redfield 1953:84-7).

Michael Kearney

Kearney (1937-) makes extensive use of Redfield's theoretical framework although he himself is a "cultural materialist" using a mildly

Marxist approach to anthropological data. Though he makes much of the supposed deficiencies of the idealist approach that Redfield and the majority of pre-contemporary anthropologists have taken, his approach is not essentially different than an idealist would take. Since we deal with Kearney's approach in chapter 5, I will not go into further detail here.

Other Input

Edward T. Hall

Though he doesn't fit easily into any of the above groupings, E. T Hall (1914-2001), has, in his fine book *The Silent Language* (1959), theorized three levels of culture, the lower (deeper) two of which cover part of what I would call surface and all of my deep level of culture (worldview). The levels are called the "technical," the "informal" and the "formal." Though I think he could have chosen better names for his categories, Hall's analysis suggests that there are three levels instead of our two (surface and deep).

The *technical* is the visible level of culture and is explicitly taught. This is what we learned through asking questions at home and through our lessons at school. Not living up to such instruction is considered a mistake. The *informal* is learned by imitation. It is "the caught," often relating more to the feelings. Mistakes at this level are considered to be bad taste. The *formal* is also implicit, at a still deeper level and learned quite unconsciously. There is a moral element to this level so that mistakes at this level are considered sin. When such mistakes are made, therefore, there is immediate retribution. When things are done right at this level, there is positive reinforcement. The formal is supported by technical and informal props. When the technical props are removed, it is harder to protect the core from individual deviations.

One implication of this approach is to recognize that change of worldview involves three important steps. The first step is the recognition of something, say an assumption, that one has been unconscious of at the deepest (formal) level. Secondly, once that assumption has been identified, it needs to be brought to the surface (technical) level to be examined, analyzed and changed or replaced. The third step, then, after a change has been made at the conscious (technical) level, is to "bury" the new assumption in the unconscious (formal) level as a replacement of the old unconscious assumption. It then operates as a new habit.

Though we will not use Hall's terms or his analysis, we do well to note this different approach to worldview material. I do, however, find the above approach to how assumptions are changed very helpful and assume that Hall's view of the process is accurate.

Thomas S. Kuhn

In his influential book *The Structure of Scientific Revolutions* (1962, rev ed 1970), Kuhn (1922-1996) introduces the concept of paradigm shift. Included, then, is the definition of paradigm as a transmittable tradition, picture or perspective on reality shared by a community. Though Kuhn has in mind communities of scientists within western societies, this use of the concept of paradigm is valuable for our purposes. As the reader will see in the preceding chapters, I have found it useful to see paradigms as important parts of worldviews.

Ian Barbour

In a very valuable book entitled, *Myths, Models and Paradigms* (1974) Ian Barbour (1923-) applies Kuhn's insights to religion. He contends that both science and religion are held to and proceed on the basis of picturings of reality called models and paradigms. Whether in science or in religion, Barbour holds, people embody their assumptions concerning the realities they are dealing with in such constructions and change, often radically (as Kuhn contended) when they switch from one model or paradigm to another.

Again, I have found this perspective on models and paradigms very helpful in attempting to discover the internal structuring of worldviews.

Diagram of the Streams of Worldview Analysis

A. The Boas Tradition

1. THE LINGUISTICS TRADITION			
Sapir-Whorf	**Pike**	**Chomsky**	**Spradley**
"tyranny of language"	"etic-emic"	"surface & deep"	"culture = knowledge"

Figure A.1 – The Linguistic Tradition

526 | WORLDVIEW FOR CHRISTIAN WITNESS

2. THE CULTURE AND PERSONALITY TRADITION (MONOTHEMATIC)		
Boas	**Sapir**	**Benedict**
"underlying pattern" "configuration"	"world outlook"	"psychological attitude"
		[**Hsu** - "core value" **Foster** - "image of limited good" **Lewis** - "culture of poverty"]

Figure A.2 – The Culture and Personality Tradition (Monothematic)

3. THE CULTURE AND PERSONALITY TRADITION (MULTITHEMATIC)		
Opler "themes"	**Hoebel** "postulates"	**The Kluckhohns** "dominant values"
[**Kroeber** - "super-styles,"]	[**Foster** - "cognitive orientations,"]	[**Hsu** - "postulates and corollaries"]

Figure A.3. The Culture and Personality Tradition (Multithematic)

B. The Redfield Tradition

Malinowski	**Redfield**	**Kearney**
"Weltanshauung"	"world view" "world view universals"	"interrelated propositions"

Figure A.4. The Redfield Tradition

Appendix B

Additional Worldview Configurations

I. Navaho Worldview (United States)
(Compiled and edited from T. R. Williams 1972:223-224
[based on Kluckhohn 1949b] and from Spradley & McCurdy
1975:482-483 [based on Kluckhohn and Leighton 1961].)

THEME I: The Universe is Orderly

SUBTHEME A: All Things Are in Power/Influence Relationships to One Another.

>*Paradigm 1*: Nature is more powerful than man.
>*Paradigm 2*: Like produces like and the part stands for the whole.

Practices Associated with Paradigm 2:
1. Because the juice of milk-weed produces milk, it can be used to help mothers who do not have sufficient milk for their infants.

SUBTHEME B: Evil and Good Are Complementary, and Both Are Ever-Present.

SUBTHEME C: The Personality is a Whole.

Practices Associated with Subtheme C:
1. Navajo curing rituals seek to treat the mind and body.

>*Paradigm 1*: Everything exists in two parts, the male and the female, which belong together and complete each other.

Practices Associated with Paradigm 1:
1. Rivers, mountains, and plants have both male and female expressions.

>*Paradigm 2*: Human nature is neither good nor evil, both qualities are blended in all persons from birth on.

SUBTHEME D: *Events, Not Actors or Qualities, Are Primary.*

> ***Paradigm 1***: *Experience is conceived as a continuum differentiated only by sense data.*

THEME II: All Events Are Caused and Interrelated

SUBTHEME A: *The Basic Quest is for Harmony.*

> ***Paradigm 1***: *Harmony can be restored only by orderly procedures.*
> ***Paradigm 2***: *One price of disorder, in human terms, is illness.*
> ***Paradigm 3***: *Knowledge is power.*

SUBTHEME B: *Causation is Identifiable in Personalized Terms.*

> ***Paradigm 1***: *The universe is full of dangers.*
> > ***Subparadigm a***: *Maintenance of orderliness in reiteration of words and ritual protects from the uncontrollable.*
> > ***Subparadigm b***: *Non-relatives cannot be trusted (supernatural protection can be used).*
> > ***Subparadigm c***: *Excesses are disorder.*
> > ***Subparadigm d***: *It's better to do nothing in a dangerous situation rather than risk making disorder worse.*

Practices Associated with Paradigm 1:
1. People fear the supernatural world, especially witches.
2. Reiteration of words and acts in ritual to provide protection.
3. Avoidance of non-relatives or use supernatural protection when contact is unavoidable.
4. Too much sex and gambling, while not wrong, can bring trouble.
5. Inactivity if the situation cannot be dealt with by ritual or customs.
6. Flight instead of fight.

THEME III: Morality is Conceived in Traditionalistic and Situational Terms Rather Than in Terms of Abstract Absolutes

SUBTHEME A: *Human Relations are Premised Upon Familistic Ties.*

SUBTHEME B: *The Integrity of the Individual is to be Respected.*

> ***Paradigm 1***: *The rights of individuals are to be respected to the fullest, even children.*
> ***Paradigm 2***: *What is said is to be taken literally.*

Practices Associated with Paradigm 2:
1. There is an absence of ambiguities and double meanings in speech.

II. Apache Worldview (United States)
(From Spradley & McCurdy 1975:472-473, [after M. Opler 1945])

THEME I: The Universe is Pervaded by Supernatural Power Accessible to Any Man or Woman Who Desires to Become a Shaman

Practices Associated with Theme I:
1. People seek power and often accept Christianity as simply another "power."

THEME II: The Members of a Kinship Group Share Responsibility or What Happens to Each Other

SUBTHEME A: The Success of a Hunt Depends on Actions of Women at Home.

SUBTHEME B: Characteristics of a Child Are Determined by Behavior of Parents Before the Birth.

THEME III: Men are Physically, Mentally, and Morally Superior to Women

SUBTHEME A: Men Are the Tribal Leaders.

SUBTHEME B: Women Are Most Likely to Do Things to Cause Family Fights.

SUBTHEME C: Women Are More Easily Tempted Sexually.

THEME IV: Long Life and Old Age are Important Goals

Practices Associated with Theme IV:
1. Puberty rituals have this as their purpose.
2. People seek supernatural help for long life.

THEME V: Active Participation in Social Life is Required for Authority and Influence

Practices Associated with Theme V:
1. As an older person's ability to participate actively wanes, the person has less influence.

===

III. Muslim Swahili Worldview
(Analysis by Dr. Caleb Kim, missionary to the Swahili and former student at Fuller School of Intercultural Studies).

THEME I: Supernaturalism: God and Spirits Exist, and They Are All Involved in Human Life

SUBTHEME A: God (Mungu, also called Mola, the Swahilization of Allah) is Almighty.

Paradigm 1: God is aware of all things in the human realm.
    Subparadigm a: He knows all human minds and activities.
Paradigm 2: God is too far away for people to access.
Paradigm 3: He has decreed and set up the rules that people should follow.
Paradigm 4: He is stern and people must not offend him by breaking his rules.
    Subparadigm a: God is ready to punish evildoers.
    Subparadigm b: God is so strict that people (especially Muslims) must keep his rules (e.g., the five pillars of Islam).
Paradigm 5: God is less concerned about human affairs than are spirits or ancestors and thus is far less actively involved in human lives.
Paradigm 6: In order for ordinary people to appeal to God, powerful beings, such as Muslim saints, Muhammad, and even ancestors must intermediate between people and God.

SUBTHEME B: God Has Decreed That Human Beings Live With Jinn; They are Unavoidable in Human Life.

Paradigm 1: Jinn are everywhere in the human world and are very near to people.
    Subparadigm a: Some animals can see jinn, but people cannot.
    Subparadigm b: Jinn are mostly invisible, but sometimes they appear in visible forms, such as snakes, cats, dogs or women.
    Subparadigm c: They may appear in people's dreams.
    Subparadigm d: Jinn resemble human beings in many ways. They are born, grow, marry, have sex, give birth, get old, and die. Therefore, they also have their own clans and origins.

Paradigm 2*: There are two kinds of jinn: good (beneficent) and bad (harmful).*
    Subparadigm a*: Normally, jinn are capricious, unpredictable, immature, selfish, malicious, and harmful to human beings.*
    Subparadigm b*:. The causes of most sicknesses and misfortunes of individuals are jinn.*
    Subparadigm c*: Even good jinn always have the potential for becoming evil.*
Paradigm 3*: People should have a peaceful relationship with jinn in order to maintain peace and health in the human community.*
    Subparadigm a*: People must be careful not to vex jinn by mistakenly intruding into their realm.*
    Subparadigm b*: It is always necessary to perform pacifying rituals for jinn, so that they may stop harming people.*
    Subparadigm c*: Ordinary people cannot manipulate and control spirits, but waganga (shamans) can do it.*
Paradigm 4*: Jinn can "rise to the head" of (possess) people.*
Paradigm 5*: The master of jinn (the shaman) alone can deal with jinn.*
    Subparadigm a*: Waganga (shamans) are powerful people.*
    Subparadigm b*: When jinn possess a person, he/she must be led to the waganga to get healing.*
    Subparadigm c*: In the process of pacifying jinn, communication is very important.*
    Subparadigm d*: Obtaining information on the names and origins of the possessing jinn empowers the waganga and helps them to deal effectively with jinn.*

SUBTHEME C: The Cause of Community Problems is Ancestors (mizimu).

Paradigm 1*: Believing in mizimu does not conflict with Islamic injunctions.*
Paradigm 2*: Mizimu is a part of the compartments that make up the spirit world.*
Paradigm 3*: Mizimu deals only with the (African) tradition of Waswahili.*
Paradigm 4*: Any problem through which the whole community goes has to do with mizimu.*

THEME II: Ancestor Veneration

SUBTHEME A: Ancestors Are a Part of the Human Community.

Paradigm 1*: Ancestors are those who have stopped existing physically yet who have entered into the realm of "ancestors" [ancestral spirits].*
Paradigm 2*: There are certain conditions or qualifications to become ancestors, such as the age on death, his/her reputation while alive, and the like.*
Paradigm 3*: Ancestors maintain their social membership as long as there remain the living who can remember them.*

Paradigm 4: Ancestors may appear in the dreams of the living, particularly of the elders or leaders of the community, in order to communicate with the living world.

SUBTHEME B: Ancestors (mizimu) Must be Venerated and Treated Properly, as Prescribed by Tradition.

Paradigm 1: Every clan has an mzimu or mizimu, which is the center for a clan.

Paradigm 2: Ancestors should be venerated regularly at the mizimuni (the place of mizimu) of each clan.

Paradigm 3: All the communal affairs of a clan must depend upon the approvals from ancestors (mizimu).

Paradigm 4: Mizimu will protect the whole community as long as people treat them properly by offering tambiko at mizimuni at proper times.

Paradigm 5: If not, ancestors will get mad at the living and will inflict various misfortunes upon the living community as punishment as well as a reminder of their duty.

THEME III: Past-Orientation: Old Things are Good, and Old People Should be Respected

SUBTHEME A: Tradition is Good and Important.

Paradigm 1: What has been made and enjoyed by ancestors in the past is good.

Paradigm 2: It is very important to remember the history of the clan (genealogy) to which one belongs.

Paradigm 3: Tradition must keep being observed and should not be replaced by foreign substitutes.
  - **Subparadigm a**: Things from non-Swahili societies can be used for traditional usage and purpose.
  - **Subparadigm b**: Modern materials should be evaluated by traditional values.

SUBTHEME B: Aging is a Good Thing That Deserves Respect and Honor.

Paradigm 1: Older people must be reverenced because they are the ones who know traditions and understand how to use them for the communal good.

Paradigm 2: Younger people should respect and obey older people.
  - **Subparadigm a**: The community should obey the aged leaders of the society. People should not argue with them.
  - **Subparadigm b**: Younger people should yield seats and good food first to older people.
  - **Subparadigm c**: Younger people should greet older people first, paying full respect to them.

> **Subparadigm d**: *Younger people should not walk in front of older people.*
>
> **Subparadigm e**: *Do not interrupt when older people speak.*

THEME IV: "Groupism" (as Opposed to Individualism)

SUBTHEME A: Community is More Important Than the Individual.

> **Paradigm 1**: *An individual is defined by the whole group to which the individual belongs.*
>
> **Paradigm 2**: *People should be proud of being who they are (of their clan or tribe).*
>
> **Paradigm 3**: *Idiosyncratic behavior is condemned by the whole community.*
>
> **Paradigm 4**: *An individual's shame is a shame for all community members; an individual's honor is an honor for the whole community.*
>
> **Paradigm 5**: *Even an individual's wealth should contribute to the welfare of the community. Otherwise, the evil eye may curse the person.*

SUBTHEME B: Cooperation Among All Members of the Society is Extremely Important.

> **Paradigm 1**: *All passage rites are to be conducted as a group; there is no individual rite of passage.*
>
> **Paradigm 2**: *Even such family ceremonies as weddings and any type of individual celebration should be announced to the whole community, and they ought to be celebrated and attended by the whole community.*
>
> **Paradigm 3**: *The whole community is responsible for educating young children.*

THEME V: Baraka: Baraka is Extremely Important for All People to Live Successfully on This Earth

SUBTHEME A: Baraka is a Spiritual Power.

> **Paradigm 1**: *Spiritual beings, such as God, ancestors, Muslim saints, and jinn, can bring about baraka.*
>
> **Paradigm 2**: *If people follow the rules set up by spiritually powerful leaders, they will receive baraka.*
>
> **Paradigm 3**: *Baraka can be transmitted via relics of those powerful, departed people.*
>
> **Paradigm 4**: *Human mediators of baraka are religious practitioners.*
>
> **Paradigm 5**: *Baraka can bring about healing.*
>
> > **Subparadigm a**: *In order to receive healing, ordinary people must appeal to those spiritual beings through human mediators.*

> **Subparadigm b**: *If one has experienced healing many times by being helped by spiritual beings, the person must have received much baraka.*
>
> **Paradigm 6**: *Baraka can also bring about material blessings.*

SUBTHEME B: Visitors/Guests Are a Baraka.

> **Paradigm 1**: *They should be well treated. This is applied even to spirits.*
> **Paradigm 2**: *The host/hostess should not make any guest leave his/her home by force.*
> **Paradigm 3**: *Guests/visitors can stay as long as they want, and the host/hostess should provide food to eat and a place to sleep in for guests/visitors.*
> **Paradigm 4**: *You can visit your relatives or friends without any advance notice or appointment.*

THEME VI: Event or People-Orientation (as Opposed to Time-Orientation)

SUBTHEME A: Hurry, Hurry, Does Not Bring You Any Baraka, But Slow is a Real Journey

> **Paradigm 1**: *Haste is no good; taking time is a virtue.*
> **Paradigm 2**: *People are more important than schedule or appointment.*
> > **Subparadigm a**: *All ceremonies begin when all people are present.*
> > **Subparadigm b**: *It is normal to wait for all people to be present. It is abnormal to start any event if those expected are not yet present.*
>
> **Paradigm 3**: *What people do and who do it is more important than how it is done or how fast it has been done.*

SUBTHEME B: Showing Kindness and Hospitality to Others (Especially to Guests/Visitors) is a Crucial Virtue in All Events of Life.

> **Paradigm 1**: *Greetings are extremely important. Greeting is a way of showing hospitality to others.*
> **Paradigm 2**: *In greeting others, one must ask about each member of their families and even their friends.*
> **Paradigm 3**: *Guests/visitors should be well treated. If you do not treat your visitors/guests well, it is a great shame on your family. You may miss the baraka that has come to you.*

IV. ASHANTI WORLDVIEW (Ghana)
(From Williams 1972:224-225, [after Hoebel 1954]).

THEME I: The Gods and Ancestral Spirits Control and Direct the Operation of All the Forces of the Universe

SUBTHEME A: *All Major Contraventions of the Will of the Ancestors or the Gods are Sins.*

> *Paradigm 1*: The ancestors will try a man in the spirit world, if he takes advantage of a miscarriage of justice here.
>> *Subparadigm a*: A man, except when he dies in battle or of natural causes, must know why he dies.
>
> *Paradigm 2*: The ancestors will punish the group as a whole, if the group does not punish a sinner and atone for his misdeed.
>> *Subparadigm a*: Men are endowed with conscious will, except when drunk or misdirected by an evil spirit in certain limited situations.
>>
>> *Subparadigm b*: Cursing with a forbidden oath is killing.

SUBTHEME B: *Past Misfortunes Are Repugnant to the Ancestral Spirits.*

SUBTHEME C: *Basic Property Belongs to the Ancestors.*

SUBTHEME D: *A Headman or Chief is the Representative of the Ancestors of the Group He Governs, and a Stool is Symbolic of the Collectivity of the Ancestors.*

> *Paradigm 1*: Men are bound to their chiefs by personal fealty as well as by kinship.
>
> *Paradigm 2*: All men must be allowed to participate, directly or indirectly, in the formulation of laws.

THEME II: The Spirit is Inherited Through the Father

SUBTHEME A: *Blood is Physical in Nature and is Inherited Through the Mother, Thereby Creating a Physical Bond of Continuity in Matrilineal Descent.*

> *Paradigm 1*: Menstruation is spiritually unclean.

SUBTHEME B: *The Sex Rights of a Husband in His Wife Are Exclusive.*

SUBTHEME C: *Incest Destroys the Universe.*

Appendix C

Additional Folklore for Discovering Worldview Myths

1. A Creation Myth

The Navajo people of the American southwest call themselves "People of the Surface of the Earth." These are the people who have arrived at the surface from one of twelve possible levels below the surface. James Downs (1972) describes their origin myth as follows. Note assumptions concerning the people's relationships with the land and with each other. They are matrilineal but the myth doesn't seem to indicate that. They are also very conscious of the spirit world. The "Holy People" of the myth are spirits.

> Before there were Earth Surface People, there were, and are, the Holy People who once lived in the lowest of twelve worlds below the present surface of the earth. The Holy People are holy because they are powerful—not because they are perfect. It was in each instance some act of mischief or malice that forced the Holy People to move into a higher world. Usually one among them practiced witchcraft against the others and forced the move.
>
> In each world there were adventures and events that still have effect on the people of today. Practices were established, knowledge was created, and even special types of people appeared. For instance, in the third or fourth world ... there appeared hermaphrodites or transvestites, men who dress and act like women. Such people today and in the past are somewhat venerated by the Navajo and considered to have potential supernatural power.
>
> In the last world but one, men and women quarreled bitterly and decided to live separately, each sex on the opposite side of the river. The men ... lived quite harmoniously, learning the skills of women and even inventing some important household implements and techniques. The women, on the other hand, after getting off to a good start, were unable to suppress their sexual urges. Details vary,

but it would seem that they engaged in homosexual intercourse and also had intercourse with monsters. From these relations there sprang a whole series of monsters who were to plague the Navajo for a long time—some of them even today.

Eventually the sexes reached a rapprochement and rejoined each other to live in traditional harmony. But soon a great flood began to fill the eleventh world, and the Holy People were forced to scramble up through a hollow reed to the surface of the earth.

On the earth, the natural objects were formed, the landscape shaped either by powers of the universe or by the Holy People themselves. Death appeared for the first time.

Prominent among the Holy People were First Man and First Woman, who were created from two ears of corn and who are felt by some to have created the Universe. ... But their important role is that of mother and father of Changing Woman, the most important figure in Navajo mythology. Her conception and birth were miraculous affairs, but the original pair raised her and trained and allowed her to mate with the Sun and with Water. This mating or matings ... produced two sons, twins, who grew up to seek out their father the Sun and receive from him weapons and knowledge that allowed them to slay the monsters plaguing the earth and The People. The record of their victories is written in the landscape of the Navajo country. Prominent mountains, lava flows, and other natural features are identified with the carcasses of slain monsters.

The Twin Monster Slayers ... serve as a model for traditional Navajo male behavior. Their mother, however, is ... a personification of the earth itself, for she is forever growing old and withered only to emerge again, as does the earth in the spring, as a young and beautiful woman.

... There are dozens of Holy People ... associated with specific natural features of the land, with other [Holy People], and with aspects of the weather, vegetation, mineral deposits, and with certain animals. ...

The [Holy People] are not in our sense gods, although we often translate the word that way. They can misbehave, make errors, and act with malice. At the same time, they can be controlled and coerced as well as persuaded by proper ritual acts, and it is these acts that form a network of behavioral guideposts for Navajo life (1972:97-98).

2. The Origin of Death

The Lunda of Africa tell the following story to explain how death entered the world:

In the beginning, Nzambi slid down to earth on a rainbow, and there created the animals and the trees. After this he also created a man and a woman, and he told them to marry and have children. Nzambi imposed only one prohibition upon men, that they should not sleep when the moon was up. If they disobeyed this command, they would be punished with death. When the first man had become old and had poor eyesight, it once happened that the moon was veiled behind the clouds, so that he could not see it shine. He went to sleep and died in his sleep. Since then all men have died, because they are unable to keep awake when the moon is up (Feldmann 1963:112).

Tales

Following are additional tales from Hausa (Kraft & Kirk-Greene 1973):

1. Endorsing Cleverness

A jackal was eating chicken when a bone lodged in his throat. He raced here and there looking for someone to dislodge the bone, promising a reward to that person. Along came the heron who stuck his beak into the jackal's mouth and extricated the bone. When heron asked for his reward, however, jackal replied, "You have already received your reward. You put your head into a jackal's mouth and are alive to tell about it!"

2. Endorsing Perseverance

Two frogs fell into a bowl of milk and could not get out. They swam and swam until one of them lost heart, gave up and drowned. The other, though, continued to swim until his movements caused the cream to congeal and form a ball. He then climbed onto the ball and escaped. God says, "Get up, let me help you."

3. A Cheater Deserves to be Cheated

A case was taken to a judge. During the trial, the judge saw the guilty one signal to him with three fingers. Assuming this meant the man would give him three goats if he judged in his favor, the judge did so. When the man got home, he sent the judge three pumpkins. So the judge called the man and berated him saying, "You hypocrite, you, you have cheated me. May God curse you!" As the man left he said, "I guess a tattooer doesn't like it when someone tattoos him!"

4. Weak Ones Need to be Wary When the Strong Ones Fight

Two frogs spied two bulls fighting each other. The one said, "This is a fearful thing. Let's get out of here." The other replied, "This is their affair. It has nothing to do with us." But the first said "Right. But eventually one of them will lose and will come charging this way. He may trample us. Then their fight will become our affair." The saying is indeed true that if the strong ones fight even common people will suffer.

Proverbs

Following are additional proverbs from Hausa (Kraft & Kirk-Greene 1973):

1. Exhorting to Proper Conduct

1. For the sake of tomorrow's meals one washes today's dishes.
2. Having two houses provides protection against a house-fire.

It was pure foolishness on the part of the goat to think he could greet the hyena without disaster.

Breaking wind won't bring a fire to flame.

If you're going on a trip early tomorrow, tie your loads together tonight.

Whatever you do, look after your own needs first.

2. Exhorting Activity

1. By means of drizzles, the river gets filled up.
2. A preventive is better than a medicine.
3. Good relationships depend on one's feet.

3. Exhorting Patience

1. Today and tomorrow you'll be able to accomplish it.
2. Doing a thing little by little made it possible for a needle to dig a well.
3. Coming with something valuable in hand is better than coming early.

4. Stating Facts of Life

1. No matter how long the night, morning will come.
2. Even silence is speech.
3. Ask one's face for news of his heart.
4. An old horse is a knowledgeable horse.
5. The barber doesn't like to be shaved.

5. Dealing With Cause and Effect

1. The maggot in the meat is also meat!
2. The vulture doesn't descend without a good reason.
3. A child doesn't know fire until it burns him.

6. Involving Comparisons

1. An elephant in another's town is only a rabbit.
2. Shooting something in the tail is better than missing altogether.
3. The body can sense things better than one's ears can.
4. Like so-and-so is not the same as being so-and-so.
5. Health is wealth.
6. Lack of knowledge is darker than night.
7. Possessing something is better than expertise in using it.

Additional proverbs from Jablow 1961:

7. On Ignorance and Knowledge

1. If there were no elephant in the bush, the bush-cow would be a great animal (Kru).
2. The stone in the water knows nothing of the hill that lies parched in the sun (Hausa).

8. Teaching That One Should Know His Place

1. There is no man clever enough to lick his own back (Kru).
2. An axe can never grow a beard (Yoruba).
3. A crab does not beget a bird (Ga).

9. On Women

1. A woman may speak ninety-nine lies, but she will betray herself with the hundredth (Hausa).
2. A mother who has twins doesn't lie on her side (Mano).
3. Women take up their market baskets and also take up gossip (Efik).

Following are additional Mexican-American proverbs (Zormeier & Samovar 2000):

10. Advocating Fatalism

1. Everywhere the ox goes he is put to plow; everywhere the poor man goes he must work.
2. He who is a parrot will be green wherever he is.
3. We are like well buckets, one goes up and the other comes down.
4. Submit to pain because it is inevitable.

Riddles

Following are a number of riddles in addition to those in chapter 13. Numbers 1-3 are from Kraft 2001, number 4 is from Jablow (1961):

1. Body Parts

1. My farm that grows quickly after I harvest it.
   Answer: my hair.
2. Something that is sharper than a sword.
   Answer: a tongue.
3. It is always with me but I can't see it.
   Answer: my back.
4. Two stallions that are always running out of sight and then returning.
   Answer: eyes.

2. Fauna and Insects

1. My girlfriend who eats, wipes her mouth and says nobody gave her anything.
   Answer: a chicken.
2. When they try to sell it, everyone refused to buy.
   Answer: a blind horse.
3. A thousand cattle travel without raising any dust.
   Answer: harvester ants.
4. Teacher, open your book.
   Answer: a butterfly.

3. Miscellany

1. My horse doesn't do well unless it has a tail.
   Answer: a needle and thread.
2. A small trader that trades in the nether world's market.
   Answer: a bucket (that goes down into a well to get water).
3. A young girl at our house who is always bathing.
   Answer: a water dipper.

   Something cries out in the bush but has no intestines.
   Answer: a drum.

   The harlot pretties herself but the men run away.
   Answer: a bow and arrow.

   You always stand close to the doorway but don't enter.
   Answer: a mat door covering.

   A young girl with a full head of hair.
   Answer: a type of sugar cane.

   I have a thousand cattle tied with a single rope.
   Answer: a broom.

   Here a thread, there a thread, with a pregnant woman between them. Answer: weaving.

   The girls in our home are very stout.
   Answer: granaries.

   The judge of the market.
   Answer: a measuring cup.

   One goes on the run but returns proudly.
   Answer: going to the bush and defecating.

4. Additional Riddles from Jablow's Collection

1. It goes past the chief's house but does not greet the chief.
   Answer: a torrent of rain (Yoruba).

   The same boiled yam journeys over the world.
   Answer: the moon (Vai).

   I have two roads open. Though I put my foot on the wrong one, I am not lost.
   Answer: a pair of trousers (Hausa).

   Wooden man, seeing death, yet plunges his head into it.
   Answer: a cooking spoon used to stir boiling soup (Gola).

   A mother hen with many chicks.
   Answer: the milky way (Yoruba).

   We tie the horse in the forest but its mane reaches the road.
   Answer: fire and smoke (Yoruba).

   My father has a garden enclosed by a white fence, and with a red cow grazing in the center.
   Answer: mouth, teeth and tongue (Temne).

   A fat wife, always busy but enclosed by a hedge of thorns.
   Answer: tongue, surrounded by teeth (Yoruba).

   I have two brothers and two sisters but cannot see any of them.   Answer: ears and eyes (Mende).

   A mouth without teeth, but it chews on a stick as big as an arm. Answer: the vagina (Bassa).

   Sugarcane, worthless without its juice.
   Answer: the penis (Bassa).

   They tell him to bathe and he bathes, they tell him to stop and he weeps.
   Answer: a sponge (Yoruba).

   The gray dove with the fat breast trades in all the markets.
   Answer: a cowry shell (formerly used as money) (Hausa).

   When it is seized, the child in its womb runs away.
   Answer: a gun (Yoruba).

   The iron is white hot but not yet sharp.
   Answer: a boy (Loma).

   The house of the youths is full of meat.
   Answer: an egg (Hausa).

Epithets

1. People

An unmarried, non-virgin: guinea corn that has rotted before ripening.

A prostitute: a rag in which disease is wrapped for carrying.

A co-wife: causer of anger.

A nursing mother: ridden by her child and by her husband too.

A grandchild: a maker poor of your grandparents.

A child born to an older mother: food at night is better than sleeping hungry.

2. Personal Characteristics

An evil person: a thorn

A headstrong person: a chicken (pays no attention when told to shoo).

A persistent person: a baby (doesn't know when to stop).

A quarrelsome person: a palm frond (prickly front, prickly back).

A miser: spoiled guineacorn with no gravy.

A hot-tempered person: a small pot (things boil quickly in it) or a crow (one sees both black and white as it turns over and over).

A sponger: a cattle egret (depends on cattle for its food).

A don Juan: a billygoat.

A malicious person: one who would sell his lame wife's donkey (which she depends on to get around) at the very time they have to flee.

An indecisive person: the market finished, he's still wandering around.

A disappointing person: a broad, shallow body of water.

A nobody: if he's here we have gravy, if he's not we still have gravy (i.e., his presence or absence makes no difference).

3. Non-material Things

A dilemma: a bachelor at weaning time.

Foolhardiness: a blind man turning his head to take a second look.

Something worthless: a bright eye that can't see,

Necessity: even an old anus must work.

Helping: the chaser away of fighting.

Buying on credit: the causer of illness.

4. Animals

Squirrel: a person with only one home is foolish.

Flea: preventer of sleep.

Calf: broken knees.

Camel: travel slowly, sleep far away.

5. Places (each major city has at least one nickname)

Katsina: fodder grass visible from afar.

The world: a pregnant woman (no one knows what it will bring forth).

A Koranic school: home of the fear of God.

A woman's thigh: a woman's drum (since they slap it when they laugh).

BIBLIOGRAPHY

Barbour, Ian G. 1974 *Myths, Models and Paradigms*. New York: Harper and Row.
Barnett, Homer G. 1953 *Innovation: Basis of Culture Change*. New York: McGraw-Hill.
Barnouw, Victor 1979 *Culture and Personality* (3rd ed, 1st ed 1963, 2nd ed 1973). Homewood, IL: Dorsey.
Beckett, Bob and Becky Wagner Sytsema 1977 *Commitment to Conquer*. Grand Rapids, MI: Chosen/Baker.
Benedict, Ruth 1934 *Patterns of Culture*. Boston: Houghton Mifflin.
Berger, Peter and Thomas Luckman 1966 *The Social Construction of Reality*. Garden City, NY: Doubleday.
Boas Franz 1911 *The Mind of Primitive Man*. NY: Macmillan.
Bohannan, Paul 1953 "Concepts of Time Among the Tiv of Nigeria." *Southwestern Journal of Anthropology*, vol. 9, no. 3, Autumn.
Brown, G. Gordon 1957 "Some Problems of Culture Contact With Illustrations from East Africa and Samoa," in *Human Organization* 16:11-14.
Brow, Robert 1966 *Religion: Origin and Ideas*. Downers Grove, IL: InterVarsity.
Burckhardt, Jacob 1860 *The Civilization of the Renaissance in Italy*. Oxford: Phaidon Press edit. 1945.
Burnett, David 1988 *Unearthly Powers*. Nashville: Oliver-Nelson.
---------------2002 *Clash of Worlds*. Revised edition, Monarch Books, distributed by Kregel Publications, Grand Rapids, MI.
Carroll, John (ed) 1956 *Language, Thought and Reality: Selected Writings of Benjamin Lee Whorf*. New York: Wiley.
Chomsky, Noam 1957 *Syntactic Structures*. The Hague: Mouton.
Clinton, J. Robert 1986 "A Comparison of Some Worldview Models," in Grant, I., *Worldview Source Book*. Pasadena, CA: Fuller Theological Seminary, M.A. thesis, pp 64-109.
Cole, Michael and John Gay, Joseph Glick and Donald Sharp 1971 *The Cultural Context of Learning and Thinking*. New York: Basic Books.
Douglas, Mary 1970 *Natural Symbols: Explorations in Cosmology*. NY: Random House.
Downs, James F., 1972 *The Navajo*. NY: Holt, Rinehart & Winston.
DuBois, Cora 1955 "The Dominant Value Profile of American Culture," in Lantis, M (ed) The U.S.A. as Anthropologists See It, *American Anthropologist* 57:1232-39.
Eliade, Mircea 1963 *Myth and Reality* (trans. by W. Trask). NY: Harper & Row.
Evans-Pritchard, E.E. 1956 *Nuer Religion*. Oxford: Clarendon Press.
Feldmann, Susan, 1963 *African Myths and Tales*. NY: Dell Publishing Co.
Foster, George M. 1969 *Applied Anthropology*. Boston: Little, Brown.
---------------1973 *Traditional Societies and Technological Change*. New York: Harper and Row.
Geertz, Clifford 1973 *The Interpretation of Cultures*. NY: Basic Books.
Goldschmidt, Walter 1966 *Comparative Functionalism*. Berkeley: Univ of Calif Press.
Hall, Edward T. 1959 *The Silent Language*. New York: Doubleday.
---------------1966 *The Hidden Dimension*. New York: Doubleday.
---------------1976 *Beyond Culture*. New York: Doubleday.
---------------1983 *The Dance of Life*. New York: Doubleday.

Hiebert, Paul G. 1983 *Cultural Anthropology* (2nd ed). Grand Rapids: Baker.
---------------1985 *Anthropological Insights for Missionaries*. Grand Rapids: Baker.
---------------1989 "Form and Meaning in Contextualization of the Gospel," Gilliland, D. (ed) *The Word Among Us*. Dallas: Word, pp 101-120.
---------------1994 *Anthropological Reflections on Missiological Issues*. Grand Rapids: Baker.
Hiebert, Paul, R. Daniel Shaw & Tite Tienou 1999 *Understanding Folk Religion*. Grand Rapids, MI: Baker Books.
Hoebel, E. Adamson 1954 *The Law of Primitive Man*. Cambridge, MA: Harvard.
--------------1972 *Anthropology: The Study of Man* (4th ed). NY: McGraw-Hill.
Honigman, John J. 1959 *The World of Man*. New York: Harper.
Hsu, Francis L. K. 1961 "American Core Values and National Character." In *Psychological Anthropology: Approaches to Culture and Personality*. Homewood, IL: Dorsey.
---------------1969 *The Study of Literate Civilizations*. NY: Holt, Rinehart, Winston.
Jablow, Alta, 1961 *Yes & No: The Intimate Folklore of Africa*. NY: Horizon Press.
Kallas, James 1966 *The Satanward View*. Philadelphia: Westminster.
Kearney, Michael 1975 "World View Theory and Study," *Annual Review of Anthropology* 4:247-70.
--------------1984 *World View*. Noveto, CA: Chandler and Sharp.
Keesing, Felix M. 1958 *Cultural Anthropology*. New York: Holt, Rinehart and Winston.
Kluckhohn, Clyde 1949a *Mirror for Man*. New York: McGraw-Hill (Fawcett Edition 1957).
---------------1949b "The Philosophy of the Navaho Indians," in F. Northrop (ed), *Ideological Differences and World Order*. New Haven: Yale, pp 356–84.
---------------1952 "Values and Value Orientations in the Theory of Action" in Parsons, T and E. Shils (eds) *Toward a General Theory of Action*. Cambridge, MA: Harvard Univ Press, pp 388-433.
---------------1955 "The Dominant Value Profile of American Culture," in M. Lantis (ed), *American Anthropologist* 57:1232–39.
Kluckhohn, C. and Dorothea Leighton 1961 *The Navaho* (revised ed.). Garden City, NY: Doubleday Anchor.
Kluckhohn, Florence and Fred Strodtbeck 1961 *Variations in Value Orientations*. Evanston, IL: Row, Peterson & Co. (reprinted 1973 by Greenwood Press, Westport, CT).
Kraft, Charles H. 1975 "Toward an Ethnography of Hausa Riddling," in *Ba Shiru: Oral Narrative* 6:2:17-24 (Reprinted in Kraft 2001:153-61).
---------------1976 "An Ethnolinguistic Study of Hausa Epithets," in *Studies in African Linguistics* 6:135-46 (Reprinted in Kraft 2001:162-70).
---------------1978 "An Anthropological Apologetic for the Homogeneous Unit Principle in Missiology," in *Occasional Bulletin of Missionary Research* 10:121–26, Reprinted in Kraft 2001.
---------------1979, 2005a *Christianity in Culture*. Maryknoll, NY: Orbis.
---------------1989 *Christianity with Power*. Eugene, OR: Wipf & Stock.
---------------1991 *Communication Theory for Christian Witness* (revised edition). Maryknoll, NY: Orbis.
---------------1994 *Behind Enemy Lines*. Eugene, OR: Wipf & Stock.
---------------1996 *Anthropology for Christian Witness*. Maryknoll, NY: Orbis.
---------------1997 *I Give You Authority*. Grand Rapids: Chosen/Baker.
---------------2001 *Culture, Communication and Christianity*. Pasadena, CA: Wm Carey Library.

---------------2005 "Appropriate Contextualization of Spiritual Power," in *Appropriate Christianity*. Pasadena, CA: Wm Carey.

Kraft, Charles H. and David DeBord 2000 *The Rules of Engagement*. Eugene, OR: Wipf & Stock.

Kraft, Charles H. and Marguerite 1993 "The Power of God for Christians Who Ride Two Horses," in Grieg, Gary S. and Kevin N. Springer, *The Kingdom and the Power* pp 345–56. Ventura, CA: Regal Books.

Kraft, Charles H. and A.H.M. Kirk-Greene 1973 *Teach Yourself Hausa*. London: English Universities' Press.

Kraft, Marguerite G. 1978 *Worldview and the Communication of the Gospel*. Pasadena, CA: William Carey.

Kroeber, Alfred 1917 "The Superorganic." Reprinted in Kroeber, A.L., *The Nature of Culture*, Chicago: Univ of Chicago Press, 1952.

---------------1948 *Anthropology*. New York: Harcourt, Brace and World.

Kuhn, Thomas S. 1970 *The Structure of Scientific Revolutions* (rev ed, 1st ed 1962). Chicago: University of Chicago Press.

Langness, L..L. 1987 *The Study of Culture*. (revised ed.) Novato, CA: Chandler and Sharp.

Leach, E. R. 1966 *Rethinking Anthropology*. New York: Humanities.

Leach, Maria 1956 *The Beginning: Creation Myths Around the World*. NY: Funk & Wagnalls Co.

Lemon, Nigel 1981 "Language and Learning," in Lloyd, Barbara and John Gay eds. *Universals of Human Thought*. New York: Cambridge Univ. Press.

Lewis, Oscar 1959 *Five Families*. NY: Basic Books.

---------------1961 *The Children of Sanchez*. NY: Random House.

Linton, Ralph 1936 *The Study of Man*. New York: Appleton, Century, Croft.

Loewen, Jacob 1968a "Socialization and Social Control," *Practical Anthropology* 15:145-56. Reprinted in Loewen 1975:211-22.

--------------- 1968b "The Indigenous Church and Resocialization," in *Practical Anthropology* 15:193-204. Reprinted in Loewen 1975:223-34.

--------------- 1969 "Socialization and Conversion in the Ongoing Church," in *Practical Anthropology* 16:1-17. Reprinted in Loewen 1975:235-51.

---------------1975 *Culture and Human Values*. Pasadena, CA: Wm Carey.

Luzbetak, Louis 1963, 1970 *The Church and Cultures*. Techny, IL: Divine Word. Reprinted, Pasadena, CA: William Carey, 1975.

---------------1988 *The Church and Cultures* (revised and enlarged). Maryknoll, NY: Orbis.

Lynd, Robert 1939 *Knowledge for What?* Princeton: Princeton Univ Press.

Malinowski, Bronislaw 1925 "Magic, Science and Religion," in Science, *Religion and Reality*, J. Needham (ed.). London (Reissued 1948 as Magic, Science and Religion. Boston: Beacon Press).

Mandelbaum, David 1949 *Selected Writings of Edward Sapir*. Berkeley: Univ of California Press.

Maurier, Henri 1968 *The Other Covenant: A Theology of Paganism*. NY: Newman Press.

McGavran, Donald and C. Peter Wagner 1990 *Understanding Church Growth* (3rd ed.) Grand Rapids: Eerdmans.

Mead, Margaret 1956 *New Lives for Old*. NY: Wm Morrow.

Menninger, Karl 1973 *Whatever Became of Sin?* NY: Hawthorn Books.

Messenger, John 1959 "The Christian Concept of Forgiveness and Anang Morality," in *Practical Anthropology* 6:97-103.

Naugle, David K. 2002 *Worldview: The History of a Concept*. Grand Rapids: Eerdmans.
Newbigin, Lesslie 1966 *Honest Religion for Secular Man*. Philadelphia: Westminster.
Nishioka, Yoshiyuki (Billy) 1997 *Rice and Bread: Metaphorical Construction of Reality—Towards a New Approach to World View*. Pasadena, CA: Fuller Theological Seminary, Ph.D. dissertation.
Opler, Morris E. 1945 "Themes as Dynamic Forces in Culture," *American Journal of Sociology* 51:198–206.
Otis, George Jr. 1997 *The Twilight Labyrinth*. Grand Rapids, MI: Chosen/Baker.
--------------- 1999 *Transformations* (a video). Lynnwood, WA: Sentinel Group.
Parrinder, Geoffrey, 1967 *African Mythology*. London: Hamlyn Publishing Group.
Parsons, Talcott and Edward Shils 1951 *Toward a General Theory of Action*. Cambridge, MA: Harvard.
Pennoyer, Douglas 1990 "In Dark Dungeons of Collective Captivity," in Wagner, C. Peter & F. Douglas Pennoyer, eds. *Wrestling With Dark Angels*. Ventura, CA: Regal.
Pike, Kenneth L. 1954 "Etic and Emic Standpoints for the Description of Behavior." Reprinted in Smith, A.G. ed, *Communication and Culture*, NY: Holt, 1966.
---------------1967 *Language in Relation to a Unified Theory of the Structure of Human Behavior* (2nd ed, 1st ed 1959). The Hague: Mouton.
Pike, Eunice V. and Florence Cowan 1959 "Mushroom Ritual Versus Christianity," *Practical Anthropology* 6:145–50.
Pozas, Ricardo 1962 *Juan the Chamula*. (Trans by L. Kemp). Berkeley, CA: University of California Press.
Redfield, Robert 1953 *The Primitive World and Its Transformations*. Ithaca, NY: Cornell University Press.
Reyburn, William 1958 "Motivations for Christianity," in *Practical Anthropology* 5:27-32. Reprinted in Smalley, William A. ed., Readings in Missionary Anthropology II. Pasadena, CA: Wm Carey, pp 73-76.
Richardson, Don 1974 *Peace Child*. Ventura, CA: Regal.
Rogers, Everett M. 1983 *Diffusion of Innovations* (3rd ed). New York: Free Press.
Sapir, Edward (see Mandelbaum).
Schaeffer, Francis 1976 *How Should We Then Live?* Old Tappan, NJ: Revell.
Schacter, Daniel 1996. *Searching for Memory*. NY: Basic.
Scupin, Raymond and Christopher R. DeCorse 1998 *Anthropology: a Global Perspective* (3rd edit.) Englewood Cliffs, NJ: Prentice Hall.
Sharp, J. Lauriston 1952 "Steel Axes for Stone Age Australians," *Human Organization* 11. (Reprinted in Practical Anthropology 7:62–73).
Shaw, R. Daniel 1988 *Transculturation*. Pasadena, CA: Wm Carey Library.
Siers, James, 1981 *Papua New Guinea*. Wellington, NZ: Millwood Press.
Sire, James 1997 *The Universe Next Door*, third edition. Downers Grove, IL: InterVarsity.
---------------2004 *Naming the Elephant*. Downers Grove, IL: InterVarsity.
Smart, Ninian 1983 *Worldviews: Crosscultural Explorations of Human Belief*s. NY: Scribner's.
Smith, A. G. ed. 1966 *Communication and Culture*. NY: Holt, Rinehart & Winston.
Spengler, Oswald 1926-28 *The Decline of the West* trans by C.F. Atkinson, 2 vols. 1939 edition NY: Alfred A. Knopf.
Spradley, James P. 1979 *The Ethnographic Interview*. New York: Holt, Rinehart and Winston.
---------------1980 *Participant Observation*. New York: Holt, Rinehart and Winston.

Spradley, James P. and David W. McCurdy 1980 *Anthropology: The Cultural Perspective*, 2nd ed (1st ed 1975). New York: John Wiley.

Taylor, John "Goods and Gods" in Swan, Tony and D. B. Rose, *Aboriginal Australians and Christian Missions*. Bedford Park, South Australia: Australian Assoc. for the Study of Religions, South Australia College of Advanced Education.

Tedlock, Barbara 1981 *Time and the Highland Maya*. Albuquerque, NM: University of New Mexico Press.

Tippett, Alan R. 1971 *People Movements in Southern Polynesia*. Chicago: Moody.

---------------1987 *Introduction to Missiology*. Pasadena, CA: William Carey.

Toffler, Alvin 1970 *Future Shock*. NY: Random House.

Turnbull, Colin 1972 *The Mountain People*. NY: Random House.

Voget, Fred W. 1975 *A History of Ethnology*. New York: Holt, Rinehart & Winston.

Wallace, Anthony F. C. 1956 "Revitalization Movements," *American Anthropologist* 58:264–81.

---------------1970 *Culture and Personality*, (2nd ed.) New York: Random House.

Welbourn, F.B. 1961 *East African Rebels*. London: SCM Press.

Whorf, Benjamin Lee (see Carroll, John).

Williams, Thomas Rhys 1972 *Introduction to Socialization*. St. Louis: C.V. Mosby.

Zadeh, Lofti A. 1965 "Fuzzy Sets," in *Information and Control* 8:338-53.

Zormeier, Shelly M. and Larry A. Samovar, 2000 "Language as a Mirror of Reality: Mexican American Proverbs," in Samovar, L.A. and R.E. Porter, *Intercultural Communication: A Reader*, 9th edition. Belmont, CA: Wadsworth Publishing Co.

INDEX

Names

A
Adams, Douglas, 80
Aristotle, 222

B
Barbour, Ian G., 57, 362, 525
Barnett, Homer, 179, 464
Barnouw, Victor, 251, 507, 518, 520
Barth, 81, 83
Beckett, Bob, 340
Beckett, Samuel, 80
Benedict, Ruth, 131, 251, 252, 508, 516–517
Berger, Peter, 57
Boas, Franz, 508, 509, 525
Bohannan, Paul, 212
Brockhoff, Eric, 278–282
Brow, Robert, 107
Brunner, 81, 83
Buber, 83
Bultmann, 83
Burckhardt, Jacob, 507
Burnett, David
    Animism, 111–112
    background, 105, 109
    Chinese worldview, 114–115
    Clash of Worlds: What Christians Can Do in a World of Cultures in Conflict, 109
    Hinduism, 112–113
    Islamic worldview, 115–116
    naturalism, 245
    secular worldview, 110–111
    Theravada Buddhism, 113–114
    worldview groupings, 109
    worldview questions, 109, 303

C
Calvin, 82
Camus, 81
Capra, 87
Castaneda, 87
Chomsky, Noam, 514–515
Crow, D. Michael, 110

D
DeCorse, Christopher, 221–222
Descartes, 80, 110
Douglas, Mary, 119

Downs, James, 537
DuBois, Cora, 266–277
Dye, Wayne, 417, 418

E
Einstein, 352
Eliade, Mircea, 304
Evans-Pritchard, E. E., 211

F
Feldmann, Susan, 310
Ferguson, 87
Foster, George M., 326, 327, 401, 402, 520–521
Foucault, 90
Franklin, Benjamin, 209

G
Geertz, Clifford, 119
Goldschmidt, Walter, 65
Graham, Billy, 364–365

H
Hall, Edward T.
   The Dance of Life, 209
   history, 524–525
   images of time, 211–212
   intimate space, 226–227
   personal distance, 227
   physical time, 210
   proxemics, 226
   sacred time, 210
   The Silent Language, 209, 524
   social distance, 227
   space assumptions, 218, 220, 223–224
   time assumptions, 208, 209, 215
Heidegger, 81
Heller, 80
Hesse, 84
Hesselgrave, David, 40
Hiebert, Paul G.
   American and Indian worldviews, 117
   Anthropological Insights for Missionaries, 117
   background, 105, 116
   critical realism, 57
   Cultural Anthropology, 117
   deep level, 173
   epistemology, 121–124
   Indian worldview, 119
   symbolic anthropology, 119, 124
   view of reality, 58
   worldview, defined, 118

worldview functions, 118
worldview model, 117, 119–120
Hiebert, Paul R., 458, 459
Hoebel, E. Adamson, 157, 159, 511–512, 535
Honigman, John J., 107
Hovey, Kevin, 417
Hsu, Francis L. K., 131–132, 251, 252, 517, 518

I
Iroijdrilik, 308–309

J
Jablow, Alta, 316–318, 320–321, 542, 543

K
Kafka, 80
Kallas, James, 334
Kardiner, Abram, 516
Kearney, Michael
    background, 98, 105, 125
    categorization, 169–170
    ethnosemantics, 176–177
    future-orientation, 214–215
    history, 523–524
    history of worldview concept, 125
    linear time, 213
    oscillating time, 212
    Other, 35
    present-orientation, 215
    Self-Not-self dichotomy, 126–128
    Self-Other, 127, 168, 169, 187
    time assumptions, 210
    understanding of worldview, 508
    universals, 126–128, 167
    Western history, 209
    World View, 125, 507
    worldview, defined, 125, 132
Keesing, F., 108
Kierkegaard, Soren, 81, 83
Kim, Caleb, 530
Kluckhohn, Clyde, 266–277, 518–519, 527
Kluckhohn, Florence, 214, 215
Kraft, Charles H.
    commitment, 354–355
    communication, 383
    dual allegiance Christianity, 336
    Homogeneous Unit Principle, 386
    paradigm shift, 362
    riddles, 320–321
    social control, 376
    worldview functions, 109

Kraft, Marguerite G.
    dual allegiance Christianity, 336
        Kamwe myths, 307–308, 310–311
        Kamwe worldview, 17, 260–265
Kroeber, Alfred L., 511
Kuhn, Thomas S., 362, 425, 525

L

La Mettrie, 80
Lalilikian, 308
Leach, E. R., 213
Leighton, Dorothea, 527
Lemon, Nigel, 510–511
Lewis, Oscar, 521
Lilly, 87
Lippmann, 80
Locke, 79, 110
Loewen, Jacob, 345
Lokomran, 308
Lorok, 308
Lowa, 308
Luther, 426
Luzbetak, Louis
    anthropology, 108
    background, 105
    classifications, 171–172
    cultural levels, 105–106
    discovering worldview, 301–302
    Middle Wahgi worldview, 255–259
    religion and philosophy, 107
    superorganicism, 107, 123
    themes and counter themes, 108–109
    time assumptions, 208
    worldview classifications, 107, 349–350
Lynd, Robert, 266–277

M

MacLaine, 87
Malinowski, Bronislaw, 521–522
Maurier, Henri, 484
Mayan, Juan, 445–447
McCurdy, David W.
    Apache worldview, 529
    family interactions, 225
    history, 522–523
    Nacirema worldview, 266–277
    Navaho worldview, 527
McGavran, Donald, 386, 479–480
Mead, Margaret, 251, 448, 516
Menninger, Karl, 65
Messenger, John, 49, 411–412

N

Naugle, David
  anti-God worldviews, 101
  background, 11, 98
  the Christian worldview, 27, 30
  goals, 99
  heart concept, 99–100
  naturalizing of worldview concept, 99
  reality concept, 103
  Redfield, summary of, 126–127
  spiritual warfare, 101
  warfare, 100
  Weltanschauung, 98, 103, 507
  worldview, defined, 102
  worldview and human thinking, 101
  worldview model, 125
  Worldview: The History of a Concept, 98
Neergaard, Jim, 278–282
Neibuhr, 83
Newbigin, Lesslie, 329
Newton, 209
Nietzsche, 90
Nishioka, Yoshiyuki (Billy), 120, 124

O

Opler, Morris E., 132, 252, 517–518, 529
Otis, George, Jr., 339, 410

P

Parrinder, Geoffrey, 306
Pennoyer, Douglas, 412
Pike, Kenneth, 513–514
Pope, 79
Pozas, Ricardo, 444

R

Radcliffe-Brown, A. R., 522
Redfield, Robert
  culture and personality tradition, 521, 522–523
  Naugle's summary of, 126–127
  Redfield tradition, 526
  religion, 132
  Self-Not-self dichotomy, 126–128
  Self-Other, 35, 127, 168, 187
  universals, 126–128, 167
  worldview, defined, 98, 132
Reyburn, William, 374
Richardson, Don, 392
Riscajche, Mariano, 410
Robertson, Pat, 409
Rorty, 90
Roszak, 87

S

Sagan, 80
Samovar, Larry, 318–319
Sapir, Edward, 510–511, 512, 516
Sartre, 81
Schacter, Daniel, 46
Schaeffer, Francis, 30
Scupin, Raymond, 221–222
Sharp, J. Lauriston, 438, 440–441, 476–477
Shaw, R. Daniel, 237, 458, 459
Simpson, G. G., 80
Sire, James
    Animism, 84–85
    Atheistic Extentialism, 81
    background, 11, 75
    categorization, 300–301
    Christian Theism, 78
    the Christian worldview, 27, 30
    Deism, 79
    Eastern Pantheistic Monism, 83–84
    fundamental orientation, 76
    Naming the Elephant, 75
    Naturalism, 80
    New Age beliefs, 86–87, 490
    Nihilism, 80
    Papua New Guinea beliefs, 312–313
    Postmodernism, 87–90
    primary concern, 75–77
    questions, 77–78
    theistic existentialism, 82–83, 494
    The Universe Next Door, 11, 75
    worldview, defined, 11–12, 76
    worldview perspectives, 77
Skinner, B. F., 53, 201
Smart, Ninian
    Animism, 96
    background, 11, 90
    blocs of belief, 92
    Buddhism, 97
    Contributions of The Past, 92–93
    Cosmos, 95–97
    dimensions of religion, 92
    global city and global civilization, 94
    Hinduism, 96
    jungle of religious landscape, 97–98
    Materialist, 97
    politics, 237–238
    Rise of Nationalism, 92
    structure of worldviews, 93
    supernaturalism, 131
    Theism, 95
    Triangle, 93–94

Twentieth-Century Secular Humanism, 93
　　worldview analysis, 91
　　worldview perspectives, 94
　　Worldviews: Cross-cultural Explorations of Human Beliefs, 11, 90
Spengler, Oswald, 507–508
Spradley, James P.
　　Apache worldview, 529
　　culture, defined, 297
　　The Ethnographic Interview, 297, 515
　　ethnosemantics, 175–176, 177, 297–298
　　family interactions, 225
　　history, 515–516
　　Nacirema worldview, 266–277
　　Navaho worldview, 527
　　Participant Observation, 297, 515
　　stage set, 522–523
Stewart, 266–277
Strodtbeck, F. L., 214, 215
Strodtbeck, Florence, 519–520
Strodtbeck, Fred, 519–520

T

Taylor, John, 438
Tedlock, Barbara, 212
Thales of Miletus, 222
Tienow, Tite, 458, 459
Tippett, Alan R., 382, 431, 434–435, 449–454, 487
Tizhe, 310
Tsang, Patrick, 283–295
Tumba, 310
Turner, Victor, 119

V

Voget, Fred W., 519–520
Voltaire, 79
Vonnegut, 80

W

Wagner, C. Peter, 386, 480
Wallace, Anthony F. C.
　　crisis situation, 476
　　reformulation of cultural system, 457
　　revitalization, 455, 457, 458, 521
　　worldview transformation, 429–430
Welbourn, F. B., 384
Whitmer, Steven M., 251
Whort, Benjamin Lee, 512–513
Williams, Thomas Rhys, 252, 266–277, 527, 535
Wimbler, John, 328

Y
Yogi, Maharaj, 339
Yogi, Mahesh, 84

Z
Zira, 310
Zormeier, Shelly, 318–319

Topics

A
Aborigine meeting times, 418
Abortion, sexual activity in African schools and, 49
Absolute idealism, 121
Absolutistic-pluralistic, 235
Acts of God, 196
Acupressure, 55
Adaptation
    patterns, 163–164
    religion, 138, 141–142
Additive modification, 425
Advocates
    ability to influence opinion leaders, 396
    advocate-implementor of transformational change, 464–465
    appeal to marginalized people, 395
    characteristics, 394–397
    contact duration and intensity, 396–397
    enthusiasm, 397
    as fault of gospel rejection, 394
    motivation, perception of, 395–396
    person/group dimensions, 371–372
    power of, 395
    prestige of donor group, 395
Affirmation of churches, 442
Africa
    advocates as fault of gospel rejection, 394
    African Mythology, 306
    animism, 242–243
    attitudes toward material, 225
    biblical teaching, 119
    bloc of belief, 92
    changing worldviews, 374, 384
    classification logic, 174
    Dinka worldview of origin of death, 309–310
    education, 48–49
    Independent Churches, 459
    missionary love for, 47–48
    myth of sin entering the world and God leaving, 309
    Nigeria. *See* Nigeria
    peripheral customs, 432–433
    proverbs, 316–318
    psychological problems as demonic, 19
    riddles, 321
    show of emotion, 41
    Time/Event, 218, 237
Alarm systems for crime prevention, 397–398
Allah as God, 278–279
Allegiance. *See also* Commitment
    changes to, 29, 353–355
    dual allegiance Christianity, 336, 338

multiple allegiances, 143
pledging, 160–162
prioritization, 161
as reason for study of worldview, 23
relationship dimension, 333, 337, 341
zhong, 292–294
Almolonga, Guatemala
case study, 340–341
material world causality, 410
America. *See also* Westerner
allegiances, 160, 161
America First Christianity, 447
American way is best assumption, 157–158
Americanizing, 436
Apache worldview, 529–530
attitudes toward material, 226
blacks and whites, barriers between, 389–390
changing worldviews, 349
classification logic, 174
commitment to assumptions, 20, 52–53
dogs, treatment of, 157
emotion, expression of, 152
equality of men and women, 184–186
future-orientation, 214
history of time, 209
Indian worldview compared, 117
individualism in religion, 135
individual-oriented society, 179
intuitive thinking, 153
land ownership, 418
mechanical model, 24
Mexican proverbs, 316–318
model of reality, 20
Nacirema, 266–277
Navajo. *See* Navajo
organization of cities, 223
organization of homes, 223–225
patterns of relating, 162–163
professors, questioning of, 184
proxemics, 227–228
psychological problems, 19
religion, terminology problems, 129–130
science as religion, 55
social climate, 377
subsystem assumptions, 136
Time/Event, 190, 217–218, 236–237
truth and love, 158
use of natural resources, 163, 190
view of Vietnam War, 21
worldview assumptions, 136
Analysis of worldview, 91

Anang Ibibio
   human world causality, 411–412
   morality, 49
Ancestor
   classification, 170
   Hakka worldview, 283–290
   importance of descent and kinship, 180–181
   Middle Wahgi worldview, 257–258
Angels
   Christian worldview, 19
   naturalistic to supernaturalistic, 405
   theism beliefs, 492–493
Anger
   awareness of problem of, 398
   worldview change factor, 373, 392
Animism
   appeasing evil spirits, 198
   assumptions underlying magical practices, 489
   beliefs, 241–242, 481–482
   of Buddhism, 114
   Burnett's overview, 111–112
   causality, 239, 240, 241–244, 249
   characteristics, 244, 249
   cosmos, view of, 93, 96
   divination, 489–490
   fears, 488
   human world causality, 412
   Monism, 15
   New Age, 87
   overview, 503–504
   paradigms, 253
   polytheism, 473
   popular classification, 407
   reincarnation, 15
   Sire's summary of, 85
   spirit guides, 84, 192
   spirit power-orientation, 486–487
   subthemes, 253
   themes, 253
   truth and deception, 243–244
   witnessing to, 482–491
Anthropology
   anthropological approaches, 105
   Anthropological Insights for Missionaries, 117
   Anthropology for Christian Witness, 325, 394
   concept of worldview, 12
   history of, 509–512
   non-anthropologist approaches, 75
   symbolic anthropology, 119
Anti-God worldview, 100–101
Antimaterialism, 233
Apache worldview, 529–530

Ape and the Crab myth, 311
Appealing to people in changing worldviews, 358–359
Art, as Christian message language, 393–394
Ashanti worldview, 535
Asia
   advocates as fault of gospel rejection, 394
   beliefs of creation of the universe, 221–222
   emotion, expression of, 153
   mother and son bond, 188
   Old Asia, 92
   South Korean animism, 486
Assigned meaning
   adapting, 163–164
   explaining, 159–160
   integrative function, 166
   pledging allegiance, 160–162
   psychological reinforcement, 165–166
   regulation of life, 164–165
   relating, 162–163
Assumptions
   assumption level, defined, 120
   beginning of life, 14–15
   cause of disease, 15–16
   Christian assumptions, 27–28
   commitment to, 20–21
   contradictory, 163–164
   critical realism, 63
   cultural assumptions, 22–23
   expected changes to worldview, 53–54
   habitual and unconscious behavior, 25
   human interpretation based on, 24–25
   learned by people and assumed to be true, 14–16
   mechanical model, 24
   perception of reality, 18–20
   personal behaving, 44
   reason for worldview study, 22–23
   shopping, 134
   as true, 14–16
   unconscious learning of, 29
   understanding people's worldview, 25–26
   use of terminology, 133
Assyria, 244
Atheism
   atheistic existentialism, 81, 93
   as meaningless worldview, 107
   naturalism, 245
   as secular worldview, 110
Attitudes, predispositions, 154–155
Australia
   meeting times, 418
   Yir Yoront cutting implements, 397–399
   Yir Yoront demoralization, 438–442, 450, 476–477

Authority structures, 420–421
Avoidance relationship, 189
Azande of the Sudan, casting of spells, 203
Aztec people, cultural submersion, 443–444

B
Balance, and transformational change, 477–478
A Basic Worldview Catalog, 11
Bat, popular classification of, 406
Batak
    conversion, 449–455
    ingatherings, 382
Beatitudes, calling people blessed, 475
Behavior
    creative behavior, 134–135
    derivative behavior, 151
    habits. *See* Habits
    primary behavior. *See* Primary behavior
    surface level culture, 105–106
Being, of people, 182
Ben-Hadad, King, 414
Bible
    authorship, 60
    Biblical societies, emphasis of, 199–200
    commandment against murder, 188–189
    commandment against stealing, 188–189
    contextual reasoning of authors, 153–154
    creation of the universe, 221
    historical accuracy, 82
    inspiration of, 60
    interpretation based on worldview assumptions, 24–25
    measuring of history, 217
    overlap of book held to, 492
    perceptions by different people, 70
    perceptual reality of human interpretation, 72
    recording of history, 217
    religiously true, 82
Big Bang theory, 95, 222
Biological time, 209–210
Black magic, 203
Blind men and elephant, reality of, 56–57, 61
Blindness as result of sin paradigm, 426, 475
Blocs of belief, 92
Borana conversion, 448
Brazil
    changing worldviews, 394
    spiritist movements, 458–459
Buddhism
    Burnett's overview, 113–115
    Chinese worldview, 114–115
    cosmos, view of, 93, 95, 97
    cultural forms, 138

folk Buddhism, 504
naturalism, 245–246
Theravada Buddhism, 113–114

C

Cali, Columbia, case study, 338–340
Cameroon, changing worldviews, 374
Cargo cult, 312–313, 458–459
Carolines, 308
Cartesian dualism, 110
Case studies, dimensions of Christianity, 338–341
Caste barriers, 389–390
Categorization
    causality, 238–241
    ethnoscience/ethnosemantics and, 176
    family and ancestor, 170
    items classified, 169–170
    of languages, 171
    logic, 172–175
    logical incompatibility, 407–408
    of motor vehicles, 171–172
    naturalistic to supernaturalistic, 405–406
    popular classification, 406–407
    of spirits, 172
    as a universal, 169–177
Category
    ideology and philosophy, 107
    irreligious worldview, 107
    meaningful worldview, 107
    meaningless worldview, 107
    religion, 107
    structural units, 106
Causality
    animistic causality, 239, 240, 241–244, 249, 503–504
    classification, 238–241
    cultural orientations, 233, 235
    defined, 194
    determinism, 201–202
    eternal God, 204–206
    Great Original Cause, 206
    habits, 412–414
    human world, 194, 196–197, 199–201, 410–412
    material world, 409–410
    natural world, 194, 199–201
    naturalistic causality, 239, 240–241, 245–247, 249
    power and, 408–414
    religious ritual and magic, 202–204
    spirit world, 414
    supernatural, 194, 198–201
    theistic causality, 239–240, 247–250
Cause/power understandings, 28
Chamula, cultural submersion of, 444–447

Chance happenings, 496–497
Change and retention, 65–67
Change begets change, 380
Changing worldviews
    appealing to people, 358–359
    belief vs. practice, 363
    change in allegiance, 353–355
    characteristics of people's worldview, 359–360
    cultural worldview-habits, 46–51
    disequilibrium, 48–51
    an exercise, 367
    expected changes, 53–54
    experience, 352–353
    exposing oneself, 365
    Holy Spirit, 357–358
    knowledge, 351–352, 355–356
    learning imperfectly, 360
    major changes, 347–348
    meanings, 357
    model in conflict with reality, 362–363
    negative consequences, 48–49
    new perspectives to commitment, 344
    not exchanges or replacements, 28–29
    openness to practice shift, 353
    overview, 343
    paradigms, 343–345
    people, 343–345
    personal change, 345–347
    person/group, 371–403
    perspectives, testing of, 361–362
    power source change, 356–357
    practice shift, 352–353
    principles to follow, 357–360
    reinterpretation, 344
    resocialization, 345
    social price, 51–53
    steps to take, 364, 364–365, 364–366, 365, 366
    strength of commitment to previous assumptions, 344–345
    teaching shortfalls, 360–361
    transmission problems, 37
    underlying factors, 360–363
    will, exercise of, 348–351
Characteristics of worldviews
    assumptions learned by people and assumed to be true, 14–16
    commitment guidance, 20–21
    cultural assumptions, 22–23
    lens, model or map, 18–20
    organized system, 16–18
Charismatics, social penalty of non-conformity, 51, 52
Cheater tale, 540
Chickens, Chinese assumptions, 401

Children
    The Children of Sanchez, 521
    respect for elders, 180
    separate rooms for, 419
China
    beliefs of creation of the universe, 221–222
    chickens, assumptions about, 401
    past-orientation, 215
    professors, questioning of, 184
    status issues, 388
    worldview, 114–115
Chiricahua Apache, 518
Chiropractic, 55
Christianity
    allegiance to God, 160–161
    angels in life experiences, 19
    assumptions, 27–28
    "Christian" as a bad word, 493
    Christian Theism, 78
    Christianity in Culture, 139–140, 354
    Christianity With Power, 328, 345
    as closed system, 60
    conversion, and change in habits, 53
    conversion and salvation, 71
    cosmos, view of, 95
    crucial dimensions, 328–329
    dimensions. *See* Dimensions of biblical Christianity
    dogmatic approach, 61
    dual allegiance Christianity, 336, 338
    as a faith, 139–140
    folk Christianity, 504
    Kingdom Christianity, 364
    as meaningful worldview, 107
    nominal Christians, 493–494
    power encounter, 382
    Sawi Christians, 392
    secular theism, 247–248
    single worldview, 30–31
    supernaturalism, 198
    worldview from faith, 27
Christopagans, 491
Church
    affirmation of, 442
    conformity of membership, 52
    demoralization, 442
    sanctuary arrangement, 219
    submersion, 447–448
The Civilization of the Renaissance in Italy, 507
Clans
    Hakka worldview, 287–290
    Middle Wahgi worldview, 255–256
Clash of Worlds: What Christians Can Do in a World of Cultures in Conflict, 109

Class barriers, 389–390
Classification. *See* Categorization
Cleverness tale, 539
Closed system, 58–60
Closeness of God and death, 472
Cognition
    conceptual, 40
    conceptual thinking and reasoning, 40
    concrete-relational, 40
    intuition, 40
    worldview perceptions, 39–41
Collaboration, for innovation, 391–392
Color classification, 171
Commitment. *See also* Allegiance
    affect on worldview, 144
    to assumptions, 20–21
    changing worldviews, 344–345
    Commitment to Conquer, 340
    directional, 354–355
    fundamental orientation, 76–77
    gossip, 376
    positional, 354–355
    to a religion, 140–142
    rituals and, 142
    worldview guidance, 20–21
Communalism, 166
Communication
    changing worldviews, 372–373, 383
    Communication Theory for Christian Witness, 364, 466
    cross-cultural, 465–466
    gossip, 376, 480
    interpretation of the reality, 69
    language. *See* Language
    postmodernism and language, 89
    two-way, for transformation change, 467
Communism
    as irreligious worldview, 107
    naturalistic causality, 498
Compatibility of innovations, 399–401
Competition
    in American society, 162–163
    in changing worldviews, 386, 390–392
    collaboration and cooperation, 391–392
    ingroup-outgroup, 386
    between men and women, 185–186
    Nacirema worldview, 271–272
    between worldviews, 146–148
Complexity of innovations, 401–402
Comprehensiveness of religion, 132
Computer formatting of babies, 36–37
Conceptual cognitive style, 40
Conceptual thinking, 40

Concrete-relational thinking, 40
Configurationalism, 516–517
Configurationism, 251
Configurations
   Egyptian Sunni Muslim worldview, 278–282
   Hakka worldview, 283–295
   internal structuring of worldviews, 251
   Kamwe, 260–265
   Middle Wahgi, 255–259
   Nacirema, 266–277
   paradigms, 252–254
   subthemes, 252–254
   themes, 252–254
Conformity
   church membership, 52
   social approval of, 51–52
   unconscious acceptance, 38
Confucianism, 114–115
Consistency of religion, 132
Constructive change. *See* Strategies for constructive change
Contextual reasoning, 153–154
Contextualization, 138–139
Contributions of The Past, 92–93
Conversion. *See also* Salvation
   Batak case, 449–455
   belief paradigm, 426–427
   biblical revelation, 71
   and change in habits, 53
   of Christianity, 453–455
   cross-cultural advocacy, 450
   heart transplant, 449
   out of control, 451–453
   in pattern of worldview change, 434–437, 448–455
   person/group, 381–382
Cooperation, for innovation, 391–392
Copernican Revolution, 425–426
Cosmos
   cosmic consciousness, 490–491
   cosmological assumptions, 159
   cosmology, 220–222
   creation of, 95
   differing perspectives, 94
   nature and functioning, 95
   structure, 93–94
Counter theme, 108
Creation
   of the cosmos, 95
   Intelligent Designer, 205
   myths, 306–309, 312
   Navajo myth, 537–539
   of the universe, 205, 220–222

Creativity
    changing of habits, 53
    creative behavior, 134–135
    personal behaving, 44
Crime, prevention with alarm systems, 397–398
Crisis rituals, 165
Crisis situation
    model of worldview change, 430
    transformational change and, 476
Critical idealism, 121
Critical realism
    advantages of this position, 73
    assumptions, 63
    children changing assumptions, 66
    conserving learned assumptions, 66
    dogmatism, 61, 73
    Hiebert's taxonomy, 122
    interpretation problems, 71–73
    learning from others, 73
    limitations of observers, 64–65
    limited to senses, 63
    Models of Reality, 67–68
    overview, 55–57, 502
    paradigm shift, 66
    pressure to change assumptions, 67
    REALITY and reality, 68–71
    screening or filtering of reality, 64–65
    selectivity of data, 64
    sinfulness, affect on perception, 65
    testing assumptions, 66
Cross-cultural witness
    change in allegiances, 29
    naive realism, 69
    negative consequences, 48
    personal activity of a Christian, 30
Crying, expression of, 152–153
Cults
    cargo cult, 312–313, 458–459
    mushroom cult, 443
    Taro Cult, 452
Culture
    assumptions, 22–23
    Cultural Anthropology, 117
    Culture and Personality school, 251
    culture and personality tradition, 516–524, 526
    culture shock, 22, 68–69, 476
    culture stress, 22, 476
    deep level, 12–13
    defined, 297
    domain, 176
    foreign cultural forms, 432

formal, 524
forms of, 155
informal, 524
interrelatedness to worldview, 477
model, 431–434
people and, 501–502
people distinguished from, 33
people thing, 13
person factor, 34–35
personal behaving and cultural structuring, 41–44
personification of, 122–123
pride, and changing worldviews, 378–379
psychological integration level, 106–107
relativity, 497–498
as a script, 34–35, 45
sociocultural specialization, 143
structural integration level, 106
structure, 13–14, 137–138
surface level. *See* Surface level culture
technical, 524
use of term, 33
Curiosity, 365, 380
Custom. *See* Habits
Cyclical time, 212

D

The Dance of Life, 209
Dead orthodoxy, 83, 494
Death, myth of origin of, 309–310, 539
Deep level assumptions, 132
Deep level culture
defined, 12–13, 120
disequilibrium of changes in worldview, 48–51
personal behaving and cultural structuring, 41–44
social climate, 377
unconscious assumptions, values and allegiances, 23
for understanding people, 25–26
Defense of model of reality, 20–21
Definition of worldview
anthropological perspective, 11
Kearney's definition, 125
Kraft's definition, 12, 13
Naugle's definition, 102
Redfield's definition, 523
Sire's definition, 11–12, 76
Smart's definition, 11
Deism, 79, 110, 247–248
Deliverances, of Muslims, 493
Demons. *See also* Satan
causality, 414
dual allegiance, 447–448
naturalistic to supernaturalistic, 405, 406

psychological problems and, 19
relating to, 193
removal of, 362
spiritual warfare, 101
theism beliefs, 492–493
Demonstration
of the Father, 467
of need to change, 385
of possibility to change, 378
Demoralization
of American Indians, 21
characteristics of, 436, 437
of churches, 442
defeat in war, 21
extinction, 436
inability to adapt and, 164
of Jews, 21
pattern of worldview change, 434–442
physical circumstances, 438
revitalization, 436
Yir Yoront, 438–442, 450, 455, 476–477
Dependency-independence scale, 233, 234
Deprivation, as motivation for change, 383
Depth perception, 419
Derivative behavior, 151
Despair, 87
Determinism, 122, 201–202, 498
Devil. *See* Satan
Dignity, barriers produced by habits, 413
Dimensions of biblical Christianity
allegiance/relationship, 331–333, 337, 341
case studies, 338–341
knowledge, 329–331, 337, 341
overview, 328–329
power/freedom, 334–337
Dimensions of religion, 92
Dinka myth on origin of death, 309–310
Direct realism, 58–61, 63
Directional commitment, 354–355
Disabled people, Hausa folktale, 314
Discovering worldview
epithets, 322–323, 546–547
folklore, 305
literature, 303–304
myths, 305, 306–313. *See also* Myths
observations, 298
proverbs, 304, 314–319, 541–543
questions to ask, 300–303
riddles, 304, 320–321, 543–545
tales, 304, 313–314, 539–541
for transformational change, 468

Disease. *See also* Healing
    cause of, 15–16
    explanatory assumptions, 159
    germ theory, 16, 397
    schizophrenia, 146–148, 163–164
Disequilibrium of changes in worldview, 48–51
Displacement, 394
Dissatisfaction, as motivation for change, 384
Dissociative Identity Disorder, 146
Divination, 489–490
Diviners, 242
Dobu of Papua New Guinea, 251, 517
Doctrinal dimension, 92
Dog, 156–157
Dogmatism
    critical realism, 73
    naive realism, 61
Doing, of people, 182
Dominant values, 518–519
Dreams, of Muslims, 493
Dual allegiance
    animism and Christianity, 488
    Cartesian dualism, 110
    Christianity, 336, 338
    Christianity and Roman Catholic, 447–448

E

Earning, rather than demanding, for transformational change, 467
Earth Surface People, 537
Easter Bunny, 37, 66
Eastern Pantheistic Monism, 83–84
Ebon, 308
Economics
    cultural subsystem, 133, 145–146
    determinism, 498
Education. *See* Schools
Efficiency assumptions, 415–416
Egalitarianism, 388
Egyptian Sunni Muslim worldview, 278–282
Elephant and blind men, reality of, 56–57, 61
Elijah and the prophets of Baal, 449
Elitism, 61
Emotion
    expressing, 41
    interpretation and structuring of, 156
    patterning use of, 152–153
Empiricism, 204–205
Empowerment of Satan, 485–486
Enemies, love for, 47
English language, 215–216
The Enlightenment, 447
Enthusiasm of advocates, 397

Environment
    commitment to issues, 144
    naturalistic causality beliefs, 498
    physical environment, 144–145
    relating to physical environment, 190
    relationship to social environment, 188–189
Epistemology
    Hiebert's taxonomy, 121
    signs and symbols, 101
Epithets, 322–323, 546–547
Equality
    of men and women, 184–186
    Nacirema worldview, 275
Eskimo, age and status, 197
Ethics
    ethical dimension, 92
    premodern, modern, postmodern contrasts, 89
    relativity, 498
Ethnic cohesion, 435, 477
Ethnocentrism
    barriers produced by habits, 413
    Christian advocacy, 453
The Ethnographic Interview, 297, 515
Ethnoscience, 176
Ethnosemantics
    beliefs of, 176
    development of, 515
    Ethnographic Interview, 515
    purpose of, 297
Europe, expression of emotion, 152
Evaluation
    intuition, 41
    patterning assignment of meaning, 156–158
    person/group, 178
Evangelical orthodoxy, 78
Event. *See* Time/Event
Evil spirits
    logical incompatibility, 408
    paradigm, 18
Evolution, 55–56, 57
Existentialism
    assumptions, 159
    atheistic existentialism, 81, 93
    theistic existentialism, 81–83, 494
Experience, in changing worldview, 352–353
Experiential dimension, 92
Experiential knowledge, 330, 351–352
Explanatory assumptions, 159–160
Exposing oneself to change worldviews, 365
Extinction, 436

F

Fables, 400
Factionalism, 391
Faith vs. religion, 140–142
Family
   classification, 170
   Egyptian Sunni Muslim worldview, 281–282
   habits, 134
   Kamwe worldview, 261
   kinship, 180–181, 182–183
   relationships, 420
Fatalism
   animism, 242
   determinism similarities, 201
   folktales, 313
   human world causality, 411
   as obstacle to change, 384, 387
Father
   emotional assumptions, 188
   God as Father, 472
Faustian culture, 507–508
Fears, in animism, 488
Feeling of need, 382–383, 397–399
Female category, 184–186
Fertility, use of white magic for, 203
Fetishes, as source of power, 385
Fish-catching miracle, 426, 472
Fit of innovations, 399–401
Focus, choice of, 39
Folk religions
   animism, 241
   Buddhism, 504
   Christianity, 504
   Jews, 491, 504
   Muslim, 491–492, 504
Folklore
   epithets, 322–323, 546–547
   language use, 216
   myths. *See* Myths
   proverbs, 541–543
   riddles, 543–545
   for studying worldview, 305
   tales. *See* Tales
Food, cultural assumptions of offering of, 22
Formal culture, 524
Forms of culture, 105–106, 140
Foundation, deep level, 120
Freedom
   dimension of Christianity, 334–337
   to pursue change, 379–380, 387–388
   security-freedom scale, 233, 234
Fulani of Nigeria, 59

Functions of worldviews, 151
    American vs. Indian contrasts, 118
    assignment of meaning, 155–158
    assumptions underlying primary behavior, 152–155
    flowchart, 167
    response to assigned meaning, 159–166
Fundamental orientation, 76–77
Funeral ritual, 432–434
Future-orientation, 214

G

Gasoline, popular classification of, 406
Generalizations as parts of closed systems, 58–60
Genesis, literalness of, 60
Geocentric universe, 425–426
Germ theory, 397
German Lutheranism, 453–455
Gestalt, 456
Ghana, Ashanti worldview, 535
Ghetto, 52
Ghost Dance, 458
Glasses, perception of reality, 56
Global city, 94
Global civilization, 94, 95
God as Father, 472
Good Samaritan parable, 470–472
Gospels, reality of reports, 56
Gossip, 376, 480
Government, logical incompatibility, 407
Great Original Cause, 206
Greeks
    beliefs of creation of the universe, 222
    images of time, 211
    knowledge, 182
Greeting gestures, 25–26
Grief, expression of, 152–153
Group. *See also* Person/group
    groupism, 232–233
    group-oriented society, 179–180
    Homogeneous Unit Principle, 386
    ingroup, 188, 385–386
    outgroup, 188, 385–386
    solidarity, 421–422
Guatemala, material world causality, 410
Guilt, for social control, 376
Guinea corn, Kamwe worldview, 17, 262

H

Habits. *See also* Rituals
    causality, 412–414
    changing worldviews, 371–372, 375

of Christian worldview, 26
  creativity and changing of, 53
  cultural change, 46–51
  cultural patterns, 44
  family, 134
  following of worldview, 25
  force of habit, 44–46
  operation of people, 39
  of people, 13
  primary behavior, 151
  shopping assumptions, 134
  subsystems, 134–135
Hakka worldview
  ancestral reverence theme, 283–287
  configurations, 283–295
  lineage/clan theme, 287–290
  materialism theme, 287–290
  reciprocity theme, 294
  virtuous and successful people, 295
  zhong theme, 292–294
Hausa
  epithets, 322–323
  folktales, 313–314
  language, 65, 216
  proverbs, 315–316, 541–543
  riddles, 320–321
  tales, 539–541
Healing
  habit causality, 413
  Kamwe beliefs, 16–17
  by magic, 203
  by miracles, 55, 56, 163
  of Muslims, 493
  naturalistic to supernaturalistic, 406
  with prayer, 55
  by spirits, 401
Health, innovations to fill gaps, 401
Heart
  anti-God worldviews, 101
  home for worldview, 99, 102
  transplant, 449
Hebrews. *See also* Jews
  attitudes toward material, 226
  importance of descent and kinship, 181
Hedonism, 110
Heliocentric universe, 425–426
Hemet, California, case study, 340
Hindu Advaita Vedanta system of Shankara, 84
Hinduism
  animism, 241, 242
  Burnett's overview, 112–113
  cosmos, view of, 93, 95, 96

cultural forms, 138
reaching peoples, 490
History
   measuring, 217
   recording, 217
   time-oriented vs. event-oriented, 216–217
History of worldview concept
   culture and personality tradition, 516–524, 526
   culture levels, 524
   general anthropology, 509–512
   linguistic tradition, 512–516, 525
   Naugle concept, 11
   overview, 507–508
   paradigm shift, 525
   religious insights, 525
Holy Spirit, 193, 357–358
Homogeneous Unit Principle, 386
Honor, Egyptian Sunni Muslim worldview, 280–281
Hopi, 251, 513
Housefly, interpretation of pictures, 419
Human causality, 194, 196–197
Human dignity, premodern, modern, postmodern contrasts, 88
Human nature, 182–183
Human Self, 126
Human world, causality and power, 194, 196–197, 199–201, 410–412
Humanism
   atheistic existentialism, 81, 93
   as irreligious worldview, 107
   Marxism, 93
   Nacirema worldview, 267–268
   naturalism, 80, 245–247
   scientific humanism, 140
   Twentieth-Century Secular Humanism, 93
Hurricanes, causality, 409–410

I

Ideal people, 392
Idealism, 61–62, 63
Identification with receptors, 466
Ideology, as Luzbetak category, 107
Idolatry, 161
Incan people, cultural submersion, 443–444
Incompatibility, 407–408
India
   animism, 241
   antimaterialism, 233
   bloc of belief, 92
   caste barriers, 389
   feeling of need for change, 383
   ingroup-outgroup, 386
   maya (material as illusion), 236

Status and openness to change, 387
status issues, 388
Indians
   American worldview compared, 117
   biblical teaching, 119
   Chiricahua Apache, 518
   communication of Christianity, 154
   demoralization of, 21
   Hopi, 251, 513
   intuitive thinking, 153
   land ownership, 418
   Monism worldview, 15
   relativism, 62
Indirect realism, 63
Individualism
   application to all areas of life, 166
   cultural orientations, 232–234
   Nacirema worldview, 268–271
   in religion, 135
Individual-oriented society, 179–180
Indonesia
   Batak case of conversion, 449–455
   ingatherings, 382
Informal culture, 524
Information overload, 468
Informed Intercession, 410
Ingatherings, 382
Ingroup, 188, 385–386
Innovations
   compatibility and fit, 399–401
   complexity, 401–402
   idea fills a gap, 397–399
   observability, 402
   timing, 402–403
Insecurity, barriers produced by habits, 413
Instrumentalism, 122
Integration
   psychological integration level, 106–107
   structural integration level, 106
   worldview function, 166
Intellect and changing worldviews, 364–365
Intellectual knowledge, 330, 351–352
Intelligent design. *See* Creation
Internal worldview change
   conversion, 434–437, 448–455
   demoralization, 434–442
   growing new subthemes, 427–428
   internal worldview change, 425–429
   model of culture, 431–434
   model of worldview change, 429–431
   modification of worldview components, 428–429

renewal, 461
  replacement, 425–427
  revitalization, 434–437, 455–461
  submersion, 434–437, 442–448
  subtheme replacement, 427
Interpretation, patterning assignment of meaning, 155–156
Intimate space, 226–227
Intuitive cognitive style, 40
Intuitive thinking, patterning, 153–154
Intuitivism, 61–62, 63
Invisible things, popular classification of, 406
Irreligious worldview, 107
Isaiah's vision of God, 472
Islam
  Burnett's overview, 115–116
  cosmos, view of, 95
  cultural forms, 138
  cultural pride, 378
  dreams, visions, healings and deliverances, 493
  Egyptian Sunni Muslim worldview, 278–282
  folk Muslim, 491–492, 504
  Islamic Crescent, 92
  Jesus Muslim, 493
  as meaningful worldview, 107
  Messianic Muslim, 493
  Mystic Sufism, 116
  revivalism, 279
  simplicity of beliefs, 401
  Sufism, 116, 492
  Swahili worldview, 530–534
Israelites. *See* Jews
Italian show of emotion, 41

J
Jaluit, 308
Japan
  allegiance prioritization, 161
  animism, 241
  bloc of belief, 92
  changing worldviews, 349, 374, 394
  cultural pride, 378–379
  group solidarity, 422
  importance of descent and kinship, 181
  organization of homes, 224
  patterning use of wills, 152
  revitalization, 458
  Saru-to-Kani myth, 311
  show of emotion, 41
  social climate, 377
  social mechanisms for influence, 480
  status issues, 388
  view of nature, 189–190

Jesus follower, 493
Jews
    animism, 243
    attitudes toward material, 226
    beginning of life, 15
    cosmos, view of, 95
    cultural forms, 138
    demoralization of, 21
    folk Jews, 491, 504
    God's judgment, 21
    importance of descent and kinship, 181
    as meaningful worldview, 107
    Messianic Jews, 493
    war with the Moabites, 485–486
Joking relationship, 189
Juan the Chamula, 444–447
Justice, premodern, modern, postmodern contrasts, 88

K

Kamwe worldview
    assumptions, 16–18
    beginning of life, 14–15
    configurations, 260–265
    funeral ritual, 432–434
    healing of disease by injections, 16–17
    ideal person, 393
    importing Christianity, 327
    land acquisition myth, 310–311
    logical incompatibility, 407
    motivation, perception of, 396
    myth of sin entering the world and God leaving, 309
    origin myths, 307–308
    space assumptions, 220
    subsystem assumptions, 136–137
    supernaturalism, 17
    themes, 16–18
    time/event efficiency, 415–416
    worldview assumptions, 136–137
Karma, 242
Kili, 308
Kingdom Christianity, 364
Kingdom Principles, 31
Kinship
    definition of person, 180–181
    Egyptian Sunni Muslim worldview, 281–282
    human nature, 182–183
Knowledge
    to change worldview, 351–352, 355–356
    dimension of Christianity, 329–331, 337, 341
    experiential, 330, 351–352
    intellectual, 330, 351–352
    observational, 330, 351–352

Koran, overlap of book held to, 492
Korea
   importance of descent and kinship, 181
   openness to changing worldviews, 379
   status issues, 388–389
Kwakiutl, 251

L

Land ownership, 418
Language. *See also* Communication
   classification, 171
   English, 215–216
   Language in Relation to a Unified Theory of the Structure of Human Behavior, 513
   postmodernism, 89
   The Silent Language, 209, 524
   space and, 219–220
   time and, 215–216
   value of, in changing worldviews, 392–394
Lateness assumptions, 415
Latin America
   advocates as fault of gospel rejection, 394
   competition, 386
   cultural submersion, 443–444
   group solidarity, 422
   organization of homes, 224–225
   use of time, 218
Latin World, 92
Law and punishment, for changing worldviews, 376
Laws of physics, 195–196
Learning a worldview, 36–37
Lens to perceive reality, 18–20, 38–39
Liberal Christianity, 493
Life
   compartmentalization, 129
   defined, 14–15
   key areas, 109
   regulation of, 164–165
Limited good, 520–521
Linear logic, 153–154
Linear time, 213
Linguistic tradition, 512–516, 525
Literacy
   and changing worldviews, 380–381
   timing of learning to read, 402–403
Literature, studying for worldview insight, 303–304
Logic
   for changing worldview, 376
   classification, 172–175
   ethnoscience/ethnosemantics and, 176
   logical incompatibility, 407–408
   naturalistic to supernaturalistic, 405–406
   patterning of, 153–154

popular classification, 406–407
as a universal, 169–177
Losing "face", barriers produced by habits, 413
Love charms, 203
Lutheranism, German, 453–455

M

Macrospace, 218
Madagascar, myth on origin of death, 310
Magic, control of power, 203–204
Male category, 184–186
Malietoa of Samoa, 487
Manus people, conversion of, 448
Map to perceive reality, 20
Marriage relationships, 474–475
Marshall Islands, 308–309
Marxism
    economic determinism, 498
    humanism, 93
    Marxist Bloc, 92
    naturalism, 80
    revitalization movement, 460
    as secular worldview, 110
Material universe and space
    attitudes toward material, 225–226
    clean space, 419
    cultural orientations, 233, 236
    innovations to fill gaps, 400–401
    land ownership, 418
    pictures, interpretation of, 419–420
    separate rooms for children, 419
    spiritual power through objects, 229
    universal, 218–219
    where to meet, 418
Materialism
    antimaterialism, 233
    attitudes toward, 225–226
    beliefs, 245
    cosmos, view of, 93, 97
    Hakka worldview, 287–290
    material world causality, 409–410
    Nacirema worldview, 272–274
    naturalism, 80
    social climate, 377
    space and, 219. *See also* Material universe and space
    status and, 388
    subsystems, 145–146
    of time, 144
Mathematics
    dogmatic approach, 60–61
    reality of, 59
Matrilineal society, 183

Maximon, 410
Mayan people, cultural submersion, 443–444
Mazateco, cultural submersion, 443–444
Mazeway Reformulation, 521
Meaning
    changing of, 357
    evaluating, 156–158
    interpreting, 155–156
    meaningful worldview, 107
    meaningless worldview, 107
    patterning assignment of, 155–158
    response to assigned meaning, 159–166
    symbolic anthropological treatment of, 124
Mechanical model of Western reality, 24
Mechanical universe, Nacirema worldview, 274
Mechanistic-personalistic scale, 233, 236
Mediated realism, 63
Medicine
    acupressure, 55
    chiropractic, 55
    disequilibrium of changes in worldview, 50
    miraculous healing, 55–56
    osteopathy, 55
Meeting times, 418
Melanesia. *See also* Papua New Guinea
    casting of spells, 203
    myths, 312–313
Men
    manliness as obstacle to conversion, 392
    status and role, 387–388
Mentality of a people, 106–107
Metaphysical time, 210
Mexico
    Juan the Chamula, cultural submersion, 444–447
    Mazateco, cultural submersion, 443–444
    proverbs, 316–318, 543
Micro time, 210
Microspace, 218–219
Middle Wahgi, configurations, 255–259
The mind, 99, 348
Miracles
    contemporary vs. biblical, 38
    fish-catching story, 426, 472
    healing, 55–56, 163
Missionaries
    anthropological approaches, 108
    Anthropological Insights for Missionaries, 117
    communication of Christianity to India, 154
Mobility of people, impact on family, 38
Models
    conflict with reality, 362–363
    culture, 431–434

Hiebert's model, 117, 119–120
mechanical, 24
Models of Reality, 67–68
patterns, 429–431
to perceive reality, 18–20
of reality, assumptions, 20
of reality, defense of, 20
Modern West, 92
Modesty, barriers produced by habits, 413
Modification internal worldview change
additive, 425
of components, 428–429
subtractive, 425
Monism
beliefs, 15, 490
Eastern Pantheistic Monism, 83–84
Shankara, 84
Monochronic time, 210
Monogamy, 50
Monotheism to polytheistic people, 407–408
Monothematic tradition, 526
Morality
Anang Ibibio, 49
relativism, 62
sexual activity in African schools, 49
Mother, emotional assumptions, 188
Motivation
advocates, perception of, 395–396
to change, 383
intuition, 41
patterning of, 154
Motor vehicle classification, 171–172
Mountain
Kamwe worldview, 17, 261
reality of, 58
MPD/DID, 146
Multiple Personality Disorder, 146
Multithematic tradition, 526
Murder, scriptural commandment, 188–189
Mushroom cult, 443
Music, as Christian message language, 393–394
Muslim. *See* Islam
Mystic Sufism, 116, 492
Myths
African Mythology, 306
cargo cult phenomenon, 312–313
cosmology, 221
defined, 303
land acquisition, 310–311
myth time, 211
mythic dimension, 92
Myths, Models and Paradigms, 525

Navajo creation myth, 537–539
need for cooperation and discipline, 311
origin myths, 306–309
origin of death, 309–310, 539
Papua New Guinea summary, 312–313
Saru-to-Kani (Ape and the Crab), 311
sin entered the world and God left, 309
for studying worldview, 303–304, 305, 306–313

N
Nacirema
    American way, 276–277
    competition theme, 271–272
    configurations, 266–277
    equality theme, 275
    humanism theme, 267–268
    individualism theme, 268–271
    materialism theme, 272–274
    mechanical universe theme, 274
    progress theme, 274–275
Naive realism
    cross-cultural witness, 69
    Hiebert's taxonomy, 121
    overview, 58–61, 63
Naming the Elephant, 75
Namorik, 308
Nationalism, 92
Natural resources, American attitudes, 163, 190
Natural world, causality and power, 194–197, 199–201
Naturalism
    beliefs, 80, 245
    biblical worldview, 99
    causality, 239, 240–241, 245–247, 249
    characteristics, 246–247, 249
    creation of the universe, 26
    cultural orientations, 232–233, 235
    New Age, 87
    paradigms, 253
    postmodernism, 89, 90
    subthemes, 253
    themes, 253
Naturalistic causality
    chance happenings, 496–497
    Communism, 107, 498
    environmentalism, 498
    non-stereotype form of Christianity, 495–496
    overview, 504
    positive relationships, 498–499
    reaching peoples, 495–499
    relativism, 497–498
    spiritual power demonstrations, 496
    unexplainable occurrences, 495

universe as closed or open, 497
Naturalistic to supernaturalistic, 405–406, 426
Navajo
    creation beliefs, 221, 537–539
    present-orientation, 215
    worldview, 527–528
Nazism, revitalization movement, 460
Necromancy, 489
Needs of people/groups, 382–385
    demonstration, 385
    deprivation, 383–384
    dissatisfaction, 384
    feeling of, 382–383, 397–399
    innovations, 397–399
    motivation for change, 383
    power, 384–385
Negative consequences of changes in worldviews, 48–49
Neighbor story, 46–47
Neighborliness, for transformational change, 470–472
Neo-orthodoxy, 83
New Age
    animism, 241
    attraction of, 86
    beliefs, 490–491
    changing worldviews, 350
    cosmic consciousness, 490–491
    dual allegiance, 448
    reaching peoples, 490–491
New Guinea. *See* Papua New Guinea
New Lives for Old, 448
New math, 59
Nigeria
    Anang Ibibio, 49, 411–412
    changing worldviews, 374, 378
    dogs, treatment of, 157
    exposing oneself to change worldviews, 365
    family relationships, 420
    fatalism, 411
    Fulani, 59
    funeral ritual, 432–434
    Hausa language, 65
    Kamwe. *See* Kamwe worldview
    offering and acceptance of things, 46
    organization of homes, 223, 225
    perceptions of the Bible, 70
    polygamy, 50
    power/freedom dimension, 334
    privacy concept, 228
    proverbs, 314
    status issues, 388
    teaching through fables, 400

Tiv, image of time, 212
transformational change, 464
Nihilism, 80, 245
Non-conformists, 38
Non-human Self, 126
Nordic show of emotion, 41
Not-self, 35, 126
Now versus not now, 416–418
Nuer of East Africa, image of time, 211
Nzambi, 539

O

Observations
discovery of themes, 297–298
observability of innovations, 402
observational knowledge, 330, 351–352
participant-observation, 298
problems in seeking information, 298–299
steps in discovering worldview assumptions, 298–300
Offering something to others, 325–328
Old Asia, 92
Onesimus, the slave, 474
Openness
to change worldview, 377–381
Japanese openness to changing worldviews, 379
Korean openness to change, 379
to practice shift, 353
social climate and, 377
Opinion leaders, 421
Organization
characteristic of worldviews, 16–18
of space, 223–225
Orientations
animism, 239, 240, 241–244, 249
causality, 231–233, 235
defined, 231
naturalism, 239, 240–241, 245–247, 249
overview, 231–232
person/group, 233–235
scales, 232–233
space, 231–233, 236
theism, 239–240, 247–250
Time/Event, 231–233, 236–237
types, 237–238
Origin myths, 306–309
Orthodoxy
beliefs, 247
Dead Orthodoxy, 83
evangelical, 78
Neo-orthodoxy, 83
Oscillating time, 212
Osteopathy, 55

Other, 35–36, 127
Outgroup, 188, 385–386
Overview of worldview, 502–503

P

Pacific bloc of belief, 92
Paganism, 483–484
Pantheism, 87
Papua New Guinea
    animism, 481–482
    Dobu, 251, 517
    image of time, 211
    Manus people, conversion of, 448
    Melanesia, 203, 312–313
    Middle Wahgi, 255–259
    myths, 312–313
    organization of homes, 225
    time concepts, 416–418
Parables. *See* Stories
Paradigm
    American, 254
    animism, 253
    changing worldviews, 343–345
    complexity of, 401–402
    configurations, 252–254
    evil spirits, 18
    of God, 17
    Kamwe, 255–259
    Middle Wahgi, 255–259
    Nacirema, 266–277
    naturalism, 253
    paradigm shift, concept of, 525
    replacement, 425–427
    shifting worldviews, 362, 425, 426
    subparadigm, 427–428
Participant Observation, 297, 515
Participant-observation, 298
Pascual Bailon, 410
Passage rituals, 165
Past-orientation, 215
Patience, in changing worldview, 366
Patrilineal society, 183
Patterns
    assignment of meaning, 156–158
    conversion, 434–437, 448–455
    cultural, 44
    demoralization, 434–442
    emotions, use of, 152–153
    internal worldview change, 425–429
    logic and reason, 153–154
    model of culture, 431–434
    model of worldview change, 429–431
    motivation, 154

predispositions, 154–155
renewal, 461
response to assigned meaning, 159–166
revitalization, 434–437, 455–461
submersion, 434–437, 442–448
wills, use of, 152

Patterns of Culture, 251, 517
Peace, need for, 494
Pendulum representation of time, 213
Pentecostals, social penalty of non-conformity, 52
People
behaving, 13–14
changing worldviews, 343–345
culture distinguished from, 33
and culture/worldview, 501–502
defined, 13
habits, 13
nonmaterial facets, 39–41
people movement, 449–450
People Movements in Southern Polynesia, 487
people thing, 13, 39–41
Perception
of advocates, 395–396
of the Bible, 70–71
cognition, 39–41
person/group, 177
of reality, 18–20, 24, 56
structure, 39
of the universe, 144–145
Peripheral customs, 432–433
Perseverance tale, 539–540
Person
defined, 180–182
person factor, 34–35
Person/Group. *See* Person/group
as Self, 35
Personal authority, 421
Personal behaving, 41–44
Personal distance, 227
Personal side of Christians, 30
Personal time, 210
Personalistic to mechanistic view, 426
Personalistic-mechanistic scale, 233, 235
Person/group
categorization, 169–178
causality, 194, 195, 196, 198
changing worldviews, 371–403
cultural orientations, 233–235
evaluation of people, 178
focus of observers, 178
natural world causality, 195
perception, 177

relating to physical environment, 190
relating to the spirit world, 192–193
relationships, 187
Self and Other, 36
social environment, 188–189
space/material universe assumptions, 219
Time/Event, 190–191, 207
understandings, 28
Perspective
heart and mind, 99–100
questions to each perspective, 77
Sire's view, 94
Pharisees
commitment, 354
intellectual knowledge, 351–352
will problems, 364
Philemon and slavery, 474
Philippines, class barriers, 390
Philosophical determinism, 201–202
Philosophy, as Luzbetak category, 107
Physical environment, 145, 190
Physical time, 210
Pictures, interpretation of, 419–420
Pigs, Middle Wahgi, 258–259
Plagiarism, 147
Poetry, for studying worldview, 304
Politeness problem, 299
Political leaders, 421
Pollutants, 38
Polychronic time, 210
Polygamy, 50, 473
Polynesia
casting of spells, 203
spirit power-orientation, 486–487
Polytheism, 472–473
Positional commitment, 354–355
Postmodernism, 87–90, 499
Postulates, 518
Power
causality and, 195, 196–197, 200–201
changing worldviews, 350, 356–357, 384–385
control by magic, 203–204
demonstrations by Jesus, 413–414
gospel presentations, 342
as motivation for change, 384–385
power encounter, 382
power/freedom dimension of Christianity, 334–337
religious ritual and magic, 202–204
spiritual power, for changing worldviews, 376
spiritual power through objects, 229
Practice shift, 353
Practicing the behavior in worldview changes, 366

Pragmatism, 122
Prayer, healing with, 55
Predispositions, patterning, 154–155
Preferences, 41
Present-orientation, 215
Prestige
    of advocates, 395
    resistance to change and, 386–389
Presuppositions, 11
Pride
    barriers produced by habits, 413
    in changing worldviews, 378–379
    Hausa folktale, 313–314
Priest, relationships with spirits, 193, 202–203
Primary behavior
    patterning logic and reason, 153–154
    patterning motivation, 154
    patterning predispositions, 154–155
    patterning use of emotions, 152–153
    patterning use of wills, 152
    worldview guidelines, 151
The Primitive World and its Transformations, 522
Privacy, 228
Privatism, 234–235
Process, deep level, 120
Profane time, 211
Progress, Nacirema worldview, 274–275
Property ownership, in defining personhood, 181
Prosperity Gospel, 447
Protestant Reformation, 426
Proverbs
    Hausa, 315–316, 541–543
    Mexican-American, 543
    for studying worldview, 304, 314–319
Proxemics
    concepts of privacy, 228
    defined, 226
    intimate space, 226–227
    personal distance, 227
    public distance, 227–228
    social distance, 227
Psychological integration level of culture, 106–107
Psychological problems as demonic, 19
Psychological reinforcement, 165–166
Public distance, 227–228
Public opinion, 422
Publicism, 234–235
Pueblo people, 251

Q

Questions
    asking, 298–299

assuming we have something to offer others, 325–328
Burnett's worldview questions, 109
to each perspective, 77
major questions, 303
principles for change, 325–328
subjects to investigate, 300–303
topics, 301–302
Quiche of Guatemala, image of time, 212

R
Radical predestination, 201
Radio waves, popular classification of, 406
Ralik chain, Marshall Islands, 308–309
Reaching peoples
  animistic causality, 481–491
  assumptions of magical practices of animists, 489
  discovering what God is already doing, 483–484
  divination, 489–490
  fear, in animism, 488
  fighting Satan with knowledge, 488–489
  Hinduism, 490
  insights into the spirit world, 485–486
  looking to God instead of spirits, 483
  naturalistic causality, 495–499
  New Age, 490–491
  postmodernism, 499
  spirit power-orientation of animists, 486–487
  theistic causality, 491–494
Reading, as source of power, 384
Reality
  blind men and elephant, 56–57, 61
  categorization, 169
  components of view, 38–39
  conceptualization of, 103
  critical realism. *See* Critical realism
  direct realism, 58–61, 63
  idealism, 61–62, 63
  indirect realism, 63
  intuitivism, 61–62, 63
  mediated realism, 63
  model of, 20, 362–363
  naive realism, 58–61, 63
  perception of, 18–20, 24, 55–56
  relativism, 61–62, 63
  unmediated realism, 58–61, 63
Reason, patterning of, 153–154
Receptor-orientation for transformational change, 468
Receptors
  communication of need for change, 382–383
  conservatism or openness, 377–381
  habits, 371–372
  person/group dimensions, 371–372

receptor-orientation for transformation change, 466–467
    relationships, 371–372
    study, for cross-cultural workers, 478–479
    will, in changing worldviews, 371–372
Reciprocity, Hakka worldview, 294
Reference group, for changing worldviews, 350–351
Reincarnation, 15, 242
Reinterpretation of worldviews, 344
Relationship
    appropriateness of witness, 338
    authority structures, 420–421
    changing worldviews, 371–372, 380
    of Christianity, 139
    deep-level assumptions, 132
    dimension of Christianity, 331–333, 337, 341
    family, 420
    group solidarity, 421–422
    ingroup, 188, 385–386
    joking relationship, 189
    outgroup, 188, 385–386
    overview, 505
    patterns of relating, 162–163
    physical environment, 190
    positive relationships, 498–499
    social environment, 188–189
    spirit world, 192–193
    subsystems, 145–146
    Time/Event, 190–191
    as a universal, 127–128, 187–193
Relativism
    naturalistic causality, 497–498
    overview, 61–62
    postmodernism, 87
    reality and, 63
Religion
    adaptation, 138, 141–142
    Christianity. *See* Christianity
    church membership, conformity of, 52
    consistency and comprehensiveness, 132
    cultural forms, 137–143
    defined, 129, 131
    dimensions of, 92
    faith vs., 140–142
    individualism, 135
    Islam. *See* Islam
    as a jungle, 97–98
    labeling, 131
    as Luzbetak category, 107
    problem of terminology, 129–130
    science, 55
    structure, 141
    subsystems, 133, 134–135

supernaturalism, 130
as surface level, 124
worldview compared, 90–91
worldview subcategory, 90–91
worldview vs., 123–124
Renaissance, civilization of, 507
Renewal, 461
Replacement internal worldview change, 425–427
Reporting discrepancies, 56
Reservoir of tension, 435–437
Resocialization, 345
Revitalization
characteristics of, 456–457
dynamics of, 459–461
examples, 458–459
implementation issues, 456
Marxism, 460
movements, 455–456
Nazism, 460
pattern of worldview change, 434–437, 455–461
pressure to stabilize, 455
process of, 455–456
reformulation stages, 457
Revival, 416
Riddles
body parts, 543
fauna and insects, 544
from Jablow, 545
miscellany, 544
for studying worldview, 304, 320–321
Right to assume we have something to offer others, 325–328
Rise of Nationalism, 92
Rituals. *See also* Habits
animism, 242
crisis rituals, 165
dickering ritual, 134
disequilibrium of changes in worldview, 50
family, 134
passage rituals, 165
religious ritual and magic, 202–204
ritual dimension, 92
as source of power, 385
subsystems, 134–135
in worship, 142
Roads
boundaries, 43
culture and, 34
driving only on the road rule, 45
organization of, in New England, 223
response after near-accident, 147–148
Roles of people, 183–184, 386–389
Roman Catholic, cultural submersion, 443–447

S

Sacred time, 210
Salvation, biblical revelation, 71. *See also* Conversion
Samoa
    acceptance of churches, 399–400
    spirit powers, 487
Santa Claus, 37, 53–54, 66
Saru-to-Kani myth, 311
Satan. *See also* Demons
    animism, 244
    anti-God worldviews, 101
    changing source of power, 356–357
    empowerment, 485–486
    father of lies, 100
    fighting with knowledge, 488–489
    magical rituals, 204
    spiritual warfare, 100–101
    territoriality, 485
Sawi Christians, 392
Schizophrenia, 146–148, 163–164
Schools
    individual vs. group orientation, 180
    knowledge-based, 329–330
    negative consequences of changes in worldview, 48–49
    plagiarism, 147
    sexual activity, 49
Science
    errors in beliefs, 55
    generalizations as parts of closed systems, 58–60
    human world causality, 412
    as a religion, 55
    scientific humanism, 140
    spiritual power vs., 496
Script of culture, 34–35, 45
Scripture. *See* Bible
Secular
    Burnett's overview, 110–111
    humanism, 80, 110, 495. *See also* Naturalistic causality
    secularism, 246
    secularization of western society, 329
    theism, 245, 247
Security
    changing worldviews and, 350
    security-freedom scale, 233, 234
Seed growth analogy, for constructive change, 469
Seeing, selective, 38
Selective seeing, 38
Self, in New Age, 490–491
Self and Other, 35–36
Self-Not-self, 126
Self-Other, 127
Semantic domains, 176

Sexual activity in African schools, 49
Shamans
    animism, 242
    dual allegiance Christianity, 336
    miserable death, 204
    relationships with spirits, 192, 193
    spiritual powers, 202–203
Shame
    Egyptian Sunni Muslim worldview, 280–281
    for social control, 376
Shankara, 84
Shinto, 190
Shoes, removal of, 419
Shona of Zimbabwe, animism, 242–243
Shopping assumptions, 134
Signs and symbols, 101. *See also* Epistemology
The Silent Language, 209, 524
Sin
    affect on perception of reality, 65
    anti-God worldviews, 100–101
    myth of sin entering the world and God leaving, 309
Single Christian worldview, 30–31
Slave, runaway, 47
Slavery, 474
Social climate, receptor conservatism or openness, 377
Social control
    to change worldview, 374–376
    gossip, 376
    law and punishment, 376
    logic, 376
    spiritual power, 376
Social convention, interpretation, 156
Social dimension, 92
Social distance, 227
Social mechanism, study and use for transformational change, 480
Social penalty
    of changing worldviews, 51–53, 54, 349, 373–374
    defined, 33
    giving God permission to work, 366
    imposed by people, 33
Social position and status, 388–389
Social regulation, 164–165
Social security
    in America, 375
    in Japan, 374
Societal comparison of natural, human and spirit realms, 199–200
Sociocultural glue, 477
Sociocultural specialization, 143
Solidarity, group, 421–422
Song lyrics, for studying worldview, 304
Sorcery, 203, 242
Soul, loss or damage as cause of disease, 16

South Korea, animism, 486
South Pacific
    attitudes toward material, 225
    demoralization of people, 437–438
    ingatherings, 382
    spiritual power through objects, 229
Space
    clean space, 419
    cosmology, 220–222
    cultural orientations, 233, 236
    dirty space, 419
    intimate space, 226–227
    land ownership, 418
    language and, 219–220
    macrospace, 218
    material universe, 218–219
    microspace, 218–219
    organizing, 223–225
    pictures, interpretation of, 419–420
    proxemics, 226–228
    relating to physical environment, 190
    separate rooms for children, 419
    where to meet, 418
Specialization, sociocultural, 143
Spells, casting, 203
Spiral representation of time, 213–214
Spirit. *See also* Supernaturalism
    animism, 85, 241–244
    causality, 194, 198–201, 414
    as cause of disease, 16
    changing source of power, 356–357
    classification, 172
    converting to God, 483
    demonstrations of power, 496
    evil spirits, 18, 408
    for healing, 401
    Holy Spirit, 193
    insights from animists, 485–486
    medical scientist beliefs, 55–56
    Papua New Guinea myths, 312–313
    power of, 200–201, 399
    power/freedom dimension, 335–336
    power-orientation of animists, 486–487
    relating to, 192–193
    religion and, 129–130
    religious ritual and magic, 202–204
    scientific reality, 57
    spirit guides, 85
    spiritual power through objects, 229
    spiritual warfare, 101
    structure by worldview assumptions, 41
    territoriality, 485

Status of people
   and changing worldviews, 386–389
   class and caste, 389–390
   overview, 183–184
Steady state
   crisis situation, 430
   model of worldview change, 429–430
   new steady state, 430–431
   process of worldview change, 435
Stealing, scriptural commandment, 189
Steel axes introduced to the Yir Yoront, 438–441
Stone axes, made by the Yir Yoront, 438–441
Stories
   blind men and elephant, 56–57, 61
   blindness as result of sin, 426, 475
   fish-catching, 426, 472
   neighbors, 46–47
   premodern, modern, postmodern contrasts, 88
   runaway slave, 47
   teaching through, 400
   wheat and tares, 474
Strategies for constructive change
   Biblical analogies, 469–476
   change and choice, 463
   cross-cultural workers, 478–480
   ethnic cohesion, 477
   interrelatedness of culture and worldview, 477
   overview, 504–505
   sense of balance, 477–478
   stress, 476–477
   transformational change, 463–468
Stress and transformational change, 476–477
Structure
   configurations, 251
   of culture, 137–138
   of perceptions, 39
   religion, 141
   structural integration level of culture, 106
   structure side of Christians, 30
   The Structure of Scientific Revolutions, 525
   subsystems, 135
   triangle, 93–94
Study of worldview, reasons for
   assumptions, values and allegiances, 22–23
   cause/power and person/group understandings, 28
   changing worldviews, 28–29
   Christian assumptions, 27–28
   Christian faith, 27
   Christian understanding of own worldview, 26
   habitual and unconscious behavior, 25
   human interpretation based on worldview assumptions, 24–25
   perceptions of reality, 24

for understanding people, 25–26
Subconscious, learning a worldview, 36
Subjectivism, 87
Submersion
　characteristics of, 442–443
　of churches, 447–448
　Juan the Chamula, 444–447
　pattern of worldview change, 434–437, 442–448
　survival mechanism, 443–444
Subparadigm, 427–428
Subsystems
　American assumptions, 136
　cultural, 133
　influence on worldview, 145–146
　internal structuring, 135
　Kamwe assumptions, 136–137
　surface level culture, 143–146
Subthemes
　American, 254
　animism, 253
　configurations, 252–254
　internal worldview change, 427–428
　Kamwe, 260–265
　Middle Wahgi, 255–259
　Nacirema, 266–277
　naturalism, 253
Subtractive modification, 425
Suffering of faithful people, 426
Sufism, 116, 492
Sun, popular classification of, 406
Supernaturalism. *See also* Spirit
　cultural orientations, 232–233, 235
　Egyptian Sunni Muslim worldview, 279–280
　Kamwe worldview, 17, 263–265
　paradigms, 253
　as religious, 130–131
　subsystems, 145–146
　subthemes, 253
　terminology, 131
　themes, 253
Supernaturalistic, naturalistic to, 405–406, 426
Superorganicism, 107, 123
Surface level culture
　assumptions, values and allegiances, 23
　defined, 12–13, 120
　disequilibrium of changes in worldview, 49–50
　forms of behavior, 105–106
　personal behaving and cultural structuring, 41–44
　social climate, 377
　subsystem influence on worldview, 145–146
　subsystems, 143–146
　worldview relationship and, 133

Survival mechanism, 443–444
Swahili worldview, 530–534
Symbolic anthropology, 119, 124
Symbols, 155

T

Taiwan, Hakka worldview, 283–295
Tales
    cheaters, 540
    endorsing cleverness, 539
    perseverance, 539–540
    for studying worldview, 304, 313–314
    weak ones need to be wary when strong ones fight, 541
Taoism, 115, 221–222
Taro Cult, 452
Teach Yourself Hausa, 313–314
Teachings
    confirmation of teachings, 38
    conformity, 38
    selective seeing, 38
    view of reality, 38–39
Technical culture, 524
Terminology, problems with, 129–130
Territoriality, 228
Theism
    belief in angels and demons, 492–493
    beliefs, 491
    causality, 239–240, 247–250
    characteristics, 248, 249
    "Christian" as a bad word, 493
    cosmos, view of, 93, 95
    dead orthodoxy vs. theistic existentialism, 494
    dreams, visions, healings and deliverances, 493
    existentialism, 81–83, 494
    focus on the High God, 492
    naturalism, 245
    need for peace, 494
    nominal Christians, 493–494
    ordinary vs. biblical theism, 250
    overlap of book held to, 492
    problem of secular Christianity, 493
    reaching peoples, 491–494
    secular theism, 245, 247
    void left by understandings of law, 492
Themes
    American, 254
    animism, 253
    changing worldviews, 343
    configurations, 252–254
    dynamic affirmations, 517–518
    Kamwe, 16–18, 260–265
    Middle Wahgi, 255–259

    Nacirema, 266–277
    naturalism, 253
    of worldviews, 108–109
Thinking, human, 101–102
Time
    biological time, 209–210
    conventional use of, 217–218
    cyclical time, 212
    future-orientation, 214
    history, 216–217
    history of Western time, 209
    images of, 211–214
    language and, 215–216
    linear time, 213
    materiality of, 144
    metaphysical time, 210
    micro time, 210
    monochronic time, 210
    myth time, 211
    oscillating time, 212
    past-orientation, 215
    pendulum representation, 213
    personal time, 210
    physical time, 210
    polychronic time, 210
    present-orientation, 215
    profane time, 211
    sacred time, 210
    spiral representation, 212–213
    time line, 417
    time-oriented vs. event-oriented history, 216–217
    worldview change factor, 373
Time/Event
    of athletic contests, 191
    cross-cultural workers, 208
    cultural orientations, 233, 236–237
    efficiency, 415–416
    lateness, 415
    now versus not now, 416–418
    relating to, 190–191
    worldview focus, 207
    worship, 208
Timing
    importance in worldview change, 365–366
    of innovations, 402–403
Tiv of Nigeria, image of time, 212
Totem, 242
Touch of the Kingdom of God, 469
Traditional Societies and Technological Change, 326
Traditions, belief in possibility of change, 378
Transformational change, 463–468
    advocate-implementor, 464–465

change of ideas, 465
cross-cultural communication, 465–466
demonstration of the Father, 467
earning, rather than demanding, 467
identification with receptors, 466
information overload, 468
inviting people to discovery, 468
receptor-orientation, 466–467, 468
specific people, 467–468
specific situations, 468
trust in receptors, 468
two-way communication, 467
Transformations video, 338–339, 410
Transmission of worldview, problem factors, 37
Triangle structure, 93–94
Truth, knowledge dimension, 330–331
Truth and love, 158
TV waves, popular classification of, 406
Twentieth-Century Secular Humanism, 93
The Twilight Labyrinth, 338–339
Twin Monster Slayers, 538
2/3 world society, 199–200
Types of orientations
    animism, 239, 240, 241–244, 249
    generally, 237–238
    naturalism, 239, 240–241, 245–247, 249
    theism, 239–240, 247–250

U

Uganda, demoralization of people, 438
Ultimate Cause, 204–206
Unconscious
    following of worldview, 25
    learning a worldview, 36
United States. *See* America
Universals
    categorization, 169–177
    causality. *See* Causality
    classification logic, 172–175
    ethnoscience, 176
    ethnosemantics, 176
    flowchart, 167
    human nature, 182–183
    individual and group, 179–180
    Kearney's universals, 127–128
    lineup, 167–168
    male and female, 184–186
    person, defined, 180–182
    person/group, 177–178
    relationship. *See also* Relationship
    Relationship, 127–128
    relationship, 187–193

Self-Not-self, 126
　　status and role, 183–184
　　Time/Event. *See* Time/Event
Universe
　　as closed or open, 497
　　creation of, 221
　　defined, 100
　　explanatory assumptions, 159
　　perception of, 144–145
　　The Universe Next Door, 11, 75
Unmediated realism, 58–61, 63
Urban sprawl, 38

V

Value orientations, 518–520
Variations in Value Orientations, 519
Vietnam War, 21
Viewer, 36
Visions, of Muslims, 493

W

War
　　defeat, 21
　　spiritual warfare, 101
　　Vietnam War, 21
　　warfare over worldviews, 100
Weak ones need to be wary when strong ones fight tale, 541
Wealth
　　in defining personhood, 181
　　Hausa folktale, 313–314
　　measuring, 236
Weltanschauung, 98, 103, 507
Westerner. *See also* America; Secular
　　age and status, 197
　　changing worldviews, 349
　　comparison of causality emphasis, 199–201
　　history of time, 209
　　knowledge, overemphasis on, 329
　　linear logic, 153–154
　　natural vs. supernatural, 242
　　perception of the universe, 144–145
　　power through science and technology, 202
　　social climate, 377
　　space assumptions, 220
　　status issues, 388
　　subsystems, 145–146
Whale, popular classification of, 406
Wheat and tares parable, 474
White magic, 203
Will
　　to change worldview, 348–351, 364, 371–372

to make choices and commitments, 41
  patterning use of, 152
Witchcraft, 203, 242
Women, as obstacle to conversion for men, 392
Worker strategy, cross-cultural, 478–480
World View, 125, 507
World War II
  cargo cult phenomenon, 312–313
  Japanese openness to changing worldviews, 379
  theistic existentialism, 81
Worldview analysis, 91, 525–526
Worldview: The History of a Concept, 98
Worldviews: Cross-cultural Explorations of Human Beliefs, 11, 90
Worship
  defined, 135
  redefining meaning of, 143–144
  Time/Event, 208
Wrestling With Dark Angels, 412

Y
Yin and yang, 221–222, 245–246
Yir Yoront
  cutting implements, 397–399
  demoralization, 438–442, 450, 455, 476–477

Z
Zhong, 292–294